LARAMIE JR. HIGH IMC

D1736308

LORD BYRON

moves into the realm of the vampire in one of his rare and revelatory excursions into fiction.

LOUISA MAY ALCOTT

shows a side of her vision far, far removed from the sunlit world of *Little Women*.

WILLIAM FAULKNER

creates a grisly image of death and rot under the burning southern sun.

ANNE SEXTON

turns a children's bedtime fairy story into a poem for adults only designed to drive away sleep.

STEPHEN KING

opens the doorway to an unforgettable chamber of horrors. *They are five of the thirty-four writers who have helped to shape—*

THE EVIL IMAGE

THE EVIL IMAGE

TWO CENTURIES OF GOTHIC SHORT FICTION AND POETRY

EDITED AND WITH AN INTRODUCTION BY

Patricia L. Skarda

AND

Nora Crow Jaffe

LARAMIE JR. HIGH IMC
1355 N. 22nd
LARAMIE, WY 82070

A MERIDIAN BOOK

NEW AMERICAN LIBRARY

TIMES MIRROR

NEW YORK AND SCARBOROUGH, ONTARIO

NAL BOOKS ARE AVAILABLE AT QUANTITY DISCOUNTS WHEN USED TO PROMOTE PRODUCTS OR SERVICES. FOR INFORMATION PLEASE WRITE TO PREMIUM MARKETING DIVISION, THE NEW AMERICAN LIBRARY, INC., 1633 BROADWAY, NEW YORK, NEW YORK 10019.

Copyright © 1981 by Patricia L. Skarda and Nora Crow Jaffe

All rights reserved

PERMISSIONS ACKNOWLEDGMENTS

A. E. Coppard, "Arabesque: *The Mouse*" from *Adam and Eve and Pinch Me* (1922) by permission of the Harold Matson Company, Inc.

William Faulkner, "A Rose for Emily." Copyright 1930 and renewed 1958 by William Faulkner. Reprinted from COLLECTED STORIES OF WILLIAM FAULKNER, by William Faulkner, by permission of Random House, Inc.

Stephen King, "Suffer the Little Children." Copyright 1972 by Dugent Publishing Corp. Reprinted by permission of the author and the author's agent, Kirby McCauley. First appeared in *Cavalier*.

Flannery O'Connor, "The River." Copyright 1953 by Flannery O'Connor. Reprinted from *A Good Man Is Hard to Find and Other Stories* by permission of Harcourt Brace Jovanovich, Inc.

Anne Sexton, "Briar Rose (Sleeping Beauty)." From TRANSFORMATIONS by Anne Sexton, published by Houghton Mifflin Company. Copyright 1971 by Anne Sexton. Reprinted by permission of the publisher.

Eudora Welty, "Clytie." Copyright 1941, 1969 by Eudora Welty. Reprinted from her volume A CURTAIN OF GREEN AND OTHER STORIES by permission of Harcourt Brace Jovanovich, Inc.

MERIDIAN TRADEMARK REG. PAT. U.S. OFF. AND FOREIGN COUNTRIES
REGISTERED TRADEMARK—MARCA REGISTRADA
HECHO EN WESTFORD, MASS., U.S.A.

SIGNET, SIGNET CLASSICS, MENTOR, PLUME, MERIDIAN and NAL BOOKS are published *in the United States* by The New American Library, Inc., 1633 Broadway, New York, New York 10019, *in Canada* by The New American Library of Canada Limited, 81 Mack Avenue, Scarborough, Ontario MIL 1M8

Library of Congress Cataloging in Publication Data
Main entry under title:

The Evil image.

Bibliography: p.
1. English literature.   2. Gothic revival (Literature)
3. American literature.   I. Skarda, Patricia L.
II. Jaffe, Nora.
PR1111.G67E9   820'.8'016   81–2180
ISBN 0-452-00636-8   AACR2

First Printing, June, 1981

3 4 5 6 7 8 9

PRINTED IN THE UNITED STATES OF AMERICA

Ruth Mortimer of the Smith College Rare Book Room has been especially kind and remarkably helpful in supplying first editions. Texts of "The Vampyre," "Transformation," and "Wandering Willie's Tale" all came from there.

From ghoulies and ghosties and long-leggety beasties
And things that go bump in the night,
     Good Lord, deliver us!

               —Anonymous Cornish Prayer

Contents

General Introduction

THE Gothic tradition in English literature began in 1764 with the publication of Horace Walpole's *Castle of Otranto*, subtitled in the second edition "A Gothic Story," but no tradition springs full-grown from one imagination, even as singular a one as Walpole's. His revival of ancient romance with improbable fantasies and his blend of realistic contemporary romance with sentimental stock characters captured the imaginations of a public prepared to delight in super-natural terrors, folkloric superstitions, medieval curiosities, and modern human horrors. Why he called his story "Gothic" and why its appeal satisfied the reading and thinking public of his time are questions whose answers explain in part the continuing fascination of Gothic romances and grotesque fiction since Walpole's time.

The term "Gothic" lacked precision even in its early application to the Germanic tribes that migrated into Spain, southwestern France, Italy, and elsewhere in the late phase of the Roman Empire. By the seventeenth century, the Goths had become confused with the Getae, a historically discrete Scandinavian people, and with the Jutes, members of several Germanic tribes who invaded Britain and settled in southern England in the fifth century. Since the Goths, Getae, and Jutes were thought responsible for creating the bastard culture of the Middle Ages in the place of the more classical or civilized one of the Roman Empire, "Gothic" came to designate bad taste in general, and outworn medieval traits and customs in particular.

Italian humanists of the Renaissance blamed the Goths for the barbarism and ignorance they saw in the Middle Ages, and they fixed on them responsibility even for the decline in handwriting and literary style. Lorenzo Valla (*ca.* 1407–1457) proved by textual criticism that the long-suspect Donation of Constantine was a forgery. His discovery led to the condemnation of the "monkish" black-letter script as "Gothic," a designation Walpole used to describe the sup-posed manuscript of *The Castle of Otranto* in his fictitious "Trans-lator's Preface" to the first edition. Valla also suggested that the Goths allowed the Latin language to decay into the clumsiness of medieval and church Latin. Later, François Rabelais (*ca.* 1494–

1553) used "Gothic" to refer to a rustic, coarse literary style by authors inadequately disciplined by Latin and Greek models.

The most familiar pejorative application of "Gothic" occurs in the architectural reflections of Giorgio Vasari (1511–1574) in *Lives of the Architects, Painters and Sculptors* (1550), in which the medieval architectural style was regarded as lavishly decorated, disorderly, common, inferior in quality, and insubstantial in appearance. The classical style in architecture, as in language and literature, remained the valid model for Vasari and others; the Gothic, with its crudeness and wildness, expressed the faulty taste of the barbaric style.

When the term was extended to literature, the architectural reference was, at first, not far from mind. In 1701 John Dennis voiced his disapproval of the state of English literature by saying: "While the French reformed the structure of their poems by the noble models of ancient architecture . . . we resolved . . . to adhere to our Gothic and barbarous manner" (*The Advancement and Reformation of Modern Poetry*). "Gothic" rhyme was "a horrid discord of jingling" opposed to the sonority of blank verse, understood to be more nearly classical (Shaftesbury, *Characteristicks*, 1711). Tasso, Ariosto, and Spenser were accused of having marred their medieval epic subjects by fanciful and chivalric elements reminiscent of Gothic taste. Joseph Addison (1672–1719) scorned the poets of the seventeenth century who displayed their wit in conceits, far-fetched extended metaphors, instead of making

> a thought shine in its own natural beauties. Poets who want this strength of genius to give that majestic simplicity to nature, which we so much admire in the works of the ancients, are forced to hunt after foreign ornaments, and not to let any piece of wit of what kind soever escape them. I look upon these writers as Goths in Poetry, who like those in architecture, not being able to come up to the beautiful simplicity of the old Greeks and Romans, have endeavored to supply its place with all the extravagances of an irregular fancy.
>
> (*Spectator*, No. 62, 1711)

For Addison, as for Marlowe, Shakespeare, Milton, and Defoe, supernatural subjects, such as "fairies, witches, magicians, demons, and departed spirits" (*Spectator*, No. 419, 1712), were appropriate for poetry. These were not labeled "Gothic," though such supernatural characters were to become the hallmark of much Gothic fiction and poetry. Like Walpole, Addison found the best treatment of "those secret terrors and apprehensions" in Shakespeare, and he recognized the appeal of their "strangeness and novelty." He encouraged poets given to what Dryden called "the fairy way of writing" to be well acquainted with the "legends and fables, antiquated romances, and the traditions of nurses and old women," which could make their ghosts, witches, and fairies seem natural. Such poetry spurred a renewed interest in folklore and medievalism and the English national past.

Before the dogma of the inferiority of Gothic architecture was seriously challenged, interest in the national past inspired a renewal of Gothic building in England, and a new confusion about the term followed. Sir Christopher Wren (1632–1723) tried to purify architectural styles, and to do so he made a distinction in his writings and in his building designs between the old Gothic and the new, or the ancient and the modern. His friend John Evelyn (1620–1706) had confused both architectural styles and their sources by mixing descriptions of Moorish style with Gothic style and by assuming that the Arabs and Moors were responsible for the introduction of the "fantastical and licentious manner of building" which had debauched the classical norm. For Evelyn, the "Gothic" described "congestions of heavy, dark, melancholy and *Monkish Piles*, without any just Proportion, Use or Beauty, compared with the truly Ancient" (*Account of Architects and Architecture*, 1697). Wren noted an essential difference between the somber spirit Evelyn described and the slender towers, abundant windows, and lacy fretwork of Salisbury Cathedral in England, Ulm in Germany, or Chartres in France—cathedrals we commonly regard as Gothic. In 1668 he called Salisbury "one of the best patterns of architecture in the age wherein it was built." But in 1713, in "On the State of Westminster Abbey," he followed Evelyn's lead and gave "Gothic" a new connotation and "Gothic" literature an additional strain—the Eastern or exotic mode. He focuses his comments on the Abbey of 1220:

> This we now call the Gothic manner of architecture (so the Italians called what was not after the Roman style), though the Goths were rather destroyers than builders; I think it should with more reason be called the Saracen style, for these people wanted neither arts nor learning: and after we in the west lost both, we borrowed again from them, out of their Arabic books, what they with great diligence had translated from the Greeks.

The "Saracenic" theory of Gothic seems to be founded on nothing except the Moorish invasions of Europe in the twelfth and thirteenth centuries, and Wren's attempt to distinguish between ancient and modern Gothic seems to refer to the round arches of the ancient and the "sharp-headed arches" of the modern in Westminster Abbey and his own St. Paul's Cathedral. His designation of "Saracenic" or "Arabic" was also called "Arabesque," which, like "grotesque" (etymologically, "grotto painting"), was later appropriated for literature, as in Poe's *Tales of the Grotesque and Arabesque* (1839).

Both "arabesque" and "grotesque" broadened in connotation to denote ornamental designs of surface decoration (sometimes in bas relief) or strangely mixed, fantastic decorative art. At first, arabesques were thought different from grotesques because they did not represent living creatures; but from Raphael (1483–1520) on, arabesques included the animation of human and animal figures, both natural and unnatural, amid flowing lines of branches, leaves, and scrollwork fancifully intertwined. Grotesques were decidedly unnatural, fantastic. Walpole, as we might expect, applauded the "neatness and taste" of the grotesque in the work of Don Julio Clovia (*Anecdotes of Painting in England*, 1762–1771), but Shaftesbury denigrated the strangeness, distortion, or exaggeration of grotesque art, both in painting and sculpture (*Characteristicks*, 1711). In time, bizarre or fantastic poetic visions, fictional characters, or literary styles came to be called "grotesque," and "arabesque" came to connote a fanciful delicacy appropriate to a ballet movement or a reverie. Hence, Coppard's "Arabesque: *The Mouse*" (1921) borrows an artistic term for its title and movement, and twentieth-century American Southern fiction recalls the unnaturalness of both art and literature in its common description as "grotesque" or "American Gothic."

The Eastern flavor of the arabesque in art can be detected in Gothic literature through the exotic atmosphere of "Sir Bertrand" and from the many references to *The Arabian Nights* (translated, 1704–1717), the popular title for the tales told by the clever Scheherazade in the *Thousand and One Nights*, a collection of ancient Persian-Indian-Arabian tales. The Oriental tale provided didactic writers with a flamboyant disguise of setting for English characters engaged in moral or philosophical reflections. By distancing fictional characters in wild, unfamiliar places, authors were free to suggest moral truths through fantastic, magical, even mystical situations. Byron borrowed his Turkish infidel, the Giaour, from the Oriental tradition, and Henry James admired *The Arabian Nights* for its fairytale qualities. Gradually, the Orientalism in fiction and the mistaken Saracenic theory of architecture resulted in the radical change of taste that reversed the prevailing sentiment against the Gothic aesthetic.

Bishop Richard Hurd (1719–1808) and other theologians, editors, and critics espoused the freer and more "natural" art of English landscaping, acclaimed the beauties and details of Gothic art, and rescued medieval manners of chivalry and enchantment from the opprobrium of classical enthusiasts. Hurd initiated a trend toward aesthetic relativism by declaring that "the Gothic architecture has it's [sic] own rules by which when it comes to be examined, it is seen to have it's [sic] own merit, as well as the Grecian" (*Letters on Chivalry and Romance*, VIII, 1762). William Gilpin (1724–1804) popularized the concept of the irregularity and variety of nature in a series of illustrated tours (1782–1800), and so established the tradition of the picturesque from which Ann Radcliffe borrowed for her travel sequences. And in 1756, Edmund Burke (1729–1797) observed that a certain "wildness" in nature and art produced an inspiring awe of high spiritual, moral, or intellectual worth (*A Philosophical Enquiry into the Origin of our Ideas of the Sublime and Beautiful*). To him, anything capable of exciting the ideas of pain and danger is a source of the sublime; beauty, he concluded, is the property which causes love, not desire. Beauty consists in relative smallness, smoothness, absence of angularity, and brightness of color; the sublime, on the other hand, moves from admiration, reverence, and respect to astonishment, fear, and terror—all with a high degree of obscurity or lack of clarity. "Poetry," he went on to say, "with all its obscurity, has a more general, as well as a more powerful dominion over the passions," than painting. And ideas of eternity and infinity, like the dark, confused, uncertain images of nature, "have a greater power on the fancy to form the grander passions, than those have which are more clear and determinate." The evocation of terror, then, requires obscurity from the author and an imaginative response from the reader. The inexplicable or the incomprehensible voice, vision, or act affects more powerfully than any clear beauty, whether seen or felt.

Burke may well have been affected himself by the melancholy poetry of the so-called "Graveyard School" of poets who sought out a graveyard in which to meditate on mortality. Thomas Parnell (1679–1718), Edward Young (1683–1765), Robert Blair (1699–1746), and Thomas Gray (1716–1771) endowed landscapes with an aura of Gothic gloom in elegies and lyrics which often capitalized on morbid details seen through the eyes of an isolated speaker. Ugly horrors of death—charnel houses, shadowy graves, and the like—combined with supernatural terrors to evoke in the poet and reader the paradoxical "joy of gloom" and "delicious fear" which characterized early Gothic fiction.

In the eighteenth century, fear of death and dying was complemented by earnest belief in ghosts and apparitions, as in Defoe's "Apparition of Mrs. Veal" and in the revival of interest in Elizabethan drama. Lurid violence and crime mixed well with supernatural visitants, as if to prove that the irrational acts of man were as impossible to understand as the mysterious acts of God. Folklore of England's mystical past was popularized in James Macpherson's supposed translation of Celtic poems in *Ossian* (1760–1763), and ballads of England's medieval past, with its religious or superstitious coloring, were made accessible in Thomas Percy's *Reliques of Ancient English Poetry* (1765). Since 1690, when John Locke (1632–1704) published his

Essay concerning Human Understanding, the value associated with sense experience was higher than that set on inherited truths, and the concrete imagery of the medieval past and the melancholy settings of the present lent themselves well to the imaginative visions of early Gothicists. To be convincing, then or now, obscure terrors require some particular, and usually macabre, details. Good and evil absolutes and the secret impulses of man must be made sufficiently real to horrify and sufficiently vague to terrify. The change of taste in late eighteenth-century England allowed for both dimensions in the art of early Gothic fiction. The tradition grew out of a rich confluence of philosophies, artistic and architectural practices, and literary influences, but the first truly Gothic masterpieces were as unique as they were popular.

Horace Walpole (1717–1797), author of the first true Gothic novel, also pioneered the revival of the Gothic in architecture. Inspired by real and imaginary medieval castles, he devised the plans for his house, Strawberry Hill, in Twickenham, ten miles from London. It was there that he had the extraordinary dream that impelled him to write *The Castle of Otranto* (1764):

> I waked one morning in the beginning of last June from a dream of which all I could recover was, that I had thought myself in an ancient castle . . . and that on the uppermost bannister of a great staircase I saw a gigantic hand in armour. In the evening I sat down and began to write, without knowing in the least what I intended to say or relate. . . . I was so engrossed with my tale, which I completed in less than two months, that one evening I wrote from the time I had drunk my tea, about six o'clock, till half an hour after one in the morning, when my hand and fingers were so weary, that I could not hold the pen to finish the sentence, but left Matilda and Isabella talking, in the middle of a paragraph.

The book tells the melodramatic story of the tyrant Manfred, who tries to force marriage on the princess Isabella in order to have sons by her and so forestall the accomplishment of a curse that will deprive him of his kingdom, Otranto. Meanwhile, Manfred's daughter, Matilda, has fallen in love with a supposed peasant, Theodore, who also holds Isabella's affections. The story was so bizarre by the conservative standards of the time that Walpole was forced to find means for making it palatable. He associated it with classical tragedy in the minds of his readers by giving it a five-part structure, a recognition scene, terror and pity as prevailing emotions, and a rather unconvincing "tragic flaw" for the thoroughly evil Manfred; and he presented the story as a translation, by one "William Marshal," of a sixteenth-century Italian manuscript written by a priest. In his preface to the second edition, he bolstered his case by citing the powerful example of

Shakespeare, and in particular the tragi-comedies that juxtaposed high and dignified characters with low and comical ones; and he self-consciously invoked the great Neo-Classical standard of "Nature" to justify this rather unnatural story. Walpole's concern was not misplaced; his friends did look askance at this evidence of his eccentricity:

> How do you think he has employed that leisure which his political frenzy has allowed of? In writing a novel, entitled the *Castle of Otranto*, and such a novel, that no boarding-school Miss of thirteen could get half through without yawning. It consists of ghosts and enchantments; pictures walk out of their frames, and are good company for half an hour together; helmets drop from the moon, and cover half a family. He says it was a dream, and I fancy one when he had some feverish disposition in him.
>
> (Sir Charles Hanbury Williams to George Selwyn,
> 19 March 1765)

But his admiring readers felt otherwise. They found in the novel a refreshing release from Neo-Classical conventions and a source of titillating fear. The growing reading public greedily snapped up the many parodies and imitations as they appeared.

By the time Ann Radcliffe published *The Mysteries of Udolpho* (1794), the public was prepared, by literary and architectural developments, to receive her novel with enthusiasm. Her book differed from Walpole's in important respects. Mrs. Radcliffe chose English protagonists to place in her exotic settings. The author, herself untraveled, elaborated them without having to deal with the distractions of fact. The hero and heroine displayed a tender sensibility that endeared them to sentimental readers. Emily St. Aubert responds to fear with fainting, to the deaths of her parents with prolonged grief, and to love with a fidelity that resists threats and seductions. Rather than validating the supernatural, as Walpole had done, Mrs. Radcliffe meticulously explained, at the end of the novel, the mundane reasons for all of the eerie happenings in the story. Both her method of dealing with the supernatural and Walpole's were admired and accepted; together, at the beginning of the Gothic tradition, these two novelists defined its eclectic nature. The writers who succeeded them exploited the sentiments, situations, and devices they had suggested. Mary Alcock's "Receipt for Writing a Novel" shows that aspects of the mode had become trite as early as 1799. But Walpole and Mrs. Radcliffe had proved to all who came after them—novelists, poets, dramatists, and storytellers—that at the very heart of the Gothic was respect for originality and eccentricity. The next major Gothic novelist had every reason to be grateful.

In his notorious novel *The Monk* (1795), Matthew Gregory

Lewis recounts several sensational stories at once. He begins by concentrating on the relationship between Ambrosio, who has been abandoned as an infant at the monastery door and whose eloquence and rigid virtue have advanced him in the church, and "Rosario," a young novice who turns out to be a woman in disguise. As Rosario, or rather "Matilda," is seducing the monk, Lewis abruptly switches to the story of Raymond and Agnes, whose love is thwarted by her enforced taking of religious vows. In the course of their story, Lewis tells of the spectral "Bleeding Nun"; her unwelcome visits to Raymond are ended only by the intervention of the "Wandering Jew," the cursed and restless figure that was to fascinate Byron. Having brought Raymond and Agnes to a point of crisis, Lewis returns to Ambrosio and Matilda, who are just completing the sexual act. He then proceeds to develop further the story of Lorenzo and Antonia, who have met in the opening pages while attending a sermon of Ambrosio's. The intertwining of the plots, with the disparate punishments meted out to the three religious characters who violate the vow of chastity, suggests that Lewis is scrutinizing the reluctant compliance, the hypocrisy, and the vice within the church; and the character of the evil Prioress, tormentor of the pregnant Agnes, reinforces the satire on hypocritical piety. The characters finally come together; and the novel ends in a flurry of matricide, rape, and incest as Ambrosio discovers his true identity, falls into the hands of the Inquisition, sells his soul to the devil, and finally despairs. Throughout the novel, the labyrinthine passages underneath the adjoining monastery and convent provide a setting for the action that reflects the twisted passions of the characters. The alternating portraits of woman as virgin, temptress, and demon; the choice offered between the passive purity of Antonia and the fallibility of the more resourceful Agnes; the jarring depiction of the effeminate "Rosario," who becomes the masculine "Matilda" when undisguised—all provide inspiration for the creators of female characters in subsequent Gothic fiction. *The Monk* is the quintessential Gothic novel. In 1795, thirty years after Walpole's more timid venture, Lewis distilled the spirit of Gothicism and served it up to readers so ready to receive it that they called the author "Monk" Lewis, bestowing the nickname as an accolade.

These three early Gothic novels contain almost all of the devices and themes of the Gothic short fiction and poetry which followed. Unfortunately, Walpole, Radcliffe, and Lewis themselves wrote no short fiction which could represent the full range of their powers. Radcliffe and Lewis, however, composed poetry, often for their novels, and selected pieces are reprinted in this collection. It was their novels, however, which set the brisk pace of the galloping tradition of the Gothic, and it is for these long, sentimental, often sensational, and sometimes sublime novels that Walpole, Radcliffe, and Lewis are best remembered.

As the tradition matured into the suggestive imagery of the Romantic poets and the stories and poems of skepticism and doubt of the Victorians, a far better balance was struck between supernatural events and natural characters than in the early Gothic novels, in which melodrama denied force to terror and ridiculous distortions compromised horror. Supernatural or marvelous effects, in the best Gothic literature, are limited in number, indefinite in cause or purpose, brief in appearance, and essentially, according to Sir Walter Scott, "different from ourselves" ("On the Supernatural in Fictitious Composition," 1827). Those works which unnecessarily exaggerated the terror or the horror seldom survived the reviewers, and became easy subjects for parody or satire.

The tradition had to mature before poets and storytellers realized the different effects of terror and horror, or, as Devendra Varma puts it, "the difference between awful apprehension and sickening realization: between the smell of death and stumbling against a corpse" (*The Gothic Flame*, 1957). Terror rises up from the chaos of feelings of doubt and uncertainty about man's place in the universe; horror frequently follows the recognition that greater powers than man can exert the force of violence and pain on him. The fear of the biblical Job, then, comes from terror; his punishment at the hand of God is horrible. Because man is human and finite, he can bear more terror than horror, more emotional feeling than actual physical pain. As a result, one gruesome detail of murder or mutilation, transformation or haunting spectre, is sufficient in a Gothic tale. For that reason, perhaps, the Romantic poets and their contemporaries refuse to describe many macabre details of past or present horrors; instead, they prefer to concentrate on the more imaginative terrors which defy sure definition. Coleridge, for example, in "Christabel," refuses to specify clearly the horror of Geraldine, but, whether vampire or sorcerer, she hypnotizes and terrifies the fair Christabel. In his criticism, Coleridge proves that he was writing suggestively on principle:

> Situations of torment, and images of naked horror, are easily conceived; and a writer in whose works they abound, deserves our gratitude almost equally with him who should drag us by way of sport through a military hospital, or force us to sit at the dissection table of a natural philosopher. . . . Figures that shock the imagination, and narratives that mangle the feelings, rarely discover *genius*, and always betray a low and vulgar *taste*.
>
> (Coleridge, *On the General Character of the Gothic*)

On this principle, a fair evaluation of the contents of this volume can be judged. The horrors are many, but the terrors are far more memorable because they are more affecting. Proving his genius, then, Byron chooses not to specify his crime against Astarte in *Manfred*, and, in "Green Tea," Le Fanu suggests that the invisible monkey does more than sit on the clergyman's Bible. Sir Walter Scott clearly echoes Coleridge's point, and, in "Wandering Willie's Tale," prefers the incidents and gloomy simplicity of his narrative to graphic descriptions of dead bodies or Satanic strangers.

Part of the Gothic writer's task is to evoke fear, whether terror, horror, or a combination of the two. Archetypal responses to evil differ dramatically from reactions to death or ghosts. Apparitions of the dead may frighten the guilty man, and death itself may scare the innocent; but the premonition of uncontrolled evil brings terrifying shudders to all men, and the recognition of the curse of human frailty often results in horror and insanity. Dorothy Scarborough's vivid distinction is too neat for most Gothic short fiction and poetry of the nineteenth and twentieth centuries: "Seeing a supernatural visitant is terrible, hearing him is direful, smelling him is loathsome, but having him touch you is the climax of horror" (*The Supernatural in Modern English Fiction*, 1917). Supernatural visitants become fewer and fewer as Gothic literature matures; in their place we find terrified and terrifying madmen and the horrors of madness itself. The source of man's fears gradually becomes more familiar throughout the nineteenth century as supernatural events in Gothic literature give way to inner dread, psychic terrors. The double or the complementary personality, which makes psychological truth a part of reality, can and does terrify because it awakens fear of real and horrid possibilities.

Byron's *Manfred* dramatizes in verse the agony of an arrogant, ambitious man who, like Monk Lewis' Ambrosio, loves incestuously; Astarte is even "like [him] in lineaments." For his unnatural love and his destruction of his beloved, he must endure the Romantic agony, which William Blake defines simply as, "By trying to be more than man, we become less." Manfred's terror comes from guilt and the disappointment of hopes for achievement, for love. His agony is a modern and timeless one. Like Napoleon, he went too far and became the victim of his own brief victory.

Killing a beloved by incest and degeneracy brings on the literal fall of Poe's House of Usher, where house and inmates are synonymous—dangerously cracked, isolated, and almost in ruins. Madness in Roderick Usher and his twin sister haunts the house and snares the narrator himself. The physical attractions of evil, seen in the vampire fictions of Coleridge, Byron, and Polidori, are here omitted, but the seductive power of psychological fragmentation brings even the narrator to the verge of collapse. The potential horror of live burial remains untapped in favor of the more obscure terror of madness.

In a reverse of the pattern, Markheim's double saves him from moral collapse in much the same way that the ugly dwarf in Mary Shelley's "Transformation" saves Guido. Monstrous guilt sometimes requires embodiment outside the self before it can be recognized. Such doubling symbolically charges simple tales and poems with sexual overtones and philosophical dimensions. "Goblin Market" suggests more than love of sisters, and "Green Tea" boasts a blasphemous monkey which is both obscene and libidinous.

Fears and their shapes are as various as the readers and writers of Gothic fiction and poetry. In the short story and narrative poem, a certain control of realism keeps the subconscious dreams from becoming living nightmares and the fictions from becoming facts. Madness is circumscribed by the form's brevity; monsters are made and act within a strictly limited series of events; and the few main characters recover, escape, die, or otherwise resolve the fiction economically, expeditiously. Contexts, such as frames for the narratives, structures for the poetry, or settings for the action, keep the air of the familiar wrapped around the unfamiliar. Le Fanu, for example, resorts to the epistolary convention in "Green Tea," and Scott inserted "Wandering Willie's Tale" into *Redgauntlet* to simplify by contrast the ambitions and social responsibilities of characters in the novel. Some of the following selections appeared first in volumes intended for Christmas readings. Dickens and M. R. James knew, as Ann Radcliffe did, that a secure setting only heightens the terrors of the ghost tale. Campers of all ages and guests at slumber parties can attest to the effectiveness of the storytelling context. Byron's challenge to his guests to write a story of their own may seem unlikely today, but the party at Diodati obviously took it quite seriously. On a chilly evening in June, amid friends with literary ambitions like her own, Mary Shelley was able to begin her *Frankenstein*, which grew out of a number of familiar themes and initiated a new one more powerful than the old. Her famous story, not incidentally, was revised by the addition of an elaborate formal frame, which constitutes a substantial story outside the story of Frankenstein's creation of the nameless monster. The other product of Byron's parlor game, Polidori's *Vampyre*, begins and ends in London where high society provides a welcome for Aubrey and, unfortunately, for the deceptive vampire himself. Evil can parade as good, Polidori implies, even amid fashionable people of wide experience. No one is protected from the problem of evil in himself and in society. The wise and the simple, the brave and the shy, the old and the young, may succumb to the evils of prejudice, as in Crane's *Monster*, or the malignancy of revenge, as in the stories by Henry James or M. R. James. The scientist, the artist, and the intellectual must confront external monsters or internal madness, the shapes of evil in the world and in the self.

Cultural confusion, social injustice, religious fervor, and scientific skepticism—all find their way into Gothic tales and poems. Whatever is traditional, conventional, or ideal can be disregarded, inverted, or distorted through imaginative fantasy. Like ghostly visitors, improbable occurrences attest to the continuing fascination with darkness and irrationality throughout the nineteenth and on into the twentieth centuries. In Dickens' "Signal-Man" and Hawthorne's "Young Goodman Brown," for example, visions and epiphanies literally transform unwitting narrators and characters into more perceptive figures or haunted ones. Thomas Hardy, whose long life spanned much of the nineteenth century and a quarter of the twentieth, suggests a reason for the proliferation of ghostly tales during his lifetime by saying poetically: "if way to the Better there be, it exacts a full look at the Worst" ("In Tenebris: II"). In one sense, ghost stories provide authors and readers with a safe means of controlling or coming to terms with the worst. Inner conflicts of doubt and faith or debatable social issues, such as technical progress and urban expansion, both require a break with the past, with older continuities, both communal and personal (Julia Briggs, *Night Visitors*, 1978). From the mid-nineteenth century on, scientific advances hold no certainty; religion is suspect; and, with some exceptions, art and architecture express the insignificance of the human form.

In 1818, in his lecture on the "General Character of the Gothic Mind in the Middle Ages," Coleridge could comment favorably on the "sense of self-annihilation" impressed on the beholder of Gothic architecture. The beholder becomes a part of the work contemplated, as Coleridge described it in his next lecture:

> The Greek art is beautiful. When I enter a Greek Church, my eye is charmed, and my mind elated; I feel exalted, and proud that I am a man. But the Gothic art is sublime. On entering a cathedral, I am filled with devotion and with awe; I am lost to the actualities that surround me, and my whole being expands into the infinite; earth and air, nature and art, all swell up into eternity, and the only sensible impression left, is 'that I am nothing!'
> ("General Character of the Gothic Literature and Art")

Amid the arching vaults of a Gothic cathedral, Coleridge recognizes something larger, greater than man; his insignificance is positive. Devotion and awe result in the sublime, whose sources he found in the vastness, magnificence, infinity, and, perhaps, the obscurity of a

Gothic cathedral. Without faith or transcendent values, Coleridge's self-annihilation would be meaningless, or, as Victor Hugo sees it, grotesque and potentially comic (Preface to *Cromwell*, 1827). Wolfgang Kayser elaborates by saying that to Hugo, the grotesque is opposed to the sublime:

> [The grotesque represents] one pole of a tension whose opposite pole is constituted by the sublime. . . . The true depth of the grotesque is revealed only by its confrontation with its opposite, the sublime. For just as the sublime (in contrast with the beautiful) guides our view toward a loftier, supernatural world, the ridiculously distorted and monstrously horrible ingredients of the grotesque point to an inhuman, nocturnal, and abysmal realm.
>
> (*The Grotesque in Art and Literature*, 1763)

In Gothic short fiction and poetry, the grotesque gradually displaces the sublime as a source of terror as evil is fixed in the consciousness of man himself and he sees himself as meaningless in an absurd universe. When the forces of science, technology, and religion cannot control or destroy the grotesque—whether vampire, misshapen dwarf, or dark monkey—then conflict becomes futile and alienation and despair naturally follow.

In twentieth-century Gothic literature, particularly in the masterpieces of Southern American fiction, the horror is self-created and the terror is as pervasive as selfishness. Everywhere we look in the fiction of Flannery O'Connor, for example, we find the anxiety, malice, narcissism, physical and mental distortions of grotesques. Mr. Paradise with his "purple bulge" is one of several idiosyncratic human beings who comprise the nightmare world of "The River." In "Suffer the Little Children," Stephen King's Robert, "phantomish, distorted," and the class full of other loveless grotesques with "heavy, smothering," staring eyes recall the flat decoration of monstrous figures twisted in frozen motion in the art of the first grotesques. In their narrative contexts, as in their artistic representation, the distinctions between these grotesques and the other normal figures are deliberately blurred. Mr. and Mrs. Ashfield are revealed to be as inhuman as their abysmal name implies; Miss Sidley "changes" almost as fearfully as any of her students. In their alienation, Miss Sidley, Harry Ashfield, and even Eudora Welty's Clytie despair, and destroy themselves. Not madness nor innocence nor loneliness can counter the *Angst* of these characters. Their sense of the emptiness of a world without love or faith, their soul sickness, their real and presumed alienation, admit violence to everyday life, a life their creators may see quite differently. When the source of terror is both within us and around us, there is no permanent escape, but the art of Gothic literature safely affords us a temporary stay against confusion.

Fortunately, it is no longer barbaric to admit drawing pleasure from literature evoking delicious fear. Identifying the sources which inspire it has become as much the task of the reader as of the writer. The works which follow participate in a tradition which is finely drawn, like the art or architecture which shares their heritage; perhaps they will suggest more than Munch's scream as a response to the evil image.

Critical Studies of the Gothic

Arvin, Newton. "Melville and the Gothic Novel," *New England Quarterly*, 22 (1949), 33–48.

Barasch, Frances K. *The Grotesque: A Study in Meanings*. The Hague: Mouton, 1971.

Birkhead, Edith. *The Tale of Terror: A Study of the Gothic Romance*. London, 1921; reprinted New York: Russell and Russell, 1963.

Briggs, Julia. *Night Visitors: The Rise and Fall of the English Ghost Story*. London: Faber, 1977.

Burke, Edmund. *A Philosophical Enquiry into the Origin of our Ideas of the Sublime and Beautiful* (1756), ed. J. T. Boulton. London: Routledge and Kegan Paul, 1958.

Clarens, Carlos. *An Illustrated History of the Horror Films*. New York: Putnam, 1967.

Clark, Kenneth McKenzie, Lord. *The Gothic Revival: An Essay in the History of Taste*. London: Constable and Co., Ltd., 1928.

Clayborough, Arthur. *The Grotesque in English Literature*. Oxford: Clarendon Press, 1965.

Coleridge, Samuel Taylor. *General Character of the Gothic Literature and Art* in *Complete Works*. New York: Harper, 1853.

Conant, Martha Pike. *The Oriental Tale in England*. New York, 1908; reprinted Octagon Books, 1967.

Cooke, Arthur L. "Some Side Lights on the Theory of the Gothic Romance." *Modern Language Quarterly*, 12 (1951), 429–436.

Dalziel, Margaret. *Popular Fiction 100 Years Ago: An Unexplored Tract of Literary History*. London: Cohen and West, 1957.

Drake, Nathan. *The Gleaner: A Series of Periodical Essays . . . From Scarce or Neglected Volumes*. 4 vols. London: W. Davies, 1811.

———. *Literary Hours, or Sketches Critical and Narrative*. London: W. Davies, 1800; reprinted New York: Garland, 1970.

Ehrenpreis, Anne Henry, ed. *The Literary Ballad*. London: Edward Arnold, 1966.

Fiedler, Leslie A. *Freaks: Myth and Image of the Secret Self*. New York: Simon and Schuster, 1978.

———. *Love and Death in the American Novel*, rev. ed. New York: Dell, 1966.

Foster, James R. *History of the Pre-Romantic Novel in England.* New York: Modern Language Association of America, 1949.

Frankl, Paul. *The Gothic: Literary Sources and Interpretations through Eight Centuries.* Princeton: Princeton University Press, 1960.

Garber, Frederick. "Meaning and Mode in Gothic Fiction," in *Studies in Eighteenth-Century Culture* (1973), 155–169, ed. Harold E. Pagliaro. Cleveland: The Press of Case Western University.

Gose, Elliott B., Jr. *Imagination Indulged: The Irrational in the Nineteenth Century Novel.* Montreal: Queen's University (McGill) Press, 1972.

Hart, Francis. "The Experience of Character in the English Gothic Novel," in *Experience in the Novel*, ed. Roy Harvey Pearce. New York: Columbia University Press, 1968.

Hays, Peter. *The Limping Hero: Grotesques in Literature.* New York: New York University Press, 1971.

Hazlitt, William. *Lectures on the English Comic Writers, and Fugitive Writings* (1819). New York: E. P. Dutton and Co., 1910.

Hoffman, Daniel G. *Form and Fable in American Fiction.* New York: Oxford University Press, 1961.

Hoffman, Frederick J. *The Art of Southern Fiction: A Study of Some Modern Novelists.* Carbondale, Ill.: Southern Illinois University Press, 1967.

Holland, Norman. *5 Readers Reading.* New Haven: Yale University Press, 1975.

Hume, Robert. "Gothic Versus Romantic: A Revaluation of the Gothic Novel," *Publications of the Modern Language Association*, 84 (March 1969), 282–290.

Hurd, Richard. *Letters on Chivalry and Romance, with the Third Elizabethan Dialogue* (1762), ed. Edith J. Morley. London: Henry Froude, 1911.

Jacobs, Robert D., ed. *Sources of Terror to the American Imagination. Studies in the Literary Imagination*, 7, 1 (Spring 1974). Eight essays.

Kayser, Wolfgang. *The Grotesque in Art and Literature*, trans. Ulrich Wiesstein. Bloomington, Ind.: University of Indiana Press, 1963; reprinted New York: McGraw-Hill, 1966.

Keech, James M. "The Survival of the Gothic Response," *Studies in the Novel*, 6 (1974), 130–144.

Kennard, Jean E. *Number and Nightmare: Forms of Fantasy in Contemporary Fiction.* Hamden, Conn.: Shoestring Press, 1975.

Kiely, Robert. *The Romantic Novel in England.* Cambridge: Harvard University Press, 1964.

Lawson, Lewis A. "The Grotesque in Recent Southern Fiction," in

Patterns of Commitment in American Literature, ed. Marston LaFrance. Toronto: University of Toronto Press, 1967, pp. 105–179.

Longueil, Alfred. "The Word 'Gothic' in Eighteenth Century Criticism," *Modern Language Notes*, 38 (1923), 453–460.

Lovecraft, H. P. *Supernatural Horror in Literature*. New York: Ben Abramson, 1945.

Lovejoy, A. O. "The First Gothic Revival and the Return to Nature," *Modern Language Notes*, 47, 7 (November 1932), 419–446.

MacAndrew, Elizabeth. *The Gothic Tradition in Fiction*. New York: Columbia University Press, 1979.

Malin, Irving. *New American Gothic*. Carbondale, Ill.: Southern Illinois University Press, 1962.

McKillop, Alan D. "Mrs. Radcliffe on the Supernatural in Poetry," *Journal of English and Germanic Philology*, 31 (1932), 352–359.

McNally, Raymond T., and Radu Florescu, *In Search of Dracula and Vampire Legends*. Greenwich, Conn.: New York Graphic Society, 1972.

Miles, Josephine. "The Language of Ballads," *Romance Philology*, 7 (1953), 1–9.

Miyoshi, Masao. *The Divided Self: A Perspective on the Literature of the Victorians*. New York: New York University Press, 1969.

Moers, Ellen. *Literary Women*. Garden City: Doubleday, 1976.

Monk, Samuel H. *The Sublime: A Study of Critical Theories in XVIII-Century England*. New York: Modern Language Association of America, 1935.

Murphy, John V. *The Dark Angel: Gothic Elements in Shelley's Works*. Cranbury, N. J.: Associated University Presses, Inc., 1975.

Nelson, Lowry, Jr. "Night Thoughts on the Gothic Novel," *Yale Review*, 52 (1963), 236–257.

Northey, Margot. *The Haunted Wilderness: The Gothic and Grotesque in Canadian Fiction*. Toronto: University of Toronto Press, 1976.

O'Connor, Flannery. *Mystery and Manners*, ed. Sally and Robert Fitzgerald. New York: Farrar, Straus, and Giroux, 1957.

O'Connor, William Van. *The Grotesque: An American Genre and Other Essays*. Carbondale, Ill.: Southern Illinois University Press, 1962.

Peckham, Morse. "Toward a Theory of Romanticism," *Publications of the Modern Language Association*, 66 (1951), 5–23.

Praz, Mario. *The Romantic Agony*, tr. Angus Davidson. London: Oxford University Press, 1933; reprinted 1970.

Punter, David. *The Literature of Terror: A History of Gothic Fictions from 1765 to the Present Day*. London and New York: Longmans, 1980.

Radcliffe, Ann. "On the Supernatural in Poetry." *The New Monthly Magazine and Literary Journal*, 16 (1826), 145–150.

Railo, Eino. *The Haunted Castle: A Study of the Elements of English Romanticism*. London: Routledge, 1927.

Rieger, James. "Dr. Polidori and the Genesis of *Frankenstein*," *Studies in English Literature*, 3 (1963), 461–472.

Rudwin, Maximilian Josef. *The Devil in Legend and Literature*. Chicago: Open Court Publishing Co., 1931.

Ruskin, John. "The Nature of Gothic," in *The Stones of Venice*. 3 vols. London: J. M. Dent, 1907.

Sadleir, Michael. " 'All Horrid?': Jane Austen and the Gothic Romance," in *Things Past*. London: Constable, 1944.

———. *The Northanger Novels: A Footnote to Jane Austen*. Oxford: Oxford University Press, 1927.

Scarborough, Dorothy. *The Supernatural in Modern English Fiction*. New York: G. P. Putnam's Sons, 1917.

Scott, Sir Walter. "On the Supernatural in Fictitious Composition," *Foreign Quarterly Review*, I (July and November 1827), 60–98.

Spacks, Patricia Meyer. *The Insistence of Horror: Aspects of the Supernatural in Eighteenth-Century Poetry*. Cambridge: Harvard University Press, 1962.

Spark, Muriel. *Child of Light: A Reassessment of Mary Shelley*. Hadleigh, Essex: Tower Bridge Publications Limited, 1951.

Sterrenburg, Lee. "The Last Man: Anatomy of Failed Revolutions," *Nineteenth-Century Fiction*, 33 (1978), 324–347.

Sullivan, Jack. *Elegant Nightmares: The English Ghost Story from Le Fanu to Blackwood*. Athens, Ohio: Ohio University Press, 1978.

Sullivan, Walter. *Death by Melancholy: Essays on Modern Southern Fiction*. Baton Rouge: Louisiana State University Press, 1972.

Summers, Montague. *A Gothic Bibliography*. London: Fortune Press, 1941.

———. *The Gothic Quest: A History of the Gothic Novel in England*. London, 1957; reissued New York: Russell and Russell, 1966.

Thompson, G. R. *Poe's Fiction: Romantic Irony in the Gothic Tales*. Madison, Wis.: University of Wisconsin Press, 1973.

———, ed. *The Gothic Imagination: Essays in Dark Romanticism*. Pullman, Wash.: Washington State University Press, 1974.

Thorslev, Peter L., Jr. "Incest as a Romantic Symbol," *Comparative Literature Studies*, 2 (1965), 41–58.

Tompkins, J. M. S. *The Popular Novel in England, 1770–1800*. London, 1932; reprinted Lincoln, Neb.: University of Nebraska Press, 1971, and Westport, Conn.: Greenwood Press, 1976.

Varma, Devendra P. *The Gothic Flame: A History of the Gothic Novel in England*. London, 1957; reissued New York: Russell and Russell, 1966.

Walker, I. M. "The 'Legitimate Sources' of Terror in 'The Fall of the House of Usher,' " *Modern Language Review*, 61 (1966), 585–592.

Watt, William W. *Shilling Shockers of the Gothic School: A Study of Chapbook Gothic Romances*. Cambridge, Mass.: Harvard University Press, 1932.

Wolff, Cynthia Griffin. "The Problem of Eighteenth-Century Secular Heroinism," *Modern Language Studies*, 4, 2 (Fall 1974), 35–42.

———. "The Radcliffean Gothic Model: A Form for Feminine Sexuality," *Modern Language Studies*, 9, 3 (Fall 1979), 98–113.

Wolff, Robert Lee. *Strange Stories, and Other Explorations in Victorian Fiction*. Boston: Gambit, 1971.

This picture of Strawberry Hill shows how Horace Walpole, working with John Chute, Richard Bentley, Thomas Pitt, and James Essex, revived the Gothic tradition in architecture in 1749, fifteen years before he published *The Castle of Otranto*. PHOTO: WAYNE ANDREWS.

Daniel Defoe
(ca. 1660-1731)

THE history of the Gothic tale in prose owes more to the psychological and sentimental novelist Samuel Richardson (1689–1761) than to those other claimants to the title of first English novelist, Henry Fielding (1707–1754) and Daniel Defoe. With his protracted and somewhat prurient stories of virgins menaced by dashing rakes, Richardson started a tradition that persists—in the form of the woman's Gothic romance—even now. The debt of Gothicists to Defoe, author of *Robinson Crusoe* (1719) and *Moll Flanders* (1722), is not negligible, however. In composing the short "Apparition of Mrs. Veal" and the lengthy *History and Reality of Apparitions* (1727), Defoe contributed to the journalistic and religious literature on the subject, which described as real the occult phenomena that Gothic novelists were later to exploit for psychological and emotional effects.

Defoe's usual technique, here and in his major novels, is impersonation: he insinuates himself into the role of a London prostitute or a man stranded on a desert island and pretends to be writing an accurate autobiographical account. It was customary in his time to disguise fiction as autobiography, history, or journalism; for, as in the case of Horace Walpole, the eighteenth-century novelist was diffident about presenting this new form of art to a conservative public.

Defoe drew heavily upon his expertise as pamphleteer, journalist, and spy for the concrete details that rendered his make-believe credible. Thus, in "The Apparition of Mrs. Veal," he documents in minute detail the progress of the discourse from Mrs. Bargrave, to a "kinswoman," to a "very sober and understanding gentleman," to a "friend in London," to a "gentleman, a justice of the peace at Maidstone, in Kent," and finally to himself. He provides the very specific and persuasive evidence of an elbow-chair, a scoured silk dress ("newly made up"), a cabinet, and a comb-box. He is punctilious about his dates and times. He inserts the titles of popular contemporary books and poems. He appears to be careful about quoting what was said. And he offers convincing justifications for all of Mrs. Veal's actions and speeches. The illusion is particularly effective when Defoe presents quotations, composed with verisimilitude, as the afterthoughts of Mrs. Bargrave.

Though the account is based on the actual existence of a Mrs. Veal and a Mrs. Bargrave, it is an example of reporting transformed by a meticulous literary imagination. If we may believe his later *History and Reality of Apparitions*, Defoe would have held that Mrs. Veal was a beneficent spirit who had assumed the appearance of the dead woman, rather than the departed soul itself. Besides the artistic motive and the sheer fun of imposing on the public, Defoe had the religious improvement of his audience in mind.

The Apparition of Mrs. Veal (1706)

THE PREFACE

This relation is matter of fact, and attended with such circumstances as may induce any reasonable man to believe it. It was sent by a gentleman, a justice of the peace at Maidstone, in Kent, and a very intelligent person, to his friend in London, as it is here worded; which discourse is attested by a very sober and understanding gentleman, who had it from his kinswoman, who lives in Canterbury, within a few doors of the house in which the within-named Mrs. Bargrave lived; and who he believes to be of so discerning a spirit, as not to be put upon by any fallacy, and who positively assured him that the whole matter as it is related and laid down is really true, and what she herself had in the same words, as near as may be, from Mrs. Bargrave's own mouth, who, she knows, had no reason to invent and publish such a story, or any design to forge and tell a lie, being a woman of much honesty and virtue, and her whole life a course, as it were, of piety. The use which we ought to make of it is to consider that there is a life to come after this, and a just God who will retribute to every one according to the deeds done in the body, and therefore to reflect upon our past course of life we have led in the world; that our time is short and uncertain; and that if we would escape the punishment of the ungodly and receive the reward of the righteous, which is the laying hold of eternal life, we ought, for the time to come to return to God by a speedy repentance, ceasing to do evil, and learning to do well; to seek after God early, if haply He may be found of us, and lead such lives for the future as may be well pleasing in His sight.

This thing is so rare in all its circumstances, and on so good authority, that my reading and conversation have not given me anything like it. It is fit to gratify the most ingenious and serious inquirer. Mrs. Bargrave is the person to whom Mrs. Veal appeared after her death; she is my intimate friend, and I can avouch for her reputation for these last fifteen or sixteen years, on my own knowledge; and I can confirm the good character she had from her youth to the time of my acquaintance; though since this relation she is calumniated by some people that are friends to the brother of Mrs. Veal who appeared, who think the relation of this appearance to be a reflection, and endeavour what they can to blast Mrs. Bargrave's reputation, and to laugh the story out of countenance. But by the circumstances thereof, and the cheerful disposition of Mrs. Bargrave, notwithstanding the ill-usage of a very wicked husband, there is not the least sign of dejection in her face; nor did I ever hear her let fall a desponding or murmuring expression; nay, not when actually under her husband's barbarity, which I have been witness to, and several other persons of undoubted reputation.

Now you must know Mrs. Veal was a maiden gentlewoman of about thirty years of age, and for some years last past had been troubled with fits, which were perceived coming on her by her going off from her discourses very abruptly to some impertinence. She was maintained by an only brother, and kept his house in Dover. She was a very pious woman, and her brother a very sober man, to all appearance; but now he does all he can to null or quash the story. Mrs. Veal was intimately acquainted with Mrs. Bargrave from her childhood. Mrs. Veal's circumstances were then mean; her father did not take care of his children as he ought, so that they were exposed to hardships; and Mrs. Bargrave in those days had as unkind a father, though she wanted neither for food nor clothing, whilst Mrs. Veal wanted for both, insomuch that she would often say, "Mrs. Bargrave, you are not only the best, but the only friend I have in the world; and no circumstance in life shall ever dissolve my friendship." They would often condole each other's adverse fortunes, and read together "Drelincourt upon Death," and other good books; and so, like two Christian friends, they comforted each other under their sorrow.

Some time after Mr. Veal's friends got him a place in the custom-house at Dover, which occasioned Mrs. Veal, by little and little, to fall off from her intimacy with Mrs. Bargrave, though there never was any such thing as a quarrel; but an indifferency came on by degrees, till at last Mrs. Bargrave had not seen her in two years and a half; though about a twelve-month of the time Mrs. Bargrave had been absent from Dover, and this last half-year had been in Canterbury about two months of the time, dwelling in a house of her own.

In this house, on the 8th of September 1705, she was sitting alone, in the forenoon, thinking over her unfortunate life, and arguing herself into a due resignation to Providence, though her condition seemed hard. "And," said she, "I have been provided for hitherto, and doubt not but I shall be still; and am well satisfied that my afflictions shall end when it is most fit for me"; and then took up her sewing-work, which she had no sooner done but she hears a knocking at the door. She went to see who was there, and this proved to be Mrs. Veal, her old friend, who was in a riding-habit; at that moment of time the clock struck twelve at noon.

"Madam," says Mrs. Bargrave, "I am surprised to see you, you have been so long a stranger"; but told her she was glad to see her, and offered to salute her, which Mrs. Veal complied with, till their lips almost touched; and then Mrs. Veal drew her hand across her own eyes and said, "I am not very well," and so waived it. She told Mrs. Bargrave she was going a journey, and had a great mind to see her first. "But," says Mrs. Bargrave, "how came you to take a journey alone? I am amazed at it, because I know you have a good brother." "Oh," says Mrs. Veal, "I gave my brother the slip, and came away, because I had so great a desire to see you before I took my journey." So Mrs. Bargrave went in with her into another room within the first, and Mrs. Veal set her down in an elbow-chair, in which Mrs. Bargrave was sitting when she heard Mrs. Veal knock. Then says Mrs. Veal, "My dear friend, I am come to renew our old friendship again, and beg your pardon for my breach of it; and if you can forgive me, you are the best of women." "Oh," says Mrs. Bargrave, "do not mention such a thing. I have not had an uneasy thought about it; I can easily forgive it." "What did you think of me?" said Mrs. Veal. Says Mrs. Bargrave, "I thought you were like the rest of the world, and that prosperity had made you forget yourself and me." Then Mrs. Veal reminded Mrs. Bargrave of the many friendly offices she did in her former days, and much of the conversation they had with each other in the times of their adversity; what books they read, and what comfort in particular they received from "Drelincourt's Book of Death," which was the best, she said, on that subject ever written. She also mentioned Dr. Sherlock, the two Dutch books which were translated, written upon Death, and several others; but Drelincourt, she said, had the clearest notions of death and of the future state of any who had handled that subject. Then she asked Mrs. Bargrave whether she had Drelincourt. She said, "Yes." Says Mrs. Veal, "Fetch it." And so Mrs. Bargrave goes upstairs and brings it down. Says Mrs. Veal, "Dear Mrs. Bargrave, if the eyes of our faith were as open as the eyes of our body, we should see numbers of angels about us for our guard. The notions we have of heaven now are nothing like to what it is, as Drelincourt says. Therefore be comforted under your afflictions, and believe that the Almighty has a particular regard to you, and that your afflictions are marks of God's favour; and when they have done the business they are sent for, they shall be removed from you. And believe me, my dear friend, believe what I say to you, one minute of future happiness will infinitely reward you for all your sufferings; for I can never believe" (and claps her hands upon her knees with great earnestness, which indeed ran through most of her discourse) "that ever God will suffer you to spend all your days in this afflicted state; but be assured that your afflictions shall leave you, or you them, in a short time." She spake in that pathetical and heavenly manner that Mrs. Bargrave wept several times, she was so deeply affected with it.

Then Mrs. Veal mentioned Dr. Horneck's "Ascetick," at the end of which he gives an account of the lives of the primitive Christians. Their pattern she recommended to our imitation, and said, "Their conversation was not like this of our age; for now," says she, "there is nothing but frothy, vain discourse, which is far different from theirs. Theirs was to edification, and to build one another up in faith; so that they were not as we are, nor are we as they were; but," said she, "we ought to do as they did. There was a hearty friendship among them; but where is it now to be found?" Says Mrs. Bargrave, "It is hard indeed to find a true friend in these days." Says Mrs. Veal, "Mr. Norris has a fine copy of verses, called 'Friendship in Perfection,' which I wonderfully admire. Have you seen the book?" says Mrs. Veal. "No," says Mrs. Bargrave, "but I have the verses of my own writing out." "Have you?" says Mrs. Veal; "then fetch them." Which she did from above-stairs, and offered them to Mrs. Veal to read, who refused, and waived the thing, saying holding down her head would make it ache; and then desired Mrs. Bargrave to read them to her, which she did. As they were admiring "Friendship" Mrs. Veal said, "Dear Mrs. Bargrave, I shall love you for ever." In these verses there is twice used the word Elysian. "Ah!" says Mrs. Veal, "these poets have such names for heaven!" She would often draw her hand across her own eyes and say, "Mrs. Bargrave, do not you think I am mightily impaired by my fits?" "No," says Mrs. Bargrave, "I think you look as well as ever I knew you."

After all this discourse, which the apparition put in much finer words than Mrs. Bargrave said she could pretend to, and as much more than she can remember, for it cannot be thought that an hour and three-quarters' conversation could be retained, though the main of it she thinks she does, she said to Mrs. Bargrave she would have her write a letter to her brother, and tell him she would have him give rings to such and such, and that there was a purse of gold in her cabinet, and that she would have two broad pieces given to her cousin Watson.

Talking at this rate, Mrs. Bargrave thought that a fit was coming upon her, and so placed herself in a chair just before her knees, to keep her from falling to the ground, if her fits should occasion it (for the elbow-chair, she thought, would keep her from falling on either side); and to divert Mrs. Veal, as she thought, took hold of her gown-sleeve several times and commended it. Mrs. Veal told her it was a scoured silk, and newly made up. But for all this, Mrs. Veal persisted in her request, and told Mrs. Bargrave that she must not deny her, and she would have her tell her brother all their conversation when she had an opportunity. "Dear Mrs. Veal," said Mrs. Bargrave, "this seems so impertinent that I cannot tell how to comply with it; and what a mortifying story will our conversation be to a young gentleman? Why," says Mrs. Bargrave, "it is much better, methinks, to do it yourself." "No," says Mrs. Veal, "though it seems impertinent to you now, you will see more reason for it hereafter." Mrs. Bargrave then, to satisfy her importunity, was going to fetch a pen and ink, but Mrs. Veal said, "Let it alone now, but do it when I am gone; but you must be sure to do it"; which was one of the last things she enjoined her at parting. So she promised her.

Then Mrs. Veal asked for Mrs. Bargrave's daughter. She said she was not at home, "But if you have a mind to see her," says Mrs. Bargrave, "I'll send for her." "Do," says Mrs. Veal. On which she left her, and went to a neighbour's to see for her; and by the time Mrs. Bargrave was returning, Mrs. Veal was got without the door into the street, in the face of the beast-market, on a Saturday (which is market-day), and stood ready to part. As soon as Mrs. Bargrave came to her, she asked her why she was in such haste. She said she must be going, though perhaps she might not go her journey until Monday; and told Mrs. Bargrave she hoped she should see her again at her cousin Watson's before she went whither she was going. Then she said she would take her leave of her, and walked from Mrs. Bargrave in her view, till a turning interrupted the sight of her, which was three-quarters after one in the afternoon.

Mrs. Veal died the 7th of September, at twelve o'clock at noon, of her fits, and had not above four hours' sense before death, in which time she received the sacrament. The next day after Mrs. Veal's appearing, being Sunday, Mrs. Bargrave was so mightily indisposed with a cold and a sore throat, that she could not go out that day; but on Monday morning she sent a person to Captain Watson's to know if Mrs. Veal was there. They wondered at Mrs. Bargrave's inquiry, and sent her word that she was not there, nor was expected. At this answer, Mrs. Bargrave told the maid she had certainly mistook the name or made some blunder. And though she was ill, she put on her hood, and went herself to Captain Watson's, though she knew none of the family, to see if Mrs. Veal was there or not. They said they wondered at her asking, for that she had not been in town; they were sure, if she had, she would have been there. Says Mrs. Bargrave, "I am sure she was with me on Saturday almost two hours." They said it was impossible; for they must have seen her, if she had. In comes Captain Watson while they are in dispute, and said that Mrs. Veal was certainly dead, and her escutcheons were making. This strangely surprised Mrs. Bargrave, when she sent to the person immediately who had the care of them, and found it true. Then she related the whole story to Captain Watson's family, and what gown she had on, and how striped, and that Mrs. Veal told her it was scoured. Then Mrs. Watson cried out, "You have seen her indeed, for none knew but Mrs. Veal and myself that the gown was scoured." And Mrs. Watson owned that she described the gown exactly; "for," said she, "I helped her to make it up." This Mrs. Watson blazed all about the town, and avouched the demonstration of the truth of Mrs. Bargrave's seeing Mrs. Veal's apparition; and Captain Watson carried two gentlemen immediately to Mrs. Bargrave's house to hear the relation from her own mouth. And when it spread so fast that gentlemen and persons of quality, the judicious and sceptical part of the world, flocked in upon her, it at last became such a task that she was forced to go out of the way; for they were in general extremely well satisfied of the truth of the thing, and plainly saw that Mrs. Bargrave was no hypochondriac, for she always appears with such a cheerful air and pleasing mien, that she has gained the favour and esteem of all the gentry, and it is thought a great favour if they can but get the relation from her own mouth. I should have told you before that Mrs. Veal told Mrs. Bargrave that her sister and brother-in-law were just come down from London to see her. Says Mrs. Bargrave, "How came you to order matters so strangely?" "It could not be helped," said Mrs. Veal. And her brother and sister did come to see her, and entered the town of Dover just as Mrs. Veal was expiring. Mrs. Bargrave asked her whether she would drink some tea. Says Mrs. Veal, "I do not care if I do; but I'll warrant you this mad fellow" (meaning Mrs. Bargrave's husband) "has broken all your trinkets." "But," says Mrs. Bargrave, "I'll get something to drink in for all that." But Mrs. Veal waived it, and said, "It is no matter; let it alone;" and so it passed.

All the time I sat with Mrs. Bargrave, which was some hours, she recollected fresh sayings of Mrs. Veal. And one material thing

more she told Mrs. Bargrave—that old Mr. Breton allowed Mrs. Veal
ten pounds a year, which was a secret, and unknown to Mrs. Bargrave till Mrs. Veal told it her. Mrs. Bargrave never varies in her
story, which puzzles those who doubt of the truth or are unwilling to
believe it. A servant in the neighbour's yard adjoining to Mrs. Bargrave's house heard her talking to somebody an hour of the time Mrs.
Veal was with her. Mrs. Bargrave went out to her next neighbour's
the very moment she parted with Mrs. Veal, and told her what ravish-
ing conversation she had with an old friend, and told the whole of it.
Drelincourt's "Book of Death" is, since this happened, bought up
strangely. And it is to be observed that, notwithstanding all the trouble and fatigue Mrs. Bargrave has undergone upon this account, she
never took the value of a farthing, nor suffered her daughter to take
anything of anybody, and therefore can have no interest in telling the
story.

But Mr. Veal does what he can to stifle the matter, and said he
would see Mrs. Bargrave; but yet it is certain matter of fact that he
has been at Captain Watson's since the death of his sister, and yet
never went near Mrs. Bargrave; and some of his friends report her to
be a liar, and that she knew of Mr. Breton's ten pounds a year. But
the person who pretends to say so has the reputation of a notorious
liar among persons whom I know to be of undoubted credit. Now,
Mr. Veal is more of a gentleman than to say she lies, but says a bad
husband has crazed her. But she neeeds only present herself and it will
effectually confute that pretence. Mr. Veal says he asked his sister on
her death-bed whether she had a mind to dispose of anything, and she
said no. Now, the things which Mrs. Veal's apparition would have
disposed of were so trifling, and nothing of justice aimed at in their
disposal, that the design of it appears to me to be only in order to
make Mrs. Bargrave so to demonstrate the truth of her appearance,
as to satisfy the world of the reality thereof as to what she had seen
and heard, and to secure her reputation among the reasonable and
understanding part of mankind. And then again Mr. Veal owns that
there was a purse of gold; but it was not found in her cabinet, but in a
comb-box. This looks improbable; for that Mrs. Watson owned that
Mrs. Veal was so very careful of the key of the cabinet that she would
trust nobody with it; and if so, no doubt she would not trust her gold
out of it. And Mrs. Veal's often drawing her hand over her eyes, and
asking Mrs. Bargrave whether her fits had not impaired her, looks to
me as if she did it on purpose to remind Mrs. Bargrave of her fits, to
prepare her not to think it strange that she should put her upon
writing to her brother to dispose of rings and gold, which looks so
much like a dying person's request; and it took accordingly with Mrs.
Bargrave, as the effects of her fits coming upon her; and was one of

the many instances of her wonderful love to her and care of her that she should not be affrighted, which indeed appears in her whole management, particularly in her coming to her in the daytime, waiving the salutation, and when she was alone, and then the manner of her parting to prevent a second attempt to salute her.

Now, why Mr. Veal should think this relation a reflection, as it is plain he does by his endeavouring to stifle it, I cannot imagine, because the generality believe her to be a good spirit, her discourse was so heavenly. Her two great errands were to comfort Mrs. Bargrave in her affliction, and to ask her forgiveness for the breach of friendship, and with a pious discourse to encourage her. So that after all to suppose that Mrs. Bargrave could hatch such an invention as this from Friday noon to Saturday noon, supposing that she knew of Mrs. Veal's death the very first moment, without jumbling circumstances, and without any interest too, she must be more witty, fortunate, and wicked too than any indifferent person, I dare say, will allow. I asked Mrs. Bargrave several times if she was sure she felt the gown. She answered modestly "If my senses are to be relied on, I am sure of it." I asked her if she heard a sound when she clapped her hands upon her knees. She said she did not remember she did, but said she appeared to be as much a substance as I did, who talked with her. "And I may," said she, "be as soon persuaded that your apparition is talking to me now as that I did not really see her; for I was under no manner of fear, and received her as a friend, and parted with her as such. I would not," says she, "give one farthing to make any one believe it; I have no interest in it. Nothing but trouble is entailed upon me for a long time, for aught I know; and had it not come to light by accident, it would never have been made public." But now she says she will make her own private use of it, and keep herself out of the way as much as she can; and so she has done since. She says she had a gentleman who came thirty miles to her to hear the relation, and that she had told it to a room full of people at a time. Several particular gentlemen have had the story from Mrs. Bargrave's own mouth.

This thing has very much affected me, and I am as well satisfied as I am of the best grounded matter of fact. And why we should dispute matter of fact because we cannot solve things of which we have no certain or demonstrative notions, seems strange to me. Mrs. Bargrave's authority and sincerity alone would have been undoubted in any other case.

Dr. John Aikin
(1746-1822)
and
Anna Laetitia Aikin Barbauld
(1743-1825)

IN "Sir Bertrand" and the essay which serves as its preface, John and Anna Laetitia Aikin identify and exemplify the principal theoretical tenets of the early Gothic tradition. The Benevolist view of man's potential for good finds expression in Sir Bertrand's instinctive rush to assist the nameless lady in the shroud. Her kiss and gentle care for her chivalric deliverer recall the protagonists of sentimental novels, the heroes and heroines of feeling and virtue. The final bright scene with music and feasting restores the harmony of the fictional universe, and the beauty of the maiden, anticipated by the demure femininity of the moon, resolves the evil symbolized by the labyrinthine castle, armed figure, and animated statues. If true to the Gothic mode, her speech would mix gratitude and explanation of horrors with tears, identification of heritage, and promises of idyllic marriage, perhaps to Sir Bertrand himself. The air of unreality in the tale diminishes neither the fear nor the suspense; instead, the remoteness of the setting and the strangeness of the events and devices intensify the reader's sympathy and heighten the suspense. Moral judgment is suspended for sympathy, making Sir Bertrand's unmotivated adventure potentially tragic and certainly heroic despite his slight characterization and the incompleteness of the tale. Pity for him and fear of his situation evoke a catharsis, here less earned and Aristotelian than magically brought about by the unexplained transformation of maiden and scene. According to the Aikins, the pleasure grows as the supernatural terror increases; natural terror satisfies only curiosity and produces more pain than pleasure. Aikin stops the narration before explaining the sources of Sir Bertrand's fear and amazement, leaving the mystery to be resolved in the imagination of his readers, in any manner they choose—sentimental, tragic, or sublime.

Dr. John Aikin is less often remembered for writing "Sir Bertrand" than for being the brother and supporter of Anna Laetitia Aikin Barbauld, who participated in writing the collection from which this essay and tale come. Her poetry and prose, essays and criticism, lessons and hymns for children, and editorial and biographical labors earned her a deserved reputation as one of the first distinguished women of letters. It is clear from her niece's memoir of Mrs. Barbauld that "Sir Bertrand" should be ascribed to Dr. John Aikin, but collaboration on the essay is likely. He insisted on publishing his sister's early poetry and continued his support and encouragement throughout Mrs. Barbauld's career. For "Sir Bertrand," Dr. John Aikin proves himself a thoughtful early admirer of Horace Walpole's manner and method in *The Castle of Otranto* (1764), and in "On the Pleasure Derived from Objects of Terror," he and his sister prepare the way for the delightful fears of later evil images.

On the Pleasure Derived from Objects of Terror; with Sir Bertrand, a Fragment (1773)

That the exercise of our benevolent feelings, as called forth by the view of human afflictions, should be a source of pleasure, cannot appear wonderful to one who considers that relation between the moral and natural system of man, which has connected a degree of satisfaction with every action or emotion productive of the general welfare. The painful sensation immediately arising from a scene of misery, is so much softened and alleviated by the reflex sense of self-approbation attending virtuous sympathy, that we find, on the whole, a very exquisite and refined pleasure remaining, which makes us desirous of again being witnesses of such scenes, instead of flying from them with disgust and horror. It is obvious how greatly such a provision must conduce to the ends of mutual support and assistance. But the apparent delight with which we dwell upon objects of pure terror, where our moral feelings are not in the least concerned, and no passion seems to be excited but the depressing one of fear, is a paradox of the heart, much more difficult of solution.

The reality of this source of pleasure seems evident from daily observation. The greediness with which the tales of ghosts and goblins, of murders, earthquakes, fires, shipwrecks, and all the most terrible disasters attending human life, are devoured by every ear, must have been generally remarked. Tragedy, the most favourite work of fiction, has taken a full share of those scenes; "it has supt full with horrors"—and has, perhaps, been more indebted to them for public admiration than to its tender and pathetic part. The ghost of Hamlet, Macbeth descending into the witches' cave, and the tent scene in Richard, command as forcibly the attention of our souls as the parting of Jaffeir and Belvidera, the fall of Wolsey, or the death of Shore. The inspiration of *terror* was by the antient critics assigned as the peculiar province of tragedy; and the Greek and Roman tragedians have introduced some extraordinary personages for this purpose: not only the shades of the dead, but the furies, and other fabulous inhabitants of the infernal regions. Collins, in his most poetical ode to Fear, has finely enforced this idea.

> Tho' gently Pity claim her mingled part,
>   Yet all the thunders of the scene are thine.

The old Gothic romance and the Eastern tale with their genii, giants, enchantments, and transformations, however a refined critic may censure them as absurd and extravagant, will ever retain a most powerful influence on the mind, and interest the reader independently of all peculiarity of taste. Thus the great Milton, who had a strong bias to these wildnesses of the imagination, has with striking effect made the stories "of forests and enchantments drear," a favourite subject with his *Penseroso*; and had undoubtedly their awakening images strong upon his mind when he breaks out,

> Call up him that left half-told
> The story of Cambuscan bold; &c.

How are we then to account for the pleasure derived from such objects? I have often been led to imagine that there is a deception in these cases; and that the avidity with which we attend is not a proof of our receiving real pleasure. The pain of suspense, and the irresistible desire of satisfying curiosity, when once raised, will acount for our eagerness to go quite through an adventure, though we suffer actual pain during the whole course of it. We rather choose to suffer the smart pang of a violent emotion than the uneasy craving of an unsatisfied desire. That this principle, in many instances, may involuntarily carry us through what we dislike, I am convinced from experience. This is the impulse which renders the poorest and most insipid narrative interesting when once we get fairly into it; and I have frequently felt it with regard to our modern novels, which, if lying on my table, and taken up in an idle hour, have led me through the most tedious and disgusting pages, while, like Pistol eating his leek, I have swallowed and execrated to the end. And it will not only force us through dullness, but through actual torture—through the relation of a Damien's execution, or an inquisitor's act of faith. When children, therefore, listen with pale and mute attention to the frightful stories of apparitions, we are not, perhaps, to imagine that they are in a state of enjoyment, any more than the poor bird which is dropping into the mouth of the rattlesnake—they are chained by the ears, and fascinated by curiosity. This solution, however, does not satisfy me with respect to the well-wrought scenes of artificial terror which are formed by a sublime and vigorous imagination. Here, though we know before-hand what to expect, we enter into them with eagerness, in quest of a pleasure already experienced. This is the pleasure constantly attached to the excitement of surprise from new and wonderful objects. A strange and unexpected event awakens the mind, and keeps it on the stretch; and where the agency of invisible beings is introduced, of "forms unseen, and mightier far than we," our imagination, darting forth, explores with rapture the new world which is laid open to its view, and rejoices in the expansion of its powers. Passion and fancy co-operating elevate the soul to its highest pitch; and the pain of terror is lost in amazement.

Hence, the more wild, fanciful, and extraordinary are the circumstances of a scene of horror, the more pleasure we receive from it; and where they are too near common nature, though violently borne by curiosity through the adventure, we cannot repeat it or reflect on it, without an over-balance of pain. In the *Arabian Nights* are many most striking examples of the terrible joined with the marvellous: the story of Aladdin and the travels of Sinbad are particularly excellent. The *Castle of Otranto* is a very spirited modern attempt upon the same plan of mixed terror, adapted to the model of Gothic romance. The best conceived, and most strongly worked-up scene of mere natural horror that I recollect, is in Smollett's *Ferdinand Count Fathom*; where the hero, entertained in a lone house in a forest, finds a corpse just slaughtered in the room where he is sent to sleep, and the door of which is locked upon him. It may be amusing for the reader to compare his feelings upon these, and from thence form his opinion of the justness of my theory. The following fragment, in which both these manners are attempted to be in some degree united, is offered to entertain a solitary winter's evening.

After this adventure, Sir Bertrand turned his steed towards the woulds, hoping to cross these dreary moors before the curfew. But ere he had proceeded half his journey, he was bewildered by the different tracks, and not being able, as far as the eye could reach, to espy any object but the brown heath surrounding him, he was at length quite uncertain which way he should direct his course. Night overtook him in this situation. It was one of those nights when the moon gives a faint glimmering of light through the thick black clouds of a lowering sky. Now and then she suddenly emerged in full splendor from her veil; and then instantly retired behind it, having just served to give the forlorn Sir Bertrand a wide extended prospect over the desolate waste. Hope and native courage a while urged him to push forwards, but at length the increasing darkness and fatigue of body and mind overcame him; he dreaded moving from the ground he stood on, for fear of unknown pits and bogs, and alighting from his horse in despair, he threw himself on the ground. He had not long continued in that posture when the sullen toll of a distant bell struck his ears—he started up, and turning towards the sound discerned a dim twinkling light. Instantly he seized his horse's bridle, and with cautious steps advanced towards it. After a painful march he was stopped by a moated ditch surrounding the place from whence the light proceeded; and by a momentary glimpse of moon-light he had a full view of a large antique mansion, with turrets at the corners, and an ample porch in the centre. The injuries of time were strongly marked on every thing about it. The roof in various places was fallen in, the battlements were half demolished, and the windows broken and dismantled. A draw-bridge, with a ruinous gate-way at each end, led to the court before the building—He entered, and instantly the light, which proceeded from a window in one of the turrets, glided along and vanished; at the same moment the moon sunk beneath a black cloud, and the night was darker than ever. All was silent—Sir Bertrand fastened his steed under a shed, and approaching the house traversed its whole front with light and slow footsteps—All was still as death—He looked in at the lower windows, but could not distinguish a single object through the impenetrable gloom. After a short parley with himself, he entered the porch, and seizing a massy iron knocker at the gate, lifted it up, and hesitating, at length struck a loud stroke. The noise resounded through the whole mansion with hollow echoes. All was still again—He repeated the strokes more boldly and louder—another interval of silence ensued—A third time he knocked, and a third time all was still. He then fell back to some distance that he might discern whether any light could be seen in the whole front—It again appeared in the same place and quickly glided away as before—at the same instant a deep sullen toll sounded from the turret. Sir Bertrand's heart made a fearful stop—He was a while motionless; then terror impelled him to make some hasty steps towards his steed—but shame stopt his flight; and urged by honour, and resistless desire of finishing the adventure, he returned to the porch; and working up his soul to a full steadiness of resolution, he drew forth his sword with one hand, and with the other lifted up the latch of the gate. The heavy door, creaking upon its hinges, reluctantly yielded to his hand—he applied his shoulder to it and forced it open—he quitted it and stept forward—the door instantly shut with a thundering clap. Sir Bertrand's blood was chilled—he turned back to find the door, and it was long ere his trembling hands could seize it—but his utmost strength could not open it again. After several ineffectual attempts, he looked behind him, and beheld, across a hall, upon a large staircase, a pale bluish flame which cast a dismal gleam of light around. He again summoned forth his courage and advanced towards it—It retired. He came to the foot of the stairs, and after a moment's deliberation ascended. He went slowly up, the flame retiring before him, till he came to a wide gallery—The flame proceeded along it, and he followed in silent horror, treading lightly, for the echoes of his footsteps startled him. It led him to the foot of another staircase, and then vanished—At the same instant another toll sounded from the turret—Sir Bertrand felt it strike upon his heart. He was now in total darkness, and with his arms extended, began to ascend the second staircase. A dead cold hand met his left hand and firmly grasped it, drawing him forcibly forwards—he endeavoured to disengage himself, but could not—he made a furious blow with his sword, and instantly a loud shriek pierced his ears, and the dead hand was left powerless in his—He dropt it, and rushed forwards with a desperate valour. The stairs were narrow and winding, and interrupted by frequent breaches, and loose fragments of stone. The staircase grew narrower and narrower, and at length terminated in a low iron grate. Sir Bertrand pushed it open—it led to an intricate winding passage, just large enough to admit a person upon his hands and knees. A faint glimmering of light served to show the nature of the place. Sir Bertrand entered—A deep hollow groan resounded from a distance through the vault—He went forwards, and proceeding beyond the first turning, he discerned the same blue flame which had before conducted him. He followed it. The vault, at length, suddenly opened into a lofty gallery, in the midst of which a figure appeared, compleatly armed, thrusting forwards the bloody stump of an arm, with a terrible frown and menacing gesture, and brandishing a sword in his hand. Sir Bertrand undauntedly sprung forwards; and aiming a fierce blow at the figure, it instantly vanished, letting fall a massy iron key. The flame now rested upon a pair of ample folding doors at the end of the gallery. Sir Bertrand went up to it, and applied the key to a brazen lock—with difficulty he turned the bolt—instantly the doors flew open, and discovered a large apartment, at the end of which was a coffin rested upon a bier, with a taper burning on each side of it. Along the room on both sides were gigantic statues of black marble, attired in the Moorish habit, and holding enormous sabres in their right hands. Each of them reared his arm, and advanced one leg forwards, as the knight entered; at the same moment the lid of the coffin flew open, and the bell tolled. The flame still glided forwards, and Sir Bertrand resolutely followed, till he arrived within six paces of the coffin. Suddenly, a lady in a shroud and black veil rose up in it, and stretched out her arms towards him—at the same time the statues clashed their sabres and advanced. Sir Bertrand flew to the lady and clasped her in his arms—she threw up her veil and kissed his lips; and instantly the whole building shook as with an earthquake, and fell asunder with a horrible crash. Sir Bertrand was thrown into a sudden trance, and on recovering, found himself seated on a velvet sofa, in the most magnificent room he had ever seen, lighted with innumerable tapers, in lustres of pure crystal. A sumptuous banquet was set in the middle. The doors opening to soft music, a lady of incomparable beauty, attired with amazing splendor entered, surrounded by a troop of gay nymphs more fair than the Graces— She advanced to the knight, and falling on her knees thanked him as her deliverer. The nymphs placed a garland of laurel upon his head, and the lady led him by the hand to the banquet, and sat beside him. The nymphs placed themselves at the table, and a numerous train of servants entering, served up the feast; delicious music playing all the time. Sir Bertrand could not speak for astonishment—he could only return their honours by courteous looks and gestures. After the banquet was finished, all retired but the lady, who leading back the knight to the sofa, addressed him in these words:

Ann Radcliffe
(1764-1823)

A S if to perpetuate the tradition that Horace Walpole had inaugu-
rated, Ann Ward—later Radcliffe—was born in 1764, almost
simultaneously with *The Castle of Otranto*. Her life was rather un-
eventful (Christina Rossetti was forced to give up a projected biogra-
phy for lack of material); but her rich imagination enabled her to
describe the scenery of southern France and Italy, which she had not
visited, the internecine strife in Italy, which had little foundation in
fact, and the lives of banditti as well as monks and nuns, which all
became somehow intertwined. Having begun her literary career with
The Castles of Athlin and Dunbayne (1789) and sharpened her
talents with *A Sicilian Romance* (1790) and *The Romance of the
Forest* (1791), she completed her magnum opus, *The Mysteries of
Udolpho*, in 1794. Here, in the course of four volumes and fifty-seven
chapters of prose and verse, Mrs. Radcliffe unraveled the story of the
sensitive and vulnerable Emily St. Aubert, her amiable but somewhat
undisciplined lover Valancourt, and their sinister foe Montoni. The
enormous popularity of this book persisted well into the nineteenth
century: Keats referred to it, Coleridge reviewed it, and Anna
Laetitia Barbauld praised it warmly in a volume she edited for the
series *The British Novelists* (1810).

Not every writer shared in the general enthusiasm. Jane Austen's
Northanger Abbey (1818), though sympathetic to the entertainment
such stories could offer, pointed up the perils of taking Gothic attitudes too seriously by contrasting imaginary, "Gothic," evils with
more mundane terrors that were "mournfully superior in reality."
Austen's heroine, Catherine Morland, praises her favorite Gothic
novels as "horrid." It is doubtful that Mrs. Radcliffe would have
approved of this term. In her essay "On the Supernatural in Poetry,"
published in *The New Monthly Magazine* in 1826, a sympathetic
speaker makes a distinction between horror and terror that relates the
latter both to the sublime and to the truly "Gothic." Besides invoking
the sublime, the essay raises many other issues of interest to Mrs.
Radcliffe's contemporaries. It shows her allegiance to the sentimental
tradition in its discussion of feeling, sympathy, melancholy, and

sensibility. It displays her taste for the picturesque in its emphasis on "scenery." In a close analysis of a scene from *Hamlet*, it shows Mrs. Radcliffe almost as much in harmony with modern methods of close reading as she is with the great concepts of her time, especially those of Edmund Burke: "Every minute circumstance of the scene . . . contributes to excite some feeling of dreariness, or melancholy, or solemnity, or expectation, in unison with, and leading on toward that high curiosity and thrilling awe with which we witness the conclusion of the scene."

The poem "The Snow-Fiend," published posthumously with *Gaston de Blondeville*, shows Mrs. Radcliffe evoking the Gothic emotion of terror by means of personification, a frequent rhetorical device for representing the supernatural in poetry, especially in the eighteenth century. Besides the Snow-Fiend himself, the personifications of Disease, Want, Fear, Danger, Woe, and Death reveal Mrs. Radcliffe's kinship with poets like William Collins, while the imagery of icy wastes, inhabited by these figures, suggests the frozen desolation in Mary Shelley's *Frankenstein* and Coleridge's "Ancient Mariner." Published in the same volume as "The Snow-Fiend," the companion poems "December's Eve, Abroad" and "December's Eve, At Home" bring up, first, means of exciting Gothic emotions and, then, means of counteracting them. The first poem describes sinister presences at work in the dead of winter and in an alien environment. The "gothic grace" of the eastern window evokes the architectural tradition to enhance the gloom of the dying year, and the other images of "requiem" and "winding sheet" anticipate Hardy's farewell to the departing century in "The Darkling Thrush" (1901). The second poem suggests that Ann Radcliffe knew the antidote to the Gothic as well as her critic Jane Austen knew it: the familiar pleasures of domestic life rob Gothic stories of their threatening power and make them, however terrifying, sources of entertainment.

The Snow-Fiend (1826)

Hark! to the Snow-Fiend's voice afar
That shrieks upon the troubled air!
Him by that shrilly call I know—
Though yet unseen, unfelt below—
And by the mist of livid grey,　　　　　　　　　　5
That steals upon his onward way.

He from the ice-peaks of the North
In sounding majesty comes forth;
Dark amidst the wondrous light,
That streams o'er all the northern night.   10
A wan rime through the airy waste
Marks where unseen his car has past;
And veils the spectre-shapes, his train,
That wait upon his vengeful reign.
Disease and Want and shuddering Fear   15
Danger and Woe and Death are there.
Around his head for ever raves
A whirlwind cold of misty waves.
But oft, the parting surge between,
His visage, keen and white, is seen;   20
His savage eye and paly glare
Beneath a helm of ice appear;
A snowy plume waves o'er the crest,
And wings of snow his form invest.
Aloft he bears a frozen wand;   25
The ice-bolt trembles in his hand;
And ever, when on sea he rides,
An iceberg for his throne provides.
As, fierce, he drives his distant way,
Agents remote his call obey,   30
From half-known Greenland's snow-piled shore
To Newfoundland and Labrador;
O'er solid seas, where nought is scanned
To mark a difference from land,
And sound itself does but explain   35
The desolation of his reign;
The moaning querulous and deep,
And the wild howl's infuriate sweep
Where'er he moves, some note of woe
Proclaims the presence of the foe;   40
While he, relentless, round him flings
The white shower from his flaky wings.
Hark! 'tis his voice:—I shun his call,
And shuddering seek the blazing hall.
O! speak of mirth; O! raise the song!   45
Hear not the fiends, that round him throng!
Of curtained rooms and firesides tell,
Bid Fancy work her genial spell,
That wraps in marvel and delight
December's long tempestuous night;   50

Makes courtly groups in summer bowers
Dance through pale Winter's midnight hours;
And July's eve its rich glow shed
On the hoar wreath, that binds his head;
Or knights on strange adventure bent,   55
Or ladies into thraldom sent;
Whatever gaiety ideal
Can substitute for troubles real.
Then let the storms of Winter sing,
And his sad veil the Snow-Fiend fling,   60
Though wailing lays are in the wind,
They reach not then the 'tranced mind;
Nor murky form, nor dismal sound
May pass the high, enchanted bound!

December's Eve, Abroad (1826)

Awful is Winter's setting sun,
    When, from beneath a sullen cloud,
He eyes his dreary course now run,
    And shrinks within his lurid shroud—

Leaving to Twilight's cold, grey sky   5
    Yon Minister's dark and lonely tower,
That seems to shun the searching eye,
    And vanish with the parting hour.

Dim is the long roof's sloping line,
    Whose airy pinnacles I trace,   10
Point over point, and o'er the shrine
    And eastern window's gothic grace.

While loud the winds, in chorus clear,
    Swell, or in sinking murmurs grieve,
The Ministers of Night I hear   15
    In requiem o'er December's Eve.

Wide o'er the plains and distant wolds
    I see her pall of darkness flow;
And all around, in mighty folds,
    Her winding sheet of new-fallen snow.   20

Farewell December's dismal night!

Appalled I hear thy shrieking breath;
And view, aghast, by glimmering light,
   Thy visage, terrible in death!
Farewell December's dismal night!   25

December's Eve, At Home (1826)

Welcome December's cheerful night,
   When the taper-lights appear;
When the piled hearth blazes bright,
   And those we love are circled there!

And, on the soft rug basking lies,   5
   Outstretched at ease, the spotted friend,
With glowing coat and half-shut eyes,
   Where watchfulness and slumber blend.

Welcome December's cheerful hour,
   When books, with converse sweet combined,   10
And music's many-gifted power
   Exalt, or soothe th' awakened mind.

Then, let the snow-wind shriek aloud,
   And menace oft the guarded sash,
And all his diapason crowd,   15
   As o'er the frame his white wings dash.

He sings of darkness and of storm,
   Of icy cold, and lonely ways;
But, gay the room, the hearth more warm,
   And brighter is the taper's blaze.   20

Then, let the merry tale go round,
   And airy songs the hours deceive;
And let our heart-felt laughs resound,
   In welcome to December's Eve!

Mary Alcock
(1742-1798)

THE slim volume of *Poems* 1799 by Mary Alcock includes a few prose pieces and a sentimental introduction written by a devoted niece, one Joanna Hughes. None of the poems, she says, was intended for the press; they were composed instead "either to amuse a leisure hour, to gratify an absent friend, or for the sublimer purpose of pouring out her heart in praises and thanksgivings to her God." Joanna Hughes obviously regarded her aunt as a kind of saint, martyred by a long illness suffered by "a soul equal to the severest trials, and capable of the sublimest efforts." Her poetry was free from the vanity of publication except in the instance of one "Fragment," which was published in a spirit of benevolent charity for the imprisoned debtors at Ilchester and Newgate. The reverence with which Joanna Hughes regarded her aunt makes understandable her dismissal of the prose pieces as "trifles," and her failure to note the lighthearted humor of her "Receipt for Writing a Novel."

Mary Alcock was the daughter of Dr. Denison Cumberland, Bishop of Kilmore, in Ireland, and of Joanna Bentley, daughter of the great scholar Richard Bentley (1662–1742), master of Trinity College, Cambridge. Her brother, Richard Cumberland (1732–1811), who lost his patrimony when forced to repay the ministry for a large debt, wrote poetry, essays, comedies, theological tracts, biographies, and novels. His many love stories attracted a large audience of female readers, perhaps because, as Sir Walter Scott comments, he threw "upon the softer sex the task of wooing."

In a prose piece called "The Scribbler, 1st Paper" at the end of the volume of *Poems*, Mary Alcock satirizes the kind of sentimental fiction her brother wrote, as well as the Gothic fiction of others. The piece recounts a scene and conversation in a circulating library, where a young lady exclaims her delight in the self-tormenting joys of seven-volume novels which destroy the appetite, prevent sleep, blind her with crying, and break her heart. Another young woman earnestly requests the last volume of *The Monk*. The "blasphemy and obscenity" and "contagion of evil" in that book tempt the speaker-critic to warn her against complying with the "follies and vices" inspired by the literary "fashions of the world." A meditation follows on the "calamities" Gothic novels inflict on their readers. The speaker recognizes the relationship between Gothic novelists and readers of Gothic fiction as a "system of distressing and terrifying on one side, and chusing to be distressed on the other." The "Receipt for Writing a Novel" among the poems is then recommended for "the advantage of young beginners."

The poem testifies to the popularity and similarity of Gothic fiction in the late eighteenth century. Love, jealousy, horror, duels, hysteria, fainting fits, sighs, groans, fevers, and madness are essential ingredients in plots replete with terrors, accidents, villains, and imprisonment. The length must run to volumes; digressions must abound; and the conclusion must surprise, perhaps with the revelation of hidden identities, and always with an eventual marriage. The recipe's brisk iambic tetrameter rhymed couplets express the same lack of variety which Alcock scorns in the novels she satirizes. The Gothic machinery she lightheartedly lists fits Ann Radcliffe's *Mysteries of Udolpho* (1794) so exactly that Alcock's poem may be regarded as a poetic anticipation of Jane Austen's more subtle parody in *Northanger Abbey* (1818). Writers of Gothic romances today, for example Daphne du Maurier and Victoria Holt, vary this recipe slightly for their confections, but the essential ingredients remain the same.

A Receipt for Writing a Novel (1799)

Would you a fav'rite novel make,
Try hard your reader's heart to break,
For who is pleas'd, if not tormented?
(Novels for that were first invented).
'Gainst nature, reason, sense, combine   5
To carry on your bold design,
And those ingredients I shall mention,
Compounded with your own invention,
I'm sure will answer my intention.
Of love take first a due proportion—   10
It serves to keep the heart in motion:
Of jealousy a powerful zest,
Of all tormenting passions best;
Of horror mix a copious share,
And duels you must never spare;   15

Hysteric fits at least a score,
Or, if you find occasion, more;
But fainting fits you need not measure,
The fair ones have them at their pleasure;
Of sighs and groans take no account,   20
But throw them in to vast amount;
A frantic fever you may add,
Most authors make their lovers mad;
Rack well your hero's nerves and heart,
And let your heroine take her part;   25
Her fine blue eyes were made to weep,
Nor should she ever taste of sleep;
Ply her with terrors day or night,
And keep her always in a fright,
But in a carriage when you get her,   30
Be sure you fairly overset her;
If she will break her bones—why let her:
Again, if e'er she walks abroad,
Of course you bring some wicked lord,
Who with three ruffians snaps his prey,   35
And to a castle speeds away;
There close confin'd in haunted tower,
You leave your captive in his power,
Till dead with horror and dismay,
She scales the walls and flies away.   40

　　Now you contrive the lovers meeting,
To set your reader's heart a beating,
But ere they've had a moment's leisure,
Be sure to interrupt their pleasure;
Provide yourself with fresh alarms   45
To tear 'em from each other's arms;
No matter by what fate they're parted,
So that you keep them broken-hearted.

　　A cruel father some prepare
To drag her by her flaxen hair;   50
Some raise a storm, and some a ghost,
Take either, which may please you most.
But this you must with care observe,
That when you've wound up every nerve
With expectation, hope and fear,   55
Hero and heroine must disappear.
Some fill one book, some two without 'em,

And ne'er concern their heads about 'em,
This greatly rests the writer's brain,
For any story, that gives pain,   60
You now throw in—no matter what,
However foreign to the plot,
So it but serves to swell the book,
You foist it in with desperate hook—
A masquerade, a murder'd peer,   65
His throat just cut from ear to ear—
A rake turn'd hermit—a fond maid
Run mad, by some false loon betray'd—
These stores supply the female pen,
Which writes them o'er and o'er again,   70
And readers likewise may be found
To circulate them round and round.

    Now at your fable's close devise
Some grand event to give surprize—
Suppose your hero knows no mother—   75
Suppose he proves the heroine's brother—
This at one stroke dissolves each tie,
Far as from east to west they fly:
At length when every woe's expended,
And your last volume's nearly ended,   80
Clear the mistake, and introduce
Some tatt'ling nurse to cut the noose,
The spell is broke—again they meet
Expiring at each other's feet;
Their friends lie breathless on the floor—   85
You drop your pen; you can no more—
And ere your reader can recover,
They're married—and your history's over.

Matthew Gregory Lewis
(1775-1818)

LEWIS closely parodies his traditional ballad "Alonzo the Brave" in his humorous rendering of "Giles Jollup the Grave." In identical structures, both ballads use familiar Gothic themes of the broken pledge, betrayed love, and the surprise appearance of the lover or his ghost at the wedding feast. Such themes and devices were often exploited by later writers of Gothic fiction, and, in some, like Irving's "Spectre Bridegroom," humorous elements color the melodrama. Here, in seventeen economical five-line stanzas, Lewis advances both stories by dialogue, tableaux, and simple action. The heavy-handed parody maintains the dramatic possibilities of the central situation, but substitutes amusing details for the macabre ones of the traditional ballad. In place of a skeleton's head behind a visor, Giles Jollup reveals a bare skull beneath a wig worn backward; potboys instead of worms run in and out; and indigestion replaces death as punishment for the heroine's moral failures, "falsehood and pride." In "Giles Jollup," Brave Alonzo's ominous ghost is reduced to a short pea-green and blue apothecary wearing a dirty apron and snuff-stained cravat and ruffles. The addition of comic details in "Giles Jollup" trivializes the serious subject of "Alonzo the Brave," lightens the tone, and modernizes the traditional medieval effects. In manner these ballads anticipate *Northanger Abbey* (1818), Jane Austen's skillful parody of Ann Radcliffe's *The Mysteries of Udolpho* (1794). Both Austen's *Northanger Abbey* and Alcock's "A Receipt for Writing a Novel" (1799) mock the assumptions behind Gothic romances, satirize their sensationalism, and comically caricature their heroes and heroines.

M. G. Lewis first published "Alonzo the Brave" in *The Monk* (1796), the wildly popular novel of questionable artistic merit which gave him his nickname. In *The Monk* the heroine, Antonia, reads this ballad from a volume of "old Spanish Ballads" just prior to a visitation from her mother's ghost (Book III, chapter 2). Out of the context of *The Monk*, "Alonzo the Brave" enjoyed a large readership and was even adapted for the stage as ballet, pantomime, and melodrama. All the necessary machinery of the Gothic romance—skeleton-knight, shrieking maiden, wealthy suitor, haunted castle, supernatural effects—combined in a unified tone, earn "Alonzo the Brave" high praise as Monk Lewis's finest ballad achievement.

Alonzo the Brave and Fair Imogine (1796)

A warrior so bold and a virgin so bright
   Conversed, as they sat on the green;
They gazed on each other with tender delight:
Alonzo the Brave was the name of the knight,
   The maid's was the Fair Imogine. 5

——"And, oh!" said the youth, "since to-morrow I go
   To fight in a far-distant land,
Your tears for my absence soon leaving to flow,
Some other will court you, and you will bestow
   On a wealthier suitor your hand."—— 10

——"Oh! hush these suspicions," Fair Imogine said,
   "Offensive to love and to me!
For, if you be living, or if you be dead,
I swear by the Virgin, that none in your stead
   Shall husband of Imogine be. 15

"And if e'er for another my heart should decide,
   Forgetting Alonzo the Brave,
God grant, that, to punish my falsehood and pride,
Your ghost at the marriage may sit by my side,
May tax me with perjury, claim me as bride, 20
   And bear me away to the grave!"——

To Palestine hasten'd the hero so bold;
   His love she lamented him sore:
But scarce had a twelvemonth elapsed, when behold,
A Baron all cover'd with jewels and gold 25
   Arrived at Fair Imogine's door.

His treasure, his presents, his spacious domain,
   Soon made her untrue to her vows:
He dazzled her eyes; he bewilder'd her brain;
He caught her affections so light and so vain, 30
   And carried her home as his spouse.

And now had the marriage been bless'd by the priest;
  The revelry now was begun:
The tables they groan'd with the weight of the feast;
Nor yet had the laughter and merriment ceased,   35
  When the bell of the castle toll'd—"one!"

Then first with amazement Fair Imogine found
  That a stranger was placed by her side:
His air was terrific; he utter'd no sound;
He spoke not, he moved not, he look'd not around,   40
  But earnestly gazed on the bride.

His vizor was closed, and gigantic his height;
  His armour was sable to view:
All pleasure and laughter were hush'd at his sight;
The dogs, as they eyed him, drew back in affright;   45
  The lights in the chamber burnt blue!

His presence all bosoms appear'd to dismay;
  The guests sat in silence and fear:
At length spoke the bride, while she trembled:—"I pray,
Sir Knight, that your helmet aside you would lay,   50
  And deign to partake of our cheer."——

The lady is silent: the stranger complies,
  His vizor he slowly unclosed:
Oh! then what a sight met Fair Imogine's eyes!
What words can express her dismay and surprise,   55
  When a skeleton's head was exposed!

All present then utter'd a terrified shout;
  All turn'd with disgust from the scene.
The worms they crept in, and the worms they crept out,
And sported his eyes and his temples about,   60
  While the spectre address'd Imogine:

"Behold me, thou false one! behold me!" he cried;
  "Remember Alonzo the Brave!
God grants, that, to punish thy falsehood and pride,
My ghost at thy marriage should sit by thy side,   65
Should tax thee with perjury, claim thee as bride,
  And bear thee away to the grave!"

Thus saying, his arms round the lady he wound,
  While loudly she shriek'd in dismay;
Then sank with his prey through the wide-yawning ground: 70
Nor ever again was Fair Imogine found,
  Or the spectre who bore her away.

Not long lived the Baron: and none since that time
   To inhabit the castle presume;
For chronicles tell, that, by order sublime,   75
There Imogine suffers the pain of her crime,
   And mourns her deplorable doom.

At midnight four times in each year does her sprite,
   When mortals in slumber are bound,
Array'd in her bridal apparel of white,   80
Appear in the hall with the skeleton-knight,
   And shriek as he whirls her around.

While they drink out of skulls newly torn from the grave,
   Dancing round them pale spectres are seen:
Their liquor is blood, and this horrible stave   85
They howl:—"To the health of Alonzo the Brave,
   And his consort, the False Imogine!"

Giles Jollup the Grave, and Brown Sally Green (1801)

*This is a Parody upon the foregoing Ballad. I must acknowledge,
however, that the lines printed in italics, and the idea of making an
apothecary of the knight, and a brewer of the baron, are taken from a
parody which appeared in one of the news-papers, under the title of
"Pil-Garlic the Brave and Brown Celestine."*

A Doctor so prim and a sempstress so tight
   Hob-a-nobb'd in some right marasquin;
They suck'd up the cordial with truest delight:
Giles Jollup the Grave *was just five feet in height,*
   And four feet the brown Sally Green.   5

——"And as," said Giles Jollup, "to-morrow I go
   To physic a feverish land,
At some sixpenny hop, or perhaps the Mayor's show,
You'll tumble in love with some smart city beau,
   And with him share your shop in the Strand."——   10

——"Lord! how can you think so?" brown Sally Green said;
   "You must know mighty little of me;
For if you be living, or if you be dead,
I swear, 'pon my honour, that none in your stead
   Shall husband of Sally Green be.   15

LARAMIE JR. HIGH IMC

LARAMIE JR. HIGH IMC

"And if e'er for another my heart should decide,
　　False to you and the faith which I gave,
God grant that, at dinner too amply supplied,
Over-eating may give me a pain in my side;
May your ghost then bring rhubarb to physic the bride,　　20
　　And send her well dosed to the grave!"——

Away went poor Giles, to what place is not told:
　　Sally wept, till she blew her nose sore!
But scarce had a twelvemonth elapsed, when behold!
A brewer, quite stylish, his gig that way roll'd,　　25
　　And stopp'd it at Sally Green's door.

His wealth, his pot-belly, and whisky of cane,
　　Soon made her untrue to her vows;
The steam of strong beer now bewildering her brain,
He caught her while tipsy! denials were vain,　　30
　　So he carried her home as his spouse.

And now the roast beef had been bless'd by the priest,
　　To cram now the guests had begun:
Tooth and nail like a wolf fell the bride on the feast;
Nor yet had the clash of her knife and fork ceased,　　35
　　When a bell—('twas a dustman's)—toll'd—"one!"

Then first with amazement brown Sally Green found
　　That a stranger was stuck by her side:
His cravat and his ruffles with snuff were embrown'd;
He ate not, he drank not, but, turning him round,　　40
　　Sent some pudding away to be fried!!!

His wig was turn'd forwards, and short was his height;
　　His apron was dirty to view:
The women (oh! wondrous) were hush'd at his sight:
The cats, as they eyed him, drew back (well they might),　　45
　　For his body was pea-green and blue!

Now, as all wish'd to speak, but none knew what to say,
　　They look'd mighty foolish and queer:
At length spoke the bride, while she trembled—"I pray,
Dear Sir, your peruke that aside you would lay,　　50
　　And partake of some strong or small beer!"——

The sempstress is silent; the stranger complies,
　　And his wig from his phiz deigns to pull.
Adzooks! what a squall Sally gave through surprize!
Like a pig that is stuck how she open'd her eyes,　　55
　　When she recognized Jollup's bare skull!

Each miss then exclaim'd, while she turn'd up her snout,
    ——"Sir, your head isn't fit to be seen!"——
The pot-boys ran in, and the pot-boys ran out,
And couldn't conceive what the noise was about,   60
    While the Doctor address'd Sally Green:

——"Behold me, thou jilt-flirt! behold me!" he cried;
    "You've broken the faith which you gave!
God grants, that, to punish your falsehood and pride,
Over-eating should give you a pain in your side: 65
Come, swallow this rhubarb! I'll physic the bride,
    And send her well-dosed to the grave!"——

Thus saying, the physic her throat he forced down,
    In spite of whate'er she could say;
Then bore to his chariot the damsel so brown;   70
Nor ever again was she seen in that town,
    Or the Doctor who whisk'd her away.

Not long liv'd the Brewer: and none since that time
    To make use of the brewhouse presume;
For 'tis firmly believed, that, by order sublime,   75
There Sally Green suffers the pain of her crime,
    And bawls to get out of the room.

At midnight four times in each year does her sprite
    With shrieks make the chamber resound:
—"I won't take the rhubarb!" she squalls in affright,   80
While, a cup in his left hand, a draught in his right,
    Giles Jollup pursues her around!

With wigs so well powder'd, their fees while they crave,
    Dancing round them twelve doctors are seen:
They drink chicken-broth, while this horrible stave   85
Is twang'd through each nose—"To Giles Jollup the Grave,
    And his patient, the sick Sally Green!"——

Edvard Munch's *Death and the Maiden* might serve to illustrate literary works like Lewis' "Alonzo the Brave" and Irving's "Spectre Bridegroom," which describe relationships between mortal women and apparitions from the grave. COURTESY MUSEUM OF FINE ARTS, BOSTON.

Samuel Taylor Coleridge
(1772-1834)

WHILE he was completing his well-known "Rime of the Ancient Mariner," Coleridge directed his poetic energy toward "Christabel," where he consciously concerned himself with the preternatural rather than the supernatural of "The Rime." This meant that he put aside "invisible things" above nature in favor of such visible things as the abnormal or exceptional. He planned two essays to clarify the distinction, but these were never written. Instead, he wrote only the brief, defensive preface to "Christabel" to explain his new accentual meter and to apologize for the lack of originality in the poem. The "celebrated poets" he mentions there are Sir Walter Scott and Lord Byron, who had both published successful works in the popular Gothic mode. From these and other Gothic masters, Coleridge borrowed for "Christabel" stock characters, superstitions, and the medieval setting with all its attendant eeriness. But Coleridge subordinates the elaborate Gothic machinery of a shocking tale to the consideration of the power of evil incarnate.

Here, as in "The Rime of the Ancient Mariner," his method is to suggest the dreadful by obscuring realities, to imply the worst by avoiding definition. Such deliberate ambiguity, especially in sexual matters, corrects the ingenious though disappointing explanations of Ann Radcliffe and the "libidinous minuteness" of M. G. Lewis, which Coleridge found objectionable. Geraldine is at once a kind of "lamia" figure, moving between mortal and immortal states in the guise of a snake; a vampire, depending on Christabel for her life through a seductive relationship; a sorcerer with a withered bosom and scaly side of ghastly hue; and a lesbian. Whatever she is, she compromises Christabel's innocence, though she does so reluctantly:

> Ah! what a stricken look was hers!
> Deep from within she seems half-way
> To lift some weight with sick assay,
> And eyes the maid and seeks delay.
> (ll. 256–259)

She triumphs in her seduction of both Christabel and Sir Leoline, and there the narrative breaks off. The inconclusive story is without overt moral, and the fear it evokes is without satisfying catharsis.

The preternatural vision seemed too grim for Coleridge to manage after he had heard Wordsworth's faint praise of "Christabel" and learned of his refusal to include it in the second edition of *Lyrical Ballads* (1800). By the time he published the fragment "Christabel" with "Kubla Khan" and "The Pains of Sleep" in 1816, he was known to be an opium addict. The preface to "Kubla Khan" made clear reference to a vision induced by an "anodyne" prescribed for illness; "The Pains of Sleep" gives an almost clinical description of an addict's dream turned nightmare. However, Coleridge does not use the excuse of illness or addiction to explain his failure to complete "Christabel"; instead, he says:

> The reason of my not finishing Christabel is not that I don't know how to do it—for I have, as I always had, the whole plan entire from beginning to end in my mind, but I fear I could not carry on with equal success the execution of the idea, an extremely subtle and difficult one.

> *(Table-Talk)*

From several of his many famous conversations, we learn that Coleridge supposedly intended to complete the story with a series of vanishings and reappearances, impersonations and magical transformations, ending with the happy marriage of Christabel and her once-absent knight and the reconciliation of father and daughter (James Gillman, *The Life of STC*, 1838). Coleridge once said that the story is partly based on the belief that the virtuous of the world save the wicked (Gillman). And yet another account absolves Geraldine of any malevolence at all, claiming that Christabel's suffering is vicarious, endured for her "lover far away" (Ernest Hartley Coleridge, "Christabel," 1907). These contradictary suggestions support the assumption that Coleridge himself, by reason of his addiction or for other cause, labored unsuccessfully to resolve the cosmic confusion of good and evil seen in the finished portion of "Christabel." Nonetheless, we cannot deny that Bard Bracy's dream allegorically identifies Geraldine as serpent and Christabel as dove. In 1804, in one of the seventy notebooks which survived his death, Coleridge used a similar image to describe his own despair:

> I have never loved Evil for its own sake; . . . nor ever sought pleasure for its own sake, but only as the means of escaping from pains that coiled round my mental powers, as a serpent around the body & wings of an Eagle!

> *(The Notebooks, 2368)*

In the "Conclusion to Part II," added to "Christabel" in 1801 and directed to his infant son Hartley, Coleridge writes of the thin line between love and hate, the contradictory nature of human emotions which informs the characters of Geraldine, Sir Leoline, and even Christabel, whose Christlike name is only one of the many masks of reality in this unfinished Gothic poem. Even in its unfinished state, the poem's fearful power and musical effectiveness intrigue and haunt the reader. When Shelley heard "Christabel" read aloud at the Villa Diodati, he rushed from the room in horror; later he confessed that he had imagined seeing eyes in the breasts of one of the ladies (probably his wife, Mary). Byron confirms the truth of this "fit of phantasy" (*Letters* and *Journals* VI, p. 126), and, so by this example of another "competent poet," we are prepared to respond with fearful intensity to the genius of Samuel Taylor Coleridge.

Christabel (1797-1801)

PREFACE

The first part of the following poem was written in the year 1797, at Stowey, in the county of Somerset. The second part, after my return from Germany, in the year 1800, at Keswick, Cumberland. It is probable that if the poem had been finished at either of the former periods, or if even the first and second part had been published in the year 1800, the impression of its originality would have been much greater than I dare at present expect. But for this I have only my own indolence to blame. The dates are mentioned for the exclusive purpose of precluding charges of plagiarism or servile imitation from myself. For there is amongst us a set of critics, who seem to hold, that every possible thought and image is traditional; who have no notion that there are such things as fountains in the world, small as well as great; and who would therefore charitably derive every rill they behold flowing, from a perforation made in some other man's tank. I am confident, however, that as far as the present poem is concerned, the celebrated poets whose writings I might be suspected of having imitated, either in particular passages, or in the tone and the spirit of the whole, would be among the first to vindicate me from the charge, and who, on any striking coincidence, would permit me to address them in this doggerel version of two monkish Latin hexameters.

'Tis mine and it is likewise yours;
But an if this will not do;
Let it be mine, good friend! for I
Am the poorer of the two.

I have only to add that the metre of Christabel is not, properly speaking, irregular, though it may seem so from its being founded on a new principle: namely, that of counting in each line the accents, not the syllables. Though the latter may vary from seven to twelve, yet in each line the accents will be found to be only four. Nevertheless, this occasional variation in number of syllables is not introduced wantonly, or for the mere ends of convenience, but in correspondence with some transition in the nature of the imagery or passion.

PART I

'Tis the middle of night by the castle clock,
And the owls have awakened the crowing cock;
Tu—whit!——Tu—whoo!
And hark, again! the crowing cock,
How drowsily it crew.   5

Sir Leoline, the Baron rich,
Hath a toothless mastiff bitch;
From her kennel beneath the rock
She maketh answer to the clock,
Four for the quarters, and twelve for the hour;   10
Ever and aye, by shine and shower,
Sixteen short howls, not over loud;
Some say, she sees my lady's shroud.

Is the night chilly and dark?
The night is chilly, but not dark.   15
The thin gray cloud is spread on high,
It covers but not hides the sky.
The moon is behind, and at the full;
And yet she looks both small and dull.
The night is chill, the cloud is gray: 20
'Tis a month before the month of May,
And the Spring comes slowly up this way.

The lovely lady, Christabel,
Whom her father loves so well,
What makes her in the wood so late,   25
A furlong from the castle gate?
She had dreams all yesternight

Of her own betrothéd knight;
And she in the midnight wood will pray
For the weal of her lover that's far away.   30

She stole along, she nothing spoke,
The sighs she heaved were soft and low,
And naught was green upon the oak
But moss and rarest misletoe:
She kneels beneath the huge oak tree,   35
And in silence prayeth she.

The lady sprang up suddenly,
The lovely lady, Christabel!
It moaned as near, as near can be,
But what it is she cannot tell.—   40
On the other side it seems to be,
Of the huge, broad-breasted, old oak tree.

The night is chill; the forest bare;
Is it the wind that moaneth bleak?
There is not wind enough in the air   45
To move away the ringlet curl
From the lovely lady's cheek—
There is not wind enough to twirl
The one red leaf, the last of its clan,
That dances as often as dance it can,   50
Hanging so light, and hanging so high,
On the topmost twig that looks up at the sky.

Hush, beating heart of Christabel!
Jesu, Maria, shield her well!
She folded her arms beneath her cloak,   55
And stole to the other side of the oak.
        What sees she there?

There she sees a damsel bright,
Drest in a silken robe of white,
That shadowy in the moonlight shone: 60
The neck that made that white robe wan,
Her stately neck, and arms were bare;
Her blue-veined feet unsandal'd were,
And wildly glittered here and there
The gems entangled in her hair.   65

I guess, 'twas frightful there to see
A lady so richly clad as she—
Beautiful exceedingly!

Mary mother, save me now!
(Said Christabel,) And who art thou?   70

The lady strange made answer meet,
And her voice was faint and sweet:—
Have pity on my sore distress,
I scarce can speak for weariness:
Stretch forth thy hand, and have no fear!   75
Said Christabel, How camest thou here?
And the lady, whose voice was faint and sweet,
Did thus pursue her answer meet:—

My sire is of a noble line,
And my name is Geraldine: 80
Five warriors seized me yestermorn,
Me, even me, a maid forlorn:
They choked my cries with force and fright,
And tied me on a palfrey white.
The palfrey was as fleet as wind,   85
And they rode furiously behind.

They spurred amain, their steeds were white:
And once we crossed the shade of night.
As sure as Heaven shall rescue me,
I have no thought what men they be;   90
Nor do I know how long it is
(For I have lain entranced I wis)
Since one, the tallest of the five,
Took me from the palfrey's back,
A weary woman, scarce alive.   95
Some muttered words his comrades spoke:
He placed me underneath this oak;
He swore they would return with haste;
Whither they went I cannot tell—
I thought I heard, some minutes past,   100
Sounds as of a castle bell.
Stretch forth thy hand (thus ended she),
And help a wretched maid to flee.

Then Christabel stretched forth her hand,
And comforted fair Geraldine: 105
O well, bright dame! may you command
The service of Sir Leoline;
And gladly our stout chivalry
Will he send forth and friends withal
To guide and guard you safe and free   110
Home to your noble father's hall.

She rose: and forth with steps they passed
That strove to be, and were not, fast.
Her gracious stars the lady blest,
And thus spake on sweet Christabel: 115
All our household are at rest,
The hall as silent as the cell;
Sir Leoline is weak in health,
And may not well awakened be,
But we will move as if in stealth,   120
And I beseech your courtesy,
This night, to share your couch with me.

They crossed the moat, and Christabel
Took the key that fitted well;
A little door she opened straight,   125
All in the middle of the gate;
The gate that was ironed within and without,
Where an army in battle array had marched out.
The lady sank, belike through pain,
And Christabel with might and main   130
Lifted her up, a weary weight,
Over the threshold of the gate:
Then the lady rose again,
And moved, as she were not in pain.

So free from danger, free from fear,   135
They crossed the court: right glad they were.
And Christabel devoutly cried
To the lady by her side,
Praise we the Virgin all divine
Who hath rescued thee from thy distress!   140
Alas, alas! said Geraldine,
I cannot speak for weariness.
So free from danger, free from fear,
They crossed the court: right glad they were.

Outside her kennel, the mastiff old   145
Lay fast asleep, in moonshine cold.
The mastiff old did not awake,
Yet she an angry moan did make!
And what can ail the mastiff bitch?
Never till now she uttered yell   150
Beneath the eye of Christabel.
Perhaps it is the owlet's scritch:
For what can ail the mastiff bitch?

They passed the hall, that echoes still,
Pass as lightly as you will!   155

The brands were flat, the brands were dying,
Amid their own white ashes lying;
But when the lady passed, there came
A tongue of light, a fit of flame;
And Christabel saw the lady's eye,   160
And nothing else saw she thereby,
Save the boss of the shield of Sir Leoline tall,
Which hung in a murky old niche in the wall.
O softly tread, said Christabel,
My father seldom sleepeth well.   165

Sweet Christabel her feet doth bare,
And jealous of the listening air
They steal their way from stair to stair,
Now in glimmer, and now in gloom,
And now they pass the Baron's room,   170
As still as death, with stifled breath!
And now have reached her chamber door;
And now doth Geraldine press down
The rushes of the chamber floor.

The moon shines dim in the open air,   175
And not a moonbeam enters here.
But they without its light can see
The chamber carved so curiously,
Carved with figures strange and sweet,
All made out of the carver's brain,   180
For a lady's chamber meet:
The lamp with twofold silver chain
Is fastened to an angel's feet.

The silver lamp burns dead and dim;
But Christabel the lamp will trim.   185
She trimmed the lamp, and made it bright,
And left it swinging to and fro,
While Geraldine, in wretched plight,
Sank down upon the floor below.

O weary lady, Geraldine,   190
I pray you, drink this cordial wine!
It is a wine of virtuous powers;
My mother made it of wild flowers.

And will your mother pity me,
Who am a maiden most forlorn?   195
Christabel answered—Woe is me!
She died the hour that I was born.
I have heard the gray-haired friar tell

How on her death-bed she did say,
That she should hear the castle-bell 200
Strike twelve upon my wedding-day.
O mother dear! that thou wert here!
I would, said Geraldine, she were!

But soon with altered voice, said she—
"Off, wandering mother! Peak and pine! 205
I have power to bid thee flee."
Alas! what ails poor Geraldine?
Why stares she with unsettled eye?
Can she the bodiless dead espy?
And why with hollow voice cries she, 210
"Off, woman, off! this hour is mine—
Though thou her guardian spirit be,
Off, woman, off! 'tis given to me."

Then Christabel knelt by the lady's side,
And raised to heaven her eyes so blue— 215
Alas! said she, this ghastly ride—
Dear lady! it hath wildered you!
The lady wiped her moist cold brow,
And faintly said, " 'tis over now!"

Again the wild-flower wine she drank: 220
Her fair large eyes 'gan glitter bright,
And from the floor whereon she sank,
The lofty lady stood upright:
She was most beautiful to see,
Like a lady of a far countrée. 225

And thus the lofty lady spake—
"All they who live in the upper sky,
Do love you, holy Christabel!
And you love them, and for their sake
And for the good which me befel, 230
Even I in my degree will try,
Fair maiden, to requite you well.
But now unrobe yourself; for I
Must pray, ere yet in bed I lie."

Quoth Christabel, So let it be! 235
And as the lady bade, did she.
Her gentle limbs did she undress,
And lay down in her loveliness.

But through her brain of weal and woe
So many thoughts moved to and fro, 240
That vain it were her lids to close;

So half-way from the bed she rose,
And on her elbow did recline
To look at the lady Geraldine.

Beneath the lamp the lady bowed,   245
And slowly rolled her eyes around;
Then drawing in her breath aloud,
Like one that shuddered, she unbound
The cincture from beneath her breast:
Her silken robe, and inner vest,   250
Dropt to her feet, and full in view,
Behold! her bosom and half her side——
A sight to dream of, not to tell!
O shield her! shield sweet Christabel!

Yet Geraldine nor speaks nor stirs;   255
Ah! what a stricken look was hers!
Deep from within she seems half-way
To lift some weight with sick assay,
And eyes the maid and seeks delay;
Then suddenly, as one defied,   260
Collects herself in scorn and pride,
And lay down by the maiden's side!——
And in her arms the maid she took,
           Ah wel-a-day!
And with low voice and doleful look   265
These words did say:
"In the touch of this bosom there worketh a spell,
Which is lord of thy utterance, Christabel!
Thou knowest to-night, and wilt know to-morrow,
This mark of my shame, this seal of my sorrow;   270
        But vainly thou warrest,
             For this is alone in
        Thy power to declare,
             That in the dim forest
        Thou heard'st a low moaning,   275
And found'st a bright lady, surpassingly fair;
And didst bring her home with thee in love and in charity,
To shield her and shelter her from the damp air."

THE CONCLUSION TO PART I

It was a lovely sight to see
The lady Christabel, when she   280

Was praying at the old oak tree.
    Amid the jagged shadows
    Of mossy leafless boughs,
    Kneeling in the moonlight,
    To make her gentle vows;   285
Her slender palms together prest,
Heaving sometimes on her breast;
Her face resigned to bliss or bale—
Her face, oh call it fair not pale,
And both blue eyes more bright than clear,   290
Each about to have a tear.

With open eyes (ah woe is me!)
Asleep, and dreaming fearfully,
Fearfully dreaming, yet, I wis,
Dreaming that alone, which is—   295
O sorrow and shame! Can this be she,
The lady, who knelt at the old oak tree?
And lo! the worker of these harms,
That holds the maiden in her arms,
Seems to slumber still and mild,   300
As a mother with her child.

A star hath set, a star hath risen,
O Geraldine! since arms of thine
Have been the lovely lady's prison.
O Geraldine! one hour was thine—   305
Thou'st had thy will! By tairn and rill,
The night-birds all that hour were still.
But now they are jubilant anew,
From cliff and tower, tu—whoo! tu—whoo!
Tu—whoo! tu—whoo! from wood and fell!   310

And see! the lady Christabel
Gathers herself from out her trance;
Her limbs relax, her countenance
Grows sad and soft; the smooth thin lids
Close o'er her eyes; and tears she sheds—   315
Large tears that leave the lashes bright!
And oft the while she seems to smile
As infants at a sudden light!

Yea, she doth smile, and she doth weep,
Like a youthful hermitess,   320
Beauteous in a wilderness,
Who, praying always, prays in sleep.

And, if she move unquietly,
Perchance, 'tis but the blood so free
Comes back and tingles in her feet. 325
No doubt, she hath a vision sweet.
What if her guardian spirit 'twere,
What if she knew her mother near?
But this she knows, in joys and woes,
That saints will aid if men will call: 330
For the blue sky bends over all!
    [1797]

PART II

Each matin bell, the Baron saith,
Knells us back to a world of death.
These words Sir Leoline first said,
When he rose and found his lady dead: 335
These words Sir Leoline will say
Many a morn to his dying day!

And hence the custom and law began
That still at dawn the sacristan,
Who duly pulls the heavy bell, 340
Five and forty beads must tell
Between each stroke—a warning knell,
Which not a soul can choose but hear
From Bratha Head to Wyndermere.

Saith Bracy the bard, So let it knell! 345
And let the drowsy sacristan
Still count as slowly as he can!
There is no lack of such, I ween,
As well fill up the space between.
In Langdale Pike and Witch's Lair, 350
And Dungeon-ghyll so foully rent,
With ropes of rock and bells of air
Three sinful sextons' ghosts are pent,
Who all give back, one after t'other,
The death-note to their living brother; 355
And oft too, by the knell offended,
Just as their one! two! three! is ended,
The devil mocks the doleful tale
With a merry peal from Borodale.

The air is still! through mist and cloud 360
That merry peal comes ringing loud;

And Geraldine shakes off her dread,
And rises lightly from the bed;
Puts on her silken vestments white,
And tricks her hair in lovely plight, 365
And nothing doubting of her spell
Awakens the lady Christabel.
"Sleep you, sweet lady Christabel?
I trust that you have rested well."

And Christabel awoke and spied 370
The same who lay down by her side—
O rather say, the same whom she
Raised up beneath the old oak tree!
Nay, fairer yet! and yet more fair!
For she belike hath drunken deep 375
Of all the blessedness of sleep!
And while she spake, her looks, her air
Such gentle thankfulness declare,
That (so it seemed) her girded vests
Grew tight beneath her heaving breasts. 380
"Sure I have sinn'd!" said Christabel,
"Now heaven be praised if all be well!"
And in low faltering tones, yet sweet,
Did she the lofty lady greet
With such perplexity of mind 385
As dreams too lively leave behind.

So quickly she rose, and quickly arrayed
Her maiden limbs, and having prayed
That He, who on the cross did groan,
Might wash away her sins unknown, 390
She forthwith led fair Geraldine
To meet her sire, Sir Leoline.

The lovely maid and the lady tall
Are pacing both into the hall,
And pacing on through page and groom, 395
Enter the Baron's presence-room.

The Baron rose, and while he prest
His gentle daughter to his breast,
With cheerful wonder in his eyes
The lady Geraldine espies, 400
And gave such welcome to the same,
As might beseem so bright a dame!

But when he heard the lady's tale,
And when she told her father's name,

Why waxed Sir Leoline so pale,   405
Murmuring o'er the name again,
Lord Roland de Vaux of Tryermaine?

Alas! they had been friends in youth;
But whispering tongues can poison truth;
And constancy lives in realms above;   410
And life is thorny; and youth is vain;
And to be wroth with one we love
Doth work like madness in the brain.
And thus it chanced, as I divine,
With Roland and Sir Leoline.   415
Each spake words of high disdain
And insult to his heart's best brother:
They parted—ne'er to meet again!
But never either found another
To free the hollow heart from paining—   420
They stood aloof, the scars remaining,
Like cliffs which had been rent asunder;
A dreary sea now flows between;—
But neither heat, nor frost, nor thunder,
Shall wholly do away, I ween,   425
The marks of that which once hath been.

Sir Leoline, a moment's space,
Stood gazing on the damsel's face:
And the youthful Lord of Tryermaine
Came back upon his heart again.   430

O then the Baron forgot his age,
His noble heart swelled high with rage;
He swore by the wounds in Jesu's side
He would proclaim it far and wide,
With trump and solemn heraldry,   435
That they, who thus had wronged the dame,
Were base as spotted infamy!
"And if they dare deny the same,
My herald shall appoint a week,
And let the recreant traitors seek   440
My tourney court—that there and then
I may dislodge their reptile souls
From the bodies and forms of men!"
He spake: his eye in lightning rolls!
For the lady was ruthlessly seized; and he kenned   445
In the beautiful lady the child of his friend!

And now the tears were on his face,
And fondly in his arms he took

Fair Geraldine, who met the embrace,
Prolonging it with joyous look.   450
Which when she viewed, a vision fell
Upon the soul of Christabel,
The vision of fear, the touch and pain!
She shrunk and shuddered, and saw again—
(Ah, woe is me! Was it for thee,   455
Thou gentle maid! such sights to see?)

Again she saw that bosom old,
Again she felt that bosom cold,
And drew in her breath with a hissing sound:
Whereat the Knight turned wildly round,   460
And nothing saw, but his own sweet maid
With eyes upraised, as one that prayed.

The touch, the sight, had passed away,
And in its stead that vision blest,
Which comforted her after-rest   465
While in the lady's arms she lay,
Had put a rapture in her breast,
And on her lips and o'er her eyes
Spread smiles like light!
                          With new surprise,
"What ails then my beloved child?"   470
The Baron said—His daughter mild
Made answer, "All will yet be well!"
I ween, she had no power to tell
Aught else: so mighty was the spell.

Yet he, who saw this Geraldine,   475
Had deemed her sure a thing divine:
Such sorrow with such grace she blended,
As if she feared she had offended
Sweet Christabel, that gentle maid!
And with such lowly tones she prayed   480
She might be sent without delay
Home to her father's mansion.
                          "Nay!

Nay, by my soul!" said Leoline.
"Ho! Bracy the bard, the charge be thine!
Go thou, with music sweet and loud,   485
And take two steeds with trappings proud,
And take the youth whom thou lov'st best
To bear thy harp, and learn thy song,
And clothe you both in solemn vest,

And over the mountains haste along,   490
Lest wandering folk, that are abroad,
Detain you on the valley road.

"And when he has crossed the Irthing flood,
My merry bard! he hastes, he hastes
Up Knorren Moor, through Halegarth Wood,   495
And reaches soon that castle good
Which stands and threatens Scotland's wastes.

"Bard Bracy! bard Bracy! your horses are fleet,
Ye must ride up the hall, your music so sweet,
More loud than your horses' echoing feet!   500
And loud and loud to Lord Roland call,
Thy daughter is safe in Langdale hall!
Thy beautiful daughter is safe and free—
Sir Leoline greets thee thus through me!
He bids thee come without delay   505
With all thy numerous array
And take thy lovely daughter home:
And he will meet thee on the way
With all his numerous array
White with their panting palfreys' foam: 510
And, by mine honour! I will say,
That I repent me of the day
When I spake words of fierce disdain
To Roland de Vaux of Tryermaine!—
—For since that evil hour hath flown,   515
Many a summer's sun hath shone;
Yet ne'er found I a friend again
Like Roland de Vaux of Tryermaine."

The lady fell, and clasped his knees,
Her face upraised, her eyes o'erflowing;   520
And Bracy replied, with faltering voice,
His gracious Hail on all bestowing!—
"Thy words, thou sire of Christabel,
Are sweeter than my harp can tell;
Yet might I gain a boon of thee,   525
This day my journey should not be,
So strange a dream hath come to me,
That I had vowed with music loud
To clear yon wood from thing unblest,
Warned by a vision in my rest!   530
For in my sleep I saw that dove,

That gentle bird, whom thou dost love,
And call'st by thy own daughter's name—
Sir Leoline! I saw the same
Fluttering, and uttering fearful moan,   535
Among the green herbs in the forest alone.
Which when I saw and when I heard,
I wonder'd what might ail the bird;
For nothing near it could I see,
Save the grass and green herbs underneath the old tree.   540

"And in my dream methought I went
To search out what might there be found;
And what the sweet bird's trouble meant,
That thus lay fluttering on the ground.
I went and peered, and could descry   545
No cause for her distressful cry;
But yet for her dear lady's sake
I stooped, methought, the dove to take,
When lo! I saw a bright green snake
Coiled around its wings and neck.   550
Green as the herbs on which it couched,
Close by the dove's its head it crouched;
And with the dove it heaves and stirs,
Swelling its neck as she swelled hers!
I woke; it was the midnight hour,   555
The clock was echoing in the tower;
But though my slumber was gone by,
This dream it would not pass away—
It seems to live upon my eye!
And thence I vowed this self-same day   560
With music strong and saintly song
To wander through the forest bare,
Lest aught unholy loiter there."

Thus Bracy said: the Baron, the while,
Half-listening heard him with a smile;   565
Then turned to Lady Geraldine,
His eyes made up of wonder and love;
And said in courtly accents fine,
"Sweet maid, Lord Roland's beauteous dove,
With arms more strong than harp or song,   570
Thy sire and I will crush the snake!"
He kissed her forehead as he spake,
And Geraldine in maiden wise
Casting down her large bright eyes,
With blushing cheek and courtesy fine   575

She turned her from Sir Leoline;
Softly gathering up her train,
That o'er her right arm fell again;
And folded her arms across her chest,
And couched her head upon her breast,   580
And looked askance at Christabel——
Jesu, Maria, shield her well!

A snake's small eye blinks dull and shy;
And the lady's eyes they shrunk in her head,
Each shrunk up to a serpent's eye,   585
And with somewhat of malice, and more of dread,
At Christabel she looked askance!—
One moment—and the sight was fled!
But Christabel in dizzy trance
Stumbling on the unsteady ground   590
Shuddered aloud, with a hissing sound;
And Geraldine again turned round,
And like a thing, that sought relief,
Full of wonder and full of grief,
She rolled her large bright eyes divine   595
Wildly on Sir Leoline.

The maid, alas! her thoughts are gone,
She nothing sees—no sight but one!
The maid, devoid of guile and sin,
I know not how, in fearful wise,   600
So deeply had she drunken in
That look, those shrunken serpent eyes,
That all her features were resigned
To this sole image in her mind:
And passively did imitate   605
That look of dull and treacherous hate!
And thus she stood, in dizzy trance,
Still picturing that look askance
With forced unconscious sympathy
Full before her father's view——   610
As far as such a look could be
In eyes so innocent and blue!

And when the trance was o'er, the maid
Paused awhile, and inly prayed:
Then falling at the Baron's feet,   615
"By my mother's soul do I entreat
That thou this woman send away!"
She said: and more she could not say:

For what she knew she could not tell,
O'er-mastered by the mighty spell. 620

Why is thy cheek so wan and wild,
Sir Leoline? Thy only child
Lies at thy feet, thy joy, thy pride,
So fair, so innocent, so mild;
The same, for whom thy lady died! 625
O by the pangs of her dear mother
Think thou no evil of thy child!
For her, and thee, and for no other,
She prayed the moment ere she died:
Prayed that the babe for whom she died, 630
Might prove her dear lord's joy and pride!
    That prayer her deadly pangs beguiled,
        Sir Leoline!
    And wouldst thou wrong thy only child,
        Her child and thine? 635

Within the Baron's heart and brain
If thoughts, like these, had any share,
They only swelled his rage and pain,
And did but work confusion there.
His heart was cleft with pain and rage, 640
His cheeks they quivered, his eyes were wild,
Dishonoured thus in his old age;
Dishonoured by his only child,
And all his hospitality
To the wronged daughter of his friend 645
By more than woman's jealousy
Brought thus to a disgraceful end—
He rolled his eye with stern regard
Upon the gentle minstrel bard,
And said in tones abrupt, austere— 650
"Why, Bracy! dost thou loiter here?
I bade thee hence!" The bard obeyed;
And turning from his own sweet maid,
The aged knight, Sir Leoline,
Led forth the lady Geraldine! 655
  [1800]

THE CONCLUSION TO PART II

A little child, a limber elf,
Singing, dancing to itself,

A fairy thing with red round cheeks,
That always finds, and never seeks,
Makes such a vision to the sight   660
As fills a father's eyes with light;
And pleasures flow in so thick and fast
Upon his heart, that he at last
Must needs express his love's excess
With words of unmeant bitterness.   665
Perhaps 'tis pretty to force together
Thoughts so all unlike each other;
To mutter and mock a broken charm,
To dally with wrong that does no harm.
Perhaps 'tis tender too and pretty   670
At each wild word to feel within
A sweet recoil of love and pity.
And what, if in a world of sin
(O sorrow and shame should this be true!)
Such giddiness of heart and brain   675
Comes seldom save from rage and pain,
So talks as it's most used to do.

George Gordon, Lord Byron
(1788-1824)

THE celebrity of Lord Byron was guaranteed at once with the publication of the first two cantos of *Childe Harold's Pilgrimage* in
1812, when, as he said, "I awoke and found myself famous." The
hero resembled Byron—aristocratic, ambitious, willful, proud, yet
burdened by a hopeless sorrow. "The Giaour" in the following year
had a similar titular hero—passionate, pessimistic, self-exiled, dark,
handsome, melancholy, and mysterious. The world-weariness of such
heroes was a legacy of Horace Walpole's and Ann Radcliffe's villains
—selfish, rash, strong, and Satanic. Such a combination of characteristics blurred the Gothic distinctions of hero and villain and made
the self-tortured superman a new Gothic hero, a Byronic hero. He
moves through wild and gloomy settings, attempts the impossible for
selfish aims, and, as a victim of destiny or fate, endures punishment
from unexplained terrors. The Gothic machinery of castles, curses,
and demons remains; but now it is complemented by a titanic nature,
an agonizing remorse, and a metaphysical morbidity. The mind of the
Byronic hero colors every perception, whether physical, emotional, or
intellectual. As Manfred himself says:

> The Mind which is immortal makes itself
> Requital for its good or evil thoughts,—
> Is its own origin of ill and end—
> And its own place and time. . . .
> (III. iv. 129–132)

The curse of Manfred and of man is to be his own "proper Hell!" (I.
i. 251) Each spirit in Manfred is almost an imaginative projection of
self confirming repeatedly what Manfred already knows: he is alone
in a comfortless life. Manfred's triumphant insistence upon the independence and power of the mind makes him a victor even in death,
the inevitable end of an apparently futile life. His death is a release
and so is not more difficult than life. In many ways Manfred exemplifies Sartre's existential paradox that man is "condemned to be free."

Byron qualifies this ambiguous position by investing energy in his verse as a testament to Manfred's strength and his own affirmation of an intense life. He displays the full range of his poetic capabilities in *Manfred*, his longest sustained work of serious poetry. His artistic achievement parallels Manfred's assertion of will, but *Manfred* is not Byron's poetic or philosophical credo, and the hero is not wholly like himself. Manfred combines characteristics of Faust, Prometheus, Cain, the Wandering Jew; and he recalls Byron's own earlier figures of the poet of *Childe Harold*, and the Giaour, the cursed vampire-like hero who avenges the murder of his beloved in the verse tale *The Giaour* (1812). Manfred is, most essentially, man, "half dust, half deity." If the voice of Manfred carries despair to a melodramatic extreme, it does so because the guilty, tortured, remorseful outcast can see no hope, can exercise no moderation. Byron, however, can and does, as proved by his satiric and ironic works: *English Bards and Scotch Reviewers* (1809), *A Vision of the Last Judgment* (1822), and *Don Juan* (1818–1824).

Byron's reviewers accused him of modeling *Manfred* on Marlowe's *Tragical History of Doctor Faustus* (1604) or Goethe's *Faust* (I, 1808; II, 1832), both of which have opening soliloquies remarkably like Byron's. In defense, Byron said: "The devil may take both the Faustus's, German and English—I have taken neither" (Letter to John Murray, 23 October 1817). He admits to having heard M. G. ("Monk") Lewis translate scenes from Goethe's *Faust* at Diodati late in the summer of 1816, but he never read or heard Marlowe's *Doctor Faustus*. The inspiration for *Manfred* Byron attributes to the majestic Alps, "the *Staubach* & the *Jungfrau*—and something else—much more than Faustus" (Letter to Murray, 7 June 1820). The same succession of ideas about mad scientists and criminals, defiant mortals, and ambitious immortals that led Mary Shelley to write *Frankenstein* led Byron to *Manfred*. The Aeschylean *Prometheus* gave him the challenging of the gods, the motif of eternal suffering for inexpiable crime, but Manfred's remorse is more like his own Giaour's than Faust's. Byron duplicates in *Manfred* the Giaour's love for Leila even to the detail of the hero's vision of his love after her death. He adds the suggestion of incest to *Manfred*, a clear reference to his affection for his half sister, Augusta Leigh. Percy Bysshe Shelley regarded a suggestion of incest as "a very poetical circumstance" whether based on fact or not. Neither love nor knowledge brings Manfred happiness, though both seem briefly to have consoled him earlier. The Chamois Hunter's primitivism and the Abbot's religion have no appeal; both require an innocence which has been lost before the poem begins. There is no salvation for Manfred beyond the assertion of his indomitable will, the will of the archetypal Byronic hero.

Manfred: A Dramatic Poem (1817)

"There are more things in heaven and earth, Horatio,
Than are dreamt of in your philosophy."
—*Hamlet*, Act i. Scene 5, Lines 166, 167.

ACT I

SCENE I

(*Manfred alone. Scene, a Gothic Gallery.—Time, Midnight.*)

Manfred. The lamp must be replenished, but even then
   It will not burn so long as I must watch:
   My slumbers—if I slumber—are not sleep,
   But a continuance of enduring thought,
   Which then I can resist not: in my heart
   There is a vigil, and these eyes but close
   To look within; and yet I live, and bear
   The aspect and the form of breathing men.
   But Grief should be the Instructor of the wise;
   Sorrow is Knowledge: they who know the most   10
   Must mourn the deepest o'er the fatal truth,
   The Tree of Knowledge is not that of Life.
   Philosophy and science, and the springs
   Of Wonder, and the wisdom of the World,
   I have essayed, and in my mind there is
   A power to make these subject to itself—
   But they avail not: I have done men good,
   And I have met with good even among men—
   But this availed not: I have had my foes,
   And none have baffled, many fallen before me—   20
   But this availed not:—Good—or evil—life—
   Powers, passions—all I see in other beings,
   Have been to me as rain unto the sands,
   Since that all-nameless hour. I have no dread,
   And feel the curse to have no natural fear,
   Nor fluttering throb, that beats with hopes or wishes,
   Or lurking love of something on the earth.
   Now to my task.—
               Mysterious Agency!
Ye Spirits of the unbounded Universe!

Whom I have sought in darkness and in light—   30
Ye, who do compass earth about, and dwell
In subtler essence—ye, to whom the tops
Of mountains inaccessible are haunts,
And Earth's and Ocean's caves familiar things—
I call upon ye by the written charm
Which gives me power upon you—Rise! Appear!

                                        (*A pause*)

They come not yet.—Now by the voice of him
Who is the first among you—by this sign,
Which makes you tremble—by the claims of him
Who is undying,—Rise! Appear!——Appear!   40
                                        (*A pause*)

If it be so.—Spirits of Earth and Air,
Ye shall not so elude me! By a power,
Deeper than all yet urged, a tyrant-spell,
Which had its birthplace in a star condemned,
The burning wreck of a demolished world,
A wandering hell in the eternal Space;
By the strong curse which is upon my Soul,
The thought which is within me and around me,
I do compel ye to my will.—Appear!
        (*A star is seen at the darker end of the gallery: it is
            stationary; and a voice is heard singing.*)

First Spirit. Mortal! to thy bidding bowed,   50
    From my mansion in the cloud,
    Which the breath of Twilight builds,
    And the Summer's sunset gilds
    With the azure and vermilion,
    Which is mixed for my pavilion;
    Though thy quest may be forbidden,
    On a star-beam I have ridden,
    To thine adjuration bowed:
    Mortal—be thy wish avowed!

Voice of the Second Spirit. Mont Blanc is the Monarch of   60
        mountains;
    They crowned him long ago
On a throne of rocks, in a robe of clouds,
    With a Diadem of snow.
Around his waist are forests braced,
    The Avalanche in his hand;
But ere it fall, that thundering ball
    Must pause for my command.

The Glacier's cold and restless mass
    Moves onward day by day;
But I am he who bids it pass,   70
    Or with its ice delay.
I am the Spirit of the place,
    Could make the mountain bow
And quiver to his caverned base—
    And what with me would'st *Thou*?

Voice of the Third Spirit. In the blue depth of the waters,
    Where the wave hath no strife,
Where the Wind is a stranger,
    And the Sea-snake hath life,
Where the Mermaid is decking   80
    Her green hair with shells,
Like the storm on the surface
    Came the sound of thy spells;
O'er my calm Hall of Coral
    The deep Echo rolled—
To the Spirit of Ocean
    Thy wishes unfold!

Fourth Spirit. Where the slumbering Earthquake
    Lies pillowed on fire,
And the lakes of bitumen   90
    Rise boilingly higher;
Where the roots of the Andes
    Strike deep in the earth,
As their summits to heaven
    Shoot soaringly forth;
I have quitted my birthplace,
    Thy bidding to bide—
Thy spell hath subdued me,
    Thy will be my guide!

Fifth Spirit. I am the Rider of the wind,   100
    The Stirrer of the storm;
The hurricane I left behind
    Is yet with lightning warm;
To speed to thee, o'er shore and sea
    I swept upon the blast:
The fleet I met sailed well—and yet
    'Twill sink ere night be past.

Sixth Spirit. My dwelling is the shadow of the Night,
    Why doth thy magic torture me with light?

Seventh Spirit. The Star which rules thy destiny   110
   Was ruled, ere earth began, by me:
   It was a World as fresh and fair
   As e'er revolved round Sun in air;
   Its course was free and regular,
   Space bosomed not a lovelier star.
   The Hour arrived—and it became
   A wandering mass of shapeless flame,
   A pathless Comet, and a curse,
   The menace of the Universe;
   Still rolling on with innate force,   120
   Without a sphere, without a course,
   A bright deformity on high,
   The monster of the upper sky!
   And Thou! beneath its influence born—
   Thou worm! whom I obey and scorn—
   Forced by a Power (which is not thine,
   And lent thee but to make thee mine)
   For this brief moment to descend,
   Where these weak Spirits round thee bend
   And parley with a thing like thee—   130
   What would'st thou, Child of Clay! with me?

The Seven Spirits. Earth—ocean—air—night—mountains—winds—
    thy Star,
   Are at thy beck and bidding, Child of Clay!
   Before thee at thy quest their Spirits are—
    What would'st thou with us, Son of mortals—say?
Manfred. Forgetfulness——
First Spirit.   Of what—of whom—and why?
Manfred. Of that which is within me; read it there—
   Ye know it—and I cannot utter it.
Spirit. We can but give thee that which we possess:
   Ask of us subjects, sovereignty, the power   140
   O'er earth—the whole, or portion—or a sign
   Which shall control the elements, whereof
   We are the dominators,—each and all,
   These shall be thine.
Manfred.   Oblivion—self-oblivion!
   Can ye not wring from out the hidden realms
   Ye offer so profusely—what I ask?
Spirit. It is not in our essence, in our skill;
   But—thou may'st die.
Manfred.   Will Death bestow it on me?
Spirit. We are immortal, and do not forget;
   We are eternal; and to us the past   150

Is, as the future, present.   Art thou answered?

Manfred. Ye mock me—but the Power which brought ye here
    Hath made you mine.   Slaves, scoff not at my will!
    The Mind—the Spirit—the Promethean spark,
    The lightning of my being, is as bright,
    Pervading, and far darting as your own,
    And shall not yield to yours, though cooped in clay!
    Answer, or I will teach you what I am.

Spirit. We answer—as we answered; our reply
    Is even in thine own words.

Manfred.   Why say ye so?   160

Spirit. If, as thou say'st, thine essence be as ours,
    We have replied in telling thee, the thing
    Mortals call death hath nought to do with us.

Manfred. I then have called ye from your realms in vain;
    Ye cannot, or ye will not, aid me.

Spirit.   Say—.
    What we possess we offer; it is thine:
    Bethink ere thou dismiss us; ask again;
    Kingdom, and sway, and strength, and length of days—

Manfred. Accursed! what have I to do with days?
    They are too long already.—Hence—begone!   170

Spirit. Yet pause: being here, our will would do thee service;
    Bethink thee, is there then no other gift
    Which we can make not worthless in thine eyes?

Manfred. No, none: yet stay—one moment, ere we part,
    I would behold ye face to face.   I hear
    Your voices, sweet and melancholy sounds,
    As Music on the waters; and I see
    The steady aspect of a clear large Star;
    But nothing more.   Approach me as ye are,
    Or one—or all—in your accustomed forms.   180

Spirit. We have no forms, beyond the elements
    Of which we are the mind and principle:
    But choose a form—in that we will appear.

Manfred. I have no choice; there is no form on earth
    Hideous or beautiful to me.   Let him,
    Who is most powerful of ye, take such aspect
    As unto him may seem most fitting—Come!

Seventh Spirit. (*Appearing in the shape of a beautiful female figure*)
        Behold!

Manfred.   Oh God! if it be thus, and *thou*
    Art not a madness and a mockery,
    I yet might be most happy.   I will clasp thee,   190
    And we again will be——

(*The figure vanishes.*)
My heart is crushed!
(*Manfred falls senseless.*)

(*A voice is heard in the Incantation which follows.*)

When the Moon is on the wave,
   And the glow-worm in the grass,
And the meteor on the grave,
   And the wisp on the morass;
When the falling stars are shooting,
And the answered owls are hooting,
And the silent leaves are still
In the shadow of the hill,
Shall my soul be upon thine,   200
With a power and with a sign.

Though thy slumber may be deep,
Yet thy Spirit shall not sleep;
There are shades which will not vanish,
There are thoughts thou canst not banish;
By a Power to thee unknown,
Thou canst never be alone;
Thou art wrapt as with a shroud,
Thou art gathered in a cloud;
And for ever shalt thou dwell   210
In the spirit of this spell.

Though thou seest me not pass by,
Thou shalt feel me with thine eye
As a thing that, though unseen,
Must be near thee, and hath been;
And when in that secret dread
Thou hast turned around thy head,
Thou shalt marvel I am not
As thy shadow on the spot,
And the power which thou dost feel   220
Shall be what thou must conceal.

And a magic voice and verse
Hath baptized thee with a curse;
And a Spirit of the air
Hath begirt thee with a snare;
In the wind there is a voice
Shall forbid thee to rejoice;
And to thee shall Night deny
All the quiet of her sky;

And the day shall have a sun,   230
Which shall make thee wish it done.

From thy false tears I did distil
An essence which hath strength to kill;
From thy own heart I then did wring
The black blood in its blackest spring;
From thy own smile I snatched the snake,
For there it coiled as in a brake;
From thy own lip I drew the charm
Which gave all these their chiefest harm;
In proving every poison known,   240
I found the strongest was thine own.

By the cold breast and serpent smile,
By thy unfathomed gulfs of guile,
By that most seeming virtuous eye,
By thy shut soul's hypocrisy;
By the perfection of thine art
Which passed for human thine own heart;
By thy delight in others' pain,
And by thy brotherhood of Cain,
I call upon thee! and compel   250
Thyself to be thy proper Hell!

And on thy head I pour the vial
Which doth devote thee to this trial;
Nor to slumber, nor to die,
Shall be in thy destiny;
Though thy death shall still seem near
To thy wish, but as a fear;
Lo! the spell now works around thee,
And the clankless chain hath bound thee;
O'er thy heart and brain together   260
Hath the word been passed—now wither!

Scene II

(*The Mountain of the Jungfrau.—Time, Morning.*)

(*Manfred alone upon the cliffs.*)

Manfred. The spirits I have raised abandon me,
   The spells which I have studied baffle me,
   The remedy I recked of tortured me;

I lean no more on superhuman aid;
It hath no power upon the past, and for
The future, till the past be gulfed in darkness,
It is not of my search.——My Mother Earth!
And thou fresh-breaking Day, and you, ye Mountains,
Why are ye beautiful?   I cannot love ye.
And thou, the bright Eye of the Universe,   10
That openest over all, and unto all
Art a delight——thou shin'st not on my heart.
And you, ye crags, upon whose extreme edge
I stand, and on the torrent's brink beneath
Behold the tall pines dwindled as to shrubs
In dizziness of distance; when a leap,
A stir, a motion, even a breath, would bring
My breast upon its rocky bosom's bed
To rest for ever——wherefore do I pause?
I feel the impulse——yet I do not plunge;   20
I see the peril——yet do not recede;
And my brain reels——and yet my foot is firm:
There is a power upon me which withholds,
And makes it my fatality to live,——
If it be life to wear within myself
This barrenness of Spirit, and to be
My own Soul's sepulchre, for I have ceased
To justify my deeds unto myself——
The last infirmity of evil.   Aye,
Thou winged and cloud-cleaving minister,   30
                    (*An Eagle passes.*)
Whose happy flight is highest into heaven,
Well may'st thou swoop so near me——I should be
Thy prey, and gorge thine eaglets; thou art gone
Where the eye cannot follow thee; but thine
Yet pierces downward, onward, or above,
With a pervading vision.——Beautiful!
How beautiful is all this visible world!
How glorious in its action and itself!
But we, who name ourselves its sovereigns, we,
Half dust, half deity, alike unfit   40
To sink or soar, with our mixed essence make
A conflict of its elements, and breathe
The breath of degradation and of pride,
Contending with low wants and lofty will,
Till our Mortality predominates,
And men are——what they name not to themselves,
And trust not to each other.   Hark! the note,

(*The Shepherd's pipe in the distance is heard.*)
The natural music of the mountain reed—
For here the patriarchal days are not
A pastoral fable—pipes in the liberal air,   50
Mixed with the sweet bells of the sauntering herd;
My soul would drink those echoes.   Oh, that I were
The viewless spirit of a lovely sound,
A living voice, a breathing harmony,
A bodiless enjoyment—born and dying
With the blest tone which made me!

(*Enter from below a Chamois Hunter.*)

Chamois Hunter.   Even so
This way the Chamois leapt: her nimble feet
Have baffled me; my gains to-day will scarce
Repay my break-neck travail.—What is here?
Who seems not of my trade, and yet hath reached   60
A height which none even of our mountaineers,
Save our best hunters, may attain: his garb
Is goodly, his mien manly, and his air
Proud as a free-born peasant's, at this distance:
I will approach him nearer.
Manfred. (*Not perceiving the other.*) To be thus—
Grey-haired with anguish, like these blasted pines,
Wrecks of a single winter, barkless, branchless,
A blighted trunk upon a cursed root,
Which but supplies a feeling to Decay—
And to be thus, eternally but thus,   70
Having been otherwise!   Now furrowed o'er
With wrinkles, ploughed by moments, not by years
And hours, all tortured into ages—hours
Which I outlive!—Ye toppling crags of ice!
Ye Avalanches, whom a breath draws down
In mountainous o'erwhelming, come and crush me!
I hear ye momently above, beneath,
Crash with a frequent conflict; but ye pass,
And only fall on things that still would live;
On the young flourishing forest, or the hut   80
And hamlet of the harmless villager.
Chamois Hunter. The mists begin to rise from up the valley;
I'll warn him to descend, or he may chance
To lose at once his way and life together.
Manfred. The mists boil up around the glaciers; clouds
Rise curling fast beneath me, white and sulphury,
Like foam from the roused ocean of deep Hell,

Whose every wave breaks on a living shore,
Heaped with the damned like pebbles.—I am giddy.

Chamois Hunter. I must approach him cautiously; if near, 90
  A sudden step will startle him, and he
  Seems tottering already.

Manfred.   Mountains have fallen,
  Leaving a gap in the clouds, and with the shock
  Rocking their Alpine brethren; filling up
  The ripe green valleys with Destruction's splinters;
  Damming the rivers with a sudden dash,
  Which crushed the waters into mist, and made
  Their fountains find another channel—thus,
  Thus, in its old age, did Mount Rosenberg—
  Why stood I not beneath it?

Chamois Hunter.   Friend! have a care, 100
  Your next step may be fatal!—for the love
  Of Him who made you, stand not on that brink!

Manfred. (*Not hearing him.*) Such would have been for me a fitting
      tomb;
  My bones had then been quiet in their depth;
  They had not then been strewn upon the rocks
  For the wind's pastime—as thus—thus they shall be—
  In this one plunge.—Farewell, ye opening Heavens!
  Look not upon me thus reproachfully—
  You were not meant for me—Earth! take these atoms!
      (*As Manfred is in act to spring from the cliff,*
          the Chamois Hunter seizes
        and retains him with a sudden grasp.)

Chamois Hunter. Hold, madman!—though aweary of thy life, 110
  Stain not our pure vales with thy guilty blood:
  Away with me——I will not quit my hold.

Manfred. I am most sick at heart—nay, grasp me not—
  I am all feebleness—the mountains whirl
  Spinning around me——I grow blind——What art thou?

Chamois Hunter. I'll answer that anon.—Away with me——
  The clouds grow thicker——there—now lean on me—
  Place your foot here—here, take this staff, and cling
  A moment to that shrub—now give me your hand,
  And hold fast by my girdle—softly—well— 120
  The Chalet will be gained within an hour:
  Come on, we'll quickly find a surer footing,
  And something like a pathway, which the torrent
  Hath washed since winter.—Come, 'tis bravely done—
  You should have been a hunter.—Follow me.
      (*As they descend the rocks with difficulty, the scene closes.*)

ACT II

SCENE I

(*A Cottage among the Bernese Alps.*)

(*Manfred and the Chamois Hunter.*)

Chamois Hunter. No—no—yet pause—thou must not yet go forth:
   Thy mind and body are alike unfit
   To trust each other, for some hours, at least;
   When thou art better, I will be thy guide—
   But whither?
Manfred. It imports not: I do know
   My route full well, and need no further guidance.
Chamois Hunter. Thy garb and gait bespeak thee of high lineage—
   One of the many chiefs, whose castled crags
   Look o'er the lower valleys—which of these
   May call thee Lord?   I only know their portals;   10
   My way of life leads me but rarely down
   To bask by the huge hearths of those old halls,
   Carousing with the vassals; but the paths,
   Which step from out our mountains to their doors,
   I know from childhood—which of these is thine?
Manfred. No matter.
Chamois Hunter.   Well, Sir, pardon me the question,
   And be of better cheer.   Come, taste my wine;
   'Tis of an ancient vintage; many a day
   'T has thawed my veins among our glaciers, now
   Let it do thus for thine—Come, pledge me fairly!   20
Manfred. Away, away! there's blood upon the brim!
   Will it then never—never sink in the earth?
Chamois Hunter. What dost thou mean? thy senses wander from thee.
Manfred. I say 'tis blood—my blood! the pure warm stream
   Which ran in the veins of my fathers, and in ours
   When we were in our youth, and had one heart,
   And loved each other as we should not love,
   And this was shed: but still it rises up,
   Colouring the clouds, that shut me out from Heaven,
   Where thou are not—and I shall never be.   30
Chamois Hunter. Man of strange words, and some half-maddening sin,
   Which makes thee people vacancy, whate'er
   Thy dread and sufferance be, there's comfort yet—
   The aid of holy men, and heavenly patience——

Manfred. Patience—and patience!   Hence—that word was made
  For brutes of burthen, not for birds of prey!
  Preach it to mortals of a dust like thine,—
  I am not of thine order.
Chamois Hunter.   Thanks to Heaven!
  I would not be of thine for the free fame
  Of William Tell; but whatsoe'er thine ill,   40
  It must be borne, and these wild starts are useless.
Manfred. Do I not bear it?—Look on me—I live.
Chamois Hunter. This is convulsion, and no healthful life.
Manfred. I tell thee, man! I have lived many years,
  Many long years, but they are nothing now
  To those which I must number: ages—ages—
  Space and eternity—and consciousness,
  With the fierce thirst of death—and still unslaked!
Chamois Hunter. Why on thy brow the seal of middle age
  Hath scarce been set; I am thine elder far.   50
Manfred. Think'st thou existence doth depend on time?
  It doth; but actions are our epochs: mine
  Have made my days and nights imperishable,
  Endless, and all alike, as sands on the shore,
  Innumerable atoms; and one desert,
  Barren and cold, on which the wild waves break,
  But nothing rests, save carcasses and wrecks,
  Rocks, and the salt-surf weeds of bitterness.
Chamois Hunter. Alas! he's mad—but yet I must not leave him.
Manfred. I would I were—for then the things I see   60
  Would be but a distempered dream.
Chamois Hunter.   What is it
  That thou dost see, or think thou look'st upon?
Manfred. Myself, and thee—a peasant of the Alps—
  Thy humble virtues, hospitable home,
  And spirit patient, pious, proud, and free;
  Thy self-respect, grafted on innocent thoughts;
  Thy days of health, and nights of sleep; thy toils,
  By danger dignified, yet guiltless; hopes
  Of cheerful old age and a quiet grave,
  With cross and garland over its green turf,   70
  And thy grandchildren's love for epitaph!
  This do I see—and then I look within—
  It matters not—my Soul was scorched already!
Chamois Hunter. And would'st thou then exchange thy lot for mine?
Manfred. No, friend!   I would not wrong thee, nor exchange
  My lot with living being: I can bear—

However wretchedly, 'tis still to bear—
In life what others could not brook to dream,
But perish in their slumber.
Chamois Hunter.   And with this—
  This cautious feeling for another's pain,   80
  Canst thou be black with evil?—say not so.
  Can one of gentle thoughts have wreaked revenge
  Upon his enemies?
Manfred.   Oh! no, no, no!
  My injuries came down on those who loved me—
  On those whom I best loved: I never quelled
  An enemy, save in my just defence—
  But my embrace was fatal.
Chamois Hunter.   Heaven give thee rest!
  And Penitence restore thee to thyself;
  My prayers shall be for thee.
Manfred.   I need them not,
  But can endure thy pity.   I depart—   90
  'Tis time—farewell!—Here's gold, and thanks for thee—
  No words—it is thy due.—Follow me not—
  I know my path—the mountain peril's past:
  And once again I charge thee, follow not!

                                        (*Exit Manfred.*)

                        SCENE II

        (*A lower Valley in the Alps.—A Cataract.*)

                    (*Enter Manfred.*)

  It is not noon—the Sunbow's rays still arch
  The torrent with the many hues of heaven,
  And roll the sheeted silver's waving column
  O'er the crag's headlong perpendicular,
  And fling its lines of foaming light along,
  And to and fro, like the pale courser's tail,
  The Giant steed, to be bestrode by Death,
  As told in the Apocalypse.   No eyes
  But mine now drink this sight of loveliness;
  I should be sole in this sweet solitude,   10
  And with the Spirit of the place divide
  The homage of these waters.—I will call her.
            (*Manfred takes some of the water into the palm*

of his hand and flings it into the air,
muttering the adjuration. After a pause,
the Witch of the Alps rises
beneath the arch of the sunbow of the torrent.)

Beautiful Spirit! with thy hair of light,
And dazzling eyes of glory, in whose form
The charms of Earth's least mortal daughters grow
To an unearthly stature, in an essence
Of purer elements; while the hues of youth,—
Carnationed like a sleeping Infant's cheek,
Rocked by the beating of her mother's heart,
Or the rose tints, which Summer's twilight leaves　　　　20
Upon the lofty Glacier's virgin snow,
The blush of earth embracing with her Heaven,—
Tinge thy celestial aspect, and make tame
The beauties of the Sunbow which bends o'er thee.
Beautiful Spirit! in thy calm clear brow,
Wherein is glassed serenity of Soul,
Which of itself shows immortality,
I read that thou wilt pardon to a Son
Of Earth, whom the abstruser powers permit
At times to commune with them—if that he　　　　30
Avail him of his spells—to call thee thus,
And gaze on thee a moment.
Witch.　　　　　　　　　　Son of Earth!
I know thee, and the Powers which give thee power!
I know thee for a man of many thoughts,
And deeds of good and ill, extreme in both,
Fatal and fated in thy sufferings:
I have expected this—what would'st thou with me?
Manfred. To look upon thy beauty—nothing further.
The face of the earth hath maddened me, and I
Take refuge in her mysteries, and pierce　　　　40
To the abodes of those who govern her—
But they can nothing aid me.　I have sought
From them what they could not bestow, and now
I search no further.
Witch.　　　　　　　What could be the quest
Which is not in the power of the most powerful,
The rulers of the invisible?
Manfred.　　　　　　　　A boon;—
But why should I repeat it? 'twere in vain.
Witch. I know not that; let thy lips utter it.
Manfred. Well, though it torture me, 'tis but the same;

My pang shall find a voice.   From my youth upwards   50
My Spirit walked not with the souls of men,
Nor looked upon the earth with human eyes;
The thirst of their ambition was not mine,
The aim of their existence was not mine;
My joys—my griefs—my passions—and my powers,
Made me a stranger; though I wore the form,
I had no sympathy with breathing flesh,
Nor midst the Creatures of Clay that girded me
Was there but One who——but of her anon.
I said with men, and with the thoughts of men,   60
I held but slight communion; but instead,
My joy was in the wilderness,—to breathe
The difficult air of the iced mountain's top,
Where the birds dare not build—nor insect's wing
Flit o'er the herbless granite; or to plunge
Into the torrent, and to roll along
On the swift whirl of the new-breaking wave
Of river-stream, or Ocean, in their flow.
In these my early strength exulted; or
To follow through the night the moving moon,   70
The stars and their development; or catch
The dazzling lightnings till my eyes grew dim;
Or to look, list'ning, on the scattered leaves,
While Autumn winds were at their evening song.
These were my pastimes, and to be alone;
For if the beings, of whom I was one,—
Hating to be so,—crossed me in my path,
I felt myself degraded back to them,
And was all clay again.   And then I dived,
In my lone wanderings, to the caves of Death,   80
Searching its cause in its effect; and drew
From withered bones, and skulls, and heaped up dust,
Conclusions most forbidden.   Then I passed
The nights of years in sciences untaught,
Save in the old-time; and with time and toil,
And terrible ordeal, and such penance
As in itself hath power upon the air,
And spirits that do compass air and earth,
Space, and the peopled Infinite, I made
Mine eyes familiar with Eternity,   90
Such as, before me, did the Magi, and
He who from out their fountain-dwellings raised
Eros and Anteros, at Gadara,

As I do thee;—and with my knowledge grew
The thirst of knowledge, and the power and joy
Of this most bright intelligence, until——

Witch. Proceed.

Manfred.　　　　　　Oh! I but thus prolonged my words,
Boasting these idle attributes, because
As I approach the core of my heart's grief—
But—to my task.　I have not named to thee　　　　　100
Father or mother, mistress, friend, or being,
With whom I wore the chain of human ties;
If I had such, they seemed not such to me—
Yet there was One——

Witch.　　　　　　　Spare not thyself—proceed.

Manfred. She was like me in lineaments—her eyes—
Her hair—her features—all, to the very tone
Even of her voice, they said were like to mine;
But softened all, and tempered into beauty:
She had the same lone thoughts and wanderings,
The quest of hidden knowledge, and a mind　　　　110
To comprehend the Universe: nor these
Alone, but with them gentler powers than mine,
Pity, and smiles, and tears—which I had not;
And tenderness—but that I had for her;
Humility—and that I never had.
Her faults were mine—her virtues were her own—
I loved her, and destroyed her!

Witch.　　　　　　　　With thy hand?

Manfred. Not with my hand, but heart, which broke her heart;
It gazed on mine, and withered.　I have shed
Blood, but not hers—and yet her blood was shed;　　120
I saw—and could not stanch it.

Witch.　　　　　　　　And for this—
A being of the race thou dost despise—
The order, which thine own would rise above,
Mingling with us and ours,—thou dost forego
The gifts of our great knowledge, and shrink'st back
To recreant mortality——Away!

Manfred. Daughter of Air!　I tell thee, since that hour—
But words are breath—look on me in my sleep,
Or watch my watchings—Come and sit by me!
My solitude is solitude no more,　　　　　　　　130
But peopled with the Furies;—I have gnashed
My teeth in darkness till returning morn,
Then cursed myself till sunset;—I have prayed

For madness as a blessing— tıs denied me.
I have affronted Death—but in the war
Of elements the waters shrunk from me,
And fatal things passed harmless; the cold hand
Of an all-pitiless Demon held me back,
Back by a single hair, which would not break.
In Fantasy, Imagination, all   140
The affluence of my soul—which one day was
A Crœsus in creation—I plunged deep,
But, like an ebbing wave, it dashed me back
Into the gulf of my unfathomed thought.
I plunged amidst Mankind—Forgetfulness
I sought in all, save where 'tis to be found—
And that I have to learn—my Sciences,
My long pursued and superhuman art,
Is mortal here: I dwell in my despair—
And live—and live for ever.
Witch.   It may be   150
    That I can aid thee.
Manfred.   To do this thy power
    Must wake the dead, or lay me low with them.
    Do so—in any shape—in any hour—
    With any torture—so it be the last.
Witch. That is not in my province; but if thou
    Wilt swear obedience to my will, and do
    My bidding, it may help thee to thy wishes.
Manfred. I will not swear—Obey! and whom? the Spirits
    Whose presence I command, and be the slave
    Of those who served me—Never!
Witch.   Is this all?   160
    Hast thou no gentler answer?—Yet bethink thee,
    And pause ere thou rejectest.
Manfred.   I have said it.
Witch. Enough! I may retire then—say!
Manfred.   Retire!
                              (*The Witch disappears.*)
Manfred. (*Alone.*) We are the fools of Time and Terror: Days
    Steal on us, and steal from us; yet we live,
    Loathing our life, and dreading still to die.
    In all the days of this detested yoke—
    This vital weight upon the struggling heart,
    Which sinks with sorrow, or beats quick with pain,
    Or joy that ends in agony or faintness—   170
    In all the days of past and future—for

In life there is no present—we can number
How few—how less than few—wherein the soul
Forbears to pant for death, and yet draws back
As from a stream in winter, though the chill
Be but a moment's.   I have one resource
Still in my science—I can call the dead,
And ask them what it is we dread to be:
The sternest answer can but be the Grave,
And that is nothing: if they answer not——   180
The buried Prophet answered to the Hag
Of Endor; and the Spartan Monarch drew
From the Byzantine maid's unsleeping spirit
An answer and his destiny—he slew
That which he loved, unknowing what he slew,
And died unpardoned—though he called in aid
The Phyxian Jove, and in Phigalia roused
The Arcadian Evocators to compel
The indignant shadow to depose her wrath,
Or fix her term of vengeance—she replied   190
In words of dubious import, but fulfilled.
If I had never lived, that which I love
Had still been living; had I never loved,
That which I love would still be beautiful,
Happy and giving happiness.   What is she?
What is she now?—a sufferer for my sins—
A thing I dare not think upon—or nothing.
Within few hours I shall not call in vain—
Yet in this hour I dread the thing I dare:
Until this hour I never shrunk to gaze   200
On spirit, good or evil—now I tremble,
And feel a strange cold thaw upon my heart.
But I can act even what I most abhor,
And champion human fears.—The night approaches.

                                              (*Exit.*)

Scene III

(*The summit of the Jungfrau Mountain.*)

(*Enter First Destiny.*)

The Moon is rising broad, and round, and bright;
And here on snows, where never human foot

Of common mortal trod, we nightly tread,
And leave no traces: o'er the savage sea,
The glassy ocean of the mountain ice,
We skim its rugged breakers, which put on
The aspect of a tumbling tempest's foam,
Frozen in a moment—a dead Whirlpool's image:
And this most steep fantastic pinnacle,
The fretwork of some earthquake—where the clouds   10
Pause to repose themselves in passing by—
Is sacred to our revels, or our vigils;
Here do I wait my sisters, on our way
To the Hall of Arimanes—for to-night
Is our great festival—'tis strange they come not.

A Voice without, singing. The Captive Usurper,
    Hurled down from the throne,
Lay buried in torpor,
    Forgotten and lone;
I broke through his slumbers,   20
    I shivered his chain,
I leagued him with numbers—
    He's Tyrant again!
With the blood of a million he'll answer my care,
With a Nation's destruction—his flight and despair!

Second Voice, without. The Ship sailed on, the Ship sailed fast,
    But I left not a sail, and I left not a mast;
There is not a plank of the hull or the deck,
And there is not a wretch to lament o'er his wreck;
Save one, whom I held, as he swam, by the hair,   30
And he was a subject well worthy my care;
A traitor on land, and a pirate at sea—
But I saved him to wreak further havoc for me!

First Destiny, answering.
    The City lies sleeping;
        The morn, to deplore it,
    May dawn on it weeping:
        Sullenly, slowly,
    The black plague flew o'er it—
        Thousands lie lowly;
    Tens of thousands shall perish;   40
        The living shall fly from
    The sick they should cherish;
        But nothing can vanquish
    The touch that they die from.
        Sorrow and anguish,

And evil and dread,
　　Envelope a nation;
The blest are the dead,
Who see not the sight
　　Of their own desolation;　　　　　　　　　　　　　50
This work of a night—
This wreck of a realm—this deed of my doing—
For ages I've done, and shall still be renewing!

　　　　　(*Enter the Second and Third Destinies.*)
The Three. Our hands contain the hearts of men,
　　Our footsteps are their graves;
We only give to take again
　　The Spirits of our slaves!

First Destiny. Welcome!—Where's Nemesis?
Second Destiny.　　　　　　　　　　　At some great work;
But what I know not, for my hands were full.
Third Destiny. Behold she cometh.

　　　　　(*Enter Nemesis.*)
First Destiny.　　　　　Say, where hast thou been?　　　60
My Sisters and thyself are slow to-night.
Nemesis. I was detained repairing shattered thrones—
Marrying fools, restoring dynasties—
Avenging men upon their enemies,
And making them repent their own revenge;
Goading the wise to madness; from the dull
Shaping out oracles to rule the world
Afresh—for they were waxing out of date,
And mortals dared to ponder for themselves,
To weigh kings in the balance—and to speak　　　　70
Of Freedom, the forbidden fruit.—Away!
We have outstayed the hour—mount we our clouds!
　　　　　　　　　　　　　　　　　(*Exeunt.*)

SCENE IV

(*The Hall of Arimanes.*)
(*Arimanes on his Throne, a Globe of Fire,
　　surrounded by the Spirits.*)

(*Hymn of the Spirits.*)
Hail to our Master!—Prince of Earth and Air!
Who walks the clouds and waters—in his hand

The sceptre of the Elements, which tear
   Themselves to chaos at his high command!
He breatheth—and a tempest shakes the sea;
   He speaketh—and the clouds reply in thunder;
He gazeth—from his glance the sunbeams flee;
   He moveth—Earthquakes rend the world asunder.
Beneath his footsteps the Volcanoes rise;
   His shadow is the Pestilence: his path   10
The comets herald through the crackling skies;
   And Planets turn to ashes at his wrath.
To him War offers daily sacrifice;
   To him Death pays his tribute; Life is his,
With all its Infinite of agonies—
   And his the Spirit of whatever is!

       (*Enter the Destinies and Nemesis.*)
First Destiny. Glory to Arimanes! on the earth
   His power increaseth—both my sisters did
   His bidding, nor did I neglect my duty!
Second Destiny. Glory to Arimanes! we who bow   20
   The necks of men, bow down before his throne!
Third Destiny. Glory to Arimanes! we await
   His nod!
Nemesis. Sovereign of Sovereigns! we are thine,
   And all that liveth, more or less, is ours,
   And most things wholly so; still to increase
   Our power, increasing thine, demands our care,
   And we are vigilant.   Thy late commands
   Have been fulfilled to the utmost.

       (*Enter Manfred.*)
A Spirit.   What is here?
   A mortal!—Thou most rash and fatal wretch,
   Bow down and worship!
Second Spirit.   I do know the man—   30
   A Magian of great power, and fearful skill!
Third Spirit. Bow down and worship, slave!—What, know'st thou not
   Thine and our Sovereign?—Tremble, and obey!
All the Spirits. Prostrate thyself, and thy condemned clay,
   Child of the Earth! or dread the worst.
Manfred.   I know it;
   And yet ye see I kneel not.
Fourth Spirit.   'Twill be taught thee.
Manfred. 'Tis taught already;—many a night on the earth,
   On the bare ground, have I bowed down my face,
   And strewed my head with ashes; I have known

The fulness of humiliation—for
I sunk before my vain despair, and knelt
To my own desolation.
Fifth Spirit.   Dost thou dare
Refuse to Arimanes on his throne
What the whole earth accords, beholding not
The terror of his Glory?—Crouch! I say.
Manfred. Bid *him* bow down to that which is above him,
The overruling Infinite—the Maker
Who made him not for worship—let him kneel,
And we will kneel together.
The Spirits.   Crush the worm!
Tear him in pieces!—
First Destiny.   Hence! Avaunt!—he's mine.   50
Prince of the Powers invisible!   This man
Is of no common order, as his port
And presence here denote: his sufferings
Have been of an immortal nature—like
Our own; his knowledge, and his powers and will,
As far as is compatible with clay,
Which clogs the ethereal essence, have been such
As clay hath seldom borne; his aspirations
Have been beyond the dwellers of the earth,
And they have only taught him what we know—   60
That knowledge is not happiness, and science
But an exchange of ignorance for that
Which is another kind of ignorance.
This is not all—the passions, attributes
Of Earth and Heaven, from which no power, nor being,
Nor breath from the worm upwards is exempt,
Have pierced his heart; and in their consequence
Made him a thing—which—I who pity not,
Yet pardon those who pity.   He is mine—
And thine it may be; be it so, or not—   70
No other Spirit in this region hath
A soul like his—or power upon his soul.
Nemesis. What doth he here then?
First Destiny.   Let *him* answer that.
Manfred. Ye know what I have known; and without power
I could not be amongst ye: but there are
Powers deeper still beyond—I come in quest
Of such, to answer unto what I seek.
Nemesis. What would'st thou?
Manfred.   *Thou* canst not reply to me.
Call up the dead—my question is for them.

Nemesis. Great Arimanes, doth thy will avouch   80
   The wishes of this mortal?
Arimanes.   Yea.
Nemesis.   Whom wouldst thou
   Uncharnel?
Manfred.   One without a tomb—call up
   Astarte.
Nemesis.
     Shadow! or Spirit!
       Whatever thou art,
     Which still doth inherit
       The whole or a part
     Of the form of thy birth,
       Of the mould of thy clay,
     Which returned to the earth,   90
       Re-appear to the day!
     Bear what thou borest,
       The heart and the form,
     And the aspect thou worest
       Redeem from the worm.
     Appear!—Appear!—Appear!
   Who sent thee there requires thee here!
     (*The Phantom of Astarte rises and stands in the midst.*)
Manfred. Can this be death? there's bloom upon her cheek;
   But now I see it is no living hue,
   But a strange hectic—like the unnatural red   100
   Which Autumn plants upon the perished leaf.
   It is the same!   Oh, God! that I should dread
   To look upon the same—Astarte!—No,
   I cannot speak to her—but bid her speak—
   Forgive me or condemn me.
Nemesis.
   By the Power which hath broken
     The grave which enthralled thee,
   Speak to him who hath spoken,
     Or those who have called thee!
Manfred.   She is silent,
   And in that silence I am more than answered.   110
Nemesis. My power extends no further.   Prince of Air!
   It rests with thee alone—command her voice.
Arimanes. Spirit—obey this sceptre!
Nemesis.   Silent still!
   She is not of our order, but belongs
   To the other powers.   Mortal! thy quest is vain,
   And we are baffled also.

Manfred.   Hear me, hear me—
  Astarte! my belovéd! speak to me:
  I have so much endured—so much endure—
  Look on me! the grave hath not changed thee more
  Than I am changed for thee.   Thou lovedst me   120
  Too much, as I loved thee: we were not made
  To torture thus each other—though it were
  The deadliest sin to love as we have loved.
  Say that thou loath'st me not—that I do bear
  This punishment for both—that thou wilt be
  One of the blesséd—and that I shall die;
  For hitherto all hateful things conspire
  To bind me in existence—in a life
  Which makes me shrink from Immortality—
  A future like the past.   I cannot rest.   130
  I know not what I ask, nor what I seek:
  I feel but what thou art, and what I am;
  And I would hear yet once before I perish
  The voice which was my music—Speak to me!
  For I have called on thee in the still night,
  Startled the slumbering birds from the hushed boughs,
  And woke the mountain wolves, and made the caves
  Acquainted with thy vainly echoed name,
  Which answered me—many things answered me—
  Spirits and men—but thou wert silent all.   140
  Yet speak to me!   I have outwatched the stars,
  And gazed o'er heaven in vain in search of thee.
  Speak to me!   I have wandered o'er the earth,
  And never found thy likeness—Speak to me!
  Look on the fiends around—they feel for me:
  I fear them not, and feel for thee alone.
  Speak to me! though it be in wrath;—but say—
  I reck not what—but let me hear thee once—
  This once—once more!
Phantom of Astarte.   Manfred!
Manfred.   Say on, say on—
  I live but in the sound—it is thy voice!   150
Phantom. Manfred!   To-morrow ends thine earthly ills.
  Farewell!
Manfred. Yet one word more—am I forgiven?
Phantom. Farewell!
Manfred.   Say, shall we meet again?
Phantom.   Farewell!
Manfred. One word for mercy!   Say thou lovest me.

Phantom. Manfred!

(*The Spirit of Astarte disappears.*)

Nemesis.   She's gone, and will not be recalled:
   Her words will be fulfilled.   Return to the earth.
A Spirit. He is convulsed—This is to be a mortal,
   And seek the things beyond mortality.
Another Spirit. Yet, see, he mastereth himself, and makes
   His torture tributary to his will.   160
   Had he been one of us, he would have made
   An awful Spirit.
Nemesis.   Hast thou further question
   Of our great Sovereign, or his worshippers?
Manfred. None.
Nemesis.   Then for a time farewell.
Manfred. We meet then!   Where?   On the earth?—
   Even as thou wilt: and for the grace accorded
   I now depart a debtor.   Fare ye well!

(*Exit Manfred.*)

(*Scene closes.*)

ACT III

SCENE I

(*A Hall in the Castle of Manfred.*)

(*Manfred and Herman.*)

Manfred. What is the hour?
Herman.   It wants but one till sunset,
   And promises a lovely twilight.
Manfred.   Say,
   Are all things so disposed of in the tower
   As I directed?
Herman.   All, my Lord, are ready:
   Here is the key and casket.
Manfred.   It is well:
   Thou mayst retire.

(*Exit Herman.*)

Manfred. (*Alone.*)   There is a calm upon me—
   Inexplicable stillness! which till now
   Did not belong to what I knew of life.
   If that I did not know Philosophy
   To be of all our vanities the motliest,   10

The merest word that ever fooled the ear
From out the schoolman's jargon, I should deem
The golden secret, the sought "Kalon," found,
And seated in my soul.   It will not last,
But it is well to have known it, though but once:
It hath enlarged my thoughts with a new sense,
And I within my tablets would note down
That there is such a feeling.   Who is there?

(*Re-enter Herman.*)

Herman. My Lord, the Abbot of St. Maurice craves
To greet your presence.

(*Enter the Abbot of St. Maurice.*)

Abbot.   Peace be with Count Manfred!   20
Manfred. Thanks, holy father! welcome to these walls;
Thy presence honours them, and blesseth those
Who dwell within them.
Abbot.   Would it were so, Count!—
But I would fain confer with thee alone.
Manfred. Herman, retire.—What would my reverend guest?
Abbot. Thus, without prelude:—Age and zeal—my office—
And good intent must plead my privilege;
Our near, though not acquainted neighbourhood,
May also be my herald.   Rumours strange,
And of unholy nature, are abroad,   30
And busy with thy name—a noble name
For centuries: may he who bears it now
Transmit it unimpaired!
Manfred.   Proceed,—I listen.
Abbot. 'Tis said thou holdest converse with the things
Which are forbidden to the search of man;
That with the dwellers of the dark abodes,
The many evil and unheavenly spirits
Which walk the valley of the Shade of Death,
Thou communest.   I know that with mankind,
Thy fellows in creation, thou dost rarely   40
Exchange thy thoughts, and that thy solitude
Is as an Anchorite's—were it but holy.
Manfred. And what are they who do avouch these things?
Abbot. My pious brethren—the scaréd peasantry—
Even thy own vassals—who do look on thee
With most unquiet eyes.   Thy life's in peril!
Manfred. Take it.

Abbot.   I come to save, and not destroy:
   I would not pry into thy secret soul;
   But if these things be sooth, there still is time
   For penitence and pity: reconcile thee   50
   With the true church, and through the church to Heaven.
Manfred. I hear thee.   This is my reply—whate'er
   I may have been, or am, doth rest between
   Heaven and myself—I shall not choose a mortal
   To be my mediator—Have I sinned
   Against your ordinances? prove and punish!
Abbot. My son! I did not speak of punishment,
   But penitence and pardon;—with thyself
   The choice of such remains—and for the last,
   Our institutions and our strong belief   60
   Have given me power to smooth the path from sin
   To higher hope and better thoughts; the first
   I leave to Heaven,—"Vengeance is mine alone!"
   So saith the Lord, and with all humbleness
   His servant echoes back the awful word.
Manfred. Old man! there is no power in holy men,
   Nor charm in prayer, nor purifying form
   Of penitence, nor outward look, nor fast,
   Nor agony—nor, greater than all these,
   The innate tortures of that deep Despair,   70
   Which is Remorse without the fear of Hell,
   But all in all sufficient to itself
   Would make a hell of Heaven—can exorcise
   From out the unbounded spirit the quick sense
   Of its own sins—wrongs—sufferance—and revenge
   Upon itself; there is no future pang
   Can deal that justice on the self-condemned
   He deals on his own soul.
Abbot.   All this is well;
   For this will pass away, and be succeeded
   By an auspicious hope, which shall look up   80
   With calm assurance to that blessed place,
   Which all who seek may win, whatever be
   Their earthly errors, so they be atoned:
   And the commencement of atonement is
   The sense of its necessity.   Say on—
   And all our church can teach thee shall be taught;
   And all we can absolve thee shall be pardoned.
Manfred. When Rome's sixth Emperor was near his last,
   The victim of a self-inflicted wound,

To shun the torments of a public death   90
From senates once his slaves, a certain soldier,
With show of loyal pity, would have stanched
The gushing throat with his officious robe;
The dying Roman thrust him back, and said—
Some empire still in his expiring glance—
"It is too late—is this fidelity?"
Abbot. And what of this?
Manfred.   I answer with the Roman—
"It is too late!"
Abbot.   It never can be so,
To reconcile thyself with thy own soul,
And thy own soul with Heaven.   Hast thou no hope?   100
'Tis strange—even those who do despair above,
Yet shape themselves some fantasy on earth,
To which frail twig they cling, like drowning men.
Manfred. Aye—father! I have had those early visions,
And noble aspirations in my youth,
To make my own the mind of other men,
The enlightener of nations; and to rise
I knew not whither—it might be to fall;
But fall, even as the mountain-cataract,
Which having leapt from its more dazzling height,   110
Even in the foaming strength of its abyss,
(Which casts up misty columns that become
Clouds raining from the re-ascended skies,)
Lies low but mighty still.—But this is past,
My thoughts mistook themselves.
Abbot.   And wherefore so?
Manfred. I could not tame my nature down; for he
Must serve who fain would sway; and soothe, and sue,
And watch all time, and pry into all place,
And be a living Lie, who would become
A mighty thing amongst the mean—and such   120
The mass are; I disdained to mingle with
A herd, though to be leader—and of wolves.
The lion is alone, and so am I.
Abbot. And why not live and act with other men?
Manfred. Because my nature was averse from life;
And yet not cruel; for I would not make,
But find a desolation.   Like the Wind,
The red-hot breath of the most lone Simoom,
Which dwells but in the desert, and sweeps o'er
The barren sands which bear no shrubs to blast,   130
And revels o'er their wild and arid waves,

And seeketh not, so that it is not sought,
But being met is deadly,—such hath been
The course of my existence; but there came
Things in my path which are no more.
Abbot.   Alas!
  I 'gin to fear that thou art past all aid
  From me and from my calling; yet so young,
  I still would——
Manfred.   Look on me! there is an order
  Of mortals on the earth, who do become
  Old in their youth, and die ere middle age,   140
  Without the violence of warlike death;
  Some perishing of pleasure—some of study—
  Some worn with toil, some of mere weariness,—
  Some of disease—and some insanity—
  And some of withered, or of broken hearts;
  For this last is a malady which slays
  More than are numbered in the lists of Fate,
  Taking all shapes, and bearing many names.
  Look upon me! for even of all these things
  Have I partaken; and of all these things,   150
  One were enough; then wonder not that I
  Am what I am, but that I ever was,
  Or having been, that I am still on earth.
Abbot. Yet, hear me still——
Manfred.   Old man! I do respect
  Thine order, and revere thine years; I deem
  Thy purpose pious, but it is in vain:
  Think me not churlish; I would spare thyself,
  Far more than me, in shunning at this time
  All further colloquy—and so—farewell.
                                    (*Exit Manfred.*)
Abbot. This should have been a noble creature: he   160
  Hath all the energy which would have made
  A goodly frame of glorious elements,
  Had they been wisely mingled; as it is,
  It is an awful chaos—Light and Darkness—
  And mind and dust—and passions and pure thoughts
  Mixed, and contending without end or order,—
  All dormant or destructive. He will perish—
  And yet he must not—I will try once more,
  For such are worth redemption; and my duty
  Is to dare all things for a righteous end.   170
  I'll follow him—but cautiously, though surely.
                                    (*Exit Abbot.*)

THE EVIL IMAGE

SCENE II

(Another Chamber.)

(Manfred and Herman.)

Herman. My lord, you bade me wait on you at sunset:
   He sinks behind the mountain.
Manfred.   Doth he so?
   I will look on him.
         (Manfred advances to the Window of the Hall.)
                Glorious Orb! the idol
   Of early nature, and the vigorous race
   Of undiseased mankind, the giant sons
   Of the embrace of Angels, with a sex
   More beautiful than they, which did draw down
   The erring Spirits who can ne'er return.—
   Most glorious Orb! that wert a worship, ere
   The mystery of thy making was revealed!   10
   Thou earliest minister of the Almighty,
   Which gladdened, on their mountain tops, the hearts
   Of the Chaldean shepherds, till they poured
   Themselves in orisons!   Thou material God!
   And representative of the Unknown—
   Who chose thee for his shadow!   Thou chief Star!
   Centre of many stars! which mak'st our earth
   Endurable, and temperest the hues
   And hearts of all who walk within thy rays!
   Sire of the seasons!   Monarch of the climes,   20
   And those who dwell in them! for near or far,
   Our inborn spirits have a tint of thee
   Even as our outward aspects;—thou dost rise,
   And shine, and set in glory.   Fare thee well!
   I ne'er shall see thee more.   As my first glance
   Of love and wonder was for thee, then take
   My latest look: thou wilt not beam on one
   To whom the gifts of life and warmth have been
   Of a more fatal nature.   He is gone—
   I follow.

                          (Exit Manfred.)

SCENE III

*(The Mountains—The Castle of Manfred at some distance—
A Terrace before a Tower.—Time, Twilight.)*

LARAMIE JR. HIGH IMC

(*Herman, Manuel, and other dependants of Manfred.*)

Herman. 'Tis strange enough! night after night, for years,
    He hath pursued long vigils in this tower,
    Without a witness.   I have been within it,—
    So have we all been oft-times; but from it,
    Or its contents, it were impossible
    To draw conclusions absolute, of aught
    His studies tend to.   To be sure, there is
    One chamber where none enter: I would give
    The fee of what I have to come these three years,
    To pore upon its mysteries.
Manuel.   'Twere dangerous;   10
    Content thyself with what thou know'st already.
Herman. Ah! Manuel! thou art elderly and wise,
    And couldst say much; thou hast dwelt within the castle—
    How many years is't?
Manuel.   Ere Count Manfred's birth,
    I served his father, whom he nought resembles.
Herman. There be more sons in like predicament!
    But wherein do they differ?
Manuel.   I speak not
    Of features or of form, but mind and habits;
    Count Sigismund was proud, but gay and free,—
    A warrior and a reveller; he dwelt not   20
    With books and solitude, nor made the night
    A gloomy vigil, but a festal time,
    Merrier than day; he did not walk the rocks
    And forests like a wolf, nor turn aside
    From men and their delights.
Herman.   Beshrew the hour,
    But those were jocund times! I would that such
    Would visit the old walls again; they look
    As if they had forgotten them.
Manuel.   These walls
    Must change their chieftain first.   Oh! I have seen
    Some strange things in them, Herman.
Herman.   Come, be friendly;   30
    Relate me some to while away our watch:
    I've heard thee darkly speak of an event
    Which happened hereabouts, by this same tower.
Manuel. That was a night indeed!   I do remember
    'Twas twilight, as it may be now, and such
    Another evening:—yon red cloud, which rests

On Eigher's pinnacle, so rested then,—
So like that it might be the same; the wind
Was faint and gusty, and the mountain snows
Began to glitter with the climbing moon;   40
Count Manfred was, as now, within his tower,—
How occupied, we knew not, but with him
The sole companion of his wanderings
And watchings—her, whom of all earthly things
That lived, the only thing he seemed to love,—
As he, indeed, by blood was bound to do,
The Lady Astarte, his——

                                   Hush! who comes here?

(*Enter the Abbot.*)

Abbot. Where is your master?
Herman.   Yonder in the tower.
Abbot. I must speak with him.
Manuel.   'Tis impossible;
He is most private, and must not be thus   50
Intruded on.
Abbot.   Upon myself I take
The forfeit of my fault, if fault there be—
But I must see him.
Herman.   Thou hast seen him once
This eve already.
Abbot.   Herman! I command thee,
Knock, and apprize the Count of my approach.
Herman. We dare not.
Abbot.   Then it seems I must be herald
Of my own purpose.
Manuel.   Reverend father, stop—
I pray you pause.
Abbot.   Why so?
Manuel.   But step this way,
And I will tell you further.

                                     (*Exeunt.*)

SCENE IV

(*Interior of the Tower.*)

(*Manfred alone.*)

The stars are forth, the moon above the tops
Of the snow-shining mountains.——Beautiful!
I linger yet with Nature, for the Night
Hath been to me a more familiar face
Than that of man; and in her starry shade
Of dim and solitary loveliness,
I learned the language of another world.
I do remember me, that in my youth,
When I was wandering,—upon such a night
I stood within the Coliseum's wall,   10
'Midst the chief relics of almighty Rome;
The trees which grew along the broken arches
Waved dark in the blue midnight, and the stars
Shone through the rents of ruin; from afar
The watch-dog bayed beyond the Tiber; and
More near from out the Cæsars' palace came
The owl's long cry, and, interruptedly,
Of distant sentinels the fitful song
Begun and died upon the gentle wind.
Some cypresses beyond the time-worn breach   20
Appeared to skirt the horizon, yet they stood
Within a bowshot.   Where the Cæsars dwelt,
And dwell the tuneless birds of night, amidst
A grove which springs through levelled battlements,
And twines its roots with the imperial hearths,
Ivy usurps the laurel's place of growth;
But the gladiators' bloody Circus stands,
A noble wreck in ruinous perfection,
While Cæsar's chambers, and the Augustan halls,
Grovel on earth in indistinct decay.——   30
And thou didst shine, thou rolling Moon, upon
All this, and cast a wide and tender light,
Which softened down the hoar austerity
Of rugged desolation, and filled up,
As 'twere anew, the gaps of centuries;
Leaving that beautiful which still was so,
And making that which was not—till the place
Became religion, and the heart ran o'er
With silent worship of the Great of old,—
The dead, but sceptred, Sovereigns, who still rule   40
Our spirits from their urns.
                                        'Twas such a night!
'Tis strange that I recall it at this time;
But I have found our thoughts take wildest flight

Even at the moment when they should array
Themselves in pensive order.

(*Enter the Abbot.*)
Abbot.   My good Lord!
  I crave a second grace for this approach;
  But yet let not my humble zeal offend
  By its abruptness—all it hath of ill
  Recoils on me; its good in the effect
  May light upon your head—could I say *heart*—   50
  Could I touch *that*, with words or prayers, I should
  Recall a noble spirit which hath wandered,
  But is not yet all lost.
Manfred.   Thou know'st me not;
  My days are numbered, and my deeds recorded:
  Retire, or 'twill be dangerous—Away!
Abbot. Thou dost not mean to menace me?
Manfred.   Not I!
  I simply tell thee peril is at hand,
  And would preserve thee.
Abbot.   What dost thou mean?
Manfred.   Look there!
  What dost thou see?
Abbot.   Nothing.
Manfred.   Look there, I say,
  And steadfastly;—now tell me what thou seest?   60
Abbot. That which should shake me,—but I fear it not:
  I see a dusk and awful figure rise,
  Like an infernal god, from out the earth;
  His face wrapt in a mantle, and his form
  Robed as with angry clouds: he stands between
  Thyself and me—but I do fear him not.
Manfred. Thou hast no cause—he shall not harm thee—but
  His sight may shock thine old limbs into palsy.
  I say to thee—Retire!
Abbot.   And I reply—
  Never—till I have battled with this fiend:—   70
  What doth he here?
Manfred.   Why—aye—what doth he here?
  I did not send for him,—he is unbidden.
Abbot. Alas! lost Mortal! what with guests like these
  Hast thou to do? I tremble for thy sake:
  Why doth he gaze on thee, and thou on him?
  Ah! he unveils his aspect: on his brow

The thunder-scars are graven; from his eye
   Glares forth the immortality of Hell—
   Avaunt!—
Manfred.   Pronounce—what is thy mission?
Spirit.   Come!
Abbot. What art thou, unknown being? answer!—speak!   80
Spirit. The genius of this mortal.—Come! 'tis time.
Manfred. I am prepared for all things, but deny
   The Power which summons me.   Who sent thee here?
Spirit. Thou'lt know anon—Come! come!
Manfred.   I have commanded
   Things of an essence greater far than thine,
   And striven with thy masters.   Get thee hence!
Spirit. Mortal! thine hour is come—Away! I say.
Manfred. I knew, and know my hour is come, but not
   To render up my soul to such as thee:
   Away! I'll die as I have lived—alone.   90
Spirit. Then I must summon up my brethren.—Rise!
             (*Other Spirits rise up.*)
Abbot. Avaunt! ye evil ones!—Avaunt! I say,—
   Ye have no power where Piety hath power,
   And I do charge ye in the name—
Spirit.   Old man!
   We know ourselves, our mission, and thine order;
   Waste not thy holy words on idle uses,
   It were in vain: this man is forfeited.
   Once more—I summon him—Away! Away!
Manfred. I do defy ye,—though I feel my soul
   Is ebbing from me, yet I do defy ye;   100
   Nor will I hence, while I have earthly breath
   To breathe my scorn upon ye—earthly strength
   To wrestle, though with spirits; what ye take
   Shall be ta'en limb by limb.
Spirit.   Reluctant mortal!
   Is this the Magian who would so pervade
   The world invisible, and make himself
   Almost our equal?   Can it be that thou
   Art thus in love with life? the very life
   Which made thee wretched?
Manfred.   Thou false fiend, thou liest!
   My life is in its last hour,—*that* I know,   110
   Nor would redeem a moment of that hour;
   I do not combat against Death, but thee
   And thy surrounding angels; my past power

Was purchased by no compact with thy crew,
But by superior science—penance, daring,
And length of watching, strength of mind, and skill
In knowledge of our Fathers—when the earth
Saw men and spirits walking side by side,
And gave ye no supremacy: I stand
Upon my strength—I do defy—deny—   120
Spurn back, and scorn ye!—
Spirit.   But thy many crimes
Have made thee——
Manfred.   What are they to such as thee?
Must crimes be punished but by other crimes,
And greater criminals?—Back to thy hell!
Thou hast no power upon me, *that* I feel;
Thou never shalt possess me, *that* I know:
What I have done is done; I bear within
A torture which could nothing gain from thine:
The Mind which is immortal makes itself
Requital for its good or evil thoughts,—   130
Is its own origin of ill and end—
And its own place and time: its innate sense,
When stripped of this mortality, derives
No colour from the fleeting things without,
But is absorbed in sufferance or in joy,
Born from the knowledge of its own desert.
Thou didst not tempt me, and thou couldst not tempt me;
I have not been thy dupe, nor am thy prey—
But was my own destroyer, and will be
My own hereafter.—Back, ye baffled fiends!—   140
The hand of Death is on me—but not yours!
                              (*The Demons disappear.*)
Abbot. Alas! how pale thou art—thy lips are white—
And thy breast heaves—and in thy gasping throat
The accents rattle: Give thy prayers to Heaven—
Pray—albeit but in thought,—but die not thus.
Manfred. 'Tis over—my dull eyes can fix thee not;
But all things swim around me, and the earth
Heaves as it were beneath me. Fare thee well—
Give me thy hand.
Abbot.   Cold—cold—even to the heart—
But yet one prayer—Alas! how fares it with thee?   150
Manfred. Old man! 'tis not so difficult to die.
                              (*Manfred expires.*)
Abbot. He's gone—his soul hath ta'en its earthless flight;
Whither? I dread to think—but he is gone.

Dr. John William Polidori
(1795-1821)

O N June 16, 1816, at the Villa Diodati near Geneva, Lord Byron challenged his guests—Claire Clairmont, Dr. John William Polidori, Percy Bysshe and Mary Shelley—to write a ghost story in imitation of those read aloud from *Fantasmagoriana* (1812), a collection of tales, originally in German, translated into French by Jean-Baptiste Benoît Eyriès. It was "a wet, ungenial summer," and the forced confinement to the house encouraged serious conversation on such topics as vampires, ghosts, reanimation, galvanism, and what Mary Shelley described as "the nature of the principle of life" (1831 Preface to *Frankenstein*). Byron's proposition engaged his guests' lively imaginations and resulted in three works of enduring interest to Gothicists: Mary Shelley's *Frankenstein; or, The Modern Prometheus*, John Polidori's *Vampyre; a Tale*, and Lord Byron's "Fragment of a Novel."

John William Polidori, Byron's twenty-year-old physician, was present out of duty and literary interest. His father had translated Walpole's *Castle of Otranto* into Italian and had served as secretary to the dramatist Alfieri. His sister would become mother of Dante Gabriel, Christina, and William Michael Rossetti. Polidori, like his family, achieved literary fame more by association than by quality of production. Tension characterized his companionship with Byron, who cited Polidori's "eternal nonsense—& tracasseries—& emptiness—& ill humor—& vanity" (Letter to John Murray, 17 June 1817) as the causes of friction. Byron dismissed the "Child and Childish Dr. Pollydolly" (Letter to John Cam Hobhouse, 23 June 1816) in September 1816, but later urged John Murray to "help him to a publisher" for a weak tragedy he had sent to Byron (Letter to Murray, 18 June 1817).

Polidori's own literary ambitions made him brash enough to pirate the plot of Byron's ghost story as he heard it that evening in 1816. In his diary Polidori recorded a summary of Byron's story of the vampire who seduces the sister of his traveling companion. Then, in 1819, working from his diary entry and his memory, Polidori developed the plot in extravagant diction and convoluted syntax and published it. *The Vampyre; a Tale* appeared almost simultaneously in

Colburn's *New Monthly Magazine* and in a pamphlet published by
the firm of Sherwood, Neely and Jones; both included a long anonymous preface, "Extract of a Letter to the Editor," which discursively
discusses and attributes the story to Byron. The pamphlet, from
which this text is here printed, also contained an inaccurate introduction to vampirism with an excerpt from Byron's verse tale "The
Giaour" (ll. 755–785) and another "Extract of a Letter," this one
"containing an account of Lord Byron's Residence in the Island of
Mitylene," a place Byron never lived. The intention of such apparatus
is clearly to ascribe *The Vampyre* to Byron and to express the speaker's high regard for Byron and his work. Polidori, who later claimed
authorship, undoubtedly wanted to assure the success of *The Vampyre* by playing on the celebrity of Byron. The tale was immediately
popular, and its continued success was guaranteed within a year by
stage and opera productions in Paris and London. Polidori responded
with a series of disclaimers giving a truer account of the tale's origin.
Byron disavowed authorship, tore his "Fragment of a Novel" from
the account book of his former wife, where he had written it in 1816,
and published it at the end of *Mazeppa* in 1819 as a rejoinder.
Fifteen years later Mary Shelley tried to correct the record by describing Polidori's original story at Diodati:

> Poor Polidori had some terrible idea about a skull-headed lady, who
> was so punished for peeping through a key-hole—what to see I for-
> get—something very shocking and wrong of course; but when she
> was reduced to a worse condition than the renowned Tom of Coven-
> try, he did not know what to do with her, and was obliged to des-
> patch her to the tomb of the Capulets, the only place for which she
> was fitted.

(1831 Preface to Frankenstein)

No written version of this disjointed tale has been found, and Mary
Shelley may well have misremembered its better details as she did
those of the tales from *Fantasmagoriana*. Polidori's desperate finances led him to suicide in 1891. He left behind several publications
of questionable value, the best of which is a novel introduced as being
the story at Diodati; *Ernestus Bechtold; or The Modern Oedipus*
(1819)—the title is reminiscent of Mary Shelley's *Frankenstein; or,
The Modern Prometheus*—describes the adventures of a Swiss soldier, a tragic Byronic egotist, whose wife proves to be his own sister.
      Polidori's version of *The Vampyre* fictionalizes Byron as the
vampire, "Lord Ruthven," the name used for a caricature of Byron
by his former mistress Lady Caroline Lamb in her novel *Glenarvon*
(1816). "Ianthe," too, derives from Byron, who dedicated *Childe
Harold's Pilgrimage* (1812–1818; the seventh edition is the first to
have the dedication) to "Ianthe," the name given to the eleven-year-

old Lady Charlotte Mary Harley (1801–1880), whose beauty charmed him and whose mother, Lady Oxford, loved him. "Ianthe" was also the name of the daughter of Percy Bysshe Shelley and his first wife, Harriet; and in Shelley's "Queen Mab," "Ianthe" is the maiden to whom the fairy grants a vision of the world. The name "Aubrey" probably comes from the antiquary John Aubrey (1636–1697), author of a collection of lives of eminent persons, published in 1813.

Despite the derivative names and the sensational provenance of *The Vampyre*, it is the first English vampire story and the model for Thomas Preskett Prest's *Varney the Vampire* (1847), Joseph Sheridan Le Fanu's "Carmilla" (1871), Bram Stoker's *Dracula* (1897), and a host of films, the most memorable being Tod Browning's version for Universal Pictures with Bela Lugosi playing the lead (1931). The Gothic subgenre of vampire stories is based on the facts and legends surrounding an authentic fifteenth-century Wallachian prince, Vlad II, Dracul (the Devil or Dragon), and his son Vlad Tepes, Dracula (1431–1476). The history was researched by Bram Stoker and more recently and accurately by Raymond T. McNally and Radu Florescu in a volume called *In Search of Dracula: A True History of Dracula and Vampire Legends* (1972).

For the Gothic tradition, Polidori's *Vampyre*, like Mary Shelley's *Frankenstein*, marks a shift of focus from the moral but passive hero to the fascinating active villain. For the proud impostor who masquerades as good and the guilty, melancholy aspirant to power reserved for God, we are indebted to Byron's heroes and, in part, to Byron himself, whom Lady Caroline Lamb petulantly described in her journal as being "Mad—bad—and dangerous to know." Byron's reputation was even more flamboyant than his life or works. Polidori recognized Byron's seductive powers and minimized the gory details of the vampire legend to ensure identification of Lord Ruthven with Byron. Polidori distracted attention from sex in his story by means of the realistic local color of London and the primitive Greek countryside; only with Le Fanu and Stoker was explicit sexuality added to vampire fiction. Polidori carried Aubrey's naiveté to a surprising extreme and strained belief further with the spellbound silence and sudden death from a broken blood vessel. Such clumsy narrative details abound, but the figure of the vampire-gentleman in the modern world provokes terror: it is the evil image in an alluring mask.

When Byron learned of the publication of *The Vampyre; a Tale*, he responded with typical vehemence: "Damn 'the Vampire,'—what do I know of Vampires? it must be some bookselling imposture" (Letter to Douglas Kinnaird, 24 April 1819). Attributing Polidori's *Vampyre* to Byron was, indeed, a "bookselling imposture," and a clever one, as early sales indicated. But Byron did know something of vampires, and, while disclaiming authorship, he admits it in a letter to the editor of Galignani's *Messenger*: "I have besides a personal dislike to 'Vampires' and the little acquaintance I have with them would by no means induce me to divulge their secrets" (27 April 1819). His own "Fragment of a Novel," published in 1819 to settle the question of the authorship of *The Vampyre*, ends before it divulges many vampire secrets, but his verse tale "The Giaour" (1812) confirms the suspicion that Byron knew a great deal about vampires, however much he disliked them. "A Fragment of a Novel," like "The Giaour," accommodates the popular taste for exotic Eastern settings, Gothic curses, melancholy moods, and fallen, passionate heroes. Stork, pelican, and snake are all images for the Giaour or Darvell, Byron's vampire-like or vampire figures. In both the verse tale and "Fragment," he experiments with the narrators, using them as participants as well as commentators on the ritualized action. Polidori's reliance on "The Giaour" for images and details makes his piracy of Byron's plot all the more offensive because it implies careful premeditation. Although Polidori's *Vampyre* has the virtue of completeness, even the brevity of Byron's "Fragment of a Novel" does not diminish the superior vitality and, of course, the unquestioned originality of Byron's version of vampire secrets.

The Vampyre; A Tale (1819)

It happened that in the midst of the dissipations attendant upon a London winter, there appeared at the various parties of the leaders of the *ton* a nobleman, more remarkable for his singularities, than his rank. He gazed upon the mirth around him, as if he could not participate therein. Apparently, the light laughter of the fair only attracted his attention, that he might by a look quell it, and throw fear into those breasts where thoughtlessness reigned. Those who felt this sensation of awe, could not explain whence it arose: some attributed it to the dead grey eye, which, fixing upon the object's face, did not seem to penetrate, and at one glance to pierce through to the inward workings of the heart; but fell upon the cheek with a leaden ray that weighed upon the skin it could not pass. His peculiarities caused him to be invited to every house; all wished to see him, and those who had been accustomed to violent excitement, and now felt the weight of *ennui*, were pleased at having something in their presence capable of engaging their attention. In spite of the deadly hue of his face, which never gained a warmer tint, either from the blush of modesty, or from the strong emotion of passion, though its form and outline were beautiful, many of the female hunters after notoriety attempted to win his attentions, and gain, at least, some marks of what they might term affection: Lady Mercer, who had been the mockery of every monster shewn in drawing-rooms since her marriage, threw herself in his way, and did all but put on the dress of a mountebank, to attract his notice—though in vain—when she stood before him, though his eyes were apparently fixed upon hers, still it seemed as if they were unperceived; even her unappalled impudence was baffled, and she left the field. But though the common adultress could not influence even the guidance of his eyes, it was not that the female sex was indifferent to him: yet such was the apparent caution with which he spoke to the virtuous wife and innocent daughter, that few knew he ever addressed himself to females. He had, however, the reputation of a winning tongue; and whether it was that it even overcame the dread of his singular character, or that they were moved by his apparent hatred of vice, he was as often among those females who form the boast of their sex from their domestic virtues, as among those who sully it by their vices.

About the same time, there came to London a young gentleman of the name of Aubrey: he was an orphan left with an only sister in the possession of great wealth, by parents who died while he was yet in childhood. Left also to himself by guardians, who thought it their duty merely to take care of his fortune, while they relinquished the more important charge of his mind to the care of mercenary subalterns, he cultivated more his imagination than his judgment. He had, hence, that high romantic feeling of honour and candour, which daily ruins so many milliners' apprentices. He believed all to sympathise with virtue, and thought that vice was thrown in by Providence merely for the picturesque effect of the scene, as we see in romances: he thought that the misery of a cottage merely consisted in the vesting of clothes, which were as warm, but which were better adapted to the painter's eye by their irregular folds and various coloured patches. He thought, in fine, that the dreams of poets were the realities of life. He was handsome, frank, and rich: for these reasons, upon his entering into the gay circles, many mothers surrounded him, striving which should describe with least truth their languishing or romping favourites: the daughters at the same time, by their brightening countenances when he approached, and by their sparkling eyes, when he opened his lips, soon led him into false notions of his talents and his merit. Attached as he was to the romance of his solitary hours, he was startled at finding, that, except in the tallow and wax candles that flickered, not from the presence of a ghost, but from want of snuffing, there was no foundation in real life for any of that congeries of pleasing pictures and descriptions contained in those volumes, from which he had formed his study. Finding, however, some compensation in his gratified vanity, he was about to relinquish his dreams, when the extraordinary being we have above described, crossed him in his career.

He watched him; and the very impossibility of forming an idea of the character of a man entirely absorbed in himself, who gave few other signs of his observation of external objects, than the tacit assent to their existence, implied by the avoidance of their contact: allowing his imagination to picture every thing that flattered its propensity to extravagant ideas, he soon formed this object into the hero of a romance, and determined to observe the offspring of his fancy, rather than the person before him. He became acquainted with him, paid him attentions, and so far advanced upon his notice, that his presence was always recognised. He gradually learnt that Lord Ruthven's affairs were embarrassed, and soon found, from the notes of preparation in ———— Street, that he was about to travel. Desirous of gaining some information respecting this singular character, who, till now, had only whetted his curiosity, he hinted to his guardians, that it was time for him to perform the tour, which for many generations has been thought necessary to enable the young to take some rapid steps in the career of vice towards putting themselves upon an equality with the aged, and not allowing them to appear as if fallen from the skies, whenever scandalous intrigues are mentioned as the subjects of pleasantry or of praise, according to the degree of skill shewn in carrying them on. They consented: and Aubrey immediately mentioning his intentions to Lord Ruthven, was surprised to receive from him a proposal to join him. Flattered by such a mark of esteem from him, who, apparently, had nothing in common with other men, he gladly accepted it, and in a few days they had passed the circling waters.

Hitherto, Aubrey had had no opportunity of studying Lord Ruthven's character, and now he found, that, though many more of his actions were exposed to his view, the results offered different conclusions from the apparent motives to his conduct. His companion was profuse in his liberality; the idle, the vagabond, and the beggar, received from his hand more than enough to relieve their immediate wants. But Aubrey could not avoid remarking, that it was not upon the virtuous, reduced to indigence by the misfortunes attendant even upon virtue, that he bestowed his alms; these were sent from the door with hardly suppressed sneers; but when the profligate came to ask something, not to relieve his wants, but to allow him to wallow in his lust, or to sink him still deeper in his iniquity, he was sent away with rich charity. This was, however, attributed by him to the greater importunity of the vicious, which generally prevails over the retiring bashfulness of the virtuous indigent. There was one circumstance about the charity of his Lordship, which was still more impressed upon his mind: all those upon whom it was bestowed, inevitably found that there was a curse upon it, for they were all either led to the scaffold, or sunk to the lowest and the most abject misery. At Brussels and other towns through which they passed, Aubrey was surprized at the apparent eagerness with which his companion sought for the centres of all fashionable vice; there he entered into all the spirit of the faro table: he betted, and always gambled with success, except where the known sharper was his antagonist, and then he lost even more than he gained; but it was always with the same unchanging face, with which he generally watched the society around: it was not, however, so when he encountered the rash youthful novice, or the luckless father of a numerous family; then his very wish seemed fortune's law—this apparent abstractedness of mind was laid aside, and his eyes sparkled with more fire than that of the cat whilst dallying with the half-dead mouse. In every town, he left the formerly affluent youth, torn from the circle he adorned, cursing, in the solitude of a dungeon, the fate that had drawn him within the reach of this fiend; whilst many a father sat frantic, amidst the speaking looks of mute hungry children, without a single farthing of his late immense wealth, wherewith to buy even sufficient to satisfy their present craving. Yet he took no money from the gambling table; but immediately lost, to the ruiner of many, the last gilder he had just snatched from the convulsive grasp of the innocent: this might but be the result of a certain degree of knowledge, which was not, however, capable of combating the cunning of the more experienced. Aubrey often wished to represent this to his friend, and beg him to resign that charity and pleasure which proved the ruin of all, and did not tend to his own profit; but he delayed it—for each day he hoped his friend would give him some opportunity of speaking frankly and openly to him; however, this never occurred. Lord Ruthven in his carriage, and amidst the various wild and rich scenes of nature, was always the same: his eye spoke less than his lip; and though Aubrey was near the object of his curiosity, he obtained no greater gratification from it than the constant excitement of vainly wishing to break that mystery, which to his exalted imagination began to assume the appearance of something supernatural.

They soon arrived at Rome, and Aubrey for a time lost sight of his companion; he left him in daily attendance upon the morning circle of an Italian countess, whilst he went in search of the memorials of another almost deserted city. Whilst he was thus engaged, letters arrived from England, which he opened with eager impatience; the first was from his sister, breathing nothing but affection; the others were from his guardians, the latter astonished him; if it had before entered into his imagination that there was an evil power resident in his companion, these seemed to give him almost sufficient reason for the belief. His guardians insisted upon his immediately leaving his friend, and urged, that his character was dreadfully vicious, for that the possession of irresistible powers of seduction, rendered his licentious habits more dangerous to society. It had been discovered, that his contempt for the adultress had not originated in hatred of her character; but that he had required, to enhance his gratification, that his victim, the partner of his guilt, should be hurled from the pinnacle of unsullied virtue, down to the lowest abyss of infamy and degradation: in fine, that all those females whom he had sought, apparently on account of their virtue, had, since his departure, thrown even the mask aside, and had not scrupled to expose the whole deformity of their vices to the public gaze.

Aubrey determined upon leaving one, whose character had not yet shown a single bright point on which to rest the eye. He resolved to invent some plausible pretext for abandoning him altogether, purposing, in the mean while, to watch him more closely, and to let no slight circumstances pass by unnoticed. He entered into the same circle, and soon perceived, that his Lordship was endeavouring to work upon the inexperience of the daughter of the lady whose house he chiefly frequented. In Italy, it is seldom that an unmarried female is met with in society; he was therefore obliged to carry on his plans in secret; but Aubrey's eye followed him in all his windings, and soon discovered that an assignation had been appointed, which would most likely end in the ruin of an innocent, though thoughtless girl. Losing no time, he entered the apartment of Lord Ruthven, and abruptly asked him his intentions with respect to the lady, informing him at the same time that he was aware of his being about to meet her that very night. Lord Ruthven answered, that his intentions were such as he supposed all would have upon such an occasion; and upon being pressed whether he intended to marry her, merely laughed. Aubrey retired; and, immediately writing a note, to say, that from that moment he must decline accompanying his Lordship in the remainder of their proposed tour, he ordered his servant to seek other apartments, and calling upon the mother of the lady, informed her of all he knew, not only with regard to her daughter, but also concerning the character of his Lordship. The assignation was prevented. Lord Ruthven next day merely sent his servant to notify his complete assent to a separation; but did not hint any suspicion of his plans having been foiled by Aubrey's interposition.

Having left Rome, Aubrey directed his steps towards Greece, and crossing the Peninsula, soon found himself at Athens. He then fixed his residence in the house of a Greek; and soon occupied himself in tracing the faded records of ancient glory upon monuments that apparently, ashamed of chronicling the deeds of freemen only before slaves, had hidden themselves beneath the sheltering soil or many coloured lichen. Under the same roof as himself, existed a being, so beautiful and delicate, that she might have formed the model for a painter, wishing to pourtray on canvass the promised hope of the faithful in Mahomet's paradise, save that her eyes spoke too much mind for any one to think she could belong to those who had no souls. As she danced upon the plain, or tripped along the mountain's side, one would have thought the gazelle a poor type of her beauties; for who would have exchanged her eye, apparently the eye of animated nature, for that sleepy luxurious look of the animal suited but to the taste of an epicure. The light step of Ianthe often accompanied Aubrey in his search after antiquities, and often would the unconscious girl, engaged in the pursuit of a Kashmere butterfly, show the whole beauty of her form, floating as it were upon the wind, to the eager gaze of him, who forgot the letters he had just decyphered upon an almost effaced tablet, in the contemplation of her sylph-like figure. Often would her tresses falling, as she flitted around, exhibit in the sun's ray such delicately brilliant and swiftly fading hues, as might well excuse the forgetfulness of the antiquary, who let escape from his mind the very object he had before thought of vital importance to the proper interpretation of a passage in Pausanias. But why attempt to describe charms which all feel, but none can appreciate? It was innocence, youth, and beauty, unaffected by crowded drawing-rooms and stifling balls. Whilst he drew those remains of which he wished to preserve a memorial for his future hours, she would stand by, and watch the magic effects of his pencil, in tracing the scenes of her native place; she would then describe to him the circling dance upon the open plain, would paint to him in all the glowing colours of youthful memory, the marriage pomp she remembered viewing in her infancy; and then, turning to subjects that had evidently made a greater impression upon her mind, would tell him all the supernatural tales of her nurse. Her earnestness and apparent belief of what she narrated, excited the interest even of Aubrey; and often as she told him the tale of the living vampyre, who had passed years amidst his friends, and dearest ties, forced every year, by feeding upon the life of a lovely female to prolong his existence for the ensuing months, his blood would run cold, whilst he attempted to laugh her out of such idle and horrible fantasies; but Ianthe cited to him the names of old men, who had at last detected one living among themselves, after several of their near relatives and children had been found marked with the stamp of the fiend's appetite; and when she found him so incredulous, she begged of him to believe her, for it had been remarked, that those who had dared to question their existence, always had some proof given, which obliged them, with grief and heartbreaking, to confess it was true. She detailed to him the traditional appearance of these monsters, and his horror was increased, by hearing a pretty accurate description of Lord Ruthven; he, however, still persisted in persuading her, that there could be no truth in her fears, though at the same time he wondered at the many coincidences which had all tended to excite a belief in the supernatural power of Lord Ruthven.

Aubrey began to attach himself more and more to Ianthe; her innocence, so contrasted with all the affected virtues of the women among whom he had sought for his vision of romance, won his heart; and while he ridiculed the idea of a young man of English habits, marrying an uneducated Greek girl, still he found himself more and more attached to the almost fairy form before him. He would tear himself at times from her, and, forming a plan for some antiquarian research, he would depart, determined not to return until his object was attained; but he always found it impossible to fix his attention upon the ruins around him, whilst in his mind he retained an image that seemed alone the rightful possessor of his thoughts. Ianthe was unconscious of his love, and was ever the same frank infantile being he had first known. She always seemed to part from him with reluctance; but it was because she had no longer any one with whom she could visit her favourite haunts, whilst her guardian was occupied in sketching or uncovering some fragment which had yet escaped the destructive hand of time. She had appealed to her parents on the subject of Vampyres, and they both, with several present, affirmed their existence, pale with horror at the very name. Soon after, Aubrey determined to proceed upon one of his excursions, which was to detain him for a few hours; when they heard the name of the place, they all at once begged of him not to return at night, as he must necessarily pass through a wood, where no Greek would ever remain, after the day had closed, upon any consideration. They described it as the resort of the vampyres in their nocturnal orgies, and denounced the most heavy evils as impending upon him who dared to cross their path. Aubrey made light of their representations, and tried to laugh them out of the idea; but when he saw them shudder at his daring thus to mock a superior, infernal power, the very name of which apparently made their blood freeze, he was silent.

Next morning Aubrey set off upon his excursion unattended; he was surprised to observe the melancholy face of his host, and was concerned to find that his words, mocking the belief of those horrible fiends, had inspired them with such terror. When he was about to depart, Ianthe came to the side of his horse and earnestly begged of him to return, ere night allowed the power of these beings to be put in action; he promised. He was, however, so occupied in his research, that he did not perceive that day-light would soon end, and that in the horizon there was one of those specks which, in the warmer climates, so rapidly gather into a tremendous mass, and pour all their rage upon the devoted country. He at last, however, mounted his horse, determined to make up by speed for his delay: but it was too late. Twilight, in these southern climates, is almost unknown; immediately the sun sets, night begins: and ere he had advanced far, the power of the storm was above—its echoing thunders had scarcely an interval of rest—its thick heavy rain forced its way through the canopying foliage, whilst the blue forked lightning seemed to fall and radiate at his very feet. Suddenly his horse took fright, and he was carried with dreadful rapidity through the entangled forest. The animal at last, through fatigue, stopped, and he found, by the glare of lightning, that he was in the neighbourhood of a hovel that hardly lifted itself up from the masses of dead leaves and brushwood which surrounded it. Dismounting, he approached, hoping to find some one to guide him to the town, or at least trusting to obtain shelter from the pelting of the storm. As he approached, the thunders, for a moment silent, allowed him to hear the dreadful shrieks of a woman mingling with the stifled, exultant mockery of a laugh, continued in one almost unbroken sound; he was startled: but, roused by the thunder which again rolled over his head, he, with a sudden effort, forced open the door of the hut. He found himself in utter darkness: the sound, however, guided him. He was apparently unperceived; for, though he called, still the sounds continued, and no notice was taken of him. He found himself in contact with some one, whom he immediately seized; when a voice cried, "Again baffled!" to which a loud laugh succeeded; and he felt himself grappled by one whose strength seemed superhuman: determined to sell his life as dearly as he could, he struggled; but it was in vain: he was lifted from his feet and hurled with enormous force against the ground: his enemy threw himself upon him, and kneeling upon his breast, had placed his hands upon his throat—when the glare of many torches penetrating through the hole that gave light in the day, disturbed him; he instantly rose, and, leaving his prey, rushed through the door, and in a moment the crashing of the branches, as he broke through the wood, was no longer heard. The storm was now still; and Aubrey, incapable of moving, was soon heard by those without. They entered; the light of their torches fell upon the mud walls, and the thatch loaded on every individual straw

with heavy flakes of soot. At the desire of Aubrey they searched for
her who had attracted him by her cries; he was again left in darkness;
but what was his horror, when the light of the torches once more burst
upon him, to perceive the airy form of his fair conductress brought in
a lifeless corpse. He shut his eyes, hoping that it was but a vision
arising from his disturbed imagination; but he again saw the same
form, when he unclosed them, stretched by his side. There was no
colour upon her cheek, not even upon her lip; yet there was a stillness
about her face that seemed almost as attaching as the life that once
dwelt there—upon her neck and breast was blood, and upon her
throat were the marks of teeth having opened the vein—to this the
men pointed, crying, simultaneously struck with horror, "A Vampyre! a Vampyre!" A litter was quickly formed, and Aubrey was laid
by the side of her who had lately been to him the object of so many
bright and fairy visions, now fallen with the flower of life that had
died within her. He knew not what his thoughts were—his mind was
benumbed and seemed to shun reflection, and take refuge in vacancy
—he held almost unconsciously in his hand a naked dagger of a
particular construction, which had been found in the hut. They were
soon met by different parties who had been engaged in the search of
her whom a mother had missed. Their lamentable cries, as they approached the city, forewarned the parents of some dreadful catastrophe. To describe their grief would be impossible; but when they
ascertained the cause of their child's death, they looked at Aubrey,
and pointed to the corse. They were inconsolable; both died broken-
hearted.

Aubrey being put to bed was seized with a most violent fever,
and was often delirious; in these intervals he would call upon Lord
Ruthven and upon Ianthe—by some unaccountable combination he
seemed to beg of his former companion to spare the being he loved.
At other times he would imprecate maledictions upon his head, and
curse him as her destroyer. Lord Ruthven chanced at this time to
arrive at Athens, and, from whatever motive, upon hearing of the state
of Aubrey, immediately placed himself in the same house, and became his constant attendant. When the latter recovered from his
delirium, he was horrified and startled at the sight of him whose
image he had now combined with that of a Vampyre; but Lord
Ruthven, by his kind words, implying almost repentance for the fault
that had caused their separation, and still more by the attention,
anxiety, and care which he showed, soon reconciled him to his presence. His lordship seemed quite changed; he no longer appeared that
apathetic being who had so astonished Aubrey; but as soon as his
convalescence began to be rapid, he again gradually retired into the
same state of mind, and Aubrey perceived no difference from the

former man, except that at times he was surprised to meet his gaze fixed intently upon him, with a smile of malicious exultation playing upon his lips: he knew not why, but this smile haunted him. During the last stage of the invalid's recovery, Lord Ruthven was apparently engaged in watching the tideless waves raised by the cooling breeze, or in marking the progress of those orbs, circling, like our world, the moveless sun; indeed, he appeared to wish to avoid the eyes of all.

Aubrey's mind, by this shock, was much weakened, and that elasticity of spirit which had once so distinguished him now seemed to have fled for ever. He was now as much a lover of solitude and silence as Lord Ruthven; but much as he wished for solitude, his mind could not find it in the neighbourhood of Athens; if he sought it amidst the ruins he had formerly frequented, Ianthe's form stood by his side—if he sought it in the woods, her light step would appear wandering amidst the underwood, in quest of the modest violet; then suddenly turning round, would show, to his wild imagination, her pale face and wounded throat, with a meek smile upon her lips. He determined to fly scenes, every feature of which created such bitter associations in his mind. He proposed to Lord Ruthven, to whom he held himself bound by the tender care he had taken of him during his illness, that they should visit those parts of Greece neither had yet seen. They travelled in every direction, and sought every spot to which a recollection could be attached: but though they thus hastened from place to place, yet they seemed not to heed what they gazed upon. They heard much of robbers, but they gradually began to slight these reports, which they imagined were only the invention of individuals, whose interest it was to excite the generosity of those whom they defended from pretended dangers. In consequence of thus neglecting the advice of the inhabitants, on one occasion they travelled with only a few guards, more to serve as guides than as a defence. Upon entering, however, a narrow defile, at the bottom of which was the bed of a torrent, with large masses of rock brought down from the neighbouring precipices, they had reason to repent their negligence; for scarcely were the whole of the party engaged in the narrow pass, when they were startled by the whistling of bullets close to their heads, and by the echoed report of several guns. In an instant their guards had left them, and, placing themselves behind rocks, had begun to fire in the direction whence the report came. Lord Ruthven and Aubrey, imitating their example, retired for a moment behind the sheltering turn of the defile: but ashamed of being thus detained by a foe, who with insulting shouts bade them advance, and being exposed to unresisting slaughter, if any of the robbers should climb above and take them in the rear, they determined at once to rush forward in search of the enemy. Hardly had they lost the shelter of the rock, when Lord Ruthven received a shot in the shoulder, which brought him to the ground. Aubrey hastened to his assistance; and, no longer heeding the contest or his own peril, was soon surprised by seeing the robbers' faces around him—his guards having, upon Lord Ruthven's being wounded, immediately thrown up their arms and surrendered.

By promises of great reward, Aubury soon induced them to convey his wounded friend to a neighbouring cabin; and having agreed upon a ransom, he was no more disturbed by their presence— they being content merely to guard the entrance till their comrade should return with the promised sum, for which he had an order. Lord Ruthven's strength rapidly decreased; in two days mortification ensued, and death seemed advancing with hasty steps. His conduct and appearance had not changed; he seemed as unconscious of pain as he had been of the objects about him: but towards the close of the last evening, his mind became apparently uneasy, and his eye often fixed upon Aubrey, who was induced to offer his assistance with more than usual earnestness—"Assist me! you may save me—you may do more than that—I mean not my life, I heed the death of my existence as little as that of the passing day; but you may save my honour, your friend's honour." "How? tell me how? I would do any thing," replied Aubrey. "I need but little—my life ebbs apace—I cannot explain the whole—but if you would conceal all you know of me, my honour were free from stain in the world's mouth—and if my death were unknown for some time in England—I—I—but life." "It shall not be known." "Swear!" cried the dying man, raising himself with exultant violence, "Swear by all your soul reveres, by all your nature fears, swear that for a year and a day you will not impart your knowledge of my crimes or death to any living being in any way, whatever may happen, or whatever you may see." His eyes seemed bursting from the sockets: "I swear!" said Aubrey; he sunk laughing upon his pillow, and breathed no more.

Aubrey retired to rest, but did not sleep; the many circumstances attending his acquaintance with this man rose upon his mind, and he knew not why; when he remembered his oath a cold shivering came over him, as if from the presentiment of something horrible awaiting him. Rising early in the morning, he was about to enter the hovel in which he had left the corpse, when a robber met him, and informed him that it was no longer there, having been conveyed by himself and comrades, upon his retiring, to the pinnacle of a neighbouring mount, according to a promise they had given his lordship, that it should be exposed to the first cold ray of the moon that rose after his death. Aubrey astonished, and taking several of the men, determined to go and bury it upon the spot where it lay. But, when he had mounted to the summit he found no trace of either the corpse or the clothes, though the robbers swore they pointed out the identical rock on which they had laid the body. For a time his mind was bewildered in conjectures, but he at last returned, convinced that they had buried the corpse for the sake of the clothes.

Weary of a country in which he had met with such terrible misfortunes, and in which all apparently conspired to heighten that superstitious melancholy that had seized upon his mind, he resolved to leave it, and soon arrived at Smyrna. While waiting for a vessel to convey him to Otranto, or to Naples, he occupied himself in arranging those effects he had with him belonging to Lord Ruthven. Amongst other things there was a case containing several weapons of offence, more or less adapted to ensure the death of the victim. There were several daggers and ataghans. Whilst turning them over, and examining their curious forms, what was his surprise at finding a sheath apparently ornamented in the same style as the dagger discovered in the fatal hut—he shuddered—hastening to gain further proof, he found the weapon, and his horror may be imagined when he discovered that it fitted, though peculiarly shaped, the sheath he held in his hand. His eyes seemed to need no further certainty—they seemed gazing to be bound to the dagger; yet still he wished to disbelieve; but the particular form, the same varying tints upon the haft and sheath were alike in splendour on both, and left no room for doubt; there were also drops of blood on each.

He left Smyrna, and on his way home, at Rome, his first inquiries were concerning the lady he had attempted to snatch from Lord Ruthven's seductive arts. Her parents were in distress, their fortune ruined, and she had not been heard of since the departure of his lordship. Aubrey's mind became almost broken under so many repeated horrors; he was afraid that this lady had fallen a victim to the destroyer of Ianthe. He became morose and silent; and his only occupation consisted in urging the speed of the postilions, as if he were going to save the life of some one he held dear. He arrived at Calais; a breeze, which seemed obedient to his will, soon wafted him to the English shores; and he hastened to the mansion of his fathers, and there, for a moment, appeared to lose, in the embraces and caresses of his sister, all memory of the past. If she before, by her infantine caresses, had gained his affection, now that the woman began to appear, she was still more attaching as a companion.

Miss Aubrey had not that winning grace which gains the gaze and applause of the drawing-room assemblies. There was none of that light brilliancy which only exists in the heated atmosphere of a crowded apartment. Her blue eye was never lit up by the levity of the mind beneath. There was a melancholy charm about it which did not seem to arise from misfortune, but from some feeling within, that appeared to indicate a soul conscious of a brighter realm. Her step was not that light footing, which strays where'er a butterfly or a colour may attract—it was sedate and pensive. When alone, her face was never frightened by the smile of joy; but when her brother breathed to her his affection, and would in her presence forget those griefs she knew destroyed his rest, who would have exchanged her smile for that of the voluptuary? It seemed as if those eyes, that face were then playing in the light of their own native sphere. She was yet only eighteen, and had not been presented to the world, it having been thought by her guardians more fit that her presentation should be delayed until her brother's return from the continent, when he might be her protector. It was now, therefore, resolved that the next drawing-room, which was fast approaching; should be the epoch of her entry into the "busy scene." Aubrey would rather have remained in the mansion of his fathers; and fed upon the melancholy which overpowered him. He could not feel interest about the frivolities of fashionable strangers, when his mind had been so torn by the events he had witnessed; but he determined to sacrifice his own comfort to the protection of his sister. They soon arrived in town, and prepared for the next day, which had been announced as a drawing-room.

The crowd was excessive—a drawing-room had not been held for a long time, and all who were anxious to bask in the smile of royalty, hastened thither. Aubrey was there with his sister. While he was standing in a corner by himself, heedless of all around him, engaged in the remembrance that the first time he had seen Lord Ruthven was in that very place—he felt himself suddenly seized by the arm, and a voice he recognized too well, sounded in his ear— "Remember your oath." He had hardly courage to turn, fearful of seeing a spectre that would blast him, when he perceived, at a little distance, the same figure which had attracted his notice on this spot upon his first entry into society. He gazed till his limbs almost refusing to bear their weight, he was obliged to take the arm of a friend, and forcing a passage through the crowd, he threw himself into his carriage, and was driven home. He paced the room with hurried steps, and fixed his hands upon his head, as if he were afraid his thoughts were bursting from his brain. Lord Ruthven again before him—circumstances started up in dreadful array—the dagger—his oath. He roused himself, he could not believe it possible—the dead rise again! He thought his imagination had conjured up the image his mind was resting upon. It was impossible that it could be real—he determined, therefore, to go again into society; for though he attempted to ask concerning Lord Ruthven, the name hung upon his lips, and he could not succeed in gaining information. He went a few nights after with his sister to the assembly of a near relation. Leaving her under the protection of a matron, he retired into a recess, and there gave himself up to his own devouring thoughts. Perceiving, at last, that many were leaving, he roused himself, and entering another room, found his sister surrounded by several, apparently in earnest conversation; he attempted to pass and get near her, when one, whom he requested to move, turned around and revealed to him those features he most abhorred. He sprang forward, seized his sister's arm, and, with hurried step, forced her towards the street: at the door he found himself impeded by the crowd of servants who were waiting for their lords; and while he was engaged in passing them, he again heard that voice whisper close to him—"Remember your oath!" He did not dare to turn, but, hurrying his sister, soon reached home.

Aubrey became almost distracted. If before his mind had been absorbed by one subject, how much more completely was it engrossed, now that the certainty of the monster's living again pressed upon his thoughts. His sister's attentions were now unheeded, and it was in vain that she intreated him to explain to her what had caused his abrupt conduct. He only uttered a few words and those terrified her. The more he thought, the more he was bewildered. His oath startled him; was he then to allow this monster to roam, bearing ruin upon his breath, amidst all he held dear, and not avert its progress? His very sister might have been touched by him. But even if he were to break his oath, and disclose his suspicions, who would believe him? He thought of employing his own hand to free the world from such a wretch; but death, he remembered, had been already mocked. For days he remained in this state; shut up in his room, he saw no one, and eat only when his sister came, who, with eyes streaming with tears, besought him, for her sake, to support nature. At last, no longer capable of bearing stillness and solitude, he left his house; roamed from street to street, anxious to fly that image which haunted him. His dress became neglected, and he wandered, as often exposed to the noon-day sun as to the midnight damps. He was no longer to be recognized; at first he returned with the evening to the house; but at last he laid him down to rest wherever fatigue overtook him. His sister, anxious for his safety, employed people to follow him; but they were soon distanced by him who fled from a pursuer swifter than any—from thought. His conduct, however, suddenly changed. Struck with the idea that he left by his absence the whole of his friends, with a fiend amongst them, of whose presence they were unconscious, he determined to enter again into society, and watch him closely, anxious to forewarn, in spite of his oath, all whom Lord Ruthven approached with intimacy. But when he entered into a room, his haggard and suspicious looks were so striking, his inward shudderings so visible, that his sister was at last obliged to beg of him to abstain from seeking, for her sake, a society which affected him so strongly. When, however,

remonstrance proved unavailing, the guardians thought proper to inter-
pose, and, fearing that his mind was becoming alienated, they thought
it high time to resume again that trust which had been before imposed
upon them by Aubrey's parents.

Desirous of saving him from the injuries and sufferings he had
daily encountered in his wanderings, and of preventing him from
exposing to the general eye those marks of what they considered
folly, they engaged a physician to reside in the house, and take constant care of him. He hardly appeared to notice it, so completely was
his mind absorbed by one terrible subject. His incoherence became at
last so great, that he was confined to his chamber. There he would
often lie for days, incapable of being roused. He had become emaciated, his eyes had attained a glassy lustre; the only sign of affection
and recollection remaining displayed itself upon the entry of his sister; then he would sometimes start, and, seizing her hands, with looks
that severely afflicted her, he would desire her not to touch him. "Oh,
do not touch him—if your love for me is aught, do not go near him!"
When, however, she inquired to whom he referred, his only answer
was, "True! true!" and again he sank into a state, whence not even
she could rouse him. This lasted many months: gradually, however,
as the year was passing, his incoherences became less frequent and
his mind threw off a portion of its gloom, whilst his guardians observed, that several times in the day he would count upon his fingers a
definite number, and then smile.

The time had nearly elapsed, when, upon the last day of the
year, one of his guardians entering his room, began to converse with
his physician upon the melancholy circumstance of Aubrey's being in
so awful a situation, when his sister was going next day to be married.
Instantly Aubrey's attention was attracted; he asked anxiously to
whom. Glad of this mark of returning intellect, of which they feared
he had been deprived, they mentioned the name of the Earl of
Marsden. Thinking this was a young Earl whom he had met with in
society, Aubrey seemed pleased, and astonished them still more by
his expressing his intention to be present at the nuptials, and desiring
to see his sister. They answered not, but in a few minutes his sister
was with him. He was apparently again capable of being affected by
the influence of her lovely smile; for he pressed her to his breast, and
kissed her cheek, wet with tears, flowing at the thought of her brother's being once more alive to the feelings of affection. He began to
speak with all his wonted warmth, and to congratulate her upon her
marriage with a person so distinguished for rank and every accomplishment; when he suddenly perceived a locket upon her breast;
opening it, what was his surprise at beholding the features of the
monster who had so long influenced his life. He seized the portrait in

a paroxysm of rage, and trampled it under foot. Upon her asking him why he thus destroyed the resemblance of her future husband, he looked as if he did not understand her—then seizing her hands, and gazing on her with a frantic expression of countenance, he bade her swear that she would never wed this monster, for he—But he could not advance—it seemed as if that voice again bade him remember his oath—he turned suddenly round, thinking Lord Ruthven was near him but saw no one. In the meantime the guardians and physician, who had heard the whole, and thought this was but a return of his disorder, entered, and forcing him from Miss Aubrey, desired her to leave him. He fell upon his knees to them, he implored, he begged of them to delay but for one day. They, attributing this to the insanity they imagined had taken possession of his mind endeavoured to pacify him, and retired.

Lord Ruthven had called the morning after the drawing-room, and had been refused with every one else. When he heard of Aubrey's ill health, he readily understood himself to be the cause of it; but when he learned that he was deemed insane, his exultation and pleasure could hardly be concealed from those among whom he had gained this information. He hastened to the house of his former companion, and, by constant attendance, and the pretence of great affection for the brother and interest in his fate, he gradually won the ear of Miss Aubrey. Who could resist his power? His tongue had dangers and toils to recount—could speak of himself as of an individual having no sympathy with any being on the crowded earth, save with her to whom he addressed himself; could tell how, since he knew her, his existence had begun to seem worthy of preservation, if it were merely that he might listen to her soothing accents; in fine, he knew so well how to use the serpent's art, or such was the will of fate, that he gained her affections. The title of the elder branch falling at length to him, he obtained an important embassy, which served as an excuse for hastening the marriage, in spite of her brother's deranged state, which was to take place the very day before his departure for the continent.

Aubrey, when he was left by the physician and his guardians, attempted to bribe the servants, but in vain. He asked for pen and paper; it was given him; he wrote a letter to his sister, conjuring her, as she valued her own happiness, her own honour, and the honour of those now in the grave, who once held her in their arms as their hope and the hope of their house, to delay but for a few hours that marriage, on which he denounced the most heavy curses. The servants promised they would deliver it; but giving it to the physician, he thought it better not to harass any more the mind of Miss Aubrey by, what he considered, the ravings of a maniac. Night passed on without rest to the busy inmates of the house; and Aubrey heard, with a horror that may more easily be conceived than described, the notes of busy preparation. Morning came, and the sound of carriages broke upon his ear. Aubrey grew almost frantic. The curiosity of the servants at last overcame their vigilance, they gradually stole away, leaving him in the custody of an helpless old woman. He seized the opportunity, with one bound was out of the room, and in a moment found himself in the apartment where all were nearly assembled. Lord Ruthven was the first to perceive him: he immediately approached, and, taking his arm by force, hurried him from the room, speechless with rage. When on the staircase, Lord Ruthven whispered in his ear—"Remember your oath, and know, if not my bride today, your sister is dishonoured. Women are frail!" So saying, he pushed him towards his attendants, who, roused by the old woman, had come in search of him. Aubrey could no longer support himself; his rage not finding vent, had broken a blood-vessel, and he was conveyed to bed. This was not mentioned to his sister, who was not present when he entered, as the physician was afraid of agitating her. The marriage was solemnized, and the bride and bridegroom left London.

Aubrey's weakness increased; the effusion of blood produced symptoms of the near approach of death. He desired his sister's guardians might be called, and when the midnight hour had struck, he related composedly what the reader has perused—he died immediately after.

The guardians hastened to protect Miss Aubrey; but when they arrived, it was too late. Lord Ruthven had disappeared, and Aubrey's sister had glutted the thirst of a Vampyre!

A Fragment of a Novel (1819)
by Byron

June 17, 1816

In the year 17—, having for some time determined on a journey through countries not hitherto much frequented by travellers, I set out, accompanied by a friend, whom I shall designate by the name of Augustus Darvell. He was a few years my elder, and a man of considerable fortune and ancient family: advantages which an extensive capacity prevented him alike from undervaluing or overrating. Some peculiar circumstances in his private history had rendered him to me an object of attention, of interest, and even of regard, which neither the reserve of his manners, nor occasional indications of an inquietude at times nearly approaching to alienation of mind, could extinguish.

I was yet young in life, which I had begun early; but my intimacy with him was of a recent date: we had been educated at the same schools and university; but his progress through these had preceded mine, and he had been deeply initiated into what is called the world, while I was yet in my novitiate. While thus engaged, I heard much both of his past and present life; and, although in these accounts there were many and irreconcilable contradictions, I could still gather from the whole that he was a being of no common order, and one who, whatever pains he might take to avoid remark, would still be remarkable. I had cultivated his acquaintance subsequently, and endeavoured to obtain his friendship, but this last appeared to be unattainable; whatever affections he might have possessed seemed now, some to have been extinguished, and others to be concentred: that his feelings were acute, I had sufficient opportunities of observing; for, although he could control, he could not altogether disguise them: still he had a power of giving to one passion the appearance of another, in such a manner that it was difficult to define the nature of what was working within him; and the expressions of his features would vary so rapidly, though slightly, that it was useless to trace them to their sources. It was evident that he was a prey to some cureless disquiet; but whether it arose from ambition, love, remorse, grief, from one or all of these, or merely from a morbid temperament akin to disease, I could not discover: there were circumstances alleged which might have justified the application to each of these causes; but, as I have before said, these were so contradictory and contradicted, that none could be fixed upon with accuracy. Where there is mystery, it is generally supposed that there must also be evil: I know not how this may be, but in him there certainly was the one, though I could not ascertain the extent of the other—and felt loth, as far as regarded himself, to believe in its existence. My advances were received with sufficient coldnesss: but I was young, and not easily discouraged, and at length succeeded in obtaining, to a certain degree, that common-place intercourse and moderate confidence of common and every-day concerns, created and cemented by similarity of pursuit and frequency of meeting, which is called intimacy, or friendship, according to the ideas of him who uses those words to express them.

Darvell had already travelled extensively; and to him I had applied for information with regard to the conduct of my intended journey. It was my secret wish that he might be prevailed on to accompany me; it was also a probable hope, founded upon the shadowy restlessness which I observed in him, and to which the animation which he appeared to feel on such subjects, and his apparent indifference to all by which he was more immediately surrounded, gave fresh strength. This wish I first hinted, and then expressed: his answer, though I had partly expected it, gave me all the pleasure of surprise— he consented; and, after the requisite arrangement, we commenced our voyages. After journeying through various countries of the south of Europe, our attention was turned towards the East, according to our original destination; and it was in my progress through those regions that the incident occurred upon which will turn what I may have to relate.

The constitution of Darvell, which must from his appearance have been in early life more than usually robust, had been for some time gradually giving way, without the intervention of any apparent disease: he had neither cough nor hectic, yet he became daily more enfeebled; his habits were temperate, and he neither declined nor complained of fatigue; yet he was evidently wasting away: he became more and more silent and sleepless, and at length so seriously altered, that my alarm grew proportionate to what I conceived to be his danger.

We had determined, on our arrival at Smyrna, on an excursion to the ruins of Ephesus and Sardis, from which I endeavoured to dissuade him in his present state of indisposition—but in vain: there appeared to be an oppression on his mind, and a solemnity in his manner, which ill corresponded with his eagerness to proceed on what I regarded as a mere party of pleasure little suited to a valetudinarian; but I opposed him no longer—and in a few days we set off together, accompanied only by a serrugee and a single janizary.

We had passed halfway towards the remains of Ephesus, leaving behind us the more fertile environs of Smyrna, and were entering upon that wild and tenantless tract through the marshes and defiles which lead to the few huts yet lingering over the broken columns of Diana—the roofless walls of expelled Christianity, and the still more recent but complete desolation of abandoned mosques—when the sudden and rapid illness of my companion obliged us to halt at a Turkish cemetery, the turbaned tombstones of which were the sole indication that human life had ever been a sojourner in this wilderness. The only caravansera we had seen was left some hours behind us, not a vestige of a town or even cottage was within sight or hope, and this "city of the dead" appeared to be the sole refuge for my unfortunate friend, who seemed on the verge of becoming the last of its inhabitants.

In this situation, I looked round for a place where he might most conveniently repose:—contrary to the usual aspect of Mahometan burial-grounds, the cypresses were in this few in number, and these thinly scattered over its extent; the tombstones were mostly fallen, and worn with age: upon one of the most considerable of these, and beneath one of the most spreading trees, Darvell supported himself, in a half-reclining posture, with great difficulty. He asked for water. I had some doubts of our being able to find any, and prepared to go in search of it with hesitating despondency: but he desired me to remain; and turning to Suleiman, our janizary, who stood by us smoking with great tranquillity, he said, "Suleiman, verbana su," (*i.e.* "bring some water,") and went on describing the spot where it was to be found with great minuteness, at a small well for camels, a few hundred yards to the right: the janizary obeyed. I said to Darvell, "How did you know this?" He replied, "From our situation; you must perceive that this place was once inhabited, and could not have been so without springs: I have also been here before."

"You have been here before! How came you never to mention this to me? and what could you be doing in a place where no one would remain a moment longer than they could help it?"

To this question I received no answer. In the mean time Suleiman returned with the water, leaving the serrugee and the horses at the fountain. The quenching of his thirst had the appearance of reviving him for a moment; and I conceived hopes of his being able to proceed, or at least to return, and I urged the attempt. He was silent —and appeared to be collecting his spirits for an effort to speak. He began—

"This is the end of my journey, and of my life; I came here to die; but I have a request to make, a command—for such my last words must be. You will observe it?"

"Most certainly; but have better hopes."

I have no hopes, nor wishes, but this—conceal my death from every human being."

"I hope there will be no occasion; that you will recover, and—"

"Peace! it must be so: promise this."

"I do."

"Swear it, by all that—" He here dictated an oath of great solemnity.

"There is no occasion for this. I will observe your request; and to doubt me is—"

"It cannot be helped—you must swear."

I took the oath, it appeared to relieve him. He removed a seal ring from his finger, on which were some Arabic characters, and presented it to me. He proceeded—

"On the ninth day of the month, at noon precisely (what month you please, but this must be the day), you must fling this ring into the salt springs which run into the Bay of Eleusis; the day after, at the same hour, you must repair to the ruins of the temple of Ceres, and wait one hour."

"Why?"

"You will see."

"The ninth day of the month, you say?"

"The ninth."

As I observed that the present was the ninth day of the month, his countenance changed, and he paused. As he sat, evidently becoming more feeble, a stork, with a snake in her beak, perched upon a tombstone near us; and, without devouring her prey, appeared to be steadfastly regarding us. I know not what impelled me to drive it away but the attempt was useless; she made a few circles in the air, and returned exactly to the same spot. Darvell pointed to it, and smiled—he spoke—I know not whether to himself or to me—but the words were only, " 'Tis well!"

"What is well? What do you mean?"

"No matter; you must bury me here this evening, and exactly where that bird is now perched. You know the rest of my injunctions."

He then proceeded to give me several directions as to the manner in which his death might be best concealed. After these were finished, he exclaimed, "You perceive that bird?"

"Certainly."

"And the serpent writhing in her beak?"

"Doubtless: there is nothing uncommon in it; it is her natural prey. But it is odd that she does not devour it."

He smiled in a ghastly manner, and said faintly, "It is not yet time!" As he spoke, the stork flew away. My eyes followed it for a moment—it could hardly be longer than ten might be counted. I felt Darvell's weight, as it were, increase upon my shoulder, and, turning to look upon his face, perceived that he was dead!

I was shocked with the sudden certainty which could not be mistaken—his countenance in a few minutes became nearly black. I should have attributed so rapid a change to poison, had I not been aware that he had no opportunity of receiving it unperceived. The day was declining, the body was rapidly altering, and nothing remained but to fulfil his request. With the aid of Suleiman's ataghan and my own sabre, we scooped a shallow grave upon the spot which Darvell had indicated: the earth easily gave way, having already received some Mahometan tenant. We dug as deeply as the time permitted us, and throwing the dry earth upon all that remained of the singular being so lately departed, we cut a few sods of greener turf from the less withered soil around us, and laid them upon his sepulchre.

Between astonishment and grief, I was tearless.

Edvard Munch's *Vampire* clearly reveals the sexuality hinted at in a poem like Coleridge's "Christabel." COLLECTION, THE MUSEUM OF MODERN ART, NEW YORK.

Mary Wollstonecraft Shelley
(1797-1851)

LITERARY achievement surrounded Mary Shelley from birth to death. Her father, William Godwin, established himself as a political theorist of revolutionary tendencies in his *Enquiry Concerning Political Justice* (1793) and as a psychological novelist in *Caleb Williams* (1794), a tragic story of guilt and pursuit. Her mother, Mary Wollstonecraft, who died from complications of Mary's birth, had achieved eminence as the author of *A Vindication of the Rights of Woman* (1792), the first sustained essay advocating the equality of women. Her husband, Percy Bysshe Shelley, poet and dramatist, encouraged and assisted Mary in her own literary efforts, most notably in *Frankenstein: or the Modern Prometheus*, written when Mary was nineteen, published in 1818. Following Shelley's death by drowning in 1822, Mary Shelley produced four novels, two travel books, five volumes of biographical sketches, twenty-five short stories, two biographical pieces on Shelley and Godwin, and an edition of her husband's poetry and prose with detailed notes.

"Transformation," published in the same year as the revised edition of *Frankenstein*, both borrows and tellingly omits many of the themes and devices of the novel that has inspired a host of imitations in opera, drama, and film. The pseudoscientific creation of the nameless monster by the student Victor Frankenstein is replaced by the light fairy-tale magic of the dwarf's sudden appearance. He, like Frankenstein's creature, is called a "monster," but Guido has none of the responsibility for him that Victor Frankenstein has for his handiwork. Mary Shelley characterizes Guido as wildly irresponsible: he sells his property to buy ephemeral pleasures; he insults his "second parent" by seeming to prefer his friends over him; and he irresponsibly gambles his body for wealth. His offenses, born of greed and pride, lack the grandeur of Frankenstein's overreaching ambitions and conscious morality. Nonetheless, Guido is true to his beloved Juliet, who, like Frankenstein's Elizabeth, grew up with him and was betrothed to him at a parent's deathbed. Juliet's beauty, goodness, and innocence echo Elizabeth's noble character, and Torella's paternal kindness and wisdom parallel the virtues of Victor Frankenstein's father. Both

Guido and Frankenstein enjoy free and happy childhoods, but betray, in different ways, the idyllic love that surrounded them in youth.

The most reverberant echo of Gothic theme from *Frankenstein* to "Transformation" is the *Doppelgänger* or "double" motif. The misshapen dwarf physically mirrors the monstrous immorality of Guido just as Frankenstein's monster mirrors the young scientist's impulses, both creative and destructive. Like Frankenstein, his is a domestic, benevolent, and intellectual character. The complications of the duality are far greater in the novel, of course, but the halves of the divided self competing for the beloved bring both fictions to an appropriate climax. The dwarf's satanic oaths and power over sea and sky owe much to Byron's *Manfred*, where the attraction to power beyond man's limits results in the death of the beloved. The impiety of "tempting Providence" clarifies the supernatural details more obviously in "Transformation" than in either *Frankenstein* or *Manfred*, where clarity of moral categories is deliberately obscured by Romantic suggestions of heroism. In the short story, Guido literally battles with himself for Juliet, as he battled a cousin earlier and as his dream foretold; and, despite the disadvantages of size, agility, and weapon, he wins. With his victory he regains his own body, his stepfather's forgiveness, and his moral and monetary inheritance. Moral reform earns Guido the title "*il Cortese*," the kind one. He becomes a fond and faithful husband with a pale cheek and a bent form to remind him of his folly in the days he was an "*enfant gâté*," a spoiled child. As in Stevenson's "Markheim," the double eventually proves to be a force for good in the most traditional sense.

"Transformation" lacks the sincerity and strong emotion of the novel; but even in its brevity and simplicity, it comments on *Frankenstein* and supports the view that the living stimulus and lively suggestions of Percy Bysshe Shelley led Mary Shelley to greater and more lasting literary achievement. "Transformation" is encumbered by overt moralizing, but the reflections of *Frankenstein* cannot be ignored.

Transformation (1831)

Forthwith this frame of mine was wrench'd
    With a woeful agony,
Which forced me to begin my tale,
    And then it set me free.

> Since then, at an uncertain hour,
> That agony returns;
> And till my ghastly tale is told
> This heart within me burns.
> —Coleridge's *Ancient Mariner*.

I have heard it said, that, when any strange, supernatural, and necromantic adventure has occurred to a human being, that being, however desirous he may be to conceal the same, feels at certain periods torn up as it were by an intellectual earthquake, and is forced to bare the inner depths of his spirit to another. I am a witness of the truth of this. I have dearly sworn to myself never to reveal to human ears the horrors to which I once, in excess of fiendly pride, delivered myself over. The holy man who heard my confession, and reconciled me to the church, is dead. None knows that once—

Why should it not be thus? Why tell a tale of impious tempting of Providence, and soul-subduing humiliation? Why? answer me, ye who are wise in the secrets of human nature! I only know that so it is; and in spite of strong resolve—of a pride that too much masters me—of shame, and even of fear, so to render myself odious to my species—I must speak.

Genoa! my birth-place—proud city! looking upon the blue waves of the Mediterranean sea—dost thou remember me in my boyhood, when thy cliffs and promontories, thy bright sky and gay vineyards, were my world? Happy time! when to the young heart the narrow-bounded universe, which leaves, by its very limitation, free scope to the imagination, enchains our physical energies, and, sole period in our lives, innocence and enjoyment are united. Yet, who can look back to childhood, and not remember its sorrows and its harrowing fears? I was born with the most imperious, haughty, tameless spirit, with which ever mortal was gifted. I quailed before my father only; and he, generous and noble, but capricious and tyrannical, at once fostered and checked the wild impetuosity of my character, making obedience necessary, but inspiring no respect for the motives which guided his commands. To be a man, free, independent; or, in better words, insolent and domineering, was the hope and prayer of my rebel heart.

My father had one friend, a wealthy Genoese noble, who in a political tumult was suddenly sentenced to banishment, and his property confiscated. The Marchese Torella went into exile alone. Like my father, he was a widower: he had one child, the almost infant Juliet, who was left under my father's guardianship. I should certainly have been an unkind master to the lovely girl, but that I was forced by my position to become her protector. A variety of childish incidents all tended to one point,—to make Juliet see in me a rock of refuge; I in her, one, who must perish through the soft sensibility of her nature too rudely visited, but for my guardian care. We grew up together. The opening rose in May was not more sweet than this dear girl. An irradiation of beauty was spread over her face. Her form, her step, her voice—my heart weeps even now, to think of all of relying, gentle, loving, and pure, that was enshrined in that celestial tenement. When I was eleven and Juliet eight years of age, a cousin of mine, much older than either—he seemed to us a man—took great notice of my playmate; he called her his bride, and asked her to marry him. She refused, and he insisted, drawing her unwillingly towards him. With the countenance and emotions of a maniac I threw myself on him—I strove to draw his sword—I clung to his neck with the ferocious resolve to strangle him: he was obliged to call for assistance to disengage himself from me. On that night I led Juliet to the chapel of our house: I made her touch the sacred relics—I harrowed her child's heart, and profaned her child's lips with an oath, that she would be mine, and mine only.

Well, those days passed away. Torella returned in a few years, and became wealthier and more prosperous than ever. When I was seventeen, my father died; he had been magnificent to prodigality; Torella rejoiced that my minority would afford an opportunity for repairing my fortunes. Juliet and I had been affianced beside my father's deathbed—Torella was to be a second parent to me.

I desired to see the world, and I was indulged. I went to Florence, to Rome, to Naples; thence I passed to Toulon, and at length reached what had long been the bourne of my wishes, Paris. There was wild work in Paris then. The poor king, Charles the Sixth, now sane, now mad, now a monarch, now an abject slave, was the very mockery of humanity. The queen, the dauphin, the Duke of Burgundy, alternately friends and foes—now meeting in prodigal feasts, now shedding blood in rivalry—were blind to the miserable state of their country, and the dangers that impended over it, and gave themselves wholly up to dissolute enjoyment or savage strife. My character still followed me. I was arrogant and self-willed; I loved display, and above all, I threw all control far from me. Who could control me in Paris? My young friends were eager to foster passions which furnished them with pleasures. I was deemed handsome—I was master of every knightly accomplishment. I was disconnected with any political party. I grew a favourite with all: my presumption and arrogance was pardoned in one so young: I became a spoiled child. Who could control me? not the letters and advice of Torella—only strong necessity visiting me in the abhorred shape of an empty purse. But there were means to refill this void. Acre after acre, estate after estate, I sold. My dress, my jewels, my horses and their caparisons, were almost unrivalled in gorgeous Paris, while the lands of my inheritance passed into possession of others.

The Duke of Orleans was waylaid and murdered by the Duke of Burgundy. Fear and terror possessed all Paris. The dauphin and the queen shut themselves up; every pleasure was suspended. I grew weary of this state of things, and my heart yearned for my boyhood's haunts. I was nearly a beggar, yet still I would go there, claim my bride, and rebuild my fortunes. A few happy ventures as a merchant would make me rich again. Nevertheless, I would not return in humble guise. My last act was to dispose of my remaining estate near Albaro for half its worth, for ready money. Then I despatched all kinds of artificers, arras, furniture of regal splendour, to fit up the last relic of my inheritance, my palace in Genoa. I lingered a little longer yet, ashamed at the part of the prodigal returned, which I feared I should play. I sent my horses. One matchless Spanish jennet I despatched to my promised bride; its caparisons flamed with jewels and cloth of gold. In every part I caused to be entwined the initials of Juliet and her Guido. My present found favour in hers and in her father's eyes.

Still to return a proclaimed spendthrift, the mark of impertinent wonder, perhaps of scorn, and to encounter singly the reproaches or taunts of my fellow-citizens, was no alluring prospect. As a shield between me and censure, I invited some few of the most reckless of my comrades to accompany me: thus I went armed against the world, hiding a rankling feeling, half fear and half penitence, by bravado and an insolent display of satisfied vanity.

I arrived in Genoa. I trod the pavement of my ancestral palace. My proud step was no interpreter of my heart, for I deeply felt that, though surrounded by every luxury, I was a beggar. The first step I took in claiming Juliet must widely declare me such. I read contempt or pity in the looks of all. I fancied, so apt is conscience to imagine what it deserves, that rich and poor, young and old, all regarded me with derision. Torella came not near me. No wonder that my second father should expect a son's deference from me in waiting first on him. But, galled and stung by a sense of my follies and demerit, I strove to throw the blame on others. We kept nightly orgies in Palazzo Carega. To sleepless, riotous nights, followed listless, supine mornings. At the Ave Maria we showed our dainty persons in the streets, scoffing at the sober citizens, casting insolent glances on the shrinking women. Juliet was not among them—no, no; if she had been there, shame would have driven me away, if love had not brought me to her feet.

I grew tired of this. Suddenly I paid the Marchese a visit. He was at his villa, one among the many which deck the suburb of San Pietro d'Arena. It was the month of May—a month of May in that garden of the world—the blossoms of the fruit trees were fading among thick, green foliage; the vines were shooting forth; the ground strewed with the fallen olive blooms; the fire-fly was in the myrtle hedge; heaven and earth wore a mantle of surpassing beauty. Torella welcomed me kindly, though seriously; and even his shade of displeasure soon wore away. Some resemblance to my father—some look and tone of youthful ingenuousness, lurking still in spite of my misdeeds, softened the good old man's heart. He sent for his daughter—he presented me to her as her betrothed. The chamber became hallowed by a holy light as she entered. Hers was that cherub look, those large, soft eyes, full dimpled cheeks, and mouth of infantine sweetness, that expresses the rare union of happiness and love. Admiration first possessed me; she is mine! was the second proud emotion, and my lips curled with haughty triumph. I had not been the *enfant gâté* of the beauties of France not to have learnt the art of pleasing the soft heart of woman. If towards men I was overbearing, the deference I paid to them was the more in contrast. I commenced my courtship by the display of a thousand gallantries to Juliet, who, vowed to me from infancy, had never admitted the devotion of others; and who, though accustomed to expressions of admiration, was uninitiated in the language of lovers.

For a few days all went well. Torella never alluded to my extravagance; he treated me as a favourite son. But the time came, as we discussed the preliminaries to my union with his daughter, when this fair face of things should be overcast. A contract had been drawn up in my father's lifetime. I had rendered this, in fact, void, by having squandered the whole of the wealth which was to have been shared by Juliet and myself. Torella, in consequence, chose to consider this bond as cancelled, and proposed another, in which, though the wealth he bestowed was immeasurably increased, there were so many restrictions as to the mode of spending it, that I, who saw independence only in free career being given to my own imperious will, taunted him as taking advantage of my situation, and refused utterly to subscribe to his conditions. The old man mildly strove to recall me to reason. Roused pride became the tyrant of my thought: I listened with indignation—I repelled him with disdain.

"Juliet, thou art mine! Did we not interchange vows in our innocent childhood? are we not one in the sight of God? and shall thy cold-hearted, cold-blooded father divide us? Be generous, my love, be just; take not away a gift, last treasure of thy Guido—retract not thy vows—let us defy the world, and setting at nought the calculations of age, find in our mutual affection a refuge from every ill."

Fiend I must have been, with such sophistry to endeavour to poison that sanctuary of holy thought and tender love. Juliet shrank from me affrighted. Her father was the best and kindest of men, and she strove to show me how, in obeying him, every good would follow. He would receive my tardy submission with warm affection; and generous pardon would follow my repentance. Profitless words for a young and gentle daughter to use to a man accustomed to make his will, law; and to feel in his own heart a despot so terrible and stern, that he could yield obedience to nought save his own imperious desires! My resentment grew with resistance; my wild companions were ready to add fuel to the flame. We laid a plan to carry off Juliet. At first it appeared to be crowned with success. Midway, on our return, we were overtaken by the agonized father and his attendants. A conflict ensued. Before the city guard came to decide the victory in favour of our antagonists, two of Torella's servitors were dangerously wounded.

This portion of my history weighs most heavily with me. Changed man as I am, I abhor myself in the recollection. May none who hear this tale ever have felt as I. A horse driven to fury by a rider armed with barbed spurs, was not more a slave than I, to the violent tyranny of my temper. A fiend possessed my soul, irritating it to madness. I felt the voice of conscience within me; but if I yielded to it for a brief interval, it was only to be a moment after torn, as by a whirlwind, away—borne along on the stream of desperate rage—the plaything of the storms engendered by pride. I was imprisoned, and, at the instance of Torella, set free. Again I returned to carry off both him and his child to France; which hapless country, then preyed on by freebooters and gangs of lawless soldiery, offered a grateful refuge to a criminal like me. Our plots were discovered. I was sentenced to banishment; and, as my debts were already enormous, my remaining property was put in the hands of commissioners for their payment. Torella again offered his mediation, requiring only my promise not to renew my abortive attempts on himself and his daughter. I spurned his offers, and fancied that I triumphed when I was thrust out from Genoa, a solitary and penniless exile. My companions were gone: they had been dismissed the city some weeks before, and were already in France. I was alone—friendless; with nor sword at my side, nor ducat in my purse.

I wandered along the sea-shore, a whirlwind of passion possessing and tearing my soul. It was as if a live coal had been set burning in my breast. At first I meditated on what *I should do*. I would join a band of freebooters. Revenge!—the word seemed balm to me: I hugged it—caressed it—till, like a serpent, it stung me. Then again I would abjure and despise Genoa, that little corner of the world. I would return to Paris, where so many of my friends swarmed; where my services would be eagerly accepted; where I would carve out fortune with my sword, and might, through success, make my paltry birth-place, and the false Torella, rue the day when they drove me, a new Coriolanus, from her walls. I would return to Paris—thus, on foot—a beggar—and present myself in my poverty to those I had formerly entertained sumptuously? There was gall in the mere thought of it.

The reality of things began to dawn upon my mind, bringing despair in its train. For several months I had been a prisoner: the evils of my dungeon had whipped my soul to madness, but they had subdued my corporeal frame. I was weak and wan. Torella had used a thousand artifices to administer to my comfort; I had detected and scorned them all—and I reaped the harvest of my obduracy. What was to be done? Should I crouch before my foe, and sue for forgiveness? Die rather ten thousand deaths! Never should they obtain that victory! Hate—I swore eternal hate! Hate from whom? to whom? From a wandering outcast—to a mighty noble. I and my feelings were nothing to them: already had they forgotten one so unworthy. And Juliet! —her angel-face and sylph-like form gleamed among the clouds of my despair with vain beauty; for I had lost her—the glory and flower of the world! Another will call her his!—that smile of paradise will bless another!

Even now my heart fails within me when I recur to this rout of grim-visaged ideas. Now subdued almost to tears, now raving in my agony, still I wandered along the rocky shore, which grew at each step wilder and more desolate. Hanging rocks and hoar precipices overlooked the tideless ocean; black caverns yawned; and for ever, among the seaworn recesses, murmured and dashed the unfruitful waters. Now my way was almost barred by an abrupt promontory, now rendered nearly impracticable by fragments fallen from the cliff. Evening was at hand, when, seaward, arose, as if on the waving of a wizard's wand, a murky web of clouds, blotting the late azure sky, and darkening and disturbing the till now placid deep. The clouds had strange fantastic shapes; and they changed, and mingled, and seemed to be driven about by a mighty spell. The waves raised their white crests; the thunder first muttered, then roared from across the waste of waters, which took a deep purple dye, flecked with foam. The spot where I stood, looked, on one side, to the wide-spread ocean; on the other, it was barred by a rugged promontory. Round this cape suddenly came, driven by the wind, a vessel. In vain the mariners tried to force a path for her to the open sea—the gale drove her on the rocks. It will perish!—all on board will perish! Would I were among them! And to my young heart the idea of death came for the first time blended with that of joy. It was an awful sight to behold that vessel struggling with her fate. Hardly could I discern the sailors, but I heard them. It was soon all over! A rock, just covered by the tossing waves, and so unperceived, lay in wait for its prey. A crash of thunder broke over my head at the moment that, with a frightful shock, the skiff dashed upon her unseen enemy. In a brief space of time she went to pieces. There I stood in safety; and there were my fellow-creatures, battling, how hopelessly, with annihilation. Methought I saw them struggling—too truly did I hear their shrieks, conquering the barking surges in their shrill agony. The dark breakers threw hither and thither the fragments of the wreck: soon it disappeared. I had been fascinated to gaze till the end: at last I sank on my knees—I covered my face with my hands: I again looked up; something was floating on the billows towards the shore. It neared and neared. Was that a human form? It grew more distinct; and at last a mighty wave, lifting the whole freight, lodged it upon a rock. A human being bestriding a sea-chest! A human being! Yet was it one? Surely never such had existed before—a misshapen dwarf, with squinting eyes, distorted features, and body deformed, till it became a horror to behold. My blood, lately warming towards a fellow-being so snatched from a watery tomb, froze in my heart. The dwarf got off his chest; he tossed his straight, straggling hair from his odious visage:

"By St. Beelzebub!" he exclaimed, "I have been well bested." He looked round and saw me. "Oh, by the fiend! here is another ally of the mighty one. To what saint did you offer prayers, friend—if not to mine? Yet I remember you not on board."

I shrank from the monster and his blasphemy. Again he questioned me, and I muttered some inaudible reply. He continued:

"Your voice is drowned by this dissonant roar. What a noise the big ocean makes! Schoolboys bursting from their prison are not louder than these waves set free to play. They disturb me. I will no more of their ill-timed brawling. Silence, hoary One! Winds, avaunt! —to your homes! Clouds, fly to the antipodes, and leave our heaven clear!"

As he spoke, he stretched out his two long lank arms, that looked like spider's claws, and seemed to embrace with them the expanse before him. Was it a miracle? The clouds became broken, and fled; the azure sky first peeped out, and then was spread a calm field of blue above us; the stormy gale was exchanged to the softly breathing west; the sea grew calm; the waves dwindled to riplets.

"I like obedience even in these stupid elements," said the dwarf. "How much more in the tameless mind of man! It was a well got up storm, you must allow—and all of my own making."

It was tempting Providence to interchange talk with this magician. But *Power*, in all its shapes, is venerable to man. Awe, curiosity, a clinging fascination, drew me towards him.

"Come, don't be frightened, friend," said the wretch: "I am good-humoured when pleased; and something does please me in your well-proportioned body and handsome face, though you look a little woe-begone. You have suffered a land—I, a sea wreck. Perhaps I can allay the tempest of your fortunes as I did my own. Shall we be friends?" And he held out his hand; I could not touch it. "Well, then, companions—that will do as well. And now, while I rest after the buffeting I underwent just now, tell me why, young and gallant as you seem, you wander thus alone and downcast on this wild sea-shore."

The voice of the wretch was screeching and horrid, and his contortions as he spoke were frightful to behold. Yet he did gain a kind of influence over me, which I could not master, and I told him my tale. When it was ended, he laughed long and loud: the rocks echoed back the sound: hell seemed yelling around me.

"Oh, thou cousin of Lucifer!" said he; "so thou too hast fallen through thy pride; and, though bright as the son of Morning, thou art ready to give up thy good looks, thy bride, and thy well-being, rather than submit thee to the tyranny of good. I honour thy choice, by my soul!—So thou hast fled, and yield the day; and mean to starve on these rocks, and to let the birds peck out thy dead eyes, while thy enemy and thy betrothed rejoice in thy ruin. They pride is strangely akin to humility, methinks."

As he spoke, a thousand fanged thoughts stung me to the heart.

"What would you that I should do?" I cried.

"I! Oh, nothing, but lie down and say your prayers before you die. But, were I you, I know the deed that should be done."

I drew near him. His supernatural powers made him an oracle in my eyes; yet a strange unearthly thrill quivered through my frame as I said—"Speak!—teach me—what act do you advise?"

"Revenge thyself, man!—humble thy enemies!—set thy foot on the old man's neck, and possess thyself of his daughter!"

"To the east and west I turn," cried I, "and see no means! Had I gold, much could I achieve; but, poor and single, I am powerless."

The dwarf had been seated on his chest as he listened to my story. Now he got off; he touched a spring; it flew open! What a mine of wealth—of blazing jewels, beaming gold, and pale silver—was displayed therein. A mad desire to possess this treasure was born within me.

"Doubtless," I said, "one so powerful as you could do all things."

"Nay," said the monster, humbly, "I am less omnipotent than I seem. Some things I possess which you may covet; but I would give them all for a small share, or even for a loan of what is yours."

"My possessions are at your service," I replied, bitterly—"my poverty, my exile, my disgrace—I make a free gift of them all."

"Good! I thank you. Add one other thing to your gift, and my treasure is yours."

"As nothing is my sole inheritance, what besides nothing would you have?"

"Your comely face and well-made limbs."

I shivered. Would this all-powerful monster murder me? I had no dagger. I forgot to pray—but I grew pale.

"I ask for a loan, not a gift," said the frightful thing: "lend me your body for three days—you shall have mine to cage your soul the while, and, in payment, my chest. What say you to the bargain? Three short days."

We are told that it is dangerous to hold unlawful talk; and well do I prove the same. Tamely written down, it may seem incredible that I should lend any ear to this proposition; but, in spite of his unnatural ugliness, there was something fascinating in a being whose voice could govern earth, air, and sea. I felt a keen desire to comply; for with that chest I could command the world. My only hesitation resulted from a fear that he would not be true to his bargain. Then, I thought, I shall soon die here on these lonely sands, and the limbs he covets will be mine no more:—it is worth the chance. And, besides, I knew that, by all the rules of art-magic, there were formula and oaths which none of its practisers dared break. I hesitated to reply; and he went on, now displaying his wealth, now speaking of the petty price he demanded, till it seemed madness to refuse. Thus is it: place our bark in the current of the stream, and down, over fall and cataract it is hurried; give up our conduct to the wild torrent of passion, and we are away, we know not whither.

He swore many an oath, and I adjured him by many a sacred name; till I saw this wonder of power, this ruler of the elements, shiver like an autumn leaf before my words; and as if the spirit spake unwillingly and per force within him, at last, he, with broken voice, revealed the spell whereby he might be obliged, did he wish to play me false, to render up the unlawful spoil. Our warm lifeblood must mingle to make and to mar the charm.

Enough of this unholy theme. I was persuaded—the thing was done. The morrow dawned upon me as I lay upon the shingles, and I knew not my own shadow as it fell from me. I felt myself changed to a shape of horror, and cursed my easy faith and blind credulity. The chest was there—there the gold and precious stones for which I had sold the frame of flesh which nature had given me. The sight a little stilled my emotions: three days would soon be gone.

They did pass. The dwarf had supplied me with a plenteous store of food. At first I could hardly walk, so strange and out of joint were all my limbs; and my voice—it was that of the fiend. But I kept silent, and turned my face to the sun, that I might not see my shadow, and counted the hours, and ruminated on my future conduct. To bring Torella to my feet—to possess my Juliet in spite of him—all this my wealth could easily achieve. During dark night I slept, and dreamt of the accomplishment of my desires. Two suns had set—the third dawned. I was agitated, fearful. Oh expectation, what a frightful thing art thou, when kindled more by fear than hope! How dost thou twist thyself round the heart, torturing its pulsations! How dost thou dart unknown pangs all through our feeble mechanism, now seeming to shiver us like broken glass, to nothingness—now giving us a fresh strength, which can *do* nothing, and so torments us by a sensation, such as the strong man must feel who cannot break his fetters, though they bend in his grasp. Slowly paced the bright, bright orb up the eastern sky; long it lingered in the zenith, and still more slowly wandered down the west: it touched the horizon's verge—it was lost! Its glories were on the summits of the cliff—they grew dun and gray. The evening star shone bright. He will soon be here.

He came not! By the living heavens, he came not!—and night dragged out its weary length, and, in its decaying age, "day began to grizzle its dark hair;" and the sun rose again on the most miserable wretch that ever upbraided its light. Three days thus I passed. The jewels and the gold—oh, how I abhorred them!

Well, well—I will not blacken these pages with demoniac ravings. All too terrible were the thoughts, the raging tumult of ideas that filled my soul. At the end of that time I slept; I had not before since the third sunset; and I dreamt that I was at Juliet's feet, and she smiled, and then she shrieked—for she saw my transformation—and again she smiled, for still her beautiful lover knelt before her. But it was not I—it was he, the fiend, arrayed in my limbs, speaking with my voice, winning her with my looks of love. I strove to warn her, but my tongue refused its office; I strove to tear him from her, but I was rooted to the ground—I awoke with the agony. There were the solitary hoar precipices—there the plashing sea, the quiet strand, and the blue sky over all. What did it mean? was my dream but a mirror of the truth? was he wooing and winning my betrothed? I would on the instant back to Genoa—but I was banished. I laughed—the dwarf's yell burst from my lips—*I* banished! O, no! they had not exiled the foul limbs I wore; I might with these enter, without fear of incurring the threatened penalty of death, my own, my native city.

I began to walk towards Genoa. I was somewhat accustomed to my distorted limbs; none were ever so ill adapted for a straightforward movement; it was with infinite difficulty that I proceeded. Then, too, I desired to avoid all the hamlets strewed here and there on the seabeach, for I was unwilling to make a display of my hideousness. I was not quite sure that, if seen, the mere boys would not stone me to death as I passed, for a monster: some ungentle salutations I did receive from the few peasants or fishermen I chanced to meet. But it was dark night before I approached Genoa. The weather was so balmy and sweet that it struck me that the Marchese and his daughter would very probably have quitted the city for their country retreat. It was from Villa Torella that I had attempted to carry off Juliet; I had spent many an hour reconnoitring the spot, and knew each inch of ground in its vicinity. It was beautifully situated, embosomed in trees, on the margin of a stream. As I drew near, it became evident that my conjecture was right; nay, moreover, that the hours were being then devoted to feasting and merriment. For the house was lighted up; strains of soft and gay music were wafted towards me by the breeze. My heart sank within me. Such was the generous kindness of Torella's heart that I felt sure that he would not have indulged in public manifestations of rejoicing just after my unfortunate banishment, but for a cause I dared not dwell upon.

The country people were all alive and flocking about; it became necessary that I should study to conceal myself; and yet I longed to address some one, or to hear others discourse, or in any way to gain intelligence of what was really going on. At length, entering the walks that were in immediate vicinity to the mansion, I found one dark enough to veil my excessive frightfulness; and yet others as well as I were loitering in its shade. I soon gathered all I wanted to know— all that first made my very heart die with horror, and then boil with indignation. To-morrow Juliet was to be given to the penitent, reformed, beloved Guido—to-morrow my bride was to pledge her vows to a fiend from hell! And I did this!—my accursed pride—my demoniac violence and wicked self-idolatry had caused this act. For if I had acted as the wretch who had stolen my form had acted—if, with a mien at once yielding and dignified, I had presented myself to Torella, saying, I have done wrong, forgive me; I am unworthy of your angel-child, but permit me to claim her hereafter, when my altered conduct shall manifest that I abjure my vices, and endeavour to become in some sort worthy of her. I go to serve against the infidels; and when my zeal for religion and my true penitence for the past shall appear to you to cancel my crimes, permit me again to call myself your son. Thus had he spoken; and the penitent was welcomed even as the prodigal son of scripture: the fatted calf was killed for him; and he, still pursuing the same path, displayed such openhearted regret for his follies, so humble a concession of all his rights, and so ardent a resolve to reacquire them by a life of contrition and virtue, that he quickly conquered the kind, old man; and full pardon, and the gift of his lovely child, followed in swift succession.

O! had an angel from Paradise whispered to me to act thus! But now, what would be the innocent Juliet's fate? Would God permit the foul union—or, some prodigy destroying it, link the dishonoured name of Carega with the worst of crimes? To-morrow at dawn they were to be married: there was but one way to prevent this—to meet mine enemy, and to enforce the ratification of our agreement. I felt that this could only be done by a mortal struggle. I had no sword—if indeed my distorted arms could wield a soldier's weapon—but I had a dagger, and in that lay my every hope. There was no time for pondering or balancing nicely the question: I might die in the attempt; but besides the burning jealousy and despair of my own heart, honour, mere humanity, demanded that I should fall rather than not destroy the machinations of the fiend.

The guests departed—the lights began to disappear; it was evident that the inhabitants of the villa were seeking repose. I hid myself among the trees—the garden grew desert—the gates were closed—I wandered round and came under a window—ah! well did I know the same!—a soft twilight glimmered in the room—the curtains were half withdrawn. It was the temple of innocence and beauty. Its magnificence was tempered, as it were, by the slight disarrangements occasioned by its being dwelt in, and all the objects scattered around displayed the taste of her who hallowed it by her presence. I saw her enter with a quick light step—I saw her approach the window—she drew back the curtain yet further, and looked out into the night. Its breezy freshness played among her ringlets, and wafted them from the transparent marble of her brow. She clasped her hands, she raised her eyes to Heaven. I heard her voice. Guido! she softly murmured, Mine own Guido! and then, as if overcome by the fulness of her own heart, she sank on her knees—her praised eyes—her negligent but graceful attitude—the beaming thankfulness that lighted up her face—oh, these are tame words! Heart of mine, thou imagest ever, though thou canst not portray, the celestial beauty of that child of light and love.

I heard a step—a quick firm step along the shady avenue. Soon I saw a cavalier, richly dressed, young and, methought, graceful to look on, advance. I hid myself yet closer. The youth approached; he paused beneath the window. She arose, and again looking out she saw him, and said—I cannot, no, at this distant time I cannot record her terms of soft silver tenderness; to me they were spoken, but they were replied to by him.

"I will not go," he cried: "here where you have been, where your memory glides like some Heaven-visiting ghost, I will pass the long hours till we meet, never, my Juliet, again, day or night, to part. But do thou, my love, retire; the cold morn and fitful breeze will make thy cheek pale, and fill with languor thy love-lighted eyes. Ah, sweetest! could I press one kiss upon them, I could, methinks, repose."

And then he approached still nearer, and methought he was about to clamber into her chamber. I had hesitated, not to terrify her; now I was no longer master of myself. I rushed forward—I threw myself on him—I tore him away—I cried, "O loathsome and foul-shaped wretch!"

I need not repeat epithets, all tending, as it appeared, to rail at a person I at present feel some partiality for. A shriek rose from Juliet's lips. I neither heard nor saw—I *felt* only mine enemy, whose throat I grasped, and my dagger's hilt; he struggled, but could not escape: at length hoarsely he breathed these words: "Do!—strike home! destroy this body—you will still live: may your life be long and merry!"

The descending dagger was arrested at the word, and he, feeling my hold relax, extricated himself and drew his sword, while the up-roar in the house, and flying of torches from one room to the other, showed that soon we should be separated—and I—oh! far better die: so that he did not survive, I cared not. In the midst of my frenzy there was much calculation: fall I might, and so that he did not survive, I cared not for the death-blow I might deal against myself. While still, therefore, he thought I paused, and while I saw the villainous resolve to take advantage of my hesitation, in the sudden thrust he made at me, I threw myself on his sword, and at the same moment plunged my dagger, with a true desperate aim, in his side. We fell together, rolling over each other, and the tide of blood that flowed from the gaping wound of each mingled on the grass. More I know not—I fainted.

Again I returned to life: weak almost to death, I found myself stretched upon a bed—Juliet was kneeling beside it. Strange! my first broken request was for a mirror. I was so wan and ghastly, that my poor girl hesitated, as she told me afterwards; but, by the mass! I thought myself a right proper youth when I saw the dear reflection of my own well-known features, I confess it is a weakness, but I avow it, I do entertain a considerable affection for the countenance and limbs I behold, whenever I look at a glass; and have more mirrors in my house, and consult them oftener than any beauty in Venice. Before you too much condemn me, permit me to say that no one better knows than I the value of his own body; no one, probably, except myself, ever having had it stolen from him.

Incoherently I at first talked of the dwarf and his crimes, and reproached Juliet for her too easy admission of his love. She thought me raving, as well she might, and yet it was some time before I could prevail on myself to admit that the Guido whose penitence had won her back for me was myself; and while I cursed bitterly the monstrous dwarf, and blest the well-directed blow that had deprived him of life, I suddenly checked myself when I heard her say—Amen! knowing that him whom she reviled was my very self. A little reflection taught me silence—a little practice enabled me to speak of that frightful night without any very excessive blunder. The wound I had given myself was no mockery of one—it was long before I recovered—and as the benevolent and generous Torella sat beside me, talking such wisdom as might win friends to repentance, and mine own dear Juliet hovered near me, administering to my wants, and cheering me by her smiles, the work of my bodily cure and mental reform went on together. I have never, indeed, wholly recovered my strength—my cheek is paler since—my person a little bent. Juliet sometimes ventures to allude bitterly to the malice that caused this change, but I kiss her on the moment, and tell her all is for the best. I am a fonder and more faithful husband—and true is this—but for that wound, never had I called her mine.

I did not revisit the sea-shore, nor seek for the fiend's treasure; yet, while I ponder on the past, I often think, and my confessor was not backward in favouring the idea, that it might be a good rather than an evil spirit, sent by my guardian angel, to show me the folly and misery of pride. So well at least did I learn this lesson, roughly taught as I was, that I am known now by all my friends and fellow-citizens by the name of Guido il Cortese.

John Keats
(1795-1821)

REFERRING to the "fine Mother Radcliff names" that he uses in "The Eve of St. Agnes" and "Isabella," Keats acknowledges his debt to Ann Radcliffe, from whom he also borrowed the dream-visions and macabre physical details in "Isabella." The story itself comes from Boccaccio's *Decameron* (Day IV, Tale 5), but Keats elaborates the narrative with echoes of Chaucer, Shakespeare's *Romeo and Juliet*, Leigh Hunt's *Story of Rimini* (1816), and other contemporary romantic novels, which led him to the thin pathos beneath the extravagant sentimentality and excessive decoration of the brief tale. In transforming Boccaccio's bold outline into sensuous romance, Keats idealizes the love between Isabella and Lorenzo, describing their lovesickness and analyzing their emotions to excess.

The story departs from Boccaccio's tale several times to digress in accordance with the convention of medieval metrical romance, but all digressions except the invocation of Boccaccio (XIX–XX) are unnecessarily rhetorical, shrill, or artificial. The merchant brothers' pride and avarice (XVI–XVIII) certainly motivate their murder of Lorenzo, but the extended criticism of their employment practices is flamboyant and inappropriate. Nonetheless, even these stanzas had impressive though sentimental admirers. George Bernard Shaw regarded stanzas XIV–XVII as potentially Marxist, and F. Scott Fitzgerald called the pretentious rhetoric of XVI "great." Charles Lamb saw the merits of the poem somewhat more clearly, identifying the exhuming scene (XLVI–XLVIII) as "more awfully simple in diction, more nakedly grand and moving in sentiment" than anything in Dante, Chaucer, or Spenser. The vivid realism of these stanzas highlights Isabella's beauty, youth, and determination as well as the horror of the situation, but infelicities remain. "Dainties" for breasts is a strange euphemism for this context, and the last couplet of XLVIII is strained in metaphor, rhetoric, and rhyme.

In the next scene, Isabella lavishes gruesome attention on Lorenzo's severed head before planting it in the basil pot. The combing of hair and lashes, cleansing with tears, and wrapping in perfumed silk testify to Keats's Gothic imagination and his characteristically sensuous expression. Repeated references to hair, tears, fragrances, and music link the exhuming and second burial to the dream-vision (XXXV–XLI), three of the high points of the poem.

In death, Lorenzo's physical appearance, voice, and sad longing for life measure the effects of the "forest tomb," and separation from life and Isabella. The mournful "Adieu!" of the visiting shade more tenderly commits Isabella to action than the quick "Goodbye!" before the murder. Apparently death grants Lorenzo an assertiveness and power of language he seldom displayed in life. In diction and rhyme, rhetoric and imagery, Lorenzo's spirit speaks elegantly, eloquently in neat *ottava rima* stanzas.

Keats himself recognized the weaknesses of "Isabella," calling it "too smokeable," naive and unphilosophical. In a letter to Woodhouse, he says: "Isabella is what I should call were I reviewer 'A weak-sided Poem' with an amusing sober-sadness about it." He preferred his "Lamia" and "The Eve of St. Agnes," but the Gothic effects in these later poems are more subtle and tangential to their central concerns. The plainer structure of "Isabella," its extensive dialogue, and vivid scenes reveal Keats's early dramatic ability, before he attempted "Hyperion" and over a year before he began the odes. "Isabella" became immensely popular in the mid-nineteenth century, particularly for the Pre-Raphaelites. One of them, William Holman Hunt, executed a splendid painting of a scene from "The Pot of Basil." In his Preface to *Poems, 1853*, Matthew Arnold went so far as to say that "Isabella" "contains, perhaps, a greater number of happy single expressions which one could quote than all the extant tragedies of Sophocles." His criticism of the structure of "Isabella" is more severe, but Arnold rightly draws attention to Keats's precise imagery and memorable phrases.

Isabella; or, The Pot of Basil (1820)

I

Fair Isabel, poor simple Isabel!
    Lorenzo, a young palmer in Love's eye!
They could not in the self-same mansion dwell
    Without some stir of heart, some malady;
They could not sit at meals but feel how well   5
    It soothed each to be the other by;

They could not, sure, beneath the same roof sleep
But to each other dream, and nightly weep.

II

With every morn their love grew tenderer,
　　With every eve deeper and tenderer still;　　　　10
He might not in house, field, or garden stir,
　　But her full shape would all his seeing fill;
And his continual voice was pleasanter
　　To her, than noise of trees or hidden rill;
Her lute-string gave an echo of his name,　　　　15
She spoilt her half-done broidery with the same.

III

He knew whose gentle hand was at the latch,
　　Before the door had given her to his eyes;
And from her chamber-window he would catch
　　Her beauty farther than the falcon spies;　　　　20
And constant as her vespers would he watch,
　　Because her face was turn'd to the same skies;
And with sick longing all the night outwear,
To hear her morning-step upon the stair.

IV

A whole long month of May in this sad plight　　　　25
　　Made their cheeks paler by the break of June:
"To-morrow will I bow to my delight,
　　To-morrow will I ask my lady's boon."—
"O may I never see another night,
　　Lorenzo, if thy lips breathe not love's tune."—　　　　30
So spake they to their pillows; but, alas,
Honeyless days and days did he let pass;

V

Until sweet Isabella's untouch'd cheek
　　Fell sick within the rose's just domain,
Fell thin as a young mother's, who doth seek　　　　35
　　By every lull to cool her infant's pain:
"How ill she is," said he, "I may not speak,
　　And yet I will, and tell my love all plain:

If looks speak love-laws, I will drink her tears,
And at the least 'twill startle off her cares."   40

VI

So said he one fair morning, and all day
   His heart beat awfully against his side;
And to his heart he inwardly did pray
   For power to speak; but still the ruddy tide
Stifled his voice, and puls'd resolve away—   45
   Fever'd his high conceit of such a bride,
Yet brought him to the meekness of a child:
Alas! when passion is both meek and wild!

VII

So once more he had wak'd and anguished
   A dreary night of love and misery,   50
If Isabel's quick eye had not been wed
   To every symbol on his forehead high;
She saw it waxing very pale and dead,
   And straight all flush'd; so, lisped tenderly,
"Lorenzo!"—here she ceas'd her timid quest,   55
But in her tone and look he read the rest.

VIII

"O Isabella, I can half perceive
   That I may speak my grief into thine ear;
If thou didst ever any thing believe,
   Believe how I love thee, believe how near   60
My soul is to its doom: I would not grieve
   Thy hand by unwelcome pressing, would not fear
Thine eyes by gazing; but I cannot live
Another night, and not my passion shrive.

IX

"Love! thou art leading me from wintry cold,   65
   Lady! thou leadest me to summer clime,
And I must taste the blossoms that unfold
   In its ripe warmth this gracious morning time."
So said, his erewhile timid lips grew bold,
   And poesied with hers in dewy rhyme: 70

Great bliss was with them, and great happiness
Grew, like a lusty flower in June's caress.

X

Parting they seem'd to tread upon the air,
   Twin roses by the zephyr blown apart
Only to meet again more close, and share   75
   The inward fragrance of each other's heart.
She, to her chamber gone, a ditty fair
   Sang, of delicious love and honey'd dart;
He with light steps went up a western hill,
And bade the sun farewell, and joy'd his fill.   80

XI

All close they met again, before the dusk
   Had taken from the stars its pleasant veil,
All close they met, all eves, before the dusk
   Had taken from the stars its pleasant veil,
Close in a bower of hyacinth and musk,   85
   Unknown of any, free from whispering tale.
Ah! better had it been for ever so,
Than idle ears should pleasure in their woe.

XII

Were they unhappy then?—It cannot be—
   Too many tears for lovers have been shed,   90
Too many sighs give we to them in fee,
   Too much of pity after they are dead,
Too many doleful stories do we see,
   Whose matter in bright gold were best be read;
Except in such a page where Theseus' spouse   95
Over the pathless waves towards him bows.

XIII

But, for the general award of love,
   The little sweet doth kill much bitterness;
Though Dido silent is in under-grove,
   And Isabella's was a great distress,   100
Though young Lorenzo in warm Indian clove
   Was not embalm'd, this truth is not the less—

Even bees, the little almsmen of spring-bowers,
Know there is richest juice in poison-flowers.

XIV

With her two brothers this fair lady dwelt,   105
    Enriched from ancestral merchandize,
And for them many a weary hand did swelt
    In torched mines and noisy factories,
And many once proud-quiver'd loins did melt
    In blood from stinging whip;—with hollow eyes   110
Many all day in dazzling river stood,
To take the rich-ored driftings of the flood.

XV

For them the Ceylon diver held his breath,
    And went all naked to the hungry shark;
For them his ears gush'd blood; for them in death   115
    The seal on the cold ice with piteous bark
Lay full of darts; for them alone did seethe
    A thousand men in troubles wide and dark:
Half-ignorant, they turn'd an easy wheel,
That set sharp racks at work, to pinch and peel.   120

XVI

Why were they proud? Because their marble founts
    Gush'd with more pride than do a wretch's tears?—
Why were they proud? Because fair orange-mounts
    Were of more soft ascent than lazar stairs?—
Why were they proud? Because red-lin'd accounts   125
    Were richer than the songs of Grecian years?—
Why were they proud? again we ask aloud,
Why in the name of Glory were they proud?

XVII

Yet were these Florentines as self-retired
    In hungry pride and gainful cowardice,   130
As two close Hebrews in that land inspired,
    Paled in and vineyarded from beggar-spies;
The hawks of ship-mast forests—the untired
    And pannier'd mules for ducats and old lies—

Quick cat's-paws on the generous stray-away,—   135
Great wits in Spanish, Tuscan, and Malay.

XVIII

How was it these same ledger-men could spy
   Fair Isabella in her downy nest?
How could they find out in Lorenzo's eye
   A straying from his toil? Hot Egypt's pest   140
Into their vision covetous and sly!
   How could these money-bags see east and west?—
Yet so they did—and every dealer fair
Must see behind, as doth the hunted hare.

XIX

O eloquent and famed Boccaccio!   145
   Of thee we now should ask forgiving boon,
And of thy spicy myrtles as they blow,
   And of thy roses amorous of the moon,
And of thy lilies, that do paler grow
   Now they can no more hear thy ghittern's tune,   150
For venturing syllables that ill beseem
The quiet glooms of such a piteous theme.

XX

Grant thou a pardon here, and then the tale
   Shall move on soberly, as it is meet;
There is no other crime, no mad assail   155
   To make old prose in modern rhyme more sweet:
But it is done—succeed the verse or fail—
   To honour thee, and thy gone spirit greet;
To stead thee as a verse in English tongue,
An echo of thee in the north-wind sung.   160

XXI

These brethren having found by many signs
   What love Lorenzo for their sister had,
And how she lov'd him too, each unconfines
   His bitter thoughts to other, well nigh mad
That he, the servant of their trade designs,   165
   Should in their sister's love be blithe and glad,

When 'twas their plan to coax her by degrees
To some high noble and his olive-trees.

XXII

And many a jealous conference had they,
   And many times they bit their lips alone,   170
Before they fix'd upon a surest way
   To make the youngster for his crime atone;
And at the last, these men of cruel clay
   Cut Mercy with a sharp knife to the bone;
For they resolved in some forest dim   175
To kill Lorenzo, and there bury him.

XXIII

So on a pleasant morning, as he leant
   Into the sun-rise, o'er the balustrade
Of the garden-terrace, towards him they bent
   Their footing through the dews; and to him said,   180
"You seem there in the quiet of content,
   Lorenzo, and we are most loth to invade
Calm speculation; but if you are wise,
Bestride your steed while cold is in the skies.

XXIV

"To-day we purpose, ay, this hour we mount   185
   To spur three leagues towards the Apennine;
Come down, we pray thee, ere the hot sun count
   His dewy rosary on the eglantine."
Lorenzo, courteously as he was wont,
   Bow'd a fair greeting to these serpents' whine;   190
And went in haste, to get in readiness,
With belt, and spur, and bracing huntsman's dress.

XXV

And as he to the court-yard pass'd along,
   Each third step did he pause, and listen'd oft
If he could hear his lady's matin-song,   195
   Or the light whisper of her footstep soft;
And as he thus over his passion hung,
   He heard a laugh full musical aloft;

When, looking up, he saw her features bright
Smile through an in-door lattice, all delight.   200

XXVI

"Love, Isabel!" said he, "I was in pain
 Lest I should miss to bid thee a good morrow:
Ah! what if I should lose thee, when so fain
 I am to stifle all the heavy sorrow
Of a poor three hours' absence? but we'll gain   205
 Out of the amorous dark what day doth borrow.
Goodbye! I'll soon be back."—"Goodbye!" said she:—
And as he went she chanted merrily.

XXVII

So the two brothers and their murder'd man
 Rode past fair Florence, to where Arno's stream   210
Gurgles through straiten'd banks, and still doth fan
 Itself with dancing bulrush, and the bream
Keeps head against the freshets.   Sick and wan
 The brothers' faces in the ford did seem,
Lorenzo's flush with love.—They pass'd the water   215
Into a forest quiet for the slaughter.

XXVIII

There was Lorenzo slain and buried in,
 There in that forest did his great love cease;
Ah! when a soul doth thus its freedom win,
 It aches in loneliness—is ill at peace   220
As the break-covert blood-hounds of such sin:
 They dipp'd their swords in the water, and did tease
Their horses homeward, with convulsed spur,
Each richer by his being a murderer.

XXIX

They told their sister how, with sudden speed,   225
 Lorenzo had ta'en ship for foreign lands,
Because of some great urgency and need
 In their affairs, requiring trusty hands.
Poor Girl! put on thy stifling widow's weed,
 And 'scape at once from Hope's accursed bands;   230

To-day thou wilt not see him, nor to-morrow,
And the next day will be a day of sorrow.

XXX

She weeps alone for pleasures not to be;
   Sorely she wept until the night came on,
And then, instead of love, O misery!   235
   She brooded o'er the luxury alone:
His image in the dusk she seem'd to see,
   And to the silence made a gentle moan,
Spreading her perfect arms upon the air,
And on her couch low murmuring "Where? O where?"   240

XXXI

But Selfishness, Love's cousin, held not long
   Its fiery vigil in her single breast;
She fretted for the golden hour, and hung
   Upon the time with feverish unrest—
Not long—for soon into her heart a throng   245
   Of higher occupants, a richer zest,
Came tragic; passion not to be subdued,
And sorrow for her love in travels rude.

XXXII

In the mid days of autumn, on their eves
   The breath of Winter comes from far away,   250
And the sick west continually bereaves
   Of some gold tinge, and plays a roundelay
Of death among the bushes and the leaves,
   To make all bare before he dares to stray
From his north cavern.   So sweet Isabel   255
By gradual decay from beauty fell,

XXXIII

Because Lorenzo came not.   Oftentimes
   She ask'd her brothers, with an eye all pale,
Striving to be itself, what dungeon climes
   Could keep him off so long?   They spake a tale   260
Time after time, to quiet her.   Their crimes
   Came on them, like a smoke from Hinnom's vale;

And every night in dreams they groan'd aloud,
To see their sister in her snowy shroud.

XXXIV

And she had died in drowsy ignorance,   265
   But for a thing more deadly dark than all;
It came like a fierce potion, drunk by chance,
   Which saves a sick man from the feather'd pall
For some few gasping moments; like a lance,
   Waking an Indian from his cloudy hall   270
With cruel pierce, and bringing him again
Sense of the gnawing fire at heart and brain.

XXXV

It was a vision.—In the drowsy gloom,
   The dull of midnight, at her couch's foot
Lorenzo stood, and wept: the forest tomb   275
   Had marr'd his glossy hair which once could shoot
Lustre into the sun, and put cold doom
   Upon his lips, and taken the soft lute
From his lorn voice, and past his loamed ears
Had made a miry channel for his tears.   280

XXXVI

Strange sound it was, when the pale shadow spake;
   For there was striving, in its piteous tongue,
To speak as when on earth it was awake,
   And Isabella on its music hung:
Languor there was in it, and tremulous shake,   285
   As in a palsied Druid's harp unstrung;
And through it moan'd a ghostly under-song,
Like hoarse night-gusts sepulchral briars among.

XXXVII

Its eyes, though wild, were still all dewy bright
   With love, and kept all phantom fear aloof   290
From the poor girl by magic of their light,
   The while it did unthread the horrid woof
Of the late darken'd time,—the murderous spite
   Of pride and avarice,—the dark pine roof

In the forest,—and the sodden turfed dell,　　　　　　　295
Where, without any word, from stabs he fell.

XXXVIII

Saying moreover, "Isabel, my sweet!
　　Red whortle-berries droop above my head,
And a large flint-stone weighs upon my feet;
　　Around me beeches and high chestnuts shed　　　300
Their leaves and prickly nuts; a sheep-fold bleat
　　Comes from beyond the river to my bed:
Go, shed one tear upon my heather-bloom,
And it shall comfort me within the tomb.

XXXIX

"I am a shadow now, alas! alas!　　　　　　　　　305
　　Upon the skirts of human-nature dwelling
Alone: I chant alone the holy mass,
　　While little sounds of life are round me knelling,
And glossy bees at noon do fieldward pass,
　　And many a chapel bell the hour is telling,　　　310
Paining me through: those sounds grow strange to me,
And thou art distant in Humanity.

XL

"I know what was, I feel full well what is,
　　And I should rage, if spirits could go mad;
Though I forget the taste of earthly bliss,　　　　315
　　That paleness warms my grave, as though I had
A Seraph chosen from the bright abyss
　　To be my spouse: thy paleness makes me glad;
Thy beauty grows upon me, and I feel
A greater love through all my essence steal."　　　320

XLI

The Spirit mourn'd "Adieu!"—dissolv'd, and left
　　The atom darkness in a slow turmoil;
As when of healthful midnight sleep bereft,
　　Thinking on rugged hours and fruitless toil,
We put our eyes into a pillowy cleft,　　　　　　325
　　And see the spangly gloom froth up and boil:

It made sad Isabella's eyelids ache,
And in the dawn she started up awake;

XLII

"Ha! ha!" said she, "I knew not this hard life,
 I thought the worst was simple misery;   330
I thought some Fate with pleasure or with strife
 Portion'd us—happy days, or else to die;
But there is crime—a brother's bloody knife!
 Sweet Spirit, thou hast school'd my infancy:
I'll visit thee for this, and kiss thine eyes,   335
And greet thee morn and even in the skies."

XLIII

When the full morning came, she had devised
 How she might secret to the forest hie;
How she might find the clay, so dearly prized,
 And sing to it one latest lullaby;   340
How her short absence might be unsurmised,
 While she the inmost of the dream would try.
Resolv'd, she took with her an aged nurse,
And went into that dismal forest-hearse.

XLIV

See, as they creep along the river side,   345
 How she doth whisper to that aged Dame,
And, after looking round the champaign wide,
 Shows her a knife.—"What feverous hectic flame
Burns in thee, child?—What good can thee betide,
 That thou should'st smile again?"—The evening came, 350
And they had found Lorenzo's earthy bed;
The flint was there, the berries at his head.

XLV

Who hath not loiter'd in a green church-yard,
 And let his spirit, like a demon-mole,
Work through the clayey soil and gravel hard,   355
 To see scull, coffin'd bones, and funeral stole;
Pitying each form that hungry Death hath marr'd,
 And filling it once more with human soul?

Ah! this is holiday to what was felt
When Isabella by Lorenzo knelt.   360

XLVI

She gaz'd into the fresh-thrown mould, as though
    One glance did fully all its secrets tell;
Clearly she saw, as other eyes would know
    Pale limbs at bottom of a crystal well;
Upon the murderous spot she seem'd to grow,   365
    Like to a native lily of the dell:
Then with her knife, all sudden, she began
To dig more fervently than misers can.

XLVII

Soon she turn'd up a soiled glove, whereon
    Her silk had play'd in purple phantasies,   370
She kiss'd it with a lip more chill than stone,
    And put it in her bosom, where it dries
And freezes utterly unto the bone
    Those dainties made to still an infant's cries:
Then 'gan she work again; nor stay'd her care,   375
But to throw back at times her veiling hair.

XLVIII

That old nurse stood beside her wondering,
    Until her heart felt pity to the core
At sight of such a dismal labouring,
    And so she kneeled, with her locks all hoar,   380
And put her lean hands to the horrid thing:
    Three hours they labour'd at this travail sore;
At last they felt the kernel of the grave,
And Isabella did not stamp and rave.

XLIX

Ah! wherefore all this wormy circumstance?   385
    Why linger at the yawning tomb so long?
O for the gentleness of old Romance,
    The simple plaining of a minstrel's song!
Fair reader, at the old tale take a glance,
    For here, in truth, it doth not well belong   390

To speak:—O turn thee to the very tale,
And taste the music of that vision pale.

L

With duller steel than the Perséan sword
   They cut away no formless monster's head,
But one, whose gentleness did well accord   395
   With death, as life.   The ancient harps have said,
Love never dies, but lives, immortal Lord:
   If Love impersonate was ever dead,
Pale Isabella kiss'd it, and low moan'd.
'Twas love; cold,—dead indeed, but not dethroned.   400

LI

In anxious secrecy they took it home,
   And then the prize was all for Isabel:
She calm'd its wild hair with a golden comb,
   And all around each eye's sepulchral cell
Pointed each fringed lash; the smeared loam   405
   With tears, as chilly as a dripping well,
She drench'd away:—and still she comb'd, and kept
Sighing all day—and still she kiss'd, and wept.

LII

Then in a silken scarf,—sweet with the dews
   Of precious flowers pluck'd in Araby,   410
And divine liquids come with odorous ooze
   Through the cold serpent-pipe refreshfully,—
She wrapp'd it up; and for its tomb did choose
   A garden-pot, wherein she laid it by,
And cover'd it with mould, and o'er it set   415
Sweet Basil, which her tears kept ever wet.

LIII

And she forgot the stars, the moon, and sun,
   And she forgot the blue above the trees,
And she forgot the dells where waters run,
   And she forgot the chilly autumn breeze;   420
She had no knowledge when the day was done,
   And the new morn she saw not: but in peace

Hung over her sweet Basil evermore,
And moisten'd it with tears unto the core.

LIV

And so she ever fed it with thin tears, 425
    Whence thick, and green, and beautiful it grew,
So that it smelt more balmy than its peers
    Of Basil-tufts in Florence; for it drew
Nurture besides, and life, from human fears,
    From the fast mouldering head there shut from view: 430
So that the jewel, safely casketed,
Came forth, and in perfumed leafits spread.

LV

O Melancholy, linger here awhile!
    O Music, Music, breathe despondingly!
O Echo, Echo, from some sombre isle, 435
    Unknown, Lethean, sigh to us—O sigh!
Spirits in grief, lift up your heads, and smile;
    Lift up your heads, sweet Spirits, heavily,
And make a pale light in your cypress glooms,
Tinting with silver wan your marble tombs. 440

LVI

Moan hither, all ye syllables of woe,
    From the deep throat of sad Melpomene!
Through bronzed lyre in tragic order go,
    And touch the strings into a mystery;
Sound mournfully upon the winds and low; 445
    For simple Isabel is soon to be
Among the dead: She withers, like a palm
Cut by an Indian for its juicy balm.

LVII

O leave the palm to wither by itself;
    Let not quick Winter chill its dying hour!— 450
It may not be—those Baälites of pelf,
    Her brethren, noted the continual shower
From her dead eyes; and many a curious elf,
    Among her kindred, wonder'd that such dower

Of youth and beauty should be thrown aside   455
By one mark'd out to be a Noble's bride.

LVIII

And, furthermore, her brethren wonder'd much
   Why she sat drooping by the Basil green,
And why it flourish'd, as by magic touch;
   Greatly they wonder'd what the thing might mean: 460
They could not surely give belief, that such
   A very nothing would have power to wean
Her from her own fair youth, and pleasures gay,
And even remembrance of her love's delay.

LIX

Therefore they watch'd a time when they might sift   465
   This hidden whim; and long they watch'd in vain;
For seldom did she go to chapel-shrift,
   And seldom felt she any hunger-pain;
And when she left, she hurried back, as swift
   As bird on wing to breast its eggs again;   470
And, patient as a hen-bird, sat her there
Beside her Basil, weeping through her hair.

LX

Yet they contriv'd to steal the Basil-pot,
   And to examine it in secret place:
The thing was vile with green and livid spot,   475
   And yet they knew it was Lorenzo's face:
The guerdon of their murder they had got,
And so left Florence in a moment's space,
Never to turn again.—Away they went,
With blood upon their heads, to banishment.   480

LXI

O Melancholy, turn thine eyes away!
   O Music, Music, breathe despondingly!
O Echo, Echo, on some other day,
   From isles Lethean, sigh to us—O sigh!
Spirits of grief, sing not your "Well-a-way!"   485
   For Isabel, sweet Isabel, will die;

Will die a death too lone and incomplete,
Now they have ta'en away her Basil sweet.

LXII

Piteous she look'd on dead and senseless things,
    Asking for her lost Basil amorously;   490
And with melodious chuckle in the strings
    Of her lorn voice, she oftentimes would cry
After the Pilgrim in his wanderings,
    To ask him where her Basil was; and why
'Twas hid from her: "For cruel 'tis," said she,   495
"To steal my Basil-pot away from me."

LXIII

And so she pined, and so she died forlorn,
    Imploring for her Basil to the last.
No heart was there in Florence but did mourn
    In pity of her love, so overcast.   500
And a sad ditty of this story born
    From mouth to mouth through all the country pass'd:
Still is the burthen sung—"O cruelty,
"To steal my Basil-pot away from me!"

William Holman Hunt's painting inspired by Keats's "Isabella; or, The Pot of Basil" demonstrates the interest of the Pre-Raphaelites in the Romantic poet's Gothicism. COURTESY TYNE AND WEAR COVENTRY COUNCIL.

Sir Walter Scott
(1771-1832)

THE past of Sir Walter Scott's native Scotland intrigued him, and its deep awareness of its own traditions led him quite naturally to rework old ballads and legends from Scotland's rich mine of folklore. Taking a cue from the Germans, he published, in 1796, translations of the ballads "Lenore" and "Der Wilde Jäger" by the German poet Gottfried August Bürger. These so greatly impressed M. G. Lewis, the famous author of *The Monk* (1796), that he invited Scott to contribute several ballads to his long-planned anthology *Tales of Wonder* (1801), where Lewis' "Alonzo the Brave and Fair Imogine" and its parody appeared. Scott met Lewis in Edinburgh, and a fast friendship followed. Lewis found a publisher for Scott's translation of Goethe's drama *Götz von Berlichingen*, and, by unnecessarily delaying publication of *Tales of Wonder*, encouraged Scott to publish more of his ballads and three of Lewis' in a little volume called *Apology for Tales of Terror*, issued in 1799. (Lewis had originally intended to call *Tales of Wonder, Tales of Terror*.) The same publisher, Ballantyne, soon brought out Scott's extraordinary collection of ballads on Scottish history and tradition, *The Minstrelsy of the Scottish Border* (3 volumes; 1802–1803), which was a significant source for all his later literary efforts. Despite the thoroughness of his research and the accuracy of the Scottish dialect in these ballads, Scott's fame was not assured until the publication of *The Lay of the Last Minstrel* (1805), a poem of love, war, and sorcery based on Coleridge's "Christabel." By 1810 Scott's literary reputation eclipsed that of Lewis. With *Waverley* (1814) and the more than thirty novels that followed, Scott became known as the most entertaining writer of his age. He praised Walpole, Radcliffe, and Mary Shelley in his *Lives of the Novelists* (1821–1824), and he befriended, encouraged, and influenced James Hogg, author of *The Private Memoirs and Confessions of a Justified Sinner* (1824). He wrote a considerable number of Gothic poems and several "goblin dramas" and compiled *Letters on Demonology and Witchcraft* (1830). He liberally sprinkled his novels with supernatural omens, spirits, and superstitions from the Scottish folklore he loved, but he bestowed unusual care on "Wandering

Willie's Tale," a ghost story told by a former retainer of the Redgauntlet family in the historical novel *Redgauntlet* (1824).

Willie's story of his grandfather is the symbolic center of the
novel, an example of the defiance to be required of the protagonists.
The tale is a kind of parable, and, as David Daiches says, a disillu-
sioned commentary on the harshness and cruelty of the violent Scottish past (*Nineteenth Century Fiction*, September 1951). Steenie
Steenson, the hero of the tale, must face hell itself to demand the
receipt for his rent, his rightful due. Justice is done to Steenie, but not
without great mental trauma and a convincing display of vigor,
courage, and caution. Willie's Scottish dialect, the earthy vernacular
of the lowlands, is Scott's way of endorsing the qualities of mind and
character which Steenie exemplifies. In the course of the story, Scott
satirizes "great men" by condemning them to hell and by giving
Willie comments on their pomposity and self-indulgence throughout
the tale. Steenie's common sense and staunch refusal to play a tune,
eat, or drink with the inmates of hell shows him to be a greater man
than his dead landlord or his landlord's powerful friends. His faith
saves him from returning to pay homage for the protection received:
"I refer mysell to God's pleasure, and not to yours," he says with
firmness. Such strong resistance to hellish demands is made all the
stronger by Steenie's hunger and thirst and appreciation for music,
even music learned from a warlock. The balance of natural and
supernatural details, rational attitudes and uncanny visions, historical
fact and romantic imagination, realistic requests and occult require-
ments, gives "Wandering Willie's Tale" the authenticity of a genuine
folk tale. Willie's dialect clothes his light sarcasm and grave seriousness with a charm best realized by reading aloud; the narration of the
blind fiddler is economical, lively, and remarkably consistent. The
verisimilitude of the tale is achieved, in part, by Scott's language, as
Stevenson's is in "Thrawn Janet" and Hogg's is in *The Private
Memoirs and Confessions of a Justified Sinner*. Unlike Hawthorne's
"Young Goodman Brown," the story requires no allegory to make
the diabolical intimacy seem real, but Scott bolstered belief in his
fiction by adding a long footnote about Sir Robert Grierson of Lagg,
the source for his depiction of Sir Robert Redgauntlet. Both are
notable bondsmen of Satan, and both have a filching monkey, Major
Weir, the name of a wizard executed in 1670 at Edinburgh. By
borrowing from Scottish tradition and demonological lore for "Wandering Willie's Tale," Scott enriches a legend about the persecutors
of the religious Covenanters. In an essay ("On the Supernatural in
Fictitious Composition," *Foreign Quarterly Review*, 1827), he remarked that the belief in ghosts "though easily capable of being
pushed into superstition and absurdity, has its origins . . . in the

facts upon which our holy religion is founded." Intuitively, Scott's
sensitive, original mediator, Wandering Willie, endorses these religious facts as he describes the human values and virtues of Scotland's cruel past.

Wandering Willie's Tale (1824)

Ye maun have heard of Sir Robert Redgauntlet of that Ilk, who
lived in these parts before the dear years. The country will lang mind
him; and our fathers used to draw breath thick if ever they heard him
named. He was out wi' the Hielandmen in Montrose's time; and again
he was in the hills wi' Glencairn in the saxteen hundred and fifty-twa;
and sae when King Charles the Second came in, wha was in sic
favour as the Laird of Redgauntlet? He was knighted at Lonon court,
wi' the King's ain sword; and being a red-hot prelatist, he came down
here, rampauging like a lion, with commissions of lieutenancy, and of
lunacy for what I ken, to put down a' the Whigs and Covenanters in
the country. Wild wark they made of it; for the Whigs were as dour as
the Cavaliers were fierce, and it was which should first tire the other.
Redgauntlet was aye for the stronghand; and his name is kenn'd as
wide in the country as Claverhouse's or Tam Dalyell's. Glen, nor
dargle, nor mountain, nor cave, could hide the puir hill-folk when
Redgauntlet was out with bugle and bloodhound after them, as if they
had been sae mony deer. And troth when they fand them, they didna
mak muckle mair ceremony than a Hielandman wi' a roe-buck—It
was just, "Will ye tak the test?"—if not, "Make ready—présent—
fire!"—and there lay the recusant.

Far and wide was Sir Robert hated and feared. Men thought he
had a direct compact with Satan—that he was proof against steel—
and that bullets happed aff his buff-coat like hail-stanes from a hearth
—that he had a mear that would turn a hare on the side of Carrifra-
gawns—and muckle to the same purpose, of whilk mair anon. The
best blessing they wared on him was, "De'il scowp wi' Redgauntlet!"
He wasna a bad master to his ain folk though, and was weel aneugh
liked by his tenants; and as for the lackies and troopers that raid out
wi' him to the persecutions, as the Whigs ca'ad these killing times,
they wad hae drunken themsels blind to his health at ony time.

Now ye are to ken that my gudesire lived on Redgauntlet's
grund—they ca' the place Primrose-Knowe. We had lived on the

grund, and under the Redgauntlets, since the riding days, and lang before. It was a pleasant bit; and I think the air is callerer and fresher there than onywhere else in the country. It's a' deserted now; and I sat on the broken door-check three days since, and was glad I couldna see the plight the place was in; but that's a' wide o' the mark. There dwelt my gudesire, Steenie Steenson, a rambling, rattling chiel' he had been in his young days, and could play weel on the pipes; he was famous at "Hoopers and Girders"—a' Cumberland couldna touch him at "Jockie Lattin"—and he had the finest finger for the back-lill between Berwick and Carlisle. The like o' Steenie wasna the sort that they made Whigs o'. And so he became a Tory, as they ca' it, which we now ca' Jacobites, just out of a kind of needcessity, that he might belang to some side or other. He had nae ill-will to the Whig bodies, and likedna to see the blude rin, though, being obliged to follow Sir Robert in hunting and hosting, watching and warding, he saw muckle mischief, and maybe did some, that he couldna avoid.

Now Steenie was a kind of favourite with his master, and kenn'd a' the folks about the castle, and was often sent for to play the pipes when they were at their merriment. Auld Dougal MacCallum, the butler, that had followed Sir Robert through gude and ill, thick and thin, pool and stream, was specially fond of the pipes, and aye gae my gudesire his gude word wi' the Laird; for Dougal could turn his master round his finger.

Weel, round came the Revolution, and it had like to have broken the hearts baith of Dougal and his master. But the change was not a'thegether sae great as they feared, and other folk thought for. The Whigs made an unca crawing what they wad do with their auld enemies, and in special wi' Sir Robert Redgauntlet. But there were ower mony great folks dipped in the same doings, to make a spick and span new warld. So Parliament passed it a' ower easy; and Sir Robert, bating that he was held to hunting foxes instead of Covenanters, remained just the man he was. His revel was as loud, and his hall as weel lighted, as ever it had been, though maybe he lacked the fines of the non-conformists, that used to come to stock larder and cellar; for it is certain he began to be keener about the rents than his tenants used to find him before, and they behoved to be prompt to the rent-day, or else the Laird wasna pleased. And he was sic an awsome body, that naebody cared to anger him; for the oaths he swore, and the rage that he used to get into, and the looks that he put on, made men sometimes think him a deevil incarnate.

Weel, my gudesire was nae manager—no that he was a very great misguider—but he hadna the saving gift, and he got twa terms rent in arrear. He got the first brash at Whitsunday put ower wi' fair words and piping; but when Martinmas came, there was a summons

from the grund-officer to come wi' the rent on a day preceese, or else
Steenie behoved to flitt. Sair wark he had to get the siller; but he was
weel-freended, and at last he got the haill scraped thegether—a thousand merks—the maist of it was from a neighbour they ca'd Laurie
Lapraik—a sly tod. Laurie had walth o' gear—could hunt wi' the
hound and rin wi' the hare—and be Whig or Tory, saunt or sinner,
as the wind stood. He was a professor in this Revolution warld, but
he liked an orra sound and a tune on the pipes weel aneugh at a bye-
time; and abune a', he thought he had gude security for the siller he
lent my gudesire over the stocking at Primrose-Knowe.

Away trots my gudesire to Redgauntlet Castle wi' a heavy purse
and a light heart, glad to be out of the Laird's danger. Weel, the first
thing he learned at the Castle was, that Sir Robert had fretted himsell
into a fit of the gout, because he did not appear before twelve o'clock.
It wasna a'thegether for sake of the money, Dougal thought; but
because he didna like to part wi' my gudesire aff the grund. Dougal
was glad to see Steenie, and brought him into the great oak parlour,
and there sat the Laird his leesome lane, excepting that he had beside
him a great, ill-favoured jack-an-ape, that was a special pet of his; a
cankered beast it was, and mony an ill-natured trick it played—ill to
please it was, and easily angered—ran about the haill castle, chattering and yowling, and pinching, and biting folk, specially before ill-
weather, or disturbances in the state. Sir Robert ca'ad it Major Weir,
after the warlock that was burned; and few folk liked either the name
or the conditions of the creature—they thought there was something
in it by ordinar—and my gudesire was not just easy in mind when the
door shut on him, and he saw himself in the room wi' naebody but
the Laird, Dougal MacAllum, and the Major, a thing that hadna
chanced to him before.

Sir Robert sat, or, I should say, lay, in a great armed chair, wi'
his grand velvet gown, and his feet on a cradle; for he had baith gout
and gravel, and his face looked as gash and ghastly as Satan's. Major
Weir sat opposite to him, in a red-laced coat, and the Laird's wig on
his head; and aye as Sir Robert girned wi' pain, the jack-an-ape girned
too, like a sheep's-head between a pair of tangs—an ill-faur'd, fearsome couple they were. The Laird's buff-coat was hung on a pin
behind him, and his broadsword and his pistols within reach; for he
keepit up the auld fashion of having the weapons ready, and a horse
saddled day and night, just as he used to do when he was able to loup
on horseback, and away after ony of the hill-folk he could get speer-
ings of. Some said it was for fear of the Whigs taking vengeance, but I
judge it was just his auld custom—he wasna gien to fear onything.
The rental-book, wi' its black cover and brass clasps, was lying beside
him; and a book of sculduddry sangs was put betwixt the leaves, to

keep it open at the place where it bore evidence against the Goodman of Primrose-Knowe, as behind the hand with his mails and duties. Sir Robert gave my gudesire a look, as if he would have withered his heart in his bosom. Ye maun ken had a way of bending his brows, that men saw the visible mark of a horse-shoe in his forehead, deep-dinted, as if it had been stamped there.

"Are ye come light-handed, ye son of a toom whistle?" said Sir Robert. "Zounds! if you are—"

My gudesire, with as gude a countenance as he could put on, made a leg, and placed the bag of money on the table wi' a dash, like a man that does something clever. The Laird drew it to him hastily—"Is it all here, Steenie, man?"

"Your honour will find it right," said my gudesire.

"Here, Dougal," said the Laird, "gie Steenie a tass of brandy down stairs, till I count the siller and write the receipt."

But they werena weel out of the room, when Sir Robert gied a yelloch that garr'd the castle rock. Back ran Dougal—in flew the livery-men—yell on yell gied the Laird, ilk ane mair awfu' than the ither. My gudesire knew not whether to stand or flee, but he ventured back into the parlour, where a' was gaun hirdy-girdie—naebody to say "come in" or "gae out." Terribly the Laird roared for cauld water to his feet, and wine to cool his throat; and, Hell, hell, hell, and its flames, was aye the word in his mouth. They brought him water, and when they plunged his swoln feet into the tub, he cried out it was burning; and folk say that it *did* bubble and sparkle like a seething cauldron. He flung the cup at Dougal's head, and said he had given him blood instead of burgundy; and, sure aneugh, the lass washed clottered blood aff the carpet the neist day. The jack-an-ape they ca'd Major Weir, it jibbered and cried as if it was mocking its master; my gudesire's head was like to turn—he forgot baith siller and receipt, and down stairs he banged; but as he ran, the shrieks came faint and fainter; there was a deep-drawn shivering groan, and word gaed through the Castle, that the Laird was dead.

Weel, away came my gudesire, wi' his finger in his mouth, and his best hope was, that Dougal had seen the money-bag, and heard the Laird speak of writing the receipt. The young Laird, now Sir John, came from Edinburgh, to see things put to rights. Sir John and his father never gree'd weel—he had been bred an advocate, and afterwards sat in the last Scots Parliament and voted for the Union, having gotten, it was thought, a rug of the compensations—if his father could have come out of his grave, he would have brained him for it on his awn hearth-stane. Some thought it was easier counting with the auld rough Knight than the fair-spoken young ane—but mair of that anon.

Dougal MacCallum, poor body, neither grat nor graned, but gaed about the house looking like a corpse, but directing, as was his duty, a' the order of the grand funeral. Now, Dougal looked aye waur and waur when night was coming, and was aye the last to gang to his bed, whilk was in a little round just opposite the chamber of dais, whilk his master occupied while he was living, and where he now lay in state as they ca'ad it, well-a-day! The night before the funeral, Dougal could keep his awn counsel nae langer; he came doun with his proud spirit, and fairly asked auld Hutcheon to sit in his room with him for an hour. When they were in the round, Dougal took ae tass of brandy to himsel, and gave another to Hutcheon, and wished him all health and lang life, and said that, for himsel, he wasna lang for this world; for that, every night since Sir Robert's death, his silver call had sounded from the state chamber, just as it used to do at nights in his lifetime, to call Dougal to help to turn him in his bed. Dougal said, that being alone with the dead on that floor of the tower, (for naebody cared to wake Sir Robert Redgauntlet like another corpse,) he had never daured to answer the call, but that now his conscience checked him for neglecting his duty; for, "though death breaks service," said MacCallum, "it shall never break my service to Sir Robert; and I will answer his next whistle, so be you will stand by me, Hutcheon."

Hutcheon had nae will to the wark, but he had stood by Dougal in battle and broil, and he wad not fail him at this pinch; so down the carles sat over a stoup of brandy, and Hutcheon, who was something of a clerk, would have read a chapter of the Bible; but Dougal would hear naething but a blaud of Davie Lindsay, whilk was the waur preparation.

When midnight came, and the house was quiet as the grave, sure aneugh the silver whistle sounded as sharp and shrill as if Sir Robert was blowing it, and up got the twa auld serving-men, and tottered into the room where the dead man lay. Hutcheon saw aneugh at the first glance; for there were torches in the room, which shewed him the foul fiend, in his ain shape, sitting on the Laird's coffin! Over he cowped as if he had been dead. He could not tell how lang he lay in a trance at the door, but when he gathered himself, he cried on his neighbour, and getting no answer, raised the house, when Dougal was found lying dead within twa steps of the bed where his master's coffin was placed. As for the whistle, it was gaen anes and aye; but mony a time was it heard on the top of the house in the bartizan, and amang the auld chimnies and turrets, where the howlets have their nests. Sir John hushed the matter up, and the funeral passed over without mair bogle-wark.

But when a' was over, and the Laird was beginning to settle his affairs, every tenant was called up for his arrears, and my gudesire for the full sum that stood against him in the rental-book. Weel, away he trots to the Castle, to tell his story, and there he is introduced to Sir John, sitting in his father's chair, in deep mourning, with weepers and hanging cravat, and a small walking rapier by his side, instead of the auld broad-sword that had a hundred-weight of steel about it, what with blade, chape, and basket-hilt. I have heard their communing so often tauld ower, that I almost think I was there mysell, though I couldna be born at the time. (In fact, Alan, my companion mimicked, with a good deal of humour, the flattering, conciliating tone of the tenant's address, and the hypocritical melancholy of the Laird's reply. His grandfather, he said, had, while he spoke, his eye fixed on the rental-book, as if it were a mastiff-dog that he was afraid would spring up and bite him.)

"I wass ye joy, sir, of the head-seat, and the white loaf, and the braid lairdship. Your father was a kind man to friends and followers; muckle grace to you, Sir John, to fill his shoon—his boots, I suld say, for he seldom wore shoon, unless it were muils when he had the gout."

"Ay, Steenie," quoth the Laird, sighing deeply, and putting his napkin to his een, "his was a sudden call, and he will be missed in the country; no time to set his house in order—weel prepared God-ward, no doubt, which is the root of the matter—but left us behind a tangled hesp to wind, Steenie.—Hem! hem! We maun go to business, Steenie; much to do, and little time to do it in."

Here he opened the fatal volume; I have heard of a thing they call Doomsday-book—I am clear it has been a rental of back-ganging tenants.

"Stephen," said Sir John, still in the same soft, sleekit tone of voice—"Stephen Stevenson, or Steenson, ye are down here for a year's rent behind the hand—due at last term."

Stephen. "Please your honour, Sir John, I paid it to your father."

Sir John. "Ye took a receipt then, doubtless, Stephen; and can produce it?"

Stephen. "Indeed I hadna time, an it like your honour; for nae sooner had I set doun the siller, and just as his honour, Sir Robert, that's gaen, drew it till him to count it, and write out the receipt, he was ta'en wi' the pains that removed him."

"That was unlucky," said Sir John, after a pause. "But ye maybe paid it in the presence of somebody. I want but a *talis qualis* evidence, Stephen. I would go ower strictly to work with no poor man."

Stephen. "Troth, Sir John, there was naebody in the room but Dougal MacCallum the butler. But, as your honour kens, he has e'en followed his auld master."

"Very unlucky again, Stephen," said Sir John, without altering his voice a single note. "The man to whom ye paid the money is dead—and the man who witnessed the payment is dead too—and the siller, which should have been to the fore, is neither seen nor heard tell of in the repositories. How am I to believe a' this?"

Stephen. "I dinna ken, your honour; but there is a bit memorandum note of the very coins; for, God help me! I had to borrow out of twenty purses; and I am sure that ilk man there set down will take his grit oath for what purpose I borrowed the money."

Sir John. "I have little doubt ye *borrowed* the money, Steenie. It is the *payment* that I want to have some proof of."

Stephen. "The siller maun be about the house, Sir John. And since your honour never got it, and his honour that was canna have taen it wi' him, maybe some of the family may have seen it."

Sir John. "We will examine the servants, Stephen; that is but reasonable."

But lackey and lass, and page and groom, all denied stoutly that they had ever seen such a bag of money as my gudesire described. What was waur, he had unluckily not mentioned to any living soul of them his purpose of paying his rent. Ae quean had noticed something under his arm, but she took it for the pipes.

Sir John Redgauntlet ordered the servants out of the room, and then said to my gudesire, "Now, Steenie, ye see you have fair play; and, as I have little doubt ye ken better where to find the siller than ony other body, I beg, in fair terms, and for your own sake, that you will end this fasherie; for, Stephen, ye maun pay or flitt."

"The Lord forgie your opinion," said Stephen, driven almost to his wits' end—"I am an honest man."

"So am I, Stephen," said his honour; "and so are all the folks in the house, I hope. But if there be a knave amongst us, it must be he that tells the story he cannot prove." He paused, and then added, mair sternly, "If I understand your trick, sir, you want to take advantage of some malicious reports concerning things in this family, and particularly respecting my father's sudden death, thereby to cheat me out of the money, and perhaps take away my character, by insinuating that I have received the rent I am demanding.—Where do you suppose this money to be?—I insist upon knowing."

My gudesire saw everything look so muckle against him, that he grew nearly desperate—however, he shifted from one foot to another, looked to every corner of the room, and made no answer.

"Speak out, sirrah," said the Laird, assuming a look of his father's, a very particular ane, which he had when he was angry—it seemed as if the wrinkless of his frown made that self-same fearful shape of a horse's shoe in the middle of his brow—"Speak out, sir! I *will* know your thoughts—do you suppose that I have this money?"

"Far be it frae me to say so," said Stephen.

"Do you charge any of my people with having taken it?"

"I wad be laith to charge them that may be innocent," said my gudesire; "and if there be any one that is guilty, I have nae proof."

"Somewhere the money must be, if there is a word of truth in your story," said Sir John; "I ask where you think it is—and demand a correct answer?"

"In hell, if you will have my thoughts of it," said my gudesire, driven to extremity—"in hell! with your father and his silver whistle."

Down the stairs he ran (for the parlour was nae place for him after such a word) and he heard the Laird swearing blood and wounds behind him, as fast as ever did Sir Robert, and roaring for the baillie and the baron-officer.

Away rode my gudesire to his chief creditor (him they ca'd Laurie Lapraik) to try if he could make onything out of him; but when he tauld his story, he got but the warst word in his wame—thief, beggar, and dyvour, were the saftest terms; and to the boot of these hard terms, Laurie brought up the auld story of his dipping his hand in the blood of God's saints, just as if a tenant could have helped riding with the Laird, and that a laird like Sir Robert Redgauntlet. My gudesire was, by this time, far beyond the bounds of patience, and, while he and Laurie were at de'il speed the liars, he was wanchancie aneugh to abuse his doctrine as weel as the man, and said things that gar'd folks flesh grew that heard them;—he wasna just himsell, and he had lived wi' a wild set in his day.

At last they parted, and my gudesire was to ride hame through the wood of Pitmarkie, that is a' fou of black firs, as they say. I ken the wood, but the firs may be black or white for what I can tell. At the entry of the wood there is a wild common, and on the edge of the common, a little lonely change-house, that was keepit then by an ostler-wife, they suld hae ca'd her Tibbie Faw, and there puir Steenie cried for a mutchkin of brandy, for he had had no refreshment the hail day. Tibbie was earnest wi' him to take a bite of meat, but he couldna think o't, nor would he take his foot out of the stirrup, and took off the brandy wholely at twa draughts, and named a toast at each: the first was, the memory of Sir Robert Redgauntlet, and might he never lie quiet in his grave till he had righted his poor bond-tenant; and the second was, a health to Man's Enemy, if he would but get him back the pock of siller, or tell him what came o't, for he saw the hail world was like to regard him as a thief and a cheat, and he took that waur than even the ruin of his house and hauld.

On he rode, little caring where. It was a dark night turned, and the trees made it yet darker, and he let the beast take its ain road through the wood; when, all of a sudden, from tired and wearied that it was before, the nag began to spring, and flee, and stend, that my gudesire could hardly keep the saddle—Upon the whilk, a horseman, suddenly riding up beside him, said, "That's a mettle beast of yours, freend; will you sell him?"—So saying, he touched the horse's neck with his riding-wand, and it fell into its auld heigh-ho of a stumbling trot; "But his spunk's soon out of him, I think," continued the stranger, "and that is like mony a man's courage, that thinks he wad do great things till he come to the proof."

My gudesire scarce listened to this, but spurred his horse, with "Gude e'en to you, freend."

But it's like the stranger was ane that does na lightly yield his point; for, ride as Steenie liked, he was aye beside him at the self-same pace. At last my gudesire, Steenie Steenson, grew half angry; and, to say the truth, half feared.

"What is it that ye want with me, freend?" he said. "If ye be a robber, I have nae money; if ye be a leal man, wanting company, I have nae heart to mirth or speaking; and if ye want to ken the road, I scarce ken it mysell."

"If you will tell me your grief," said the stranger, "I am one that, though I have been sair miscaa'd in the world, am the only hand for helping my friends."

So my gudesire, to ease his ain heart, mair than from any hope of help, told him the story from beginning to end.

"It's a hard pinch," said the stranger; "but I think I can help you."

"If you could lend the money, sir, and take a lang day—I ken nae other help on earth," said my gudesire.

"But there may be some under the earth," said the stranger. "Come, I'll be frank wi' you; I could lend you the money on bond, but you would maybe scruple my terms. Now, I can tell you, that your auld Laird is disturbed in his grave by your curses, and the wailing of your family, and—if ye daur venture to go to see him, he will give you the receipt."

My gudesire's hair stood on end at this proposal, but he thought his companion might be some humoursome chield that was trying to frighten him, and might end with lending him the money. Besides, he was bauld wi' brandy, and desperate wi' distress; and he said, he had courage to go to the gate of hell, and a step farther, for that receipt. The stranger laughed.

Weel, they rode on through the thickest of the wood, when, all of a sudden, the horse stopped at the door of a great house; and, but that he knew the place was ten miles off, my father would have thought he was at Redgauntlet Castle. They rode into the outer court-yard, through the muckle faulding yetts, and aneath the auld port-cullis; and the whole front of the house was lighted, and there were pipes and fiddles, and as much dancing and deray within as used to be in Sir Robert's house at Pace and Yule, and such high seasons. They lap off, and my gudesire, as seemed to him, fastened his horse to the very ring he had tied him to that morning, when he gaed to wait on the young Sir John.

"God!" said my father, "if Sir Robert's death be but a dream!"

He knocked at the ha' door, just as he wont, and his auld ac-quaintance, Dougal MacCallum, just after his wont, too,—came to open the door, and said, "Piper Steenie, are ye there, lad? Sir Robert has been crying for you."

My gudesire was like a man in a dream—he looked for the stranger, but he was gaen for the time. At last, he just tried to say, "Ha! Dougal Driveower, are ye living? I thought ye had been dead."

"Never fash yoursell wi' me," said Dougal, "but look to your-sell; and see ya tak naething frae onybody here, neither meat, drink, or siller, except just the receipt that is your ain."

So saying, he led the way out through halls and trances that were weel kenn'd to my gudesire, and into the auld oak parlour; and there was as much singing of profane sangs, and birling of red wine, and speaking blasphemy and sculduddry, as had ever been in Red-gauntlet Castle when it was at the blythest.

But, Lord take us in keeping! what a set of ghastly revellers they were that sat round that table!—My gudesire kenn'd mony that had long before gane to their place. There was the fierce Middleton, and the dissolute Rothes, and the crafty Lauderdale; and Dalyell, with his bald head and a beard to his girdle; and Earlshall, with Cameron's blude on his hand; and wild Bonshaw, that tied blessed Mr. Cargill's limbs till the blude sprung; and Dumbarton Douglas, the twice-turned traitor baith to country and king. There was the Bluidy Advocate MacKenyie, who, for his worldly wit and wisdom, had been to the rest as a god. And there was Claverhouse, as beautiful as when he lived, with his long, dark, curled locks, streaming down to his laced buff-coat, and his left hand always on his right spule-blade, to hide the wound that the silver bullet had made. He sat apart from them all, and looked at them with a melancholy, haughty countenance; while the rest hallooed, and sung, and laughed, that the room rang. But their smiles were fearfully contorted from time to time; and their laughter passed into such wild sounds, as made my gudesire's very nails grow blue, and chilled the marrow in his banes.

They that waited at the table were just the wicked serving-men and troopers, that had done their work and wicked bidding on earth. There was the Lang Lad of the Nethertown, that helped to take

Argyle; and the Bishop's summoner, that they called the De'il's Rattle-bag; and the wicked guardsmen, in their laced coats; and the savage Highland Amorites, that shed blood like water; and many a proud serving-man, haughty of heart and bloody of hand, cringing to the rich, and making them wickeder than they would be; grinding the poor to powder, when the rich had broken them to fragments. And mony, mony mair were coming and ganging, a' as busy in their vocation as if they had been alive.

Sir Robert Redgauntlet, in the midst of a' this fearful riot, cried, wi' a voice like thunder, on Steenie Piper, to come to the board-head where he was sitting; his legs stretched out before him, and swathed up with flannel, with his holster pistols aside him, and the great broadsword rested against his chair, just as my gudesire had seen him the last time upon earth—the very cushion for the jack-an-ape was close to him, but the creature itsell was not there—it wasna its hour, it's likely; for he heard them say as he came forward, "Is not the Major come yet?" And another answered, "The jack-an-ape will be here betimes the morn." And when my gudesire came forward, Sir Robert, or his ghaist, or the deevil in his likeness, said, "Weel, piper, hae ye settled wi' my son for the year's rent?"

With much ado my father gat breath to say, that Sir John would not settle without his honour's receipt.

"Ye shall hae that for a tune of the pipes, Steenie," said the appearance of Sir Robert—"Play us up 'Weel hoddled, Luckie.' "

Now this was a tune my gudesire learned frae a warlock, that heard it when they were worshipping Satan at their meetings; and my gudesire had sometimes played it at the ranting suppers in Redgauntlet Castle, but never very willingly; and now he grew cauld at the very name of it, and said, for excuse, he hadna his pipes wi' him.

"MacCallum, ye limb of Beelzebub," said the fearfu' Sir Robert, "bring Steenie the pipes that I am keeping for him!"

MacCallum brought a pair of pipes might have served the piper of Donald of the Isles. But he gave my gudesire a nudge as he offered them; and looking secretly and closely, Steenie saw that the chanter was of steel, and heated to a white heat; so he had fair warning not to trust his fingers with it. So he excused himself again, and said, he was faint and frightened, and had not wind aneugh to fill the bag.

"Then ye maun eat and drink, Steenie," said the figure; "for we do little else here; and it's ill speaking between a fou man and a fasting."

Now these were the very words that the bloody Earl of Douglas said to keep the King's messenger in hand, while he cut the head off

MacLellan of Bombie, at the Threave Castle; and that put Steenie mair and mair on his guard. So he spoke up like a man, and said he came neither to eat, or drink, or make minstrelsy; but simply for his ain—to ken what was come o' the money he had paid, and to get a discharge for it; and he was so stout-hearted by this time, that he charged Sir Robert for conscience-sake—(he had no power to say the holy name)—and as he hoped for peace and rest, to spread no snares for him, but just to give him his ain.

The appearance gnashed its teeth and laughed, but it took from a large pocket-book the receipt, and handed it to Steenie. "Here is your receipt, ye pitiful cur; and for the money, my dog-whelp of a son may go look for it in the Cat's Cradle."

My gudesire uttered mony thanks, and was about to retire, when Sir Robert roared aloud, "Stop though, thou sack-doudling son of a whore! I am not done with thee. Here we do nothing for nothing; and you must return on this very day twelvemonth, to pay your master the homage that you owe me for my protection."

My father's tongue was loosed of a suddenty, and he said aloud, "I refer mysell to God's pleasure, and not to yours."

He had no sooner uttered the word than all was dark around him; and he sunk on the earth with such a sudden shock, that he lost both breath and sense.

How lang Steenie lay there, he could not tell; but when he came to himsell, he was lying in the auld kirkyard of Redgauntlet parishine, just at the door of the family aisle, and the scutcheon of the auld knight, Sir Robert, hanging over his head. There was a deep morning fog on grass and gravestone around him, and his horse was feeding quietly beside the minister's twa cows. Steenie would have thought the whole was a dream, but he had the receipt in his hand, fairly written and signed by the auld Laird; only the last letters of his name were a little disorderly, written like one seized with sudden pain.

Sorely troubled in his mind, he left that dreary place, rode through the mist to Redgauntlet Castle, and with much ado he got speech of the Laird. "Well, you dyvour bankrupt," was the first word, "have you brought me my rent?"

"No," answered my gudesire, "I have not; but I have brought your honour Sir Robert's receipt for it."

"How, sirrah?—Sir Robert's receipt!—You told me he had not given you one."

"Will your honour please to see if that bit line is right?"

Sir John looked at every line, and at every letter, with much attention; and at last, at the date, which my gudesire had not observed,—*"From my appointed place,"* he read, *"this twenty-fifth of*

November."—"What! That is yesterday!—Villain, thou must have gone to hell for this!"

"I got it from your honour's father—whether he be in heaven or hell, I know not," said Steenie.

"I will delate you for a warlock to the Privy Council!" said Sir John. "I will send you to your master, the devil, with the help of a tar-barrel and a torch!"

"I intend to delate mysell to the Presbytery," said Steenie, "and tell them all I have seen last night, whilk are things fitter for them to judge of than a borrel man like me."

Sir John paused, composed himsell, and desired to hear the full history; and my gudesire told it him from point to point, as I have told it you—word for word, neither more nor less.

Sir John was silent again for a long time, and at last he said, very composedly, "Steenie, this story of yours concerns the honour of many a noble family besides mine; and if it be a leasing-making, to keep yourself out of my danger, the least you can expect is to have a red-hot iron driven through your tongue, and that will be as bad as scauding your fingers wi' a red-hot chanter. But yet it may be true, Steenie; and if the money cast up, I will not know what to think of it.—But where shall we find the Cat's Cradle? There are cats enough about the old house, but I think they kitten without the ceremony of bed or cradle."

"We were best ask Hutcheon," said my gudesire; "he kens a' the odd corners about as weel as—another serving-man that is now gane, and that I wad not like to name."

Aweel, Hutcheon, when he was asked, told them, that a ruinous turret, lang disused, next to the clock-house, only accessible by a ladder, for the opening was on the outside, and far above the battlements, was called of old the Cat's Cradle.

"There will I go immediately," said Sir John; and he took (with what purpose, Heaven kens) one of his father's pistols from the hall-table, where they had lain since the night he died, and hastened to the battlements.

It was a dangerous place to climb, for the ladder was auld and frail, and wanted ane or twa rounds. However, up got Sir John, and entered at the turret door, where his body stopped the only little light that was in the bit turret. Something flees at him wi' a vengeance, maist dang him back ower—bang gaed the knight's pistol, and Hutcheon, that held the ladder, and my gudesire that stood beside him, hears a loud skelloch. A minute after, Sir John flings the body of the jack-an-ape down to them, and cries that the siller is fund, and that they should come up and help him. And there was the bag of siller sure aneugh, and mony orra things besides, that had been missing for mony a day. And Sir John, when he had riped the turret weel, led my gudesire into the dining-parlour, and took him by the hand, and spoke kindly to him, and said he was sorry he should have doubted his word, and that he would hereafter be a good master to him, to make amends.

"And now, Steenie," said Sir John, "although this vision of yours tends, on the whole, to my father's credit, as an honest man, that he should, even after his death, desire to see justice done to a poor man like you, yet you are sensible that ill-dispositioned men might make bad constructions upon it, concerning his soul's health. So, I think, we had better lay the hail dirdum on that ill-deedie creature, Major Weir, and say naething about your dream in the wood of Pitmurkie. You had taken ower mickle brandy to be very certain about onything; and, Steenie, this receipt (his hand shook while he held it out)—it's but a queer kind of document, and we will do best, I think, to put it quietly in the fire."

"Od, but for as queer as it is, it's a' the voucher I have for my rent," said my gudesire, who was afraid, it may be, of losing the benefit of Sir Robert's discharge.

"I will bear the contents to your credit in the rental-book, and give you a discharge under my own hand," said Sir John, "and that on the spot. And, Steenie, if you can hold your tongue about this matter, you shall sit, from this term downward, at an easier rent."

"Mony thanks to your honour," said Steenie, who saw easily in what corner the wind sat; "doubtless I will be conformable to all your honour's commands; only I would willingly speak wi' some powerful minister on the subject, for I do not like the sort of soumons of appointment whilk your honour's father——"

"Do not call the phantom my father!" said Sir John, interrupting him.

"Weel, then, the thing that was so like him," said my gudesire; "he spoke of my coming back to him this time twelvemonth, and it's a weight on my conscience."

"Aweel, then," said Sir John, "if you be so much distressed in mind, you may speak to our minister of the parish; he is a douce man, regards the honour of our family, and the mair that he may look for some patronage from me."

Wi' that, my father readily agreed that the receipt should be burnt, and the Laird threw it into the chimney with his ain hand. Burn it would not for them, though; but away it flew up the lumm, wi' a lang train of sparks at its tail, and a hissing noise like a squib.

My gudesire gaed down to the Manse, and the minister, when he had heard the story, said, it was his real opinion, that though my gudesire had gaen very far in tampering with dangerous matters, yet, as he had refused the devil's arles (for such was the offer of meat and drink) and had refused to do homage by piping at his bidding, he hoped, that if he held a circumspect walk hereafter, Satan could take little advantage by what was come and gane. And, indeed, my gude-sire, of his ain accord, lang forswore baith the pipes and the brandy —it was not even till the year was out, and the fatal day passed, that he would so much as take the fiddle, or drink usquebaugh or tip-penny.

Sir John made up his story about the jack-an-ape as he liked himsell; and some believe till this day there was no more in the matter than the filching nature of the brute. Indeed ye'll no hinder some to threap, that it was nane o' the Auld Enemy that Dougal and my gudesire saw in the Laird's room, but only that wanchancy crea-ture, the Major, capering on the coffin; and that, as to the blawing on the Laird's whistle that was heard after he was dead, the filthy brute could do that as weel as the Laird himsell, if no better. But Heaven kens the truth, whilk first came out by the minister's wife, after Sir John and her ain gudeman were baith in the moulds. And then my gudesire, wha was failed in his limbs, but not in his judgment or memory—at least nothing to speak of—was obliged to tell the real narrative to his friends, for the credit of his gude name. He might else have been charged for a warlock.

Washington Irving
(1783-1859)

THE first professional writer of the American Republic, Washington Irving, delighted his English contemporaries with the burlesque and the epic grandeur of his earliest book, *A History of New York* (1809). Referring to Irving by his pseudonym, Sir Walter Scott hailed the young American by noting his English models: "I have never read anything so closely resembling the style of Dean Swift as the annals of Diedrich Knickerbocker. . . . I think, too, there are passages which indicate that the author possesses power of a different kind, and has some touches which remind me of Sterne." When the first number of *The Sketch Book* was published in 1819, Irving became, along with Scott and Byron, one of the three great idols of the English reading public. His later works—including *The Conquest of Granada* (1829), *The Alhambra* (1832), and the *Life of George Washington* (1885–1859)—won admiration as monumental accomplishments performed with felicity, gaiety, and grace. But he is best loved and most remembered now for his earlier work in *The Sketch Book*, where posing as one "Geoffrey Crayon, Gent.," he recounted such stories as "Rip Van Winkle" and "The Legend of Sleepy Hollow."

These, the most famous of the stories in *The Sketch Book*, take as their setting the Hudson River Valley of Irving's boyhood. "The Spectre Bridegroom," on the other hand, shows the writer responding to the allure of German Romanticism—the same movement that had earlier inspired M. G. Lewis and Sir Walter Scott to translate ballads and to write their own in imitation. The history of the goblin horseman who carries away the fair Leonora—the story the baron tells to frighten the ladies into hysterics—is probably the one that inspires Sir Herman Von Starkenfaust's ruse. It was the most celebrated of the Gothic ballads, Gottfried August Bürger's "Lenore," translated by Lewis, whose own "Alonzo the Brave" demonstrates the same incongruous combination of wedding festivities and apparitions from the grave that fascinated Irving.

Irving's witty prose variation on the story of Leonora shows how successfully he can put the Gothic to comic use. Such humor marks his work at its best. Moreover, the plump and dimpled heroine, with her heaving bosom and dreamy eye, might be another incarnation of Katrina Van Tassel in "The Legend of Sleepy Hollow"; the sumptuous banquet and the banquet hall have their counterparts in Balt Van Tassel's hospitable home; and Sir Herman's knightly prank is altogether worthy of a Brom Bones. The mystery, resolved in the manner of Ann Radcliffe, still has the light touch of the American storyteller and humorist; and though the setting is Germanic, his style and spirit are the same as in his best-known tales. The good things to eat and drink, the comfortable furnishings, and the willing lovers suggest that his inspiration is the cheerful promise and tempting abundance of life itself, as everywhere the comic writer sees it.

The Spectre Bridegroom.
A Traveller's Tale* (1819-1820)

> He that supper for is dight,
> He lyes full cold, I trow, this night!
> Yestreen to chamber I him led,
> This night Gray-Steel has made his bed.
> —*Sir Eger, Sir Grahame, and Sir Gray-Steel*

On the summit of one of the heights of the Odenwald, a wild and romantic tract of Upper Germany, that lies not far from the confluence of the Main and the Rhine, there stood, many, many years since, the Castle of the Baron Von Landshort. It is now quite fallen to decay, and almost buried among beech trees and dark firs; above which, however, its old watch-tower may still be seen, struggling, like the former possessor I have mentioned, to carry a high head, and look down upon the neighboring country.

The baron was a dry branch of the great family of Katzenellenbogen,† and inherited the relics of the property, and all the pride of his ancestors. Though the warlike disposition of his predecessors had much impaired the family possessions, yet the baron still endeavored to keep up some show of former state. The times were peaceable, and

---

* The erudite reader, well versed in good-for-nothing lore, will perceive that the above Tale must have been suggested to the old Swiss by a little French anecdote, a circumstance said to have taken place at Paris.

† *i. e.*, CAT'S-ELBOW. The name of a family of those parts very powerful in former times. The appellation, we are told, was given in compliment to a peerless dame of the family, celebrated for her fine arm.

the German nobles, in general, had abandoned their inconvenient old castles, perched like eagles' nests among the mountains, and had built more convenient residences in the valleys: still the baron remained proudly drawn up in his little fortress, cherishing, with hereditary inveteracy, all the old family feuds; so that he was on ill terms with some of his nearest neighbors, on account of disputes that had happened between their great-great-grandfathers.

The baron had but one child, a daughter; but nature, when she grants but one child, always compensates by making it a prodigy; and so it was with the daughter of the baron. All the nurses, gossips, and country cousins, assured her father that she had not her equal for beauty in all Germany; and who should know better than they? She had, moreover, been brought up with great care under the superintendence of two maiden aunts, who had spent some years of their early life at one of the little German courts, and were skilled in all the branches of knowledge necessary to the education of a fine lady. Under their instructions she became a miracle of accomplishments. By the time she was eighteen, she could embroider to admiration, and had worked whole histories of the saints in tapestry, with such strength of expression in their countenances, that they looked like so many souls in purgatory. She could read without great difficulty, and had spelled her way through several church legends, and almost all the chivalric wonders of the Heldenbuch. She had even made considerable proficiency in writing; could sign her own name without missing a letter, and so legibly, that her aunts could read it without spectacles. She excelled in making little elegant good-for-nothing ladylike nicknacks of all kinds; was versed in the most abstruse dancing of the day; played a number of airs on the harp and guitar; and knew all the tender ballads of the Minnelieders by heart.

Her aunts, too, having been great flirts and coquettes in their younger days, were admirably calculated to be vigilant guardians and strict censors of the conduct of their niece; for there is no duenna so rigidly prudent, and inexorably decorous, as a superannuated coquette. She was rarely suffered out of their sight; never went beyond the domains of the castle, unless well attended, or rather well watched; had continual lectures read to her about strict decorum and implicit obedience; and, as to the men—pah!—she was taught to hold them at such a distance, and in such absolute distrust, that, unless properly authorized, she would not have cast a glance upon the handsomest cavalier in the world—no, not if he were even dying at her feet.

The good effects of this system were wonderfully apparent. The young lady was a pattern of docility and correctness. While others were wasting their sweetness in the glare of the world, and liable to be plucked and thrown aside by every hand, she was coyly blooming into fresh and lovely womanhood under the protection of those immaculate spinsters, like a rose-bud blushing forth among guardian thorns. Her aunts looked upon her with pride and exultation, and vaunted that though all the other young ladies in the world might go astray, yet, thank Heaven, nothing of the kind could happen to the heiress of Katzenellenbogen.

But, however scantily the Baron Von Landshort might be provided with children, his household was by no means a small one; for Providence had enriched him with abundance of poor relations. They, one and all, possessed the affectionate disposition common to humble relatives; were wonderfully attached to the baron, and took every possible occasion to come in swarms and enliven the castle. All family festivals were commemorated by these good people at the baron's expense; and when they were filled with good cheer, they would declare that there was nothing on earth so delightful as these family meetings, these jubilees of the heart.

The baron, though a small man, had a large soul, and it swelled with satisfaction at the consciousness of being the greatest man in the little world about him. He loved to tell long stories about the dark old warriors whose portraits looked grimly down from the walls around, and he found no listeners equal to those that fed at his expense. He was much given to the marvellous, and a firm believer in all those supernatural tales with which every mountain and valley in Germany abounds. The faith of his guests exceeded even his own: they listened to every tale of wonder with open eyes and mouth, and never failed to be astonished, even though repeated for the hundredth time. Thus lived the Baron Von Landshort, the oracle of his table, the absolute monarch of his little territory, and happy, above all things, in the persuasion that he was the wisest man of the age.

At the time of which my story treats, there was a great family gathering at the castle, on an affair of the utmost importance: it was to receive the destined bridegroom of the baron's daughter. A negotiation had been carried on between the father and an old nobleman of Bavaria, to unite the dignity of their houses by the marriage of their children. The preliminaries had been conducted with proper punctilio. The young people were betrothed without seeing each other; and the time was appointed for the marriage ceremony. The young Count Von Altenburg had been recalled from the army for the purpose, and was actually on his way to the baron's to receive his bride. Missives had even been received from him, from Wurtzburg, where he was accidentally detained, mentioning the day and hour when he might be expected to arrive.

The castle was in a tumult of preparation to give him a suitable welcome. The fair bride had been decked out with uncommon care. The two aunts had superintended her toilet, and quarrelled the whole morning about every article of her dress. The young lady had taken advantage of their contest to follow the bent of her own taste; and fortunately it was a good one. She looked as lovely as youthful bridegroom could desire; and the flutter of expectation heightened the lustre of her charms.

The suffusions that mantled her face and neck, the gentle heaving of the bosom, the eye now and then lost in reverie, all betrayed the soft tumult that was going on in her little heart. The aunts were continually hovering around her; for maiden aunts are apt to take great interest in affairs of this nature. They were giving her a world of staid counsel how to deport herself, what to say, and in what manner to receive the expected lover.

The baron was no less busied in preparations. He had, in truth, nothing exactly to do; but he was naturally a fuming bustling little man, and could not remain passive when all the world was in a hurry. He worried from top to bottom of the castle with an air of infinite anxiety; he continually called the servants from their work to exhort them to be diligent; and buzzed about every hall and chamber, as idly restless and importunate as a blue-bottle fly on a warm summer's day.

In the mean time the fatted calf had been killed; the forests had rung with the clamor of the huntsmen; the kitchen was crowded with good cheer; the cellars had yielded up whole oceans of *Rhein-wein* and *Ferne-wein*; and even the great Heidelburg tun had been laid under contribution. Every thing was ready to receive the distinguished guest with *Saus und Braus* in the true spirit of German hospitality—but the guest delayed to make his appearance. Hour rolled after hour. The sun, that had poured his downward rays upon the rich forest of the Odenwald, now just gleamed along the summits of the mountains. The baron mounted the highest tower, and strained his eyes in hope of catching a distant sight of the count and his attendants. Once he thought he beheld them; the sound of horns came floating from the valley, prolonged by the mountain echoes. A number of horsemen were seen far below, slowly advancing along the road; but when they had nearly reached the foot of the mountain, they suddenly struck off in a different direction. The last ray of sunshine departed—the bats began to flit by in the twilight—the road grew dimmer and dimmer to the view; and nothing appeared stirring in it but now and then a peasant lagging homeward from his labor.

While the old castle of Landshort was in this state of perplexity, a very interesting scene was transacting in a different part of the Odenwald.

The young Count Von Altenburg was tranquilly pursuing his route in that sober jog-trot way, in which a man travels toward matrimony when his friends have taken all the trouble and uncertainty of courtship off his hands, and a bride is waiting for him, as certainly as a dinner at the end of his journey. He had encountered at Wurtzburg, a youthful companion in arms, with whom he had seen some service on the frontiers; Herman Von Starkenfaust, one of the stoutest hands, and worthiest hearts, of German chivalry, who was now returning from the army. His father's castle was not far distant from the old fortress of Landshort, although an hereditary feud rendered the families hostile, and strangers to each other.

In the warm-hearted moment of recognition, the young friends related all their past adventures and fortunes, and the count gave the whole history of his intended nuptials with a young lady whom he had never seen, but of whose charms he had received the most enrapturing descriptions.

As the route of the friends lay in the same direction, they agreed to perform the rest of their journey together; and, that they might do it the more leisurely, set off from Wurtzburg at a nearly hour, the count having given directions for his retinue to follow and overtake him.

They beguiled their wayfaring with recollections of their military scenes and adventures; but the count was apt to be a little tedious, now and then, about the reputed charms of his bride, and the felicity that awaited him.

In this way they had entered among the mountains of the Odenwald, and were traversing one of its most lonely and thickly-wooded passes. It is well known that the forests of Germany have always been as much infested by robbers as its castles by spectres; and, at this time, the former were particularly numerous, from the hordes of disbanded soldiers wandering about the country. It will not appear extraordinary, therefore, that the cavaliers were attacked by a gang of these stragglers, in the midst of the forest. They defended themselves with bravery, but were nearly overpowered, when the count's retinue arrived to their assistance. At sight of them the robbers fled, but not until the count had received a mortal wound. He was slowly and carefully conveyed back to the city of Wurtzburg, and a friar summoned from a neighboring convent, who was famous for his skill in administering to both soul and body; but half of his skill was superfluous; the moments of the unfortunate count were numbered.

With his dying breath he entreated his friend to repair instantly to the castle of Landshort, and explain the fatal cause of his not keeping his appointment with his bride. Though not the most ardent of lovers, he was one of the most punctilious of men, and appeared earnestly solicitous that his mission should be speedily and courteously executed. "Unless this is done," said he, "I shall not sleep quietly in my grave!" He repeated these last words with peculiar solemnity. A request, at a moment so impressive, admitted no hesitation. Starkenfaust endeavored to soothe him to calmness; promised faithfully to execute his wish, and gave him his hand in solemn pledge. The dying man pressed it in acknowledgment, but soon lapsed into delirium—raved about his bride—his engagements—his plighted word; ordered his horse, that he might ride to the castle of Landshort; and expired in the fancied act of vaulting into the saddle.

Starkenfaust bestowed a sigh and a soldier's tear on the untimely fate of his comrade; and then pondered on the awkward mission he had undertaken. His heart was heavy, and his head perplexed; for he was to present himself an unbidden guest among hostile people, and to damp their festivity with tidings fatal to their hopes. Still there were certain whisperings of curiosity in his bosom to see this far-famed beauty of Katzenellenbogen, so cautiously shut up from the world; for he was a passionate admirer of the sex, and there was a dash of eccentricity and enterprise in his character that made him fond of all singular adventure.

Previous to his departure he made all due arrangements with the holy fraternity of the convent for the funeral solemnities of his friend, who was to be buried in the cathedral of Wurtzburg, near some of his illustrious relatives; and the mourning retinue of the count took charge of his remains.

It is now high time that we should return to the ancient family of Katzenellenbogen, who were impatient for their guest, and still more for their dinner; and to the worthy little baron, whom we left airing himself on the watch-tower.

Night closed in, but still no guest arrived. The baron descended from the tower in despair. The banquet, which had been delayed from hour to hour, could no longer be postponed. The meats were already overdone; the cook in an agony; and the whole household had the look of a garrison that had been reduced by famine. The baron was obliged reluctantly to give orders for the feast without the presence of the guest. All were seated at table, and just on the point of commencing, when the sound of a horn from without the gate gave notice of the approach of a stranger. Another long blast filled the old courts of the castle with its echoes, and was answered by the warder from the walls. The baron hastened to receive his future son-in-law.

The drawbridge had been let down, and the stranger was before the gate. He was a tall, gallant cavalier, mounted on a black steed. His countenance was pale, but he had a beaming, romantic eye, and an air of stately melancholy. The baron was a little mortified that he should have come in this simple, solitary style. His dignity for a moment was ruffled, and he felt disposed to consider it a want of proper respect for the important occasion, and the important family with which he was to be connected. He pacified himself, however, with the conclusion, that it must have been youthful impatience which had induced him thus to spur on sooner than his attendants.

"I am sorry," said the stranger, "to break in upon you thus unseasonably——"

Here the baron interrupted him with a world of compliments and greetings; for, to tell the truth, he prided himself upon his courtesy and eloquence. The stranger attempted, once or twice, to stem the torrent of words, but in vain, so he bowed his head and suffered it to flow on. By the time the baron had come to a pause, they had reached the inner court of the castle; and the stranger was again about to speak, when he was once more interrupted by the appearance of the female part of the family, leading forth the shrinking and blushing bride. He gazed on her for a moment as one entranced; it seemed as if his whole soul beamed forth in the gaze, and rested upon that lovely form. One of the maiden aunts whispered something in her ear; she made an effort to speak; her moist blue eye was timidly raised; gave a shy glance of inquiry on the stranger; and was cast again to the ground. The words died away; but there was a sweet smile playing about her lips, and a soft dimpling of the cheek that showed her glance had not been unsatisfactory. It was impossible for a girl of the fond age of eighteen, highly predisposed for love and matrimony, not to be pleased with so gallant a cavalier.

The late hour at which the guest had arrived left no time for parley. The baron was peremptory, and deferred all particular conversation until the morning, and led the way to the untasted banquet.

It was served up in the great hall of the castle. Around the walls hung the hard-favored portraits of the heroes of the house of Katzenellenbogen, and the trophies which they had gained in the field and in the chase. Hacked corslets, splintered jousting spears, and tattered banners, were mingled with the spoils of sylvan warfare; the jaws of the wolf, and the tusks of the boar, grinned horribly among crossbows and battle-axes, and a huge pair of antlers branched immediately over the head of the youthful bridegroom.

The cavalier took but little notice of the company or the entertainment. He scarcely tasted the banquet, but seemed absorbed in admiration of his bride. He conversed in a low tone that could not be overheard—for the language of love is never loud; but where is the female ear so dull that it cannot catch the softest whisper of the lover? There was a mingled tenderness and gravity in his manner, that appeared to have a powerful effect upon the young lady. Her color came and went as she listened with deep attention. Now and then she made some blushing reply, and when his eye was turned away, she would steal a sidelong glance at his romantic countenance, and heave a gentle sigh of tender happiness. It was evident that the young couple were completely enamored. The aunts, who were deeply versed in the mysteries of the heart, declared that they had fallen in love with each other at first sight.

The feast went on merrily, or at least noisily, for the guests were all blessed with those keen appetites that attend upon light purses and mountain air. The baron told his best and longest stories, and never had he told them so well, or with such great effect. If there was any thing marvellous, his auditors were lost in astonishment; and if any thing facetious, they were sure to laugh exactly in the right place. The baron, it is true, like most great men, was too dignified to utter any joke but a dull one; it was always enforced, however, by a bumper of excellent Hockheimer; and even a dull joke, at one's own table, served up with jolly old wine, is irresistible. Many good things were said by poorer and keener wits, that would not bear repeating, except on similar occasions; many sly speeches whispered in ladies' ears, that almost convulsed them with suppressed laughter; and a song or two roared out by a poor, but merry and broad-faced cousin of the baron, that absolutely made the maiden aunts hold up their fans.

Amidst all this revelry, the stranger guest maintained a most singular and unseasonable gravity. His countenance assumed a deeper cast of dejection as the evening advanced; and, strange as it may appear, even the baron's jokes seemed only to render him the more melancholy. At times he was lost in thought, and at times there was a perturbed and restless wandering of the eye that bespoke a mind but ill at ease. His conversations with the bride became more and more earnest and mysterious. Lowering clouds began to steal over the fair serenity of her brow, and tremors to run through her tender frame.

All this could not escape the notice of the company. Their gayety was chilled by the unaccountable gloom of the bridegroom; their spirits were infected; whispers and glances were interchanged, accompanied by shrugs and dubious shakes of the head. The song and the laugh grew less and less frequent; there were dreary pauses in the conversation, which were at length succeeded by wild tales and supernatural legends. One dismal story produced another still more dismal, and the baron nearly frightened some of the ladies into hysterics with the history of the goblin horseman that carried away the fair Leonora; a dreadful story, which has since been put into excellent verse, and is read and believed by all the world.

The bridegroom listened to this tale with profound attention. He kept his eyes steadily fixed on the baron, and, as the story drew to a close, began gradually to rise from his seat, growing taller and taller, until, in the baron's entranced eye, he seemed almost to tower into a giant. The moment the tale was finished, he heaved a deep sigh, and took a solemn farewell of the company. They were all amazement. The baron was perfectly thunder-struck.

"What! going to leave the castle at midnight? why, every thing was prepared for his reception; a chamber was ready for him if he wished to retire."

The stranger shook his head mournfully and mysteriously; "I must lay my head in a different chamber tonight!"

There was something in this reply, and the tone in which it was uttered, that made the baron's heart misgive him; but he rallied his forces, and repeated his hospitable entreaties.

The stranger shook his head silently, but positively, at every offer; and, waving his farewell to the company, stalked slowly out of the hall. The maiden aunts were absolutely petrified—the bride hung her head, and a tear stole to her eye.

The baron followed the stranger to the great court of the castle, where the black charger stood pawing the earth, and snorting with impatience. When they had reached the portal, whose deep archway was dimly lighted by a cresset, the stranger paused, and addressed the baron in a hollow tone of voice, which the vaulted roof rendered still more sepulchral.

"Now that we are alone," said he, "I will impart to you the reason of my going. I have a solemn, an indispensable engagement—"

"Why," said the baron, "cannot you send some one in your place?"

"It admits of no substitute—I must attend it in person—I must away to Wurtzburg cathedral—"

"Ay," said the baron, plucking up spirit, "but not until tomorrow—to-morrow you shall take your bride there."

"No! No!" replied the stranger, with tenfold solemnity, "my engagement is with no bride—the worms! the worms expect me! I am a dead man—I have been slain by robbers—my body lies at Wurtzburg—at midnight I am to be buried—the grave is waiting for me—I must keep my appointment!"

He sprang on his black charger, dashed over the drawbridge, and the clattering of his horse's hoofs was lost in the whistling of the night blast.

The baron returned to the hall in the utmost consternation, and related what had passed. Two ladies fainted outright, others sickened at the idea of having banqueted with a spectre. It was the opinion of some, that this might be the wild huntsman, famous in German legend. Some talked of mountain sprites, of wood-demons, and of other supernatural beings, with which the good people of Germany have been so grievously harassed since time immemorial. One of the poor relations ventured to suggest that it might be some sportive evasion of the young cavalier, and that the very gloominess of the caprice seemed to accord with so melancholy a personage. This, however, drew on him the indignation of the whole company, and especially of the baron, who looked upon him as little better than an infidel; so that he was fain to abjure his heresy as speedily as possible, and come into the faith of the true believers.

But whatever may have been the doubts entertained, they were completely put to an end by the arrival, next day, of regular missives, confirming the intelligence of the young count's murder, and his interment in Wurtzburg cathedral.

The dismay at the castle may well be imagined. The baron shut himself up in his chamber. The guests, who had come to rejoice with him, could not think of abandoning him in his distress. They wandered about the courts, or collected in groups in the hall, shaking their heads and shrugging their shoulders, at the troubles of so good a man; and sat longer than ever at table, and ate and drank more stoutly than ever, by way of keeping up their spirits. But the situation of the widowed bride was the most pitiable. To have lost a husband before she had even embraced him—and such a husband! if the very spectre could be so gracious and noble, what must have been the living man. She filled the house with lamentations.

On the night of the second day of her widowhood, she had retired to her chamber, accompanied by one of her aunts, who insisted on sleeping with her. The aunt, who was one of the best tellers of ghost stories in all Germany, had just been recounting one of her longest, and had fallen asleep in the very midst of it. The chamber was remote, and overlooked a small garden. The niece lay pensively gazing at the beams of the rising moon, as they trembled on the leaves of an aspen-tree before the lattice. The castle-clock had just tolled midnight, when a soft strain of music stole up from the garden. She rose hastily from her bed, and stepped lightly to the window. A tall figure stood among the shadows of the trees. As it raised its head, a beam of moonlight fell upon the countenance. Heaven and earth! she beheld the Spectre Bridegroom! A loud shriek at that moment burst upon her ear, and her aunt, who had been awakened by the music, and had followed her silently to the window, fell into her arms. When she looked again, the spectre had disappeared.

Of the two females, the aunt now required the most soothing, for she was perfectly beside herself with terror. As to the young lady, there was something, even in the spectre of her lover, that seemed endearing. There was still the semblance of manly beauty; and though the shadow of a man is but little calculated to satisfy the affections of a love-sick girl, yet, where the substance is not to be had, even that is consoling. The aunt declared she would never sleep in that chamber again; the niece, for once, was refractory, and declared as strongly that she would sleep in no other in the castle: the consequence was, that she had to sleep in it alone: but she drew a promise from her aunt not to relate the story of the spectre, lest she should be denied the only melancholy pleasure left her on earth—that of inhabiting the chamber over which the guardian shade of her lover kept its nightly vigils.

How long the good old lady would have observed this promise is uncertain, for she dearly loved to talk of the marvellous, and there is a triumph in being the first to tell a frightful story; it is, however, still quoted in the neighborhood, as a memorable instance of female secrecy, that she kept it to herself for a whole week; when she was suddenly absolved from all further restraint, by intelligence brought to the breakfast table one morning that the young lady was not to be found. Her room was empty—the bed had not been slept in—the window was open, and the bird had flown!

The astonishment and concern with which the intelligence was received, can only be imagined by those who have witnessed the agitation which the mishaps of a great man cause among his friends. Even the poor relations paused for a moment from the indefatigable labors of the trencher; when the aunt, who had at first been struck speechless, wrung her hands, and shrieked out, "The goblin! the goblin! she's carried away by the goblin."

In a few words she related the fearful scene of the garden, and concluded that the spectre must have carried off his bride. Two of the domestics corroborated the opinion, for they had heard the clattering of a horse's hoofs down the mountain about midnight, and had no doubt that it was the spectre on his black charger, bearing her away to the tomb. All present were struck with the direful probability; for events of the kind are extremely common in Germany, as many well authenticated histories bear witness.

What a lamentable situation was that of the poor baron! What a heart-rending dilemma for a fond father, and a member of the great family of Katzenellenbogen! His only daughter had either been rapt away to the grave, or he was to have some wood-demon for a son-in-law, and, perchance, a troop of goblin grandchildren. As usual, he was completely bewildered, and all the castle in an uproar. The men were ordered to take horse, and scour every road and path and glen of the Odenwald. The baron himself had just drawn on his jack-boots, girded on his sword, and was about to mount his steed to sally forth on the doubtful quest, when he was brought to a pause by a new apparition. A lady was seen approaching the castle, mounted on a palfrey, attended by a cavalier on horseback. She galloped up to the gate, sprang from her horse, and falling at the baron's feet, embraced his knees. It was his lost daughter, and her companion—the Spectre Bridegroom! The baron was astounded. He looked at his daughter, then at the spectre, and almost doubted the evidence of his senses. The latter, too, was wonderfully improved in his appearance since his visit to the world of spirits. His dress was splendid, and set off a noble figure of manly symmetry. He was no longer pale and melancholy. His fine countenance was flushed with the glow of youth, and joy rioted in his large dark eye.

The mystery was soon cleared up. The cavalier (for, in truth, as you must have known all the while, he was no goblin) announced himself as Sir Herman Von Starkenfaust. He related his adventure with the young count. He told how he had hastened to the castle to deliver the unwelcome tidings, but that the eloquence of the baron had interrupted him in every attempt to tell his tale. How the sight of the bride had completely captivated him, and that to pass a few hours near her, he had tacitly suffered the mistake to continue. How he had been sorely perplexed in what way to make a decent retreat, until the baron's goblin stories had suggested his eccentric exit. How, fearing the feudal hostility of the family, he had repeated his visits by stealth —had haunted the garden beneath the young lady's window—had wooed—had won—had borne away in triumph—and, in a word, had wedded the fair.

Under any other circumstances the baron would have been inflexible, for he was tenacious of paternal authority, and devoutly obstinate in all family feuds; but he loved his daughter; he had lamented her as lost; he rejoiced to find her still alive; and, though her husband was of a hostile house, yet, thank Heaven, he was not a goblin. There was something, it must be acknowledged, that did not exactly accord with his notions of strict veracity, in the joke the knight had passed upon him of his being a dead man; but several old friends present, who had served in the wars, assured him that every stratagem was excusable in love, and that the cavalier was entitled to especial privilege, having lately served as a trooper.

Matters, therefore, were happily arranged. The baron pardoned the young couple on the spot. The revels at the castle were resumed. The poor relations overwhelmed this new member of the family with loving kindness; he was so gallant, so generous—and so rich. The aunts, it is true, were somewhat scandalized that their system of strict seclusion, and passive obedience should be so badly exemplified, but attributed it all to their negligence in not having the windows grated. One of them was particularly mortified at having her marvellous story marred, and that the only spectre she had ever seen should turn out a counterfeit; but the niece seemed perfectly happy at having found him substantial flesh and blood—and so the story ends.

Edgar Allan Poe
(1809-1849)

NO American writer has been more maligned and more misunderstood than Edgar Allan Poe. His character and fiction invited a host of legends which, until rather recently, obscured the facts of his life and a fair evaluation of his work. His enduring influence on such writers as Charles Baudelaire, Stéphane Mallarmé, French symbolist poets, Dante Gabriel Rossetti, Robert Louis Stevenson, Wilkie Collins, and Oscar Wilde have returned him to the attention of America and Americans, where his original genius justifiably fascinates adolescent readers and mature novelists, poets, and short-story writers alike. At last he has taken his well-deserved place as an American pioneer of detective and science fiction and of aesthetic and literary criticism; always he is remembered as an artistic explorer of the minds of men obsessed with irrational fears and impulses. Allen Tate was speaking for American writers when he said: "Poe . . . discovered our great subject, the disintegration of the modern personality" (*Kenyon Review*, Summer 1952).

Poe was orphaned at age two and adopted by John Allan of Richmond, Virginia, who provided him with an English education and one year at the University of Virginia. His adopted father refused to pay the drinking and gambling debts Poe incurred there, and he was forced to leave the university to make his own way. In Boston, his birthplace, he paid to have his first volume published: *Tamerlane and Other Poems* (1827). A brief military career, including a year at West Point, did not satisfy the restless young Poe. Two more collections of poetry, *Al Aaraaf, Tamerlane, and Minor Poems* (1829) and *Poems* (1831), however, launched his literary career and gave him peace in a profession he enjoyed. Although never far from poverty, Poe managed to support himself and his wife and cousin, Virginia Clemm, as an editor, reviewer, poet, and writer of tales, in Baltimore, Richmond, Philadelphia, and New York. He sold his poetry and short fiction to magazines and newspapers before collecting it in several editions, among them *Tales of the Grotesque and Arabesque* (1839) and *The Raven and Other Poems* (1845). Poe's criticism and reviews lack the sensational appeal of the murderers and madmen of his fiction and the melancholy subjects of his poetry, but his indebtedness to Coleridge's principles is as consistent in his essays as Gothic devices are in his tales.

In "The Fall of the House of Usher," Poe's unity of design, atmospheric effects, and Gothic subject present his art at its most controlled. The exact location of the house is unspecified to concentrate the focus on the mental anguish of Roderick Usher and the first-person narrator. The isolation of the house, the autumnal season, and the gloomy dusk cast an aura of dread about the speaker-visitor, whose usual empirical approach fails to dispel his feelings of "iciness, a sinking, a sickening of the heart." Unfamiliar "fancies" of presentiment cannot raise him to sublime contemplation; mystery surrounds him and the almost animate house with "eye-like windows." The grotesque mansion houses grotesque inhabitants who are so alike that the mind and heart of one reflect the other's as nearly as the tarn reflects their family home. Decay, discoloration, instability, and "a barely perceptible fissure" characterize the family and the House of Usher. Poe charges his language with emotion to highlight the fatal and parallel flaws amid the oppressive, pervasive gloom of a nightmare world without surface meaning or apparent value. Beneath the vivid details, Poe creates a dreamy preternatural enclosure descriptive of states of mind. Even the poem, "The Haunted Palace," at the story's core, reflects the coherent incoherence of Roderick Usher's mind and dwelling. The narrator enters as deeply into the house as into Usher's mind until he himself feels "the wild influences of Usher's own fantastic yet impressive superstitions." Poe's use of poetry, painting, and the romance "Mad Trist," duplicates the action of his story and further complicates his portrayal of Usher's confused life and mind. The suggestion of incest, twinship, family likeness, and Usher's belief in the "sentience of all vegetable things" heighten the circumscription of house, family, inmates, and narrator. An absolutely closed system of art and mind, love and sympathy, the animate and the inanimate, give "The Fall of the House of Usher" the "totality of effect" which is the aim of Poe's art.

The Fall of the House of Usher (1839)

> Son cœur est un luth suspendu;
> Sitôt qu'on le touche il résonne.
> —De Béranger.

During the whole of a dull, dark, and soundless day in the autumn of the year, when the clouds hung oppressively low in the heavens, I had been passing alone, on horseback, through a singularly dreary tract of country; and at length found myself, as the shades of the evening drew on, within view of the melancholy House of Usher. I know not how it was—but, with the first glimpse of the building, a sense of insufferable gloom pervaded my spirit. I say insufferable; for the feeling was unrelieved by any of that half-pleasurable, because poetic, sentiment, with which the mind usually receives even the sternest natural images of the desolate or terrible. I looked upon the scene before me—upon the mere house, and the simple landscape features of the domain—upon the bleak walls—upon the vacant eye-like windows—upon a few rank sedges—and upon a few white trunks of decayed trees—with an utter depression of soul which I can compare to no earthly sensation more properly than to the after-dream of the reveller upon opium—the bitter lapse into everyday life—the hideous dropping off of the veil. There was an iciness, a sinking, a sickening of the heart—an unredeemed dreariness of thought which no goading of the imagination could torture into aught of the sublime. What was it—I paused to think—what was it that so unnerved me in the contemplation of the House of Usher? It was a mystery all insoluble; nor could I grapple with the shadowy fancies that crowded upon me as I pondered. I was forced to fall back upon the unsatisfactory conclusion, that while, beyond doubt, there *are* combinations of very simple natural objects which have the power of thus affecting us, still the analysis of this power lies among considerations beyond our depth. It was possible, I reflected, that a mere different arrangement of the particulars of the scene, of the details of the picture, would be sufficient to modify, or perhaps to annihilate its capacity for sorrowful impression; and, acting upon this idea, I reined my horse to the precipitous brink of a black and lurid tarn that lay in unruffled lustre by the dwelling, and gazed down—but with a shudder even more thrilling than before—upon the remodelled and inverted images of the gray sedge, and the ghastly tree-stems, and the vacant and eye-like windows.

Nevertheless, in this mansion of gloom I now proposed to myself a sojourn of some weeks. Its proprietor, Roderick Usher, had been one of my boon companions in boyhood; but many years had elapsed since our last meeting. A letter, however, had lately reached me in a distant part of the country—a letter from him—which, in its wildly importunate nature, had admitted of no other than a personal reply. The MS. gave evidence of nervous agitation. The writer spoke of acute bodily illness—of a mental disorder which oppressed him—and of an earnest desire to see me, as his best, and indeed his only personal friend, with a view of attempting, by the cheerfulness of my society, some alleviation of his malady. It was the manner in which all this, and much more, was said—it was the apparent *heart* that went with his request—which allowed me no room for hesitation; and I accordingly obeyed forthwith what I still considered a very singular summons.

Although, as boys, we had been even intimate associates, yet I really knew little of my friend. His reserve had been always excessive and habitual. I was aware, however, that his very ancient family had been noted, time out of mind, for a peculiar sensibility of temperament, displaying itself, through long ages, in many works of exalted art, and manifested, of late, in repeated deeds of munificent yet unobtrusive charity, as well as in a passionate devotion to the intricacies, perhaps even more than to the orthodox and easily recognisable beauties, of musical science. I had learned, too, the very remarkable fact, that the stem of the Usher race, all time-honoured as it was, had put forth, at no period, any enduring branch; in other words, that the entire family lay in the direct line of descent, and had always, with very trifling and very temporary variation, so lain. It was this deficiency, I considered, while running over in thought the perfect keeping of the character of the premises with the accredited character of the people, and while speculating upon the possible influence which the one, in the long lapse of centuries, might have exercised upon the other—it was this deficiency, perhaps, of collateral issue, and the consequent undeviating transmission, from sire to son, of the patrimony with the name, which had, at length, so identified the two as to merge the original title of the estate in the quaint and equivocal appellation of the "House of Usher"—an appellation which seemed to include, in the minds of the peasantry who used it, both the family and the family mansion.

I have said that the sole effect of my somewhat childish experiment—that of looking down within the tarn—had been to deepen the first singular impression. There can be no doubt that the consciousness of the rapid increase of my superstition—for why should I not so term it?—served mainly to accelerate the increase itself. Such, I have long known, is the paradoxical law of all sentiments having terror as a basis. And it might have been for this reason only, that, when I again uplifted my eyes to the house itself, from its image in the pool, there grew in my mind a strange fancy—a fancy so ridiculous, indeed, that I but mention it to show the vivid force of the sensations which oppressed me. I had so worked upon my imagination as really to believe that about the whole mansion and domain there hung an atmosphere peculiar to themselves and their immediate vicinity—an atmosphere which had no affinity with the air of heaven, but which had reeked up from the decayed trees, and the gray wall, and the silent tarn—a pestilent and mystic vapour, dull, sluggish, faintly discernible, and leaden-hued.

Shaking off from my spirit what *must* have been a dream, I scanned more narrowly the real aspect of the building. Its principal feature seemed to be that of an excessive antiquity. The discoloration of ages had been great. Minute fungi overspread the whole exterior, hanging in a fine tangled web-work from the eaves. Yet all this was apart from any extraordinary dilapidation. No portion of the masonry had fallen; and there appeared to be a wild inconsistency between its still perfect adaptation of parts, and the crumbling condition of the individual stones. In this there was much that reminded me of the specious totality of old wood-work which has rotted for long years in some neglected vault, with no disturbance from the breath of the external air. Beyond this indication of extensive decay, however, the fabric gave little token of instability. Perhaps the eye of a scrutinising observer might have discovered a barely perceptible fissure, which, extending from the roof of the building in front, made its way down the wall in a zigzag direction, until it became lost in the sullen waters of the tarn.

Noticing these things, I rode over a short causeway to the house. A servant in waiting took my horse, and I entered the Gothic arch-way of the hall. A valet, of stealthy step, thence conducted me, in silence, through many dark and intricate passages in my progress to the *studio* of his master. Much that I encountered on the way contributed, I know not how, to heighten the vague sentiments of which I have already spoken. While the objects around me—while the carvings of the ceilings, the sombre tapestries of the walls, the ebon blackness of the floors, and the phantasmagoric armorial trophies which rattled as I strode, were but matters to which, or to such as which, I had been accustomed from my infancy—while I hesitated not to acknowledge how familiar was all this—I still wondered to find how unfamiliar were the fancies which ordinary images were stirring up. On one of the staircases, I met the physician of the family. His countenance, I thought, wore a mingled expression of low cunning and perplexity. He accosted me with trepidation and passed on. The valet now threw open a door and ushered me into the presence of his master.

The room in which I found myself was very large and lofty. The windows were long, narrow, and pointed, and at so vast a distance from the black oaken floor as to be altogether inaccessible from within. Feeble gleams of encrimsoned light made their way through the trellised panes, and served to render sufficiently distinct the more prominent objects around; the eye, however, struggled in vain to reach the remoter angles of the chamber, or the recesses of the vaulted and fretted ceiling. Dark draperies hung upon the walls. The general furniture was profuse, comfortless, antique, and tattered. Many books and musical instruments lay scattered about, but failed to give any vitality to the scene. I felt that I breathed an atmosphere of sorrow. An air of stern, deep, and irredeemable gloom hung over and pervaded all.

Upon my entrance, Usher arose from a sofa on which he had been lying at full length, and greeted me with a vivacious warmth which had much in it, I at first thought, of an overdone cordiality—of the constrained effort of the *ennuyé* man of the world. A glance, however, at his countenance, convinced me of his perfect sincerity. We sat down; and for some moments, while he spoke not, I gazed upon him with a feeling half of pity, half of awe. Surely, man had never before so terribly altered, in so brief a period, as had Roderick Usher! It was with difficulty that I could bring myself to admit the identity of the wan being before me with the companion of my early boyhood. Yet the character of his face had been at all times remarkable. A cadaverousness of complexion; an eye large, liquid, and luminous beyond comparison; lips somewhat thin and very pallid, but of a surpassingly beautiful curve; a nose of a delicate Hebrew model, but with a breadth of nostril unusual in similar formations; a finely moulded chin, speaking, in its want of prominence, of a want of moral energy; hair of a more than web-like softness and tenuity; these features, with an inordinate expansion above the regions of the temple, made up altogether a countenance not easily to be forgotten. And now in the mere exaggeration of the prevailing character of these features, and of the expression they were wont to convey, lay so much of change that I doubted to whom I spoke. The now ghastly pallor of the skin, and the now miraculous lustre of the eye, above all things startled and even awed me. The silken hair, too, had been suffered to grow all unheeded, and as, in its wild gossamer texture, it floated rather than fell about the face, I could not, even with effort, connect its Arabesque expression with any idea of simple humanity.

In the manner of my friend I was at once struck with an incoherence—an inconsistency; and I soon found this to arise from a series of feeble and futile struggles to overcome an habitual trepidancy—an excessive nervous agitation. For something of this nature I had indeed been prepared, no less by his letter, than by reminiscences of certain boyish traits, and by conclusions deduced from his peculiar physical conformation and temperament. His action was alternately vivacious and sullen. His voice varied rapidly from a tremulous indecision (when the animal spirits seemed utterly in abeyance) to that species of energetic concision—that abrupt, weighty, unhurried, and hollow-sounding enunciation—that leaden, self-balanced and perfectly modulated guttural utterance, which may be observed in the lost drunkard, or the irreclaimable eater of opium, during the periods of his most intense excitement.

It was thus that he spoke of the object of my visit, of his earnest desire to see me, and of the solace he expected me to afford him. He entered, at some length, into what he conceived to be the nature of his malady. It was, he said, a constitutional and a family evil, and one for which he despaired to find a remedy—a mere nervous affection, he immediately added, which would undoubtedly soon pass off. It displayed itself in a host of unnatural sensations. Some of these, as he detailed them, interested and bewildered me; although, perhaps, the terms, and the general manner of the narration had their weight. He suffered much from a morbid acuteness of the senses; the most insipid food was alone endurable; he could wear only garments of certain texture; the odours of all flowers were oppressive; his eyes were tortured by even a faint light; and there were but peculiar sounds, and these from stringed instruments, which did not inspire him with horror.

To an anomalous species of terror I found him a bounden slave. "I shall perish," said he, "I *must* perish in this deplorable folly. Thus, thus, and not otherwise, shall I be lost. I dread the events of the future, not in themselves, but in their results. I shudder at the thought of any, even the most trivial, incident, which may operate upon this intolerable agitation of soul. I have, indeed, no abhorrence of danger, except in its absolute effect—in terror. In this unnerved—in this pitiable condition—I feel that the period will sooner or later arrive when I must abandon life and reason together, in some struggle with the grim phantasm, FEAR."

I learned, moreover, at intervals, and through broken and equivocal hints, another singular feature of his mental condition. He was enchained by certain superstitious impressions in regard to the dwelling which he tenanted, and whence, for many years, he had never ventured forth—in regard to an influence whose supposititious force was conveyed in terms too shadowy here to be re-stated—an influence which some peculiarities in the mere form and substance of his family mansion, had, by dint of long sufferance, he said, obtained over his spirit—an effect which the *physique* of the gray walls and turrets, and of the dim tarn into which they all looked down, had, at length, brought about upon the *morale* of his existence.

He admitted, however, although with hesitation, that much of the peculiar gloom which thus afflicted him could be traced to a more natural and far more palpable origin—to the severe and long-continued illness—indeed to the evidently approaching dissolution of a tenderly beloved sister—his sole companion for long years—his last and only relative on earth. "Her decease," he said, with a bitterness which I can never forget, "would leave him (him the hopeless and the frail) the last of the ancient race of the Ushers." While he spoke, the lady Madeline (for so was she called) passed slowly through a remote portion of the apartment, and, without having noticed my presence, disappeared. I regarded her with an utter astonishment not unmingled with dread—and yet I found it impossible to account for such feelings. A sensation of stupor oppressed me, as my eyes followed her retreating steps. When a door, at length, closed upon her, my glance sought instinctively and eagerly the countenance of the brother—but he had buried his face in his hands, and I could only perceive that a far more than ordinary wanness had overspread the emaciated fingers through which trickled many passionate tears.

The disease of the lady Madeline had long baffled the skill of her physicians. A settled apathy, a gradual wasting away of the person, and frequent although transient affections of a partially cataleptical character, were the unusual diagnosis. Hitherto she had steadily borne up against the pressure of her malady, and had not betaken herself finally to bed; but, on the closing in of the evening of my arrival at the house, she succumbed (as her brother told me at night with inexpressible agitation) to the prostrating power of the destroyer; and I learned that the glimpse I had obtained of her person would thus probably be the last I should obtain—that the lady, at least while living, would be seen by me no more.

For several days ensuing, her name was unmentioned by either Usher or myself: and during this period I was busied in earnest endeavours to alleviate the melancholy of my friend. We painted and read together; or I listened, as if in a dream, to the wild improvisations of his speaking guitar. And thus, as a closer and still closer intimacy admitted me more unreservedly into the recesses of his spirit, the more bitterly did I perceive the futility of all attempt at cheering a mind from which darkness, as if an inherent positive quality, poured forth upon all objects of the moral and physical universe, in one unceasing radiation of gloom.

I shall ever bear about me a memory of the many solemn hours I thus spent alone with the master of the House of Usher. Yet I should fail in any attempt to convey an idea of the exact character of the studies, or of the occupations, in which he involved me, or led me the way. An excited and highly distempered ideality threw a sulphureous lustre over all. His long improvised dirges will ring forever in my ears. Among other things, I hold painfully in mind a certain singular perversion and amplification of the wild air of the last waltz of Von Weber. From the paintings over which his elaborate fancy brooded, and which grew, touch by touch, into vaguenesses at which I shuddered the more thrillingly, because I shuddered knowing not why;—from these paintings (vivid as their images now are before me) I would in vain endeavour to educe more than a small portion which should lie within the compass of merely written words. By the utter simplicity, by the nakedness of his designs, he arrested and overawed attention. If ever mortal painted an idea, that mortal was Roderick Usher. For me at least—in the circumstances then surrounding me—there arose out of the pure abstractions which the hypochondriac contrived to throw upon his canvas, an intensity of intolerable awe, no shadow of which felt I ever yet in the contemplation of the certainly glowing yet too concrete reveries of Fuseli.

One of the phantasmagoric conceptions of my friend, partaking not so rigidly of the spirit of abstraction, may be shadowed forth, although feebly, in words. A small picture presented the interior of an immensely long and rectangular vault or tunnel, with low walls, smooth, white, and without interruption or device. Certain accessory points of the design served well to convey the idea that this excavation lay at an exceeding depth below the surface of the earth. No outlet was observed in any portion of its vast extent, and no torch, or other artificial source of light was discernible; yet a flood of intense rays rolled throughout, and bathed the whole in a ghastly and inappropriate splendour.

I have just spoken of that morbid condition of the auditory nerve which rendered all music intolerable to the sufferer, with the exception of certain effects of stringed instruments. It was, perhaps, the narrow limits to which he thus confined himself upon the guitar, which gave birth, in great measure, to the fantastic character of his performances. But the fervid *facility* of his *impromptus* could not be so accounted for. They must have been, and were, in the notes, as well as in the words of his wild fantasias (for he not unfrequently accompanied himself with rhymed verbal improvisations), the result of that intense mental collectedness and concentration to which I have previously alluded as observable only in particular moments of the highest artificial excitement. The words of one of these rhapsodies I have easily remembered. I was, perhaps, the more forcibly impressed with it, as he gave it, because, in the under or mystic current of its meaning, I fancied that I perceived, and for the first time, a full consciousness on the part of Usher, of the tottering of his lofty reason upon her throne. The verses, which were entitled "The Haunted Palace," ran very nearly, if not accurately, thus:

I

In the greenest of our valleys,
  By good angels tenanted,
Once a fair and stately palace—
  Radiant palace—reared its head.
In the monarch Thought's dominion—
  It stood there!
Never seraph spread a pinion
  Over fabric half so fair.

II

Banners yellow, glorious, golden,
　　On its roof did float and flow;
(This—all this—was in the olden
　　Time long ago)
And every gentle air that dallied,
　　In that sweet day,
Along the ramparts plumed and pallid,
　　A winged odour went away.

III

Wanderers in that happy valley
　　Through two luminous windows saw
Spirits moving musically
　　To a lute's well-tunèd law,
Round about a throne, where sitting
　　(Porphyrogene!)
In state his glory well befitting,
　　The ruler of the realm was seen.

IV

And all with pearl and ruby glowing
　　Was the fair palace door,
Through which came flowing, flowing, flowing
　　And sparkling evermore,
A troop of Echoes whose sweet duty
　　Was but to sing,
In voices of surpassing beauty,
　　The wit and wisdom of their king.

V

But evil things, in robes of sorrow,
　　Assailed the monarch's high estate;
(Ah, let us mourn, for never morrow
　　Shall dawn upon him, desolate!)
And, round about his home, the glory
　　That blushed and bloomed
Is but a dim-remembered story
　　Of the old time entombed.

VI

And travellers now within that valley,
　　Through the red-litten windows, see
Vast forms that move fantastically
　　To a discordant melody;
While, like a rapid ghastly river,

Through the pale door,
A hideous throng rush out forever,
And laugh—but smile no more.

I well remember that suggestions arising from this ballad, led us into a train of thought wherein there became manifest an opinion of Usher's which I mention not so much on account of its novelty (for other men have thought thus) as on account of the pertinacity with which he maintained it. This opinion, in its general form, was that of the sentience of all vegetable things. But, in his disordered fancy, the idea had assumed a more daring character, and trespassed, under certain conditions, upon the kingdom of inorganization. I lack words to express the full extent, or the earnest *abandon* of his persuasion. The belief, however, was connected (as I have previously hinted) with the gray stones of the home of his forefathers. The conditions of the sentience had been here, he imagined, fulfilled in the method of collocation of these stones—in the order of their arrangement, as well as in that of the many *fungi* which overspread them, and of the decayed trees which stood around—above all, in the long undisturbed endurance of this arrangement, and in its reduplication in the still waters of the tarn. Its evidence—the evidence of the sentience—was to be seen, he said, (and I here started as he spoke,) in the gradual yet certain condensation of an atmosphere of their own about the waters and the walls. The result was discoverable, he added, in that silent, yet importunate and terrible influence which for centuries had moulded the destinies of his family, and which made *him* what I now saw him—what he was. Such opinions need no comment, and I will make none.

Our books—the books which, for years, had formed no small portion of the mental existence of the invalid—were, as might be supposed, in strict keeping with this character of phantasm. We pored together over such works as the Ververt et Chartreuse of Gresset; the Belphegor of Machiavelli; the Heaven and Hell of Swedenborg; the Subterranean Voyage of Nicholas Klimm by Holberg; the Chiromancy of Robert Flud, of Jean D'Indaginé, and of De la Chambre; the Journey into the Blue Distance of Tieck; and the City of the Sun of Campanella. One favourite volume was a small octavo edition of the *Directorium Inquisitorum*, by the Dominican Eymeric de Gironne; and there were passages in Pomponius Mela, about the old African Satyrs and Aegipans, over which Usher would sit dreaming for hours. His chief delight, however, was found in the perusal of an exceedingly rare and curious book in quarto Gothic—the manual of a forgotten church—the *Vigiliae Mortuorum secundum Chorum Ecclesiae Maguntinae.*

I could not help thinking of the wild ritual of this work, and of its probable influence upon the hypochondriac, when, one evening, having informed me abruptly that the lady Madeline was no more, he stated his intention of preserving her corpse for a fortnight (previously to its final interment) in one of the numerous vaults within the main walls of the building. The worldly reason, however, assigned for this singular proceeding, was one which I did not feel at liberty to dispute. The brother had been led to his resolution (so he told me) by consideration of the unusual character of the malady of the deceased, of certain obtrusive and eager inquiries on the part of her medical men, and of the remote and exposed situation of the burial-ground of the family. I will not deny that when I called to mind the sinister countenance of the person whom I met upon the staircase, on the day of my arrival at the house, I had no desire to oppose what I regarded as at best but a harmless, and by no means an unnatural, precaution.

At the request of Usher, I personally aided him in the arrangements for the temporary entombment. The body having been encoffined, we two alone bore it to its rest. The vault in which we placed it (and which had been so long unopened that our torches, half smothered in its oppressive atmosphere, gave us little opportunity for investigation) was small, damp, and entirely without means of admission for light; lying, at great depth, immediately beneath that portion of the building in which was my own sleeping apartment. It had been used, apparently, in remote feudal times, for the worst purposes of a donjon-keep, and, in later days, as a place of deposit for powder, or some other highly combustible substance, as a portion of its floor, and the whole interior of a long archway through which we reached it, were carefully sheathed wtth copper. The door, of massive iron, had been, also, similarly protected. Its immense weight caused an unusually sharp grating sound, as it moved upon its hinges.

Having deposited our mournful burden upon tressels within this region of horror, we partially turned aside the yet unscrewed lid of the coffin, and looked upon the face of the tenant. A striking similitude between the brother and sister now first arrested my attention; and Usher, divining, perhaps, my thoughts, murmured out some few words from which I learned that the deceased and himself had been twins, and that sympathies of a scarcely intelligible nature had always existed between them. Our glances, however, rested not long upon the dead—for we could not regard her unawed. The disease which had thus entombed the lady in the maturity of youth, had left, as usual in all maladies of a strictly cataleptical character, the mockery of a faint blush upon the bosom and the face, and that suspiciously lingering smile upon the lip which is so terrible in death. We replaced and screwed down the lid, and, having secured the door of iron, made our way, with toil, into the scarcely less gloomy apartments of the upper portion of the house.

And now, some days of bitter grief having elapsed, an observable change came over the features of the mental disorder of my friend. His ordinary manner had vanished. His ordinary occupations were neglected or forgotten. He roamed from chamber to chamber with hurried, unequal, and objectless step. The pallor of his countenance had assumed, if possible, a more ghastly hue—but the luminousness of his eye had utterly gone out. The once occasional huskiness of his tone was heard no more; and a tremulous quaver, as if of extreme terror, habitually characterized his utterance. There were times, indeed, when I thought his unceasingly agitated mind was labouring with some oppressive secret, to divulge which he struggled for the necessary courage. At times, again, I was obliged to resolve all into the mere inexplicable vagaries of madness, for I beheld him gazing upon vacancy for long hours, in an attitude of the profoundest attention, as if listening to some imaginary sound. It was no wonder that his condition terrified—that it infected me. I felt creeping upon me, by slow yet certain degrees, the wild influences of his own fantastic yet impressive superstitions.

It was, especially, upon retiring to bed late in the night of the seventh or eighth day after the placing of the lady Madeline within the donjon, that I experienced the full power of such feelings. Sleep came not near my couch—while the hours waned and waned away. I struggled to reason off the nervousness which had dominion over me. I endeavoured to believe that much, if not all of what I felt, was due to the bewildering influence of the gloomy furniture of the room—of the dark and tattered draperies, which, tortured into motion by the breath of a rising tempest, swayed fitfully to and fro upon the walls, and rustled uneasily about the decorations of the bed. But my efforts were fruitless. An irrepressible tremour gradually pervaded my frame; and, at length, there sat upon my very heart an incubus of utterly causeless alarm. Shaking this off with a gasp and a struggle, I uplifted myself upon the pillows, and, peering earnestly within the intense darkness of the chamber, hearkened—I know not why, except that an instinctive spirit prompted me—to certain low and indefinite sounds which came, through the pauses of the storm, at long intervals, I knew not whence. Overpowered by an intense sentiment of horror, unaccountable yet unendurable, I threw on my clothes with haste (for I felt that I should sleep no more during the night), and endeavoured to arouse myself from the pitiable condition into which I had fallen, by pacing rapidly to and fro through the apartment.

I had taken but few turns in this manner, when a light step on an adjoining staircase arrested my attention. I presently recognised it as that of Usher. In an instant afterward he rapped, with a gentle touch, at my door, and entered, bearing a lamp. His countenance was, as usual, cadaverously wan—but, moreover, there was a species of mad hilarity in his eyes—an evidently restrained *hysteria* in his whole demeanour. His air appalled me—but anything was preferable to the solitude which I had so long endured, and I even welcomed his presence as a relief.

"And you have not seen it?" he said abruptly, after having stared about him for some moments in silence—"you have not then seen it?—but, stay! you shall." Thus speaking, and having carefully shaded his lamp, he hurried to one of the casements, and threw it freely open to the storm.

The impetuous fury of the entering gust nearly lifted us from our feet. It was, indeed, a tempestuous yet sternly beautiful night, and one wildly singular in its terror and its beauty. A whirlwind had apparently collected its force in our vicinity; for there were frequent and violent alterations in the direction of the wind; and the exceeding density of the clouds (which hung so low as to press upon the turrets of the house) did not prevent our perceiving the life-like velocity with which they flew careering from all points against each other, without passing away into the distance. I say that even their exceeding density did not prevent our perceiving this—yet we had no glimpse of the moon or stars—nor was there any flashing forth of the lightning. But the under surfaces of the huge masses of agitated vapour, as well as all terrestrial objects immediately around us, were glowing in the unnatural light of a faintly luminous and distinctly visible gaseous exhalation which hung about and enshrouded the mansion.

"You must not—you shall not behold this!" said I, shudderingly, to Usher, as I led him, with a gentle violence, from the window to a seat. "These appearances, which bewilder you, are merely electrical phenomena not uncommon—or it may be that they have their ghastly origin in the rank miasma of the tarn. Let us close this casement;—the air is chilling and dangerous to your frame. Here is one of your favourite romances. I will read, and you shall listen; and so we will pass away this terrible night together."

The antique volume which I had taken up was the "Mad Trist" of Sir Launcelot Canning; but I had called it a favourite of Usher's more in sad jest than in earnest; for, in truth, there is little in its uncouth and unimaginative prolixity which could have had interest for the lofty and spiritual ideality of my friend. It was, however, the only book immediately at hand; and I indulged a vague hope that the excitement which now agitated the hypochondriac, might find relief (for the history of mental disorder is full of similar anomalies) even in the extremeness of the folly which I should read. Could I have judged, indeed, by the wild overstrained air of vivacity with which he hearkened, or apparently hearkened, to the words of the tale, I might well have congratulated myself upon the success of my design.

I had arrived at that well-known portion of the story where Ethelred, the hero of the Trist, having sought in vain for peaceable admission into the dwelling of the hermit, proceeds to make good an entrance by force. Here, it will be remembered, the words of the narrative run thus:

"And Ethelred, who was by nature of a doughty heart, and who was now mighty withal, on account of the powerfulness of the wine which he had drunken, waited no longer to hold parley with the hermit, who, in sooth, was of an obstinate and maliceful turn, but, feeling the rain upon his shoulders, and fearing the rising of the tempest, uplifted his mace outright, and, with blows, made quickly room in the plankings of the door for his gauntleted hand; and now pulling therewith sturdily, he so cracked, and ripped, and tore all asunder, that the noise of the dry and hollow-sounding wood alarumed and reverberated throughout the forest."

At the termination of this sentence I started, and for a moment, paused; for it appeared to me (although I at once concluded that my excited fancy had deceived me)—it appeared to me that, from some very remote portion of the mansion, there came, indistinctly, to my ears, what might have been, in its exact similarity of character, the echo (but a stifled and dull one certainly) of the very cracking and ripping sound which Sir Launcelot had so particularly described. It was, beyond doubt, the coincidence alone which had arrested my attention; for, amid the rattling of the sashes of the casements, and the ordinary commingled noises of the still increasing storm, the sound, in itself, had nothing, surely, which should have interested or disturbed me. I continued the story:

"But the good champion Ethelred, now entering within the door, was sore enraged and amazed to perceive no signal of the maliceful hermit; but, in the stead thereof, a dragon of a scaly and prodigious demeanour, and of a fiery tongue, which sate in guard before a palace of gold, with a floor of silver; and upon the wall there hung a shield of shining brass with this legend enwritten—

Who entereth herein, a conqueror hath bin;
Who slayeth the dragon, the shield he shall win;

And Ethelred uplifted his mace, and struck upon the head of the dragon, which fell before him, and gave up his pesty breath, with a shriek so horrid and harsh, and withal so piercing, that Ethelred had fain to close his ears with his hands against the dreadful noise of it, the like whereof was never before heard."

Here again I paused abruptly, and now with a feeling of wild amazement—for there could be no doubt whatever that, in this instance, I did actually hear (although from what direction it proceeded I found it impossible to say) a low and apparently distant, but harsh, protracted, and most unusual screaming or grating sound—the exact counterpart of what my fancy had already conjured up for the dragon's unnatural shriek as described by the romancer.

Oppressed, as I certainly was, upon the occurrence of the second and most extraordinary coincidence, by a thousand conflicting sensations, in which wonder and extreme terror were predominant, I still retained sufficient presence of mind to avoid exciting, by any observation, the sensitive nervousness of my companion. I was by no means certain that he had noticed the sounds in question; although, assuredly, a strange alteration had, during the last few minutes, taken place in his demeanour. From a position fronting my own, he had gradually brought round his chair, so as to sit with his face to the door of the chamber; and thus I could but partially perceive his features, although I saw that his lips trembled as if he were murmuring inaudibly. His head had dropped upon his breast—yet I knew that he was not asleep, from the wide and rigid opening of the eye as I caught a glance of it in profile. The motion of his body, too, was at variance with this idea—for he rocked from side to side with a gentle yet constant and uniform sway. Having rapidly taken notice of all this, I resumed the narrative of Sir Launcelot, which thus proceeded:

"And now, the champion, having escaped from the terrible fury of the dragon, bethinking himself of the brazen shield, and of the breaking up of the enchantment which was upon it, removed the carcass from out of the way before him, and approached valorously over the silver pavement of the castle to where the shield was upon the wall; which in sooth tarried not for his full coming, but fell down at his feet upon the silver floor, with a mighty great and terrible ringing sound."

No sooner had these syllables passed my lips, than—as if a shield of brass had indeed, at the moment, fallen heavily upon a floor of silver—I became aware of a distinct, hollow, metallic, and clangorous, yet apparently muffled reverberation. Completely unnerved, I leaped to my feet; but the measured rocking movement of Usher was undisturbed. I rushed to the chair in which he sat. His eyes were bent fixedly before him, and throughout his whole countenance there reigned a stony rigidity. But, as I placed my hand upon his shoulder, there came a strong shudder over his whole person; a sickly smile quivered about his lips; and I saw that he spoke in a low, hurried, and gibbering murmur, as if unconscious of my presence. Bending closely over him, I at length drank in the hideous import of his words.

"Not hear it?—yes, I hear it, and *have* heard it. Long—long—long—many minutes, many hours, many days, have I heard it—yet I dared not—oh, pity me, miserable wretch that I am!—I dared not—I *dared* not speak! *We have put her living in the tomb!* Said I not that my senses were acute? I *now* tell you that I heard her first feeble movements in the hollow coffin. I heard them—many, many days ago—yet I dared not—*I dared not speak!* And now—to-night—Ethelred—ha! ha!—the breaking of the hermit's door, and the death-cry of the dragon, and the clangour of the shield!—say, rather, the rending of her coffin, and the grating of the iron hinges of her prison, and her struggles within the coppered archway of the vault! Oh whither shall I fly? Will she not be here anon? Is she not hurrying to upbraid me for my haste? Have I not heard her footstep on the stair? Do I not distinguish that heavy and horrible beating of her heart? MADMAN!" here he sprang furiously to his feet, and shrieked out his syllables, as if in the effort he were giving up his soul—"MADMAN! I TELL YOU THAT SHE NOW STANDS WITHOUT THE DOOR!"

As if in the superhuman energy of his utterance there had been found the potency of a spell—the huge antique panels to which the speaker pointed, threw slowly back, upon the instant, their ponderous and ebony jaws. It was the work of the rushing gust—but then without those doors there DID stand the lofty and enshrouded figure of the lady Madeline of Usher. There was blood upon her white robes, and the evidence of some bitter struggle upon every portion of her emaciated frame. For a moment she remained trembling and reeling to and fro upon the threshold, then, with a low moaning cry, fell heavily inward upon the person of her brother, and in her violent and now final death-agonies, bore him to the floor a corpse, and a victim to the terrors he had anticipated.

From that chamber, and from that mansion, I fled aghast. The storm was still abroad in all its wrath as I found myself crossing the old causeway. Suddenly there shot along the path a wild light, and I turned to see whence a gleam so unusual could have issued; for the vast house and its shadows were alone behind me. The radiance was that of the full, setting, and blood-red moon which now shone vividly through that once barely-discernible fissure of which I have before spoken as extending from the roof of the building, in a zigzag direction, to the base. While I gazed, this fissure rapidly widened—there came a fierce breath of the whirlwind—the entire orb of the satellite burst at once upon my sight—my brain reeled as I saw the mighty walls rushing asunder—there was a long tumultuous shouting sound like the voice of a thousand waters—and the deep and dank tarn at my feet closed sullenly and silently over the fragments of the "HOUSE OF USHER."

Nathaniel Hawthorne
(1804-1864)

MUCH as writers of the Southern Gothic were later to draw upon the present circumstances and past history of the region they knew best, so Nathaniel Hawthorne, a century earlier, gathered the materials for his fiction from New England towns like Concord and Salem, site of the infamous witch trials of the seventeenth century. *The Scarlet Letter* (1850) takes place in Salem. *The Blithedale Romance* (1852) centers around Brook Farm, in what is now West Roxbury. The sketches contained in *Mosses from an Old Manse* (1846) have immortalized the sprawling house in Concord, where guides still point out to reverent visitors the inscriptions Hawthorne and his wife Sophia carved with a diamond in the windowpane. The original for *The House of Seven Gables* (1851) in Salem attracts many tourists from abroad, who hear with disbelief that rooms were painted with a concoction of rust and sour milk. The short story "Young Goodman Brown," with its background of witchery, black masses, suspicion of Quakers, and Puritan rigor, derives from a history that is still very much alive to the people of Salem.

Though "Young Goodman Brown" is an allegory, the characters and events it describes do not have clear and exact equivalents; and the story resists final interpretation. The young wife Faith is a representation of Goodman Brown's religious faith, but she is also a human being who survives his death. Goodman Brown is a Calvinist Everyman, who ventures deep into a forest of doubt and sin; he is also a pitiable human being, with memories of his childhood and tender affection for his bride. The Satanic guide with the snakelike walking stick is surely the Devil; but like a *Doppelgänger* or a relative, he resembles Goodman Brown himself.

In the lurid, flame-lit forest, Goodman Brown both loses and finds his faith. Thinking that he can entertain ideas of evil without relinquishing his religion, he undergoes a repetition of the Fall of Man, perceives evil where he saw none before, and dies a gloomy, despairing death. All those whom he formerly respected or adored—his father and grandfather, his instructors in religion, his civil superiors, and his bride—appear irredeemably tainted with sin and corruption. On the other hand, he has found Faith herself at the hellish altar, or at least he thinks he has; and that faith is the rigid Calvinism that allows for damnation before birth and insists upon the utter depravity of men. The problem of interpretation is further complicated by unresolved mysteries in the story. Goodman Brown tells Faith to look to Heaven and save herself, but he does not know whether she has done so. Her pink ribbons fall from the cloud of evil, but she is wearing her ribbons when she meets him on his return. The action has all taken place during one night, and Hawthorne suggests that Goodman Brown may have dreamed the whole experience. If that is true, then Goodman Brown's perception of evil in the human beings whom he has loved is really proof of his own corruption; and his frenzied revulsion and self-imposed loneliness are the punishments meted out to him for his failure of love and his inhumane endeavor to see beneath the surface.

Many writers have been stimulated by religious beliefs to use Gothic devices and conventions to evoke the supernatural. Minor writers and motion-picture makers have often exploited religion for insincere and superficial horrific effects. For other writers, like the Roman Catholic Flannery O'Connor, faith is at the core of what they want to say and lends seriousness of purpose to their use of Gothic devices. It is characteristic of Hawthorne, with his Puritan heritage and his deep sense of sin, that his Gothic allegory draws strength from his religious concerns.

Young Goodman Brown (1835)

Young Goodman Brown came forth, at sunset, into the street of Salem village, but put his head back, after crossing the threshold, to exchange a parting kiss with his young wife. And Faith, as the wife was aptly named, thrust her own pretty head into the street, letting the wind play with the pink ribbons of her cap, while she called to Goodman Brown.

"Dearest heart," whispered she, softly and rather sadly, when her lips were close to his ear, "pr'y thee, put off your journey until sunrise, and sleep in your own bed to-night. A lone woman is troubled with such dreams and such thoughts, that she's afeard of herself, sometimes. Pray, tarry with me this night, dear husband, of all nights in the year!"

"My love and my Faith," replied young Goodman Brown, "of

all nights in the year, this one night must I tarry away from thee. My journey, as thou callest it, forth and back again, must needs be done 'twixt now and sunrise. What, my sweet, pretty wife, dost thou doubt me already, and we but three months married!"

"Then, God bless you!" said Faith, with the pink ribbons, "and may you find all well, when you come back."

"Amen!" cried Goodman Brown. "Say thy prayers, dear Faith, and go to bed at dusk, and no harm will come to thee."

So they parted; and the young man pursued his way, until, being about to turn the corner by the meeting-house, he looked back, and saw the head of Faith still peeping after him, with a melancholy air, in spite of her pink ribbons.

"Poor little Faith!" thought he, for his heart smote him. "What a wretch am I, to leave her on such an errand! She talks of dreams, too. Methought, as she spoke, there was trouble in her face, as if a dream had warned her what work is to be done to-night. But, no, no! 't would kill her to think it. Well; she's a blessed angel on earth; and after this one night, I'll cling to her skirts and follow her to Heaven."

With this excellent resolve for the future, Goodman Brown felt himself justified in making more haste on his present evil purpose. He had taken a dreary road, darkened by all the gloomiest trees of the forest, which barely stood aside to let the narrow path creep through, and closed immediately behind. It was all as lonely as could be; and there is this peculiarity in such a solitude, that the traveler knows not who may be concealed by the innumerable trunks and the thick boughs overhead; so that, with lonely footsteps, he may yet be passing through an unseen multitude.

"There may be a devilish Indian behind every tree," said Goodman Brown, to himself; and he glanced fearfully behind him, as he added, "What if the devil himself should be at my very elbow!"

His head being turned back, he passed a crook of the road, and looking forward again, beheld the figure of a man, in grave and decent attire, seated at the foot of an old tree. He arose, at Goodman Brown's approach, and walked onward, side by side with him.

"You are late, Goodman Brown," said he. "The clock of the Old South was striking as I came through Boston; and that is full fifteen minutes agone."

"Faith kept me back awhile," replied the young man, with a tremor in his voice, caused by the sudden appearance of his companion, though not wholly unexpected.

It was now deep dusk in the forest, and deepest in that part of it where these two were journeying. As nearly as could be discerned, the second traveler was about fifty years old, apparently in the same rank of life as Goodman Brown, and bearing a considerable resemblance to him, though perhaps more in expression than features. Still, they might have been taken for father and son. And yet, though the elder person was as simply clad as the younger, and as simple in manner too, he had an indescribable air of one who knew the world, and would not have felt abashed at the governor's dinner-table, or in King William's court, were it possible that his affairs should call him thither. But the only thing about him, that could be fixed upon as remarkable, was his staff, which bore the likeness of a great black snake, so curiously wrought, that it might almost be seen to twist and wriggle itself, like a living serpent. This, of course, must have been an ocular deception, assisted by the uncertain light.

"Come, Goodman Brown!" cried his fellow-traveler, "this is a dull pace for the beginning of a journey. Take my staff, if you are so soon weary."

"Friend," said the other, exchanging his slow pace for a full stop, "having kept covenant by meeting thee here, it is my purpose now to return whence I came. I have scruples, touching the matter thou wot'st of."

"Sayest thou so?" replied he of the serpent, smiling apart. "Let us walk on, nevertheless, reasoning as we go, and if I convince thee not, thou shalt turn back. We are but a little way in the forest, yet."

"Too far, too far!" exclaimed the goodman, unconsciously resuming his walk. "My father never went into the woods on such an errand, nor his father before him. We have been a race of honest men and good Christians, since the days of the martyrs. And shall I be the first of the name of Brown, that ever took this path, and kept—"

"Such company, thou wouldst say," observed the elder person, interpreting his pause. "Good, Goodman Brown! I have been as well acquainted with your family as with ever a one among the Puritans; and that's no trifle to say. I helped your grandfather, the constable, when he lashed the Quaker woman so smartly through the streets of Salem. And it was I that brought your father a pitch-pine knot, kindled at my own hearth, to set fire to an Indian village, in King Philip's war. They were my good friends, both; and many a pleasant walk have we had along this path, and returned merrily after midnight. I would fain be friends with you, for their sake."

"If it be as thou sayest," replied Goodman Brown, "I marvel they never spoke of these matters. Or, verily, I marvel not, seeing that the least rumor of the sort would have driven them from New-England. We are a people of prayer, and good works, to boot, and abide no such wickedness."

"Wickedness or not," said the traveler with the twisted staff, "I have a very general acquaintance here in New-England. The deacons of many a church have drunk the communion wine with me; the selectmen, of divers towns, make me their chairman; and a majority of the Great and General Court are firm supporters of my interest. The governor and I, too—but these are state-secrets."

"Can this be so!" cried Goodman Brown, with a stare of amazement at his undisturbed companion. "Howbeit, I have nothing to do with the governor and council; they have their own ways, and are no rule for a simple husbandman, like me. But, were I to go on with thee, how should I meet the eye of that good old man, our minister, at Salem village? Oh, his voice would make me tremble, both Sabbathday and lecture-day!"

Thus far, the elder traveler had listened with due gravity, but now burst into a fit of irrepressible mirth, shaking himself so violently, that his snake-like staff actually seemed to wriggle in sympathy.

"Ha! ha! ha!" shouted he, again and again; then composing himself, "Well, go on, Goodman Brown, go on; but, pr'y thee, don't kill me with laughing!"

"Well, then, to end the matter at once," said Goodman Brown, considerably nettled, "there is my wife, Faith. It would break her dear little heart; and I'd rather break my own!"

"Nay, if that be the case," answered the other, "e'en go thy ways, Goodman Brown. I would not, for twenty old women like the one hobbling before us, that Faith should come to any harm."

As he spoke, he pointed his staff at a female figure on the path, in whom Goodman Brown recognized a very pious and exemplary dame, who had taught him his catechism, in youth, and was still his moral and spiritual adviser, jointly with the minister and Deacon Gookin.

"A marvel, truly, that Goody Cloyse should be so far in the wilderness, at night-fall!" said he. "But, with your leave, friend, I shall take a cut through the woods, until we have left this Christian woman behind. Being a stranger to you, she might ask whom I was consorting with, and whither I was going."

"Be it so," said his fellow-traveler. "Betake you to the woods, and let me keep the path."

Accordingly, the young man turned aside, but took care to watch his companion, who advanced softly along the road, until he had come within a staff's length of the old dame. She, meanwhile, was making the best of her way, with singular speed for so aged a woman, and mumbling some indistinct words, a prayer, doubtless, as she went. The traveler put forth his staff, and touched her withered neck with what seemed the serpent's tail.

"The devil!" screamed the pious old lady.

"Then Goody Cloyse knows her old friend?" observed the traveler, confronting her, and leaning on his writhing stick.

"Ah, forsooth, and is it your worship, indeed?" cried the good dame. "Yea, truly is it, and in the very image of my old gossip, Goodman Brown, the grandfather of the silly fellow that now is. But, would your worship believe it? my broomstick hath strangely disappeared, stolen, as I suspect, by that unhanged witch, Goody Cory, and that, too, when I was all anointed with the juice of smallage and cinque-foil and wolf's-bane—"

"Mingled with fine wheat and the fat of a new-born babe," said the shape of old Goodman Brown.

"Ah, your worship knows the receipt," cried the old lady, cackling aloud. "So, as I was saying, being all ready for the meeting, and no horse to ride on, I made up my mind to foot it; for they tell me, there is a nice young man to be taken into communion to-night. But now your good worship will lend me your arm, and we shall be there in a twinkling."

"That can hardly be," answered her friend. "I may not spare you my arm, Goody Cloyse, but here is my staff, if you will."

So saying, he threw it down at her feet, where, perhaps, it assumed life, being one of the rods which its owner had formerly lent to the Egyptian Magi. Of this fact, however, Goodman Brown could not take cognizance. He had cast up his eyes in astonishment, and looking down again, beheld neither Goody Cloyse nor the serpentine staff, but his fellow-traveler alone, who waited for him as calmly as if nothing had happened.

"That old woman taught me my catechism!" said the young man; and there was a world of meaning in this simple comment.

They continued to walk onward, while the elder traveler exhorted his companion to make good speed and persevere in the path, discoursing so aptly, that his arguments seemed rather to spring up in the bosom of his auditor, than to be suggested by himself. As they went, he plucked a branch of maple, to serve for a walking-stick, and began to strip it of the twigs and little boughs, which were wet with evening dew. The moment his fingers touched them, they became strangely withered and dried up, as with a week's sunshine. Thus the pair proceeded, at a good free pace, until suddenly, in a gloomy hollow of the road, Goodman Brown sat himself down on the stump of a tree, and refused to go any farther.

"Friend," said he, stubbornly, "my mind is made up. Not another step will I budge on this errand. What if a wretched old woman do choose to go to the devil, when I thought she was going to Heaven! Is that any reason why I should quit my dear Faith, and go after her?"

"You will think better of this, by-and-by," said his acquaintance, composedly. "Sit here and rest yourself awhile; and when you feel like moving again, there is my staff to help you along."

Without more words, he threw his companion the maple stick, and was as speedily out of sight, as if he had vanished into the deepening gloom. The young man sat a few moments, by the road-side, applauding himself greatly, and thinking with how clear a conscience he should meet the minister, in his morning-walk, nor shrink from the eye of good old Deacon Gookin. And what calm sleep would be his, that very night, which was to have been spent so wickedly, but purely and sweetly now, in the arms of Faith! Amidst these pleasant and praiseworthy meditations, Goodman Brown heard the tramp of horses along the road, and deemed it advisable to conceal himself within the verge of the forest, conscious of the guilty purpose that had brought him thither, though now so happily turned from it.

On came the hoof-tramps and the voices of the riders, two grave old voices, conversing soberly as they drew near. These mingled sounds appeared to pass along the road, within a few yards of the young man's hiding-place; but owing, doubtless, to the depth of the gloom, at that particular spot, neither the travelers nor their steeds were visible. Though their figures brushed the small boughs by the way-side, it could not be seen that they intercepted, even for a moment, the faint gleam from the strip of bright sky, athwart which they must have passed. Goodman Brown alternately crouched and stood on tip-toe, pulling aside the branches, and thrusting forth his head as far as he durst, without discerning so much as a shadow. It vexed him the more, because he could have sworn, were such a thing possible, that he recognized the voices of the minister and Deacon Gookin, jogging along quietly, as they were wont to do, when bound to some ordination or ecclesiastical council. While yet within hearing, one of the riders stopped to pluck a switch.

"Of the two, reverend Sir," said the voice like the deacon's, "I had rather miss an ordination-dinner than to-night's meeting. They tell me that some of our community are to be here from Falmouth and beyond, and others from Connecticut and Rhode-Island; besides several of the Indian powows, who, after their fashion, know almost as much deviltry as the best of us. Moreover, there is a goodly young woman to be taken into communion."

"Mighty well, Deacon Gookin!" replied the solemn old tones of the minister. "Spur up, or we shall be late. Nothing can be done, you know, until I get on the ground."

The hoofs clattered again, and the voices, talking so strangely in the empty air, passed on through the forest, where no church had ever been gathered, nor solitary Christian prayed. Whither, then, could these holy men be journeying, so deep into the heathen wilderness? Young Goodman Brown caught hold of a tree, for support, being ready to sink down on the ground, faint and overburthened with the heavy sickness of his heart. He looked up to the sky, doubting whether there really was a Heaven above him. Yet, there was the blue arch, and the stars brightening in it.

"With Heaven above, and Faith below, I will yet stand firm against the devil!" cried Goodman Brown.

While he still gazed upward, into the deep arch of the firmament, and had lifted his hands to pray, a cloud, though no wind was stirring, hurried across the zenith, and hid the brightening stars. The blue sky was still visible, except directly overhead, where this black mass of cloud was sweeping swiftly northward. Aloft in the air, as if from the depths of the cloud, came a confused and doubtful sound of voices. Once, the listener fancied that he could distinguish the accents of town's-people of his own, men and women, both pious and ungodly, many of whom he had met at the communion-table, and had seen others rioting at the tavern. The next moment, so indistinct were the sounds, he doubted whether he had heard aught but the murmur of the old forest, whispering without a wind. Then came a stronger swell of those familiar tones, heard daily in the sunshine, at Salem village, but never, until now, from a cloud of night. There was one voice, of a young woman, uttering lamentations, yet with an uncertain sorrow, and entreating for some favor, which, perhaps, it would grieve her to obtain. And all the unseen multitude, both saints and sinners, seemed to encourage her onward.

"Faith!" shouted Goodman Brown, in a voice of agony and desperation; and the echoes of the forest mocked him, crying— "Faith! Faith!" as if bewildered wretches were seeking her, all through the wilderness.

The cry of grief, rage, and terror, was yet piercing the night, when the unhappy husband held his breath for a response. There was a scream, drowned immediately in a louder murmur of voices, fading into far-off laughter, as the dark cloud swept away, leaving the clear and silent sky above Goodman Brown. But something fluttered lightly down through the air, and caught on the branch of a tree. The young man seized it, and beheld a pink ribbon.

"My Faith is gone!" cried he, after one stupefied moment. "There is no good on earth; and sin is but a name. Come, devil! for to thee is this world given."

And maddened with despair, so that he laughed loud and long, did Goodman Brown grasp his staff and set forth again, at such a rate, that he seemed to fly along the forest-path, rather than to walk or run. The road grew wilder and drearier, and more faintly traced, and vanished at length, leaving him in the heart of the dark wilderness, still rushing onward, with the instinct that guides mortal man to evil. The whole forest was peopled with frightful sounds; the creaking of the trees, the howling of wild beasts, and the yell of Indians; while, sometimes, the wind tolled like a distant church-bell, and sometimes gave a broad roar around the traveler, as if all Nature were laughing him to scorn. But he was himself the chief horror of the scene, and shrank not from its other horrors.

"Ha! ha! ha!" roared Goodman Brown, when the wind laughed at him. "Let us hear which will laugh loudest! Think not to frighten me with your deviltry! Come witch, come wizard, come Indian powow, come devil himself! and here comes Goodman Brown. You may as well fear him as he fear you!"

In truth, all through the haunted forest, there could be nothing more frightful than the figure of Goodman Brown. On he flew, among the black pines, brandishing his staff with frenzied gestures, now giving vent to an inspiration of horrid blasphemy, and now shouting forth such laughter, as set all the echoes of the forest laughing like demons around him. The fiend in his own shape is less hideous, than when he rages in the breast of man. Thus sped the demoniac on his course, until, quivering among the trees, he saw a red light before him, as when the felled trunks and branches of a clearing have been set on fire, and throw up their lurid blaze against the sky, at the hour of midnight. He paused, in a lull of the tempest that had driven him onward, and heard the swell of what seemed a hymn, rolling solemnly from a distance, with the weight of many voices. He knew the tune; it was a familiar one in the choir of the village meeting-house. The verse died heavily away, and was lengthened by a chorus, not of human voices, but of all the sounds of the benighted wilderness, pealing in awful harmony together. Goodman Brown cried out; and his cry was lost to his own ear, by its unison with the cry of the desert.

In the interval of silence, he stole forward, until the light glared full upon his eyes. At one extremity of an open space, hemmed in by the dark wall of the forest, arose a rock, bearing some rude, natural resemblance either to an altar or a pulpit, and surrounded by four blazing pines, their tops aflame, their stems untouched, like candles at an evening meeting. The mass of foliage, that had overgrown the summit of the rock, was all on fire, blazing high into the night, and fitfully illuminating the whole field. Each pendent twig and leafy festoon was in a blaze. As the red light arose and fell, a numerous congregation alternately shone forth, then disappeared in shadow, and again grew, as it were, out of the darkness, peopling the heart of the solitary woods at once.

"A grave and dark-clad company!" quoth Goodman Brown.

In truth, they were such. Among them, quivering to-and-fro, between gloom and splendor, appeared faces that would be seen, next day, at the council-board of the province, and others which, Sabbath after Sabbath, looked devoutly heavenward, and benignantly over the crowded pews, from the holiest pulpits in the land. Some affirm, that the lady of the governor was there. At least, there were high dames well known to her, and wives of honored husbands, and widows, a great multitude, and ancient maidens, all of excellent repute, and fair young girls, who trembled, lest their mothers should espy them. Either the sudden gleams of light, flashing over the obscure field, bedazzled Goodman Brown, or he recognized a score of the church-members of Salem village, famous for their especial sanctity. Good old Deacon Gookin had arrived, and waited at the skirts of that venerable saint, his revered pastor. But, irreverently consorting with these grave, reputable, and pious people, these elders of the church, these chaste dames and dewy virgins, there were men of dissolute lives and women of spotted fame, wretches given over to all mean and filthy vice, and suspected even of horrid crimes. It was strange to see, that the good shrank not from the wicked, nor were the sinners abashed by the saints. Scattered, also, among their pale-faced enemies, were the Indian priests, or powows, who had often scared their native forest with more hideous incantations than any known to English witchcraft.

"But, where is Faith?" thought Goodman Brown; and, as hope came into his heart, he trembled.

Another verse of the hymn arose, a slow and solemn strain, such as the pious love, but joined to words which expressed all that our nature can conceive of sin, and darkly hinted at far more. Unfathomable to mere mortals is the lore of fiends. Verse after verse was sung, and still the chorus of the desert swelled between, like the deepest tone of a mighty organ. And, with the final peal of that dreadful anthem, there came a sound, as if the roaring wind, the rushing streams, the howling beasts, and every other voice of the unconverted wilderness, were mingling and according with the voice of guilty man, in homage to the prince of all. The four blazing pines threw up a loftier flame, and obscurely discovered shapes and visages of horror on the smoke-wreaths, above the impious assembly. At the same moment, the fire on the rock shot redly forth, and formed a glowing arch above its base, where now appeared a figure. With reverence be it spoken, the apparition bore no slight similitude, both in garb and manner, to some grave divine of the New-England churches.

"Bring forth the converts!" cried a voice, that echoed through the field and rolled into the forest.

At the word, Goodman Brown stept forth from the shadow of

the trees, and approached the congregation, with whom he felt a loathful brotherhood, by the sympathy of all that was wicked in his heart. He could have well nigh sworn, that the shape of his own dead father beckoned him to advance, looking downward from a smoke-wreath, while a woman, with dim features of despair, threw out her hand to warn him back. Was it his mother? But he had no power to retreat one step, nor to resist, even in thought, when the minister and good old Deacon Gookin, seized his arms, and led him to the blazing rock. Thither came also the slender form of a veiled female, led between Goody Cloyse, that pious teacher of the catechism, and Martha Carrier, who had received the devil's promise to be queen of hell. A rampant hag was she! And there stood the proselytes, beneath the canopy of fire.

"Welcome, my children," said the dark figure, "to the communion of your grave! Ye have found, thus young, your nature and your destiny. My children, look behind you!"

They turned; and flashing forth, as it were, in a sheet of flame, the fiend-worshippers were seen; the smile of welcome gleamed darkly on every visage.

"There," resumed the sable form, "are all whom ye have reverenced from youth. Ye deemed them holier than yourselves, and shrank from your own sin, contrasting it with their lives of righteousness, and prayerful aspirations heavenward. Yet, here are they all, in my worshipping assembly! This night it shall be granted you to know their secret deeds; how hoary-bearded elders of the church have whispered wanton words to the young maids of their households; how many a woman, eager for widow's weeds, has given her husband a drink at bed-time, and let him sleep his last sleep in her bosom; how beardless youths have made haste to inherit their fathers' wealth; and how fair damsels—blush not, sweet ones!—have dug little graves in the garden, and bidden me, the sole guest, to an infant's funeral. By the sympathy of your human hearts for sin, ye shall scent out all the places—whether in church, bed-chamber, street, field, or forest—where crime has been committed, and shall exult to behold the whole earth one stain of guilt, one mighty blood-spot. Far more than this! It shall be yours to penetrate, in every bosom, the deep mystery of sin, the fountain of all wicked arts, and which, inexhaustibly supplies more evil impulses than human power—than my power, at its utmost!—can make manifest in deeds. And now, my children, look upon each other."

They did so; and, by the blaze of the hell-kindled torches, the wretched man beheld his Faith, and the wife her husband, trembling before that unhallowed altar.

"Lo! there ye stand, my children," said the figure, in a deep and solemn tone, almost sad, with its despairing awfulness, as if his once angelic nature could yet mourn for our miserable race. "Depending upon one another's hearts, ye had still hoped, that virtue were not all a dream. Now are ye undeceived! Evil is the nature of mankind. Evil must be your only happiness. Welcome, again, my children, to the communion of your race!"

"Welcome!" repeated the fiend-worshippers, in one cry of despair and triumph.

And there they stood, the only pair, as it seemed, who were yet hesitating on the verge of wickedness, in this dark world. A basin was hollowed, naturally, in the rock. Did it contain water, reddened by the lurid light? or was it blood? or, perchance, a liquid flame? Herein did the Shape of Evil dip his hand, and prepare to lay the mark of baptism upon their foreheads, that they might be partakers of the mystery of sin, more conscious of the secret guilt of others, both in deed and thought, than they could now be of their own. The husband cast one look at his pale wife, and Faith at him. What polluted wretches would the next glance shew them to each other, shuddering alike at what they disclosed and what they saw!

"Faith! Faith!" cried the husband. "Look up to Heaven, and resist the Wicked One!"

Whether Faith obeyed, he knew not. Hardly had he spoken, when he found himself amid calm night and solitude, listening to a roar of the wind, which died heavily away through the forest. He staggered against the rock and felt it chill and damp, while a hanging twig, that had been all on fire, besprinkled his cheek with the coldest dew.

The next morning, young Goodman Brown came slowly into the street of Salem village, staring around him like a bewildered man. The good old minister was taking a walk along the graveyard, to get an appetite for breakfast and meditate his sermon, and bestowed a blessing, as he passed, on Goodman Brown. He shrank from the venerable saint, as if to avoid an anathema. Old Deacon Gookin was at domestic worship, and the holy words of his prayer were heard through the open window. "What God doth the wizard pray to?" quoth Goodman Brown. Goody Cloyse, that excellent old Christian, stood in the early sunshine, at her own lattice, catechising a little girl, who had brought her a pint of morning's milk. Goodman Brown snatched away the child, as from the grasp of the fiend himself. Turning the corner by the meeting-house, he spied the head of Faith, with the pink ribbons, gazing anxiously forth, and bursting into such joy at sight of him, that she skipt along the street, and almost kissed her husband before the whole village. But, Goodman Brown looked sternly and sadly into her face, and passed on without a greeting.

Had Goodman Brown fallen asleep in the forest, and only dreamed a wild dream of a witch-meeting?

Be it so, if you will. But, alas! it was a dream of evil omen for young Goodman Brown. A stern, a sad, a darkly meditative, a distrustful, if not a desperate man, did he become, from the night of that fearful dream. On the Sabbath-day, when the congregation were singing a holy psalm, he could not listen, because an anthem of sin rushed loudly upon his ear, and drowned all the blessed strain. When the minister spoke from the pulpit, with power and fervid eloquence, and, with his hand on the open Bible, of the sacred truths of our religion, and of saint-like lives and triumphant deaths, and of future bliss or misery unutterable, then did Goodman Brown turn pale, dreading, lest the roof should thunder down upon the gray blasphemer and his hearers. Often, awaking suddenly at midnight, he shrank from the bosom of Faith, and at morning or eventide, when the family knelt down at prayer, he scowled, and muttered to himself, and gazed sternly at his wife, and turned away. And when he had lived long, and was borne to his grave, a hoary corpse, followed by Faith, an aged woman, and children and grand-children, a goodly procession, besides neighbors, not a few, they carved no hopeful verse upon his tomb-stone; for his dying hour was gloom.

Charlotte Brontë
(1816-1855)
and
Emily Brontë
(1818-1848)

AMID the moors of Yorkshire, Charlotte and Emily Brontë drew on their limited experience and fertile imaginations to create the indomitable morality of *Jane Eyre* (1847) and the violent love and revenge in *Wuthering Heights* (1848). The powerful and irrational effects of these novels on readers mark the intensity of feeling that went into them—an intensity that demands a sophisticated response. In writing poetry, these two remarkable novelists trained themselves to focus on the terrors of real life without diminishing emotion even when disappointed in love, burdened by the early deaths of their mother and two sisters, and separated from their close family at Haworth Parsonage in 1842–1844. Shortly after their reunion in 1846, Charlotte discovered Emily's poetic manuscripts, recognized their lyric power and metaphysical depth, and set out to have them published. Their careers as authors were thus launched with a slim volume of sixty-one poems, nineteen by Charlotte, twenty-one by Emily, and twenty-one by their younger sister, Anne. The clever pseudonyms, Currer, Ellis, and Acton Bell, concealed their sex without explicitly denying it.

Contemporary reviewers admired most Emily's "Fine quaint spirit" (*Athenaeum*, July 1846), noting her abstract ideas, beauty of bare truth and insight, and musical plainness. Charlotte was dismissed as "indifferent at verse" (*Cento of Poetry*, 30 December 1848). These distinctions remained valid even after Charlotte's several revisions (1845, 1850) and her painstaking editing of the manuscripts.

"Rochester's Song to Jane Eyre" was published in the first edition of *Jane Eyre*, but was later eliminated because Jane's view of him, in Charlotte's memorable prose, offered a more sensitive picture. The poem disappoints admirers of Mr. Rochester, whose speech in the novel contains a far more original command of language and image than the monotonous regularity of rhythm, heavy rhymes, and hackneyed metaphors of the poem. The bold personifications, reminiscent of Ann Radcliffe's, do reflect, however, Mr. Rochester's early defiance of obstacles to his marriage and support the reading that moral maturity and Christian charity must underlie lasting romantic love.

In "Retrospection," Charlotte frees herself from poetic conventions to tell of the fearful loss of the Brontë world of shadows. The "web in childhood" specifically refers to Gondal and Angria, the imaginary kingdoms created in 1826 and sustained in lyrics, dramas, and tales until 1840. This extensive juvenilia has aroused considerable interest, particularly that of Fannie E. Ratchford, who evaluates all the texts in her book, *The Brontës' Web of Childhood* (1941).

Emily's poem "R. Alcona to J. Brenzaida," often called "Remembrance," describes the grief of Rosina of Alcona, Queen of Gondal, for her beloved Prince Julius of Brenzaida of the Gondalan house of Angora, two characters from the childhood epic. The lament certainly anticipates Heathcliff's passion for Catherine as he expressed it in his last conversation with her: "would *you* like to live with your soul in the grave?" (*Wuthering Heights*, chapter XV). The tone of the poem is anguished, grim, yet softer than in the novel. Its strength lies in the successful blend of the natural landscape with the speaker's spiritual state. Repetition and syntactical balance keep the feeling from becoming maudlin. Emily's personifications, rhythms, and rhymes are far more subtle and more skillful than Charlotte's.

Charlotte thought "No Coward Soul Is Mine" to be "the last lines Emily ever wrote." Though not the last, they are certainly among the best. Faith and defiance of death raise the poem to metaphysical heights. A heroic spirit, serene and selfless, here comments on the paradoxical relation of the soul to God. Though the subject would not have suited Catherine and Heathcliff, the mood of spirited defiance is very much like theirs.

Charlotte Brontë

Rochester's Song to Jane Eyre (1847)

The truest love that ever heart
   Felt at its kindled core
Did through each vein, in quickened start,
   The tide of being pour.

Her coming was my hope each day, 5
   Her parting was my pain;
The chance that did her steps delay
   Was ice in every vein.

I dreamed it would be nameless bliss,
   As I loved, loved to be; 10
And to this object did I press
   As blind as eagerly.

But wide as pathless was the space
   That lay our lives between,
And dangerous as the foamy race 15
   Of ocean-surges green.

And haunted as a robber-path
   Through wilderness or wood;
For Right and Might, and Woe and Wrath,
   Between our spirits stood. 20

I dangers dared; I hindrance scorned;
   I omens did defy:
Whatever menaced, harassed, warned,
   I passed impetuous by.

On sped my rainbow, fast as light; 25
   I flew as in a dream;
For glorious rose upon my sight
   The child of Shower and Gleam.

Still bright on clouds of suffering dim
   Shines that soft, solemn joy; 30
Nor care I now, how dense and grim
   Disasters gather nigh.

I care not in this moment sweet,
   Though all I have rushed o'er
Should come on pinion, strong and fleet, 35
   Proclaiming vengeance sore:

Though haughty Hate should strike me down,
   Right, bar approach to me,
And grinding Might, with furious frown,
   Swear endless enmity. 40

My love has placed her little hand
   With noble faith in mine,
And vowed that wedlock's sacred band
   Our nature shall entwine.

My love has sworn, with sealing kiss,   45
   With me to live—to die;
I have at last my nameless bliss:
   As I love—loved am I!

Retrospection (1835)

We wove a web in childhood,
   A web of sunny air;
We dug a spring in infancy
   Of water pure and fair;

We sowed in youth a mustard seed,   5
   We cut an almond rod;
We are now grown up to riper age:
   Are they withered in the sod?

Are they blighted, failed and faded,
   Are they mouldered back to clay?   10
For life is darkly shaded,
   And its joys fleet fast away!

Emily Brontë

R. Alcona to J. Brenzaida (1845)

Cold in the earth, and the deep snow piled above thee!
Far, far removed, cold in the dreary grave!
Have I forgot, my Only Love, to love thee,
Severed at last by Time's all-wearing wave?

Now, when alone, do my thoughts no longer hover   5
Over the mountains on Angora's shore;
Resting their wings where heath and fern-leaves cover
That noble heart for ever, ever more?

Cold in the earth, and fifteen wild Decembers
From those brown hills have melted into spring—   10
Faithful indeed is the spirit that remembers
After such years of change and suffering!

Sweet Love of youth, forgive if I forget thee
While the World's tide is bearing me along:
Sterner desires and darker hopes beset me,   15
Hopes which obscure but cannot do thee wrong.

No other Sun has lightened up my heaven;
No other Star has ever shone for me:
All my life's bliss from thy dear life was given—
All my life's bliss is in the grave with thee.   20

But when the days of golden dreams had perished
And even Despair was powerless to destroy,
Then did I learn how existence could be cherished,
Strengthened and fed without the aid of joy;

Then did I check the tears of useless passion,   25
Weaned my young soul from yearning after thine;
Sternly denied its burning wish to hasten
Down to that tomb already more than mine!

And even yet, I dare not let it languish,
Dare not indulge in Memory's rapturous pain;   30
Once drinking deep of that divinest anguish,
How could I seek the empty world again?

No Coward Soul Is Mine (1846)

No coward soul is mine
No trembler in the world's storm-troubled sphere
I see Heaven's glories shine
And Faith shines equal arming me from Fear

O God within my breast   5
Almighty ever-present Deity
Life, that in me hast rest
As I Undying Life, have power in Thee

Vain are the thousand creeds
That move men's hearts, unutterably vain,   10

Worthless as withered weeds
Or idlest froth amid the boundless main

To waken doubt in one
Holding so fast by thy infinity
So surely anchored on　　　　　　　　　　　　　15
The steadfast rock of Immortality

With wide-embracing love
Thy spirit animates eternal years
Pervades and broods above,
Changes, sustains, dissolves, creates and rears　　　20

Though Earth and moon were gone
And suns and universes ceased to be
And thou wert left alone
Every Existence would exist in thee

There is not room for Death　　　　　　　　　　25
Nor atom that his might could render void
Since thou art Being and Breath
And what thou art may never be destroyed.

Charles Dickens
(1812-1870)

IN 1850 Charles Dickens wrote to the Reverend James White inviting him to contribute to the first Christmas number of *Household Words*:

> We are now getting our Christmas Extra Number together, and I think you are the boy to do, if you will, one of the stories. I propose to give the number some fireside name, and to make it consist of short stories supposed to be told by a family sitting around the fire. *I don't care about their referring to Christmas at all*, nor do I design to connect them together, otherwise than by their names.

These Christmas numbers, first of *Household Words* and then of its continuation *All the Year Round*, proved to be extremely popular: the circulation grew from the 80,000 copies of "The Seven Poor Travellers" (1854) to the 300,000 copies of "No Thoroughfare" (1867). By 1868 Dickens had grown tired of the exacting work required in putting out these Christmas numbers and used the beginning of a new series of *All the Year Round* as an opportunity for discontinuing them: "The Extra Christmas Number has been so extensively, and regularly, and often imitated, that it is in very great danger of becoming tiresome. I have therefore resolved . . . to abolish it at the highest tide of its success."

The story "The Signal-Man," from the Christmas number "Mugby Junction" of *All the Year Round*, makes no reference to Christmas. It is nonetheless easy to understand the peculiar charm of imagining such a story told around a Christmas fire. Hearing a ghost story at the season of Christian rebirth and redemption gives it, as Henry James would say, "another turn of the screw." In fact, James's own tale by that name is a Christmas story, as is Robert Louis Stevenson's "Markheim." Dickens' own special sense of the suitability of ghost stories for the Christmas season had led him, in 1843, to write the famous *Christmas Carol*, in which the ghosts of past, present, and future Christmases appear to the mirthless and uncharitable Ebenezer Scrooge.

Scrooge was a flat version of a type that was to occupy much of Dickens' attention: the grasping, cold-hearted capitalist, responsible for much of the progress and many of the problems of Victorian

England. Mr. Dombey of the novel *Dombey and Son* (1846–1848) embodied these tendencies in a more complicated manner. In that novel, as in "The Signal-Man," Dickens made the railroad a symbol of the technological advances that pleased and troubled the Victorians. *Dombey and Son* sets the railroad against all the qualities of the heart. "The Signal-Man" contrasts the railroad, and all whom it fascinates, with the simple beliefs of those who accept what cannot be rationally understood. The skeptical and empirical-minded narrator is impelled by his curiosity to pry into the signal-man's secrets; he tries to discredit what he thinks is a superstitious faith in prophetic warnings; and he resolves to betray the signal-man's confidences to "the wisest medical practitioner we could hear of," if not to officials of the railroad. The end of the story validates the signal-man's acceptance of the occult and suggests that his premonitions contain a truth beyond medicine and technology. Ironically, he dies; his death, it is implied, may bring about a change of heart in the narrator. At the same time, with the image of the railroad ever-present in "The Signal-Man," the Gothic story enters the modern world.

The Signal-Man (1866)

"Halloa! Below there!"

When he heard a voice thus calling to him, he was standing at the door of his box, with a flag in his hand, furled round its short pole. One would have thought, considering the nature of the ground, that he could not have doubted from what quarter the voice came; but, instead of looking up to where I stood on the top of the steep cutting nearly over his head, he turned himself about and looked down the Line. There was something remarkable in his manner of doing so, though I could not have said for my life what. But I know it was remarkable enough to attract my notice, even though his figure was foreshortened and shadowed, down in the deep trench, and mine was high above him, so steeped in the glow of an angry sunset, that I had shaded my eyes with my hand before I saw him at all.

"Halloa! Below!"

From looking down the Line, he turned himself about again, and, raising his eyes, saw my figure high above him.

"Is there any path by which I can come down and speak to you?"

He looked up at me without replying, and I looked down at him without pressing him too soon with a repetition of my idle question.

Just then there came a vague vibration in the earth and air, quickly changing into a violent pulsation, and an on-coming rush that caused me to start back, as though it had force to draw me down. When such vapour as rose to my height from this rapid train had passed me, and was skimming away over the landscape, I looked down again, and saw him refurling the flag he had shown while the train went by.

I repeated my inquiry. After a pause, during which he seemed to regard me with fixed attention, he motioned with his rolled-up flag towards a point on my level, some two or three hundred yards distant. I called down to him, "All right!" and made for that point. There, by dint of looking closely about me, I found a rough zigzag descending path notched out, which I followed.

The cutting was extremely deep, and unusually precipitate. It was made through a clammy stone, that became oozier and wetter as I went down. For these reasons, I found the way long enough to give me time to recall a singular air of reluctance or compulsion with which he had pointed out the path.

When I came down low enough upon the zigzag descent to see him again, I saw that he was standing between the rails on the way by which the train had lately passed, in an attitude as if he were waiting for me to appear. He had his left hand at his chin, and that left elbow rested on his right hand, crossed over his breast. His attitude was one of such expectation and watchfulness, that I stopped a moment, wondering at it.

I resumed my downward way, and stepping out upon the level of the railroad, and drawing nearer to him, saw that he was a dark sallow man, with a dark beard and rather heavy eyebrows. His post was in as solitary and dismal a place as ever I saw. On either side, a dripping wet wall of jagged stone, excluding all view but a strip of sky; the perspective one way only a crooked prolongation of this great dungeon; the shorter perspective in the other direction terminating in a gloomy red light, and the gloomier entrance to a black tunnel, in whose massive architecture there was a barbarous, depressing, and forbidding air. So little sunlight ever found its way to this spot, that it had an earthy, deadly smell; and so much cold wind rushed through it, that it struck chill to me, as if I had left the natural world.

Before he stirred, I was near enough to him to have touched him. Not even then removing his eyes from mine, he stepped back one step, and lifted his hand.

This was a lonesome post to occupy (I said), and it had riveted my attention when I looked down from up yonder. A visitor was a rarity, I should suppose; not an unwelcome rarity, I hoped? In me he merely saw a man who had been shut up within narrow limits all his life, and who, being at last set free, had a newly awakened interest in these great works. To such purpose I spoke to him; but I am far from sure of the terms I used; for, besides that I am not happy in opening any conversation, there was something in the man that daunted me.

He directed a most curious look towards the red light near the tunnel's mouth, and looked all about it, as if something were missing from it, and then looked at me.

That light was part of his charge? Was it not?

He answered in a low voice, "Don't you know it is?"

The monstrous thought came into my mind, as I perused the fixed eyes and the saturnine face, that this was a spirit, not a man. I have speculated since whether there may have been infection in his mind.

In my turn, I stepped back. But, in making the action, I detected in his eyes some latent fear of me. This put the monstrous thought to flight.

"You look at me," I said, forcing a smile, "as if you had a dread of me."

"I was doubtful," he returned, "whether I had seen you before."

"Where?"

He pointed to the red light he had looked at.

"There?" I said.

Intently watchful of me, he replied (but without sound), "Yes."

"My good fellow, what should I do there? However, be that as it may, I never was there, you may swear."

"I think I may," he rejoined. "Yes; I am sure I may."

His manner cleared, like my own. He replied to my remarks with readiness, and in well-chosen words. Had he much to do there? Yes; that was to say, he had enough responsibility to bear; but exactness and watchfulness were what was required of him, and of actual work—manual labour—he had next to none. To change that signal, to trim those lights, and to turn this iron handle now and then, was all he had to do under that head. Regarding those many long and lonely hours of which I seemed to make so much, he could only say that the routine of his life had shaped itself into that form, and he had grown used to it. He had taught himself a language down here—if only to know it by sight, and to have formed his own crude ideas of its pronunciation, could be called learning it. He had also worked at fractions and decimals, and tried a little algebra; but he was, and had been as a boy, a poor hand at figures. Was it necessary for him when on duty always to remain in that channel of damp air, and could he never rise into the sunshine from between those high stone walls? Why, that depended upon times and circumstances. Under some conditions there would be less upon the Line than under others, and the same held good as to certain hours of the day and night. In bright weather he did choose occasions for getting a little above these lower shadows; but being at all times liable to be called by his electric bell, and at such times listening for it with redoubled anxiety, the relief was less than I would suppose.

He took me into his box, where there was a fire, a desk for an official book in which he had to make certain entries, a telegraphic instrument with its dial, face, and needles, and the little bell of which he had spoken. On my trusting that he would excuse the remark that he had been well educated, and (I hoped I might say without offence) perhaps educated above that station, he observed that instances of slight incongruity in such wise would rarely be found wanting among large bodies of men; that he had heard it was so in work-houses, in the police force, even in that last desperate resource, the army; and that he knew it was so, more or less, in any great railway staff. He had been, when young (if I could believe it, sitting in that hut—he scarcely could), a student of natural philosophy, and had attended lectures; but he had run wild, misused his opportunities, gone down, and never risen again. He had no complaint to offer about that. He had made his bed, and he lay upon it. It was far too late to make another.

All that I have condensed he said in a quiet manner, with his grave dark regards divided between me and the fire. He threw in the word "Sir" from time to time, and especially when he referred to his youth—as though to request me to understand that he claimed to be nothing but what I found him. He was several times interrupted by the little bell, and had to read off messages and send replies. Once he had to stand without the door, and display a flag as a train passed, and made some verbal communication to the driver. In the discharge of his duties, I observed him to be remarkably exact and vigilant, breaking off his discourse at a syllable, and remaining silent until what he had to do was done.

In a word, I should have set this man down as one of the safest of men to be employed in that capacity, but for the circumstance that while he was speaking to me he twice broke off with a fallen colour, turned his face towards the little bell when it did *not* ring, opened the door of the hut (which was kept shut to exclude the unhealthy damp), and looked out towards the red light near the mouth of the tunnel. On both of those occasions he came back to the fire with the inexplicable air upon him which I had remarked, without being able to define, when we were so far asunder.

Said I, when I rose to leave him, "You almost make me think that I have met with a contented man."

(I am afraid I must acknowledge that I said it to lead him on.)

"I believe I used to be so," he rejoined in the low voice in which he had first spoken; "but I am troubled, sir, I am troubled."

He would have recalled the words if he could. He had said them, however, and I took them up quickly.

"With what? What is your trouble?"

"It is very difficult to impart, sir. It is very, very difficult to speak of. If ever you make me another visit, I will try to tell you."

"But I expressly intend to make you another visit. Say, when shall it be?"

"I go off early in the morning, and I shall be on again at ten to-morrow night, sir."

"I will come at eleven."

He thanked me, and went out at the door with me. "I'll show my white light, sir," he said in his peculiar low voice, "till you have found the way up. When you have found it, don't call out! And when you are at the top, don't call out!"

His manner seemed to make the place strike colder to me, but I said no more than, "Very well."

"And when you come down to-morrow night, don't call out! Let me ask you a parting question. What made you cry, 'Halloa! Below there!' to-night?"

"Heaven knows," said I. "I cried something to that effect—"

"Not to that effect, sir. Those were the very words. I know them well."

"Admit those were the very words. I said them, no doubt, because I saw you below."

"For no other reason?"

"What other reason could I possibly have?"

"You had no feeling that they were conveyed to you in any supernatural way?"

"No."

He wished me good night, and held up his light. I walked by the side of the down Line of rails (with a very disagreeable sensation of a train coming behind me) until I found the path. It was easier to mount than to descend, and I got back to my inn without any adventure.

Punctual to my appointment, I placed my foot on the first notch of the zigzag next night as the distant clocks were striking eleven. He was waiting for me at the bottom, with his white light on. "I have not called out," I said when we came close together; "may I speak now?" "By all means, sir." "Good night, then, and here's my hand." "Good night, sir, and here's mine." With that we walked side by side to his box, entered it, closed the door, and sat down by the fire.

"I have made up my mind, sir," he began, bending forward as soon as we were seated, and speaking in a tone but a little above a whisper, "that you shall not have to ask me twice what troubles me. I took you for some one else yesterday evening. That troubles me."

"That mistake?"

"No. That some one else."

"Who is it?"

"I don't know."

"Like me?"

"I don't know. I never saw the face. The left arm is across the face, and the right arm is waved—violently waved. This way."

I followed his action with my eyes, and it was the action of an arm gesticulating, with the utmost passion and vehemence, "For God's sake, clear the way!"

"One moonlight night," said the man, "I was sitting here, when I heard a voice cry, 'Halloa! Below there!' I started up, looked from that door, and saw this Some one else standing by the red light near the tunnel, waving as I just now showed you. The voice seemed hoarse with shouting, and it cried, 'Look out! Look out!' And then again, 'Halloa! Below there! Look out!' I caught up my lamp, turned it on red, and ran towards the figure, calling, 'What's wrong? What has happened? Where?' It stood just outside the blackness of the tunnel. I advanced so close upon it that I wondered at its keeping the sleeve across its eyes. I ran right up at it, and had my hand stretched out to pull the sleeve away, when it was gone."

"Into the tunnel?" said I.

"No. I ran on into the tunnel, five hundred yards. I stopped, and held my lamp above my head, and saw the figures of the measured distance, and saw the wet stains stealing down the walls and trickling through the arch. I ran out again faster than I had run in (for I had a mortal abhorrence of the place upon me), and I looked all round the red light with my own red light, and I went up the iron ladder to the gallery atop of it, and I came down again, and ran back here. I telegraphed both ways, 'An alarm has been given. Is anything wrong?' The answer came back, both ways, 'All well.' "

Resisting the slow touch of a frozen finger tracing out my spine, I showed him how that this figure must be a deception of his sense of sight; and how that figures, originating in disease of the delicate nerves that minister to the functions of the eye, were known to have often troubled patients, some of whom had become conscious of the nature of their affliction, and had even proved it by experiments upon themselves. "As to an imaginary cry," said I, "do but listen for a moment to the wind in this unnatural valley while we speak so low, and to the wild harp it makes of the telegraph wires!"

That was all very well, he returned, after we had sat listening for a while, and he ought to know something of the wind and the wires— he who so often passed long winter nights there, alone and watching. But he would beg to remark that he had not finished.

I asked his pardon, and he slowly added these words, touching my arm:

"Within six hours after the Appearance, the memorable accident on this Line happened, and within ten hours the dead and wounded were brought along through the tunnel over the spot where the figure had stood."

A disagreeable shudder crept over me, but I did my best against it. It was not to be denied, I rejoined, that this was a remarkable coincidence, calculated deeply to impress his mind. But it was unquestionable that remarkable coincidences did continually occur, and they must be taken into account in dealing with such a subject. Though to be sure I must admit, I added (for I thought I saw that he was going to bring the objection to bear upon me), men of common sense did not allow much for coincidences in making the ordinary calculations of life.

He again begged to remark that he had not finished.

I again begged his pardon for being betrayed into interruptions.

"This," he said, again laying his hand upon my arm, and glancing over his shoulder with hollow eyes, "was just a year ago. Six or seven months passed, and I had recovered from the surprise and shock, when one morning, as the day was breaking, I, standing at the door, looked towards the red light, and saw the spectre again." He stopped with a fixed look at me.

"Did it cry out?"

"No. It was silent."

"Did it wave its arm?"

"No. It leaned against the shaft of the light, with both hands before the face. Like this."

Once more I followed his action with my eyes. It was an action of mourning. I have seen such an attitude in stone figures on tombs.

"Did you go up to it?"

"I came in and sat down, partly to collect my thoughts, partly because it had turned me faint. When I went to the door again, daylight was above me, and the ghost was gone."

"But nothing followed? Nothing came of this?"

He touched me on the arm with his forefinger twice or thrice, giving a ghastly nod each time.

"That very day, as a train came out of the tunnel, I noticed, at a carriage window on my side, what looked like a confusion of hands and heads, and something waved. I saw it just in time to signal the driver, Stop! He shut off, and put his brake on, but the train drifted past here a hundred and fifty yards or more. I ran after it, and, as I went along, heard terrible screams and cries. A beautiful young lady had died instantaneously in one of the compartments, and was brought in here, and laid down on this floor between us."

Involuntarily I pushed my chair back, as I looked from the boards at which he pointed to himself.

"True, sir. True. Precisely as it happened, so I tell it you."

I could think of nothing to say to any purpose, and my mouth was very dry. The wind and the wires took up the story with a long lamenting wail.

He resumed. "Now, sir, mark this, and judge how my mind is troubled. The spectre came back a week ago. Ever since, it has been there, now and again, by fits and starts."

"At the light?"

"At the danger-light."

"What does it seem to do?"

He repeated, if possible with increased passion and vehemence, that former gesticulation of, "For God's sake, clear the way!"

Then he went on. "I have no peace or rest for it. It calls to me, for many minutes together, in an agonised manner, 'Below there! Look out! Look out!' It stands waving to me. It rings my little bell—"

I caught at that. "Did it ring your bell yesterday evening when I was here, and you went to the door?"

"Twice."

"Why, see," said I, "how your imagination misleads you! My eyes were on the bell, and my ears were open to the bell, and, if I am a living man, it did *not* ring at those times. No, nor at any other time, except when it was rung in the natural course of physical things by the station communicating with you."

He shook his head. "I have never made a mistake as to that yet, sir. I have never confused the spectre's ring with the man's. The ghost's ring is a strange vibration in the bell that it derives from nothing else, and I have not asserted that the bell stirs to the eye. I don't wonder that you failed to hear it. But *I* heard it."

"And did the spectre seem to be there when you looked out?"

"It *was* there."

"Both times?"

He repeated firmly: "Both times."

"Will you come to the door with me, and look for it now?"

He bit his under lip as though he were somewhat unwilling, but arose. I opened the door, and stood on the step, while he stood in the doorway. There was the danger-light. There was the dismal mouth of the tunnel. There were the high, wet stone walls of the cutting. There were the stars above them.

"Do you see it?" I asked him, taking particular note of his face. His eyes were prominent and strained, but not very much more so, perhaps, than my own had been when I had directed them earnestly towards the same spot.

"No," he answered. "It is not there."

"Agreed," said I.

We went in again, shut the door, and resumed our seats. I was thinking how best to improve this advantage, if it might be called one, when he took up the conversation in such a matter of course way, so assuming that there could be no serious question of fact between us, that I felt myself placed in the weakest of positions.

"By this time you will fully understand, sir," he said, "that what troubles me so dreadfully is the question, What does the spectre mean?"

I was not sure, I told him, that I did fully understand.

"What is its warning against?" he said, ruminating, with his eyes on the fire, and only by times turning them on me. "What is the danger? Where is the danger? There is danger overhanging somewhere on the Line. Some dreadful calamity will happen. It is not to be doubted this third time after what has gone before. But surely this is a cruel haunting of *me*. What can *I* do?"

He pulled out his handkerchief, and wiped the drops from his heated forehead.

"If I telegraph Danger on either side of me, or on both, I can give no reason for it," he went on, wiping the palms of his hands. "I should get into trouble, and do no good. They would think I was mad. This is the way it would work—Message: 'Danger! Take care!' Answer: 'What Danger? Where?' Message: 'Don't know. But, for God's sake, take care!' They would displace me. What else could they do?"

His pain of mind was most pitiable to see. It was the mental torture of a conscientious man, oppressed beyond endurance by an unintelligible responsibility involving life.

"When it first stood under the danger-light," he went on, putting his dark hair back from his head, and drawing his hands outward across and across his temples in an extremity of feverish distress, "why not tell me where that accident was to happen, if it must happen? Why not tell me how it could be averted, if it could have been averted? When on its second coming it hid its face, why not tell me, instead, 'She is going to die. Let them keep her at home'? If it came, on those two occasions, only to show me that its warnings were true, and so to prepare me for the third, why not warn me plainly now? And I, Lord help me! A mere poor signal-man on this solitary station! Why not go to somebody with credit to be believed, and power to act?"

When I saw him in this state, I saw that for the poor man's sake, as well as for the public safety, what I had to do for the time was to compose his mind. Therefore, setting aside all question of reality or unreality between us, I represented to him that whoever thoroughly discharged his duty must do well, and that at least it was his comfort that he understood his duty, though he did not understand these confounding Appearances. In this effort I succeeded far better than in the attempt to reason him out of his conviction. He became calm; the occupations incidental to his post as the night advanced began to make larger demands on his attention; and I left him at two in the morning. I had offered to stay through the night, but he would not hear of it.

That I more than once looked back at the red light as I ascended the pathway, that I did not like the red light, and that I should have slept but poorly if my bed had been under it, I see no reason to conceal. Nor did I like the two sequences of the accident and the dead girl. I see no reason to conceal that either.

But what ran most in my thoughts was the consideration, how ought I to act, having become the recipient of this disclosure? I had proved the man to be intelligent, vigilant, painstaking, and exact; but how long might he remain so, in his state of mind? Though in a subordinate position, still he held a most important trust, and would I (for instance) like to stake my own life on the chances of his continuing to execute it with precision?

Unable to overcome a feeling that there would be something treacherous in my communicating what he had told me to his superiors in the Company, without first being plain with himself and proposing a middle course to him, I ultimately resolved to offer to accompany him (otherwise keeping his secret for the present) to the wisest medical practitioner we could hear of in those parts, and to take his opinion. A change in his time of duty would come round next night, he had apprised me, and he would be off an hour or two after sunrise, and on again soon after sunset. I had appointed to return accordingly.

Next evening was a lovely evening, and I walked out early to enjoy it. The sun was not yet quite down when I traversed the field path near the top of the deep cutting. I would extend my walk for an hour, I said to myself, half an hour on and half an hour back, and it would then be time to go to my signal-man's box.

Before pursuing my stroll, I stepped to the brink, and mechanically looked down, from the point from which I had first seen him. I cannot describe the thrill that seized upon me when, close at the mouth of the tunnel, I saw the appearance of a man, with his left sleeve across his eyes, passionately waving his right arm.

The nameless horror that oppressed me passed in a moment, for in a moment I saw that this appearance of a man was a man indeed, and that there was a little group of other men, standing at a short distance, to whom he seemed to be rehearsing the gesture he made. The danger-light was not yet lighted. Against its shaft, a little low hut, entirely new to me, had been made of some wooden supports and tarpaulin. It looked no bigger than a bed.

With an irresistible sense that something was wrong—with a flashing, self-reproachful fear that fatal mischief had come of my leaving the man there, and causing no one to be sent to overlook or correct what he did—I descended the notched path with all the speed I could make.

"What is the matter?" I asked the men.

"Signal-man killed this morning, sir."

"Not the man belonging to that box?"

"Yes, sir."

"Not the man I know?"

"You will recognise him, sir, if you knew him," said the man who spoke for the others, solemnly uncovering his own head, and raising an end of the tarpaulin, "for his face is quite composed."

"Oh, how did this happen, how did this happen?" I asked, turning from one to another as the hut closed in again.

"He was cut down by an engine, sir. No man in England knew his work better. But somehow he was not clear of the outer rail. It was just at broad day. He had struck the light, and had the lamp in his hand. As the engine came out of the tunnel, his back was towards her, and she cut him down. That man drove her, and was showing how it happened. Show the gentleman, Tom."

The man, who wore a rough dark dress, stepped back to his former place at the mouth of the tunnel.

"Coming round the curve in the tunnel, sir," he said, "I saw him at the end, like as if I saw him down a perspective-glass. There was no time to check speed, and I knew him to be very careful. As he didn't seem to take heed of the whistle, I shut it off when we were running down upon him, and called to him as loud as I could call."

"What did you say?"

"I said, 'Below there! Look out! Look out! For God's sake, clear the way!'"

I started.

"Ah! it was a dreadful time, sir. I never left off calling to him. I put this arm before my eyes not to see, and I waved this arm to the last; but it was no use."

Without prolonging the narrative to dwell on any one of its curious circumstances more than on any other, I may, in closing it, point out the coincidence that the warning of the engine-driver included, not only the words which the unfortunate signal-man had repeated to me as haunting him, but also the words which I myself—not he—had attached, and that only in my own mind, to the gesticulation he had imitated.

Dante Gabriel Rossetti
(1828-1882)

A devotion to decorative and religious beauty, love of medieval subject and archaic diction, and realism of sight and sound characterized the poetry of the middle nineteenth century to such a degree that it has often been given the label "Pre-Raphaelite." This epithet, like the term "grotesque," was borrowed from visual art to describe a literary style. Initially it was applied principally to the painting of the young William Holman Hunt, John Everett Millais, Dante Gabriel Rossetti, and other rebellious students at the Royal Academy's art school. Casually at first and then more seriously, they jeered at Sir Joshua Reynolds' portraits, rejected historical painting, and espoused the honesty, simplicity, and beauty of art before Raphael (1483–1520). The idea of a Brotherhood was suggested by Dante Gabriel Rossetti, painter and poet and major contributor to the Pre-Raphaelite Brotherhood's short-lived magazine, *The Germ* (1850). "Pre-Raphaelite" was first confusingly applied to two arts; it was soon extended to the artistic movement which had as its vague principle the redemption of English art from decline. Rossetti proved to be the most powerful force in both the Brotherhood (1848–1854) and the later Pre-Raphaelite Movement (1856–1872), which expanded to include William Morris, George Meredith, Algernon Charles Swinburne, and Rossetti's brother William and sister Christina. His training for such a role began at his birth into a family with literary associations: his father had written librettos for Rossini's operas, and his uncle, John Polidori, had been Byron's personal physician and author of *The Vampyre* (1819). The Rossettis' library, conversation, and visitors encouraged the literary and artistic ambitions of all four children. At age five, Dante Gabriel wrote a chivalric romance, and, when he was seven, his long poem "Sir Hugh the Heron," written in imitation of Sir Walter Scott, was published by his grandfather Polidori. Gothic novels, ballads, romances, Dante's love poetry, and the Romantic poetry of Blake, Byron, and Keats cultivated in the precocious Dante Gabriel Rossetti an appreciation for the supernatural, the occult, and the erotic—all reflected in his splendid literary ballad "Sister Helen."

Rossetti borrowed his themes of betrayed love, revenge, and black magic from the popular translations of German folk tales and the medieval ballads found in Thomas Percy's *Reliques of Ancient English Poetry* (1765), standard reading in the nineteenth century. His Pre-Raphaelite fellowship probably inspired his particularizing of precise details, the evocation of sensory vividness, and the invocation of Mary in the refrain. The psychological tension, complex dialogue, and three-part refrain, however, are peculiarly Rossetti's.

The tortured mind of Helen, seen in her one-line responses to her little brother's questions and reports, reveals itself through heavy irony, narrative commentary, and sisterly instruction. Her bitterness and predetermined revenge escape the notice of the naive child-reporter, whose curiosity is easily satisfied by declarations of fact. Helen's questions goad him into describing the petitioners and their requests, the evening gloom and chilly wind. As Helen melts the wax image of Keith of Ewern, her brother describes the effects of her witchery from his vantage point on the balcony above all the action. His innocence highlights her concentrated revenge even as the family relationship keeps her more human than witchlike. Her awareness of her own inevitable damnation for her curse does not dissuade her from melting her waxen man; as the wax melts, she guarantees her own destruction.

The third voice in the ballad consistently repeats the heavenly invocation "O Mother, Mary Mother," to contrast the demonic sister with spiritual motherhood. Also repeated without change is "between Hell and Heaven," the place of earth between eternal extremes in the medieval world view. The incremental repetition in the middle third of the refrain creates a feeling of ominous suspense through its subtle variations. The changes in wording, like the refrains with their exclamations and questions, alternate sympathy for Helen with judgment. The effect is like that of the chorus in Greek tragedy, and, like a choric ode, the refrain blends incantation with prayer. The repetition slows the pace of the poem and gives each stanza a poetic formality, especially in the dialogue. Commenting on each stanza, the refrain varies in purpose as the occasion demands. The haunting music of the refrain heightens the horror of the voodoo-like witchery by reminding us always of the standards against which Sister Helen must be judged. She cannot have her revenge with impunity.

Helen's anguish is presented with a psychological realism uncommon in earlier folk ballads. Browning's dramatic monologues may have suggested her obsessive vengeance to Rossetti, but the representation of tensions in the ballad form was Rossetti's idea. He recognized the force of his rendering and revised the poem several times; for his last edition of 1881, he added the stanzas of the bride's silent petition (st. 30-35). By reworking the ballad, he improved the drama by humanizing Helen and "lifting the tragedy to a yet sterner height" (T. H. Caine, *Recollections of Dante Gabriel Rossetti,* 1898). "Sister Helen" marks another step toward the psychological Gothic and goes far toward explaining Rossetti's delight in the work of Edgar Allan Poe.

Sister Helen (1853-1881)

"Why did you melt your waxen man,
             Sister Helen?
To-day is the third since you began."
"The time was long, yet the time ran,
             Little brother."   5
          (*O Mother, Mary Mother,*
Three days to-day, between Hell and Heaven!)

"But if you have done your work aright,
             Sister Helen,
You'll let me play, for you said I might."   10
"Be very still in your play to-night,
             Little brother."
          (*O Mother, Mary Mother,*
Third night, to-night, between Hell and Heaven!)

"You said it must melt ere vesper-bell,   15
             Sister Helen;
If now it be molten, all is well."
"Even so,—nay, peace! you cannot tell,
             Little brother."
          (*O Mother, Mary Mother,*   20
O what is this, between Hell and Heaven?)

"Oh the waxen knave was plump to-day,
             Sister Helen;
How like dead folk he has dropped away!"
"Nay now, of the dead what can you say,   25
             Little brother?"
          (*O Mother, Mary Mother,*
What of the dead, between Hell and Heaven?)

"See, see, the sunken pile of wood,
             Sister Helen,   30

Shines through the thinned wax red as blood!"
"Nay now, when looked you yet on blood,
                    Little brother?"
              (*O Mother, Mary Mother,*
How pale she is, between Hell and Heaven!)   35

"Now close your eyes, for they're sick and sore,
                    Sister Helen,
And I'll play without the gallery door."
"Aye, let me rest,—I'll lie on the floor,
                    Little brother."   40
              (*O Mother, Mary Mother,*
What rest to-night, between Hell and Heaven?)

"Here high up in the balcony,
                    Sister Helen,
The moon flies face to face with me."   45
"Aye, look and say whatever you see,
                    Little brother."
              (*O Mother, Mary Mother,*
What sight to-night, between Hell and Heaven?)

"Outside it's merry in the wind's wake,   50
                    Sister Helen;
In the shaken trees the chill stars shake."
Hush, heard you a horse-tread as you spake,
                    Little brother?"
              (*O Mother, Mary Mother,*   55
What sound to-night, between Hell and Heaven?)

"I hear a horse-tread, and I see,
                    Sister Helen,
Three horsemen that ride terribly."
"Little brother, whence come the three,   60
                    Little brother?"
              (*O Mother, Mary Mother,*
Whence should they come, between Hell and Heaven?)

"They come by the hill-verge from Boyne Bar,
                    Sister Helen,   65
And one draws nigh, but two are afar."
"Look, look, do you know them who they are,
                    Little brother?"
              (*O Mother, Mary Mother,*
Who should they be, between Hell and Heaven?)   70

"Oh, it's Keith of Eastholm rides so fast,
                    Sister Helen,

For I know the white mane on the blast."
"The hour has come, has come at last,
             Little brother!"   75
           (*O Mother, Mary Mother,*
Her hour at last, between Hell and Heaven!)

"He has made a sign and called Halloo!
             Sister Helen,
And he says that he would speak with you."   80
"Oh tell him I fear the frozen dew,
             Little brother."
           (*O Mother, Mary Mother,*
Why laughs she thus, between Hell and Heaven?)

"The wind is loud, but I hear him cry,   85
             Sister Helen,
That Keith of Ewern's like to die."
"And he and thou, and thou and I,
             Little brother."
           (*O Mother, Mary Mother,*   90
And they and we, between Hell and Heaven!)

"Three days ago, on his marriage-morn,
             Sister Helen,
He sickened, and lies since then forlorn."
"For bridegroom's side is the bride a thorn,   95
             Little brother?"
           (*O Mother, Mary Mother,*
Cold bridal cheer, between Hell and Heaven!)

"Three days and nights he has lain abed,
             Sister Helen,   100
And he prays in torment to be dead."
"The thing may chance, if he have prayed,
             Little brother!"
           (*O Mother, Mary Mother,*
If he have prayed, between Hell and Heaven!)   105

"But he has not ceased to cry to-day,
             Sister Helen,
That you should take your curse away."
"*My* prayer was heard,—he need but pray,
             Little brother!"   110
           (*O Mother, Mary Mother,*
Shall God not hear, between Hell and Heaven?)

"But he says, till you take back your ban,
             Sister Helen,

His soul would pass, yet never can."   115
"Nay then, shall I slay a living man,
    Little brother?"
   (*O Mother, Mary Mother,*
A living soul, between Hell and Heaven!)

"But he calls for ever on your name,   120
    Sister Helen,
And says that he melts before a flame."
"My heart for his pleasure fared the same,
    Little brother."
   (*O Mother, Mary Mother,*   125
Fire at the heart, between Hell and Heaven!)

"Here's Keith of Westholm riding fast,
    Sister Helen,
For I know the white plume on the blast."
"The hour, the sweet hour I forecast,   130
    Little brother!"
   (*O Mother, Mary Mother,*
Is the hour sweet, between Hell and Heaven?)

"He stops to speak, and he stills his horse,
    Sister Helen;   135
But his words are drowned in the wind's course."
"Nay hear, nay hear, you must hear perforce,
    Little brother!"
   (*O Mother, Mary Mother,*
What word now heard, between Hell and Heaven?)   140

"Oh he says that Keith of Ewern's cry,
    Sister Helen,
Is ever to see you ere he die."
"In all that his soul sees, there am I,
    Little brother!"   145
   (*O Mother, Mary Mother,*
The soul's one sight, between Hell and Heaven!)

"He sends a ring and a broken coin,
    Sister Helen,
And bids you mind the banks of Boyne."   150
"What else he broke will he ever join,
    Little brother?"
   (*O Mother, Mary Mother,*
No, never joined, between Hell and Heaven!)

"He yields you these and craves full fain,   155
    Sister Helen,

You pardon him in his mortal pain."
"What else he took will he give again,
          Little brother?"
             (*O Mother, Mary Mother,*
Not twice to give, between Hell and Heaven!)   160

"He calls your name in an agony,
          Sister Helen,
That even dead Love must weep to see."
"Hate, born of Love, is blind as he,   165
          Little brother!"
             (*O Mother, Mary Mother,*
Love turned to hate, between Hell and Heaven!)

"Oh it's Keith of Keith now that rides fast,
          Sister Helen,   170
For I know the white hair on the blast."
"The short, short hour will soon be past,
          Little brother!"
             (*O Mother, Mary Mother,*
Will soon be past, between Hell and Heaven!)   175

"He looks at me and he tries to speak,
          Sister Helen,
But oh! his voice is sad and weak!"
"What here should the mighty Baron seek,
          Little brother?"   180
             (*O Mother, Mary Mother,*
Is this the end, between Hell and Heaven?)

"Oh his son still cries, if you forgive,
          Sister Helen,
The body dies, but the soul shall live."   185
"Fire shall forgive me as I forgive,
          Little brother!"
             (*O Mother, Mary Mother,*
As she forgives, between Hell and Heaven!)

"Oh he prays you, as his heart would rive,   190
          Sister Helen,
To save his dear son's soul alive."
"Fire cannot slay it, it shall thrive,
          Little brother!"
             (*O Mother, Mary Mother,*   195
Alas, alas, between Hell and Heaven!)

"He cries to you, kneeling in the road,
          Sister Helen,

To go with him for the love of God!"
"The way is long to his son's abode,
   Little brother."
   (*O Mother, Mary Mother,*
The way is long, between Hell and Heaven!)   200

"A lady's here, by a dark steed brought,
   Sister Helen,
So darkly clad, I saw her not."   205
"See her now or never see aught,
   Little brother!"
   (*O Mother, Mary Mother,*
What more to see, between Hell and Heaven?)   210

"Her hood falls back, and the moon shines fair,
   Sister Helen,
On the Lady of Ewern's golden hair."
"Blest hour of my power and her despair,
   Little brother!"   215
   (*O Mother, Mary Mother,*
Hour blest and bann'd, between Hell and Heaven!)

"Pale, pale her cheeks, that in pride did glow,
   Sister Helen,
'Neath the bridal-wreath three days ago."   220
"One morn for pride and three days for woe,
   Little brother!"
   (*O Mother, Mary Mother,*
Three days, three nights, between Hell and Heaven!)

"Her clasped hands stretch from her bending head,   225
   Sister Helen;
With the loud wind's wail her sobs are wed."
"What wedding-strains hath her bridal-bed,
   Little brother?"
   (*O Mother, Mary Mother,*   230
What strain but death's, between Hell and Heaven?)

"She may not speak, she sinks in a swoon,
   Sister Helen,—
She lifts her lips and gasps on the moon."
"Oh! might I but hear her soul's blithe tune,   235
   Little brother!"
   (*O Mother, Mary Mother,*
Her woe's dumb cry, between Hell and Heaven!)

"They've caught her to Westholm's saddle-bow,
   Sister Helen,   240

And her moonlit hair gleams white in its flow."
"Let it turn whiter than winter snow,
           Little brother!"
              (*O Mother, Mary Mother,*
Woe-withered gold, between Hell and Heaven!)   245

"O Sister Helen, you heard the bell,
           Sister Helen!
More loud than the vesper-chime it fell."
"No vesper-chime, but a dying knell,
           Little brother!"   250
              (*O Mother, Mary Mother,*
His dying knell, between Hell and Heaven!)

"Alas! but I fear the heavy sound,
           Sister Helen;
Is it in the sky or in the ground?"   255
"Say, have they turned their horses round,
           Little brother?"
              (*O Mother, Mary Mother,*
What would she more, between Hell and Heaven?)

"They have raised the old man from his knee,   260
           Sister Helen,
And they ride in silence hastily."
"More fast the naked soul doth flee,
           Little brother!"
              (*O Mother, Mary Mother,*   265
The naked soul, between Hell and Heaven!)

"Flank to flank are the three steeds gone,
           Sister Helen,
But the lady's dark steed goes alone."
"And lonely her bridegroom's soul hath flown,   270
           Little brother."
              (*O Mother, Mary Mother,*
The lonely ghost, between Hell and Heaven!)

"Oh the wind is sad in the iron chill,
           Sister Helen,   275
And weary sad they look by the hill."
"But he and I are sadder still,
           Little brother!"
              (*O Mother, Mary Mother,*
Most sad of all, between Hell and Heaven!)   280

"See, see, the wax has dropped from its place,
           Sister Helen,

And the flames are winning up apace!"
"Yet here they burn but for a space,
                Little brother!"   285
         (*O Mother, Mary Mother,*
Here for a space, between Hell and Heaven!)

"Ah! what white thing at the door has cross'd,
                Sister Helen?
Ah! what is this that sighs in the frost?"   290
"A soul that's lost as mine is lost,
                Little brother!"
         (*O Mother, Mary Mother,*
Lost, lost, all lost, between Hell and Heaven!)

Christina Georgina Rossetti
(1830-1894)

AS Dante Gabriel Rossetti chose to describe a close relationship between a brother and a sister in his ballad "Sister Helen," so his
own sister Christina took as her subject for "Goblin Market" another
strong family tie—this time between two sisters. The Rossetti family
included their brother William Michael, who edited Christina's poems
and Polidori's diary, and their sister Maria, to whom "Goblin Market" is dedicated. The critic Ellen Moers, in "Female Gothic: Monsters, Goblins, Freaks," has speculated that the poem is about "the
erotic life of children" and that it describes "the night side of the
Victorian nursery—a world where childish cruelty and childish sexuality come to the fore." Her interpretation would account for the
chaste but suggestive closeness of Laura and Lizzie; it would help to
explain the peculiar importance of infantlike sucking in the poem;
and it would throw light on the division between the two sisters and
their tormentors, the goblin "brothers":

> Leering at each other,
> Brother with queer brother;
> Signalling each other,
> Brother with sly brother.

Though Laura and Lizzie grow up to become wives and mothers,
Christina herself remained unmarried, and her sister Maria became
an Anglican nun. The fruit that tempts and almost destroys Laura is
clearly the fruit of forbidden sexual pleasure. Her salvation lies in
intimacy with her sister—an intimacy presented as above reproach.

Christina's devout Anglicanism and her reputation as a Christian poet suggest an alternate interpretation that was, no doubt, more
satisfactory to her Victorian contemporaries: Laura's temptation and
sin are redeemed by Lizzie's vicarious suffering. Such a Christian
reading of the poem would relate it to other tales of sin and redemption, for example Coleridge's "Ancient Mariner." Less useful is the
interpretation of "Goblin Market" as a poem about the divided self:
seeing Laura and Lizzie as symbolic of profane and sacred love or

sensuality and reason does little to illuminate the perverse intensity of the poem.

Although the goblin fruit that tempts and destroys is reminiscent of other fairy foods (see Scott's "Wandering Willie's Tale"), the goblins themselves are original creations. They are grotesque and monstrous combinations of animal and human:

> One had a cat's face,
> One whisked a tail,
> One tramped at a rat's pace,
> One crawled like a snail, . . .

Such nightmarish distortions of the human shape are the special legacy of women writing in the Gothic tradition. Encouraged to view their mothers, their sisters, and themselves as somehow inferior or even incomplete, these women wrote with fascination of the freakish and grotesque. Sometimes, like the monster in *Frankenstein*, such a fantastic creation became a sympathetic character; at other times, as in "Goblin Market," the grotesques embodied all the sinister and seductive fantasies that self-doubt could engender. Christina Rossetti and her literary sisters, Emily Brontë and Mary Shelley, saw the evil image through the prism of their womanhood.

Goblin Market (1859)

Morning and evening
Maids heard the goblins cry:
"Come buy our orchard fruits,
Come buy, come buy:
Apples and quinces,   5
Lemons and oranges,
Plump unpecked cherries,
Melons and raspberries,
Bloom-down-cheeked peaches,
Swart-headed mulberries,   10
Wild free-born cranberries,
Crab-apples, dewberries,
Pine-apples, blackberries,
Apricots, strawberries;—
All ripe together   15
In summer weather,—

Morns that pass by,
Fair eves that fly;
Come buy, come buy:
Our grapes fresh from the vine,   20
Pomegranates full and fine,
Dates and sharp bullaces,
Rare pears and greengages,
Damsons and bilberries,
Taste them and try: 25
Currants and gooseberries,
Bright-fire-like barberries,
Figs to fill your mouth,
Citrons from the South,
Sweet to tongue and sound to eye;   30
Come buy, come buy."

   Evening by evening
Among the brookside rushes,
Laura bowed her head to hear,
Lizzie veiled her blushes: 35
Crouching close together
In the cooling weather,
With clasping arms and cautioning lips,
With tingling cheeks and finger-tips.
"Lie close," Laura said,   40
Pricking up her golden head:
"We must not look at goblin men,
We must not buy their fruits:
Who knows upon what soil they fed
Their hungry thirsty roots?"   45
"Come buy," call the goblins
Hobbling down the glen.
"O," cried Lizzie, "Laura, Laura,
You should not peep at goblin men."
Lizzie covered up her eyes,   50
Covered close lest they should look;
Laura reared her glossy head,
And whispered like the restless brook:
"Look, Lizzie, look, Lizzie,
Down the glen tramp little men.   55
One hauls a basket,
One bears a plate,
One lugs a golden dish
Of many pounds' weight.
How fair the vine must grow   60

Whose grapes are so luscious;
How warm the wind must blow
Through those fruit bushes."
"No," said Lizzie, "no, no, no;
Their offers should not charm us,   65
Their evil gifts would harm us."
She thrust a dimpled finger
In each ear, shut eyes and ran:
Curious Laura chose to linger
Wondering at each merchant man.   70
One had a cat's face,
One whisked a tail,
One tramped at a rat's pace,
One crawled like a snail,
One like a wombat prowled obtuse and furry,   75
One like a ratel tumbled hurry-scurry.
She heard a voice like voice of doves
Cooing all together:
They sounded kind and full of loves
In the pleasant weather.   80

   Laura stretched her gleaming neck
Like a rush-imbedded swan,
Like a lily from the beck,
Like a moonlit poplar branch,
Like a vessel at the launch   85
When its last restraint is gone.

   Backwards up the mossy glen
Turned and trooped the goblin men,
With their shrill repeated cry,
"Come buy, come buy."   90
When they reached where Laura was
They stood stock still upon the moss,
Leering at each other,
Brother with queer brother;
Signalling each other,   95
Brother with sly brother.
One set his basket down,
One reared his plate;
One began to weave a crown
Of tendrils, leaves, and rough nuts brown   100
(Men sell not such in any town);
One heaved the golden weight
Of dish and fruit to offer her:

"Come buy, come buy," was still their cry.
Laura stared but did not stir,   105
Longed but had no money:
The whisk-tailed merchant bade her taste
In tones as smooth as honey,
The cat-faced purr'd,
The rat-paced spoke a word   110
Of welcome, and the snail-paced even was heard;
One parrot-voiced and jolly
Cried "Pretty Goblin" still for "Pretty Polly";—
One whistled like a bird.

But sweet-tooth Laura spoke in haste: 115
"Good folk, I have no coin;
To take were to purloin:
I have no copper in my purse,
I have no silver either,
And all my gold is on the furze   120
That shakes in windy weather
Above the rusty heather."
"You have much gold upon your head,"
They answered altogether:
"Buy from us with a golden curl."   125
She clipped a precious golden lock,
She dropped a tear more rare than pearl,
Then sucked their fruit globes fair or red:
Sweeter than honey from the rock,
Stronger than man-rejoicing wine,   130
Clearer than water flowed that juice;
She never tasted such before,
How should it cloy with length of use?
She sucked and sucked and sucked the more
Fruits which that unknown orchard bore;   135
She sucked until her lips were sore;
Then flung the emptied rinds away,
But gathered up one kernel stone,
And knew not was it night or day
As she turned home alone.   140

Lizzie met her at the gate
Full of wise upbraidings:
"Dear, you should not stay so late,
Twilight is not good for maidens;
Should not loiter in the glen   145
In the haunts of goblin men.

Do you not remember Jeanie,
How she met them in the moonlight,
Took their gifts both choice and many,
Ate their fruits and wore their flowers   150
Plucked from bowers
Where summer ripens at all hours?
But ever in the noonlight
She pined and pined away;
Sought them by night and day,   155
Found them no more, but dwindled and grew gray;
Then fell with the first snow,
While to this day no grass will grow
Where she lies low:
I planted daisies there a year ago   160
That never blow.
You should not loiter so."
"Nay, hush," said Laura:
"Nay, hush, my sister:
I ate and ate my fill,   165
Yet my mouth waters still;
To-morrow night I will
Buy more,"—and kissed her.
"Have done with sorrow;
I'll bring you plums to-morrow   170
Fresh on their mother twigs,
Cherries worth getting;
You cannot think what figs
My teeth have met in,
What melons icy-cold   175
Piled on a dish of gold
Too huge for me to hold,
What peaches with a velvet nap,
Pellucid grapes without one seed:
Odorous indeed must be the mead   180
Whereon they grow, and pure the wave they drink,
With lilies at the brink,
And sugar-sweet their sap."

   Golden head by golden head,
Like two pigeons in one nest   185
Folded in each other's wings,
They lay down in their curtained bed:
Like two blossoms on one stem,
Like two flakes of new fallen snow,
Like two wands of ivory   190

Tipped with gold for awful kings.
Moon and stars gazed in at them,
Wind sang to them lullaby,
Lumbering owls forbore to fly,
Not a bat flapped to and fro   195
Round their rest:
Cheek to cheek and breast to breast
Locked together in one nest.

   Early in the morning
When the first cock crowed his warning,   200
Neat like bees, as sweet and busy,
Laura rose with Lizzie:
Fetched in honey, milked the cows,
Aired and set to rights the house,
Kneaded cakes of whitest wheat,   205
Cakes for dainty mouths to eat,
Next churned butter, whipped up cream,
Fed their poultry, sat and sewed;
Talked as modest maidens should:
Lizzie with an open heart,   210
Laura in an absent dream,
One content, one sick in part;
One warbling for the mere bright day's delight,
One longing for the night.

   At length slow evening came: 215
They went with pitchers to the reedy brook;
Lizzie most placid in her look,
Laura most like a leaping flame.
They drew the gurgling water from its deep;
Lizzie plucked purple and rich golden flags,   220
Then turning homeward said: "The sunset flushes
Those furthest loftiest crags;
Come, Laura, not another maiden lags,
No wilful squirrel wags,
The beasts and birds are fast asleep."   225
But Laura loitered still among the rushes
And said the bank was steep.

   And said the hour was early still,
The dew not fallen, the wind not chill:
Listening ever, but not catching   230
The customary cry,
"Come buy, come buy,"
With its iterated jingle

Of sugar-baited words:
Not for all her watching   235
Once discerning even one goblin
Racing, whisking, tumbling, hobbling;
Let alone the herds
That used to tramp along the glen,
In groups or single,   240
Of brisk fruit-merchant men.

     Till Lizzie urged: "O Laura, come;
I hear the fruit-call, but I dare not look:
You should not loiter longer at this brook:
Come with me home.   245
The stars rise, the moon bends her arc,
Each glow-worm winks her spark,
Let us get home before the night grows dark;
For clouds may gather
Though this is summer weather,   250
Put out the lights and drench us through;
Then if we lost our way what should we do?"

     Laura turned cold as stone
To find her sister heard that cry alone,
That goblin cry,   255
"Come buy our fruits, come buy."
Must she then buy no more such dainty fruit?
Must she no more such succous pasture find,
Gone deaf and blind?
Her tree of life drooped from the root: 260
She said not one word in her heart's sore ache;
But peering thro' the dimness, naught discerning,
Trudged home, her pitcher dripping all the way;
So crept to bed, and lay
Silent till Lizzie slept;   265
Then sat up in a passionate yearning,
And gnashed her teeth for balked desire, and wept
As if her heart would break.

     Day after day, night after night,
Laura kept watch in vain,   270
In sullen silence of exceeding pain.
She never caught again the goblin cry:
"Come buy, come buy";—
She never spied the goblin men
Hawking their fruits along the glen: 275
But when the noon waxed bright

Her hair grew thin and gray;
She dwindled, as the fair full moon doth turn
To swift decay, and burn
Her fire away.   280

   One day remembering her kernel-stone
She set it by a wall that faced the south;
Dewed it with tears, hoped for a root,
Watched for a waxing shoot,
But there came none;   285
It never saw the sun,
It never felt the trickling moisture run:
While with sunk eyes and faded mouth
She dreamed of melons, as a traveller sees
False waves in desert drouth   290
With shade of leaf-crowned trees,
And burns the thirstier in the sandful breeze.

   She no more swept the house,
Tended the fowls or cows,
Fetched honey, kneaded cakes of wheat,   295
Brought water from the brook:
But sat down listless in the chimney-nook
And would not eat.

   Tender Lizzie could not bear
To watch her sister's cankerous care,   300
Yet not to share.
She night and morning
Caught the goblins' cry:
"Come buy our orchard fruits,
Come buy, come buy."   305
Beside the brook, along the glen,
She heard the tramp of goblin men,
The voice and stir
Poor Laura could not hear;
Longed to buy fruit to comfort her,   310
But feared to pay too dear.
She thought of Jeanie in her grave,
Who should have been a bride;
But who for joys brides hope to have
Fell sick and died   315
In her gay prime,
In earliest winter-time,
With the first glazing rime,
With the first snow-fall of crisp winter-time.

Till Laura, dwindling,   320
Seemed knocking at Death's door:
Then Lizzie weighed no more
Better and worse,
But put a silver penny in her purse,
Kissed Laura, crossed the heath with clumps of furze   325
At twilight, halted by the brook;
And for the first time in her life
Began to listen and look.

Laughed every goblin
When they spied her peeping: 330
Came towards her hobbling,
Flying, running, leaping,
Puffing and blowing,
Chuckling, clapping, crowing,
Clucking and gobbling,   335
Mopping and mowing,
Full of airs and graces,
Pulling wry faces,
Demure grimaces,
Cat-like and rat-like,   340
Ratel and wombat-like,
Snail-paced in a hurry,
Parrot-voiced and whistler,
Helter-skelter, hurry-skurry,
Chattering like magpies,   345
Fluttering like pigeons,
Gliding like fishes,—
Hugged her and kissed her;
Squeezed and caressed her;
Stretched up their dishes,   350
Panniers and plates:
"Look at our apples
Russet and dun,
Bob at our cherries,
Bite at our peaches,   355
Citrons and dates,
Grapes for the asking,
Pears red with basking
Out in the sun,
Plums on their twigs;   360
Pluck them and suck them,
Pomegranates, figs."

"Good folk," said Lizzie,
Mindful of Jeanie,
"Give me much and many";—   365
Held out her apron,
Tossed them her penny.
"Nay, take a seat with us,
Honor and eat with us,"
They answered grinning: 370
"Our feast is but beginning.
Night yet is early,
Warm and dew-pearly,
Wakeful and starry:
Such fruits as these   375
No man can carry;
Half their bloom would fly,
Half their dew would dry,
Half their flavor would pass by.
Sit down and feast with us,   380
Be welcome guest with us,
Cheer you and rest with us."
"Thank you," said Lizzie; "but one waits
At home alone for me:
So, without further parleying,   385
If you will not sell me any
Of your fruits though much and many,
Give me back my silver penny
I tossed you for a fee."
They began to scratch their pates,   390
No longer wagging, purring,
But visibly demurring,
Grunting and snarling.
One called her proud,
Cross-grained, uncivil;   395
Their tones waxed loud,
Their looks were evil.
Lashing their tails
They trod and hustled her,
Elbowed and jostled her,   400
Clawed with their nails,
Barking, mewing, hissing, mocking,
Tore her gown and soiled her stocking,
Twitched her hair out by the roots,
Stamped upon her tender feet,   405

Held her hands and squeezed their fruits
Against her mouth to make her eat.

    White and golden Lizzie stood,
Like a lily in a flood,—
Like a rock of blue-veined stone   410
Lashed by tides obstreperously,—
Like a beacon left alone
In a hoary roaring sea,
Sending up a golden fire,—
Like a fruit-crowned orange-tree   415
White with blossoms honey-sweet
Sore beset by wasp and bee,—
Like a royal virgin town
Topped with gilded dome and spire
Close beleaguered by a fleet   420
Mad to tug her standard down.

    One may lead a horse to water,
Twenty cannot make him drink.
Though the goblins cuffed and caught her,
Coaxed and fought her,   425
Bullied and besought her,
Scratched her, pinched her black as ink,
Kicked and knocked her,
Mauled and mocked her,
Lizzie uttered not a word;   430
Would not open lip from lip
Lest they should cram a mouthful in;
But laughed in heart to feel the drip
Of juice that syrupped all her face,
And lodged in dimples of her chin,   435
And streaked her neck which quaked like curd.
At last the evil people,
Worn out by her resistance,
Flung back her penny, kicked their fruit
Along whichever road they took,   440
Not leaving root or stone or shoot.
Some writhed into the ground,
Some dived into the brook
With ring and ripple,
Some scudded on the gale without a sound,   445
Some vanished in the distance.

    In a smart, ache, tingle,
Lizzie went her way;

Knew not was it night or day;
Sprang up the bank, tore through the furze,   450
Threaded copse and dingle,
And heard her penny jingle
Bouncing in her purse,—
Its bounce was music to her ear.
She ran and ran   455
As if she feared some goblin man
Dogged her with gibe or curse
Or something worse:
But not one goblin skurried after,
Nor was she pricked by fear;   460
The kind heart made her windy-paced
That urged her home quite out of breath with haste
And inward laughter.

    She cried "Laura," up the garden,
"Did you miss me?   465
Come and kiss me.
Never mind my bruises,
Hug me, kiss me, suck my juices
Squeezed from goblin fruits for you,
Goblin pulp and goblin dew.   470
Eat me, drink me, love me;
Laura, make much of me:
For your sake I have braved the glen
And had to do with goblin merchant men."

    Laura started from her chair,   475
Flung her arms up in the air,
Clutched her hair:
"Lizzie, Lizzie, have you tasted
For my sake the fruit forbidden?
Must your light like mine be hidden,   480
Your young life like mine be wasted,
Undone in mine undoing
And ruined in my ruin,
Thirsty, cankered, goblin-ridden?"
She clung about her sister,   485
Kissed and kissed and kissed her:
Tears once again
Refreshed her shrunken eyes,
Dropping like rain
After long sultry drouth;   490
Shaking with aguish fear, and pain,
She kissed and kissed her with a hungry mouth.

    Her lips began to scorch,
That juice was wormwood to her tongue,
She loathed the feast: 495
Writhing as one possessed she leaped and sung,
Rent all her robe, and wrung
Her hands in lamentable haste,
And beat her breast.
Her locks streamed like the torch   500
Borne by a racer at full speed,
Or like the mane of horses in their flight,
Or like an eagle when she stems the light
Straight toward the sun,
Or like a caged thing freed,   505
Or like a flying flag when armies run.

    Swift fire spread through her veins, knocked at her heart,
Met the fire smouldering there
And overbore its lesser flame;
She gorged on bitterness without a name: 510
Ah! fool, to choose such part
Of soul-consuming care!
Sense failed in the mortal strife:
Like the watch-tower of a town
Which an earthquake shatters down,   515
Like a lightning-stricken mast,
Like a wind-uprooted tree
Spun about,
Like a foam-topped water-spout
Cast down headlong in the sea,   520
She fell at last;
Pleasure past and anguish past,
Is it death or is it life?

    Life out of death.
That night long Lizzie watched by her,   525
Counted her pulse's flagging stir,
Felt for her breath,
Held water to her lips, and cooled her face
With tears and fanning leaves:
But when the first birds chirped about their eaves,   530
And early reapers plodded to the place
Of golden sheaves,
And dew-wet grass
Bowed in the morning winds so brisk to pass,
And new buds with new day   535

Opened of cup-like lilies on the stream,
Laura awoke as from a dream,
Laughed in the innocent old way,
Hugged Lizzie but not twice or thrice;
Her gleaming locks showed not one thread of gray, 540
Her breath was sweet as May,
And light danced in her eyes.

 Days, weeks, months, years
Afterwards, when both were wives
With children of their own; 545
Their mother-hearts beset with fears,
Their lives bound up in tender lives;
Laura would call the little ones
And tell them of her early prime,
Those pleasant days long gone 550
Of not-returning time:
Would talk about the haunted glen,
The wicked, quaint fruit-merchant men,
Their fruits like honey to the throat,
But poison in the blood; 555
(Men sell not such in any town;)
Would tell them how her sister stood
In deadly peril to do her good,
And win the fiery antidote:
Then joining hands to little hands 560
Would bid them cling together,
"For there is no friend like a sister,
In calm or stormy weather,
To cheer one on the tedious way,
To fetch one if one goes astray, 565
To lift one if one totters down,
To strengthen whilst one stands."

Joseph Sheridan Le Fanu
(1814-1873)

IN her book *Night Visitors: The Rise and Fall of the English Ghost Story* (1977), Julia Briggs explores the reasons for the profusion of ghostly tales published between 1850 and 1930 and provides an explanation for the apparent decline of interest in the genre: the impact of the First World War combined with the currency of Freudian theory to make the ghost story seem obsolescent. Thirty years earlier, in 1947, V. S. Pritchett had raised the same issues in his preface to *In a Glass Darkly: Stories by Sheridan Le Fanu*:

> Nightmares make us get up and take notes; if a bodiless hand appears on the door we consult the psychiatrist; our re-discovery of the unconscious has, in itself, meant a quick contraction in the activity of the mysterious for it has led to the fatal discovery that we are the ghosts and that we haunt ourselves.

But the obituaries written about the ghost story go back even further. In 1923, in his preface to *Madam Crowl's Ghost and Other Tales of Mystery* by Le Fanu, Montague Rhodes James declares that the ghost story is old-fashioned; but he finds in Le Fanu a style complementary to the form:

> I do not think it is merely the fact of my being past middle age that leads me to regard the leisureliness of his style a merit; for I am by no means inappreciative of the more modern efforts in this branch of fiction. No, it has to be recognized, I am sure, that the ghost-story is in itself a slightly old-fashioned form; it needs some deliberateness in the telling: we listen to it the more readily if the narrator poses as elderly, or throws back his experience to "some thirty years ago."

In fact, it was the Anglo-Irish Le Fanu who brought new vitality to the tradition of the English ghost story and helped to ensure that it would survive the social and psychological revolutions soon to come about. He is, as James says, leisurely in his manner; and he relies on the elderly Dr. Martin Hesselius to present, in framed narrations, many of his best tales. At the same time, he is, as Pritchett says, a psychologist, who comes closer to our own taste than to that of the Victorians. His methods are at once conservative and radically new, and so he inspires later writers, like James himself, to adapt this old-fashioned form to the temper of modern times.

Of all Le Fanu's ghost stories, "Green Tea" best exemplifies his blend of primitive terror with modern psychological insight. Since Mr. Jennings is working on a study of pagan metaphysics when the monkey first appears, one could interpret "Green Tea" as a story about loss of faith. The clergyman, shaken in his beliefs, becomes subject to the visitations of an infernal agent; he then must turn for help to a medical doctor, the "materialistic" Dr. Harley, who is not capable of ministering to the soul. Such an interpretation would link "Green Tea" with other tales of mistaken reliance on medical or scientific knowledge, for example Mary Shelley's *Frankenstein* and Stevenson's *Dr. Jekyll and Mr. Hyde*; but it would not fully account for the peculiar relationship that develops between Mr. Jennings and his visitor. A shy, gentle clergyman is constantly distracted by a shaggy, grinning ape—a debased and deformed version of a human shape—that squats on his book in church and prevents him from reading, sings blasphemies in his head to interrupt his prayers, and finally drives him to suicide. That may not be all the monkey does: Dr. Hesselius doubts that Mr. Jennings ever gave him "his full and unreserved confidence." Pritchett sums it up: "Dark and hairy with original sin—a piece of sexual symbolism if there ever was one—the monkey of 'Green Tea' skips out of the unchaste jungle of a pious bachelor's unconscious. . . ."

After Mr. Jennings has died, Dr. Hesselius explains his possession with a curious bipartite diagnosis: on the one hand, the vision of the monkey was the result of the opening of an interior eye, brought about by drinking green tea; on the other, the death was the result of "hereditary suicidal mania." The first part of the diagnosis requires our belief in a traditional world of supernatural beings, a belief that Mr. Jennings has trifled with in studying paganism and one very much in accord with the teachings of Emanuel Swedenborg (1688–1772), the Swedish philosopher and mystic whose writings heavily influenced the English Romantics. The second part of the diagnosis postulates the existence of a mental disorder and suggests Le Fanu's interest in the workings of the troubled mind.

This double diagnosis agrees with the dualities of Dr. Hesselius himself, who is both a medical practitioner and a student of "Metaphysical Medicine," who acknowledges the high reputation of the ineffectual Dr. Harley while admitting respect for Swedenborg, and who alternates between writing as a doctor and writing as an "intelligent layman." The wide range of his sympathies makes him an especially reliable narrator, even though his story encloses that of Mr. Jennings and is itself transmitted by a mysterious, restless colleague.

Poised between these two rather dubious speakers, Dr. Hesselius gradually unfolds his impressions in letters that sustain our suspense. From moment to moment, we cannot know more about Mr. Jennings than the doctor himself knows. Le Fanu was looking back to such eighteenth-century writers as Samuel Richardson (1689–1761) in using this epistolary device. At the same time, in scrutinizing the tortured Mr. Jennings, he was anticipating modern discoveries about repressed sexuality and obsessive thinking. "Green Tea" shows how the ghost story—that "old-fashioned" way of representing the evil image—can continue to haunt the well-defended and resistant minds of present-day readers.

Green Tea
A Case Reported by Martin Hesselius, the German Physician. (1869)

PREFACE

Though carefully educated in medicine and surgery, I have never practised either. The study of each continues, nevertheless, to interest me profoundly. Neither idleness nor caprice caused my secession from the honourable profession which I had just entered. The cause was a very trifling scratch inflicted by a dissecting-knife. This trifle cost me the loss of two fingers, amputated promptly, and the more painful loss of my health, for I have never been quite well since, and have seldom been twelve months together in the same place.

In my wanderings I became acquainted with Dr. Martin Hesselius, a wanderer like myself, like me a physician, and like me an enthusiast in his profession. Unlike me in this, that his wanderings were voluntary, and he a man, if not of fortune, as we estimate fortune in England, at least in what our forefathers used to term "easy circumstances."

In Dr. Martin Hesselius I found my master. His knowledge was immense, his grasp of a case was an intuition. He was the very man to inspire a young enthusiast, like me, with awe and delight. My admiration has stood the test of time and survived the separation of death. I am sure it was well-founded.

For nearly twenty years I acted as his medical secretary. His immense collection of papers he has left in my care, to be arranged, indexed, and bound. His treatment of some of these cases is curious. He writes in two distinct characters. He describes what he saw and heard as an intelligent layman might, and when in this style of narrative he has seen the patient either through his own hall-door, to the light of day, or through the gates of darkness to the caverns of the dead, he returns upon the narrative, and in the terms of his art, and with all the force and originality of genius, proceeds to the work of analysis, diagnosis, and illustration.

Here and there a case strikes me as of a kind to amuse or horrify a lay reader with an interest quite different from the peculiar one which it may possess for an expert. With slight modifications, chiefly of language, and of course a change of names, I copy the following. The narrator is Dr. Martin Hesselius. I find it among the voluminous notes of cases which he made during a tour in England about fifty-four years ago.

It is related in a series of letters to his friend Professor Van Loo of Leyden. The professor was not a physician, but a chemist, and a man who read history and metaphysics and medicine, and had, in his day, written a play.

The narrative is therefore, if somewhat less valuable as a medical record, necessarily written in a manner more likely to interest an unlearned reader.

These letters, from a memorandum attached, appear to have been returned on the death of the professor, in 1819, to Dr. Hesselius. They are written, some in English, some in French, but the greater part in German. I am a faithful, though I am conscious, by no means a graceful, translator, and although, here and there, I omit some passages, and shorten others, and disguise names, I have interpolated nothing.

CHAPTER I.
DR. HESSELIUS RELATES HOW HE MET THE REV. MR. JENNINGS.

The Rev. M. Jennings is tall and thin. He is middle-aged, and dresses with a natty, old-fashioned, high-church precision. He is naturally a little stately, but not at all stiff. His features, without being handsome, are well formed, and their expression extremely kind, but also shy.

I met him one evening at Lady Mary Heyduke's. The modesty and benevolence of his countenance are extremely prepossessing.

We were but a small party, and he joined agreeably enough in the conversation. He seems to enjoy listening very much more than contributing to the talk; but what he says is always to the purpose and well said. He is a great favourite of Lady Mary's, who, it seems, consults him upon many things, and thinks him the most happy and blessed person on earth. Little knows she about him.

The Rev. Mr. Jennings is a bachelor, and has, they say, sixty thousand pounds in the funds. He is a charitable man. He is most anxious to be actively employed in his sacred profession, and yet, though always tolerably well elsewhere, when he goes down to his vicarage in Warwickshire, to engage in the active duties of his sacred calling, his health soon fails him, and in a very strange way. So says Lady Mary.

There is no doubt that Mr. Jennings's health does break down in, generally, a sudden and mysterious way, sometimes in the very act of officiating in his old and pretty church at Kenlis. It may be his heart, it may be his brain. But so it has happened three or four times, or oftener, that after proceeding a certain way in the service, he has on a sudden stopped short, and after a silence, apparently quite unable to resume, he has fallen into solitary, inaudible prayer, his hands and eyes uplifted, and then pale as death, and in the agitation of a strange shame and horror, descended trembling, got into the vestry-room, and left his congregation, without explanation, to themselves. This occurred when his curate was absent. When he goes down to Kenlis, now, he always takes care to provide a clergyman to share his duty, and to supply his place on the instant, should he become thus suddenly incapacitated.

When Mr. Jennings breaks down quite, and beats a retreat from the vicarage, and returns to London, where, in a dark street off Piccadilly, he inhabits a very narrow house, Lady Mary says that he is always perfectly well. I have my own opinion about that. There are degrees of course. We shall see.

Mr. Jennings is a perfectly gentleman-like man. People, however, remark something odd. There is an impression a little ambiguous. One thing which certainly contributes to it, people, I think, don't remember—perhaps, distinctly remark. But I did, almost immediately. Mr. Jennings has a way of looking sidelong upon the carpet, as if his eye followed the movements of something there. This, of course, is not always. It occurs only now and then. But often enough to give a certain oddity as I have said to his manner, and in this glance travelling along the floor, there is something both shy and anxious.

A medical philosopher, as you are good enough to call me, elaborating theories by the aid of cases sought out by himself, and by him watched and scrutinised with more time at command, and consequently infinitely more minuteness than the ordinary practitioner can afford, falls insensibly into habits of observation which accompany him everywhere, and are exercised, as some people would say, impertinently, upon every subject that presents itself with the least likelihood of rewarding inquiry.

There was a promise of this kind in this slight, timid, kindly, but reserved gentleman, whom I met for the first time at this agreeable little evening gathering. I observed, of course, more than I here set down; but I reserve all that borders on the technical for a strictly scientific paper.

I may remark, that when I here speak of medical science, I do so as I hope some day to see it more generally understood, in a much more comprehensive sense than its generally material treatment would warrant. I believe that the entire natural world is but the ultimate expression of that spiritual world from which, and in which alone, it has its life. I believe that the essential man is a spirit, that the spirit is an organised substance, but as different in point of material from what we ordinarily understand by matter, as light or electricity is; that the material body is, in the most literal sense, a vesture, and death consequently no interruption of the living man's existence, but simply his extrication from the natural body—a process which commences at the moment of what we term death, and the completion of which, at furthest, a few days later, is the resurrection "in power."

The person who weighs the consequences of these positions will probably see their practical bearing upon medical science. This is, however, by no means the proper place for displaying the proofs and discussing the consequences of this too generally unrecognised state of facts.

In pursuance of my habit, I was covertly observing Mr. Jennings, with all my caution—I think he perceived it—and I saw plainly that he was as cautiously observing me. Lady Mary happening to address me by my name, as Dr. Hesselius, I saw that he glanced at me more sharply, and then became thoughtful for a few minutes.

After this, as I conversed with a gentleman at the other end of the room, I saw him look at me more steadily, and with an interest which I thought I understood. I then saw him take an opportunity of chatting with Lady Mary, and was, as one always is, perfectly aware of being the subject of a distant inquiry and answer.

This tall clergyman approached me by-and-by: and in a little time we had got into conversation. When two people, who like reading, and know books and places, having travelled, wish to converse, it is very strange if they can't find topics. It was not accident that brought him near me, and led him into conversation. He knew German, and had read my Essays on Metaphysical Medicine, which suggest more than they actually say.

This courteous man, gentle, shy, plainly a man of thought and reading, who moving and talking among us, was not altogether of us, and whom I already suspected of leading a life whose transactions and alarms were carefully concealed, with an impenetrable reserve from, not only the world, but his best beloved friends—was cautiously weighing in his own mind the idea of taking a certain step with regard to me.

I penetrated his thoughts without his being aware of it, and was careful to say nothing which could betray to his sensitive vigilance my suspicions respecting his position, or my surmises about his plans respecting myself.

We chatted upon indifferent subjects for a time; but at last he said:

"I was very much interested by some papers of yours, Dr. Hesselius, upon what you term Metaphysical Medicine—I read them in German, ten or twelve years ago—have they been translated?"

"No, I'm sure they have not—I should have heard. They would have asked my leave, I think."

"I asked the publishers here, a few months ago, to get the book for me in the original German; but they tell me it is out of print."

"So it is, and has been for some years; but it flatters me as an author to find that you have not forgotten my little book, although," I added, laughing, "ten or twelve years is a considerable time to have managed without it; but I suppose you have been turning the subject over again in your mind, or something has happened lately to revive your interest in it."

At this remark, accompanied by a glance of inquiry, a sudden embarrassment disturbed Mr. Jennings, analogous to that which makes a young lady blush and look foolish. He dropped his eyes, and folded his hands together uneasily, and looked oddly, and you would have said, guilty for a moment.

I helped him out of his awkwardness in the best way, by appearing not to observe it, and going straight on, I said: "Those revivals of interest in a subject happen to me often; one book suggests another, and often sends me back a wild-goose chase over an interval of twenty years. But if you still care to possess a copy, I shall be only too happy to provide you; I have still got two or three by me—and if you allow me to present one I shall be very much honoured."

"You are very good indeed," he said, quite at his ease again, in a moment: "I almost despaired—I don't know how to thank you."

"Pray don't say a word; the thing is really so little worth that I am only ashamed of having offered it, and if you thank me any more I shall throw it into the fire in a fit of modesty."

Mr. Jennings laughed. He inquired where I was staying in London, and after a little more conversation on a variety of subjects, he took his departure.

CHAPTER II.
THE DOCTOR QUESTIONS LADY MARY, AND SHE ANSWERS.

"I like your vicar so much, Lady Mary," said I, so soon as he was gone. "He has read, travelled, and thought, and having also suffered, he ought to be an accomplished companion."

"So he is, and, better still, he is a really good man," said she. "His advice is invaluable about my schools, and all my little undertakings at Dawlbridge, and he's so painstaking, he takes so much trouble—you have no idea—wherever he thinks he can be of use: he's so good-natured and so sensible."

"It is pleasant to hear so good an account of his neighbourly virtues. I can only testify to his being an agreeable and gentle companion, and in addition to what you have told me, I think I can tell you two or three things about him," said I.

"Really!"

"Yes, to begin with, he's unmarried."

"Yes, that's right—go on."

"He has been writing, that is he *was*, but for two or three years, perhaps, he has not gone on with his work, and the book was upon some rather abstract subject—perhaps theology."

"Well, he was writing a book, as you say; I'm not quite sure what it was about, but only that it was nothing that I cared for, very likely you are right, and he certainly did stop—yes."

"And although he only drank a little coffee here to-night, he likes tea, at least, did like it, extravagantly."

"Yes; that's *quite* true."

"He drank green tea, a good deal, didn't he?" I pursued.

"Well, that's very odd! Green tea was a subject on which we used almost to quarrel."

"But he has quite given that up," I continued.

"So he has."

"And, now, one more fact. His mother, or his father, did you know them?"

"Yes, both; his father is only ten years dead, and their place is near Dawlbridge. We knew them very well," she answered.

"Well, either his mother or his father—I should rather think his father—saw a ghost," said I.

"Well, you really are a conjurer, Doctor Hesselius."

"Conjurer or no, haven't I said right?" I answered, merrily.

"You certainly have, and it *was* his father: he was a silent, whimsical man, and he used to bore my father about his dreams, and at last he told him a story about a ghost he had seen and talked with, and a very odd story it was. I remember it particularly because I was so afraid of him. This story was long before he died—when I was quite a child—and his ways were so silent and moping, and he used to drop in, sometimes, in the dusk, when I was alone in the drawing-room, and I used to fancy there were ghosts about him."

I smiled and nodded.

"And now having established my character as a conjurer I think I must say good-night," said I.

"But how *did* you find it out?"

"By the planets of course, as the gipsies do," I answered, and so, gaily, we said good-night.

Next morning I sent the little book he had been inquiring after, and a note to Mr. Jennings, and on returning late that evening, I found that he had called and left his card. He asked whether I was at home, and asked at what hour he would be most likely to find me.

Does he intend opening his case, and consulting me "professionally," as they say? I hope so. I have already conceived a theory about him. It is supported by Lady Mary's answers to my parting questions. I should like much to ascertain from his own lips. But what can I do consistently with good breeding to invite a confession? Nothing. I rather think he meditates one. At all events, my dear Van L., I shan't make myself difficult of access; I mean to return his visit tomorrow. It will be only civil in return for his politeness, to ask to see him. Perhaps something may come of it. Whether much, little, or nothing, my dear Van L., you shall hear.

CHAPTER III.
DR. HESSELIUS PICKS UP SOMETHING IN LATIN BOOKS.

Well, I have called at Blank-street.

On inquiring at the door, the servant told me that Mr. Jennings was engaged very particularly with a gentleman, a clergyman from Kenlis, his parish in the country. Intending to reserve my privilege and to call again, I merely intimated that I should try another time, and had turned to go, when the servant begged my pardon, and asked me, looking at me a little more attentively than well-bred persons of his order usually do, whether I was Dr. Hesselius, and, on learning that I was, he said, "Perhaps then, sir, you would allow me to mention it to Mr. Jennings, for I am sure he wishes to see you."

The servant returned in a moment, with a message from Mr. Jennings, asking me to go into his study, which was in effect his back drawing-room, promising to be with me in a very few minutes.

This was really a study—almost a library. The room was lofty, with two tall slender windows, and rich dark curtains. It was much larger than I had expected, and stored with books on every side, from the floor to the ceiling. The upper carpet—for to my tread it felt that there were two or three—was a Turkey carpet. My steps fell noiselessly. The book-cases standing out, placed the windows, particularly narrow ones, in deep recesses. The effect of the room was, although extremely comfortable, and even luxurious, decidedly gloomy, and aided by the silence, almost oppressive. Perhaps, however, I ought to have allowed something for association. My mind had connected peculiar ideas with Mr. Jennings. I stepped into this perfectly silent room, of a very silent house, with a peculiar foreboding; and its darkness, and solemn clothing of books, for except where two narrow looking-glasses were set in the wall, they were everywhere, helped this sombre feeling.

While awaiting Mr. Jennings's arrival, I amused myself by looking into some of the books with which his shelves were laden. Not among these, but immediately under them, with their backs upward, on the floor, I lighted upon a complete set of Swedenborg's Arcana Cælestia, in the original Latin, a very fine folio set, bound in the natty livery which theology affects, pure vellum, namely, gold letters, and carmine edges. There were paper markers in several of these volumes. I raised and placed them, one after the other, upon the table, and opening where these papers were placed, I read in the solemn Latin phraseology, a series of sentences indicated by a pencilled line at the margin. Of these I copy here a few, translating them into English.

"When man's interior sight is opened, which is that of his spirit, then there appear the things of another life, which cannot possibly be made visible to the bodily sight. . . .

"By the internal sight it has been granted me to see the things that are in the other life, more clearly than I see those that are in the world. From these considerations, it is evident that external vision exists from interior vision, and this from a vision still more interior, and so on. . . .

"There are with every man at least two evil spirits. . . .

"With wicked genii there is also a fluent speech, but harsh and grating. There is also among them, a speech which is not fluent, wherein the dissent of the thoughts is perceived as something secretly creeping along within it. . . .

"The evil spirits associated with man are, indeed, from the hells, but when with man they are not then in hell, but are taken out thence. The place where they then are is in the midst between heaven and hell, and is called the world of spirits—when the evil spirits who are with man, are in that world, they are not in any infernal torment, but in every thought and affection of the man, and so, in all that the man himself enjoys. But when they are remitted into their hell, they return to their former state. . . .

"If evil spirits could perceive that they were associated with man, and yet that they were spirits separate from him, and if they could flow in into the things of his body, they would attempt by a thousand means to destroy him; for they hate man with a deadly hatred. . . .

"Knowing, therefore, that I was a man in the body, they were continually striving to destroy me, not as to the body only, but especially as to the soul; for to destroy any man or spirit is the very delight of the life of all who are in hell; but I have been continually protected by the Lord. Hence it appears how dangerous it is for man to be in a living consort with spirits, unless he be in the good of faith. . . .

"Nothing is more carefully guarded from the knowledge of associate spirits than their being thus conjoint with a man, for if they knew it they would speak to him, with the intention to destroy him. . . .

"The delight of hell is to do evil to man, and to hasten his eternal ruin."

A long note, written with a very sharp and fine pencil, in Mr. Jennings's neat hand, at the foot of the page, caught my eye. Expecting his criticism upon the text, I read a word or two, and stopped, for it was something quite different, and began with these words, Deus misereatur mei—"May God compassionate me." Thus warned of its private nature, I averted my eyes, and shut the book, replacing all the volumes as I had found them, except one which interested me, and in which, as men studious and solitary in their habits will do, I grew so absorbed as to take no cognisance of the outer world, nor to remember where I was.

I was reading some pages which refer to "representatives" and "correspondents," in the technical language of Swedenborg, and had arrived at a passage, the substance of which is, that evil spirits, when seen by other eyes than those of their infernal associates, present themselves, by "correspondence," in the shape of the beast (fera) which represents their particular lust and life in aspect direful and atrocious. This is a long passage, and particularises a number of those bestial forms.

CHAPTER IV.
FOUR EYES WERE READING THE PASSAGE.

I was running the head of my pencil-case along the line as I read it, and something caused me to raise my eyes.

Directly before me was one of the mirrors I have mentioned, in which I saw reflected the tall shape of my friend Mr. Jennings leaning over my shoulder, and reading the page at which I was busy, and with a face so dark and wild that I should hardly have known him.

I turned and rose. He stood erect also, and with an effort laughed a little, saying:

"I came in and asked you how you did, but without succeeding in awaking you from your book; so I could not restrain my curiosity, and very impertinently, I'm afraid, peeped over your shoulder. This is not your first time of looking into those pages. You have looked into Swedenborg, no doubt, long ago?"

"Oh dear, yes! I owe Swedenborg a great deal; you will discover traces of him in the little book on Metaphysical Medicine, which you were so good as to remember."

Although my friend affected a gaiety of manner, there was a slight flush in his face, and I could perceive that he was inwardly much perturbed.

"I'm scarcely yet qualified, I know so little of Swedenborg. I've only had them a fortnight," he answered, "and I think they are rather likely to make a solitary man nervous—that is, judging from the very little I have read—I don't say that they have made me so," he laughed; "and I'm so very much obliged for the book. I hope you got my note?"

I made all proper acknowledgments and modest disclaimers.

"I never read a book that I go with so entirely as that of yours," he continued. "I saw at once there is more in it than is quite unfolded. Do you know Dr. Harley?" he asked, rather abruptly.

In passing, the editor remarks that the physician here named was one of the most eminent who ever practised in England.

I did, having had letters to him, and had experienced from him great courtesy and considerable assistance during my visit to England.

"I think that man one of the very greatest fools I ever met in my life," said Mr. Jennings.

This was the first time I had ever heard him say a sharp thing of anybody, and such a term applied to so high a name a little startled me.

"Really! and in what way?" I asked.

"In his profession," he answered.

I smiled.

"I mean this," he said: "he seems to me, one half, blind—I mean one half of all he looks at is dark—preternaturally bright and vivid all the rest; and the worst of it is, it seems *wilful*. I can't get him—I mean he won't—I've had some experience of him as a physician, but I look on him as, in that sense, no better than a paralytic mind, an intellect half dead. I'll tell you—I know I shall some time—all about it," he said, with a little agitation. "You stay some months longer in England. If I should be out of town during your stay for a little time, would you allow me to trouble you with a letter?"

"I should be only too happy," I assured him.

"Very good of you. I am so utterly dissatisfied with Harley."

"A little leaning to the materialistic school," I said.

"A *mere* materialist," he corrected me; "you can't think how that sort of thing worries one who knows better. You won't tell any one—any of my friends you know—that I am hippish; now, for instance, no one knows—not even Lady Mary—that I have seen Dr. Harley, or any other doctor. So pray don't mention it; and, if I should have any threatening of an attack, you'll kindly let me write, or, should I be in town, have a little talk with you."

I was full of conjecture, and unconsciously I found I had fixed my eyes gravely on him, for he lowered his for a moment, and he said:

"I see you think I might as well tell you now, or else you are forming a conjecture; but you may as well give it up. If you were guessing all the rest of your life, you will never hit on it."

He shook his head smiling, and over that wintry sunshine a black cloud suddenly came down, and he drew his breath in, through his teeth, as men do in pain.

"Sorry, of course, to learn that you apprehend occasion to consult any of us; but, command me when and how you like, and I need not assure you that your confidence is sacred."

He then talked of quite other things, and in a comparatively cheerful way; and, after a little time, I took my leave.

CHAPTER V.
DOCTOR HESSELIUS IS SUMMONED TO RICHMOND.

We parted cheerfully, but he was not cheerful, nor was I. There are certain expressions of that powerful organ of spirit—the human face—which, although I have seen them often, and possess a doctor's nerve, yet disturb me profoundly. One look of Mr. Jennings haunted me. It had seized my imagination with so dismal a power that I changed my plans for the evening, and went to the opera, feeling that I wanted a change of ideas.

I heard nothing of or from him for two or three days, when a note in his hand reached me. It was cheerful, and full of hope. He said that he had been for some little time so much better—quite well, in fact—that he was going to make a little experiment, and run down for a month or so to his parish, to try whether a little work might not quite set him up. There was in it a fervent religious expression of gratitude for his restoration, as he now almost hoped he might call it.

A day or two later I saw Lady Mary, who repeated what his note had announced, and told me that he was actually in Warwickshire, having resumed his clerical duties at Kenlis; and she added, "I begin to think that he is really perfectly well, and that there never was anything the matter, more than nerves and fancy; we are all nervous, but I fancy there is nothing like a little hard work for that kind of weakness, and he has made up his mind to try it. I should not be surprised if he did not come back for a year."

Notwithstanding all this confidence, only two days later I had this note, dated from his house off Piccadilly:

"Dear sir. I have returned disappointed. If I should feel at all able to see you, I shall write to ask you kindly to call. At present I am too low, and, in fact, simply unable to say all I wish to say. Pray don't mention my name to my friends. I can see no one. By-and-by, please God, you shall hear from me. I mean to take a run into Shropshire, where some of my people are. God bless you! May we, on my return, meet more happily than I can now write."

About a week after this I saw Lady Mary at her own house, the last person, she said, left in town, and just on the wing for Brighton, for the London season was quite over. She told me that she had heard from Mr. Jennings's niece, Martha, in Shropshire. There was nothing to be gathered from her letter, more than that he was low and nervous. In those words, of which healthy people think so lightly, what a world of suffering is sometimes hidden!

Nearly five weeks passed without any further news of Mr. Jennings. At the end of that time I received a note from him. He wrote:

"I have been in the country, and have had change of air, change of scene, change of faces, change of everything and in everything— but *myself*. I have made up my mind, so far as the most irresolute creature on earth can do it, to tell my case fully to you. If your engagements will permit, pray come to me to-day, to-morrow, or the next day; but, pray defer as little as possible. You know not how much I need help. I have a quiet house at Richmond, where I now am. Perhaps you can manage to come to dinner, or to luncheon, or even to tea. You shall have no trouble in finding me out. The servant at Blank-street, who takes this note, will have a carriage at your door at any hour you please; and I am always to be found. You will say that I ought not to be alone. I have tried everything. Come and see."

I called up the servant, and decided on going out the same evening, which accordingly I did.

He would have been much better in a lodging-house, or a hotel, I thought, as I drove up through a short double row of sombre elms to a very old-fashioned brick house, darkened by the foliage of these trees, which over-topped, and nearly surrounded it. It was a perverse choice, for nothing could be imagined more triste and silent. The house, I found, belonged to him. He had stayed for a day or two in town, and, finding it for some cause insupportable, had come out here, probably because being furnished and his own, he was relieved of the thought and delay of selection, by coming here.

The sun had already set, and the red reflected light of the western sky illuminated the scene with the peculiar effect with which we are all familiar. The hall seemed very dark, but, getting to the back drawing-room, whose windows command the west, I was again in the same dusky light. I sat down, looking out upon the richly-wooded landscape that glowed in the grand and melancholy light which was every moment fading. The corners of the room were already dark; all was growing dim, and the gloom was insensibly toning my mind, already prepared for what was sinister. I was waiting alone for his arrival, which soon took place. The door communicating with the front room opened, and the tall figure of Mr. Jennings, faintly seen in the ruddy twilight, came, with quiet stealthy steps, into the room.

We shook hands, and, taking a chair to the window, where there was still light enough to enable us to see each other's faces, he sat down beside me, and, placing his hand upon my arm, with scarcely a word of preface, began his narrative.

CHAPTER VI.
HOW MR. JENNINGS MET HIS COMPANION.

The faint glow of the west, the pomp of the then lonely woods of Richmond, were before us, behind and about us the darkening room, and on the stony face of the sufferer—for the character of his face, though still gentle and secret, was changed—rested that dim, odd glow which seemed to descend and produce, where it touches, lights, sudden though faint, which are lost, almost without gradation, in darkness. The silence, too, was utter; not a distant wheel, or bark, or whistle from without; and within the depressing stillness of an invalid bachelor's house.

I guessed well the nature, though not even vaguely the particulars, of the revelations I was about to receive, from that fixed face of suffering that, so oddly flushed, stood out, like a portrait of Schalken's, before its background of darkness.

"It began," he said, "on the 15th of October, three years and eleven weeks ago, and two days—I keep very accurate count, for every day is torment. If I leave anywhere a chasm in my narrative tell me.

"About four years ago I began a work, which had cost me very much thought and reading. It was upon the religious metaphysics of the ancients."

"I know," said I; "the actual religion of educated and thinking paganism, quite apart from symbolic worship? A wide and very interesting field."

"Yes; but not good for the mind—the Christian mind, I mean. Paganism is all bound together in essential unity and with evil sympathy, their religion involves their art, and both their manners, and the subject is a degrading fascination and the nemesis sure. God forgive me!

"I wrote a great deal; I wrote late at night. I was always thinking on the subject, walking about, wherever I was, everywhere. It thoroughly infected me. You are to remember that all the material ideas connected with it were more or less of the beautiful, the subject itself delightfully interesting, and I, then, without a care."

He sighed heavily.

"I believe that every one who sets about writing in earnest does his work, as a friend of mine phrased it, *on* something—tea, or coffee, or tobacco. I suppose there is a material waste that must be hourly supplied in such occupations, or that we should grow too abstracted, and the mind, as it were, pass out of the body, unless it were reminded often of the connexion by actual sensation. At all events, I felt the want, and I supplied it. Tea was my companion—at first the ordinary black tea, made in the usual way, not too strong; but I drank a great deal, and increased its strength as I went on. I never experienced an uncomfortable symptom from it. I began to take a little green tea. I found the effect pleasanter, it cleared and intensified the power of thought so. I had come to take it frequently, but not stronger than one might take it for pleasure. I wrote a great deal out here, it was so quiet, and in this room. I used to sit up very late, and it became a habit with me to sip my tea—green tea—every now and then as my work proceeded. I had a little kettle on my table, that swung over a lamp, and made tea two or three times between eleven o'clock and two or three in the morning, my hours of going to bed. I used to go into town every day. I was not a monk, and, although I often spent an hour or two in a library, hunting up authorities and looking out lights upon my theme, I was in no morbid state, so far as I can judge. I met my friends pretty much as usual, and enjoyed their society, and on the whole, existence had never been, I think, so pleasant before.

"I had met with a man who had some odd old books, German editions in mediæval Latin, and I was only too happy to be permitted access to them. This obliging person's books were in the City, a very out-of-the-way part of it. I had rather out-stayed my intended hour, and, on coming out, seeing no cab near, I was tempted to get into the omnibus which used to drive past this house. It was darker than this by the time the 'bus had reached an old house, you may have remarked, with four poplars at each side of the door, and there the last passenger but myself got out. We drove along rather faster. It was twilight now. I leaned back in my corner next the door ruminating pleasantly.

"The interior of the omnibus was nearly dark. I had observed in the corner opposite to me at the other side, and at the end next the horses, two small circular reflections, as it seemed to me, of a reddish light. They were about two inches apart, and about the size of those small brass buttons that yachting men used to put upon their jackets. I began to speculate as listless men will upon this trifle, as it seemed. From what centre did that faint but deep red light come, and from what—glass beads, buttons, toy decorations—was it reflected? We were lumbering along gently, having nearly a mile still to go. I had not solved the puzzle, and it became in another minute more odd for these two luminous points, with a sudden jerk, descended nearer the floor, keeping still their relative distance and horizontal position, and then, as suddenly, they rose to the level of the seat on which I was sitting, and I saw them no more.

"My curiosity was now really excited, and, before I had time to think, I saw again these two dull lamps, again together near the floor; again they disappeared, and again in their old corner I saw them.

"So, keeping my eyes upon them, I edged quietly up my own side, towards the end at which I still saw these tiny discs of red.

"There was very little light in the 'bus. It was nearly dark. I leaned forward to aid my endeavour to discover what these little circles really were. They shifted their position a little as I did so. I began now to perceive an outline of something black, and I soon saw with tolerable distinctness the outline of a small black monkey, pushing its face forward in mimicry to meet mine; those were its eyes, and I now dimly saw its teeth grinning at me.

"I drew back, not knowing whether it might not meditate a spring. I fancied that one of the passengers had forgot this ugly pet, and wishing to ascertain something of its temper, though not caring to trust my fingers to it, I poked my umbrella softly towards it. It remained immovable—up to it—*through* it! For through it, and back and forward, it passed, without the slightest resistance.

"I can't, in the least, convey to you the kind of horror that I felt. When I had ascertained that the thing was an illusion, as I then supposed, there came a misgiving about myself and a terror that fascinated me in impotence to remove my gaze from the eyes of the brute for some moments. As I looked, it made a little skip back, quite into the corner, and I, in a panic, found myself at the door, having put my head out, drawing deep breaths of the outer air, and staring at the lights and trees we were passing, too glad to reassure myself of reality.

"I stopped the 'bus, and got out. I perceived the man look oddly at me as I paid him. I dare say there was something unusual in my looks and manner, for I had never felt so strangely before."

CHAPTER VII.
THE JOURNEY: FIRST STAGE.

"When the omnibus drove on, and I was alone upon the road, I looked carefully round to ascertain whether the monkey had followed me. To my indescribable relief I saw it nowhere. I can't describe easily what a shock I had received, and my sense of genuine gratitude on finding myself, as I supposed, quite rid of it.

"I had got out a little before we reached this house, two or three hundred steps away. A brick wall runs along the footpath, and inside the wall is a hedge of yew or some dark evergreen of that kind, and within that again the row of fine trees which you may have remarked as you came.

"This brick wall is about as high as my shoulder, and happening to raise my eyes I saw the monkey, with that stooping gait, on all fours, walking or creeping, close beside me on top of the wall. I stopped, looking at it with a feeling of loathing and horror. As I stopped so did it. It sat up on the wall with its long hands on its knees looking at me. There was not light enough to see it much more than in outline, nor was it dark enough to bring the peculiar light of its eyes into strong relief. I still saw, however, that red foggy light plainly enough. It did not show its teeth, nor exhibit any sign of irritation, but seemed jaded and sulky, and was observing me steadily.

"I drew back into the middle of the road. It was an unconscious recoil, and there I stood, still looking at it. It did not move.

"With an instinctive determination to try something—anything, I turned about and walked briskly towards town with askance look, all the time watching the movements of the beast. It crept swiftly along the wall, at exactly my pace.

"Where the wall ends, near the turn of the road, it came down and with a wiry spring or two brought itself close to my feet, and continued to keep up to me, as I quickened my pace. It was at my left side, so close to my leg that I felt every moment as if I should tread upon it.

"The road was quite deserted and silent, and it was darker every moment. I stopped dismayed and bewildered, turning as I did so, the other way—I mean, towards this house, away from which I had been walking. When I stood still, the monkey drew back to a distance of, I suppose, about five or six yards, and remained stationary, watching me.

"I had been more agitated than I have said. I had read, of course, as every one has, something about 'spectral illusions,' as you physicians term the phenomena of such cases. I considered my situation and looked my misfortune in the face.

"These affections, I had read, are sometimes transitory and sometimes obstinate. I had read of cases in which the appearance, at first harmless, had, step by step, degenerated into something direful and insupportable, and ended by wearing its victim out. Still as I stood there, but for my bestial companion, quite alone, I tried to comfort myself by repeating again and again the assurance, 'the thing is purely disease, a well-known physical affection, as distinctly as small-pox or neuralgia. Doctors are all agreed on that, philosophy demonstrates it. I must not be a fool. I've been sitting up too late, and I dare say my digestion is quite wrong, and with God's help, I shall be all right, and this is but a symptom of nervous dyspepsia.' Did I believe all this? Not one word of it, no more than any other miserable being ever did who is once seized and riveted in this satanic captivity. Against my convictions, I might say my knowledge, I was simply bullying myself into a false courage.

"I now walked homeward. I had only a few hundred yards to go. I had forced myself into a sort of resignation, but I had not got over the sickening shock and the flurry of the first certainty of my misfortune.

"I made up my mind to pass the night at home. The brute moved close beside me, and I fancied there was the sort of anxious drawing toward the house, which one sees in tired horses or dogs, sometimes as they come toward home.

"I was afraid to go into town—I was afraid of any one's seeing and recognising me. I was conscious of an irrepressible agitation in my manner. Also, I was afraid of any violent change in my habits, such as going to a place of amusement, or walking from home in order to fatigue myself. At the hall-door it waited till I mounted the steps, and when the door was opened entered with me.

"I drank no tea that night. I got cigars and some brandy-and-water. My idea was that I should act upon my material system, and by living for a while in sensation apart from thought, send myself forcibly, as it were, into a new groove. I came up here to this drawing-room. I sat just here. The monkey got upon a small table that then stood *there*. It looked dazed and languid. An irrepressible uneasiness as to its movements kept my eyes always upon it. Its eyes were half-closed, but I could see them glow. It was looking steadily at me. In all situations, at all hours, it is awake and looking at me. That never changes.

"I shall not continue in detail my narrative of this particular night. I shall describe, rather, the phenomena of the first year, which never varied, collectively. I shall describe the monkey as it appeared in daylight. In the dark, as you shall presently hear, there are peculiarities. It is a small monkey, perfectly black. It had only one peculiarity—a character of malignity—unfathomable malignity. During the first year it looked sullen and sick. But this character of intense malice and vigilance was always underlying that surly languor. During all that time it acted as if on a plan of giving me as little trouble as was consistent with watching me. Its eyes were never off me. I have never lost sight of it, except in my sleep, light or dark, day or night, since it came here, excepting when it withdraws for some weeks at a time, unaccountably.

"In total dark it is visible as in daylight. I do not mean merely its eyes. It is *all* visible distinctly in a halo that resembles a glow of red embers, and which accompanies it in all its movements.

"When it leaves me for a time, it is always at night, in the dark, and in the same way. It grows at first uneasy, and then furious, and then advances towards me, grinning and shaking its paws clenched, and, at the same time, there comes the appearance of fire in the grate. I never have any fire. I can't sleep in the room where there is any, and it draws nearer and nearer to the chimney, quivering, it seems, with rage, and when its fury rises to the highest pitch, it springs into the grate, and up the chimney, and I see it no more.

"When first this happened I thought I was released. I was a new man. A day passed—a night—and no return, and a blessed week—a week—another week. I was always on my knees, Dr. Hesselius always, thanking God and praying. A whole month passed of liberty, but on a sudden, it was with me again."

CHAPTER VIII.
THE SECOND STAGE.

"It was with me, and the malice which before was torpid under a sullen exterior, was now active. It was perfectly unchanged in every other respect. This new energy was apparent in its activity and its looks, and soon in other ways.

"For a time, you will understand, the change was shown only in an increased vivacity, and an air of menace, as if it was always brooding over some atrocious plan. Its eyes, as before, were never off me."

"Is it here now?" I asked.

"No," he replied, "it has been absent exactly a fortnight and a day—fifteen days. It has sometimes been away so long as nearly two months, once for three. Its absence always exceeds a fortnight, although it may be but by a single day. Fifteen days having past since I saw it last, it may return now at any moment."

"Is its return," I asked, "accompanied by any peculiar manifestation?"

"Nothing—no," he said. "It is simply with me again. On lifting my eyes from a book, or turning my head, I see it, as usual, looking at me, and then it remains, as before, for its appointed time. I have never told so much and so minutely before to any one."

I perceived that he was agitated, and looking like death, and he repeatedly applied his handkerchief to his forehead, and I suggested that he might be tired, and told him that I would call, with pleasure, in the morning, but he said:

"No, if you don't mind hearing it all now. I have got so far, and I should prefer making one effort of it. When I spoke to Dr. Harley, I had nothing like so much to tell. You are a philosophic physician. You give spirit its proper rank. If this thing is real—"

He paused, looking at me with agitated inquiry.

"We can discuss it by-and-by, and very fully. I will give you all I think," I answered, after an interval.

"Well—very well. If it is anything real, I say, it is prevailing, little by little, and drawing me more interiorly into hell. Optic nerves, he talked of. Ah! well—there are other nerves of communication. May God Almighty help me! You shall hear.

"Its power of action, I tell you, had increased. Its malice became, in a way, aggressive. About two years ago, some questions that were pending between me and the bishop, having been settled, I went down to my parish in Warwickshire, anxious to find occupation in my profession. I was not prepared for what happened, although I have since thought I might have apprehended something like it. The reason of my saying so, is this—"

He was beginning to speak with a great deal more effort and reluctance, and sighed often, and seemed at times nearly overcome. But at this time his manner was not agitated. It was more like that of a sinking patient, who has given himself up.

"Yes, but I will first tell you about Kenlis, my parish.

"It was with me when I left this for Dawlbridge. It was my silent travelling companion, and it remained with me at the vicarage. When I entered on the discharge of my duties, another change took place. The thing exhibited an atrocious determination to thwart me. It was with me in the church—in the reading-desk—in the pulpit—within the communion-rails. At last, it reached this extremity, that while I was reading to the congregation, it would spring upon the open book and squat there, so that I was unable to see the page. This happened more than once.

"I left Dawlbridge for a time. I placed myself in Dr. Harley's hands. I did everything he told me. He gave my case a great deal of thought. It interested him, I think. He seemed successful. For nearly three months I was perfectly free from a return. I began to think I was safe. With his full assent I returned to Dawlbridge.

"I travelled in a chaise. I was in good spirits. I was more—I was happy and grateful. I was returning, as I thought, delivered from a dreadful hallucination, to the scene of duties which I longed to enter upon. It was a beautiful sunny evening, everything looked serene and cheerful, and I was delighted. I remember looking out of the window to see the spire of my church at Kenlis among the trees, at the point where one has the earliest view of it. It is exactly where the little stream that bounds the parish, passes under the road by a culvert, and where it emerges at the road-side, a stone with an old inscription is placed. As we passed this point, I drew my head in and sat down, and in the corner of the chaise was the monkey.

"For a moment I felt faint, and then quite wild with despair and horror. I called to the driver, and got out, and sat down the road-side, and prayed to God silently for mercy. A despairing resignation supervened. My companion was with me as I re-entered the vicarage. The same persecution followed. After a short struggle I submitted, and soon I left the place.

"I told you," he said, "that the beast has before this become in certain ways aggressive. I will explain a little. It seemed to be actuated by intense and increasing fury, whenever I said my prayers, or even meditated prayer. It amounted at last to a dreadful interruption. You will ask, how could a silent immaterial phantom effect that? It was thus, whenever I meditated praying; it was always before me, and nearer and nearer.

"It used to spring on a table, on the back of a chair, on the chimney-piece, and slowly to swing itself from side to side, looking at me all the time. There is in its motion an indefinable power to dissipate thought, and to contract one's attention to that monotony, till the ideas shrink, as it were, to a point, and at last to nothing—and unless I had started up, and shook off the catalepsy I have felt as if my mind were on the point of losing itself. There are other ways," he sighed heavily; "thus, for instance, while I pray with my eyes closed, it comes closer and closer, and I see it. I know it is not to be accounted for physically, but I do actually see it, though my lids are closed, and so it rocks my mind, as it were, and overpowers me, and I am obliged to rise from my knees. If you had ever yourself known this, you would be acquainted with desperation."

CHAPTER IX.
THE THIRD STAGE.

"I see, Dr. Hesselius, that you don't lose one word of my statement. I need not ask you to listen specially to what I am now going to tell you. They talk of the optic nerves, and of spectral illusions, as if the organ of sight was the only point assailable by the influences that have fastened upon me—I know better. For two years in my direful case that limitation prevailed. But as food is taken in softly at the lips, and then brought under the teeth, as the tip of the little finger caught in a mill crank will draw in the hand, and the arm, and the whole body, so the miserable mortal who has been once caught firmly by the end of the finest fibre of his nerve, is drawn in and in, by the enormous machinery of hell, until he is as I am. Yes, Doctor, as *I* am, for a while I talk to you, and implore relief, I feel that my prayer is for the impossible, and my pleading with the inexorable."

I endeavoured to calm his visibly increasing agitation, and told him that he must not despair.

While we talked the night had overtaken us. The filmy moonlight was wide over the scene which the window commanded, and I said:

"Perhaps you would prefer having candles. This light, you know, is odd. I should wish you, as much as possible, under your usual conditions while I make my diagnosis, shall I call it—otherwise I don't care."

"All lights are the same to me," he said; "except when I read or write, I care not if night were perpetual. I am going to tell you what happened about a year ago. The thing began to speak to me."

"Speak! How do you mean—speak as a man does, do you mean?"

"Yes; speak in words and consecutive sentences with perfect coherence and articulation; but there is a peculiarity. It is not like the tone of a human voice. It is not by my ears it reaches me—it comes like a singing through my head.

"This faculty, the power of speaking to me, will be my undoing. It won't let me pray, it interrupts me with dreadful blasphemies. I dare not go on, I could not. Oh! doctor, can the skill, and thought, and prayer of man avail me nothing!"

"You must promise me, my dear sir, not to trouble yourself with unnecessarily exciting thoughts; confine yourself strictly to the narrative of *facts*; and recollect, above all, that even if the thing that infests you be as you seem to suppose, a reality with an actual independent life and will, yet it can have no power to hurt you, unless it be given from above: its access to your senses depends mainly upon your physical condition—this is, under God, your comfort and reliance: we are all alike environed. It is only that in your case, the 'paries,' the veil of the flesh, the screen, is a little out of repair, and sights and sounds are transmitted. We must enter on a new course, sir—be encouraged. I'll give to-night to the careful consideration of the whole case."

"You are very good, sir; you think it worth trying, you don't give me quite up; but, sir, you don't know, it is gaining such an influence over me: it orders me about, it is such a tyrant, and I'm growing so helpless. May God deliver me!"

"It orders you about—of course you mean by speech?"

"Yes, yes; it is always urging me to crimes, to injure others, or myself. You see, doctor, the situation is urgent, it is indeed. When I was in Shropshire, a few weeks ago" (Mr. Jennings was speaking rapidly and trembling now, holding my arm with one hand, and looking in my face), "I went out one day with a party of friends for a walk: my persecutor, I tell you, was with me at the time. I lagged behind the rest: the country near the Dee, you know, is beautiful. Our path happened to lie near a coal mine, and at the verge of the wood is a perpendicular shaft, they say, a hundred and fifty feet deep. My niece had remained behind with me—she knows, of course, nothing of the nature of my sufferings. She knew, however, that I had been ill, and was low, and she remained to prevent my being quite alone. As we loitered slowly on together the brute that accompanied me was urging me to throw myself down the shaft. I tell you now—

oh, sir, think of it! the one consideration that saved me from that hideous death was the fear lest the shock of witnessing the occurrence should be too much for the poor girl. I asked her to go on and take her walk with her friends, saying that I could go no further. She made excuses, and the more I urged her the firmer she became. She looked doubtful and frightened. I suppose there was something in my looks or manner that alarmed her; but she would not go, and that literally saved me. You had no idea, sir, that a living man could be made so abject a slave of Satan," he said, with a ghastly groan and a shudder.

There was a pause here, and I said, "You *were* preserved nevertheless. It was the act of God. You are in his hands and in the power of no other being: be therefore confident for the future."

CHAPTER X.
HOME.

I made him have candles lighted, and saw the room looking cheery and inhabited before I left him. I told him that he must regard his illness strictly as one dependent on physical, though subtle physical, causes. I told him that he had evidence of God's care and love in the deliverance which he had just described, and that I had perceived with pain that he seemed to regard its peculiar features as indicating that he had been delivered over to spiritual reprobation. Than such a conclusion nothing could be, I insisted, less warranted; and not only so, but more contrary to facts, as disclosed in his mysterious deliverance from that murderous influence during his Shropshire excursion. First, his niece had been retained by his side without his intending to keep her near him; and, secondly, there had been infused into his mind an irresistible repugnance to execute the dreadful suggestion in her presence.

As I reasoned this point with him, Mr. Jennings wept. He seemed comforted. One promise I exacted, which was that should the monkey at any time return, I should be sent for immediately; and, repeating my assurance that I would give neither time nor thought to any other subject until I had thoroughly investigated his case, and that to-morrow he should hear the result, I took my leave.

Before getting into the carriage I told the servant that his master was far from well, and that he should make a point of frequently looking into his room.

My own arrangements I made with a view to being quite secure from interruptions.

I merely called at my lodgings, and, with a travelling-desk and carpet-bag, set off in a hackney carriage for an inn about two miles out of town, called The Horns, a very quiet and comfortable house, with good thick walls. And there I resolved, without the possibility of intrusion or distraction, to devote some hours of the night, in my comfortable sitting-room, to Mr. Jennings's case, and so much of the morning as it might require.

(There occurs here a careful note of Dr. Hesselius's opinion upon the case, and of the habits, dietary, and medicines which he prescribed. It is curious—some people would say mystical. But on the whole I doubt whether it would sufficiently interest a reader of the kind I am likely to meet with to warrant its being here reprinted. This whole letter was plainly written at the inn in which he had hid himself for the occasion. The next letter is dated from his town lodgings.)

I left town for the inn where I slept last night at half-past nine, and did not arrive at my room in town until one o'clock this afternoon. I found a letter in Mr. Jennings's hand upon my table. It had not come by post, and on inquiry, I learned that Mr. Jennings's servant had brought it, and on learning that I was not to return until to-day, and that no one could tell him my address, he seemed very uncomfortable, and said that his orders from his master were that he was not to return without an answer.

I opened the letter, and read:

"Dear Dr. Hesselius. It is here. You had not been an hour gone when it returned. It is speaking. It knows all that has happened. It knows everything—it knows you, and is frantic and atrocious. It reviles. I send you this. It knows every word I have written—I write. This I promised, and I therefore write, but I fear very confused, very incoherently. I am so interrupted, disturbed.

"Ever yours, sincerely yours,
"ROBERT LYNDER JENNINGS."

"When did this come?" I asked.

"About eleven last night; the man was here again, and has been here three times to-day. The last time is about an hour since."

Thus answered, and with the notes I had made upon his case in my pocket, I was, in a few minutes, driving out to Richmond, to see Mr. Jennings.

I by no means, as you perceive, despaired of Mr. Jennings's case. He had himself remembered and applied, though quite in a mistaken way, the principle which I lay down in my Metaphysical Medicine, and which governs all such cases. I was about to apply it in earnest. I was profoundly interested, and very anxious to see and examine him while the "enemy" was actually present.

I drove up to the sombre house, and ran up the steps, and knocked. The door, in a little time, was opened by a tall woman in black silk. She looked ill, and as if she had been crying. She curtseyed, and heard my question, but she did not answer. She turned her face away, extending her hand hurriedly towards two men who were coming down-stairs; and thus having, as it were, tacitly made me over to them, she passed through a side-door hastily and shut it.

The man who was nearest the hall, I at once accosted, but being now close to him, I was shocked to see that both his hands were covered with blood.

I drew back a little, and the man passing down-stairs merely said in a low tone, "Here's the servant, sir."

The servant had stopped on the stairs, confounded and dumb at seeing me. He was rubbing his hands in a handkerchief, and it was steeped in blood.

"Jones, what is it, what has happened?" I asked, while a sickening suspicion overpowered me.

The man asked me to come up to the lobby. I was beside him in a moment, and frowning and pallid, with contracted eyes, he told me the horror which I already half guessed.

His master had made away with himself.

I went up-stairs with him to the room—what I saw there I won't tell you. He had cut his throat with his razor. It was a frightful gash. The two men had laid him upon the bed and composed his limbs. It had happened, as the immense pool of blood on the floor declared, at some distance between the bed and the window. There was carpet round his bed, and a carpet under his dressing-table, but none on the rest of the floor, for the man said he did not like carpet on his bedroom. In this sombre, and now terrible room, one of the great elms that darkened the house was slowly moving the shadow of one of its great boughs upon this dreadful floor.

I beckoned to the servant and we went down stairs together. I turned, off the hall, into an old-fashioned panelled room, and there standing, I heard all the servant had to tell. It was not a great deal.

"I concluded, sir, from your words, and looks, sir, as you left last night, that you thought my master seriously ill. I thought it might be that you were afraid of a fit, or something. So I attended very close to your directions. He sat up late, till past three o'clock. He was not writing or reading. He was talking a great deal to himself, but that was nothing unusual. At about that hour I assisted him to undress, and left him in his slippers and dressing-gown. I went back softly in about half an hour. He was in his bed, quite undressed, and a pair of candles lighted on the table beside his bed. He was leaning on his elbow and looking out at the other side of the bed when I came in. I asked him if he wanted anything, and he said no.

"I don't know whether it was what you said to me, sir, or something a little unusual about him, but I was uneasy, uncommon uneasy, about him last night.

"In another half hour, or it might be a little more, I went up again. I did not hear him talking as before. I opened the door a little. The candles were both out, which was not usual. I had a bedroom candle, and I let the light in, a little bit, looking softly round. I saw him sitting in that chair beside the dressing-table with his clothes on again. He turned round and looked at me. I thought it strange he should get up and dress, and put out the candles to sit in the dark, that way. But I only asked him again if I could do anything for him. He said, no, rather sharp, I thought. I asked if I might light the candles, and he said, 'Do as you like, Jones.' So I lighted them, and I lingered a little about the room, and he said, 'Tell me truth, Jones, why did you come again—you did not hear any one cursing?' 'No sir,' I said, wondering what he could mean.

" 'No,' said he, after me, 'of course, no'; and I said to him, 'Wouldn't it be well, sir, you went to bed? It's just five o'clock'; and he said nothing but, 'Very likely: good-night, Jones.' So I went, sir, but in less than an hour I came again. The door was fast, and he heard me, and called as I thought from the bed to know what I wanted, and he desired me not to disturb him again. I lay down and slept for a little. It must have been between six and seven when I went up again. The door was still fast, and he made no answer, so I did not like to disturb him, and thinking he was alseep, I left him till nine. It was his custom to ring when he wished me to come, and I had no particular hour for calling him. I tapped very gently, and getting no answer, I stayed away a good while, supposing he was getting some rest then. It was not till eleven o'clock I grew really uncomfortable about him—for at the latest he was never that I could remember, later than half-past ten. I got no answer. I knocked and called, and still no answer. So not being able to force the door, I called Thomas from the stables, and together we forced it, and found him in the shocking way you saw."

Jones had no more to tell. Poor Mr. Jennings was very gentle, and very kind. All his people were fond of him. I could see that the servant was very much moved.

So, dejected and agitated, I passed from that terrible house, and its dark canopy of elms, and I hope I shall never see it more. While I write to you I feel like a man who has but half waked from a frightful and monotonous dream. My memory rejects the picture with incredulity and horror. Yet I know it is true. It is the story of the process of a poison, a poison which excites the reciprocal action of spirit and nerve, and paralyses the tissue that separates those cognate functions of the senses, the external and the interior. Thus we find strange bed-fellows, and the mortal and immortal prematurely make acquaintance.

CONCLUSION.
A WORD FOR THOSE WHO SUFFER.

My dear Van L., you have suffered from an affection similar to that which I have just described. You twice complained of a return of it.

Who, under God, cured you? Your humble servant, Martin Hesselius. Let me rather adopt the more emphasised piety of a certain good old French surgeon of three hundred years ago: "I treated, and God cured you."

Come, my friend, you are not to be hippish. Let me tell you a fact.

I have met with, and treated, as my book shows, fifty-seven cases of this kind of vision, which I term indifferently "sublimated," "precocious," and "interior."

There is another class of affections which are truly termed— though commonly confounded with those which I describe—spectral illusions. These latter I look upon as being no less simply curable than a cold in the head or a trifling dyspepsia.

It is those which rank in the first category that test our promptitude of thought. Fifty-seven such cases have I encountered, neither more nor less. And in how many of these have I failed? In no one single instance.

There is no one affliction of mortality more easily and certainly reducible, with a little patience, and a rational confidence in the physician. With these simple conditions, I look upon the cure as absolutely certain.

You are to remember that I had not even commenced to treat Mr. Jennings's case. I have not any doubt that I should have cured him perfectly in eighteen months, or possibly it might have extended to two years. Some cases are very rapidly curable, others extremely tedious. Every intelligent physician who will give thought and diligence to the task, will effect a cure.

You know my tract on The Cardinal Functions of the Brain. I there, by the evidence of innumerable facts, prove, as I think, the high probability of a circulation arterial and venous in its mechanism, through the nerves. Of this system, thus considered, the brain is the heart. The fluid, which is propagated hence through one class of nerves, returns in an altered state through another, and the nature of that fluid is spiritual, though not immaterial, any more than, as I before remarked, light or electricity are so.

By various abuses, among which the habitual use of such agents as green tea is one, this fluid may be affected as to its quality, but it is more frequently disturbed as to equilibrium. This fluid being that which we have in common with spirits, a congestion found upon the masses of brain or nerve, connected with the interior sense, forms a surface unduly exposed, on which disembodied spirits may operate: communication is thus more or less effectually established. Between this brain circulation and the heart circulation there is an intimate sympathy. The seat, or rather the instrument of exterior vision, is the eye. The seat of interior vision is the nervous tissue and brain, immediately about and above the eyebrow. You remember how effectually I dissipated your pictures by the simple application of iced eau-de-cologne. Few cases, however can be treated exactly alike with anything like rapid success. Cold acts powerfully as a repellant of the nervous fluid. Long enough continued it will even produce that permanent insensibility which we call numbness, and a little longer, muscular as well as sensational paralysis.

I have not, I repeat, the slightest doubt that I should have first dimmed and ultimately sealed that inner eye which Mr. Jennings had inadvertently opened. The same senses are opened in delirium tremens, and entirely shut up again when the overaction of the cerebral heart, and the prodigious nervous congestions that attend it, are terminated by a decided change in the state of the body. It is by acting steadily upon the body, by a simple process, that this result is produced—and inevitably produced—I have never yet failed.

Poor Mr. Jennings made away with himself. But that catastrophe was the result of a totally different malady, which, as it were, projected itself upon that disease which was established. His case was in the distinctive manner a complication, and the complaint under which he really succumbed, was hereditary suicidal mania. Poor Mr. Jennings I cannot call a patient of mine, for I had not even begun to treat his case, and he had not yet given me, I am convinced, his full and unreserved confidence. If the patient do not array himself on the side of the disease, his cure is certain.

Louisa May Alcott
(1832-1888)

LIKE her character Jo March, who contributed sensational stories to the *Weekly Volcano* to bolster the family finances, Louisa May Alcott, author of *Little Women* (1868–1869), published "blood-and-thunder tales" in such popular magazines as *The Flag of Our Union* and *Frank Leslie's Illustrated Newspaper.* Since she was reluctant to acknowledge her authorship of these stories, she adopted a pseudonym, or first issued them under her initials. Only recently has the research of Madeleine Stern and Leona Rosthenberg brought to light these bloodcurdling contributions to the Gothic tradition. Their volumes of Alcott stories, *Behind a Mask* (1975) and *Plots and Counterplots* (1978), force a reevaluation of a writer usually regarded as domestic and genteel.

In a conversation with a contemporary female writer, L. C. Pickett, Alcott explained the necessity for maintaining a disguise:

> I think my natural ambition is for the lurid style. I indulge in gorgeous fantasies and wish that I dared inscribe them upon my pages and set them before the public. . . . How should I dare to interfere with the proper grayness of old Concord? The dear old town has never known a startling hue since the redcoats were there. Far be it from me to inject an inharmonious color into the neutral tint. And my favorite characters! Suppose they went to cavorting at their own sweet will, to the infinite horror of dear Mr. Emerson, who never imagined a Concord person as walking off a plumb line stretched between two pearly clouds in the empyrean. . . . No, my dear, I shall always be a wretched victim to the respectable traditions of Concord.

Just as Horace Walpole had earlier adopted a false identity to forestall the ridicule that he feared would greet *The Castle of Otranto*, so the New England spinster and bluestocking hesitated to jeopardize her reputation for propriety with her father's literary friends, Emerson and Hawthorne.

One senses that the disguise freed her, that it permitted her to experiment vicariously with the forbidden pleasures of sex. Many writers of the modern woman's Gothic romance have followed her practice, adopting pseudonyms as they brush, with tantalizing closeness, by the subjects of rape and sadism. Outright pornography would scandalize and repel their readers by making fantasy too explicit. But the bored housewife and the lovesick teenager can safely indulge in lascivious reverie when their Gothic romance merely hints at the enticing dangers. The darkly handsome count, or master, or cavalier, who conceals a tragic secret behind his slightly contemptuous and cruel smile, offers the thrill of sexual adventure that the author is careful to contain by means of a domestic or moralistic ending. Victoria Holt, Norah Lofts, Catherine Cookson, and Mary Stewart are old hands at this kind of teasing; and even Daphne du Maurier, for example in *Rebecca* (1938), flirts with the possibilities.

In Alcott's "Perilous Play," the flavor of sexual drama is enhanced with the spice of hashish. The usually reliable Mark Done, his passion inflamed by the nefarious drug, threatens to force his love on the beautiful but marble-cold Rose St. Just. Since she, too, has eaten the bean-shaped comfits, the civilized self-restraint of both is imperiled; and animal instinct menaces their peace almost as much as the raging storm. The drug that thus plays havoc with their manners has the benefit of permitting them to declare their mutual love, and the story ends with a bold tribute to the releasing powers of hashish. Louisa May Alcott, in these recently republished stories, has anticipated her modern successors and even outdone them in daring. As the world turns, they will probably try to match her.

Perilous Play (1863)

"If some one does not propose a new and interesting amusement I shall die of *ennui*," said pretty Belle Daventry, in a tone of despair. "I have read all my books, used up all my Berlin wools, and it's too warm to go to town for more. No one can go sailing yet, as the tide is out; we are all nearly tired to death of cards, croquet, and gossip, so what shall we do to while away this endless afternoon? Dr. Meredith, I command you to invent and propose a new game in five minutes."

"To hear is to obey," replied the young man, who lay in the grass at her feet, as he submissively slapped his forehead and fell a-thinking with all his might.

Holding up her finger to preserve silence, Belle pulled out her watch, and waited with an expectant smile. The rest of the young party, who were indolently scattered about under the elms, drew nearer, and brightened visibly, for Dr. Meredith's inventive powers were well-known, and something refreshingly novel might be expected from him.

One gentleman did not stir, but, then, he lay within earshot, and merely turned his fine eyes from the sea to the group before him. His glance rested a moment on Belle's piquant figure, for she looked very pretty with her bright hair blowing in the wind, one plump, white hand extended to keep order, and one little foot, in a distracting slipper, just visible below the voluminous folds of her dress.

Then the glance passed to another figure, sitting somewhat apart in a cloud of white muslin, for an airy burnoose floated from head and shoulders, showing only a singularly charming face. Pale, and yet brilliant, for the Southern eyes were magnificent, and clear olive cheeks contrasted with darkest hair; lips like a pomegranate flower, and delicate, straight brows, as mobile as the lips. A cluster of crimson flowers, half falling from the loose black braids, and a golden bracelet of Arabian coins on the slender wrist, were the only ornaments she wore, and became her better than the fashionable frippery of her companions.

A book lay on her lap, but her eyes, full of a passionate melancholy, were fixed on the sea, which glittered round an island green and flowery as a Summer paradise. Rose St. Just was as beautiful as her Spanish mother, but had inherited the pride and reserve of her English father; and this pride was the thorn which repelled lovers from the human flower.

Mark Done sighed as he looked, and, as if the sigh, low as it was, roused her from her reverie, Rose flashed a quick glance at him, took up her book, and went on reading the legend of "The Lotus Eaters."

"Time is up now, doctor," cried Belle, pocketing her watch with a flourish.

"Ready to report," answered Meredith, sitting up, and producing a little box of tortoise-shell and gold.

"How mysterious! What is it? Let me see, first!" And Belle removed the cover, looking like an inquisitive child. "Only bonbons; how stupid! That won't do, sir. We don't want to be fed with sugar-plums. We demand to be amused."

"Eat six of these despised bonbons, and you *will* be amused in a new, delicious, and wonderful manner," said the young doctor, laying half-a-dozen on a green leaf, and offering them to her.

"Why, what are they?" she asked, looking at them askance.

"Hasheesh; did you ever hear of it?"

"Oh, yes; it's that Indian stuff which brings one fantastic visions, isn't it? I've always wanted to see and taste it, and now I will," cried Belle, nibbling at one of the bean-shaped comfits with its green heart.

"I advise you not to try it. People do all sorts of queer things when they take it. I wouldn't for the world," said a prudent young lady, warningly, as all examined the box and its contents.

"Six can do no harm, I give you my word. I take twenty before I can enjoy myself, and some people even more. I've tried many experiments, both on the sick and the well, and nothing ever happened amiss, though the demonstrations were immensely interesting," said Meredith, eating his sugar-plums with a tranquil air, which was very convincing to others.

"How shall I feel?" asked Belle, beginning on her second comfit.

"A heavenly dreaminess comes over one, in which they move as if on air. Everything is calm and lovely to them; no pain, no care, no fear of anything, and while it lasts one feels like an angel half asleep."

"But if one takes too much, how then?" said a deep voice behind the doctor.

"Hum! Well, that's not so pleasant, unless one likes phantoms, frenzies, and a touch of nightmare, which seems to last a thousand years. Ever try it, Done?" replied Meredith, turning toward the speaker, who was now leaning on his arm, and looking interested.

"Never. I'm not a good subject for experiments. Too nervous a temperament to play pranks with."

"I should say ten would be about your number. Less than that seldom affects men. Ladies go off sooner, and don't need so many. Miss St. Just, may I offer you a taste of Elysium? I owe my success to you," said the doctor, approaching her deferentially.

"To me! And how?" she asked, lifting her large eyes with a slight smile.

"I was in the depths of despair when my eye caught the title of your book, and I was saved. For I remembered that I had hasheesh in my pocket."

"Are you a lotus-eater?" she said, permitting him to lay the six charmed bonbons on the page.

"My faith, no! I use it for my patients. It is very efficacious in nervous disorders, and is getting to be quite a pet remedy with us."

"I do not want to forget the past, but to read the future. Will hasheesh help me to do that?" asked Rose, with an eager look, which made the young man flush, wondering if he bore any part in her hopes of that veiled future.

"Alas, no. I wish it could, for I, too, long to know my fate," he answered, very low, as he looked into the lovely face before him.

The soft glance changed to one of cool indifference, and Rose gently brushed the hasheesh off her book, saying, with a little gesture of dismissal:

"Then I have no desire to taste Elysium."

The white morsels dropped into the grass at her feet; but Dr. Meredith let them lie, and turning sharply, went back to sun himself in Belle's smiles.

"I've eaten all mine, and so has Evelyn. Mr. Norton will see

goblins, I know, for he has taken quantities. I'm glad of it, for he
don't believe in it, and I want to have him convinced by making a
spectacle of himself for our amusement," said Belle, in great spirits at
the new plan.

"When does the trance come on?" asked Evelyn, a shy girl
already rather alarmed at what she had done.

"About three hours after you take your dose, though the time
varies with different people. Your pulse will rise, heart beat quickly,
eyes darken and dilate, and an uplifted sensation will pervade you
generally. Then these symptoms change, and the bliss begins. I've
seen people sit or lie in one position for hours, rapt in a delicious
dream, and wake from it as tranquil as if they had not a nerve in their
bodies."

"How charming! I'll take some every time I'm worried. Let me
see. It's now four, so our trances will come about seven, and we will
devote the evening to manifestations," said Belle.

"Come, Done, try it. We are all going in for the fun. Here's your
dose," and Meredith tossed him a dozen bonbons, twisted up in a bit
of paper.

"No, thank you; I know myself too well to risk it. If you are all
going to turn hasheesh-eaters, you'll need some one to take care of
you, so I'll keep sober," tossing the little parcel back.

It fell short, and the doctor, too lazy to pick it up, let it lie,
merely saying, with a laugh:

"Well, I advise any bashful man to take hasheesh when he wants
to offer his heart to any fair lady, for it will give him the courage of a
hero, the eloquence of a poet, and the ardor of an Italian. Remember
that, gentlemen, and come to me when the crisis approaches."

"Does it conquer the pride, rouse the pity, and soften the hard
hearts of the fair sex?" asked Done.

"I dare say now is your time to settle the fact, for here are two
ladies who have imbibed, and in three hours will be in such a seraphic
state of mind that 'No' will be an impossibility to them."

"Oh, mercy on us; what *have* we done? If that's the case, I shall
shut myself up till my foolish fit is over. Rose, you haven't taken any;
I beg you to mount guard over me, and see that I don't disgrace
myself by any nonsense. Promise me you will," cried Belle, in half
real, half feigned alarm at the consequences of her prank.

"I promise," said Rose, and floated down the green path as noiselessly as a white cloud, with a curious smile on her lips.

"Don't tell any of the rest what we have done, but after tea let
us go into the grove and compare notes," said Norton, as Done
strolled away to the beach, and the voices of approaching friends
broke the Summer quiet.

At tea, the initiated glanced covertly at one another, and saw, or fancied they saw, the effects of the hasheesh, in a certain suppressed excitement of manner, and unusually brilliant eyes. Belle laughed often, a silvery ringing laugh, pleasant to hear; but when complimented on her good spirits, she looked distressed, and said she could not help her merriment; Meredith was quite calm, but rather dreamy; Evelyn was pale, and her next neighbor heard her heart beat; Norton talked incessantly, but as he talked uncommonly well, no one suspected anything. Done and Miss St. Just watched the others with interest, and were very quiet, especially Rose, who scarcely spoke, but smiled her sweetest, and looked very lovely.

The moon rose early, and the experimenters slipped away to the grove, leaving the outsiders on the lawn as usual. Some bold spirit asked Rose to sing, and she at once complied, pouring out Spanish airs in a voice that melted the hearts of her audience, so full of fiery sweetness or tragic pathos was it. Done seemed quite carried away, and lay with his face in the grass, to hide the tears that would come; till, afraid of openly disgracing himself, he started up and hurried down to the little wharf, where he sat alone, listening to the music with a countenance which plainly revealed to the stars the passion which possessed him. The sound of loud laughter from the grove, followed by entire silence, caused him to wonder what demonstrations were taking place, and half resolved to go and see. But that enchanting voice held him captive, even when a boat put off mysteriously from a point near by, and sailed away like a phantom through the twilight.

Half an hour afterward, a white figure came down the path, and Rose's voice broke in on his midsummer night's dream. The moon shone clearly now, and showed him the anxiety in her face as she said, hurriedly: "Where is Belle?"

"Gone sailing, I believe."

"How could you let her go? She was not fit to take care of herself?"

"I forgot that."

"So did I; but I promised to watch over her, and I must. Which way did they go?" demanded Rose, wrapping the white mantle about her, and running her eye over the little boats moored below.

"You will follow her?"

"Yes."

"I'll be your guide, then. They went toward the lighthouse; it is too far to row; I am at your service. Oh, say yes," cried Done, leaping into his own skiff, and offering his hand persuasively.

She hesitated an instant and looked at him. He was always pale, and the moonlight seemed to increase this pallor, but his hat-brim hid his eyes, and his voice was very quiet. A loud peal of laughter floated over the water, and, as if the sound decided her, she gave him her hand and entered the boat. Done smiled triumphantly as he shook out the sail, which caught the freshening wind, and sent the boat dancing along a path of light.

How lovely it was! All the indescribable allurements of a perfect Summer night surrounded them; balmy airs, enchanting moonlight, distant music, and, close at hand, the delicious atmosphere of love, which made itself felt in the eloquent silences that fell between them. Rose seemed to yield to the subtle charm, and leaned back on the cushioned seat, with her beautiful head uncovered, her face full of dreamy softness, and her hands lying loosely clasped before her. She seldom spoke, showed no further anxiety for Belle, and seemed to forget the object of her search, so absorbed was she in some delicious thought which wrapped her in its peace.

Done sat opposite, flushed now, restless, and excited, for his eyes glittered; the hand on the rudder shook, and his voice sounded intense and passionate, even in the utterance of the simplest words. He talked continually and with unusual brilliancy, for, though a man of many accomplishments, he was too indolent or too fastidious to exert himself, except among his peers. Rose seemed to look without seeing, to listen without hearing, and, though she smiled blissfully, the smiles were evidently not for him.

On they sailed, scarcely heeding the bank of black cloud piled up in the horizon, the rising wind, or the silence which proved their solitude. Rose moved once or twice, and lifted her hand as if to speak, but sank back mutely, and the hand fell again, as if it had not energy enough to enforce her wish. A cloud sweeping over the moon, a distant growl of thunder, and the slight gust that struck the sail, seemed to rouse her. Done was singing now like one inspired, his hat at his feet, hair in disorder, and a strangely rapturous expression in his eyes, which were fixed on her. She started, shivered, and seemed to recover herself with an effort.

"Where are they?" she asked, looking vainly for the island heights and the other boat.

"They have gone to the beach, I fancy, but we will follow." As Done leaned forward to speak, she saw his face, and shrank back with a sudden flush, for in it she read clearly what she had felt, yet doubted until now. He saw the tell-tale blush and gesture, and said impetuously: "You know it now; you cannot deceive me longer, nor daunt me with your pride! Rose, I love you, and dare tell you so tonight!"

"Not now—not here—I will not listen. Turn back, and be silent, I entreat you, Mr. Done," she said, hurriedly.

He laughed a defiant laugh, and took her hand in his, which was burning and throbbing with the rapid beat of his pulse.

"No. I *will* have my answer here, and now, and never turn back till you give it; you have been a thorny Rose, and given me many wounds. I'll be paid for my heartache with sweet words, tender looks, and frank confessions of love, for, proud as you are, you do love me, and dare not deny it."

Something in his tone terrified her; she snatched her hand away, and drew beyond his reach, trying to speak calmly, and to meet coldly the ardent glances of the eyes which were strangely darkened and dilated with uncontrollable emotion.

"You forget yourself. I shall give no answer to an avoval made in such terms. Take me home instantly," she said in a tone of command.

"Confess you love me, Rose."

"Never!"

"Ah! I'll have a kinder answer, or—" Done half rose and put out his hand to grasp and draw her to him, but the cry she uttered seemed to arrest him with a sort of shock. He dropped into his seat, passed his hand over his eyes, and shivered nervously, as he muttered in an altered tone: "I meant nothing; it's the moonlight; sit down, I'll control myself—upon my soul I will!"

"If you do not, I shall go overboard. Are you mad, sir?" cried Rose, trembling with indignation.

"Then, I shall follow you, for I *am* mad, Rose, with love— hasheesh!"

His voice sank to a whisper, but the last word thrilled along her nerves, as no sound of fear had ever done before. An instant she regarded him with a look which took in every sign of unnatural excitement, then she clasped her hands with an imploring gesture, saying, in a tone of despair:

"Why did I come! How will it end? Oh, Mark, take me home before it is too late!"

"Hush! Be calm; don't thwart me, or I may get wild again. My thoughts are not clear, but I understand you. There, take my knife, and if I forget myself, kill me. Don't go overboard; you are too beautiful to die, my Rose!"

He threw her the slender hunting-knife he wore, looked at her a moment with a far-off look, and trimmed the sail like one moving in a dream. Rose took the weapon, wrapped her cloak closely about her, and, crouching as far away as possible, kept her eye on him, with a face in which watchful terror contended with some secret trouble and bewilderment more powerful than her fear.

The boat moved round, and began to beat up against wind and tide; spray flew from her bow, the sail bent and strained in the gusts that struck it with perilous fitfulness. The moon was nearly hidden by scudding clouds, and one-half the sky was black with the gathering storm. Rose looked from threatening heavens to treacherous sea, and tried to be ready for any danger, but her calm had been sadly broken, and she could not recover it. Done sat motionless, uttering no word of encouragement, though the frequent flaws almost tore the rope from his hand, and the water often dashed over him.

"Are we in any danger?" asked Rose, at last, unable to bear the silence, for he looked like a ghostly helmsman, seen by the fitful night, pale now, wild-eyed, and speechless.

"Yes, great danger."

"I thought you were a skillful boatman."

"I am when I am myself; now I am rapidly losing the control of my will, and the strange quiet is coming over me. If I had been alone I should have given up sooner, but for your sake I kept on."

"Can't you work the boat?" asked Rose, terror-struck by the changed tone of his voice, the slow, uncertain movements of his hands.

"No; I see everything through a thick cloud; your voice sounds far away, and my desire is to lay my head down and sleep."

"Let me steer—I can, I must!" she cried, springing toward him, and laying her hand on the rudder.

He smiled, and kissed the little hand, saying, dreamily:

"You could not hold it a minute; sit by me, love; let us turn the boat again, and drift away together—anywhere, anywhere out of the world."

"Oh, Heaven, what will become of us!" and Rose wrung her hands in real despair. "Mr. Done—Mark—dear Mark, rouse yourself and listen to me. Turn, as you say, for it is certain death to go on so. Turn, and let us drift to the lighthouse; they will hear and help us. Quick, take down the sail, get out the oars, and let us try to reach there before the storm breaks."

As Rose spoke, he obeyed her like a dumb animal; love for her was stronger even than the instinct of self-preservation, and for her sake he fought against the treacherous lethargy which was swiftly overpowering him. The sail was lowered, the boat brought round, and, with little help from the ill-pulled oars, it drifted rapidly out to sea with the ebbing tide.

As she caught her breath after this dangerous manœuvre was accomplished, Rose asked, in a quiet tone, she vainly tried to render natural: "How much hasheesh did you take?"

"All that Meredith threw me. Too much; but I was possessed to do it, so I hid the roll and tried it," he answered, peering at her with a weird laugh.

"Let us talk; our safety lies in keeping awake, and I dare not let you sleep," continued Rose, dashing water on her own hot forehead with a sort of desperation.

"Say you love me; that would wake me up from my last sleep, I think. I have hoped and feared, waited and suffered so long. Be pitiful, and answer, Rose."

"I do; but I should not own it now."

So low was the soft reply, he scarcely heard it, but he felt it, and made a strong effort to break from the hateful spell that bound him. Leaning forward, he tried to read her face in a ray of moonlight breaking through the clouds; he saw a new and tender warmth in it, for all the pride was gone, and no fear marred the eloquence of those soft, Southern eyes.

"Kiss me, Rose, then I shall believe it. I feel lost in a dream, and you, so changed, so kind, may be only a fair phantom. Kiss me, love, and make it real."

As if swayed by a power more potent than her will, Rose bent to meet his lips. But the ardent pressure seemed to startle her from a momentary oblivion of everything but love. She covered up her face, and sank down, as if overwhelmed with shame, sobbing through her passionate tears.

"Ah, what am I doing? I am mad, for I, too, have taken hasheesh," she exclaimed vehemently.

What he answered she never heard, for a rattling peal of thunder drowned his voice, and then the storm broke loose. Rain fell in torrents, the wind blew fiercely, sky and sea were black as ink, and the boat tossed from wave to wave almost at their mercy.

Giving herself up for lost, Rose crept to her lover's side and clung there, conscious only that they would bide together through the perils their own folly brought them. Done's excitement was quite gone now; he sat like a statue, shielding the frail creature whom he loved, with a smile on his face, which looked awfully emotionless when the lightning gave her glimpses of its white immobility.

Drenched, exhausted, and half senseless with danger, fear, and exposure, Rose saw at last a welcome glimmer through the gloom, and roused herself to cry for help.

"Mark, wake and help me! Shout, for God's sake—shout and call them, for we are lost if we drift by!" she cried, lifting his head from his breast, and forcing him to see the brilliant beacons streaming far across the troubled waters.

He understood her, and, springing up, uttered shout after shout, like one demented. Fortunately, the storm had lulled a little; the lighthouse keeper heard and answered. Rose seized the helm, Done the oars, and, with one frantic effort, guided the boat into quieter waters, where it was met by the keeper, who towed it to the rocky nook which served as a harbor.

The moment a strong, steady face met her eyes, and a gruff, cheery voice hailed her, Rose gave way, and was carried up to the house, looking more like a beautiful drowned Ophelia than a living woman.

"Here, Sally, see to the poor thing; she's had a rough time on't. I'll take care of her sweetheart—and a nice job I'll have, I reckon, for if he ain't mad or drunk, he's had a stroke of lightnin', and looks as if he wouldn't get his hearin' in a hurry," said the old man, as he housed his unexpected guests, and stood staring at Done, who looked about him like one dazed. "You jest turn in yonder and sleep it off, mate. We'll see to the lady, and right your boat in the morning," the old man added.

"Be kind to Rose. I frightened her. I'll not forget you. Yes, let me sleep and get over this cursed folly as soon as possible," muttered this strange visitor.

Done threw himself down on the rough couch and tried to sleep, but every nerve was over-strained, every pulse beating like a trip-hammer, and everything about him was intensified and exaggerated with awful power. The thunder-shower seemed a wild hurricane, the quaint room a wilderness peopled with tormenting phantoms, and all the events of his life passed before him in an endless procession, which nearly maddened him. The old man looked weird and gigantic, his own voice sounded shrill and discordant, and the ceaseless murmur of Rose's incoherent wanderings haunted him like parts of a grotesque but dreadful dream.

All night he lay motionless, with staring eyes, feverish lips, and a mind on the rack, for the delicate machinery which had been tampered with, revenged the wrong by torturing the foolish experimenter. All night Rose wept and sung, talked and cried for help in a piteous state of nervous excitement, for with her the trance came first, and the after-agitation was increased by the events of the evening. She slept at last, lulled by the old woman's motherly care, and Done was spared one tormenting fear, for he dreaded the consequences of this folly on her, more than upon himself.

As day dawned he rose, haggard and faint, and staggered out. At the door he met the keeper, who stopped him to report that the boat was in order, and a fair day coming. Seeing doubt and perplexity in the old man's eye, Done told him the truth, and added that he was going to the beach for a plunge, hoping by that simple tonic to restore his unstrung nerves.

He came back feeling like himself again, except for a dull headache, and a heavy sense of remorse weighing on his spirits, for he distinctly recollected all the events of the night. The old woman made him eat and drink, and in an hour he felt ready for the homeward trip.

Rose slept late, and when she woke, soon recovered herself, for her dose had been a small one. When she had breakfasted and made a hasty toilet, she professed herself anxious to return at once. She dreaded, yet longed, to see Done, and when the time came, armed herself with pride, feeling all a woman's shame at what had passed, and resolving to feign forgetfulness of the incidents of the previous night.

Pale and cold as a statue she met him; but the moment he began to say, humbly, "Forgive me, Rose," she silenced him with an imperious gesture and the command:

"Don't speak of it; I only remember that it was very horrible, and wish to forget it all as soon as possible."

"All, Rose?" he asked, significantly.

"Yes, *all!* No one would care to recall the follies of a hasheesh dream," she answered, turning hastily to hide the scarlet flush that would rise, and the eyes that would fall before his own.

"*I* never can forget, but I will be silent if you bid me."

"I do. Let us go. What will they think at the island? Mr. Done, give me your promise to tell no one, now or ever, that I tried that dangerous experiment. I will guard your secret also."

She spoke eagerly, and looked up imploringly.

"I promise"; and he gave her his hand, holding her own with a wistful glance, till she drew it away, and begged him to take her home.

Leaving hearty thanks and a generous token of their gratitude, they sailed away with a fair wind, finding in the freshness of the morning a speedy cure for tired bodies and excited minds.

They said little, but it was impossible for Rose to preserve her coldness. The memory of the past night broke down her pride, and Done's tender glances touched her heart. She half hid her face behind her hand, and tried to compose herself for the scene to come, for, as she approached the island, she saw Belle and her party waiting for them on the shore.

"Oh, Mr. Done, screen me from their eyes and questions as much as you can! I'm so worn out and nervous, I shall betray myself. You will help me?" and she turned to him with a confiding look, strangely at variance with her usual calm self-possession.

"I'll shield you with my life, if you will tell me why you took the hasheesh," he said, bent on knowing his fate.

"I hoped it would make me soft and lovable, like other women. I'm tired of being a lonely statue," she faltered, as if the truth was wrung from her by a power stronger than her will.

"And I took it to gain courage to tell my love. Rose, we have been near death together, let us share life together, and neither of us be any more lonely or afraid?"

He stretched his hand to her with his heart in his face, and she gave him hers with a look of tender submission, as he said, ardently:

"Heaven bless hasheesh, if its dreams end like this!"

Henry James
(1843-1916)

IN the course of the same illustrious career that produced *Portrait of a Lady* (1879), *The Aspern Papers* (1888), *The Spoils of Poynton* (1896), *The Wings of the Dove* (1902), *The Ambassadors* (1903), and *The Golden Bowl* (1904), Henry James also wrote eighteen ghostly tales, including the well-known *Turn of the Screw* (1898). In that short novel, an unnamed governess, daughter of a poor and eccentric country vicar, agrees to take care of the wards of the dashing "master in Harley Street," to whom she is very much attracted. She decides that the children, Miles and Flora, are haunted by the ghosts of the former governess, Miss Jessel, and the valet, Peter Quint; and she resolves, for the salvation of the children's souls, to challenge the ghosts. Since she herself narrates the story, it is impossible to determine whether the ghosts are real apparitions, like Defoe's Mrs. Veal, or figments of her rich imagination and starved sexuality. James worked to involve the reader in the creative act by means of what he called his "process of *adumbration*"; that is, he refused to make clear the nature of the evil he was describing.

Through the same narrative device, "The Ghostly Rental" calls upon the reader's powers to analyze and understand, or rest content with mystery. At the end of the story, we cannot tell for certain what we are to believe about the reality of ghosts. The young theology student who narrates the tale, however well-intentioned, is somewhat unreliable: he is self-congratulating about his cool fair-mindedness, oblivious to the humor of his "dying of curiosity," and heedless of Captain Diamond's dying request that he treat his daughter politely. Despite the narrator's "cheerful views of the supernatural," we have some reason to believe that the captain's ghost would haunt him—for his "violence"—as well as haunting his own daughter, for the trick that "wears him out." Whatever we are to make of the ending, however, we do agree with the narrator's early judgment that the house is "spiritually blighted," if only because Captain Diamond's guilt has blinded him to any but an occult explanation of events. Ironically, the captain's daughter, ghostly inmate of the house, becomes guiltier and more haunted than he. James's psychological definition of what a haunted house is throws new light on other ghost stories, for example Shirley Jackson's *The Haunting of Hill House* (1959).

At the end of *The Turn of the Screw*, the reader is left wondering, as the governess herself wonders in the story, "Was there a 'secret' at Bly—a mystery of Udolpho or an insane, an unmentionable relative kept in unsuspected confinement?" These allusions to Ann Radcliffe's and Charlotte Brontë's novels establish the Gothic context of *The Turn of the Screw*. Similarly, in "The Ghostly Rental," the narrator's description of himself as a figure from *The Arabian Nights* places the story firmly in the Gothic tradition. The mention of E. T. A. Hoffmann, the German romancer who influenced Poe and provided the starting point for Freud's famous essay on "The 'Uncanny' " (1919), likewise calls attention to the background of the tale. Captain Diamond's fixed and "glittering" eyes summon up the picture of Coleridge's Ancient Mariner, who is also compelled, in spite of himself, to rehearse his misfortunes. The captain's "grotesqueness," and that of related images like the gig, reinforce these Gothic associations. James was reading Baudelaire at the time he wrote "The Ghostly Rental." The influence of Poe's translator and promoter may account for echoes from such stories as "The Fall of the House of Usher" (1839). Certainly the ending, which shows the interconnectedness of house and inhabitants, proves James's interest in the kind of psychological issue that Poe had raised.

Most importantly, Miss Deborah's reference to Blue Beard, in her warning to the narrator, establishes a connection with fairy tales. In fact, as Leon Edel points out in his introduction to *The Ghostly Tales of Henry James* (1948), "For Henry James the ghostly narrative could be neither clinical nor analytic; it had to have all the richness of life and all the terror, wonder, excitement, curiosity, the mind is capable of evoking; in a word the ghostly tale was 'the most possible form of the fairy tale.' " James saw the ghost story as an opportunity to enjoy all the "wonder" of the fairy tale without its accompanying "silliness." Like Anne Sexton, he was interested in exploring Gothic variations on themes and motifs usually associated with children's literature.

The details of the setting in "The Ghostly Rental" derive from James's brief attendance at Harvard Law School in 1862–1863. His personal reasons for writing such stories as this may include some terrifying psychological experiences endured by his father, the first Henry James, by his sister Alice, and by his brother, the well-known psychologist William James. His relatives tended to interpret these experiences as confrontations with the occult. Their son and brother, who had no recorded ghostly encounters of his own, translated these tendencies into literature.

The Ghostly Rental (1876)

I was in my twenty-second year, and I had just left college. I was at liberty to choose my career, and I chose it with much promptness. I afterward renounced it, in truth, with equal ardor, but I have never regretted those two youthful years of perplexed and excited, but also of agreeable and fruitful experiment. I had a taste for theology, and during my college term I had been an admiring reader of Dr. Channing. This was theology of a grateful and succulent savor; it seemed to offer one the rose of faith delightfully stripped of its thorns. And then (for I rather think this had something to do with it), I had taken a fancy to the old Divinity School. I have always had an eye to the back scene in the human drama, and it seemed to me that I might play my part with a fair chance of applause (from myself at least), in that detached and tranquil home of mild casuistry, with its respectable avenue on one side, and its prospect of green fields and contact with acres of woodland on the other. Cambridge, for the lovers of woods and fields, has changed for the worse since those days, and the precinct in question has forfeited much of its mingled pastoral and scholastic quietude. It was then a College-hall in the woods—a charming mixture. What it is now has nothing to do with my story; and I have no doubt that there are still doctrine-haunted young seniors who, as they stroll near it in the summer dusk, promise themselves, later, to taste of its fine leisurely quality. For myself, I was not disappointed. I established myself in a great square, low-browed room, with deep window-benches; I hung prints from Overbeck and Ary Scheffer on the walls; I arranged my books, with great refinement of classification, in the alcoves beside the high chimney-shelf, and I began to read Plotinus and St. Augustine. Among my companions were two or three men of ability and of good fellowship, with whom I occasionally brewed a fireside bowl; and with adventurous reading, deep discourse, potations conscientiously shallow, and long country walks, my initiation into the clerical mystery progressed agreeably enough.

With one of my comrades I formed an especial friendship, and we passed a great deal of time together. Unfortunately he had a chronic weakness of one of his knees, which compelled him to lead a very sedentary life, and as I was a methodical pedestrian, this made some difference in our habits. I used often to stretch away for my daily ramble, with no companion but the stick in my hand or the book in my pocket. But in the use of my legs and the sense of unstinted open air, I have always found company enough. I should, perhaps, add that in the enjoyment of a very sharp pair of eyes, I found something of a social pleasure. My eyes and I were on excellent terms; they were indefatigable observers of all wayside incidents, and so long as they were amused I was contented. It is, indeed, owing to their inquisitive habits that I came into possession of this remarkable story. Much of the country about the old College town is pretty now, but it was prettier thirty years ago. That multitudinous eruption of domiciliary pasteboard which now graces the landscape, in the direction of the low, blue Waltham Hills, had not yet taken place; there were no genteel cottages to put the shabby meadows and scrubby orchards to shame—a juxtaposition by which, in later years, neither element of the contrast has gained. Certain crooked cross-roads, then, as I remember them, were more deeply and naturally rural, and the solitary dwellings on the long grassy slopes beside them, under the tall, customary elm that curved its foliage in mid-air like the outward dropping ears of a girdled wheat-sheaf, sat with their shingled hoods well pulled down on their ears, and no prescience whatever of the fashion of French roofs—weather-wrinkled old peasant women, as you might call them, quietly wearing the native coif, and never dreaming of mounting bonnets, and indecently exposing their venerable brows. That winter was what is called an "open" one; there was much cold, but little snow; the roads were firm and free, and I was rarely compelled by the weather to forego my exercise. One gray December afternoon I had sought it in the direction of the adjacent town of Medford, and I was retracing my steps at an even pace, and watching the pale, cold tints—the transparent amber and faded rose-color—which curtained, in wintry fashion, the western sky, and reminded me of a sceptical smile on the lips of a beautiful woman. I came, as dusk was falling, to a narrow road which I had never traversed and which I imagined offered me a short cut homeward. I was about three miles away; I was late, and would have been thankful to make them two. I diverged, walked some ten minutes, and then perceived that the road had a very unfrequented air. The wheel-ruts looked old; the stillness seemed peculiarly sensible. And yet down the road stood a house, so that it must in some degree have been a thoroughfare. On one side was a high, natural embankment, on the top of which was perched an apple-orchard, whose tangled boughs made a stretch of coarse black lace-work, hung across the coldly rosy west. In a short time I came to the house, and I immediately found myself interested in it. I stopped in front of it gazing hard, I hardly knew why, but with a vague mixture of curiosity and timidity. It was a house like most of the houses thereabouts, except that it was decidedly a handsome specimen of its class. It stood on a grassy slope, it had its tall, impartially drooping elm beside it, and its old black well-cover at its shoulder. But it was of very large proportions, and it had a striking look of solidity and stoutness of timber. It had lived to a good old age, too, for the wood-work on its door-way and under its eaves, carefully and abundantly carved, referred it to the middle, at the latest, of the last century. All this had once been painted white, but the broad back of time, leaning against the door-posts for a hundred years, had laid bare the grain of the wood. Behind the house stretched an orchard of apple-trees, more gnarled and fantastic than usual, and wearing, in the deepening dusk, a blighted and exhausted aspect. All the windows of the house had rusty shutters, without slats, and these were closely drawn. There was no sign of life about it; it looked blank, bare and vacant, and yet, as I lingered near it, it seemed to have a familiar meaning—an audible eloquence. I have always thought of the impression made upon me at first sight, by that gray colonial dwelling, as a proof that induction may sometimes be near akin to divination; for after all, there was nothing on the face of the matter to warrant the very serious induction that I made. I fell back and crossed the road. The last red light of the sunset disengaged itself, as it was about to vanish, and rested faintly for a moment on the time-silvered front of the old house. It touched, with perfect regularity, the series of small panes in the fan-shaped window above the door, and twinkled there fantastically. Then it died away, and left the place more intensely somber. At this moment, I said to myself with the accent of profound conviction—"The house is simply haunted!"

Somehow, immediately, I believed it, and so long as I was not shut up inside, the idea gave me pleasure. It was implied in the aspect of the house, and it explained it. Half an hour before, if I had been asked, I would have said, as befitted a young man who was explicitly cultivating cheerful views of the supernatural, that there were no such things as haunted houses. But the dwelling before me gave a vivid meaning to the empty words; it had been spiritually blighted.

The longer I looked at it, the intenser seemed the secret that it held. I walked all round it, I tried to peep here and there, through a crevice in the shutters, and I took a puerile satisfaction in laying my hand on the door-knob and gently turning it. If the door had yielded, would I have gone in?—would I have penetrated the dusty stillness? My audacity, fortunately, was not put to the test. The portal was admirably solid, and I was unable even to shake it. At last I turned away, casting many looks behind me. I pursued my way, and, after a longer walk than I had bargained for, reached the high-road. At a certain distance below the point at which the long lane I have mentioned entered it, stood a comfortable, tidy dwelling, which might have offered itself as the model of the house which is in no sense haunted—which has no sinister secrets, and knows nothing but blooming prosperity. Its clean white paint stared placidly through the dusk, and its vine-covered porch had been dressed in straw for the winter. An old, one-horse chaise, freighted with two departing visitors, was leaving the door, and through the undraped windows, I saw the lamp-lit sitting-room, and the table spread with the early "tea," which had been improvised for the comfort of the guests. The mistress of the house had come to the gate with her friends; she lingered there after the chaise had wheeled creakingly away, half to watch them down the road, and half to give me, as I passed in the twilight, a questioning look. She was a comely, quick young woman, with a sharp, dark eye, and I ventured to stop and speak to her.

"That house down that side-road," I said, "about a mile from here—the only one—can you tell me whom it belongs to?"

She stared at me a moment, and, I thought, colored a little. "Our folks never go down that road," she said, briefly.

"But it's a short way to Medford," I answered.

She gave a little toss of her head. "Perhaps it would turn out a long way. At any rate, we don't use it."

This was interesting. A thrifty Yankee household must have good reasons for this scorn of time-saving processes. "But you know the house, at least?" I said.

"Well, I have seen it."

"And to whom does it belong?"

She gave a little laugh and looked away, as if she were aware that, to a stranger, her words might seem to savor of agricultural superstition. "I guess it belongs to them that are in it."

"But is there any one in it? It is completely closed."

"That makes no difference. They never come out, and no one ever goes in." And she turned away.

But I laid my hand on her arm, respectfully. "You mean," I said, "that the house is haunted?"

She drew herself away, colored, raised her finger to her lips, and hurried into the house, where, in a moment, the curtains were dropped over the windows.

For several days, I thought repeatedly of this little adventure, but I took some satisfaction in keeping it to myself. If the house was not haunted, it was useless to expose my imaginative whims, and if it was, it was agreeable to drain the cup of horror without assistance. I determined, of course, to pass that way again; and a week later—it was the last day of the year—I retraced my steps. I approached the house from the opposite direction, and found myself before it at about the same hour as before. The light was failing, the sky low and gray; the wind wailed along the hard, bare ground, and made slow eddies of the frost-blackened leaves. The melancholy mansion stood there, seeming to gather the winter twilight around it, and mask itself in it, inscrutably. I hardly knew on what errand I had come, but I had a vague feeling that if this time the door-knob were to turn and the door to open, I should take my heart in my hands, and let them close behind me. Who were the mysterious tenants to whom the good woman at the corner had alluded? What had been seen or heard— what was related? The door was as stubborn as before, and my impertinent fumblings with the latch caused no upper window to be thrown open, nor any strange, pale face to be thrust out. I ventured even to raise the rusty knocker and give it half-a-dozen raps, but they made a flat, dead sound, and aroused no echo. Familiarity breeds contempt; I don't know what I should have done next, if, in the distance, up the road (the same one I had followed), I had not seen a solitary figure advancing. I was unwilling to be observed hanging about this ill-famed dwelling, and I sought refuge among the dense shadows of a grove of pines near by, where I might peep forth, and yet remain invisible. Presently, the new-comer drew near, and I perceived that he was making straight for the house. He was a little, old man, the most striking feature of whose appearance was a voluminous cloak, of a sort of military cut. He carried a walking-stick, and advanced in a slow, painful, somewhat hobbling fashion, but with an air of extreme resolution. He turned off from the road, and followed the vague wheel-track, and within a few yards of the house he paused. He looked up at it, fixedly and searchingly, as if he were counting the windows, or noting certain familiar marks. Then he took off his hat, and bent over slowly and solemnly, as if he were performing an obeisance. As he stood uncovered, I had a good look at him. He was, as I have said, a diminutive old man, but it would have been hard to decide whether he belonged to this world or to the other. His head reminded me, vaguely, of the portraits of Andrew Jackson. He had a crop of grizzled hair, as stiff as a brush, a lean, pale, smooth-shaven face, and an eye of intense brilliancy, surmounted with thick brows, which had remained perfectly black. His face, as well as his cloak, seemed to belong to an old soldier; he looked like a retired military man of a modest rank; but he struck me as exceeding the classic privilege of even such a personage to be eccentric and grotesque. When he had finished his salute, he advanced to the door, fumbled in the folds of his cloak, which hung down much further in front than behind, and produced a key. This he slowly and carefully inserted into the lock, and then, apparently, he turned it. But the door did not immediately open; first he bent his head, turned his ear, and stood listening, and then he looked up and down the road. Satisfied or re-assured, he applied his aged shoulder to one of the deep-set panels, and pressed a moment. The door yielded—opening into perfect darkness. He stopped again on the threshold, and again removed his hat and made his bow. Then he went in, and carefully closed the door behind him.

Who in the world was he, and what was his errand? He might have been a figure out of one of Hoffmann's tales. Was he vision or a reality—an inmate of the house, or a familiar, friendly visitor? What had been the meaning, in either case, of his mystic genuflexions, and how did he propose to proceed, in that inner darkness? I emerged from my retirement, and observed narrowly, several of the windows. In each of them, at an interval, a ray of light became visible in the chink between the two leaves of the shutters. Evidently, he was lighting up; was he going to give a party—a ghostly revel? My curiosity grew intense, but I was quite at a loss how to satisfy it. For a moment I thought of rapping peremptorily at the door; but I dismissed this idea as unmannerly, and calculated to break the spell, if spell there was. I walked round the house and tried, without violence, to open one of the lower windows. It resisted, but I had better fortune, in a moment, with another. There was a risk, certainly, in the trick I was playing—a risk of being seen from within, or (worse) seeing, myself, something that I should repent of seeing. But curiosity, as I say, had become an inspiration, and the risk was highly agreeable. Through the parting of the shutters I looked into a lighted room—a room lighted by two candles in old brass flambeaux, placed upon the mantel-shelf. It was apparently a sort of back parlor, and it had retained all its furniture. This was of a homely, old-fashioned pattern, and consisted of hair-cloth chairs and sofas, spare mahogany tables, and framed samplers hung upon the walls. But although the room was furnished, it had a strangely uninhabited look; the tables and chairs were in rigid positions, and no small, familiar objects were visible. I could not see everything, and I could only guess at the existence, on my right, of a large folding-door. It was apparently open, and the light of the neighboring room passed through it. I waited for some time, but the room remained empty. At last I became conscious that a large shadow was projected upon the wall opposite the folding-door—the shadow, evidently, of a figure in the adjoining room. It was tall and grotesque, and seemed to represent a person sitting perfectly motionless, in profile. I thought I recognized the perpendicular bristles and far-arching nose of my little old man. There was a strange fixedness in his posture; he appeared to be seated, and looking intently at something. I watched the shadow a long time, but it never stirred. At last, however, just as my patience began to ebb, it moved slowly, rose to the ceiling, and became indistinct. I don't know what I should have seen next, but by an irresistible impulse, I closed the shutter. Was it delicacy?—was it pusillanimity? I can hardly say. I lingered, nevertheless, near the house, hoping that my friend would re-appear. I was not disappointed; for he at last emerged, looking just as when he had gone in, and taking his leave in the same ceremonious fashion. (The lights, I had already observed, had disappeared from the crevice of each of the windows.) He faced about before the door, took off his hat, and made an obsequious bow. As he turned away I had a hundred minds to speak to him, but I let him depart in peace. This, I may say, was pure delicacy;—you will answer, perhaps, that it came too late. It seemed to me that he had a right to resent my observation; though my own right to exercise it (if ghosts were in the question) struck me as equally positive. I continued to watch him as he hobbled softly down the bank, and along the lonely road. Then I musingly retreated in the opposite direction. I was tempted to follow him, at a distance, to see what became of him; but this, too, seemed indelicate; and I confess, moreover, that I felt the inclination to coquet a little, as it were, with my discovery—to pull apart the petals of the flower one by one.

I continued to smell the flower, from time to time, for its oddity of perfume had fascinated me. I passed by the house on the cross-road again, but never encountered the old man in the cloak or any other way-farer. It seemed to keep observers at a distance, and I was careful not to gossip about it: one inquirer, I said to myself, may edge his way into the secret, but there is no room for two. At the same time, of course, I would have been thankful for any chance side-light that might fall across the matter—though I could not well see whence it was to come. I hoped to meet the old man in the cloak elsewhere, but as the days passed by without his re-appearing, I ceased to expect it. And yet I reflected that he probably lived in that neighborhood, inasmuch as he had made his pilgrimage to the vacant house on foot. If he had come from a distance, he would have been sure to arrive in some old deep-hooded gig with yellow wheels—a vehicle as venerably grotesque as himself. One day I took a stroll in Mount Auburn cemetery—an institution at that period in its infancy, and full of a sylvan charm which it has now completely forfeited. It contained more maple and birch than willow and cypress, and the sleepers had ample elbow room. It was not a city of the dead, but at the most a village, and a meditative pedestrian might stroll there without too importunate reminder of the grotesque side of our claims to posthumous consideration. I had come out to enjoy the first fore-taste of Spring—one of those mild days of late winter, when the torpid earth seems to draw the first long breath that marks the rup-ture of the spell of sleep. The sun was veiled in haze, and yet warm, and the frost was oozing from its deepest lurking-places. I had been treading for half an hour the winding ways of the cemetery, when suddenly I perceived a familiar figure seated on a bench against a

southward-facing evergreen hedge. I call the figure familiar, because I
had seen it often in memory and in fancy; in fact, I had beheld it but
once. Its back was turned to me, but it wore a voluminous cloak,
which there was no mistaking. Here, at last, was my fellow-visitor at
the haunted house, and here was my chance, if I wished to approach
him! I made a circuit, and came toward him from in front. He saw
me, at the end of the alley, and sat motionless, with his hands on
the head of his stick, watching me from under his black eyebrows as I
drew near. At a distance these black eyebrows looked formidable;
they were the only thing I saw in his face. But on a closer view I was
re-assured, simply because I immediately felt that no man could really be as fantastically fierce as this poor old gentleman looked. His
face was a kind of caricature of martial truculence. I stopped in front
of him, and respectfully asked leave to sit and rest upon his bench.
He granted it with a silent gesture, of much dignity, and I placed
myself beside him. In this position I was able, covertly, to observe
him. He was quite as much an oddity in the morning sunshine, as
he had been in the dubious twilight. The lines in his face were as rigid
as if they had been hacked out of a block by a clumsy wood-carver.
His eyes were flamboyant, his nose terrific, his mouth implacable.
And yet, after awhile, when he slowly turned and looked at me,
fixedly, I perceived that in spite of this portentous mask, he was a
very mild old man. I was sure he even would have been glad to smile,
but, evidently, his facial muscles were too stiff—they had taken a
different fold, once for all. I wondered whether he was demented, but
I dismissed the idea; the fixed glitter in his eye was not that of
insanity. What his face really expressed was deep and simple sadness;
his heart perhaps was broken, but his brain was intact. His dress was
shabby but neat, and his old blue cloak had known half a century's
brushing.

I hastened to make some observation upon the exceptional softness of the day, and he answered me in a gentle, mellow voice, which
it was almost startling to hear proceed from such bellicose lips.

"This is a very comfortable place," he presently added.

"I am fond of walking in graveyards," I rejoined deliberately;
flattering myself that I had struck a vein that might lead to something.

I was encouraged; he turned and fixed me with his duskily glowing eyes. Then very gravely,—"Walking, yes. Take all your exercise
now. Some day you will have to settle down in a graveyard in a fixed
position."

"Very true," said I. "But you know there are some people who
are said to take exercise even after that day."

He had been looking at me still; at this he looked away.

"You don't understand?" I said, gently.

He continued to gaze straight before him.

"Some people, you know, walk about after death," I went on.

At last he turned, and looked at me more portentously than ever. "You don't believe that," he said simply.

"How do you know I don't?"

"Because you are young and foolish." This was said without acerbity—even kindly; but in the tone of an old man whose consciousness of his own heavy experience made everything else seem light.

"I am certainly young," I answered; "but I don't think that, on the whole, I am foolish. But say I don't believe in ghosts—most people would be on my side."

"Most people are fools!" said the old man.

I let the question rest, and talked of other things. My companion seemed on his guard, he eyed me defiantly, and made brief answers to my remarks; but I nevertheless gathered an impression that our meeting was an agreeable thing to him, and even a social incident of some importance. He was evidently a lonely creature, and his opportunities for gossip were rare. He had had troubles, and they had detached him from the world, and driven him back upon himself; but the social chord in his antiquated soul was not entirely broken, and I was sure he was gratified to find that it could still feebly resound. At last, he began to ask questions himself; he inquired whether I was a student.

"I am a student of divinity," I answered.

"Of divinity?"

"Of theology. I am studying for the ministry."

At this he eyed me with peculiar intensity—after which his gaze wandered away again. "There are certain things you ought to know, then," he said at last.

"I have a great desire for knowledge," I answered. "What things do you mean?"

He looked at me again awhile, but without heeding my question. "I like your appearance," he said. "You seem to me a sober lad."

"Oh, I am perfectly sober!" I exclaimed—yet departing for a moment from my soberness.

"I think you are fair-minded," he went on.

"I don't any longer strike you as foolish, then?" I asked.

"I stick to what I said about people who deny the power of departed spirits to return. They *are* fools!" And he rapped fiercely with his staff on the earth.

I hesitated a moment, and then, abruptly, "You have seen a ghost!" I said.

He appeared not at all startled.

"You are right, sir!" he answered with great dignity. "With me it's not a matter of cold theory—I have not had to pry into old books to learn what to believe. *I know!* With these eyes I have beheld the departed spirit standing before me as near as you are!" And his eyes, as he spoke, certainly looked as if they had rested upon strange things.

I was irresistibly impressed—I was touched with credulity.

"And was it very terrible?" I asked.

"I am an old soldier—I am not afraid!"

"When was it?—where was it?" I asked.

He looked at me mistrustfully, and I saw that I was going too fast.

"Excuse me from going into particulars," he said. "I am not at liberty to speak more fully. I have told you so much, because I cannot bear to hear this subject spoken of lightly. Remember in future, that you have seen a very honest old man who told you—on his honor—that he had seen a ghost!" And he got up, as if he thought he had said enough. Reserve, shyness, pride, the fear of being laughed at, the memory, possibly, of former strokes of sarcasm—all this, on one side, had its weight with him; but I suspected that on the other, his tongue was loosened by the garrulity of old age, the sense of solitude, and the need of sympathy—and perhaps, also, by the friendliness which he had been so good as to express toward myself. Evidently it would be unwise to press him, but I hoped to see him again.

"To give greater weight to my words," he added, "let me mention my name—Captain Diamond, sir. I have seen service."

"I hope I may have the pleasure of meeting you again," I said.

"The same to you, sir!" And brandishing his stick portentously—though with the friendliest intentions—he marched stiffly away.

I asked two or three persons—selected with discretion—whether they knew anything about Captain Diamond, but they were quite unable to enlighten me. At last, suddenly, I smote my forehead, and, dubbing myself a dolt, remembered that I was neglecting a source of information to which I had never applied in vain. The excellent person at whose table I habitually dined, and who dispensed hospitality to students at so much a week, had a sister as good as herself, and of conversational powers more varied. This sister, who was known as Miss Deborah, was an old maid in all the force of the term. She was deformed, and she never went out of the house; she sat all day at the window, between a bird-cage and a flower-pot, stitching small linen articles—mysterious bands and frills. She wielded, I was assured, an exquisite needle, and her work was highly prized. In spite of her deformity and her confinement, she had a little, fresh, round face, and an imperturbable serenity of spirit. She had also a very quick little wit of her own, she was extremely observant, and she had a high relish for a friendly chat. Nothing pleased her so much as to have you— especially, I think, if you were a young divinity student—move your chair near her sunny window, and settle yourself for twenty minutes' "talk." "Well, sir," she used always to say "what is the latest monstrosity in Biblical criticism?"—for she used to pretend to be horrified at the rationalistic tendency of the age. But she was an inexorable little philosopher, and I am convinced that she was a keener rationalist than any of us, and that, if she had chosen, she could have propounded questions that would have made the boldest of us wince. Her window commanded the whole town—or rather, the whole country. Knowledge came to her as she sat singing, with her little, cracked voice, in her low rocking-chair. She was the first to learn everything, and the last to forget it. She had the town gossip at her fingers' ends, and she knew everything about people she had never seen. When I asked her how she had acquired her learning, she said simply—"Oh, I observe!" "Observe closely enough," she once said, "and it doesn't matter where you are. You may be in a pitch-dark closet. All you want is something to start with; one thing leads to another, and all things are mixed up. Shut me up in a dark closet and I will observe after a while, that some places in it are darker than others. After that (give me time), and I will tell you what the President of the United States is going to have for dinner." Once I paid her a compliment. "Your observation," I said, "is as fine as your needle, and your statements are as true as your stitches."

Of course Miss Deborah had heard of Captain Diamond. He had been much talked about many years before, but he had survived the scandal that attached to his name.

"What was the scandal?" I asked.

"He killed his daughter."

"Killed her?" I cried; "how so?"

"Oh, not with a pistol, or a dagger, or a dose of arsenic! With his tongue. Talk of women's tongues! He cursed her—with some horrible oath—and she died!"

"What had she done?"

"She had received a visit from a young man who loved her, and whom he had forbidden the house."

"The house," I said—"ah yes! The house is out in the country, two or three miles from here, on a lonely cross-road."

Miss Deborah looked sharply at me, as she bit her thread.

"Ah, you know about the house?" she said.

"A little," I answered; "I have seen it. But I want you to tell me more."

But here Miss Deborah betrayed an incommunicativeness which was most unusual.

"You wouldn't call me superstitious, would you?" she asked.

"You?—you are the quintessence of pure reason."

"Well, every thread has its rotten place, and every needle its grain of rust. I would rather not talk about that house."

"You have no idea how you excite my curiosity!" I said.

"I can feel for you. But it would make me very nervous."

"What harm can come to you?" I asked.

"Some harm came to a friend of mine." And Miss Deborah gave a very positive nod.

"What had your friend done?"

"She had told me Captain Diamond's secret, which he had told her with a mighty mystery. She had been an old flame of his, and he took her into his confidence. He bade her tell no one, and assured her that if she did, something dreadful would happen to her."

"And what happened to her?"

"She died."

"Oh, we are all mortal!" I said. "Had she given him a promise?"

"She had not taken it seriously, she had not believed him. She repeated the story to me, and three days afterward, she was taken with inflammation of the lungs. A month afterward, here where I sit now, I was stitching her grave-clothes. Since then, I have never mentioned what she told me."

"Was it very strange?"

"It was strange, but it was ridiculous too. It is a thing to make you shudder and to make you laugh, both. But you can't worry it out of me. I am sure that if I were to tell you, I should immediately break a needle in my finger, and die the next week of lock-jaw."

I retired, and urged Miss Deborah no further; but every two or three days, after dinner, I came and sat down by her rocking chair. I made no further allusion to Captain Diamond; I sat silent, clipping tape with her scissors. At last, one day, she told me I was looking poorly. I was pale.

"I am dying of curiosity," I said. "I have lost my appetite. I have eaten no dinner."

"Remember Bluebeard's wife!" said Miss Deborah.

"One may as well perish by the sword as by famine!" I answered.

Still she said nothing, and at last I rose with a melo-dramatic sigh and departed. As I reached the door she called me and pointed to the chair I had vacated. "I never was hard-hearted," she said. "Sit down, and if we are to perish, may we at least perish together." And then, in very few words, she communicated what she knew of Captain

Diamond's secret. "He was a very high-tempered old man, and
though he was very fond of his daughter, his will was law. He had
picked out a husband for her, and given her due notice. Her mother
was dead, and they lived alone together. The house had been Mrs.
Diamond's own marriage portion; the Captain, I believe, hadn't a
penny. After his marriage they had come to live there, and he had
begun to work the farm. The poor girl's lover was a young man with
whiskers from Boston. The Captain came in one evening and found
them together; he collared the young man, and hurled a terrible curse
at the poor girl. The young man cried that she was his wife, and he
asked her if it was true. She said, No! Thereupon Captain Diamond,
his fury growing fiercer, repeated his imprecation, ordered her out of
the house, and disowned her forever. She swooned away, but her
father went raging off and left her. Several hours later, he came back
and found the house empty. On the table was a note from the young
man telling him that he had killed his daughter, repeating the assurance that she was his own wife, and declaring that he himself claimed
the sole right to commit her remains to earth. He had carried the
body away in a gig! Captain Diamond wrote him a dreadful note in
answer, saying that he didn't believe his daughter was dead, but that,
whether or no, she was dead to him. A week later, in the middle of
the night, he saw her ghost. Then, I suppose, he was convinced. The
ghost re-appeared several times, and finally began regularly to haunt
the house. It made the old man very uncomfortable, for little by little
his passion had passed away, and he was given up to grief. He determined at last to leave the place, and tried to sell it or rent it; but
meanwhile the story had gone abroad, the ghost had been seen by
other persons, the house had a bad name, and it was impossible to
dispose of it. With the farm, it was the old man's only property, and
his only means of subsistence; if he could neither live in it nor rent it
he was beggared. But the ghost had no mercy, as he had had none.
He struggled for six months, and at last he broke down. He put on his
old blue cloak and took up his staff, and prepared to wander away
and beg his bread. Then the ghost relented, and proposed a compromise. 'Leave the house to me!' it said; 'I have marked it for my
own. Go off and live elsewhere. But to enable you to live, I will be
your tenant, since you can find no other. I will hire the house of you
and pay you a certain rent.' And the ghost named a sum. The old
man consented, and he goes every quarter to collect his rent!"

I laughed at this recital, but I confess I shuddered too, for my
own observation had exactly confirmed it. Had I not been witness of
one of the Captain's quarterly visits, had I not all but seen him sit
watching his spectral tenant count out the rent-money, and when he
trudged away in the dark, had he not a little bag of strangely gotten

coin hidden in the folds of his old blue cloak? I imparted none of these reflections to Miss Deborah, for I was determined that my observations should have a sequel, and I promised myself the pleasure of treating her to my story in its full maturity. "Captain Diamond," I asked, "has no other known means of subsistence?"

"None whatever. He toils not, neither does he spin—his ghost supports him. A haunted house is valuable property!"

"And in what coin does the ghost pay?"

"In good American gold and silver. It has only this peculiarity— that the pieces are all dated before the young girl's death. It's a strange mixture of matter and spirit!"

"And does the ghost do things handsomely; is the rent large?"

"The old man, I believe, lives decently, and has his pipe and his glass. He took a little house down by the river; the door is sidewise to the street, and there is a little garden before it. There he spends his days, and has an old colored woman to do for him. Some years ago, he used to wander about a good deal, he was a familiar figure in the town, and most people knew his legend. But of late he has drawn back into his shell; he sits over his fire, and curiosity has forgotten him. I suppose he is falling into his dotage. But I am sure, I trust," said Miss Deborah in conclusion, "that he won't outlive his faculties or his powers of locomotion, for, if I remember rightly, it was part of the bargain that he should come in person to collect his rent."

We neither of us seemed likely to suffer any especial penalty for Miss Deborah's indiscretion; I found her, day after day, singing over her work, neither more nor less active than usual. For myself, I boldly pursued my observations. I went again, more than once, to the great graveyard, but I was disappointed in my hope of finding Captain Diamond there. I had a prospect, however, which afforded me compensation. I shrewdly inferred that the old man's quarterly pilgrimages were made upon the last day of the old quarter. My first sight of him had been on the 31st of December, and it was probable that he would return to his haunted home on the last day of March. This was near at hand; at last it arrived. I betook myself late in the afternoon to the old house on the cross-road, supposing that the hour of twilight was the appointed season. I was not wrong. I had been hovering about for a short time, feeling very much like a restless ghost myself, when he appeared in the same manner as before, and wearing the same costume. I again concealed myself, and saw him enter the house with the ceremonial which he had used on the former occasion. A light appeared successively in the crevice of each pair of shutters, and I opened the window which had yielded to my importunity before. Again I saw the great shadow on the wall, motionless and solemn. But I saw nothing else. The old man re-appeared at last, made his fantastic salaam before the house, and crept away into the dusk.

One day, more than a month after this, I met him again at Mount Auburn. The air was full of the voice of Spring; the birds had come back and were twittering over their Winter's travels, and a mild west wind was making a thin murmur in the raw verdure. He was seated on a bench in the sun, still muffled in his enormous mantle, and he recognized me as soon as I approached him. He nodded at me as if he were an old Bashaw giving the signal for my decapitation, but it was apparent that he was pleased to see me.

"I have looked for you here more than once," I said. "You don't come often."

"What did you want of me?" he asked.

"I wanted to enjoy your conversation. I did so greatly when I met you here before."

"You found me amusing?"

"Interesting!" I said.

"You didn't think me cracked?"

"Cracked?—My dear sir—!" I protested.

"I'm the sanest man in the country. I know that is what insane people always say; but generally they can't prove it. I can!"

"I believe it," I said. "But I am curious to know how such a thing can be proved."

He was silent awhile.

"I will tell you. I once committed, unintentionally, a great crime. Now I pay the penalty. I give up my life to it. I don't shirk it; I face it squarely, knowing perfectly what it is. I haven't tried to bluff it off; I haven't begged off from it; I haven't run away from it. The penalty is terrible, but I have accepted it. I have been a philosopher!

"If I were a Catholic, I might have turned monk, and spent the rest of my life in fasting and praying. That is no penalty; that is an evasion. I might have blown my brains out—I might have gone mad. I wouldn't do either. I would simply face the music, take the consequences. As I say, they are awful! I take them on certain days, four times a year. So it has been these twenty years; so it will be as long as I last. It's my business; it's my avocation. That's the way I feel about it. I call that reasonable!"

"Admirably so!" I said. "But you fill me with curiosity and with compassion."

"Especially with curiosity," he said, cunningly.

"Why," I answered, "if I know exactly what you suffer I can pity you more."

"I'm much obliged. I don't want your pity; it won't help me. I'll tell you something, but it's not for myself; it's for your own sake."

He paused a long time and looked all round him, as if for chance eaves-droppers. I anxiously awaited his revelation, but he disappointed me. "Are you still studying theology?" he asked.

"Oh, yes," I answered, perhaps with a shade of irritation. "It's a thing one can't learn in six months."

"I should think not, so long as you have nothing but your books. Do you know the proverb, 'A grain of experience is worth a pound of precept?' I'm a great theologian."

"Ah, you have had experience," I murmured sympathetically.

"You have read about the immortality of the soul; you have seen Jonathan Edwards and Dr. Hopkins chopping logic over it, and deciding, by chapter and verse, that it is true. But I have seen it with these eyes; I have touched it with these hands!" And the old man held up his rugged old fists and shook them portentously. "That's better!" he went on; "but I have bought it dearly. You had better take it from the books—evidently you always will. You are a very good young man; you will never have a crime on your conscience."

I answered with some juvenile fatuity, that I certainly hoped I had my share of human passions, good young man and prospective Doctor of Divinity as I was.

"Ah, but you have a nice, quiet little temper," he said. "So have I—now! But once I was very brutal—very brutal. You ought to know that such things are. I killed my own child."

"Your own child?"

"I struck her down to the earth and left her to die. They could not hang me, for it was not with my hand I struck her. It was with foul and damnable words. That makes a difference; it's a grand law we live under! Well, sir, I can answer for it that *her* soul is immortal. We have an appointment to meet four times a year, and then I catch it!"

"She has never forgiven you?"

"She has forgiven me as the angels forgive! That's what I can't stand—the soft, quiet way she looks at me. I'd rather she twisted a knife about in my heart—O Lord, Lord, Lord!" and Captain Diamond bowed his head over his stick, and leaned his forehead on his crossed hands.

I was impressed and moved, and his attitude seemed for the moment a check to further questions. Before I ventured to ask him anything more, he slowly rose and pulled his old cloak around him. He was unused to talking about his troubles, and his memories overwhelmed him. "I must go my way," he said; "I must be creeping along."

"I shall perhaps meet you here again," I said.

"Oh, I'm a stiff-jointed old fellow," he answered, "and this is rather far for me to come. I have to reserve myself. I have sat sometimes a month at a time smoking my pipe in my chair. But I should like to see you again." And he stopped and looked at me, terribly and kindly. "Some day, perhaps, I shall be glad to be able to lay my hand on a young, unperverted soul. If a man can make a friend, it is always something gained. What is your name?"

I had in my pocket a small volume of Pascal's "Thoughts," on the fly-leaf of which were written my name and address. I took it out and offered it to my old friend. "Pray keep this little book," I said. "It is one I am very fond of, and it will tell you something about me."

He took it and turned it over slowly, then looking up at me with a scowl of gratitude, "I'm not much of a reader," he said; "but I won't refuse the first present I shall have received since—my troubles; and the last. Thank you, sir!" And with the little book in his hand he took his departure.

I was left to imagine him for some weeks after that sitting solitary in his arm-chair with his pipe. I had not another glimpse of him. But I was awaiting my chance, and on the last day of June, another quarter having elapsed, I deemed that it had come. The evening dusk in June falls late, and I was impatient for its coming. At last, toward the end of a lovely summer's day, I revisited Captain Diamond's property. Everything now was green around it save the blighted orchard in its rear, but its own immitigable grayness and sadness were as striking as when I had first beheld it beneath a December sky. As I drew near it, I saw that I was late for my purpose, for my purpose had simply been to step forward on Captain Diamond's arrival, and bravely ask him to let me go in with him. He had preceded me, and there were lights already in the windows. I was unwilling, of course, to disturb him during his ghostly interview, and I waited till he came forth. The lights disappeared in the course of time; then the door opened and Captain Diamond stole out. That evening he made no bow to the haunted house, for the first object he beheld was his fair-minded young friend planted, modestly but firmly, near the door-step. He stopped short, looking at me, and this time his terrible scowl was in keeping with the situation.

"I knew you were here," I said. "I came on purpose."

He seemed dismayed, and looked round at the house uneasily.

"I beg your pardon if I have ventured too far," I added, "but you know you have encouraged me."

"How did you know I was here?"

"I reasoned it out. You told me half your story, and I guessed the other half. I am a great observer, and I had noticed this house in passing. It seemed to me to have a mystery. When you kindly confided to me that you saw spirits, I was sure that it could only be here that you saw them."

"You are mighty clever," cried the old man. "And what brought you here this evening?"

I was obliged to evade this question.

"Oh, I often come; I like to look at the house—it fascinates me."

He turned and looked up at it himself. "It's nothing to look at outside." He was evidently quite unaware of its peculiar outward appearance, and this odd fact, communicated to me thus in the twilight, and under the very brow of the sinister dwelling, seemed to make his vision of the strange things within more real.

"I have been hoping," I said, "for a chance to see the inside. I thought I might find you here, and that you would let me go in with you. I should like to see what you see."

He seemed confounded by my boldness, but not altogether displeased. He laid his hand on my arm. "Do you know what I see?" he asked.

"How can I know, except as you said the other day, by experience? I want to have the experience. Pray, open the door and take me in."

Captain Diamond's brilliant eyes expanded beneath their dusky brows, and after holding his breath a moment, he indulged in the first and last apology for a laugh by which I was to see his solemn visage contorted. It was profoundly grotesque, but it was perfectly noiseless. "Take you in?" he softly growled. "I wouldn't go in again before my time's up for a thousand times that sum." And he thrust out his hand from the folds of his cloak and exhibited a small agglommeration of coin, knotted into the corner of an old silk pocket-handkerchief. "I stick to my bargain no less, but no more!"

"But you told me the first time I had the pleasure of talking with you that it was not so terrible."

"I don't say it's terrible—now. But it's damned disagreeable!"

This adjective was uttered with a force that made me hesitate and reflect. While I did so, I thought I heard a slight movement of one of the window-shutters above us. I looked up, but everything seemed motionless. Captain Diamond, too, had been thinking; suddenly he turned toward the house. "If you will go in alone," he said, "you are welcome."

"Will you wait for me here?"

"Yes, you will not stop long."

"But the house is pitch dark. When you go you have lights."

He thrust his hand into the depths of his cloak and produced some matches. "Take take," he said. "You will find two candlesticks with candles on the table in the hall. Light them, take one in each hand and go ahead."

"Where shall I go?"

"Anywhere—everywhere. You can trust the ghost to find you."

I will not pretend to deny that by this time my heart was beating. And yet I imagine I motioned the old man with a sufficiently dignified gesture to open the door. I had made up my mind that there was in fact a ghost. I had conceded the premise. Only I had assured myself that once the mind was prepared, and the thing was not a surprise, it was possible to keep cool. Captain Diamond turned the lock, flung open the door, and bowed low to me as I passed in. I stood in the darkness, and heard the door close behind me. For some moments, I stirred neither finger nor toe; I stared bravely into the impenetrable dusk. But I saw nothing and heard nothing, and at last I struck a match. On the table were two old brass candlesticks rusty from disuse. I lighted the candles and began my tour of exploration.

A wide staircase rose in front of me, guarded by an antique balustrade of that rigidly delicate carving which is found so often in old New England houses. I postponed ascending it, and turned into the room on my right. This was an old-fashioned parlor, meagerly furnished, and musty with the absence of human life. I raised my two lights aloft and saw nothing but its empty chairs and its blank walls. Behind it was the room into which I had peeped from without, and which, in fact, communicated with it, as I had supposed, by folding doors. Here, too, I found myself confronted by no menacing specter. I crossed the hall again, and visited the rooms on the other side; a dining-room in front, where I might have written my name with my finger in the deep dust of the great square table; a kitchen behind with its pots and pans eternally cold. All this was hard and grim, but it was not formidable. I came back into the hall, and walked to the foot of the staircase, holding up my candles; to ascend required a fresh effort, and I was scanning the gloom above. Suddenly, with an inexpressible sensation, I became aware that this gloom was animated; it seemed to move and gather itself together. Slowly—I say slowly, for to my tense expectancy the instants appeared ages—it took the shape of a large, definite figure, and this figure advanced and stood at the top of the stairs. I frankly confess that by this time I was conscious of a feeling to which I am in duty bound to apply the vulgar name of fear. I may poetize it and call it Dread, with a capital letter; it was at any rate the feeling that makes a man yield ground. I measured it as it grew, and it seemed perfectly irresistible; for it did not appear to come from within but from without, and to be embodied in the dark image at the head of the staircase. After a fashion I reasoned—I remember reasoning. I said to myself, "I had always thought ghosts were white and transparent; this is a thing of thick shadows, densely opaque." I reminded myself that the occasion was momentous, and that if fear were to overcome me I should gather all possible impressions while my wits remained. I stepped back, foot behind foot, with my eyes still on the figure and placed my candles on the table. I was perfectly conscious that the proper thing was to ascend the stairs resolutely, face to face with the image, but the soles of my shoes seemed suddenly to have been transformed into leaden weights. I had got what I wanted; I was seeing the ghost. I tried to look at the figure distinctly so that I could remember it, and fairly claim, afterward, not to have lost my self-possession. I even asked myself how long it was expected I should stand looking, and how soon I could honorably retire. All this, of course, passed through my mind with extreme rapidity, and it was checked by a further movement on the part of the figure. Two white hands appeared in the dark perpendicular mass, and were slowly raised to what seemed to be the level of the head. Here they were pressed together, over the region of the face, and then they were removed, and the face was disclosed. It was dim, white, strange, in every way ghostly. It looked down at me for an instant, after which one of the hands was raised again, slowly, and waved to and fro before it. There was something very singular in this gesture; it seemed to denote resentment and dismissal, and yet it had a sort of trivial, familiar motion. Familiarity on the part of the haunting Presence had not entered into my calculations, and did not strike me pleasantly. I agreed with Captain Diamond that it was "damned disagreeable." I was pervaded by an intense desire to make an orderly, and, if possible, a graceful retreat. I wished to do it gallantly, and it seemed to me that it would be gallant to blow out my candles. I turned and did so, punctiliously, and then I made my way to the door, groped a moment and opened it. The outer light, almost extinct as it was, entered for a moment, played over the dusty depths of the house and showed me the solid shadow.

Standing on the grass, bent over his stick, under the early glimmering stars, I found Captain Diamond. He looked up at me fixedly for a moment, but asked no questions, and then he went and locked the door. This duty performed, he discharged the other—made his obeisance like the priest before the altar—and then without heeding me further, took his departure.

A few days later, I suspended my studies and went off for the summer's vacation. I was absent for several weeks, during which I had plenty of leisure to analyze my impressions of the supernatural. I took some satisfaction in the reflection that I had not been ignobly terrified; I had not bolted nor swooned—I had proceeded with dignity. Nevertheless, I was certainly more comfortable when I had put thirty miles between me and the scene of my exploit, and I continued for many days to prefer the daylight to the dark. My nerves had been powerfully excited; of this I was particularly conscious when, under the influence of the drowsy air of the sea-side, my excitement began slowly to ebb. As it disappeared, I attempted to take a sternly rational view of my experience. Certainly I had seen *something*—that was not fancy; but what had I seen? I regretted extremely now that I had not been bolder, that I had not gone nearer and inspected the apparition more minutely. But it was very well to talk; I had done as much as any man in the circumstances would have dared; it was indeed a physical impossibility that I should have advanced. Was not this paralyzation of my powers in itself a supernatural influence? Not necessarily, perhaps, for a sham ghost that one accepted might do as much execution as a real ghost. But why had I so easily accepted the sable phantom that waved its hand? Why had it so impressed itself? Unquestionably, true or false, it was a very clever phantom. I greatly preferred that it should have been true—in the first place because I did not care to have shivered and shaken for nothing, and in the second place because to have seen a well-authenticated goblin is, as things go, a feather in a quiet man's cap. I tried, therefore, to let my vision rest and to stop turning it over. But an impulse stronger than my will recurred at intervals and set a mocking question on my lips. Granted that the apparition was Captain Diamond's daughter; if it was she it certainly was her spirit. But was it not her spirit and something more?

The middle of September saw me again established among the theologic shades, but I made no haste to revisit the haunted house.

The last of the month approached—the term of another quarter with poor Captain Diamond—and found me indisposed to disturb his pilgrimage on this occasion; though I confess that I thought with a good deal of compassion of the feeble old man trudging away, lonely, in the autumn dusk, on his extraordinary errand. On the thirtieth of September, at noonday, I was drowsing over a heavy octavo, when I heard a feeble rap at my door. I replied with an invitation to enter, but as this produced no effect I repaired to the door and opened it. Before me stood an elderly negress with her head bound in a scarlet turban, and a white handkerchief folded across her bosom. She looked at me intently and in silence; she had that air of supreme gravity and decency which aged persons of her race so often wear. I stood interrogative, and at last, drawing her hand from her ample pocket, she held up a little book. It was the copy of Pascal's "Thoughts" that I had given to Captain Diamond.

"Please, sir," she said, very mildly, "do you know this book?"

"Perfectly," said I, "my name is on the fly-leaf."

"It is your name—no other?"

"I will write my name if you like, and you can compare them," I answered.

She was silent a moment and then, with dignity—"It would be useless, sir," she said, "I can't read. If you will give me your word that is enough. I come," she went on, "from the gentleman to whom you gave the book. He told me to carry it as a token—a token—that is what he called it. He is right down sick, and he wants to see you."

"Captain Diamond—sick?" I cried. "Is his illness serious?"

"He is very bad—he is all gone."

I expressed my regret and sympathy, and offered to go to him immediately, if his sable messenger would show me the way. She assented deferentially, and in a few moments I was following her along the sunny streets, feeling very much like a personage in the Arabian Nights, led to a postern gate by an Ethiopian slave. My own conductress directed her steps toward the river and stopped at a decent little yellow house in one of the streets that descend to it. She quickly opened the door and led me in, and I very soon found myself in the presence of my old friend. He was in bed, in a darkened room, and evidently in a very feeble state. He lay back on his pillow staring before him, with his bristling hair more erect than ever, and his intensely dark and bright old eyes touched with the glitter of fever. His apartment was humble and scrupulously neat, and I could see that my dusky guide was a faithful servant. Captain Diamond, lying there rigid and pale on his white sheets, resembled some ruggedly carven figure on the lid of a Gothic tomb. He looked at me silently, and my companion withdrew and left us alone.

"Yes, it's you," he said, at last, "it's you, that good young man. There is no mistake, is there?"

"I hope not; I believe I'm a good young man. But I am very sorry you are ill. What can I do for you?"

"I am very bad, very bad; my poor old bones ache so!" and, groaning portentously, he tried to turn toward me.

I questioned him about the nature of his malady and the length of time he had been in bed, but he barely heeded me; he seemed impatient to speak of something else. He grasped my sleeve, pulled me toward him, and whispered quickly:

"You know my time's up!"

"Oh, I trust not," I said, mistaking his meaning. "I shall certainly see you on your legs again."

"God knows!" he cried. "But I don't mean I'm dying; not yet a bit. What I mean is, I'm due at the house. This is rent-day."

"Oh, exactly! But you can't go."

"I can't go. It's awful. I shall lose my money. If I am dying, I want it all the same. I want to pay the doctor. I want to be buried like a respectable man."

"It is this evening?" I asked.

"This evening at sunset, sharp."

He lay staring at me, and, as I looked at him in return, I suddenly understood his motive in sending for me. Morally, as it came into my thought, I winced. But, I suppose I looked unperturbed, for he continued in the same tone. "I can't lose my money. Some one else must go. I asked Belinda; but she won't hear of it."

"You believe the money will be paid to another person?"

"We can try, at least. I have never failed before and I don't know. But, if you say I'm as sick as a dog, that my old bones ache, that I'm dying, perhaps she'll trust you. She don't want me to starve!"

"You would like me to go in your place, then?"

"You have been there once; you know what it is. Are you afraid?"

I hesitated.

"Give me three minutes to reflect," I said, "and I will tell you." My glance wandered over the room and rested on the various objects that spoke of the threadbare, decent poverty of its occupant. There seemed to be a mute appeal to my pity and my resolution in their cracked and faded sparseness. Meanwhile Captain Diamond continued, feebly:

"I think she'd trust you, as I have trusted you; she'll like your face; she'll see there is no harm in you. It's a hundred and thirty-three dollars, exactly. Be sure you put them into a safe place."

"Yes," I said at last, "I will go, and, so far as it depends upon me, you shall have the money by nine o'clock to-night."

He seemed greatly relieved; he took my hand and faintly pressed it, and soon afterward I withdrew. I tried for the rest of the day not to think of my evening's work, but, of course, I thought of nothing else. I will not deny that I was nervous; I was, in fact, greatly excited, and I spent my time in alternately hoping that the mystery should prove less deep than it appeared, and yet fearing that it might prove too shallow. The hours passed very slowly, but, as the afternoon began to wane, I started on my mission. On the way, I stopped at Captain Diamond's modest dwelling, to ask how he was doing, and to receive such last instructions as he might desire to lay upon me. The old negress, gravely and inscrutably placid, admitted me, and, in answer to my inquiries, said that the Captain was very low; he had sunk since the morning.

"You must be right smart," she said, "if you want to get back before he drops off."

A glance assured me that she knew of my projected expedition, though, in her own opaque black pupil, there was not a gleam of self-betrayal.

"But why should Captain Diamond drop off?" I asked. "He certainly seems very weak; but I cannot make out that he has any definite disease."

"His disease is old age," she said, sententiously.

"But he is not so old as that; sixty-seven or sixty-eight, at most."

She was silent a moment.

"He's worn out; he's used up; he can't stand it any longer."

"Can I see him a moment?" I asked; upon which she led me again to his room.

He was lying in the same way as when I had left him, except that his eyes were closed. But he seemed very "low," as she had said, and he had very little pulse. Nevertheless, I further learned the doctor had been there in the afternoon and professed himself satisfied. "He don't know what's been going on," said Belinda, curtly.

The old man stirred a little, opened his eyes, and after some time recognized me.

"I'm going, you know," I said. "I'm going for your money. Have you anything more to say?" He raised himself slowly, and with a painful effort, against his pillows; but he seemed hardly to understand me. "The house, you know," I said. "Your daughter."

He rubbed his forehead, slowly, awhile, and at last, his comprehension awoke. "Ah, yes," he murmured, "I trust you. A hundred and thirty-three dollars. In old pieces—all in old pieces." Then he added more vigorously, and with a brightening eye: "Be very respectful—be very polite. If not—if not—" and his voice failed again.

"Oh, I certainly shall be," I said, with a rather forced smile. "But, if not?"

"If not, I shall know it!" he said, very gravely. And with this, his eyes closed and he sunk down again.

I took my departure and pursued my journey with a sufficiently resolute step. When I reached the house, I made a propitiatory bow in front of it, in emulation of Captain Diamond. I had timed my walk so as to be able to enter without delay; night had already fallen. I turned the key, opened the door and shut it behind me. Then I struck a light, and found the two candlesticks I had used before, standing on the tables in the entry. I applied a match to both of them, took them up and went into the parlor. It was empty, and though I waited awhile, it remained empty. I passed then into the other rooms on the same floor, and no dark image rose before me to check my steps. At last, I came out into the hall again, and stood weighing the question of going upstairs. The staircase had been the scene of my discomfiture before, and I approached it with profound mistrust. At the foot, I paused, looking up, with my hand on the balustrade. I was acutely expectant, and my expectation was justified. Slowly, in the darkness above, the black figure that I had seen before took shape. It was not an illusion; it was a figure, and the same. I gave it time to define itself, and watched it stand and look down at me with its hidden face. Then, deliberately, I lifted up my voice and spoke.

"I have come in place of Captain Diamond, at his request," I said. "He is very ill; he is unable to leave his bed. He earnestly begs that you will pay the money to me; I will immediately carry it to him." The figure stood motionless, giving no sign. "Captain Diamond would have come if he were able to move," I added, in a moment, appealingly; "but, he is utterly unable."

At this the figure slowly unveiled its face and showed me a dim, white mask; then it began slowly to descend the stairs. Instinctively I fell back before it, retreating to the door of the front sitting-room. With my eyes still fixed on it, I moved backward across the threshold; then I stopped in the middle of the room and set down my lights. The figure advanced; it seemed to be that of a tall woman, dressed in vaporous black crape. As it drew near, I saw that it had a perfectly human face, though it looked extremely pale and sad. We stood gazing at each other; my agitation had completely vanished; I was only deeply interested.

"Is my father dangerously ill?" said the apparition.

At the sound of its voice—gentle, tremulous, and perfectly human—I started forward; I felt a rebound of excitement. I drew a long breath, I gave a sort of cry, for what I saw before me was not a disembodied spirit, but a beautiful woman, an audacious actress. Instinctively, irresistibly, by the force of reaction against my credulity, I stretched out my hand and seized the long veil that muffled her head. I gave it a violent jerk, dragged it nearly off, and stood staring at a large fair person, of about five-and-thirty. I comprehended her at a glance; her long black dress, her pale, sorrow-worn face, painted to look paler, her very fine eyes,—the color of her father's,—and her sense of outrage at my movement.

"My father, I suppose," she cried, "did not send you here to insult me!" and she turned away rapidly, took up one of the candles and moved toward the door. Here she paused, looked at me again, hesitated, and then drew a purse from her pocket and flung it down on the floor. "There is your money!" she said, majestically.

I stood there, wavering between amazement and shame, and saw her pass out into the hall. Then I picked up the purse. The next moment, I heard a loud shriek and a crash of something dropping, and she came staggering back into the room without her light.

"My father—my father!" she cried; and with parted lips and dilated eyes, she rushed toward me.

"Your father—where?" I demanded.

"In the hall, at the foot of the stairs."

I stepped forward to go out, but she seized my arm.

"He is in white," she cried, "in his shirt. It's not he!"

"Why, your father is in his house, in his bed, extremely ill," I answered.

She looked at me fixedly, with searching eyes.

"Dying?"

"I hope not," I stuttered.

She gave a long moan and covered her face with her hands.

"Oh, heavens, I have seen his ghost!" she cried.

She still held my arm; she seemed too terrified to release it. "His ghost!" I echoed, wondering.

"It's the punishment of my long folly!" she went on.

"Ah," said I, "it's the punishment of my indiscretion—of my violence!"

"Take me away, take me away!" she cried, still clinging to my arm. "Not there"—as I was turning toward the hall and the front door—"not there, for pity's sake! By this door—the back entrance." And snatching the other candles from the table, she led me through the neighboring room into the back part of the house. Here was a door opening from a sort of scullery into the orchard. I turned the rusty lock and we passed out and stood in the cool air, beneath the stars. Here my companion gathered her black drapery about her, and stood for a moment, hesitating. I had been infinitely flurried, but my curiosity touching her was uppermost. Agitated, pale, picturesque, she looked, in the early evening light, very beautiful.

"You have been playing all these years a most extraordinary game," I said.

She looked at me somberly, and seemed disinclined to reply. "I came in perfect good faith," I went on. "The last time—three months ago—you remember?—you greatly frightened me."

"Of course it was an extraordinary game," she answered at last. "But it was the only way."

"Had he not forgiven you?"

"So long as he thought me dead, yes. There have been things in my life he could not forgive."

I hesitated and then—"And where is your husband?" I asked.

"I have no husband—I have never had a husband."

She made a gesture which checked further questions, and moved rapidly away. I walked with her round the house to the road, and she kept murmuring—"It was he—it was he!" When we reached the road she stopped, and asked me which way I was going. I pointed to the road by which I had come, and she said—"I take the other. You are going to my father's?" she added.

"Directly," I said.

"Will you let me know to-morrow what you have found?"

"With pleasure. But how shall I communicate with you?"

She seemed at a loss, and looked about her. "Write a few words," she said, "and put them under that stone." And she pointed to one of the lava slabs that bordered the old well. I gave her my promise to comply, and she turned away. "I know my road," she said. "Everything is arranged. It's an old story."

She left me with a rapid step, and as she receded into the darkness, resumed, with the dark flowing lines of her drapery, the phantasmal appearance with which she had at first appeared to me. I watched her till she became invisible, and then I took my own leave of the place. I returned to town at a swinging pace, and marched straight to the little yellow house near the river. I took the liberty of entering without a knock, and, encountering no interruption, made my way to Captain Diamond's room. Outside the door, on a low bench, with folded arms, sat the sable Belinda.

"How is he?" I asked.

"He's gone to glory."

"Dead?" I cried.

She rose with a sort of tragic chuckle.

"He's as big a ghost as any of them now!"

I passed into the room and found the old man lying there irredeemably rigid and still. I wrote that evening a few lines which I proposed on the morrow to place beneath the stone, near the well; but my promise was not destined to be executed. I slept that night very ill—it was natural—and in my restlessness left my bed to walk about the room. As I did so I caught sight, in passing my window, of a red glow in the north-western sky. A house was on fire in the country, and evidently burning fast. It lay in the same direction as the scene of my evening's adventures, and as I stood watching the crimson horizon I was startled by a sharp memory. I had blown out the candle which lighted me, with my companion, to the door through which we escaped, but I had not accounted for the other light, which she had carried into the hall and dropped—heaven knew where—in her consternation. The next day I walked out with my folded letter and turned into the familiar cross-road. The haunted house was a mass of charred beams and smoldering ashes; the well cover had been pulled off, in quest of water, by the few neighbors who had had the audacity to contest what they must have regarded as a demon-kindled blaze, the loose stones were completely displaced, and the earth had been trampled into puddles.

William Butler Yeats
(1865-1939)

YEATS is the greatest lyric poet that Ireland has produced and the acknowledged leader of the Irish Literary Renaissance, which aimed at reviving ancient Irish folklore, legends, and tradition. He called himself one of the "last romantics" ("Coole Park and Bally-lee," 1931), and, like Wordsworth and Coleridge, celebrated the natural man in ballads. Song characterizes his work, and themes of music, dance, and singing recur frequently. The simplicity of his syntax and diction often hides the complexity of his insights, but his haunting rhythms and vibrant images live in memory like a folksong, yielding new significance with each singing.

As a child, Yeats often visited his maternal grandparents in Sligo, in the west of Ireland. There he first learned the Irish songs, legends, superstitions, and traditions which provided him the material for his poetry. Yeats said he made "a new religion, almost an infallible Church of poetic tradition, of a fardel of stories, and of personages, and of emotions . . . passed on from generation to generation by poets and painters with some help from philosophers and theologians" (*Autobiographies*, 1926). He practiced this religion by writing poetry, drama, a few short stories, essays, and his mystic book *A Vision* (1925), which blended the disparate elements of his belief into a new system. Throughout his life, he was fascinated with the supernatural and the occult—he visited mediums, participated in seances, founded the Dublin Hermetic Society, and joined Madame Blavatsky's Theosophical Society and the Rosicrucian Order of the Golden Dawn. These societies for occult research and mysticism flourished in the nineties, and Yeats knew them all. With the president of the Order of the Golden Dawn, Aleister Crowley, who was reputed to be a sinister magician, Yeats collected and examined the folklore of County Sligo; the results of their research constitute the essays in *The Celtic Twilight* (1893). In his essay "Magic," Yeats firmly expresses his belief in "the evocation of spirits," in magic; he could not reject it:

> I often think I would put this belief in magic from me if I could, for I have come to see or to imagine, in men and women, in houses, in handicrafts, in nearly all sights and sounds, a certain evil, a cer-

tain ugliness, that comes from the slow perishing through the centuries of a quality of mind that made this belief and its evidences common over the world.

Indian philosophy seemed to represent the vast extension of belief throughout the world; for Yeats, the Brahmin Mohini J. Chatterjee and the Indian sage Shri Purohit Swami furthered his belief in the individual self as distinct from the universal self, maker of past and future. The poet's task, he came to believe, is to make the personal universal and hence more meaningful for all men.

Even in his early poetry Yeats works by image and symbol toward truth. In "The Stolen Child," a piece resembling "Goblin Market" in its appeal to children, the domestic images of the final stanza become symbolic of the human peace and human joy which the child loses when he joins the faeries. Calves on the hillside, mice round the oatmeal-chest, kettles on the hob—all the sights and sounds of the cozy human world—are left behind. Mortality, as Keats knew too, has its own pleasures; he who sacrifices them in search of a magical ideal often sacrifices the highest good. The child's choice is between the freedom from weeping and the more ambivalent freedom from human delights.

The child goes "solemn-eyed" to an uneasy world, a "leafy island" with "drowsy water rats," "dim gray sands," and "pools among the rushes." It is a mysteriously sad world described in subtle metaphors of somnolence and even of death. Escape to the wooded island with tearful ferns is made attractive by the refrain, itself a little self-contained stanza, a haunting song, wild and menacing and subtly terrifying.

The subtlety of Yeats's poetry recalls the Romantic poets and others who explored the implied terrors and evils in the world and in the imagination of man. The poet's is "a mysterious art," Yeats wrote to the Irish patriot Lady Gregory, "always reminding and half-reminding those who understand it of dearly loved things, doing its work by suggestion, not by direct statement, a complexity of rhythm, colour, gesture, not space-pervading like the intellect but a memory and a prophecy."

The Stolen Child (1886)

Where dips the rocky highland
Of Sleuth Wood in the lake,
There lies a leafy island

Where flapping herons wake
The drowsy water rats;   5
There we've hid our faery vats.
Full of berries,
And of reddest stolen cherries.
Come away, O human child!
To the waters and the wild   10
With a faery, hand in hand,
For the world's more full of weeping than you can understand.

Where the wave of moonlight glosses
The dim gray sands with light,
Far off by furthest Rosses   15
We foot it all the night,
Weaving olden dances,
Mingling hands and mingling glances
Till the moon has taken flight;
To and fro we leap   20
And chase the frothy bubbles,
While the world is full of troubles
And is anxious in its sleep.
Come away, O human child!
To the waters and the wild   25
With a faery, hand in hand,
For the world's more full of weeping than you can understand.

Where the wandering water gushes
From the hills above Glen-Car,
In pools among the rushes   30
That scarce could bathe a star,
We seek for slumbering trout,
And whispering in their ears
Give them unquiet dreams;
Leaning softly out   35
From ferns that drop their tears
Over the young streams.
Come away, O human child!
To the waters and the wild
With a faery, hand in hand,   40
For the world's more full of weeping than you can understand.

Away with us he's going,
The solemn-eyed:
He'll hear no more the lowing
Of the calves on the warm hillside;   45

Or the kettle on the hob
Sing peace into his breast,
Or see the brown mice bob
Round and round the oatmeal-chest.
For he comes, the human child,   50
To the waters and the wild
With a faery, hand in hand,
From a world more full of weeping than he can understand.

Robert Louis Stevenson
(1850-1894)

IN this story of a criminal, Stevenson dramatizes Markheim's inner conflict through a nameless visitant, the double or *Doppelgänger* who is his counterpart or alter ego. Stevenson used the theme earlier in his famous novella *The Strange Case of Dr. Jekyll and Mr. Hyde* (1886), where the duality of good and evil is so carefully drawn that the characters have become familiar abbreviations for the divided self. The idea for *Dr. Jekyll* came to Stevenson in a nightmare (as have many other Gothic stories to other authors) and was later informed by his reading of a pre-Freudian paper on the subconscious mind found in a French scientific journal. "Markheim" undoubtedly builds on the same sources of inspiration as *Dr. Jekyll*, but whereas the novella treats the concept of the divided self as universal and inevitable, the short story uses a violent crime as the occasion of the division. This difference reduces the similarity substantially.

The murder of the pawnbroker recalls Dostoevsky's *Crime and Punishment* (1866; read by Stevenson in the first French edition), and Markheim, like Raskolnikov, finally surrenders himself to legal authorities. With resignation and full awareness that his punishment will be hanging, Markheim thus surrenders his very life: "Life," Stevenson writes, "tempted him no longer." Markheim's double responds triumphantly to this renunciation of evil and so identifies himself as conscience or even ethical Christianity rather than the devil or spirit of evil Markheim first believes him to be. The Christmas Day setting and the three-o'clock hour suggest a conflation of moral rebirth and death consistent with Christ's nativity and crucifixion, but there the Christology ends.

Markheim's panic after the murder echoes Macbeth's after killing Duncan. "Time was that when the brains were out" in "Markheim" recalls Macbeth's memory of a more innocent time: "The time has been/ That when the brains were out, the man would die,/ And there an end" (III.iv.78–80). Guilt born of fear of discovery makes both dead men live in every sight and sound perceived by the murderers. Macbeth sees the ghost of Banquo; Markheim hears the maddening ticking of the pawnbroker's clocks. Earlier in *Macbeth* and later in "Markheim" the knocking at the door brings a new fear of waking the dead. Both murderers become understandably paranoid, but Markheim fears even his own reflections, and, unlike Macbeth, has occasion to speak to no one. Stevenson's concentration on the murderer's obsessive view of his own "interesting hell" illustrates the theories of Thomas De Quincey in his essays "On Murder Considered as One of the Fine Arts" and "On the Knocking at the Gate in *Macbeth*," from which Stevenson drew inspiration for the several allusions to *Macbeth*. His characterization of Markheim as a child, however, is peculiarly his own and is reminiscent of his *A Child's Garden of Verses* (1885), in which shadows and sounds are often misperceived as concrete realities. Like a feverish child, Markheim sees "an army of spies" in the mirrors, hears "presences" in the upper chambers, and imagines "footsteps and sighs" in the pattering rain. A montage of reflections, both literal and figurative, makes a symbol of the mirror suggested as the Christmas gift for the fictitious lady and prepares for the mirroring of Markheim's soul in the conversation with the ghostly visitant, summoned by memories of the childhood church.

The indistinct stranger is simultaneously both self and other, conscience and devil. The ambiguity of the double may have derived from James Hogg's *Private Memoirs and Confessions of a Justified Sinner* (1824), in which hypocrisy and ignorance of self confuse the Sinner, and multiple narrators and the shifting identity of the double keep absolute moral categories unrealized. Through the dialogue with his unknown self, Markheim becomes both participant and observer of himself, "like an actor on a stage," "a travesty," a "disguise." Evil acts have masked a good soul, one trained in the middle-class Calvinism of Stevenson's own youth, the same rigid theology that betrays James Hogg's Sinner. In Stevenson's story the mysterious visitor first seems a tormentor, but, by eliciting acknowledgment of evil, the double forces Markheim to see himself as he really is. The human mirror, then, reveals all and confession follows.

The visitant becomes the most significant "hand-conscience" for Markheim, though the pawnbroker's cluttered chamber and clock-filled shop also mirror the protagonist's agony of self-deception and disorder. The character of the place and the awareness of time reawaken the resolve to be and do good. Like the saints he mentions, Markheim has taken on "the tone of his surroundings"; external objects and impressions reflect his troubled mind and bear on his self-examination. In speaking of *Dr. Jekyll*, Henry James, who was Stevenson's close friend from the summer of 1885 till Stevenson's death in 1894, notices the same method that Stevenson uses here: "even inanimate objects have a kind of wicked look." The tight pattern of symbolism and imagery in "Markheim" heightens the suspense and portrays the anguish of the disordered mind. Little is wasted in this

psychological portrayal of a criminal whose good and evil impulses
are represented in one image.

Markheim (1887)

"Yes," said the dealer, "our windfalls are of various kinds.
Some customers are ignorant, and then I touch a dividend on my
superior knowledge. Some are dishonest," and here he held up the
candle, so that the light fell strongly on his visitor, "and in that case,"
he continued, "I profit by my virtue."

Markheim had but just entered from the daylight streets, and his
eyes had not yet grown familiar with the mingled shine and darkness
in the shop. At these pointed words, and before the near presence of
the flame, he blinked painfully and looked aside.

The dealer chuckled. "You come to me on Christmas Day," he
resumed, "when you know that I am alone in my house, put up my
shutters, and make a point of refusing business. Well, you will have
to pay for that; you will have to pay for my loss of time, when I
should be balancing my books; you will have to pay, besides, for a
kind of manner that I remark in you to-day very strongly. I am the
essence of discretion, and ask no awkward questions; but when a
customer cannot look me in the eye, he has to pay for it." The
dealer once more chuckled; and then, changing to his usual business
voice, though still with a note of irony, "You can give, as usual, a
clear account of how you came into the possession of the object?" he
continued. "Still your uncle's cabinet? A remarkable collector, sir!"

And the little pale, round-shouldered dealer stood almost on tip-
toe, looking over the top of his gold spectacles, and nodding his head
with every mark of disbelief. Markheim returned his gaze with one of
infinite pity, and a touch of horror.

"This time," said he, "you are in error. I have not come to sell,
but to buy. I have no curios to dispose of; my uncle's cabinet is bare
to the wainscot; even were it still intact, I have done well on the Stock
Exchange, and should more likely add to it than otherwise, and my
errand to-day is simplicity itself. I seek a Christmas present for a
lady," he continued, waxing more fluent as he struck into the speech
he had prepared; "and certainly I owe you every excuse for thus
disturbing you upon so small a matter. But the thing was neglected
yesterday; I must produce my little compliment at dinner; and, as you
very well know, a rich marriage is not a thing to be neglected."

There followed a pause, during which the dealer seemed to

weigh this statement incredulously. The ticking of many clocks among the curious lumber of the shop, and the faint rushing of the cabs in a near thoroughfare, filled up the interval of silence.

"Well, sir," said the dealer, "be it so. You are an old customer after all; and if, as you say, you have the chance of a good marriage, far be it from me to be an obstacle. Here is a nice thing for a lady now," he went on, "this hand glass—fifteenth century, warranted; comes from a good collection, too; but I reserve the name, in the interests of my customer, who was just like yourself, my dear sir, the nephew and sole heir of a remarkable collector."

The dealer, while he thus ran on in his dry and biting voice, had stooped to take the object from its place; and, as he had done so, a shock had passed through Markheim, a start both of hand and foot, a sudden leap of many tumultuous passions to the face. It passed as swiftly as it came, and left no trace beyond a certain trembling of the hand that now received the glass.

"A glass," he said hoarsely, and then paused, and repeated it more clearly. "A glass? For Christmas? Surely not?"

"And why not?" cried the dealer. "Why not a glass?"

Markheim was looking upon him with an indefinable expression. "You ask me why not?" he said. "Why, look here—look in it—look at yourself! Do you like to see it? No! nor I—nor any man."

The little man had jumped back when Markheim had so suddenly confronted him with the mirror; but now, perceiving there was nothing worse on hand, he chuckled. "Your future lady, sir, must be pretty hard favoured," said he.

"I ask you," said Markheim, "for a Christmas present, and you give me this—this damned reminder of years, and sins and follies—this hand-conscience! Did you mean it? Had you a thought in your mind? Tell me. It will be better for you if you do. Come, tell me about yourself. I hazard a guess now, that you are in secret a very charitable man?"

The dealer looked closely at his companion. It was very odd, Markheim did not appear to be laughing; there was something in his face like an eager sparkle of hope, but nothing of mirth.

"What are you driving at?" the dealer asked.

"Not charitable?" returned the other, gloomily. "Not charitable; not pious; not scrupulous; unloving, unbeloved; a hand to get money, a safe to keep it. Is that all? Dear God, man, is that all?"

"I will tell you what it is," began the dealer, with some sharpness, and then broke off again into a chuckle. "But I see this is a love match of yours, and you have been drinking the lady's health."

"Ah!" cried Markheim, with a strange curiosity. "Ah, have you been in love? Tell me about that."

"I," cried the dealer. "I in love! I never had the time, nor have I the time to-day for all this nonsense. Will you take the glass?"

"Where is the hurry?" returned Markheim. "It is very pleasant to stand here talking; and life is so short and insecure that I would not hurry away from any pleasure—no, not even from so mild a one as this. We should rather cling, cling to what little we can get, like a man at a cliff's edge. Every second is a cliff, if you think upon it—a cliff a mile high—high enough, if we fall, to dash us out of every feature of humanity. Hence it is best to talk pleasantly. Let us talk of each other; why should we wear this mask? Let us be confidential. Who knows, we might become friends?"

"I have just one word to say to you," said the dealer. "Either make your purchase, or walk out of my shop."

"True, true," said Markheim. "Enough fooling. To business. Show me something else."

The dealer stooped once more, this time to replace the glass upon the shelf, his thin blond hair falling over his eyes as he did so. Markheim moved a little nearer, with one hand in the pocket of his greatcoat; he drew himself up and filled his lungs; at the same time many different emotions were depicted together on his face—terror, horror, and resolve, fascination and a physical repulsion; and through a haggard lift of his upper lip, his teeth looked out.

"This, perhaps, may suit," observed the dealer; and then, as he began to re-arise, Markheim bounded from behind upon his victim. The long, skewerlike dagger flashed and fell. The dealer struggled like a hen, striking his temple on the shelf, and then tumbled on the floor in a heap.

Time had some score of small voices in that shop, some stately and slow as was becoming to their great age; others garrulous and hurried. All these told out the seconds in an intricate chorus of tickings. Then the passage of a lad's feet, heavily running on the pavement, broke in upon these smaller voices and startled Markheim into the consciousness of his surroundings. He looked about him awfully. The candle stood on the counter, its flame solemnly wagging in a draught; and by that inconsiderable movement, the whole room was filled with noiseless bustle and kept heaving like a sea: the tall shadows nodding, the gross blots of darkness swelling and dwindling as with respiration, the faces of the portraits and the china gods changing and wavering like images in water. The inner door stood ajar, and peered into that leaguer of shadows with a long slit of daylight like a pointing finger.

From these fear-stricken rovings, Markheim's eyes returned to the body of his victim, where it lay both humped and sprawling, incredibly small and strangely meaner than in life. In these poor,

miserly clothes, in that ungainly attitude, the dealer lay like so much
sawdust. Markheim had feared to see it, and, lo! it was nothing. And
yet, as he gazed, this bundle of old clothes and pool of blood began to
find eloquent voices. There it must lie; there was none to work the
cunning hinges or direct the miracle of locomotion—there it must lie
till it was found. Found! ay, and then? Then would this dead flesh lift
up a cry that would ring over England, and fill the world with the
echoes of pursuit. Ay, dead or not, this was still the enemy. "Time
was that when the brains were out," he thought; and the first word
struck into his mind. Time, now that the deed was accomplished—
time, which had closed for the victim, had become instant and momentous for the slayer.

The thought was yet in his mind, when, first one and then another, with every variety of pace and voice—one deep as the bell
from a cathedral turret, another ringing on its treble notes the prelude
of a waltz—the clocks began to strike the hour of three in the afternoon.

The sudden outbreak of so many tongues in that dumb chamber
staggered him. He began to bestir himself, going to and fro with the
candle, beleaguered by moving shadows, and startled to the soul by
chance reflections. In many rich mirrors, some of home designs, some
from Venice or Amsterdam, he saw his face repeated and repeated,
as it were an army of spies; his own eyes met and detected him; and
the sound of his own steps, lightly as they fell, vexed the surrounding
quiet. And still as he continued to fill his pockets, his mind accused
him, with a sickening iteration, of the thousand faults of his design.
He should have chosen a more quiet hour; he should have prepared
an alibi; he should not have used a knife; he should have been more
cautious, and only bound and gagged the dealer, and not killed him;
he should have been more bold, and killed the servant also; he should
have done all things otherwise; poignant regrets, weary, incessant
toiling of the mind to change what was unchangeable, to plan what
was now useless, to be the architect of the irrevocable past. Meanwhile, and behind all this activity, brute terrors, like the scurrying of
rats in a deserted attic, filled the more remote chambers of his brain
with riot; the hand of the constable would fall heavy on his shoulder,
and his nerves would jerk like a hooked fish; or he beheld, in galloping defile, the dock, the prison, the gallows, and the black coffin.

Terror of the people in the street sat down before his mind like a
besieging army. It was impossible, he thought, but that some rumour
of the struggle must have reached their ears and set on edge their
curiosity; and now, in all the neighbouring houses, he divined them
sitting motionless and with uplifted ear—solitary people, condemned
to spend Christmas dwelling alone on memories of the past, and now

startlingly recalled from that tender exercise; happy family parties, struck into silence round the table, the mother still with raised finger: every degree and age and humour, but all, by their own hearts, prying and hearkening and weaving the rope that was to hang him. Sometimes it seemed to him he could not move too softly; the clink of the tall Bohemian goblets rang out loudly like a bell; and alarmed by the bigness of the ticking, he was tempted to stop the clocks. And then, again, with a swift transition of his terrors, the very silence of the place appeared a source of peril, and a thing to strike and freeze the passer-by; and he would step more boldly, and bustle aloud among the contents of the shop, and imitate, with elaborate bravado, the movements of a busy man at ease in his own house.

But he was now so pulled about by different alarms that, while one portion of his mind was still alert and cunning, another trembled on the brink of lunacy. One hallucination in particular took a strong hold on his credulity. The neighbour hearkening with white face beside his window, the passer-by arrested by a horrible surmise on the pavement—these could at worst suspect, they could not know; through the brick walls and shuttered windows only sounds could penetrate. But here, within the house, was he alone? He knew he was; he had watched the servant set forth sweethearting, in her poor best, "out for the day" written in every ribbon and smile. Yes, he was alone, of course; and yet, in the bulk of empty house above him, he could surely hear a stir of delicate footing—he was surely conscious, inexplicably conscious of some presence. Ay, surely; to every room and corner of the house his imagination followed it; and now it was a faceless thing, and yet had eyes to see with; and again it was a shadow of himself; and yet again behold the image of the dead dealer, reinspired with cunning and hatred.

At times, with a strong effort, he would glance at the open door which still seemed to repel his eyes. The house was tall, the skylight small and dirty, the day blind with fog; and the light that filtered down to the ground storey was exceedingly faint, and showed dimly on the threshold of the shop. And yet, in that strip of doubtful brightness, did there not hang wavering a shadow?

Suddenly, from the street outside, a very jovial gentleman began to beat with a staff on the shop-door, accompanying his blows with shouts and railleries in which the dealer was continually called upon by name. Markheim, smitten into ice glanced at the dead man. But no! he lay quite still; he was fled away far beyond earshot of these blows and shoutings; he was sunk beneath seas of silence; and his name, which would once have caught his notice above the howling of a storm, had become an empty sound. And presently the jovial gentleman desisted from his knocking and departed.

Here was a broad hint to hurry what remained to be done, to get forth from this accusing neighbourhood, to plunge into a bath of London multitudes, and to reach, on the other side of day, that haven of safety and apparent innocence—his bed. One visitor had come: at any moment another might follow and be more obstinate. To have done the deed, and yet not to reap the profit, would be too abhorrent a failure. The money, that was now Markheim's concern; and as a means to that, the keys.

He glanced over his shoulder at the open door, where the shadow was still lingering and shivering; and with no conscious repugnance of the mind, yet with a tremour of the belly, he drew near the body of his victim. The human character had quite departed. Like a suit half-stuffed with bran, the limbs lay scattered, the trunk doubled, on the floor; and yet the thing repelled him. Although so dingy and inconsiderable to the eye, he feared it might have more significance to the touch. He took the body by the shoulders, and turned it on its back. It was strangely light and supple, and the limbs, as if they had been broken, fell into the oddest postures. The face was robbed of all expression; but it was as pale as wax, and shockingly smeared with blood about one temple. That was, for Markheim, the one displeasing circumstance. It carried him back, upon the instant, to a certain fair day in a fishers' village: a gray day, a piping wind, a crowd upon the street, the blare of brasses, the booming of drums, the nasal voice of a ballad singer; and a boy going to and fro, buried over head in the crowd and divided between interest and fear, until, coming out upon the chief place of concourse, he beheld a booth and a great screen with pictures, dismally designed, garishly coloured: Brownrigg with her apprentice; the Mannings with their murdered guest; Weare in the death-grip of Thurtell; and a score besides of famous crimes. The thing was as clear as an illusion; he was once again that little boy; he was looking once again, and with the same sense of physical revolt, at these vile pictures; he was still stunned by the thumping of the drums. A bar of that day's music returned upon his memory; and at that, for the first time, a qualm came over him, a breath of nausea, a sudden weakness of the joints, which he must instantly resist and conquer.

He judged it more prudent to confront than to flee from these considerations; looking the more hardily in the dead face, bending his mind to realise the nature and greatness of his crime. So little a while ago that face had moved with every change of sentiment, that pale mouth had spoken, that body had been all on fire with governable energies; and now, and by his act, that piece of life had been arrested, as the horologist, with interjected finger, arrests the beating of the clock. So he reasoned in vain; he could rise to no more remorseful consciousness; the same heart which had shuddered before the painted effigies of crime, looked on its reality unmoved. At best, he felt a gleam of pity for one who had been endowed in vain with all those faculties that can make the world a garden of enchantment, one who had never lived and who was now dead. But of penitence, no, not a tremour.

With that, shaking himself clear of these considerations, he found the keys and advanced towards the open door of the shop. Outside, it had begun to rain smartly; and the sound of the shower upon the roof had banished silence. Like some dripping cavern, the chambers of the house were haunted by an incessant echoing, which filled the ear and mingled with the ticking of the clocks. And, as Markheim approached the door, he seemed to hear, in answer to his own cautious tread, the steps of another foot withdrawing up the stair. The shadow still palpitated loosely on the threshold. He threw a ton's weight of resolve upon his muscles, and drew back the door.

The faint, foggy daylight glimmered dimly on the bare floor and stairs; on the bright suit of armour posted, halbert in hand, upon the landing; and on the dark wood-carvings, and framed pictures that hung against the yellow panels of the wainscot. So loud was the beating of the rain through all the house that, in Markheim's ears, it began to be distinguished into many different sounds. Footsteps and sighs, the tread of regiments marching in the distance, the chink of money in the counting, and the creaking of doors held stealthily ajar, appeared to mingle with the patter of the drops upon the cupola and the gushing of the water in the pipes. The sense that he was not alone grew upon him to the verge of madness. On every side he was haunted and begirt by presences. He heard them moving in the upper chambers; from the shop, he heard the dead man getting to his legs; and as he began with a great effort to mount the stairs, feet fled quietly before him and followed stealthily behind. If he were but deaf, he thought, how tranquilly he would possess his soul! And then again, and hearkening with ever fresh attention, he blessed himself for that unresting sense which held the outposts and stood a trusty sentinel upon his life. His head turned continually on his neck; his eyes, which seemed starting from their orbits, scouted on every side, and on every side were half-rewarded as with the tail of something nameless vanishing. The four-and-twenty steps to the first floor were four-and-twenty agonies.

On that first storey, the doors stood ajar, three of them like three ambushes, shaking his nerves like the throats of cannon. He could never again, he felt, be sufficiently immured and fortified from men's observing eyes; he longed to be home, girt in by walls, buried among bedclothes, and invisible to all but God. And at that thought he wondered a little, recollecting tales of other murderers and the fear they were said to entertain of heavenly avengers. It was not so, at least, with him. He feared the laws of nature, lest, in their callous and immutable procedure, they should preserve some damning evidence of his crime. He feared tenfold more, with a slavish, superstitious terror, some scission in the continuity of man's experience, some wilful illegality of nature. He played a game of skill, depending on the rules, calculating consequence from cause; and what if nature, as the defeated tyrant overthrew the chess-board, should break the mould of their succession? The like had befallen Napoleon (so writers said) when the winter changed the time of its appearance. The like might befall Markheim: the solid walls might become transparent and reveal his doings like those of bees in a glass hive; the stout planks might yield under his foot like quicksands and detain him in their clutch; ay, and there were soberer accidents that might destroy him: if, for instance, the house should fall and imprison him beside the body of his victim; or the house next door should fly on fire, and the firemen invade him from all sides. These things he feared; and, in a sense, these things might be called the hands of God reached forth against sin. But about God himself he was at ease; his act was doubtless exceptional, but so were his excuses, which God knew; it was there, and not among men, that he felt sure of justice.

When he had got safe into the drawing-room, and shut the door behind him, he was aware of a respite from alarms. The room was quite dismantled, uncarpeted besides, and strewn with packing-cases and incongruous furniture; several great pier-glasses, in which he beheld himself at various angles, like an actor on a stage; many pictures, framed and unframed, standing, with their faces to the wall; a fine Sheraton sideboard, a cabinet of marquetry, and a great old bed, with tapestry hangings. The windows opened to the floor; but by great good fortune the lower part of the shutters had been closed, and this concealed him from the neighbours. Here, then, Markheim drew in a packing-case before the cabinet, and began to search among the keys. It was a long business, for there were many; and it was irksome, besides; for, after all, there might be nothing in the cabinet, and time was on the wing. But the closeness of the occupation sobered him. With the tail of his eye he saw the door—even glanced at it from time to time directly, like a besieged commander pleased to verify the good estate of his defences. But in truth he was at peace. The rain falling in the street sounded natural and pleasant. Presently, on the other side, the notes of a piano were wakened to the music of a hymn, and the voices of many children took up the air and words. How stately, how comfortable was the melody! How fresh the youthful voices! Markheim gave ear to it smilingly, as he sorted out the keys; and his mind was thronged with answerable ideas and images; church-going children and the pealing of the high organ; children afield, bathers by the brookside, ramblers on the brambly common, kite-fliers in the windy and cloud-navigated sky; and then, at another cadence of the hymn, back again to church, and the somnolence of summer Sundays, and the high genteel voice of the parson (which he smiled a little to recall) and the painted Jacobean tombs, and the dim lettering of the Ten Commandments in the chancel.

And as he sat thus, at once busy and absent, he was startled to his feet. A flash of ice, a flash of fire, a bursting gush of blood, went over him, and then he stood transfixed and thrilling. A step mounted the stair slowly and steadily, and presently a hand was laid upon the knob, and the lock clicked, and the door opened.

Fear held Markheim in a vice. What to expect he knew not, whether the dead man walking, or the official ministers of human justice, or some chance witness blindly stumbling in to consign him to the gallows. But when a face was thrust into the aperture, glanced round the room, looked at him, nodded and smiled as if in friendly recognition, and then withdrew again, and the door closed behind it, his fear broke loose from his control in a hoarse cry. At the sound of this the visitant returned.

"Did you call me?" he asked, pleasantly, and with that he entered the room and closed the door behind him.

Markheim stood and gazed at him with all his eyes. Perhaps there was a film upon his sight, but the outlines of the new comer seemed to change and waver like those of the idols in the wavering candle-light of the shop; and at times he thought he knew him; and at times he thought he bore a likeness to himself; and always, like a lump of living terror, there lay in his bosom the conviction that this thing was not of the earth and not of God.

And yet the creature had a strange air of the commonplace, as he stood looking on Markheim with a smile; and when he added: "You are looking for the money, I believe?" it was in the tones of everyday politeness.

Markheim made no answer.

"I should warn you," resumed the other, "that the maid has left her sweetheart earlier than usual and will soon be here. If Mr. Markheim be found in this house, I need not describe to him the consequences."

"You know me?" cried the murderer.

The visitor smiled. "You have long been a favourite of mine," he said; "and I have long observed and often sought to help you."

"What are you?" cried Markheim: "the devil?"

"What I may be," returned the other, "cannot affect the service I propose to render you."

"It can," cried Markheim; "it does! Be helped by you? No, never; not by you! You do not know me yet; thank God, you do not know me!"

"I know you," replied the visitant, with a sort of kind severity or rather firmness. "I know you to the soul."

"Know me!" cried Markheim. "Who can do so? My life is but a travesty and slander on myself. I have lived to belie my nature. All men do; all men are better than this disguise that grows about and stifles them. You see each dragged away by life, like one whom bravos have seized and muffled in a cloak. If they had their own control—if you could see their faces, they would be altogether different, they would shine out for heroes and saints! I am worse than most; my self is more overlaid; my excuse is known to me and God. But, had I the time, I could disclose myself."

"To me?" inquired the visitant.

"To you before all," returned the murderer. "I supposed you were intelligent. I thought—since you exist—you would prove a reader of the heart. And yet you would propose to judge me by my acts! Think of it; my acts! I was born and I have lived in a land of giants; giants have dragged me by the wrists since I was born out of my mother—the giants of circumstance. And you would judge me by my acts! But can you not look within? Can you not understand that evil is hateful to me? Can you not see within me the clear writing of conscience, never blurred by any wilful sophistry, although too often disregarded? Can you not read me for a thing that surely must be common as humanity—the unwilling sinner?"

"All this is very feelingly expressed," was the reply, "but it regards me not. These points of consistency are beyond my province, and I care not in the least by what compulsion you may have been dragged away, so as you are but carried in the right direction. But time flies; the servant delays, looking in the faces of the crowd and at the pictures on the hoardings, but still she keeps moving nearer; and remember, it is as if the gallows itself was striding towards you through the Christmas streets! Shall I help you; I, who know all? Shall I tell you where to find the money?"

"For what price?" asked Markheim.

"I offer you the service for a Christmas gift," returned the other.

Markheim could not refrain from smiling with a kind of bitter triumph. "No," said he, "I will take nothing at your hands; if I were dying of thirst, and it was your hand that put the pitcher to my lips, I should find the courage to refuse. It may be credulous, but I will do nothing to commit myself to evil."

"I have no objection to a death-bed repentance," observed the visitant.

"Because you disbelieve their efficacy!" Markheim cried.

"I do not say so," returned the other; "but I look on these things from a different side, and when the life is done my interest falls. The man has lived to serve me, to spread black looks under colour of religion, or to sow tares in the wheat-field, as you do, in a course of weak compliance with desire. Now that he draws so near to his deliverance, he can add but one act of service—to repent, to die smiling, and thus to build up in confidence and hope the more timorous of my surviving followers. I am not so hard a master. Try me. Accept my help. Please yourself in life as you have done hitherto; please yourself more amply, spread your elbows at the board; and when the night begins to fall and the curtains to be drawn, I tell you, for your greater comfort, that you will find it even easy to compound your quarrel with your conscience, and to make a truckling peace with God. I came but now from such a death-bed, and the room was full of sincere mourners, listening to the man's last words: and when I looked into that face, which had been set as a flint against mercy, I found it smiling with hope."

"And do you, then, suppose me such a creature?" asked Markheim. "Do you think I have no more generous aspirations than to sin, and sin, and sin, and, at last, sneak into heaven? My heart rises at the thought. Is this, then, your experience of mankind? or is it because you find me with red hands that you presume such baseness? and is this crime of murder indeed so impious as to dry up the very springs of good?"

"Murder is to me no special category," replied the other. "All sins are murder, even as all life is war. I behold your race, like starving mariners on a raft, plucking crusts out of the hands of famine and feeding on each other's lives. I follow sins beyond the moment of their acting; I find in all that the last consequence is death; and to my eyes, the pretty maid who thwarts her mother with such taking graces on a question of a ball, drips no less visibly with human gore than such a murderer as yourself. Do I say that I follow sins? I follow virtues also; they differ not by the thickness of a nail, they are both scythes for the reaping angel of Death. Evil, for which I live, consists not in action but in character. The bad man is dear to me; not the bad act, whose fruits, if we could follow them far enough down the hurtling cataract of the ages, might yet be found more blessed than those of the rarest virtues. And it is not because you have killed a dealer, but because you are Markheim, that I offered to forward your escape."

"I will lay my heart open to you," answered Markheim. "This

crime on which you find me is my last. On my way to it I have learned many lessons; itself is a lesson, a momentous lesson. Hitherto I have been driven with revolt to what I would not; I was a bond-slave to poverty, driven and scourged. There are robust virtues that can stand in these temptations; mine was not so: I had a thirst of pleasure. But to-day, and out of this deed, I pluck both warning and riches—both the power and a fresh resolve to be myself. I become in all things a free actor in the world; I begin to see myself all changed, these hands the agents of good, this heart at peace. Something comes over me out of the past; something of what I have dreamed on Sabbath evenings to the sound of the church organ, of what I forecast when I shed tears over noble books, or talked, an innocent child, with my mother. There lies my life; I have wandered a few years, but now I see once more my city of destination."

"You are to use this money on the Stock Exchange, I think?" remarked the visitor; "and there, if I mistake not, you have already lost some thousands?"

"Ah," said Markheim, "but this time I have a sure thing."

"This time, again, you will lose," replied the visitor quietly.

"Ah, but I keep back the half!" cried Markheim.

"That also you will lose," said the other.

The sweat started upon Markheim's brow. "Well, then, what matter?" he exclaimed. "Say it be lost, say I am plunged again in poverty, shall one part of me, and that the worst, continue until the end to override the better? Evil and good run strong in me, haling me both ways. I do not love the one thing, I love all. I can conceive great deeds, renunciations, martyrdoms; and though I be fallen to such a crime as murder, pity is no stranger to my thoughts. I pity the poor; who knows their trials better than myself? I pity and help them; I prize love, I love honest laughter; there is no good thing nor true thing on earth but I love it from my heart. And are my vices only to direct my life, and my virtues to lie without effect, like some passive lumber of the mind? Not so; good, also, is a spring of acts."

But the visitant raised his finger. "For six-and-thirty years that you have been in this world," said he, "through many changes of fortune and varieties of humour, I have watched you steadily fall. Fifteen years ago you would have started at a theft. Three years back you would have blenched at the name of murder. Is there any crime, is there any cruelty or meanness, from which you still recoil?—five years from now I shall detect you in the fact! Downward, downward, lies your way; nor can anything but death avail to stop you."

"It is true," Markheim said huskily, "I have in some degree complied with evil. But it is so with all: the very saints, in the mere exercise of living, grow less dainty, and take on the tone of their surroundings."

"I will propound to you one simple question," said the other; "and as you answer, I shall read to you your moral horoscope. You have grown in many things more lax; possibly you do right to be so; and at any account, it is the same with all men. But granting that, are you in any one particular, however trifling, more difficult to please with your own conduct, or do you go in all things with a looser rein?"

"In any one?" repeated Markheim, with an anguish of consideration. "No," he added, with despair, "in none! I have gone down in all."

"Then," said the visitor, "content yourself with what you are, for you will never change; and the words of your part on this stage are irrevocably written down."

Markheim stood for a long while silent, and indeed it was the visitor who first broke the silence. "That being so," he said, "shall I show you the money?"

"And grace?" cried Markheim.

"Have you not tried it?" returned the other. "Two or three years ago, did I not see you on the platform of revival meetings, and was not your voice the loudest in the hymn?"

"It is true," said Markheim; "and I see clearly what remains for me by way of duty. I thank you for these lessons from my soul; my eyes are opened, and I behold myself at last for what I am."

At this moment, the sharp note of the door-bell rang through the house; and the visitant, as though this were some concerted signal for which he had been waiting, changed at once in his demeanour.

"The maid!" he cried. "She has returned, as I forewarned you, and there is now before you one more difficult passage. Her master, you must say, is ill; you must let her in, with an assured but rather serious countenance—no smiles, no overacting, and I promise you success! Once the girl within, and the door closed, the same dexterity that has already rid you of the dealer will relieve you of this last danger in your path. Thenceforward you have the whole evening— the whole night, if needful—to ransack the treasures of the house and to make good your safety. This is help that comes to you with the mask of danger. Up!" he cried: "up, friend; your life hangs trembling in the scales: up, and act!"

Markheim steadily regarded his counsellor. "If I be condemned to evil acts," he said, "there is still one door of freedom open—I can cease from action. If my life be an ill thing, I can lay it down. Though I be, as you say truly, at the beck of every small temptation, I can yet, by one decisive gesture, place myself beyond the reach of all. My love of good is damned to barrenness; it may, and let it be! But I have still my hatred of evil; and from that, to your galling disappointment, you shall see that I can draw both energy and courage."

The features of the visitor began to undergo a wonderful and lovely change: they brightened and softened with a tender triumph; and, even as they brightened, faded and dislimned. But Markheim did not pause to watch or understand the transformation. He opened the door and went downstairs very slowly, thinking to himself. His past went soberly before him; he beheld it as it was, ugly and strenuous like a dream, random as chance-medley—a scene of defeat. Life, as he thus reviewed it, tempted him no longer; but on the further side he perceived a quiet haven for his bark. He paused in the passage, and looked into the shop, where the candle still burned by the dead body. It was strangely silent. Thoughts of the dealer swarmed into his mind, as he stood gazing. And then the bell once more broke out into impatient clamour.

He confronted the maid upon the threshold with something like a smile.

"You had better go for the police," said he: "I have killed your master."

Thomas Hardy
(1840-1928)

THOMAS Hardy would have appreciated the irony of being buried in the Poets' Corner of Westminster Abbey, for, a few years before his death, he had requested that a memorial to Byron be placed there; the Abbey refused Byron the honor on the grounds that he had been a most immoral writer. Hardy responded in "A Refusal," a poem in the form of an imaginary monologue by the Dean of Westminster, speaking intentional doggerel. Beneath the polished insult lies the simple truth that Hardy too had been accused of immorality in his last two major novels—*Tess of the D'Urbervilles* (1891) and *Jude the Obscure* (1896). The reviewers of his day had found "smut" where Hardy had intended honesty of emotion and passion; they had seen eager exploitation of "every unclean situation" where he had provided only frank treatment of sex and religion. *Jude the Obscure* was banned from public libraries and burned by a bishop before the world was ready to acknowledge the genius of a man once called an "amateur of filth." Following such an inhospitable reception, Hardy resolved to write no more fiction and turned exclusively to poetry in the last third of his life.

Fortunately, writers and scholars of the twentieth century have been fairer in their assessment of Hardy's work. A. E. Coppard admits modeling his short stories on those in *Life's Little Ironies* (1894), a collection which characterizes, with dry humor and anecdotal reminiscence, the disillusion and stoic bitterness of an artist who was helpless to stop the flow of progress, a progress he saw ironically as inevitable and, in some ways, as admirable.

Hardy's poetry, like his fiction, expresses a grim tolerance for the new ways of a new century. In poetry, he could express more directly what haunted him, in a place, in a memory. His pessimism and irony and what he called his "meliorism" inspire his use of Gothic images to represent effortlessly the naturalness of the Romantics, the stoicism of the Victorians, the vividness of the Pre-Raphaelites, and the profound skepticism of the Moderns—the sweep of literary movements of his long life.

"The Darkling Thrush" was first published in the *Graphic* under the title "By the Century's Deathbed," a melancholy description of the speaker's position in time and space. Leaning "upon a coppice gate" at dusk in winter, the speaker finds in the bleak, lonely landscape appropriate images for the passing century, the dying Victorian age. Images of death abound in the "spectre-gray" Frost, the "dregs" of Winter. The century's corpse has a "cloudy" crypt, a windy "death-lament," and a pulse which is "shrunken hard and dry." "Fervourless" is an understated description of the man, his fellow spirits, and the onetime passions of the age.

Out of the same desolate situation, another voice sings "Of joy illimited" in a carol with religious overtones noted in the vesper by the term "evensong." The voice of the thrush counters that of the despairing speaker, and, like Keats's nightingale, suggests by its cheerful song a new perspective. The thrush is "darkling," shrouded in darkness, yet happy; flinging "his soul/ Upon the growing gloom," he becomes a symbol for tolerance and patience and "Some blessed Hope." The speaker remains unconvinced, however, and draws no explicit consolation from the brave bird in the ever-growing gloom at the end of the year.

The same is true of the speaker's recovery from "A Wasted Illness": he will have to endure the same pain again before death, or so he thinks. The recovery makes the illness a "wasted" one, for only death can end physical suffering and the mental tortures of serious illness. Hardy was once dangerously ill, with internal bleeding, and was confined to bed from October 1880 to May 1881—the period during which this poem was written. He added "(Overheard)" to the title when the poem was reprinted in the Wessex Edition to distance his own experience.

Hardy's architectural training and his knowledge of Gothic churches, in particular, give the "vaults" and "galleries" and "aisles" of torment a realism even Poe would have approved. The feverish descent and the piercing, pounding pain are made all the more ghastly by the alliterative effects and the companionship of "webby waxing things and waning things/ As on I went." It is easy to see why the reviewers of his time accused him of a morbid temperament, but it is even easier to join today's critics in their applause for his macabre imagination and suggestions of supernatural agency.

The Darkling Thrush (1901)

I leant upon a coppice gate
  When Frost was spectre-gray,
And Winter's dregs made desolate

The weakening eye of day.
The tangled bine-stems scored the sky   5
    Like strings from broken lyres,
And all mankind that haunted nigh
    Had sought their household fires.

The land's sharp features seemed to be
    The Century's corpse outleant,   10
His crypt the cloudy canopy,
    The wind his death-lament.
The ancient pulse of germ and birth
    Was shrunken hard and dry,
And every spirit upon earth   15
    Seemed fervourless as I.

At once a voice outburst among
    The bleak twigs overhead
In a full-hearted evensong
    Of joy illimited;   20
An aged thrush, frail, gaunt, and small,
    In blast-beruffled plume,
Had chosen thus to fling his soul
    Upon the growing gloom.

So little cause for carollings   25
    Of such ecstatic sound
Was written on terrestrial things
    Afar or nigh around,
That I could think there trembled through
    His happy good-night air   30
Some blessed Hope, whereof he knew
    And I was unaware.

A Wasted Illness (1901)

    Through vaults of pain,
Enribbed and wrought with groins of ghastliness,
I passed, and garish spectres moved my brain
    To dire distress.

    And hammerings,   5
And quakes, and shoots, and stifling hotness, blent

With webby waxing things and waning things
    As on I went.

    "Where lies the end
To this foul way?" I asked with weakening breath.   10
Thereon ahead I saw a door extend—
    The door to death.

    It loomed more clear:
"At last!" I cried. "The all-delivering door!"
And then, I knew not how, it grew less near   15
    Than theretofore.

    And back slid I
Along the galleries by which I came,
And tediously the day returned, and sky,
    And life—the same.   20

    And all was well:
Old circumstance resumed its former show,
And on my head the dews of comfort fell
    As ere my woe.

    I roam anew,   25
Scarce conscious of my late distress. . . . And yet
Those backward steps through pain I cannot view
    Without regret.

    For that dire train
Of waxing shapes and waning, passed before,   30
And those grim aisles, must be traversed again
    To reach that door.

Stephen Crane
(1871-1900)

FROM the title, with its rich ambiguity, to the searing beauty of the fire, to the unused, empty teacups at the end, Stephen Crane's novella *The Monster* everywhere presents multiple meanings and invites a variety of responses. Little Jimmy, playing train, destroys a flower. He cannot revive it; he cannot restore the dead to life. He looks to his father, who is godlike both to him and to the black hostler Henry Johnson. But Dr. Trescott is far from understanding the problem that the crushed flower poses, and even farther from grasping the solution. Is he right or wrong in restoring Henry to life as a faceless and mindless monster? He certainly owes Henry his best effort as a doctor. Yet the description of his drive toward his burning home suggests that his intuition is limited, and the images of magic and witchcraft associated with the house he builds after the fire give him the aura of a sorcerer. As Judge Hagenthorpe says, in discussing with Dr. Trescott the ethics of saving Henry's life, "It is hard for a man to know what to do." Is the judge, then, the spokesman for Crane? Perhaps, and yet his wife is among those who refuse their sympathy and support to Mrs. Trescott.

Presumptuous as Dr. Trescott may be, unfeeling as the judge is, they are surely less at fault than most of the townspeople in Whilomville. (The name "Whilomville" suggests a "town that once has been.") Crane scrutinizes every social echelon in its appropriate setting. In Watermelon Alley, the opportunistic Bella first announces that she was engaged to Henry and then, when confronted with the maimed man, crawls babbling away. Henry's friend Alek sets a price on his mercy, while his wife—in an ironic anticipation of the ending —laments her loss of lady callers. The barber-shop customers, like a Greek chorus commenting on the action, pronounce their judgment that Henry should have been allowed to die. Their obscene joking about his facelessness shows that mercy is not their motive. At the gracious home of Theresa Page, a little girl becomes frightened, so beginning a cycle of vicious rumors. In the household of Martha Goodwin, spinster and gossip, the ladies collect slander while Martha seems to support the doctor out of sheer perverseness.

If Dr. Trescott is monster-like in his proud defiance of nature's law, society is monster-like in its crude reactions to the preternatural. As Eric Solomon writes in *Stephen Crane* (1966): "What is monstrous about Henry is his inability to comprehend the effect of his altered appearance. This opacity society can never forgive, for Henry's weakminded refusal to accept appearances calls into question the social and religious hypocrisies that order men's lives."

In being unaware of his deformity, Henry has an advantage over Mary Shelley's monster, whose story in *Frankenstein* anticipated his. Both monsters are created by men whose motives are dubious, Dr. Trescott's more complexly so than Frankenstein's. Both are shunned by society, even by children, who might be thought free from prejudice. Both bring disaster to their creators. To the psychological insight and moral exploration of *Frankenstein*, however, Crane added the element of social commentary. His analysis of such social issues as the position of blacks in America, small-town conformity, and suspicion of the intellectual helps give the story the energy and power that almost conceal from view the subtle craft. Crane judged *The Monster* the best of his works, even better than *The Red Badge of Courage* (1895). His judgment gives plausibility to the notion that the Gothic is a versatile mode—one hospitable to a social conscience.

The Monster (1899)

I

Little Jim was, for the time, engine Number 36, and he was making the run between Syracuse and Rochester. He was fourteen minutes behind time, and the throttle was wide open. In consequence, when he swung around the curve at the flower-bed, a wheel of his cart destroyed a peony. Number 36 slowed down at once and looked guiltily at his father, who was mowing the lawn. The doctor had his back to this accident, and he continued to pace slowly to and fro, pushing the mower.

Jim dropped the tongue of the cart. He looked at his father and at the broken flower. Finally he went to the peony and tried to stand it on its pins, resuscitated, but the spine of it was hurt, and it would only hang limply from his hand. Jim could do no reparation. He looked again toward his father.

He went on to the lawn, very slowly, and kicking wretchedly at the turf. Presently his father came along with the whirring machine, while the sweet, new grass blades spun from the knives. In a low voice, Jim said, "Pa!"

The doctor was shaving this lawn as if it were a priest's chin. All during the season he had worked at it in the coolness and peace of the evenings after supper. Even in the shadow of the cherry-trees the grass was strong and healthy. Jim raised his voice a trifle. "Pa!"

The doctor paused, and with the howl of the machine no longer occupying the sense, one could hear the robins in the cherry-trees arranging their affairs. Jim's hands were behind his back, and sometimes his fingers clasped and unclasped. Again he said, "Pa!" The child's fresh and rosy lip was lowered.

The doctor stared down at his son, thrusting his head forward and frowning attentively. "What is it, Jimmie?"

"Pa!" repeated the child at length. Then he raised his finger and pointed at the flower-bed. "There!"

"What?" said the doctor, frowning more. "What is it, Jim?"

After a period of silence, during which the child may have undergone a severe mental tumult, he raised his finger and repeated his former word—"There!" The father had respected this silence with perfect courtesy. Afterwards his glance carefully followed the direction indicated by the child's finger, but he could see nothing which explained to him. "I don't understand what you mean, Jimmie," he said.

It seemed that the importance of the whole thing had taken away the boy's vocabulary. He could only reiterate, "There!"

The doctor mused upon the situation, but he could make nothing of it. At last he said, "Come, show me."

Together they crossed the lawn toward the flower-bed. At some yards from the broken peony Jimmie began to lag. "There!" The word came almost breathlessly.

"Where?" said the doctor.

Jimmie kicked at the grass. "There!" he replied.

The doctor was obliged to go forward alone. After some trouble he found the subject of the incident, the broken flower. Turning then, he saw the child lurking at the rear and scanning his countenance.

The father reflected. After a time he said, "Jimmie, come here." With an infinite modesty of demeanor the child came forward. "Jimmie, how did this happen?"

The child answered, "Now—I was playin' train—and—now—I runned over it."

"You were doing what?"

"I was playin' train."

The father reflected again. "Well, Jimmie," he said, slowly, "I guess you had better not play train any more to-day. Do you think you had better?"

"No, sir," said Jimmie.

During the delivery of the judgment the child had not faced his father, and afterwards he went away, with his head lowered, shuffling his feet.

II

It was apparent from Jimmie's manner that he felt some kind of desire to efface himself. He went down to the stable. Henry Johnson, the negro who cared for the doctor's horses, was sponging the buggy. He grinned fraternally when he saw Jimmie coming. These two were pals. In regard to almost everything in life they seemed to have minds precisely alike. Of course there were points of emphatic divergence. For instance, it was plain from Henry's talk that he was a very handsome negro, and he was known to be a light, a weight, and an eminence in the suburb of the town, where lived the larger number of the negroes, and obviously this glory was over Jimmie's horizon; but he vaguely appreciated it and paid deference to Henry for it mainly because Henry appreciated it and deferred to himself. However, on all points of conduct as related to the doctor, who was the moon, they were in complete but unexpressed understanding. Whenever Jimmie became the victim of an eclipse he went to the stable to solace himself with Henry's crimes. Henry, with the elasticity of his race, could usually provide a sin to place himself on a footing with the disgraced one. Perhaps he would remember that he had forgotten to put the hitching-strap in the back of the buggy on some recent occasion, and had been reprimanded by the doctor. Then these two would commune subtly and without words concerning their moon, holding themselves sympathetically as people who had committed similar treasons. On the other hand, Henry would sometimes choose to absolutely repudiate this idea, and when Jimmie appeared in his shame would bully him most virtuously, preaching with assurance the precepts of the doctor's creed, and pointing out to Jimmie all his abominations. Jimmie did not discover that this was odious in his comrade. He accepted it and lived in its shadow with humility, merely trying to conciliate the saintly Henry with acts of deference. Won by this attitude, Henry would sometimes allow the child to enjoy the felicity of squeezing the sponge over a buggy-wheel, even when Jimmie was still gory from unspeakable deeds.

Whenever Henry dwelt for a time in sackcloth, Jimmie did not patronize him at all. This was a justice of his age, his condition. He did not know. Besides, Henry could drive a horse, and Jimmie had a full sense of this sublimity. Henry personally conducted the moon during the splendid journeys through the country roads, where farms spread on all sides, with sheep, cows, and other marvels abounding.

"Hello, Jim!" said Henry, poising his sponge. Water was dripping from the buggy. Sometimes the horses in the stalls stamped thunderingly on the pine floor. There was an atmosphere of hay and of harness.

For a minute Jimmie refused to take an interest in anything. He was very downcast. He could not even feel the wonders of wagon-washing. Henry, while at his work, narrowly observed him.

"Your pop done wallop yer, didn't he?" he said at last.

"No," said Jimmie, defensively; "he didn't."

After this casual remark Henry continued his labor, with a scowl of occupation. Presently he said: "I done tol' yer many's th' time not to go a-foolin' an' a-projjeckin' with them flowers. Yer pop don' like it nohow." As a matter of fact, Henry had never mentioned flowers to the boy.

Jimmie preserved a gloomy silence, so Henry began to use seductive wiles in this affair of washing a wagon. It was not until he began to spin a wheel on the tree, and the sprinkling water flew everywhere, that the boy was visibly moved. He had been seated on the sill of the carriage-house door, but at the beginning of this ceremony he arose and circled towards the buggy, with an interest that slowly consumed the remembrance of a late disgrace.

Johnson could then display all the dignity of a man whose duty it was to protect Jimmie from a splashing. "Look out, boy! look out! You done gwi' spile yer pants. I raikon your mommer don' 'low this foolishness, she know it. I ain't gwi' have you round yere spilin' yer pants, an' have Mis' Trescott light on me pressen'ly. 'Deed I ain't."

He spoke with an air of great irritation, but he was not annoyed at all. This tone was merely a part of his importance. In reality he was always delighted to have the child there to witness the business of the stable. For one thing, Jimmie was invariably overcome with reverence when he was told how beautifully a harness was polished or a horse groomed. Henry explained each detail of this kind with unction, procuring great joy from the child's admiration.

III

After Johnson had taken his supper in the kitchen, he went to his loft in the carriage-house and dressed himself with much care. No belle of a court circle could bestow more mind on a toilet than did Johnson. On second thought, he was more like a priest arraying himself for some parade of the church. As he emerged from his room and sauntered down the carriage-drive, no one would have suspected him of ever having washed a buggy.

It was not altogether a matter of the lavender trousers, nor yet the straw hat with its bright silk band. The change was somewhere far in the interior of Henry. But there was no cake-walk hyperbole in it. He was simply a quiet, well-bred gentleman of position, wealth, and other necessary achievements out for an evening stroll, and he had never washed a wagon in his life.

In the morning, when in his working-clothes, he had met a friend—"Hello, Pete!" "Hello, Henry!" Now, in his effulgence, he encountered this same friend. His bow was not at all haughty. If it expressed anything, it expressed consummate generosity—"Good-evenin', Misteh Washington." Pete, who was very dirty, being at work in a potato-patch, responded in a mixture of abasement and appreciation—"Good-evenin', Misteh Johnsing."

The shimmering blue of the electric arc-lamps was strong in the main street of the town. At numerous points it was conquered by the orange glare of the outnumbering gaslights in the windows of shops. Through this radiant lane moved a crowd, which culminated in a throng before the post-office, awaiting the distribution of the evening mails. Occasionally there came into it a shrill electric street-car, the motor singing like a cageful of grasshoppers, and possessing a great gong that clanged forth both warnings and simple noise. At the little theatre, which was a varnish and red-plush miniature of one of the famous New York theatres, a company of strollers was to play "East Lynne." The young men of the town were mainly gathered at the corners, in distinctive groups, which expressed various shades and lines of chumship, and had little to do with any social gradations. There they discussed everything with critical insight, passing the whole town in review as it swarmed in the street. When the gongs of the electric cars ceased for a moment to harry the ears, there could be heard the sound of the feet of the leisurely crowd on the bluestone pavement, and it was like the peaceful evening lashing at the shore of a lake. At the foot of the hill, where two lines of maples sentinelled the way, an electric lamp glowed high among the embowering branches, and made most wonderful shadow-etchings on the road below it.

When Johnson appeared amid the throng a member of one of the profane groups at a corner instantly telegraphed news of this extraordinary arrival to his companions. They hailed him. "Hello, Henry! Going to walk for a cake to-night?"

"Ain't he smooth?"

"Why, you've got that cake right in your pocket, Henry!"

"Throw out your chest a little more."

Henry was not ruffled in any way by these quiet admonitions and compliments. In reply he laughed a supremely good-natured, chuckling laugh, which nevertheless expressed an underground complacency of superior metal.

Young Griscom, the lawyer, was just emerging from Reifsnyder's barber shop, rubbing his chin contentedly. On the steps he dropped his hand and looked with wide eyes into the crowd. Suddenly he bolted back into the shop. "Wow!" he cried to the parliament; "you ought to see the coon that's coming!"

Reifsnyder and his assistant instantly poised their razors high and turned towards the window. Two belathered heads reared from the chairs. The electric shine in the street caused an effect like water to them who looked through the glass from the yellow glamour of Reifsnyder's shop. In fact, the people without resembled the inhabitants of a great aquarium that here had a square pane in it. Presently into this frame swam the graceful form of Henry Johnson.

"Chee!" said Reifsnyder. He and his assistant with one accord threw their obligations to the winds, and leaving their lathered victims helpless, advanced to the window. "Ain't he a taisy?" said Reifsnyder, marvelling.

But the man in the first chair, with a grievance in his mind, had found a weapon. "Why, that's only Henry Johnson, you blamed idiots! Come on now, Reif, and shave me. What do you think I am—a mummy?"

Reifsnyder turned, in a great excitement. "I bait you any money that vas not Henry Johnson! Henry Johnson! Rats!" The scorn put into this last word made it an explosion. "That man was a Pullman-car porter or someding. How could that be Henry Johnson?" he demanded, turbulently. "You vas crazy."

The man in the first chair faced the barber in a storm of indignation. "Didn't I give him those lavender trousers?" he roared.

And young Griscom, who had remained attentively at the window, said: "Yes, I guess that was Henry. It looked like him."

"Oh, vell," said Reifsnyder, returning to his business, "if you think so! Oh, vell!" He implied that he was submitting for the sake of amiability.

Finally the man in the second chair, mumbling from a mouth made timid by adjacent lather, said: "That was Henry Johnson all right. Why, he always dresses like that when he wants to make a front! He's the biggest dude in town—anybody knows that."

"Chinger!" said Reifsnyder.

Henry was not at all oblivious of the wake of wondering ejaculation that streamed out behind him. On other occasions he had reaped this same joy, and he always had an eye for the demonstration. With a face beaming with happiness he turned away from the scene of his victories into a narrow side street, where the electric light still hung high, but only to exhibit a row of tumble-down houses leaning together like paralytics.

The saffron Miss Bella Farragut, in a calico frock, had been crouched on the front stoop, gossiping at long range, but she espied her approaching caller at a distance. She dashed around the corner of the house, galloping like a horse. Henry saw it all, but he preserved the polite demeanor of a guest when a waiter spills claret down his cuff. In this awkward situation he was simply perfect.

The duty of receiving Mr. Johnson fell upon Mrs. Farragut, because Bella, in another room, was scrambling wildly into her best gown. The fat old woman met him with a great ivory smile, sweeping back with the door, and bowing low. "Walk in, Misteh Johnson, walk in. How is you dis ebenin', Misteh Johnson—how is you?"

Henry's face showed like a reflector as he bowed and bowed, bending almost from his head to his ankles. "Good-evenin', Mis' Fa'gut; good-evenin'. How is you dis evenin'? Is all you' folks well, Mis' Fa'gut?"

After a great deal of kowtow, they were planted in two chairs opposite each other in the living-room. Here they exchanged the most tremendous civilities, until Miss Bella swept into the room, when there was more kowtow on all sides, and a smiling show of teeth that was like an illumination.

The cooking-stove was of course in this drawing-room, and on the fire was some kind of a long-winded stew. Mrs. Farragut was obliged to arise and attend to it from time to time. Also young Sim came in and went to bed on his pallet in the corner. But to all these domesticities the three maintained an absolute dumbness. They bowed and smiled and ignored and imitated until a late hour, and if they had been the occupants of the most gorgeous salon in the world they could not have been more like three monkeys.

After Henry had gone, Bella, who encouraged herself in the appropriation of phrases, said, "Oh, ma, isn't he divine?"

IV

A Saturday evening was a sign always for a larger crowd to parade the thoroughfare. In summer the band played until ten o'clock in the little park. Most of the young men of the town affected to be superior to this band, even to despise it; but in the still and fragrant evenings they invariably turned out in force, because the girls were sure to attend this concert, strolling slowly over the grass, linked closely in pairs, or preferably in threes, in the curious public dependence upon one another which was their inheritance. There was no particular social aspect to this gathering, save that group regarded group with interest, but mainly in silence. Perhaps one girl would nudge another girl and suddenly say, "Look! there goes Gertie Hodgson and her sister!" And they would appear to regard this as an event of importance.

On a particular evening a rather large company of young men were gathered on the sidewalk that edged the park. They remained thus beyond the borders of the festivities because of their dignity, which would not exactly allow them to appear in anything which was so much fun for the younger lads. These latter were careering madly through the crowd, precipitating minor accidents from time to time, but usually fleeing like mist swept by the wind before retribution could lay hands upon them.

The band played a waltz which involved a gift of prominence to the bass horn, and one of the young men on the sidewalk said that the music reminded him of the new engines on the hill pumping water into the reservoir. A similarity of this kind was not inconceivable, but the young man did not say it because he disliked the band's playing. He said it because it was fashionable to say that manner of thing concerning the band. However, over in the stand, Billie Harris, who played the snare-drum, was always surrounded by a throng of boys, who adored his every whack.

After the mails from New York and Rochester had been finally distributed, the crowd from the post-office added to the mass already in the park. The wind waved the leaves of the maples, and, high in the air, the blue-burning globes of the arc lamps caused the wonderful traceries of leaf shadows on the ground. When the light fell upon the upturned face of a girl, it caused it to glow with a wonderful pallor. A policeman came suddenly from the darkness and chased a gang of obstreperous little boys. They hooted him from a distance. The leader of the band had some of the mannerisms of the great musicians, and during a period of silence the crowd smiled when they saw him raise his hand to his brow, stroke it sentimentally, and glance upward with a look of poetic anguish. In the shivering light, which gave to the park an effect like a great vaulted hall, the throng swarmed, with a gentle murmur of dresses switching the turf, and with a steady hum of voices.

Suddenly, without preliminary bars, there arose from afar the great hoarse roar of a factory whistle. It raised and swelled to a sinister note, and then it sang on the night wind one long call that held the crowd in the park immovable, speechless. The band-master had been about to vehemently let fall his hand to start the band on a thundering career through a popular march, but, smitten by this giant voice from the night, his hand dropped slowly to his knee, and, his mouth agape, he looked at his men in silence. The cry died away to a wail and then to stillness. It released the muscles of the company of young men on the sidewalk, who had been like statues, posed eagerly, lithely, their ears turned. And then they wheeled upon each other simultaneously, and, in a single explosion, they shouted, "One!"

Again the sound swelled in the night and roared its long

ominous cry, and as it died away the crowd of young men wheeled upon each other and, in chorus, yelled, "Two!"

There was a moment of breathless waiting. Then they bawled, "Second district!" In a flash the company of indolent and cynical young men had vanished like a snowball disrupted by dynamite.

V

Jake Rogers was the first man to reach the home of Tuscarora Hose Company Number Six. He had wrenched his key from his pocket as he tore down the street, and he jumped at the spring-lock like a demon. As the doors flew back before his hands he leaped and kicked the wedges from a pair of wheels, loosened a tongue from its clasp, and in the glare of the electric light which the town placed before each of its hose-houses the next comers beheld the spectacle of Jake Rogers bent like hickory in the manfulness of his pulling, and the heavy cart was moving slowly towards the doors. Four men joined him at the time, and as they swung with the cart out into the street, dark figures sped towards them from the ponderous shadows back of the electric lamps. Some set up the inevitable question, "What district?"

"Second," was replied to them in a compact howl. Tuscarora Hose Company Number Six swept on a perilous wheel into Niagara Avenue, and as the men, attached to the cart by the rope which had been paid out from the windlass under the tongue, pulled madly in their fervor and abandon, the gong under the axle clanged incitingly. And sometimes the same cry was heard, "What district?"

"Second."

On a grade Johnnie Thorpe fell, and exercising a singular muscular ability, rolled out in time from the track of the on-coming wheel, and arose, dishevelled and aggrieved, casting a look of mournful disenchantment upon the black crowd that poured after the machine. The cart seemed to be the apex of a dark wave that was whirling as if it had been a broken dam. Back of the lad were stretches of lawn, and in that direction front-doors were banged by men who hoarsely shouted out into the clamorous avenue, "What district?"

At one of these houses a woman came to the door bearing a lamp, shielding her face from its rays with her hands. Across the cropped grass the avenue represented to her a kind of black torrent, upon which, nevertheless, fled numerous miraculous figures upon bicycles. She did not know that the towering light at the corner was continuing its nightly whine.

Suddenly a little boy somersaulted around the corner of the

house as if he had been projected down a flight of stairs by a catapul-tian boot. He halted himself in front of the house by dint of a rather extraordinary evolution with his legs. "Oh, ma," he gasped, "can I go? Can I, ma?"

She straightened with the coldness of the exterior mother-judg-ment, although the hand that held the lamp trembled slightly. "No, Willie; you had better come to bed."

Instantly he began to buck and fume like a mustang. "Oh, ma," he cried, contorting himself—"oh, ma, can't I go? Please, ma, can't I go? Can't I go, ma?"

"It's half-past nine now, Willie."

He ended by wailing out a compromise: "Well, just down to the corner, ma? Just down to the corner?"

From the avenue came the sound of rushing men who wildly shouted. Somebody had grappled the bell-rope in the Methodist church, and now over the town rang this solemn and terrible voice, speaking from the clouds. Moved from its peaceful business, this bell gained a new spirit in the portentous night, and it swung the heart to and fro, up and down, with each peal of it.

"Just down to the corner, ma?"

"Willie, it's half-past nine now."

VI

The outlines of the house of Dr. Trescott had faded quietly into the evening, hiding a shape such as we call Queen Anne against the pall of the blackened sky. The neighborhood was at this time so quiet, and seemed so devoid of obstructions, that Hannigan's dog thought it a good opportunity to prowl in forbidden precincts, and so came and pawed Trescott's lawn, growling, and considering himself a formidable beast. Later, Peter Washington strolled past the house and whistled, but there was no dim light shining from Henry's loft, and presently Peter went his way. The rays from the street, creeping in silvery waves over the grass, caused the row of shrubs along the drive to throw a clear, bold shade.

A wisp of smoke came from one of the windows at the end of the house and drifted quietly into the branches of a cherry-tree. Its companions followed it in slowly increasing numbers, and finally there was a current controlled by invisible banks which poured into the fruit-laden boughs of the cherry-tree. It was no more to be noted than if a troop of dim and silent gray monkeys had been climbing a grapevine into the clouds.

After a moment the window brightened as if the four panes of it had been stained with blood, and a quick ear might have been led to imagine the fire-imps calling and calling, clan joining clan, gathering to the colors. From the street, however, the house maintained its dark quiet, insisting to a passer-by that it was the safe dwelling of people who chose to retire early to tranquil dreams. No one could have heard this low droning of the gathering clans.

Suddenly the panes of the red window tinkled and crashed to the ground, and at other windows there suddenly reared other flames, like bloody spectres at the apertures of a haunted house. This outbreak had been well planned, as if by professional revolutionists.

A man's voice suddenly shouted: "Fire! Fire! Fire!" Hannigan had flung his pipe frenziedly from him because his lungs demanded room. He tumbled down from his perch, swung over the fence, and ran shouting towards the front-door of the Trescotts'. Then he hammered on the door, using his fists as if they were mallets. Mrs. Trescott instantly came to one of the windows on the second floor. Afterwards she knew she had been about to say, "The doctor is not at home, but if you will leave your name, I will let him know as soon as he comes."

Hannigan's bawling was for a minute incoherent, but she understood that it was not about croup.

"What?" she said, raising the window swiftly.

"Your house is on fire! You're all ablaze! Move quick if—" His cries were resounding in the street as if it were a cave of echoes. Many feet pattered swiftly on the stones. There was one man who ran with an almost fabulous speed. He wore lavender trousers. A straw hat with a bright silk band was held half crumpled in his hand.

As Henry reached the front-door, Hannigan had just broken the lock with a kick. A thick cloud of smoke poured over them, and Henry, ducking his head, rushed into it. From Hannigan's clamor he knew only one thing, but it turned him blue with horror. In the hall a lick of flame had found the cord that supported "Signing the Declaration." The engraving slumped suddenly down at one end, and then dropped to the floor, where it burst with the sound of a bomb. The fire was already roaring like a winter wind among the pines.

At the head of the stairs Mrs. Trescott was waving her arms as if they were two reeds. "Jimmie! Save Jimmie!" she screamed in Henry's face. He plunged past her and disappeared, taking the long-familiar routes among these upper chambers, where he had once held office as a sort of second assistant house-maid.

Hannigan had followed him up the stairs, and grappled the arm of the maniacal woman there. His face was black with rage. "You must come down," he bellowed.

She would only scream at him in reply: "Jimmie! Jimmie! Save Jimmie!" But he dragged her forth while she babbled at him.

As they swung out into the open air a man ran across the lawn, and seizing a shutter, pulled it from its hinges and flung it far out upon the grass. Then he frantically attacked the other shutters one by one. It was a kind of temporary insanity.

"Here, you," howled Hannigan, "hold Mrs. Trescott— And stop—"

The news had been telegraphed by a twist of the wrist of a neighbor who had gone to the fire-box at the corner, and the time when Hannigan and his charge struggled out of the house was the time when the whistle roared its hoarse night call, smiting the crowd in the park, causing the leader of the band, who was about to order the first triumphal clang of a military march, to let his hand drop slowly to his knees.

VII

Henry pawed awkwardly through the smoke in the upper halls. He had attempted to guide himself by the walls, but they were too hot. The paper was crimpling, and he expected at any moment to have a flame burst from under his hands.

"Jimmie!"

He did not call very loud, as if in fear that the humming flames below would overhear him.

"Jimmie! Oh, Jimmie!"

Stumbling and panting, he speedily reached the entrance to Jimmie's room and flung open the door. The little chamber had no smoke in it at all. It was faintly illuminated by a beautiful rosy light reflected circuitously from the flames that were consuming the house. The boy had apparently just been aroused by the noise. He sat in his bed, his lips apart, his eyes wide, while upon his little white-robed figure played caressingly the light from the fire. As the door flew open he had before him this apparition of his pal, a terror-stricken negro, all tousled and with wool scorching, who leaped upon him and bore him up in a blanket as if the whole affair were a case of kidnapping by a dreadful robber chief. Without waiting to go through the usual short but complete process of wrinkling up his face, Jimmie let out a gorgeous bawl, which resembled the expression of a calf's deepest terror. As Johnson, bearing him, reeled into the smoke of the hall, he flung his arms about his neck and buried his face in the blanket. He called twice in muffled tones: "Mam-ma! Mam-ma!"

When Johnson came to the top of the stairs with his burden, he took a quick step backward. Through the smoke that rolled to him he could see that the lower hall was all ablaze. He cried out then in a howl that resembled Jimmie's former achievement. His legs gained a frightful faculty of bending sideways. Swinging about precariously on these reedy legs, he made his way back slowly, back along the upper hall. From the way of him then, he had given up almost all idea of escaping from the burning house, and with it the desire. He was submitting, submitting because of his fathers, bending his mind in a most perfect slavery to this conflagration.

He now clutched Jimmie as unconsciously as when, running toward the house, he had clutched the hat with the bright silk band.

Suddenly he remembered a little private staircase which led from a bedroom to an apartment which the doctor had fitted up as a laboratory and work-house, where he used some of his leisure, and also hours when he might have been sleeping, in devoting himself to experiments which came in the way of his study and interest.

When Johnson recalled this stairway the submission to the blaze departed instantly. He had been perfectly familiar with it, but his confusion had destroyed the memory of it.

In his sudden momentary apathy there had been little that resembled fear, but now, as a way of safety came to him, the old frantic terror caught him. He was no longer creature to the flames, and he was afraid of the battle with them. It was a singular and swift set of alternations in which he feared twice without submission, and submitted once without fear.

"Jimmie!" he wailed, as he staggered on his way. He wished this little inanimate body at his breast to participate in his tremblings. But the child had lain limp and still during these headlong charges and countercharges, and no sign came from him.

Johnson passed through two rooms and came to the head of the stairs. As he opened the door great billows of smoke poured out, but gripping Jimmie closer, he plunged down through them. All manner of odors assailed him during this flight. They seemed to be alive with envy, hatred, and malice. At the entrance to the laboratory he confronted a strange spectacle. The room was like a garden in the region where might be burning flowers. Flames of violet, crimson, green, blue, orange, and purple were blooming everywhere. There was one blaze that was precisely the hue of a delicate coral. In another place was a mass that lay merely in phosphorescent inaction like a pile of emeralds. But all these marvels were to be seen dimly through clouds of heaving, turning, deadly smoke.

Johnson halted for a moment on the threshold. He cried out again in the negro wail that had in it the sadness of the swamps. Then he rushed across the room. An orange-colored flame leaped like a panther at the lavender trousers. This animal bit deeply into Johnson. There was an explosion at one side, and suddenly before him there reared a delicate, trembling sapphire shape like a fairy lady. With a quiet smile she blocked his path and doomed him and Jimmie. Johnson shrieked, and then ducked in the manner of his race in fights. He aimed to pass under the left guard of the sapphire lady. But she was swifter than eagles, and her talons caught in him as he plunged past her. Bowing his head as if his neck had been struck, Johnson lurched forward, twisting this way and that way. He fell on his back. The still form in the blanket flung from his arms, rolled to the edge of the floor and beneath the window.

Johnson had fallen with his head at the base of an old-fashioned desk. There was a row of jars upon the top of this desk. For the most part, they were silent amid this rioting, but there was one which seemed to hold a scintillant and writhing serpent.

Suddenly the glass splintered, and a ruby-red snakelike thing poured its thick length out upon the top of the old desk. It coiled and hesitated, and then began to swim a languorous way down the mahogany slant. At the angle it waved its sizzling molten head to and fro over the closed eyes of the man beneath it. Then, in a moment, with a mystic impulse, it moved again, and the red snake flowed directly down into Johnson's upturned face.

Afterwards the trail of this creature seemed to reek, and amid flames and low explosions drops like red-hot jewels pattered softly down it at leisurely intervals.

VIII

Suddenly all roads led to Dr. Trescott's. The whole town flowed towards one point. Chippeway Hose Company Number One toiled desperately up Bridge Street Hill even as the Tuscaroras came in an impetuous sweep down Niagara Avenue. Meanwhile the machine of the hook-and-ladder experts from across the creek was spinning on its way. The chief of the fire department had been playing poker in the rear room of Whiteley's cigar-store, but at the first breath of the alarm he sprang through the door like a man escaping with the kitty.

In Whilomville, on these occasions, there was always a number of people who instantly turned their attention to the bells in the churches and school-houses. The bells not only emphasized the alarm, but it was the habit to send these sounds rolling across the sky in a stirring brazen uproar until the flames were practically vanquished. There was also a kind of rivalry as to which bell should be made to produce the greatest din. Even the Valley Church, four miles away among the farms, had heard the voices of its brethren, and immediately added a quaint little yelp.

Dr. Trescott had been driving homeward, slowly smoking a cigar, and feeling glad that this last case was now in complete obedience to him, like a wild animal that he had subdued, when he heard the long whistle, and chirped to his horse under the unlicensed but perfectly distinct impression that a fire had broken out in Oakhurst, a new and rather high-flying suburb of the town which was at least two miles from his own home. But in the second blast and in the ensuing silence he read the designation of his own district. He was then only a few blocks from his house. He took out the whip and laid it lightly on the mare. Surprised and frightened at this extraordinary action, she leaped forward, and as the reins straightened like steel bands, the doctor leaned backward a trifle. When the mare whirled him up to the closed gate he was wondering whose house could be afire. The man who had rung the signal-box yelled something at him, but he already knew. He left the mare to her will.

In front of his door was a maniacal woman in a wrapper. "Ned!" she screamed at sight of him. "Jimmie! Save Jimmie!"

Trescott had grown hard and chill. "Where?" he said. "Where?"

Mrs. Trescott's voice began to bubble. "Up—up—up—" She pointed at the second-story windows.

Hannigan was already shouting: "Don't go in that way! You can't go in that way!"

Trescott ran around the corner of the house and disappeared from them. He knew from the view he had taken of the main hall that it would be impossible to ascend from there. His hopes were fastened now to the stairway which led from the laboratory. The door which opened from this room out upon the lawn was fastened with a bolt and lock, but he kicked close to the lock and then close to the bolt. The door with a loud crash flew back. The doctor recoiled from the roll of smoke, and then bending low, he stepped into the garden of burning flowers. On the floor his stinging eyes could make out a form in a smouldering blanket near the window. Then, as he carried his son towards the door, he saw that the whole lawn seemed now alive with men and boys, the leaders in the great charge that the whole town was making. They seized him and his burden, and overpowered him in wet blankets and water.

But Hannigan was howling: "Johnson is in there yet! Henry Johnson is in there yet! He went in after the kid! Johnson is in there yet!"

These cries penetrated to the sleepy senses of Trescott, and he struggled with his captors, swearing, unknown to him and to them, all the deep blasphemies of his medical-student days. He rose to his feet and went again towards the door of the laboratory. They endeavored to restrain him, although they were much affrighted at him.

But a young man who was a brakeman on the railway, and lived in one of the rear streets near the Trescotts, had gone into the laboratory and brought forth a thing which he laid on the grass.

IX

There were hoarse commands from in front of the house. "Turn on your water, Five!" "Let 'er go, One!" The gathering crowd swayed this way and that way. The flames, towering high, cast a wild red light on their faces. There came the clangor of a gong from along some adjacent street. The crowd exclaimed at it. "Here comes Number Three!" "That's Three a-comin'!" A panting and irregular mob dashed into view, dragging a hose-cart. A cry of exultation arose from the little boys. "Here's Three!" The lads welcomed Never-Die Hose Company Number Three as if it was composed of a chariot dragged by a band of gods. The perspiring citizens flung themselves into the fray. The boys danced in impish joy at the displays of prowess. They acclaimed the approach of Number Two. They welcomed Number Four with cheers. They were so deeply moved by this whole affair that they bitterly guyed the late appearance of the hook and ladder company, whose heavy apparatus had almost stalled them on the Bridge Street hill. The lads hated and feared a fire, of course. They did not particularly want to have anybody's house burn, but still it was fine to see the gathering of the companies, and amid a great noise to watch their heroes perform all manner of prodigies.

They were divided into parties over the worth of different companies, and supported their creeds with no small violence. For instance, in that part of the little city where Number Four had its home it would be most daring for a boy to contend the superiority of any other company. Likewise, in another quarter, where a strange boy was asked which fire company was the best in Whilomville, he was expected to answer "Number One." Feuds, which the boys forgot and remembered according to chance or the importance of some recent event, existed all through the town.

They did not care much for John Shipley, the chief of the department. It was true that he went to a fire with the speed of a falling angel, but when there he invariably lapsed into a certain still mood, which was almost a preoccupation, moving leisurely around the burning structure and surveying it, puffing meanwhile at a cigar. This quiet man, who even when life was in danger seldom raised his voice, was not much to their fancy. Now old Sykes Huntington, when he was chief, used to bellow continually like a bull and gesticulate in a sort of delirium. He was much finer as a spectacle than this Shipley, who viewed a fire with the same steadiness that he viewed a raise in a large jack-pot. The greater number of the boys could never understand why the members of these companies persisted in re-electing Shipley, although they often pretended to understand it, because "My father says" was a very formidable phrase in argument, and the fathers seemed almost unanimous in advocating Shipley.

At this time there was considerable discussion as to which company had gotten the first stream of water on the fire. Most of the boys claimed that Number Five owned that distinction, but there was a determined minority who contended for Number One. Boys who were the blood adherents of other companies were obliged to choose between the two on this occasion, and the talk waxed warm.

But a great rumor went among the crowds. It was told with hushed voices. Afterwards a reverent silence fell even upon the boys. Jimmie Trescott and Henry Johnson had been burned to death, and Dr. Trescott himself had been most savagely hurt. The crowd did not even feel the police pushing at them. They raised their eyes, shining now with awe, towards the high flames.

The man who had information was at his best. In low tones he described the whole affair. "That was the kid's room—in the corner there. He had measles or somethin', and this coon—Johnson—was a-settin' up with 'im, and Johnson got sleepy or somethin' and upset the lamp, and the doctor he was down in his office, and he came running up, and they all got burned together till they dragged 'em out."

Another man, always preserved for the deliverance of the final judgment, was saying: "Oh, they'll die sure. Burned to flinders. No chance. Hull lot of 'em. Anybody can see." The crowd concentrated its gaze still more closely upon these flags of fire which waved joyfully against the black sky. The bells of the town were clashing unceasingly.

A little procession moved across the lawn and towards the street. There were three cots, borne by twelve of the firemen. The police moved sternly, but it needed no effort of theirs to open a lane for this slow cortège. The men who bore the cots were well known to the crowd, but in this solemn parade during the ringing of the bells and the shouting, and with the red glare upon the sky, they seemed utterly foreign, and Whilomville paid them a deep respect. Each man in this stretcher party had gained a reflected majesty. They were footmen to death, and the crowd made subtle obeisance to this august dignity derived from three prospective graves. One woman turned away with a shriek at sight of the covered body on the first stretcher, and people faced her suddenly in silent and mournful indignation. Otherwise there was barely a sound as these twelve important men with measured tread carried their burdens through the throng.

The little boys no longer discussed the merits of the different fire companies. For the greater part they had been routed. Only the more courageous viewed closely the three figures veiled in yellow blankets.

X

Old Judge Denning Hagenthorpe, who lived nearly opposite the Trescotts, had thrown his door wide open to receive the afflicted family. When it was publicly learned that the doctor and his son and the negro were still alive, it required a specially detailed policeman to prevent people from scaling the front porch and interviewing these sorely wounded. One old lady appeared with a miraculous poultice, and she quoted most damning Scripture to the officer when he said that she could not pass him. Throughout the night some lads old enough to be given privileges or to compel them from their mothers remained vigilantly upon the kerb in anticipation of a death or some such event. The reporter of the *Morning Tribune* rode thither on his bicycle every hour until three o'clock.

Six of the ten doctors in Whilomville attended at Judge Hagenthorpe's house.

Almost at once they were able to know that Trescott's burns were not vitally important. The child would possibly be scarred badly, but his life was undoubtedly safe. As for the negro Henry Johnson, he could not live. His body was frightfully seared, but more than that, he now had no face. His face had simply been burned away.

Trescott was always asking news of the two other patients. In the morning he seemed fresh and strong, so they told him that Johnson was doomed. They then saw him stir on the bed, and sprang quickly to see if the bandages needed readjusting. In the sudden glance he threw from one to another he impressed them as being both leonine and impracticable.

The morning paper announced the death of Henry Johnson. It contained a long interview with Edward J. Hannigan, in which the latter described in full the performance of Johnson at the fire. There was also an editorial built from all the best words in the vocabulary of the staff. The town halted in its accustomed road of thought, and turned a reverent attention to the memory of this hostler. In the breasts of many people was the regret that they had not known enough to give him a hand and a lift when he was alive, and they judged themselves stupid and ungenerous for this failure.

The name of Henry Johnson became suddenly the title of a saint to the little boys. The one who thought of it first could, by quoting it in an argument, at once overthrow his antagonist, whether it applied to the subject or whether it did not.

"Nigger, nigger, never die.
Black face and shiny eye."

Boys who had called this odious couplet in the rear of Johnson's march buried the fact at the bottom of their hearts.

Later in the day Miss Bella Farragut, of No. 7 Watermelon Alley, announced that she had been engaged to marry Mr. Henry Johnson.

XI

The old judge had a cane with an ivory head. He could never think at his best until he was leaning slightly on this stick and smoothing the white top with slow movements of his hands. It was also to him a kind of narcotic. If by any chance he mislaid it, he grew at once very irritable, and was likely to speak sharply to his sister, whose mental incapacity he had patiently endured for thirty years in the old mansion on Ontario Street. She was not at all aware of her brother's opinion of her endowments, and so it might be said that the judge had successfully dissembled for more than a quarter of a century, only risking the truth at the times when his cane was lost.

On a particular day the judge sat in his armchair on the porch. The sunshine sprinkled through the lilac-bushes and poured great coins on the boards. The sparrows disputed in the trees that lined the pavements. The judge mused deeply, while his hands gently caressed the ivory head of his cane.

Finally he arose and entered the house, his brow still furrowed in a thoughtful frown. His stick thumped solemnly in regular beats. On the second floor he entered a room where Dr. Trescott was working about the bedside of Henry Johnson. The bandages on the negro's head allowed only one thing to appear, an eye, which unwinkingly stared at the judge. The latter spoke to Trescott on the condition of the patient. Afterward he evidently had something further to say, but he seemed to be kept from it by the scrutiny of the unwinking eye, at which he furtively glanced from time to time.

When Jimmie Trescott was sufficiently recovered, his mother had taken him to pay a visit to his grandparents in Connecticut. The doctor had remained to take care of his patients, but as a matter of truth he spent most of his time at Judge Hagenthorpe's house, where lay Henry Johnson. Here he slept and ate almost every meal in the long nights and days of his vigil.

At dinner, and away from the magic of the unwinking eye, the judge said, suddenly, "Trescott, do you think it is—" As Trescott paused expectantly, the judge fingered his knife. He said, thoughtfully, "No one wants to advance such ideas, but somehow I think that that poor fellow ought to die."

There was in Trescott's face at once a look of recognition, as if in this tangent of the judge he saw an old problem. He merely sighed and answered, "Who knows?" The words were spoken in a deep tone that gave them an elusive kind of significance.

The judge retreated to the cold manner of the bench. "Perhaps we may not talk with propriety of this kind of action, but I am induced to say that you are performing a questionable charity in preserving this negro's life. As near as I can understand, he will hereafter be a monster, a perfect monster, and probably with an affected brain. No man can observe you as I have observed you and not know that it was a matter of conscience with you, but I am afraid, my friend, that it is one of the blunders of virtue." The judge had delivered his views with his habitual oratory. The last three words he spoke with a particular emphasis, as if the phrase was his discovery.

The doctor made a weary gesture. "He saved my boy's life."

"Yes," said the judge, swiftly—"yes, I know!"

"And what am I to do?" said Trescott, his eyes suddenly lighting like an outburst from smouldering peat. "What am I to do? He gave himself for—for Jimmie. What am I to do for him?"

The judge abased himself completely before these words. He lowered his eyes for a moment. He picked at his cucumbers.

Presently he braced himself straightly in his chair. "He will be your creation, you understand. He is purely your creation. Nature has very evidently given him up. He is dead. You are restoring him to life. You are making him, and he will be a monster, and with no mind."

"He will be what you like, judge," cried Trescott, in sudden, polite fury. "He will be anything, but, by God! he saved my boy."

The judge interrupted in a voice trembling with emotion: "Trescott! Trescott! Don't I know?"

Trescott had subsided to a sullen mood. "Yes, you know," he answered, acidly; "but you don't know all about your own boy being saved from death." This was a perfectly childish allusion to the judge's bachelorhood. Trescott knew that the remark was infantile, but he seemed to take desperate delight in it.

But it passed the judge completely. It was not his spot.

"I am puzzled," said he, in profound thought. "I don't know what to say."

Trescott had become repentant. "Don't think I don't appreciate what you say, judge. But—"

"Of course!" responded the judge, quickly. "Of course."

"It—" began Trescott.

"Of course," said the judge.

In silence they resumed their dinner.

"Well," said the judge, ultimately, "it is hard for a man to know what to do."

"It is," said the doctor, fervidly.

There was another silence. It was broken by the judge:

"Look here, Trescott; I don't want you to think——"

"No, certainly not," answered the doctor, earnestly.

"Well, I don't want you to think I would say anything to—— It was only that I thought that I might be able to suggest to you that——perhaps——the affair was a little dubious."

With an appearance of suddenly disclosing his real mental perturbation, the doctor said: "Well, what would you do? Would you kill him?" he asked, abruptly and sternly.

"Trescott, you fool," said the old man, gently.

"Oh, well, I know, judge, but then——" He turned red, and spoke with new violence: "Say, he saved my boy—do you see? He saved my boy."

"You bet he did," cried the judge, with enthusiasm. "You bet he did." And they remained for a time gazing at each other, their faces illuminated with memories of a certain deed.

After another silence, the judge said, "It is hard for a man to know what to do."

XII

Late one evening Trescott, returning from a professional call, paused his buggy at the Hagenthorpe gate. He tied the mare to the old tin-covered post, and entered the house. Ultimately he appeared with a companion—a man who walked slowly and carefully, as if he were learning. He was wrapped to the heels in an old-fashioned ulster. They entered the buggy and drove away.

After a silence only broken by the swift and musical humming of the wheels on the smooth road, Trescott spoke. "Henry," he said, "I've got you a home here with old Alek Williams. You will have everything you want to eat and a good place to sleep, and I hope you will get along there all right. I will pay all your expenses, and come to see you as often as I can. If you don't get along, I want you to let me know as soon as possible, and then we will do what we can to make it better."

The dark figure at the doctor's side answered with a cheerful laugh. "These buggy wheels don' look like I washed 'em yesterday, docteh," he said.

Trescott hesitated for a moment, and then went on insistently, "I am taking you to Alek Williams, Henry, and I——"

The figure chuckled again. "No, 'deed! No, seh! Alek Williams don' know a hoss! 'Deed he don't. He don' know a hoss from a pig." The laugh that followed was like the rattle of pebbles.

Trescott turned and looked sternly and coldly at the dim form in the gloom from the buggy-top. "Henry," he said, "I didn't say anything about horses. I was saying——"

"Hoss? Hoss?" said the quavering voice from these near shadows. "Hoss? 'Deed I don' know all erbout a hoss! 'Deed I don't." There was a satirical chuckle.

At the end of three miles the mare slackened and the doctor leaned forward, peering, while holding tight reins. The wheels of the buggy bumped often over out-cropping boulders. A window shone forth, a simple square of topaz on a great black hill-side. Four dogs charged the buggy with ferocity, and when it did not promptly retreat, they circled courageously around the flanks, baying. A door opened near the window in the hill-side, and a man came and stood on a beach of yellow light.

"Yah! yah! You Roveh! You Susie! Come yah! Come yah this minit!"

Trescott called across the dark sea of grass, "Hello, Alek!"

"Hello!"

"Come down here and show me where to drive."

The man plunged from the beach into the surf, and Trescott could then only trace his course by the fervid and polite ejaculations of a host who was somewhere approaching. Presently Williams took the mare by the head, and uttering cries of welcome and scolding the swarming dogs, led the equipage towards the lights. When they halted at the door and Trescott was climbing out, Williams cried, "Will she stand, docteh?"

"She'll stand all right, but you better hold her for a minute. Now, Henry." The doctor turned and held both arms to the dark figure. It crawled to him painfully like a man going down a ladder. Williams took the mare away to be tied to a little tree, and when he returned he found them awaiting him in the gloom beyond the rays from the door.

He burst out then like a siphon pressed by a nervous thumb. "Hennery! Hennery, ma ol' frien'. Well, if I ain' glade. If I ain' glade!"

Trescott had taken the silent shape by the arm and led it forward into the full revelation of the light. "Well, now, Alek, you can take Henry and put him to bed, and in the morning I will——"

Near the end of this sentence old Williams had come front to front with Johnson. He gasped for a second, and then yelled the yell of a man stabbed in the heart.

For a fraction of a moment Trescott seemed to be looking for epithets. Then he roared: "You old black chump! You old black—— Shut up! Shut up! Do you hear?"

Williams obeyed instantly in the matter of his screams, but he continued in a lowered voice: "Ma Lode amassy! Who'd ever think? Ma Lode amassy!"

Trescott spoke again in the manner of a commander of a battalion. "Alek!"

The old negro again surrendered, but to himself he repeated in a whisper, "Ma Lode!" He was aghast and trembling.

As these three points of widening shadows approached the golden doorway a hale old negress appeared there, bowing. "Good-evenin', docteh! Good-evenin'! Come in! come in!" She had evidently just retired from a tempestuous struggle to place the room in order, but she was now bowing rapidly. She made the effort of a person swimming.

"Don't trouble yourself, Mary," said Trescott, entering. "I've brought Henry for you to take care of, and all you've got to do is to carry out what I tell you." Learning that he was not followed, he faced the door, and said, "Come in, Henry."

Johnson entered. "Whee!" shrieked Mrs. Williams. She almost achieved a back somersault. Six young members of the tribe of Williams made a simultaneous plunge for a position behind the stove, and formed a wailing heap.

XIII

"You know very well that you and your family lived usually on less than three dollars a week, and now that Dr. Trescott pays you five dollars a week for Johnson's board, you live like millionaires. You haven't done a stroke of work since Johnson began to board with you—everybody knows that—and so what are you kicking about?"

The judge sat in his chair on the porch, fondling his cane, and gazing down at old Williams, who stood under the lilac-bushes. "Yes, I know, jedge," said the negro, wagging his head in a puzzled manner. " 'Tain't like as if I didn't 'preciate what the docteh done, but—but—well, yeh see, jedge," he added, gaining a new impetus, "it's—it's hard wuk. This ol' man nev' did wuk so hard. Lode, no."

"Don't talk such nonsense, Alek," spoke the judge, sharply. "You have never really worked in your life—anyhow, enough to support a family of sparrows, and now when you are in a more prosperous condition than ever before, you come around talking like an old fool."

The negro began to scratch his head. "Yeh see, jedge," he said at last, "my ol' 'ooman she cain't 'ceive no lady callahs, nohow."

"Hang lady callers!" said the judge, irascibly. "If you have flour in the barrel and meat in the pot, your wife can get along without receiving lady callers, can't she?"

"But they won't come ainyhow, jedge," replied Williams, with an air of still deeper stupefaction. "Noner ma wife's frien's ner noner ma frien's 'll come near ma res'dence."

"Well, let them stay home if they are such silly people."

The old negro seemed to be seeking a way to elude this argument, but evidently finding none, he was about to shuffle meekly off. He halted, however. "Jedge," said he, "ma ol' 'ooman's near driv' abstracted."

"Your old woman is an idiot," responded the judge.

Williams came very close and peered solemnly through a branch of lilac. "Jedge," he whispered, "the chillens."

"What about them?"

Dropping his voice to funereal depths, Williams said, "They—they cain't eat."

"Can't eat!" scoffed the judge, loudly. "Can't eat! You must think I am as big an old fool as you are. Can't eat—the little rascals! What's to prevent them from eating?"

In answer, Williams said, with mournful emphasis, "Hennery." Moved with a kind of satisfaction at his tragic use of the name, he remained staring at the judge for a sign of its effect.

The judge made a gesture of irritation. "Come, now, you old scoundrel, don't beat around the bush any more. What are you up to? What do you want? Speak out like a man, and don't give me any more of this tiresome rigamarole."

"I ain't er-beatin' round 'bout nuffin, jedge," replied Williams, indignantly. "No, seh; I say whatter got to say right out. 'Deed I do."

"Well, say it, then."

"Jedge," began the negro, taking off his hat and switching his knee with it, "Lode knows I'd do jes 'bout as much fer five dollehs er week as ainy cul'd man, but—but this yere business is awful, jedge. I raikon 'ain't been no sleep in—in my house sence docteh done fetch 'im."

"Well, what do you propose to do about it?"

Williams lifted his eyes from the ground and gazed off through the trees. "Raikon I got good appetite, an' go' sleep jes like er dog, but he—he's done broke me all up. 'Tain't no good, nohow. I wake up in the night; I hear 'im, mebbe, er-whimperin' an' er-whimperin', an' I sneak an' I sneak until I try th' do' to see if he locked in. An' he keep me er-puzzlin' an' er-quakin' all night long. Don't know how'll do in th' winter. Can't let 'im out where th' chillen is. He'll done freeze where he is now." Williams spoke these sentences as if he were talking to himself. After a silence of deep reflection he continued: "Folks go round sayin' he ain't Hennery Johnson at all. They say he's er devil!"

"What?" cried the judge.

"Yesseh," repeated Williams, in tones of injury, as if his veracity had been challenged. "Yesseh. I'm er-tellin' it to yeh straight, jedge. Plenty cul'd people folks up my way say it is a devil."

"Well, you don't think so yourself, do you?"

"No. 'Tain't no devil. It's Hennery Johnson."

"Well, then, what is the matter with you? You don't care what a lot of foolish people say. Go on 'tending to your business, and pay no attention to such idle nonsense."

" 'Tis nonsense, jedge; but he *looks* like er devil."

"What do you care what he looks like?" demanded the judge.

"Ma rent is two dollehs and er half er month," said Williams, slowly.

"It might just as well be ten thousand dollars a month," responded the judge. "You never pay it, anyhow."

"Then, anoth' thing," continued Williams, in his reflective tone. "If he was all right in his haid I could stan' it; but, jedge, he's crazier 'n er loon. Then when he looks like er devil, an' done skears all ma frien's away, an' ma chillens cain't eat, an' ma ole 'ooman jes raisin' Cain all the time, an' ma rent two dollehs an' er half er month, an' him not right in his haid, it seems like five dollehs er week—"

The judge's stick came down sharply and suddenly upon the floor of the porch. "There," he said, "I thought that was what you were driving at."

Williams began swinging his head from side to side in the strange racial mannerism. "Now hol' on a minnet, jedge," he said, defensively. " 'Tain't like as if I didn't 'preciate what the docteh done. 'Tain't that. Docteh Trescott is er kind man, an' 'tain't like as if I didn't 'preciate what he done; but—but—"

"But what? You are getting painful, Alek. Now tell me this: did you ever have five dollars a week regularly before in your life?"

Williams at once drew himself up with great dignity, but in the pause after that question he drooped gradually to another attitude. In the end he answered, heroically: "No, jedge, I 'ain't. An' 'tain't like as if I was er-sayin' five dollehs wasn't er lot er money for a man like me. But, jedge, what er man oughter git fer this kinder wuk is er salary. Yesseh, jedge," he repeated, with a great impressive gesture; "fer this kinder wuk er man oughter git er salary." He laid a terrible emphasis upon the final word.

The judge laughed. "I know Dr. Trescott's mind concerning this affair, Alek; and if you are dissatisfied with your boarder, he is quite ready to move him to some other place; so, if you care to leave word with me that you are tired of the arrangement and wish it changed, he will come and take Johnson away."

Williams scratched his head again in deep perplexity. "Five dollehs is er big price fer bo'd, but 'tain't no big price fer the bo'd of er crazy man," he said, finally.

"What do you think you ought to get?" asked the judge.

"Well," answered Alek, in the manner of one deep in a balancing of the scales, "he looks like er devil, an' done skears e'rybody, an' ma chillens cain't eat, an' I cain't sleep, an' he ain't right in his haid, an'—"

"You told me all those things."

After scratching his wool, and beating his knee with his hat, and gazing off through the trees and down at the ground, Williams said, as he kicked nervously at the gravel, "Well, jedge, I think it is wuth—" He stuttered.

"Worth what?"

"Six dollehs," answered Williams, in a desperate outburst.

The judge lay back in his great arm-chair and went through all the motions of a man laughing heartily, but he made no sound save a slight cough. Williams had been watching him with apprehension.

"Well," said the judge, "do you call six dollars a salary?"

"No, seh," promptly responded Williams. " 'Tain't a salary. No, 'deed! 'Tain't a salary." He looked with some anger upon the man who questioned his intelligence in this way.

"Well, supposing your children can't eat?"

"I—"

"And supposing he looks like a devil? And supposing all those things continue? Would you be satisfied with six dollars a week?"

Recollections seemed to throng in Williams's mind at these interrogations, and he answered dubiously. "Of co'se a man who ain't right in his haid, an' looks like er devil— But six dollehs—" After these two attempts at a sentence Williams suddenly appeared as an orator, with a great shiny palm waving in the air. "I tell yeh, jedge, six dollehs is six dollehs, but if I git six dollehs for bo'ding Hennery Johnson, I uhns it! I uhns it!"

"I don't doubt that you earn six dollars for every week's work you do," said the judge.

"Well, if I bo'd Hennery Johnson fer six dollehs er week, I uhns it! I uhns it!" cried Williams, wildly.

XIV

Reifsnyder's assistant had gone to his supper, and the owner of the shop was trying to placate four men who wished to be shaved at once. Reifsnyder was very garrulous—a fact which made him rather remarkable among barbers, who, as a class, are austerely speechless, having been taught silence by the hammering reiteration of a tradition. It is the customers who talk in the ordinary event.

As Reifsnyder waved his razor down the cheek of a man in the chair, he turned often to cool the impatience of the others with pleasant talk, which they did not particularly heed.

"Oh, he should have let him die," said Bainbridge, a railway engineer, finally replying to one of the barber's orations. "Shut up, Reif, and go on with your business!"

Instead, Reifsnyder paused shaving entirely, and turned to front the speaker. "Let him die?" he demanded. "How vas that? How can you let a man die?"

"By letting him die, you chump," said the engineer. The others laughed a little, and Reifsnyder turned at once to his work, sullenly, as a man overwhelmed by the derision of numbers.

"How vas that?" he grumbled later. "How can you let a man die when he vas done so much for you?"

" 'When he vas done so much for you?' " repeated Bainbridge. "You better shave some people. How vas that? Maybe this ain't a barber shop?"

A man hitherto silent now said, "If I had been the doctor, I would have done the same thing."

"Of course," said Reifsnyder. "Any man vould do it. Any man that vas not like you, you—old—flint-hearted—fish." He had sought the final words with painful care, and he delivered the collection triumphantly at Bainbridge. The engineer laughed.

The man in the chair now lifted himself higher, while Reifsnyder began an elaborate ceremony of anointing and combing his hair. Now free to join comfortably in the talk, the man said: "They say he is the most terrible thing in the world. Young Johnnie Bernard—that drives the grocery wagon—saw him up at Alek Williams's shanty, and he says he couldn't eat anything for two days."

"Chee!" said Reifsnyder.

"Well, what makes him so terrible?" asked another.

"Because he hasn't got any face," replied the barber and the engineer in duet.

"Hasn't got any face!" repeated the man. "How can he do without any face?"

"He has no face in the front of his head,
In the place where his face ought to grow."

Bainbridge sang these lines pathetically as he arose and hung his hat on a hook. The man in the chair was about to abdicate in his favor. "Get a gait on you now," he said to Reifsnyder. "I go out at 7.31."

As the barber foamed the lather on the cheeks of the engineer he seemed to be thinking heavily. Then suddenly he burst out. "How would you like to be with no face?" he cried to the assemblage.

"Oh, if I had to have a face like yours—" answered one customer.

Bainbridge's voice came from a sea of lather. "You're kicking because if losing faces became popular, you'd have to go out of business."

"I don't think it will become so much popular," said Reifsnyder.

"Not if it's got to be taken off in the way his was taken off," said another man. "I'd rather keep mine, if you don't mind."

"I guess so!" cried the barber. "Just think!"

The shaving of Bainbridge had arrived at a time of comparative liberty for him. "I wonder what the doctor says to himself?" he observed. "He may be sorry he made him live."

"It was the only thing he could do," replied a man. The others seemed to agree with him.

"Supposing you were in his place," said one, "and Johnson had saved your kid. What would you do?"

"Certainly!"

"Of course! You would do anything on earth for him. You'd take all the trouble in the world for him. And spend your last dollar on him. Well, then?"

"I wonder how it feels to be without any face?" said Reifsnyder, musingly.

The man who had previously spoken, feeling that he had expressed himself well, repeated the whole thing. "You would do anything on earth for him. You'd take all the trouble in the world for him. And spend your last dollar on him. Well, then?"

"No, but look," said Reifsnyder; "supposing you don't got a face!"

XV

As soon as Williams was hidden from the view of the old judge he began to gesture and talk to himself. An elation had evidently penetrated to his vitals, and caused him to dilate as if he had been filled with gas. He snapped his fingers in the air, and whistled fragments of triumphal music. At times, in his progress towards his shanty, he indulged in a shuffling movement that was really a dance. It was to be learned from the intermediate monologue that he had emerged from his trials laurelled and proud. He was the unconquerable Alexander Williams. Nothing could exceed the bold self-reliance of his manner. His kingly stride, his heroic song, the derisive flourish of his hands—all betokened a man who had successfully defied the world.

On his way he saw Zeke Paterson coming to town. They hailed each other at a distance of fifty yards.

"How do, Broth' Paterson?"

"How do, Broth' Williams?"

They were both deacons.

"Is you' folks well, Broth' Paterson?"

"Middlin', middlin'. How's you' folks, Broth' Williams?"

Neither of them had slowed his pace in the smallest degree. They had simply begun this talk when a considerable space separated them, continued it as they passed, and added polite questions as they drifted steadily apart. Williams's mind seemed to be a balloon. He had been so inflated that he had not noticed that Paterson had definitely shied into the dry ditch as they came to the point of ordinary contact.

Afterwards, as he went a lonely way, he burst out again in song and pantomimic celebration of his estate. His feet moved in prancing steps.

When he came in sight of his cabin, the fields were bathed in a blue dusk, and the light in the window was pale. Cavorting and gesticulating, he gazed joyfully for some moments upon this light. Then suddenly another idea seemed to attack his mind, and he stopped, with an air of being suddenly dampened. In the end he approached his home as if it were the fortress of an enemy.

Some dogs disputed his advance for a loud moment, and then discovering their lord, slunk away embarrassed. His reproaches were addressed to them in muffled tones.

Arriving at the door, he pushed it open with the timidity of a new thief. He thrust his head cautiously sideways, and his eyes met the eyes of his wife, who sat by the table, the lamp-light defining a half of her face. " 'Sh!" he said, uselessly. His glance travelled swiftly to the inner door which shielded the one bed-chamber. The pickaninnies, strewn upon the floor of the living-room, were softly snoring. After a hearty meal they had promptly dispersed themselves about the place and gone to sleep. " 'Sh!" said Williams again to his motionless and silent wife. He had allowed only his head to appear. His wife, with one hand upon the edge of the table and the other at her knee, was regarding him with wide eyes and parted lips as if he were a spectre. She looked to be one who was living in terror, and even the familiar face at the door had thrilled her because it had come suddenly.

Williams broke the tense silence. "Is he all right?" he whispered, waving his eyes towards the inner door. Following his glance timorously, his wife nodded, and in a low tone answered:

"I raikon he's done gone t' sleep."

Williams then slunk noiselessly across his threshold.

He lifted a chair, and with infinite care placed it so that it faced the dreaded inner door. His wife moved slightly, so as to also squarely face it. A silence came upon them in which they seemed to be waiting for a calamity, pealing and deadly.

Williams finally coughed behind his hand. His wife started, and looked upon him in alarm. " 'Pears like he done gwine keep quiet ter-night," he breathed. They continually pointed their speech and their looks at the inner door, paying it the homage due to a corpse or a phantom. Another long stillness followed this sentence. Their eyes shone white and wide. A wagon rattled down the distant road. From their chairs they looked at the window, and the effect of the light in the cabin was a presentation of an intensely black and solemn night. The old woman adopted the attitude used always in church at funerals. At times she seemed to be upon the point of breaking out in prayer.

"He mighty quiet ter-night," whispered Williams. "Was he good ter-day?" For answer his wife raised her eyes to the ceiling in the supplication of Job. Williams moved restlessly. Finally he tiptoed to the door. He knelt slowly and without a sound, and placed his ear near the key-hole. Hearing a noise behind him, he turned quickly. His wife was staring at him aghast. She stood in front of the stove, and her arms were spread out in the natural movement to protect all her sleeping ducklings.

But Williams arose without having touched the door. "I raikon he er-sleep," he said, fingering his wool. He debated with himself for some time. During this interval his wife remained, a great fat statue of a mother shielding her children.

It was plain that his mind was swept suddenly by a wave of temerity. With a sounding step he moved towards the door. His fingers were almost upon the knob when he swiftly ducked and dodged away, clapping his hands to the back of his head. It was as if the portal had threatened him. There was a little tumult near the stove, where Mrs. Williams's desperate retreat had involved her feet with the prostrate children.

After the panic Williams bore traces of a feeling of shame. He returned to the charge. He firmly grasped the knob with his left hand, and with his other hand turned the key in the lock. He pushed the door, and as it swung portentously open he sprang nimbly to one side like the fearful slave liberating the lion. Near the stove a group had formed, the terror-stricken mother, with her arms stretched, and the aroused children clinging frenziedly to her skirts.

The light streamed after the swinging door, and disclosed a room six feet one way and six feet the other way. It was small enough to enable the radiance to lay it plain. Williams peered warily around the corner made by the door-post.

Suddenly he advanced, retired, and advanced again with a howl. His palsied family had expected him to spring backward, and at his howl they heaped themselves wondrously. But Williams simply stood in the little room emitting his howls before an open window. "He's gone! He's gone! He's gone!" His eye and his hand had speedily proved the fact. He had even thrown open a little cupboard.

Presently he came flying out. He grabbed his hat, and hurled the outer door back upon its hinges. Then he tumbled headlong into the night. He was yelling: "Docteh Trescott! Docteh Trescott!" He ran wildly through the fields, and galloped in the direction of town. He continued to call to Trescott, as if the latter was within easy hearing. It was as if Trescott was poised in the contemplative sky over the running negro, and could heed this reaching voice—"Docteh Trescott!"

In the cabin, Mrs. Williams, supported by relays from the battalion of children, stood quaking watch until the truth of daylight came as a reinforcement and made them arrogant, strutting, swashbuckler children, and a mother who proclaimed her illimitable courage.

XVI

Theresa Page was giving a party. It was the outcome of a long series of arguments addressed to her mother, which had been overheard in part by her father. He had at last said five words, "Oh, let her have it." The mother had then gladly capitulated.

Theresa had written nineteen invitations, and distributed them at recess to her schoolmates. Later her mother had composed five large cakes, and still later a vast amount of lemonade.

So the nine little girls and the ten little boys sat quite primly in the dining-room, while Theresa and her mother plied them with cake and lemonade, and also with ice-cream. This primness sat now quite strangely upon them. It was owing to the presence of Mrs. Page. Previously in the parlor alone with their games they had overturned a chair; the boys had let more or less of their hoodlum spirit shine forth. But when circumstances could be possibly magnified to warrant it, the girls made the boys victims of an insufferable pride, snubbing them mercilessly. So in the dining-room they resembled a class at Sunday-school, if it were not for the subterranean smiles, gestures, rebuffs, and poutings which stamped the affair as a children's party.

Two little girls of this subdued gathering were planted in a settle with their backs to the broad window. They were beaming lovingly upon each other with an effect of scorning the boys.

Hearing a noise behind her at the window, one little girl turned to face it. Instantly she screamed and sprang away, covering her face with her hands. "What was it? What was it?" cried every one in a roar. Some slight movement of the eyes of the weeping and shuddering child informed the company that she had been frightened by an appearance at the window. At once they all faced the imperturbable window, and for a moment there was a silence. An astute lad made an immediate census of the other lads. The prank of slipping out and looming spectrally at a window was too venerable. But the little boys were all present and astonished.

As they recovered their minds they uttered warlike cries, and through a side door sallied rapidly out against the terror. They vied with each other in daring.

None wished particularly to encounter a dragon in the darkness of the garden, but there could be no faltering when the fair ones in the dining-room were present. Calling to each other in stern voices, they went dragooning over the lawn, attacking the shadows with ferocity, but still with the caution of reasonable beings. They found, however, nothing new to the peace of the night. Of course there was a lad who told a great lie. He described a grim figure, bending low and slinking off along the fence. He gave a number of details, rendering his lie more splendid by a repetition of certain forms which he recalled from romances. For instance, he insisted that he had heard the creature emit a hollow laugh.

Inside the house the little girl who had raised the alarm was still shuddering and weeping. With the utmost difficulty was she brought to a state approximating calmness by Mrs. Page. Then she wanted to go home at once.

Page entered the house at this time. He had exiled himself until he concluded that this children's party was finished and gone. He was obliged to escort the little girl home because she screamed again when they opened the door and she saw the night.

She was not coherent even to her mother. Was it a man? She didn't know. It was simply a thing, a dreadful thing.

XVII

In Watermelon Alley the Farraguts were spending their evening as usual on the little rickety porch. Sometimes they howled gossip to other people on other rickety porches. The thin wail of a baby arose from a near house. A man had a terrific altercation with his wife, to which the alley paid no attention at all.

There appeared suddenly before the Farraguts a monster making a low and sweeping bow. There was an instant's pause, and then occurred something that resembled the effect of an upheaval of the earth's surface. The old woman hurled herself backward with a dreadful cry. Young Sim had been perched gracefully on a railing. At sight of the monster he simply fell over it to the ground. He made no sound, his eyes stuck out, his nerveless hands tried to grapple the rail to prevent a tumble, and then he vanished. Bella, blubbering, and with her hair suddenly and mysteriously dishevelled, was crawling on her hands and knees fearsomely up the steps.

Standing before this wreck of a family gathering, the monster continued to bow. It even raised a deprecatory claw. "Don' make no botheration 'bout me, Miss Fa'gut," it said, politely. "No, 'deed. I jes drap in ter ax if yer well this evenin', Miss Fa'gut. Don' make no botheration. No, 'deed. I gwine ax you to go to er daince with me, Miss Fa'gut, I ax you if I can have the magnifercent gratitude of you' company on that 'casion, Miss Fa'gut."

The girl cast a miserable glance behind her. She was still crawling away. On the ground beside the porch young Sim raised a strange bleat, which expressed both his fright and his lack of wind. Presently the monster, with a fashionable amble, ascended the steps after the girl.

She grovelled in a corner of the room as the creature took a chair. It seated itself very elegantly on the edge. It held an old cap in both hands. "Don' make no botheration, Miss Fa'gut. Don' make no botherations. No, 'deed. I jes drap in ter ax you if you won' do me the proud of acceptin' ma humble invitation to er daince, Miss Fa'gut."

She shielded her eyes with her arms and tried to crawl past it, but the genial monster blocked the way. "I jes drap in ter ax you 'bout er daince, Miss Fa'gut. I ax you if I kin have the magnifercent gratitude of you' company on that 'casion, Miss Fa'gut."

In a last outbreak of despair, the girl, shuddering and wailing, threw herself face downward on the floor, while the monster sat on the edge of the chair gabbling courteous invitations, and holding the old hat daintily to his stomach.

At the back of the house, Mrs. Farragut, who was of enormous weight, and who for eight years had done little more than sit in an arm-chair and describe her various ailments, had with speed and agility scaled a high board fence.

XVIII

The black mass in the middle of Trescott's property was hardly allowed to cool before the builders were at work on another house. It had sprung upward at a fabulous rate. It was like a magical composition born of the ashes. The doctor's office was the first part to be completed, and he had already moved in his new books and instruments and medicines.

Trescott sat before his desk when the chief of police arrived. "Well, we found him," said the latter.

"Did you?" cried the doctor. "Where?"

"Shambling around the streets at daylight this morning. I'll be blamed if I can figure on where he passed the night."

"Where is he now?"

"Oh, we jugged him. I didn't know what else to do with him. That's what I want you to tell me. Of course we can't keep him. No charge could be made, you know."

"I'll come down and get him."

The official grinned retrospectively. "Must say he had a fine career while he was out. First thing he did was to break up a children's party at Page's. Then he went to Watermelon Alley. Whoo! He stampeded the whole outfit. Men, women, and children running pell-mell, and yelling. They say one old woman broke her leg, or something, shinning over a fence. Then he went right out on the main street, and an Irish girl threw a fit, and there was a sort of a riot. He began to run, and a big crowd chased him, firing rocks. But he gave them the slip somehow down there by the foundry and in the railroad yard. We looked for him all night, but couldn't find him."

"Was he hurt any? Did anybody hit him with a stone?"

"Guess there isn't much of him to hurt any more, is there? Guess he's been hurt up to the limit. No. They never touched him. Of course nobody really wanted to hit him, but you know how a crowd gets. It's like—it's like—"

"Yes, I know."

For a moment the chief of the police looked reflectively at the floor. Then he spoke hesitatingly. "You know Jake Winter's little girl was the one that he scared at the party. She is pretty sick, they say."

"Is she? Why, they didn't call me. I always attend the Winter family."

"No? Didn't they?" asked the chief, slowly. "Well—you know —Winter is—well, Winter has gone clean crazy over this business. He wanted—he wanted to have you arrested."

"Have me arrested? The idiot! What in the name of wonder could he have me arrested for?"

"Of course. He is a fool. I told him to keep his trap shut. But then you know how he'll go all over town yapping about the thing. I thought I'd better tip you."

"Oh, he is of no consequence; but then, of course, I'm obliged to you, Sam."

"That's all right. Well, you'll be down tonight and take him out, eh? You'll get a good welcome from the jailer. He don't like his job for a cent. He says you can have your man whenever you want him. He's got no use for him."

"But what is this business of Winter's about having me arrested?"

"Oh, it's a lot of chin about your having no right to allow this—this—this man to be at large. But I told him to tend to his own business. Only I thought I'd better let you know. And I might as well say right now, doctor, that there is a good deal of talk about this thing. If I were you, I'd come to the jail pretty late at night, because there is likely to be a crowd around the door, and I'd bring a—er—mask, or some kind of a veil, anyhow."

XIX

Martha Goodwin was single, and well along into the thin years. She lived with her married sister in Whilomville. She performed nearly all the house-work in exchange for the privilege of existence. Every one tacitly recognized her labor as a form of penance for the early end of her betrothed, who had died of small-pox, which he had not caught from her.

But despite the strenuous and unceasing workaday of her life, she was a woman of great mind. She had adamantine opinions upon the situation in Armenia, the condition of women in China, the flirtation between Mrs. Minster of Niagara Avenue and young Griscom, the conflict in the Bible class of the Baptist Sunday-school, the duty of the United States towards the Cuban insurgents, and many other colossal matters. Her fullest experience of violence was gained on an occasion when she had seen a hound clubbed, but in the plan which she had made for the reform of the world she advocated drastic measures. For instance, she contended that all the Turks should be pushed into the sea and drowned, and that Mrs. Minster and young Griscom should be hanged side by side on twin gallows. In fact, this woman of peace, who had seen only peace, argued constantly for a creed of illimitable ferocity. She was invulnerable on these questions, because eventually she overrode all opponents with a sniff. This sniff was an active force. It was to her antagonists like a bang over the head, and none was known to recover from this expression of exalted contempt. It left them windless and conquered. They never again came forward as candidates for suppression. And Martha walked her kitchen with a stern brow, an invincible being like Napoleon.

Nevertheless her acquaintances, from the pain of their defeats, had been long in secret revolt. It was in no wise a conspiracy, because they did not care to state their open rebellion, but nevertheless it was understood that any woman who could not coincide with one of Martha's contentions was entitled to the support of others in the small circle. It amounted to an arrangement by which all were required to disbelieve any theory for which Martha fought. This, however, did not prevent them from speaking of her mind with profound respect.

Two people bore the brunt of her ability. Her sister Kate was visibly afraid of her, while Carrie Dungen sailed across from her kitchen to sit respectfully at Martha's feet and learn the business of the world. To be sure, afterwards, under another sun, she always laughed at Martha and pretended to deride her ideas, but in the presence of the sovereign she always remained silent or admiring. Kate, the sister, was of no consequence at all. Her principal delusion was that she did all the work in the up-stairs rooms of the house, while Martha did it down-stairs. The truth was seen only by the husband, who treated Martha with a kindness that was half banter, half deference. Martha herself had no suspicion that she was the only pillar of the domestic edifice. The situation was without definitions. Martha made definitions, but she devoted them entirely to the Armenians and Griscom and the Chinese and other subjects. Her dreams, which in early days had been of love of meadows and the shade of trees, of the face of a man, were now involved otherwise, and they were companioned in the kitchen curiously, Cuba, the hot-water kettle, Armenia, the washing of the dishes, and the whole thing being jumbled. In regard to social misdemeanors, she who was simply the mausoleum of a dead passion was probably the most savage critic in town. This unknown woman, hidden in a kitchen as in a well, was sure to have a considerable effect of the one kind or the other in the life of the town. Every time it moved a yard, she had personally contributed an inch. She could hammer so stoutly upon the door of a proposition that it would break from its hinges and fall upon her, but at any rate it moved. She was an engine, and the fact that she did not know that she was an engine contributed largely to the effect. One reason that she was formidable was that she did not even imagine that she was formidable. She remained a weak, innocent, and pigheaded creature, who alone would defy the universe if she thought the universe merited this proceeding.

One day Carrie Dungen came across from her kitchen with speed. She had a great deal of grist. "Oh," she cried, "Henry Johnson got away from where they was keeping him, and came to town last night, and scared everybody almost to death."

Martha was shining a dish-pan, polishing madly. No reasonable person could see cause for this operation, because the pan already glistened like silver. "Well!" she ejaculated. She imparted to the word a deep meaning. "This, my prophecy, has come to pass." It was a habit.

The overplus of information was choking Carrie. Before she could go on she was obliged to struggle for a moment. "And, oh, little Sadie Winter is awful sick, and they say Jake Winter was around this morning trying to get Doctor Trescott arrested. And poor old Mrs. Farragut sprained her ankle in trying to climb a fence. And there's a crowd around the jail all the time. They put Henry in jail because they didn't know what else to do with him, I guess. They say he is perfectly terrible."

Martha finally released the dish-pan and confronted the head-long speaker. "Well!" she said again, poising a great brown rag. Kate had heard the excited new-comer, and drifted down from the novel in her room. She was a shivery little woman. Her shoulder-blades seemed to be two panes of ice, for she was constantly shrug-ging and shrugging. "Serves him right if he was to lose all his patients," she said suddenly, in blood-thirsty tones. She snipped her words out as if her lips were scissors.

"Well, he's likely to," shouted Carrie Dungen. "Don't a lot of people say that they won't have him any more? If you're sick and nervous, Doctor Trescott would scare the life out of you, wouldn't he? He would me. I'd keep thinking."

Martha, stalking to and fro, sometimes surveyed the two other women with a contemplative frown.

XX

After the return from Connecticut, little Jimmie was at first much afraid of the monster who lived in the room over the carriage-house. He could not identify it in any way. Gradually, however, his fear dwindled under the influence of a weird fascination. He sidled into closer and closer relations with it.

One time the monster was seated on a box behind the stable basking in the rays of the afternoon sun. A heavy crêpe veil was swathed about its head.

Little Jimmie and many companions came around the corner of the stable. They were all in what was popularly known as the baby class, and consequently escaped from school a half-hour before the other children. They halted abruptly at sight of the figure on the box. Jimmie waved his hand with the air of a proprietor.

"There he is," he said.

"O-o-o!" murmured all the little boys—"o-o-o!" They shrank

back, and grouped according to courage or experience, as at the sound the monster slowly turned its head. Jimmie had remained in the van alone. "Don't be afraid! I won't let him hurt you," he said, delighted.

"Huh!" they replied, contemptuously. "We ain't afraid."

Jimmie seemed to reap all the joys of the owner and exhibitor of one of the world's marvels, while his audience remained at a distance —awed and entranced, fearful and envious.

One of them addressed Jimmie gloomily. "Bet you dassent walk right up to him." He was an older boy than Jimmie, and habitually oppressed him to a small degree. This new social elevation of the smaller lad probably seemed revolutionary to him.

"Huh!" said Jimmie, with deep scorn. "Dassent I? Dassent I, hey? Dassent I?"

The group was immensely excited. It turned its eyes upon the boy that Jimmie addressed. "No, you dassent," he said, stolidly, facing a moral defeat. He could see that Jimmie was resolved. "No, you dassent," he repeated, doggedly.

"Ho?" cried Jimmie. "You just watch!—you just watch!"

Amid a silence he turned and marched towards the monster. But possibly the palpable wariness of his companions had an effect upon him that weighed more than his previous experience, for suddenly, when near to the monster, he halted dubiously. But his playmates immediately uttered a derisive shout, and it seemed to force him forward. He went to the monster and laid his hand delicately on its shoulder. "Hello, Henry," he said, in a voice that trembled a trifle. The monster was crooning a weird line of negro melody that was scarcely more than a thread of sound, and it paid no heed to the boy.

Jimmie strutted back to his companions. They acclaimed him and hooted his opponent. Amid this clamor the larger boy with difficulty preserved a dignified attitude.

"I dassent, dassent I?" said Jimmie to him. "Now, you're so smart, let's see you do it!"

This challenge brought forth renewed taunts from the others. The larger boy puffed out his cheeks. "Well, I ain't afraid," he explained, sullenly. He had made a mistake in diplomacy, and now his small enemies were tumbling his prestige all about his ears. They crowed like roosters and bleated like lambs, and made many other noises which were supposed to bury him in ridicule and dishonor. "Well, I ain't afraid," he continued to explain through the din.

Jimmie, the hero of the mob, was pitiless. "You ain't afraid, hey?" he sneered. "If you ain't afraid, go do it, then."

"Well, I would if I wanted to," the other retorted. His eyes wore an expression of profound misery, but he preserved steadily other portions of a pot-valiant air. He suddenly faced one of his persecutors. "If you're so smart, why don't you go do it?" This persecutor sank promptly through the group to the rear. The incident gave the badgered one a breathing-spell, and for a moment even turned the derision in another direction. He took advantage of his interval. "I'll do it if anybody else will," he announced, swaggering to and fro.

Candidates for the adventure did not come forward. To defend themselves from this counter-charge, the other boys again set up their crowing and bleating. For a while they would hear nothing from him. Each time he opened his lips their chorus of noises made oratory impossible. But at last he was able to repeat that he would volunteer to dare as much in the affair as any other boy.

"Well, you go first," they shouted.

But Jimmie intervened to once more lead the populace against the large boy. "You're mighty brave, ain't you?" he said to him. "You dared me to do it, and I did—didn't I? Now who's afraid?" The others cheered this view loudly, and they instantly resumed the baiting of the large boy.

He shamefacedly scratched his left shin with his right foot. "Well, I ain't afraid." He cast an eye at the monster. "Well, I ain't afraid." With a glare of hatred at his squalling tormentors, he finally announced a grim intention. "Well, I'll do it, then, since you're so fresh. Now!"

The mob subsided as with a formidable countenance he turned towards the impassive figure on the box. The advance was also a regular progression from high daring to craven hesitation. At last, when some yards from the monster, the lad came to a full halt, as if he had encountered a stone wall. The observant little boys in the distance promptly hooted. Stung again by these cries, the lad sneaked two yards forward. He was crouched like a young cat ready for a backward spring. The crowd at the rear, beginning to respect this display, uttered some encouraging cries. Suddenly the lad gathered himself together, made a white and desperate rush forward, touched the monster's shoulder with a far-outstretched finger, and sped away, while his laughter rang out wild, shrill, and exultant.

The crowd of boys reverenced him at once, and began to throng into his camp, and look at him, and be his admirers. Jimmie was discomfited for a moment, but he and the larger boy, without agreement or word of any kind, seemed to recognize a truce, and they swiftly combined and began to parade before the others.

"Why, it's just as easy as nothing," puffed the larger boy. "Ain't it, Jim?"

"Course," blew Jimmie. "Why, it's as e-e-easy."

They were people of another class. If they had been decorated for courage on twelve battle-fields, they could not have made the other boys more ashamed of the situation.

Meanwhile they condescended to explain the emotions of the excursion, expressing unqualified contempt for any one who could hang back. "Why, it ain't nothin'. He won't do nothin' to you," they told the others, in tones of exasperation.

One of the very smallest boys in the party showed signs of a wistful desire to distinguish himself, and they turned their attention to him, pushing at his shoulders while he swung away from them, and hesitated dreamily. He was eventually induced to make furtive expedition, but it was only for a few yards. Then he paused, motionless, gazing with open mouth. The vociferous entreaties of Jimmie and the large boy had no power over him.

Mrs. Hannigan had come out on her back porch with a pail of water. From this coign she had a view of the secluded portion of the Trescott grounds that was behind the stable. She perceived the group of boys, and the monster on the box. She shaded her eyes with her hand to benefit her vision. She screeched then as if she was being murdered. "Eddie! Eddie! You come home this minute!"

Her son querulously demanded, "Aw, what for?"

"You come home this minute. Do you hear?"

The other boys seemed to think this visitation upon one of their number required them to preserve for a time the hang-dog air of a collection of culprits, and they remained in guilty silence until the little Hannigan, wrathfully protesting, was pushed through the door of his home. Mrs. Hannigan cast a piercing glance over the group, stared with a bitter face at the Trescott house, as if this new and handsome edifice was insulting her, and then followed her son.

There was wavering in the party. An inroad by one mother always caused them to carefully sweep the horizon to see if there were more coming. "This is my yard," said Jimmie, proudly. "We don't have to go home."

The monster on the box had turned its black crêpe countenance towards the sky, and was waving its arms in time to a religious chant. "Look at him now," cried a little boy. They turned, and were transfixed by the solemnity and mystery of the indefinable gestures. The wail of the melody was mournful and slow. They drew back. It seemed to spellbind them with the power of a funeral. They were so absorbed that they did not hear the doctor's buggy drive up to the stable. Trescott got out, tied his horse, and approached the group. Jimmie saw him first, and at his look of dismay the others wheeled.

"What's all this, Jimmie?" asked Trescott, in surprise.

The lad advanced to the front of his companions, halted, and said nothing. Trescott's face gloomed slightly as he scanned the scene.

"What were you doing, Jimmie?"

"We was playin'," answered Jimmie, huskily.

"Playing at what?"

"Just playin'."

Trescott looked gravely at the other boys, and asked them to please go home. They proceeded to the street much in the manner of frustrated and revealed assassins. The crime of trespass on another boy's place was still a crime when they had only accepted the other boy's cordial invitation, and they were used to being sent out of all manner of gardens upon the sudden appearance of a father or a mother. Jimmie had wretchedly watched the departure of his companions. It involved the loss of his position as a lad who controlled the privileges of his father's grounds, but then he knew that in the beginning he had no right to ask so many boys to be his guests.

Once on the sidewalk, however, they speedily forgot their shame as trespassers, and the large boy launched forth in a description of his success in the late trial of courage. As they went rapidly up the street, the little boy who had made the furtive expedition cried out confidently from the rear, "Yes, and I went almost up to him, didn't I, Willie?"

The large boy crushed him in a few words. "Huh!" he scoffed. "You only went a little way. I went clear up to him."

The pace of the other boys was so manly that the tiny thing had to trot, and he remained at the rear, getting entangled in their legs in his attempts to reach the front rank and become of some importance, dodging this way and that way, and always piping out his little claim to glory.

XXI

"By-the-way, Grace," said Trescott, looking into the dining-room from his office door, "I wish you would send Jimmie to me before school-time."

When Jimmie came, he advanced so quietly that Trescott did not at first note him. "Oh," he said, wheeling from a cabinet, "here you are, young man."

"Yes, sir."

Trescott dropped into his chair and tapped the desk with a thoughtful finger. "Jimmie, what were you doing in the back garden yesterday—you and the other boys—to Henry?"

"We weren't doing anything, pa."

Trescott looked sternly into the raised eyes of his son. "Are you sure you were not annoying him in any way? Now what were you doing, exactly?"

"Why, we—why, we—now—Willie Dalzel said I dassent go right up to him, and I did; and then he did; and then—the other boys were 'fraid; and then—you comed."

Trescott groaned deeply. His countenance was so clouded in sorrow that the lad, bewildered by the mystery of it, burst suddenly forth in dismal lamentations. "There, there. Don't cry, Jim," said Trescott, going round the desk. "Only—" He sat in a great leather reading-chair, and took the boy on his knee. "Only I want to explain to you—"

After Jimmie had gone to school, and as Trescott was about to start on his round of morning calls, a message arrived from Doctor Moser. It set forth that the latter's sister was dying in the old homestead, twenty miles away up the valley, and asked Trescott to care for his patients for the day at least. There was also in the envelope a little history of each case and of what had already been done. Trescott replied to the messenger that he would gladly assent to the arrangement.

He noted that the first name on Moser's list was Winter, but this did not seem to strike him as an important fact. When its turn came, he rang the Winter bell. "Good-morning, Mrs. Winter," he said, cheerfully, as the door was opened. "Doctor Moser has been obliged to leave town to-day, and he has asked me to come in his stead. How is the little girl this morning?"

Mrs. Winter had regarded him in stony surprise. At last she said: "Come in! I'll see my husband." She bolted into the house. Trescott entered the hall, and turned to the left into the sitting-room.

Presently Winter shuffled through the door. His eyes flashed towards Trescott. He did not betray any desire to advance far into the room. "What do you want?" he said.

"What do I want? What do I want?" repeated Trescott, lifting his head suddenly. He had heard an utterly new challenge in the night of the jungle.

"Yes, that's what I want to know," snapped Winter. "What do you want?"

Trescott was silent for a moment. He consulted Moser's memoranda. "I see that your little girl's case is a trifle serious," he remarked. "I would advise you to call a physician soon. I will leave you a copy of Dr. Moser's record to give to any one you may call." He paused to transcribe the record on a page of his note-book. Tearing out the leaf, he extended it to Winter as he moved towards the door. The latter shrunk against the wall. His head was hanging as he reached for the paper. This caused him to grasp air, and so Trescott simply let the paper flutter to the feet of the other man.

"Good-morning," said Trescott from the hall. This placid retreat seemed to suddenly arouse Winter to ferocity. It was as if he had then recalled all the truths which he had formulated to hurl at Trescott. So he followed him into the hall, and down the hall to the door, and through the door to the porch, barking in fiery rage from a respectful distance. As Trescott imperturbably turned the mare's head down the road, Winter stood on the porch, still yelping. He was like a little dog.

XXII

"Have you heard the news?" cried Carrie Dungen, as she sped towards Martha's kitchen. "Have you heard the news?" Her eyes were shining with delight.

"No," answered Martha's sister Kate, bending forward eagerly. "What was it? What was it?"

Carrie appeared triumphantly in the open door. "Oh, there's been an awful scene between Doctor Trescott and Jake Winter. I never thought that Jake Winter had any pluck at all, but this morning he told the doctor just what he thought of him."

"Well, what did he think of him?" asked Martha.

"Oh, he called him everything. Mrs. Howarth heard it through her front blinds. It was terrible, she says. It's all over town now. Everybody knows it."

"Didn't the doctor answer back?"

"No! Mrs. Howarth—she says he never said a word. He just walked down to his buggy and got in, and drove off as co-o-o-l. But Jake gave him jinks, by all accounts."

"But what did he say?" cried Kate, shrill and excited. She was evidently at some kind of a feast.

"Oh, he told him that Sadie had never been well since that night Henry Johnson frightened her at Theresa Page's party, and he held him responsible, and how dared he cross his threshold—and—and—and—"

"And what?" said Martha.

"Did he swear at him?" said Kate, in fearsome glee.

"No—not much. He did swear at him a little, but not more than a man does anyhow when he is real mad, Mrs. Howarth says."

"O-oh!" breathed Kate. "And did he call him any names?"

Martha, at her work, had been for a time in deep thought. She now interrupted the others. "It don't seem as if Sadie Winter had been sick since that time Henry Johnson got loose. She's been to school almost the whole time since then, hasn't she?"

They combined upon her in immediate indignation. "School? School? I should say not. Don't think for a moment. School!"

Martha wheeled from the sink. She held an iron spoon, and it seemed as if she was going to attack them. "Sadie Winter has passed here many a morning since then carrying her school-bag. Where was she going? To a wedding?"

The others, long accustomed to a mental tyranny, speedily surrendered.

"Did she?" stammered Kate. "I never saw her."

Carrie Dungen made a weak gesture.

"If I had been Doctor Trescott," exclaimed Martha, loudly, "I'd have knocked that miserable Jake Winter's head off."

Kate and Carrie, exchanging glances, made an alliance in the air. "I don't see why you say that, Martha," replied Carrie, with considerable boldness, gaining support and sympathy from Kate's smile. "I don't see how anybody can be blamed for getting angry when their little girl gets almost scared to death and gets sick from it, and all that. Besides, everybody says—"

"Oh, I don't care what everybody says," said Martha.

"Well, you can't go against the whole town," answered Carrie, in sudden sharp defiance.

"No, Martha, you can't go against the whole town," piped Kate, following her leader rapidly.

" 'The whole town,' " cried Martha. "I'd like to know what you call 'the whole town.' Do you call these silly people who are scared of Henry Johnson 'the whole town'?"

"Why, Martha," said Carrie, in a reasoning tone, "you talk as if you wouldn't be scared of him!"

"No more would I," retorted Martha.

"O-oh, Martha, how you talk!" said Kate. "Why, the idea! Everybody's afraid of him."

Carrie was grinning. "You've never seen him, have you?" she asked, seductively.

"No," admitted Martha.

"Well, then, how do you know that you wouldn't be scared?"

Martha confronted her. "Have you ever seen him? No? Well, then, how do you know you *would* be scared?"

The allied forces broke out in chorus: "But, Martha, everybody says so. Everybody says so."

"Everybody says what?"

"Everybody that's seen him say they were frightened almost to death. 'Tisn't only women, but it's men too. It's awful."

Martha wagged her head solemnly. "I'd try not to be afraid of him."

"But supposing you could not help it?" said Kate.

"Yes, and look here," cried Carrie. "I'll tell you another thing. The Hannigans are going to move out of the house next door."

"On account of him?" demanded Martha.

Carrie nodded. "Mrs. Hannigan says so herself."

"Well, of all things!" ejaculated Martha. "Going to move, eh? You don't say so! Where they going to move to?"

"Down on Orchard Avenue."

"Well, of all things! Nice house?"

"I don't know about that. I haven't heard. But there's lots of nice houses on Orchard."

"Yes, but they're all taken," said Kate. "There isn't a vacant house on Orchard Avenue."

"Oh yes, there is," said Martha. "The old Hampstead house is vacant."

"Oh, of course," said Kate. "But then I don't believe Mrs. Hannigan would like it there. I wonder where they can be going to move to?"

"I'm sure I don't know," sighed Martha. "It must be to some place we don't know about."

"Well," said Carrie Dungen, after a general reflective silence, "it's easy enough to find out, anyhow."

"Who knows—around here?" asked Kate.

"Why, Mrs. Smith, and there she is in her garden," said Carrie, jumping to her feet. As she dashed out of the door, Kate and Martha crowded at the window. Carrie's voice rang out from near the steps. "Mrs. Smith! Mrs. Smith! Do you know where the Hannigans are going to move to?"

XXIII

The autumn smote the leaves, and the trees of Whilomville were panoplied in crimson and yellow. The winds grew stronger, and in the melancholy purple of the nights the home shine of a window became a finer thing. The little boys, watching the sear and sorrowful leaves drifting down from the maples, dreamed of the near time when they could heap bushels in the streets and burn them during the abrupt evenings.

Three men walked down the Niagara Avenue. As they approached Judge Hagenthorpe's house he came down his walk to meet them in the manner of one who has been waiting.

"Are you ready, judge?" one said.

"All ready," he answered.

The four then walked to Trescott's house. He received them in his office, where he had been reading. He seemed surprised at this visit of four very active and influential citizens, but he had nothing to say of it.

After they were all seated, Trescott looked expectantly from one face to another. There was a little silence. It was broken by John Twelve, the wholesale grocer, who was worth $400,000, and reported to be worth over a million.

"Well, doctor," he said, with a short laugh, "I suppose we might as well admit at once that we've come to interfere in something which is none of our business."

"Why, what is it?" asked Trescott, again looking from one face to another. He seemed to appeal particularly to Judge Hagenthorpe, but the old man had his chin lowered musingly to his cane, and would not look at him.

"It's about what nobody talks of—much," said Twelve. "It's about Henry Johnson."

Trescott squared himself in his chair. "Yes?" he said.

Having delivered himself of the title, Twelve seemed to become more easy. "Yes," he answered, blandly, "we wanted to talk to you about it."

"Yes?" said Trescott.

Twelve abruptly advanced on the main attack. "Now see here, Trescott, we like you, and we have come to talk right out about this business. It may be none of our affairs and all that, and as for me, I don't mind if you tell me so; but I am not going to keep quiet and see you ruin yourself. And that's how we all feel."

"I am not ruining myself," answered Trescott.

"No, maybe you are not exactly ruining yourself," said Twelve, slowly, "but you are doing yourself a great deal of harm. You have changed from being the leading doctor in town to about the last one. It is mainly because there are always a large number of people who are very thoughtless fools, of course, but then that doesn't change the condition."

A man who had not heretofore spoken said, solemnly, "It's the women."

"Well, what I want to say is this," resumed Twelve: "Even if there are a lot of fools in the world, we can't see any reason why you should ruin yourself by opposing them. You can't teach them anything, you know."

"I am not trying to teach them anything." Trescott smiled wearily. "I—It is a matter of—well—"

"And there are a good many of us that admire you for it immensely," interrupted Twelve; "but that isn't going to change the minds of all those ninnies."

"It's the women," stated the advocate of this view again.

"Well, what I want to say is this," said Twelve. "We want you to get out of this trouble and strike your old gait again. You are simply killing your practice through your infernal pig-headedness. Now this thing is out of the ordinary, but there must be ways to—to beat the game somehow, you see. So we've talked it over—about a dozen of us—and, as I say, if you want to tell us to mind our own business, why, go ahead; but we've talked it over, and we've come to the conclusion that the only way to do is to get Johnson a place somewhere off up the valley, and—"

Trescott wearily gestured. "You don't know, my friend. Everybody is so afraid of him, they can't even give him good care. Nobody can attend to him as I do myself."

"But I have a little no-good farm up beyond Clarence Mountain that I was going to give to Henry," cried Twelve, aggrieved. "And if you—and if you—if you—through your house burning down, or anything—why, all the boys were prepared to take him right off your hands, and—and—"

Trescott arose and went to the window. He turned his back upon them. They sat waiting in silence. When he returned he kept his face in the shadow. "No, John Twelve," he said, "it can't be done."

There was another stillness. Suddenly a man stirred on his chair. "Well, then, a public institution—" he began.

"No," said Trescott; "public institutions are all very good, but he is not going to one."

In the background of the group old Judge Hagenthorpe was thoughtfully smoothing the polished ivory head of his cane.

XXIV

Trescott loudly stamped the snow from his feet and shook the flakes from his shoulders. When he entered the house he went at once to the dining-room, and then to the sitting-room. Jimmie was there, reading painfully in a large book concerning giraffes and tigers and crocodiles.

"Where is your mother, Jimmie?" asked Trescott.

"I don't know, pa," answered the boy. "I think she is up-stairs."

Trescott went to the foot of the stairs and called, but there came no answer. Seeing that the door of the little drawing-room was open, he entered. The room was bathed in the half-light that came from the four dull panes of mica in the front of the great stove. As his eyes grew used to the shadows he saw his wife curled in an arm-chair. He went to her. "Why, Grace," he said, "didn't you hear me calling you?"

She made no answer, and as he bent over the chair he heard her trying to smother a sob in the cushion.

"Grace!" he cried. "You're crying!"

She raised her face. "I've got a headache, a dreadful headache, Ned."

"A headache?" he repeated, in surprise and incredulity.

He pulled a chair close to hers. Later, as he cast his eye over the zone of light shed by the dull red panes, he saw that a low table had been drawn close to the stove, and that it was burdened with many small cups and plates of uncut tea-cake. He remembered that the day was Wednesday, and that his wife received on Wednesdays.

"Who was here to-day, Gracie?" he asked.

From his shoulder there came a mumble, "Mrs. Twelve."

"Was she—um," he said. "Why—didn't Anna Hagenthorpe come over?"

The mumble from his shoulder continued, "She wasn't well enough."

Glancing down at the cups, Trescott mechanically counted them. There were fifteen of them. "There, there," he said. "Don't cry, Grace. Don't cry."

The wind was whining round the house, and the snow beat aslant upon the windows. Sometimes the coal in the stove settled with a crumbling sound, and the four panes of mica flashed a sudden new crimson. As he sat holding her head on his shoulder, Trescott found himself occasionally trying to count the cups. There were fifteen of them.

This still from James Whale's movie *Frankenstein* (1931), adapted from Mary Shelley's novel of 1818 and starring Boris Karloff, proves that images of evil continue to fascinate a wide audience in the twentieth century. COURTESY UNIVERSAL CITY STUDIOS, INC.

Montague Rhodes James
(1862-1936)

M. R. ("Monty") James is far more often remembered for his ghost stories than for his scholarship as a bibliographer, iconographer, and theologian, though he brought his academic experience and his inveterate antiquarian curiosity into many of his tales. His eye for detail and habit of careful documentation and even his profession give Mr. Williams in "The Mezzotint" perhaps more credibility than he deserves, for his conscientious routine describes the man rather than the man the routine. Like James, Williams takes more pleasure in his work than in his play; in fact, his play is his work. If Williams had played by writing ghost stories, he, too, would have applied well-defined principles carefully, arranged his details properly, and articulated his sentiments with gentlemanly understatement.

James's rules were explicitly laid out in the prefaces to the many collected editions which followed his first, *Ghost Stories of an Antiquary* (1904). "The setting," he said, "should be fairly familiar and the majority of the characters and their talk such as you may meet or hear any day" (Preface to *More Ghost Stories of an Antiquary*, 1911). The surprising appearance, occurrence, or mysterious fact should startle the reader into exclaiming, " 'If I'm not very careful, something of this kind may happen to me!' " (Preface, 1911). Being careful may not, of course, ward off the evil ghost, and neither may being good, but being an imaginative and curious reader guarantees the effectiveness of the tale. James aimed to amuse. He read his stories to his friends during the Christmas season, and published his collections in time for Christmas readings before hearths other than his own. When he was provost of King's College (1905–1918) and Eton (1918–1936), he entertained the choristers with revengeful ghosts or modern Faust figures before they sang at the midnight service (*Eton and King's*, memoir, 1926). This ritual never became merely routine; walking corpses, one of his other favorite devices, seldom are.

For his living dead, James admitted the influence of Sheridan Le Fanu, but for the animated engravings in "The Mezzotint," he had as models Oscar Wilde's *Picture of Dorian Gray*, Poe's "Oval Portrait," and even Walpole's *Castle of Otranto*. He also knew stories and legends of Christian saints whose painted, sculptured, or printed images become animate on particular occasions for specific purposes. At an early age, James, son of a clergyman, wrote the lives of nineteen northern saints, and the iconographical studies of his mature years gave him many opportunities to review saintly facts and fictions.

The moving figure in the mezzotint is no saint, however. He's a poacher, "like the man in *Tess o' the Durbervilles*," and, like Hardy's Tess herself, he is hanged for murder. James's Essex poacher wears the white cross of righteousness on "a strange black garment," short enough to expose his "horribly thin," skeleton legs. The description fits that of a priest's chasuble in a color reserved for a funeral liturgy. His name, "Gawdy," suggests both the grotesque ornamentation of "gaudy" and the vengeance of an angry God. In the university setting where a "gaudy" is an annual dinner, the real and supposed reactions to the mysterious engraving reveal even more than the accurate and vivid description of objects and occupations, people and places, in "The Mezzotint."

Kidnapping a child is a familiar Gothic theme of ballads and fairy tales. It recurs with significant variation in Yeats's "Stolen Child." But recording the crime in a rather ordinary engraving of a country house and documenting it by reliable witnesses and revealing photographs are inventions of a delightfully entertaining modern antiquary with an unusual flair for detection.

The Mezzotint (1904)

Some time ago I believe I had the pleasure of telling you the story of an adventure which happened to a friend of mine by the name of Dennistoun, during his pursuit of objects of art for the museum at Cambridge.

He did not publish his experiences very widely upon his return to England; but they could not fail to become known to a good many of his friends, and among others to the gentleman who at that time presided over an art museum at another University. It was to be expected that the story should make a considerable impression on the mind of a man whose vocation lay in lines similar to Dennistoun's, and that he should be eager to catch at any explanation of the matter which tended to make it seem improbable that he should ever be called upon to deal with so agitating an emergency. It was, indeed, somewhat consoling to him to reflect that he was not expected to acquire ancient MSS. for his institution; that was the business of the Shelburnian Library. The authorities of that institution might, if they pleased, ransack obscure corners of the Continent for such matters. He was glad to be obliged at the moment to confine his attention to enlarging the already unsurpassed collection of English topographical drawings and engravings possessed by his museum. Yet, as it turned out, even a department so homely and familiar as this may have its dark corners, and to one of these Mr. Williams was unexpectedly introduced.

Those who have taken even the most limited interest in the acquisition of topographical pictures are aware that there is one London dealer whose aid is indispensable to their researches. Mr. J. W. Britnell publishes at short intervals very admirable catalogues of a large and constantly changing stock of engravings, plans, and old sketches of mansions, churches, and towns in England and Wales. These catalogues were, of course, the ABC of his subject to Mr. Williams: but as his museum already contained an enormous accumulation of topographical pictures, he was a regular, rather than a copious, buyer; and he rather looked to Mr. Britnell to fill up gaps in the rank and file of his collection than to supply him with rarities.

Now, in February of last year there appeared upon Mr. Williams's desk at the museum a catalogue from Mr. Britnell's emporium, and accompanying it was a typewritten communication from the dealer himself. This latter ran as follows:

"DEAR SIR,
    "We beg to call your attention to No. 978 in our accompanying catalogue, which we shall be glad to send on approval.
                                                    "Yours faithfully,
                                                        "J. W. BRITNELL."

To turn to No. 978 in the accompanying catalogue was with Mr. Williams (as he observed to himself) the work of a moment, and in the place indicated he found the following entry:

"978.—*Unknown*. Interesting mezzotint: View of a manor-house, early part of the century. 15 by 10 inches; black frame. £2 2s."

It was not specially exciting, and the price seemed high. However, as Mr. Britnell, who knew his business and his customer, seemed to set store by it, Mr. Williams wrote a postcard asking for the article to be sent on approval, along with some other engravings and sketches which appeared in the same catalogue. And so he passed without much excitement of anticipation to the ordinary labours of the day.

A parcel of any kind always arrives a day later than you expect it, and that of Mr. Britnell proved, as I believe the right phrase goes, no exception to the rule. It was delivered at the museum by the afternoon post of Saturday, after Mr. Williams had left his work, and it was accordingly brought round to his rooms in college by the attendant, in order that he might not have to wait over Sunday before looking through it and returning such of the contents as he did not propose to keep. And here he found it when he came in to tea, with a friend.

The only item with which I am concerned was the rather large, black-framed mezzotint of which I have already quoted the short description given in Mr. Britnell's catalogue. Some more details of it will have to be given, though I cannot hope to put before you the look of the picture as clearly as it is present to my own eye. Very nearly the exact duplicate of it may be seen in a good many old inn parlours, or in the passages of undisturbed country mansions at the present moment. It was a rather indifferent mezzotint, and an indifferent mezzotint is, perhaps, the worst form of engraving known. It presented a full-face view of a not very large manor-house of the last century, with three rows of plain sashed windows with rusticated masonry about them, a parapet with balls or vases at the angles, and a small portico in the centre. On either side were trees, and in front a considerable expanse of lawn. The legend "A.W.F. sculpsit" was engraved on the narrow margin; and there was no further inscription. The whole thing gave the impression that it was the work of an amateur. What in the world Mr. Britnell could mean by affixing the price of £2 2s. to such an object was more than Mr. Williams could imagine. He turned it over with a good deal of contempt; upon the back was a paper label, the left-hand half of which had been torn off. All that remained were the ends of two lines of writing: the first had the letters —ngley Hall; the second, —ssex.

It would, perhaps, be just worth while to identify the place represented, which he could easily do with the help of a gazetteer, and then he would send it back to Mr. Britnell, with some remarks reflecting upon the judgment of that gentleman.

He lighted the candles, for it was now dark, made the tea, and supplied the friend with whom he had been playing golf (for I believe the authorities of the University I write of indulge in that pursuit by way of relaxation), and tea was taken to the accompaniment of a discussion which golfing persons can imagine for themselves, but which the conscientious writer has no right to inflict upon any non-golfing persons.

The conclusion arrived at was that certain strokes might have been better, and that in certain emergencies neither player had experienced that amount of luck which a human being has a right to expect. It was now that the friend—let us call him Professor Binks— took up the framed engraving, and said:

"What's this place, Williams?"

"Just what I am going to try to find out," said Williams, going to the shelf for a gazetteer. "Look at the back. Something-ley Hall, either in Sussex or Essex. Half the name's gone, you see. You don't happen to know it, I suppose?"

"It's from that man Britnell, I suppose, isn't it?" said Binks. "Is it for the museum?"

"Well, I think I should buy it if the price was five shillings," said Williams; "but for some unearthly reason he wants two guineas for it. I can't conceive why. It's a wretched engraving, and there aren't even any figures to give it life."

"It's not worth two guineas, I should think," said Binks; "but I don't think it's so badly done. The moonlight seems rather good to me; and I should have thought there *were* figures, or at least a figure, just on the edge in front."

"Let's look," said Williams. "Well, it's true the light is rather cleverly given. Where's your figure? Oh yes! Just the head, in the very front of the picture."

And indeed there was—hardly more than a black blot on the extreme edge of the engraving—the head of a man or woman, a good deal muffled up, the back turned to the spectator, and looking towards the house.

Williams had not noticed it before.

"Still," he said, "though it's a cleverer thing than I thought, I can't spend two guineas of museum money on a picture of a place I don't know."

Professor Binks had his work to do, and soon went; and very nearly up to Hall time Williams was engaged in a vain attempt to identify the subject of his picture. "If the vowel before the *ng* had only been left, it would have been easy enough," he thought; "but as it is, the name may be anything from Guestingley to Langley, and there are many more names ending like this than I thought; and this rotten book has no index of terminations."

Hall in Mr. Williams's college was at seven. It need not be dwelt upon; the less so as he met there colleagues who had been playing golf during the afternoon, and words with which we have no concern were freely bandied across the table—merely golfing words, I would hasten to explain.

I suppose an hour or more to have been spent in what is called common-room after dinner. Later in the evening some few retired to Williams's room, and I have little doubt that whist was played and tobacco smoked. During a lull in these operations Williams picked up the mezzotint from the table without looking at it, and handed it to a person mildly interested in art, telling him where it had come from, and the other particulars which we already know.

The gentleman took it carelessly, looked at it, then said, in a tone of some interest:

"It's really a very good piece of work, Williams; it has quite a feeling of the romantic period. The light is admirably managed, it seems to me, and the figure, though it's rather too grotesque, is somehow very impressive."

"Yes, isn't it?" said Williams, who was just then busy giving whisky-and-soda to others of the company, and was unable to come across the room to look at the view again.

It was by this time rather late in the evening, and the visitors were on the move. After they went Williams was obliged to write a letter or two and clear up some odd bits of work. At last, some time past midnight, he was disposed to turn in, and he put out his lamp after lighting his bedroom candle. The picture lay face upwards on the table where the last man who looked at it had put it, and it caught his eye as he turned the lamp down. What he saw made him very nearly drop the candle on the floor, and he declares now that if he had been left in the dark at that moment he would have had a fit. But, as that did not happen, he was able to put down the light on the table and take a good look at the picture. It was indubitable—rankly impossible, no doubt, but absolutely certain. In the middle of the lawn in front of the unknown house there was a figure where no figure had been at five o'clock that afternoon. It was crawling on all-fours towards the house, and it was muffled in a strange black garment with a white cross on the back.

I do not know what is the ideal course to pursue in a situation of this kind. I can only tell you what Mr. Williams did. He took the picture by one corner and carried it across the passage to a second set of rooms which he possessed. There he locked it up in a drawer, sported the doors of both sets of rooms, and retired to bed; but first he wrote out and signed an account of the extraordinary change which the picture had undergone since it had come into his possession.

Sleep visited him rather late; but it was consoling to reflect that the behaviour of the picture did not depend upon his own unsupported testimony. Evidently the man who had looked at it the night before had seen something of the same kind as he had, otherwise he might have been tempted to think that something gravely wrong was happening either to his eyes or his mind. This possibility being fortunately precluded, two matters awaited him on the morrow. He must take stock of the picture very carefully, and call in a witness for the purpose, and he must make a determined effort to ascertain what house it was that was represented. He would therefore ask his neighbour Nisbet to breakfast with him, and he would subsequently spend a morning over the gazetteer.

Nisbet was disengaged, and arrived about 9.30. His host was not quite dressed, I am sorry to say, even at this late hour. During breakfast nothing was said about the mezzotint by Williams, save that he had a picture on which he wished for Nisbet's opinion. But those who are familiar with University life can picture for themselves the wide and delightful range of subjects over which the conversation of two Fellows of Canterbury College is likely to extend during a Sunday morning breakfast. Hardly a topic was left unchallenged, from golf to lawn-tennis. Yet I am bound to say that Williams was rather distraught; for his interest naturally centred in that very strange picture which was now reposing, face downwards, in the drawer in the room opposite.

The morning pipe was at last lighted, and the moment had arrived for which he looked. With very considerable—almost tremulous —excitement, he ran across, unlocked the drawer, and, extracting the picture—still face downwards—ran back, and put it into Nisbet's hands.

"Now," he said, "Nisbet, I want you to tell me exactly what you see in that picture. Describe it, if you don't mind, rather minutely. I'll tell you why afterwards."

"Well," said Nisbet, "I have here a view of a country-house— English, I presume—by moonlight."

"Moonlight? You're sure of that?"

"Certainly. The moon appears to be on the wane, if you wish for details, and there are clouds in the sky."

"All right. Go on. I'll swear," added Williams in an aside, "there was no moon when I saw it first."

"Well, there's not much more to be said," Nisbet continued. "The house has one—two—three rows of windows, five in each row, except at the bottom, where there's a porch instead of the middle one, and—"

"But what about figures?" said Williams, with marked interest.

"There aren't any," said Nisbet; "but—"

"What! No figure on the grass in front?"

"Not a thing."

"You'll swear to that?"

"Certainly I will. But there's just one other thing."

"What?"

"Why, one of the windows on the ground-floor—left of the door —is open."

"Is it really so? My goodness! He must have got in," said Williams, with great excitement; and he hurried to the back of the sofa on which Nisbet was sitting, and, catching the picture from him, verified the matter for himself.

It was quite true. There was no figure, and there was the open window. Williams, after a moment of speechless surprise, went to the writing-table and scribbled for a short time. Then he brought two papers to Nisbet, and asked him first to sign one—it was his own description of the picture, which you have just heard—and then to read the other, which was Williams's statement written the night before.

"What can it all mean?" said Nisbet.

"Exactly," said Williams. "Well, one thing I must do—or three things, now I think of it. I must find out from Garwood"—this was his last night's visitor—"what he saw, and then I must get the thing photographed before it goes further, and then I must find out what the place is."

"I can do the photographing myself," said Nisbet, "and I will. But, you know, it looks very much as if we were assisting at the working out of a tragedy somewhere. The question is, Has it happened already, or is it going to come off? You must find out what the place is. Yes," he said, looking at the picture again, "I expect you're right: he has got in. And if I don't mistake there'll be the devil to pay in one of the rooms upstairs."

"I'll tell you what," said Williams: "I'll take the picture across to old Green" (this was the senior Fellow of the college, who had been Bursar for many years). "It's quite likely he'll know it. We have property in Essex and Sussex, and he must have been over the two counties a lot in his time."

"Quite likely he will," said Nisbet; "but just let me take my photograph first. But look here, I rather think Green isn't up to-day. He wasn't in Hall last night, and I think I heard him say he was going down for the Sunday."

"That's true, too," said Williams; "I know he's gone to Brighton. Well, if you'll photograph it now, I'll go across to Garwood and get his statement, and you keep an eye on it while I'm gone. I'm beginning to think two guineas is not a very exorbitant price for it now."

In a short time he had returned, and brought Mr. Garwood with him. Garwood's statement was to the effect that the figure, when he had seen it, was clear of the edge of the picture, but had not got far across the lawn. He remembered a white mark on the back of its drapery, but could not have been sure it was a cross. A document to this effect was then drawn up and signed, and Nisbet proceeded to photograph the picture.

"Now what do you mean to do?" he said. "Are you going to sit and watch it all day?"

"Well, no, I think not," said Williams. "I rather imagine we're meant to see the whole thing. You see, between the time I saw it last night and this morning there was time for lots of things to happen, but the creature only got into the house. It could easily have got through its business in the time and gone to its own place again; but the fact of the window being open, I think, must mean that it's in there now. So I feel quite easy about leaving it. And, besides, I have a kind of idea that it wouldn't change much, if at all, in the daytime. We might go out for a walk this afternoon, and come in to tea, or whenever it gets dark. I shall leave it out on the table here, and sport the door. My skip can get in, but no one else."

The three agreed that this would be a good plan; and, further, that if they spent the afternoon together they would be less likely to talk about the business to other people; for any rumour of such a transaction as was going on would bring the whole of the Phasmatological Society about their ears.

We may give them a respite until five o'clock.

At or near that hour the three were entering Williams's staircase. They were at first slightly annoyed to see that the door of his rooms was unsported; but in a moment it was remembered that on Sunday the skips came for orders an hour or so earlier than on weekdays. However, a surprise was awaiting them. The first thing they saw was the picture leaning up against a pile of books on the table, as it had been left, and the next thing was Williams's skip, seated on a chair opposite, gazing at it with undisguised horror. How was this? Mr. Filcher (the name is not my own invention) was a servant of considerable standing, and set the standard of etiquette to all his own college and to several neighbouring ones, and nothing could be more alien to his practice than to be found sitting on his master's chair, or appearing to take any particular notice of his master's furniture or pictures. Indeed, he seemed to feel this himself. He started violently when the three men were in the room, and got up with a marked effort. Then he said:

"I ask your pardon, sir, for taking such a freedom as to set down."

"Not at all, Robert," interposed Mr. Williams. "I was meaning to ask you some time what you thought of that picture."

"Well, sir, of course I don't set up my opinion again yours, but it ain't the pictur I should 'ang where my little girl could see it, sir."

"Wouldn't you, Robert? Why not?"

"No, sir. Why, the pore child, I recollect once she see a Door Bible, with pictures not 'alf what that is, and we 'ad to set up with her three or four nights afterwards, if you'll believe me; and if she was to ketch a sight of this skelinton here, or whatever it is, carrying off the pore baby, she would be in a taking. You know 'ow it is with children; 'ow nervish they git with a little thing and all. But what I should say, it don't seem a right pictur to be laying about, sir, not where anyone that's liable to be startled could come on it. Should you be wanting anything this evening, sir? Thank you, sir."

With these words the excellent man went to continue the round of his masters, and you may be sure the gentlemen whom he left lost no time in gathering round the engraving. There was the house, as before, under the waning moon and the drifting clouds. The window that had been open was shut, and the figure was once more on the lawn: but not this time crawling cautiously on hands and knees. Now it was erect and stepping swiftly, with long strides, towards the front of the picture. The moon was behind it, and the black drapery hung down over its face so that only hints of that could be seen, and what was visible made the spectators profoundly thankful that they could see no more than a white dome-like forehead and a few straggling hairs. The head was bent down, and the arms were tightly clasped over an object which could be dimly seen and identified as a child, whether dead or living it was not possible to say. The legs of the appearance alone could be plainly discerned, and they were horribly thin.

From five to seven the three companions sat and watched the picture by turns. But it never changed. They agreed at last that it would be safe to leave it, and that they would return after Hall and await further developments.

When they assembled again, at the earliest possible moment, the engraving was there, but the figure was gone, and the house was quiet under the moonbeams. There was nothing for it but to spend the evening over gazetteers and guide-books. Williams was the lucky one at last, and perhaps he deserved it. At 11.30 p.m. he read from Murray's *Guide to Essex* the following lines:

"16½ miles, *Anningley*. The church has been an interesting building of Norman date, but was extensively classicized in the last century. It contains the tomb of the family of Francis, whose mansion, Anningley Hall, a solid Queen Anne house, stands immediately beyond the churchyard in a park of about 80 acres. The family is now extinct, the last heir having disappeared mysteriously in infancy in the year 1802. The father, Mr. Arthur Francis, was locally known as a talented amateur engraver in mezzotint. After his son's disappearance he lived in complete retirement at the Hall, and was found dead in his studio on the third anniversary of the disaster, having just completed an engraving of the house, impressions of which are of considerable rarity."

This looked like business, and, indeed, Mr. Green on his return at once identified the house as Anningley Hall.

"Is there any kind of explanation of the figure, Green?" was the question which Williams naturally asked.

"I don't know, I'm sure, Williams. What used to be said in the place when I first knew it, which was before I came up here, was just this: old Francis was always very much down on these poaching fellows, and whenever he got a chance he used to get a man whom he suspected of it turned off the estate, and by degrees he got rid of them all but one. Squires could do a lot of things then that they daren't think of now. Well, this man that was left was what you find pretty often in that country—the last remains of a very old family. I believe they were Lords of the Manor at one time. I recollect just the same thing in my own parish."

"What, like the man in *Tess o' the Durbervilles?*" Williams put in.

"Yes, I dare say; it's not a book I could ever read myself. But this fellow could show a row of tombs in the church there that belonged to his ancestors, and all that went to sour him a bit; but Francis, they said, could never get at him—he always kept just on the right side of the law—until one night the keepers found him at it in a wood right at the end of the estate. I could show you the place now; it marches with some land that used to belong to an uncle of mine. And you can imagine there was a row; and this man Gawdy (that was the name, to be sure—Gawdy; I thought I should get it—Gawdy), he was unlucky enough, poor chap! to shoot a keeper. Well, that was what Francis wanted, and grand juries—you know what they would have been then—and poor Gawdy was strung up in double-quick time; and I've been shown the place he was buried in, on the north side of the church—you know the way in that part of the world: anyone that's been hanged or made away with themselves, they bury them that side. And the idea that there was some friend of Gawdy's—not a relation, because he had none, poor devil! he was the last of his line: kind of *spes ultima gentis*—must have planned to get hold of Francis's boy and put an end to *his* line, too. I don't know—it's rather an out-of-the-way thing for an Essex poacher to think of—but, you know, I should say now it looks more as if old Gawdy had managed the job himself. Booh! I hate to think of it! have some whisky, Williams!"

The facts were communicated by Williams to Dennistoun, and by him to a mixed company, of which I was one, and the Sadducean Professor of Ophilogy another. I am sorry to say that the latter, when asked what he thought of it, only remarked: "Oh, those Bridgeford people will say anything"—a sentiment which met with the reception it deserved.

I have only to add that the picture is now in the Ashelian Museum; that it has been treated with a view to discovering whether sympathetic ink has been used in it, but without effect; that Mr. Britnell knew nothing of it save that he was sure it was uncommon; and that, though carefully watched, it has never been known to change again.

A. E. Coppard
(1878-1957)

IN addition to over one hundred short stories and five volumes of poetry, A. E. Coppard wrote an autobiography, entitled with characteristic pride *It's Me, O Lord!* (1957), and a descriptive bibliography of his own works (1931). He was determined, it seems, not to be forgotten by capricious posterity. Although he has not been forgotten, he has frequently been overlooked by the scholars and critics of Gothic short fiction of recent days. He called his short stories "modern folk tales" and admitted the presence of his own "fictive self" in his accounts of puzzling encounters, mysterious incidents, and marvelous characters. Although A. E. Coppard had none of the advantages most writers expect, he left a large legacy of poetry and fiction and a clear record of his achievement as a self-educated, self-sufficient, and self-promoting writer.

In "Arabesque: *The Mouse*," Coppard thinly masks himself as Filip, a spelling appropriate to the sensitive child, the confused adolescent, and the compassionate man "reading Russian novels until he thought he was mad." A "fillip" is both a snap of the finger and thumb—with which he considers killing the mutilated mouse—and also a slight goad or stimulus—which is all Filip requires for his reverie. The house "in the main street" at the top of "four flights of long dim echoing stairs" is Coppard's Cornmarket flat in Oxford (*It's Me, O Lord!*), and Filip's "crude dislike" of the "engaging little mouse" is also the author's. In his autobiography he makes his "repulsion" to mice gruesomely clear even as he notes his "tolerant interest" in them: "I loathe the creatures with their disproportionate heads and repugnant feet, but they always stir my compassion" (*It's Me, O Lord!*).

The story fails, finally, to be compassionate. Filip resets the mouse trap in the cupboard in an emotionless anticlimax after the emotional horror subsides. Earlier, he ends the daydream of Cassia with the "snap of the trap" or "the clack of the bolt" in another anticlimax. Even the sight of his mother's "stumps of arms" is denied him. Filip is characterized as a man in flight from a world which denies him understanding. He is the Jungian prototype of a man "caught, sucked in, enveloped, and devoured" by his mother (C. G. Jung, "The

Syzygy: Anima and Animus," 1959). He makes no more than a series of fitful starts at embracing the earth or touching reality because the image of his mother interrupts his efforts and confuses his perceptions of himself and others. Both Cassia and the mouse become images of his mother in a frightening series of projections. The Japanese print continually reminds him of his childhood fear when he sees his mother expressing milk from her breasts; Cassia's hand on his breast recalls the motherly love he has no longer; and the mutilated mouse duplicates his mother's fatal accident with horrifying accuracy. Smells of "dried apples and mice" in the present are redolent of the "ripe apples" of the past; his mother's injunction to let his heart always beat truly is echoed by Cassia's coy question: "does it beat truly—and for whom?" Filip's heart beats for his mother and only for his mother, whom he has lost only in the physical sense.

The mixture of fairy glamour with earthy grotesque crudity in this modern folk tale achieves the "unity, verisimilitude, and completeness of contour" which Coppard set for himself (Preface to *The Collected Tales*, 1927). His prose is poetic, but the conversation has the naturalness of the colloquial to give the reader "an impression that he is being spoken to, rather than written at" (*A Bibliography of the Writings*, 1931). Ford Madox Ford praised Coppard extravagantly when he compared his fancy, imagination, wisdom, piety, and beauty of phrase to that of Donne or Herbert, but some likeness can be seen. His sardonic cynicism and bold sensuousness do remind us of the great metaphysical poets, but his keen interest in the ugly and the revolting startle us more than they delight. The delicacy of this "arabesque" is intertwined with horror.

Arabesque: *The Mouse* (1920)

In the main street amongst tall establishments of mart and worship was a high narrow house pressed between a coffee factory and a bootmaker's. It had four flights of long dim echoing stairs, and at the top, in a room that was full of the smell of dried apples and mice, a man in the middle age of life had sat reading Russian novels until he thought he was mad. Late was the hour, the night outside black and freezing, the pavements below empty and undistinguishable when he closed his book and sat motionless in front of the glowing but flameless fire. He felt he was very tired yet he could not rest. He stared at a picture on the wall until he wanted to cry; it was a colour print by Utamaro of a suckling child caressing its mother's breasts as she sits in front of a blackbound mirror. Very chaste and decorative it was, in spite of its curious anatomy. The man gazed, empty of sight though not of mind, until the sighing of the gas jet maddened him. He got up, put out the light, and sat down again in the darkness trying to compose his mind before the comfort of the fire. And he was just about to begin a conversation with himself when a mouse crept from a hole in the skirting near the fireplace and scurried into the fender. The man had the crude dislike for such sly nocturnal things, but this mouse was so small and bright, its antics so pretty, that he drew his feet carefully from the fender and sat watching it almost with amusement. The mouse moved along the shadows of the fender, out upon the hearth, and sat before the glow, rubbing its head, ears, and tiny belly with its paws as if it were bathing itself with the warmth, until, sharp and sudden, the fire sank, an ember fell, and the mouse flashed into its hole.

The man reached forward to the mantelpiece and put his hand upon a pocket lamp. Turning on the beam, he opened the door of a cupboard beside the fireplace. Upon one of the shelves there was a small trap baited with cheese, a trap made with a wire spring, one of those that smashed down to break the back of ingenuous and unwary mice.

"Mean—so mean," he mused, "to appeal to the hunger of any living thing just in order to destroy it."

He picked up the empty trap as if to throw it in the fire.

"I suppose I had better leave it though—the place swarms with them." He still hesitated. "I hope that little beastie won't go and do anything foolish." He put the trap back quite carefully, closed the door of the cupboard, sat down again and extinguished the lamp.

Was there any one else in the world so squeamish and foolish about such things! Even his mother, mother so bright and beautiful, even she had laughed at his childish horrors. He recalled how once in his childhood, not long after his sister Yosine was born, a friendly neighbour had sent him home with a bundle of dead larks tied by the feet "for supper." The pitiful inanimity of the birds had brought a gush of tears; he had run weeping home and into the kitchen, and there he had found the strange thing doing. It was dusk; mother was kneeling before the fire. He dropped the larks.

"Mother!" he exclaimed softly. She looked at his tearful face.

"What's the matter, Filip?" she asked, smiling too at his astonishment.

"Mother! What you doing?"

Her bodice was open and she was squeezing her breasts; long thin streams of milk spurted into the fire with a plunging noise.

"Weaning your little sister," laughed mother. She took his inquisitive face and pressed it against the delicate warmth of her bosom, and he forgot the dead birds behind him.

"Let me do it, mother," he cried, and doing so he discovered the throb of the heart in his mother's breast. Wonderful it was for him to experience it, although she could not explain it to him.

"Why does it do that?"

"If it did not beat, little son, I should die and the Holy Father would take me from you."

"God?"

She nodded. He put his hand upon his own breast. "Oh feel it, Mother!" he cried. Mother unbuttoned his little coat and felt the gentle *tick tick* with her warm palm.

"Beautiful!" she said.

"Is it a good one?"

She kissed his upsmiling lips. "It is good if it beats truly. Let it always beat truly, Filip, let it always beat truly."

There was the echo of a sigh in her voice, and he had divined some grief, for he was very wise. He kissed her bosom in his tiny ecstasy and whispered soothingly: "Little mother! little mother!" In such joys he forgot his horror of the dead larks; indeed he helped mother to pluck them and spit them for supper.

It was a black day that succeeded, and full of tragedy for the child. A great bay horse with a tawny mane had knocked down his mother in the lane, and a heavy cart had passed over her, crushing both her hands. She was borne away moaning with anguish to the surgeon who cut off the two hands. She died in the night. For years the child's dreams were filled with the horror of the stumps of arms, bleeding unendingly. Yet he had never seen them, for he was sleeping when she died.

While this old woe was come vividly before him he again became aware of the mouse. His nerves stretched upon him in repulsion, but he soon relaxed to a tolerant interest, for it was really a most engaging little mouse. It moved with curious staccato scurries, stopping to rub its head or flicker with its ears; they seemed almost transparent ears. It spied a red cinder and skipped innocently up to it. . . . sniffing. . . . sniffing . . . until it jumped back scorched. It would crouch as a cat does, blinking in the warmth, or scamper madly as if dancing, and then roll upon its side rubbing its head with those pliant paws. The melancholy man watched it until it came at last to rest and squatted meditatively upon its haunches, hunched up, looking curiously wise, a pennyworth of philosophy; then once more the coals sank with a rattle and again the mouse was gone.

The man sat on before the fire and his mind filled again with

unaccountable sadness. He had grown into manhood with a burning
generosity of spirit and rifts of rebellion in him that proved too
exacting for his fellows and seemed mere wantonness to men of
casual rectitudes. "Justice and Sin," he would cry, "Property and
Virtue—incompatibilities! There can be no sin in a world of justice,
no property in a world of virtue!" With an engaging extravagance and
a certain clear-eyed honesty of mind he had put his two and two
together and seemed then to rejoice, as in some topsy-turvy dream, in
having rendered unto Caesar, as you might say, the things that were
due to Napoleon! But this kind of thing could not pass unexpiated in
a world of men living an infinite regard for Property and a pride in
their traditions of Virtue and Justice. They could indeed forgive him
his sins but they could not forgive him his compassions. So he had to
go seek for more melodious-minded men and fair unambiguous
women. But rebuffs can deal more deadly blows than daggers; he
became timid—a timidity not of fear but of pride—and grew with the
years into misanthropy, susceptible to trivial griefs and despairs, a
vessel of emotion that emptied as easily as it filled, until he came at
last to know that his griefs were half deliberate, his despairs half
unreal, and to live but for beauty—which is tranquillity—to put her
wooing hand upon him.

Now, while the mouse hunts in the cupboard, one fair recollection stirs in the man's mind—of Cassia and the harmony of their only
meeting, Cassia who had such rich red hair, and eyes, yes, her eyes
were full of starry enquiry like the eyes of mice. It was so long ago
that he had forgotten how he came to be in it, that unaccustomed
orbit of vain vivid things—a village festival, all oranges and houp-là.
He could not remember how he came to be there, but at night, in
the court hall, he had danced with Cassia—fair and unambiguous
indeed!—who had come like the wind from among the roses and
swept into his heart.

"It is easy to guess," he had said to her, "what you like most in
the world."

She laughed; "To dance? Yes, and you . . .?"

"To find a friend."

"I know, I know," she cried, caressing him with recognitions.
"Ah, at times I quite love my friends—until I begin to wonder how
much they hate me!"

He had loved at once that cool pale face, the abundance of her
strange hair as light as the autumn's clustered bronze, her lilac dress
and all the sweetness about her like a bush of lilies. How they had
laughed at the two old peasants whom they had overheard gabbling of
trifles like sickness and appetite!

"There's a lot of nature in a parsnip," said one, a fat person of the kind that swells grossly when stung by a bee, "a lot of nature when it's young, but when it's old it's like everything else."

"True it is."

"And I'm very fond of vegetables, yes, and I'm very fond of bread."

"Come out with me," whispered Cassia to Filip, and they walked out in the blackness of midnight into what must have been a garden.

"Cool it is here," she said, "and quiet, but too dark even to see your face—can you see mine?"

"The moon will not rise until after dawn," said he, "it will be white in the sky when the starlings whistle in your chimney."

They walked silently and warily about until they felt the chill of the air. A dull echo of the music came to them through the walls, then stopped, and they heard the bark of a fox away in the woods.

"You are cold," he whispered, touching her bare neck with timid fingers. "Quite, quite cold," drawing his hand tenderly over the curves of her chin and face. "Let us go in," he said, moving with discretion from the rapture he desired. "We will come out again," said Cassia.

But within the room the ball was just at an end, the musicians were packing up their instruments and the dancers were flocking out and homewards, or to the buffet which was on a platform at one end of the room. The two old peasants were there, munching hugely.

"I tell you," said one of them, "there's nothing in the world for it but the grease of an owl's liver. That's it, that's it! Take something on your stomach now, just to offset the chill of the dawn!"

Filip and Cassia were beside them, but there were so many people crowding the platform that Filip had to jump down. He stood then looking up adoringly at Cassia, who had pulled a purple cloak around her.

"For Filip, Filip, Filip," she said, pushing the last bite of her sandwich into his mouth, and pressing upon him her glass of Loupiac. Quickly he drank it with a great gesture, and, flinging the glass to the wall, took Cassia into his arms, shouting: "I'll carry you home, the whole way home, yes, I'll carry you!"

"Put me down!" she cried, beating his head and pulling his ears, as they passed among the departing dancers. "Put me down, you wild thing!"

Dark, dark was the lane outside, and the night an obsidian net, into which he walked carrying the girl. But her arms were looped around him, she discovered paths for him, clinging more tightly as he staggered against a wall, stumbled upon a gulley, or when her sweet hair was caught in the boughs of a little lime tree.

"Do not loose me, Filip, will you, do not loose me," Cassia said, putting her lips against his temple.

His brain seemed bursting, his heart rocked within him, but he adored the rich grace of her limbs against his breast. "Here it is," she murmured, and he carried her into a path that led to her home in a little lawned garden where the smell of ripe apples upon the branches and the heavy lustre of roses stole upon the air. Roses and apples! Roses and apples! He carried her right into the porch before she slid down and stood close to him with her hands still upon his shoulders. He could breathe happily at the release, standing silent and looking round at the sky sprayed with wondrous stars but without a moon.

"You are stronger than I thought you, stronger than you look, you are really very strong," she whispered, nodding her head to him. Opening the buttons of his coat she put her palm against his breast.

"Oh, how your heart does beat: does it beat truly—and for whom?"

He had seized her wrists in a little fury of love, crying: "Little mother, little mother!"

"What are you saying?" asked the girl; but before he could continue there came a footstep sounding behind the door, and the clack of a bolt. . . .

What was that? Was that really a bolt or was it . . . was it . . . the snap of the trap? The man sat up in his room intently listening, with nerves quivering again, waiting for the trap to kill the little philosopher. When he felt it was all over he reached guardedly in the darkness for the lantern, turned on the beam, and opened the door of the cupboard. Focussing the light upon the trap he was amazed to see the mouse sitting on its haunches before it, uncaught. Its head was bowed, but its bead-like eyes were full of brightness, and it sat blinking, it did not flee.

"Shoosh!" said the man, but the mouse did not move. "Why doesn't it go? Shoosh!" he said again, and suddenly the reason of the mouse's strange behaviour was made clear. The trap had not caught it completely, but it had broken off both its forefeet, and the thing crouched there holding out its two bleeding stumps humanly, too stricken to stir.

Horror flooded the man, and conquering his repugnance he plucked the mouse up quickly by the neck. Immediately the little thing fastened its teeth in his finger; the touch was no more than the slight prick of a pin. The man's impulse then exhausted itself. What should he do with it? He put his hand behind him, he dared not look, but there was nothing to be done except kill it at once, quickly, quickly. Oh, how should he do it? He bent towards the fire as if to drop the mouse into its quenching glow; but he paused and shuddered, he would hear its cries, he would have to listen. Should he crush it with finger and thumb? A glance towards the window decided him. He opened the sash with one hand and flung the wounded mouse far into the dark street. Closing the window with a crash he sank into a chair, limp with pity too deep for tears.

So he sat for two minutes, five minutes, ten minutes. Anxiety and shame filled him with heat. He opened the window again, and the freezing air poured in and cooled him. Seizing his lantern he ran down the echoing stairs, into the dark empty street, searching long and vainly for the little philosopher until he had to desist and return to his room, shivering, frozen to his very bones.

When he had recovered some warmth he took the trap from its shelf. The two feet dropped into his hand; he cast them into the fire. Then he once more set the trap and put it back carefully into the cupboard.

William Faulkner
(1897-1962)

IN writing about the works of Nathaniel Hawthorne, Henry James compares the richness of European tradition with the spareness of American culture and enumerates the institutions and experiences that American writers do not have available as sources of inspiration:

> No state, in the European sense of the word, and indeed barely a specific national name. No sovereign, no court, no personal loyalty, no aristocracy, no church, no clergy, no army, no diplomatic service, no country gentlemen, no palaces, no castles, nor manors, nor old country-houses, no parsonages, nor thatched cottages, nor ivied ruins; no cathedrals, nor abbeys, nor little Norman churches; no great Universities nor public schools—no Oxford, nor Eton, nor Harrow; no literature, no novels, no museums, no pictures, no political society, no sporting class—No Epsom nor Ascot! Some such list as that might be drawn up of the absent things in American life . . . the effect of which, upon an English or a French imagination, would probably as a general thing, be appalling. The natural remark, in the almost lurid light of such an indictment, would be that if these things are left out, everything is left out.
>
> (*Hawthorne*, 1879.)

Everything is certainly left out that English writers had relied upon in creating Gothic fiction and poetry. Just as a qualified exception might be made for Hawthorne's Salem, however, so William Faulkner's South provided American equivalents for some of the features of European culture that James listed. In place of national patriotism, there is the intense feeling of belonging to a particular region. In place of titled nobility, there is a true hereditary aristocracy demanding veneration and service. In place of ivied ruins, there are magnolias and swampland. In place of castles and manors, there are great white plantation houses. The thoroughbred horses, the Jeffersonian University of Virginia, and the Southern Baptist religion supply the lack of Epsom, Eton, and Anglicanism. Like parts of New England, the South of William Faulkner, Truman Capote, Tennessee Williams, Carson McCullers, Eudora Welty, and Flannery O'Connor provides fecund ground for the generation of folklore, superstition, and myth. These, combined with the decadent and the grotesque, have produced the special terrors of the Southern Gothic.

Faulkner's "mythical kingdom," as Malcolm Cowley has called

Yoknapatawpha County, is located in northern Mississippi on the border between the sand hills and the river bottoms. It has a population of 15,611 persons—mostly farmers and woodsmen and a few plantation owners—and an area of 2,400 square miles. Faulkner's best-known novels—*The Sound and the Fury* (1929), *As I Lay Dying* (1930), *Sanctuary* (1931), *Light in August* (1932), and *Absalom, Absalom!* (1936)—deal with Yoknapatawpha County and its inhabitants, the Compsons, the Sutpens, the Snopses. Jefferson, where "A Rose for Emily" takes place, is the county seat; and the mayor whom Emily remembers, Colonel Sartoris, is from the family whose story is told in *Sartoris* (1929), the first book in the Yoknapatawpha series.

Critical understanding of "A Rose for Emily" has been made richer and more complicated by the publication, in 1975, of Norman N. Holland's *5 Readers Reading*, which claims that "a reader responds to a literary work by using it to re-create his own characteristic psychological processes." The work he chooses to test his theory is "A Rose for Emily." Since the atmosphere of controversy surrounding the story at present makes any attempt at a definitive reading foolhardy, it seems desirable to ask some questions that have commonly concerned critics. What is the "rose" of the title? What is Faulkner implying about the contrast between past and present? between conservatism and change? between North and South? between the genteel and the lower class? between reality and illusion? between men and women? What is Faulkner saying about social and legal repression? How and why does Emily come to reflect the characteristics of her father? What is the relationship between the "stubborn and coquettish" house—with its nearly impassable entrance and its secret room—and Emily herself? What happened between Homer and Emily on the night Homer died? What has been happening ever since? Other questions can be asked, of course; but speculation on these will bring us face to face with the most horrific and perverse aspects of the Southern Gothic—aspects of the tradition made even more disturbing by Faulkner's deliberate refusal to clarify the evidence and provide the answers.

A Rose for Emily (1930)

I

When Miss Emily Grierson died, our whole town went to her funeral: the men through a sort of respectful affection for a fallen monument, the women mostly out of curiosity to see the inside of her house, which no one save an old manservant—a combined gardener and cook—had seen in at least ten years.

It was a big, squarish frame house that had once been white, decorated with cupolas and spires and scrolled balconies in the heavily lightsome style of the seventies, set on what had once been our most select street. But garages and cotton gins had encroached and obliterated even the august names of that neighborhood; only Miss Emily's house was left, lifting its stubborn and coquettish decay above the cotton wagons and the gasoline pumps—an eyesore among eyesores. And now Miss Emily had gone to join the representatives of those august names where they lay in the cedar-bemused cemetery among the ranked and anonymous graves of Union and Confederate soldiers who fell at the battle of Jefferson.

Alive, Miss Emily had been a tradition, a duty, and a care; a sort of hereditary obligation upon the town, dating from that day in 1894 when Colonel Sartoris, the mayor—he who fathered the edict that no Negro woman should appear on the streets without an apron —remitted her taxes, the dispensation dating from the death of her father on into perpetuity. Not that Miss Emily would have accepted charity. Colonel Sartoris invented an involved tale to the effect that Miss Emily's father had loaned money to the town, which the town, as a matter of business, preferred this way of repaying. Only a man of Colonel Sartoris' generation and thought could have invented it, and only a woman could have believed it.

When the next generation, with its more modern ideas, became mayors and aldermen, this arrangement created some little dissatisfaction. On the first of the year they mailed her a tax notice. February came, and there was no reply. They wrote her a formal letter, asking her to call at the sheriff's office at her convenience. A week later the mayor wrote her himself, offering to call or to send his car for her, and received in reply a note on paper of an archaic shape, in a thin, flowing calligraphy in faded ink, to the effect that she no longer went out at all. The tax notice was also enclosed, without comment.

They called a special meeting of the Board of Aldermen. A deputation waited upon her, knocked at the door through which no visitor had passed since she ceased giving china-painting lessons eight or ten years earlier. They were admitted by the old Negro into a dim hall from which a stairway mounted into still more shadow. It smelled of dust and disuse—a close, dank smell. The Negro led them into the parlor. It was furnished in heavy, leather-covered furniture. When the Negro opened the blinds of one window, they could see that the leather was cracked; and when they sat down, a faint dust rose sluggishly about their thighs, spinning with slow motes in the single sun-ray. On a tarnished gilt easel before the fireplace stood a crayon portrait of Miss Emily's father.

They rose when she entered—a small, fat woman in black, with a thin gold chain descending to her waist and vanishing into her belt, leaning on an ebony cane with a tarnished gold head. Her skeleton was small and spare; perhaps that was why what would have been merely plumpness in another was obesity in her. She looked bloated, like a body long submerged in motionless water, and of that pallid hue. Her eyes, lost in the fatty ridges of her face, looked like two small pieces of coal pressed into a lump of dough as they moved from one face to another while the visitors stated their errand.

She did not ask them to sit. She just stood in the door and listened quietly until the spokesman came to a stumbling halt. Then they could hear the invisible watch ticking at the end of the gold chain.

Her voice was dry and cold. "I have no taxes in Jefferson. Colonel Sartoris explained it to me. Perhaps one of you can gain access to the city records and satisfy yourselves."

"But we have. We are the city authorities, Miss Emily. Didn't you get a notice from the sheriff, signed by him?"

"I received a paper, yes," Miss Emily said. "Perhaps he considers himself the sheriff . . . I have no taxes in Jefferson."

"But there is nothing on the books to show that, you see. We must go by the——"

"See Colonel Sartoris. I have no taxes in Jefferson."

"But, Miss Emily——"

"See Colonel Sartoris." (Colonel Sartoris had been dead almost ten years.) "I have no taxes in Jefferson. Tobe!" The Negro appeared. "Show these gentlemen out."

II

So she vanquished them, horse and foot, just as she had vanquished their fathers thirty years before about the smell. That was two years after her father's death and a short time after her sweetheart—the one we believed would marry her—had deserted her. After her father's death she went out very little; after her sweetheart went away, people hardly saw her at all. A few of the ladies had the temerity to call, but were not received, and the only sign of life about the place was the Negro man—a young man then—going in and out with a market basket.

"Just as if a man—any man—could keep a kitchen properly," the ladies said; so they were not surprised when the smell developed. It was another link between the gross, teeming world and the high and mighty Griersons.

A neighbor, a woman, complained to the mayor, Judge Stevens, eighty years old.

"But what will you have me do about it, madam?" he said.

"Why, send her word to stop it," the woman said. "Isn't there a law?"

"I'm sure that won't be necessary," Judge Stevens said. "It's probably just a snake or a rat that nigger of hers killed in the yard. I'll speak to him about it."

The next day he received two more complaints, one from a man who came in diffident deprecation. "We really must do something about it, Judge. I'd be the last one in the world to bother Miss Emily, but we've got to do something." That night the Board of Aldermen met—three graybeards and one younger man, a member of the rising generation.

"It's simple enough," he said. "Send her word to have her place cleaned up. Give her a certain time to do it in, and if she don't . . ."

"Dammit, sir," Judge Stevens said, "will you accuse a lady to her face of smelling bad?"

So the next night, after midnight, four men crossed Miss Emily's lawn and slunk about the house like burglars, sniffing along the base of the brickwork and at the cellar openings while one of them performed a regular sowing motion with his hand out of a sack slung from his shoulder. They broke open the cellar door and sprinkled lime there, and in all the outbuildings. As they recrossed the lawn, a window that had been dark was lighted and Miss Emily sat in it, the light behind her, and her upright torso motionless as that of an idol. They crept quietly across the lawn and into the shadow of the locusts that lined the street. After a week or two the smell went away.

That was when people had begun to feel really sorry for her. People in our town, remembering how old lady Wyatt, her great-aunt, had gone completely crazy at last, believed that the Griersons held themselves a little too high for what they really were. None of the young men were quite good enough for Miss Emily and such. We had long thought of them as a tableau, Miss Emily a slender figure in white in the background, her father a spraddled silhouette in the foreground, his back to her and clutching a horsewhip, the two of them framed by the back-flung front door. So when she got to be thirty and was still single, we were not pleased exactly, but vindicated; even with insanity in the family she wouldn't have turned down all of her chances if they had really materialized.

When her father died, it got about that the house was all that was left to her; and in a way, people were glad. At last they could pity Miss Emily. Being left alone, and a pauper, she had become humanized. Now she too would know the old thrill and the old despair of a penny more or less.

The day after his death all the ladies prepared to call at the house and offer condolence and aid, as is our custom. Miss Emily met them at the door, dressed as usual and with no trace of grief on her face. She told them that her father was not dead. She did that for three days, with the ministers calling on her, and the doctors, trying to persuade her to let them dispose of the body. Just as they were about to resort to law and force, she broke down, and they buried her father quickly.

We did not say she was crazy then. We believed she had to do that. We remembered all the young men her father had driven away, and we knew that with nothing left, she would have to cling to that which had robbed her, as people will.

III

She was sick for a long time. When we saw her again, her hair was cut short, making her look like a girl, with a vague resemblance to those angels in colored church windows—sort of tragic and serene.

The town had just let the contracts for paving the sidewalks, and in the summer after her father's death they began the work. The construction company came with niggers and mules and machinery, and a foreman named Homer Barron, a Yankee—a big, dark, ready man, with a big voice and eyes lighter than his face. The little boys would follow in groups to hear him cuss the niggers, and the niggers singing in time to the rise and fall of picks. Pretty soon he knew everybody in town. Whenever you heard a lot of laughing anywhere about the square, Homer Barron would be in the center of the group. Presently we began to see him and Miss Emily on Sunday afternoons driving in the yellow-wheeled buggy and the matched team of bays from the livery stable.

At first we were glad that Miss Emily would have an interest, because the ladies all said, "Of course a Grierson would not think seriously of a Northerner, a day laborer." But there were still others, older people, who said that even grief could not cause a real lady to forget *noblesse oblige*—without calling it *noblesse oblige*. They just said, "Poor Emily. Her kinsfolk should come to her." She had some kin in Alabama; but years ago her father had fallen out with them over the estate of old lady Wyatt, the crazy woman, and there was no communication between the two families. They had not even been represented at the funeral.

And as soon as the old people said, "Poor Emily," the whispering began. "Do you suppose it's really so?" they said to one another. "Of course it is. What else could . . ." This behind their hands; rustling of craned silk and satin behind jalousies closed upon the sun of Sunday afternoon as the thin, swift clop-clop-clop of the matched team passed: "Poor Emily."

She carried her head high enough—even when we believed that she was fallen. It was as if she demanded more than ever the recognition of her dignity as the last Grierson; as if it had wanted that touch of earthiness to reaffirm her imperviousness. Like when she bought the rat poison, the arsenic. That was over a year after they had begun to say "Poor Emily," and while the two female cousins were visiting her.

"I want some poison," she said to the druggist. She was over thirty then, still a slight woman, though thinner than usual, with cold, haughty black eyes in a face the flesh of which was strained across the temples and about the eyesockets as you imagine a lighthouse-keeper's face ought to look. "I want some poison," she said.

"Yes, Miss Emily. What kind? For rats and such? I'd recom—"

"I want the best you have. I don't care what kind."

The druggist named several. "They'll kill anything up to an elephant. But what you want is—"

"Arsenic," Miss Emily said. "Is that a good one?"

"Is . . . arsenic? Yes, ma'am. But what you want—"

"I want arsenic."

The druggist looked down at her. She looked back at him, erect, her face like a strained flag. "Why, of course," the druggist said. "If that's what you want. But the law requires you to tell what you are going to use it for."

Miss Emily just stared at him, her head tilted back in order to look him eye for eye, until he looked away and went and got the arsenic and wrapped it up. The Negro delivery boy brought her the package; the druggist didn't come back. When she opened the package at home there was written on the box, under the skull and bones: "For rats."

IV

So the next day we all said, "She will kill herself"; and we said it would be the best thing. When she had first begun to be seen with Homer Barron, we had said, "She will marry him." Then we said, "She will persuade him yet," because Homer himself had remarked— he liked men, and it was known that he drank with the younger men in the Elks' Club—that he was not a marrying man. Later we said, "Poor Emily" behind the jalousies as they passed on Sunday afternoon in the glittering buggy, Miss Emily with her head high and Homer Barron with his hat cocked and a cigar in his teeth, reins and whip in a yellow glove.

Then some of the ladies began to say that it was a disgrace to the town and a bad example to the young people. The men did not want to interfere, but at last the ladies forced the Baptist minister— Miss Emily's people were Episcopal—to call upon her. He would never divulge what happened during that interview, but he refused to go back again. The next Sunday they again drove about the streets, and the following day the minister's wife wrote to Miss Emily's relations in Alabama.

So she had blood-kin under her roof again and we sat back to watch developments. At first nothing happened. Then we were sure that they were to be married. We learned that Miss Emily had been to the jeweler's and ordered a man's toilet set in silver, with the letters H. B. on each piece. Two days later we learned that she had bought a complete outfit of men's clothing, including a nightshirt, and we said, "They are married." We were really glad. We were glad because the two female cousins were even more Grierson than Miss Emily had ever been.

So we were not surprised when Homer Barron—the streets had been finished some time since—was gone. We were a little disappointed that there was not a public blowing-off, but we believed that he had gone on to prepare for Miss Emily's coming, or to give her a chance to get rid of the cousins. (By that time it was a cabal, and we were all Miss Emily's allies to help circumvent the cousins.) Sure enough, after another week they departed. And, as we had expected all along, within three days Homer Barron was back in town. A neighbor saw the Negro man admit him at the kitchen door at dusk one evening.

And that was the last we saw of Homer Barron. And of Miss Emily for some time. The Negro man went in and out with the market basket, but the front door remained closed. Now and then we would see her at a window for a moment, as the men did that night when they sprinkled the lime, but for almost six months she did not appear on the streets. Then we knew that this was to be expected too; as if that quality of her father which had thwarted her woman's life so many times had been too virulent and too furious to die.

When we next saw Miss Emily, she had grown fat and her hair was turning gray. During the next few years it grew grayer and grayer until it attained an even pepper-and-salt iron-gray, when it ceased turning. Up to the day of her death at seventy-four it was still that vigorous iron-gray, like the hair of an active man.

From that time on her front door remained closed, save for a period of six or seven years, when she was about forty, during which she gave lessons in china-painting. She fitted up a studio in one of the downstairs rooms, where the daughters and granddaughters of Colonel Sartoris' contemporaries were sent to her with the same regularity and in the same spirit that they were sent to church on Sundays with a twenty-five-cent piece for the collection plate. Meanwhile her taxes had been remitted.

Then the newer generation became the backbone and the spirit of the town, and the painting pupils grew up and fell away and did not send their children to her with boxes of color and tedious brushes and pictures cut from the ladies' magazines. The front door closed upon the last one and remained closed for good. When the town got free postal delivery, Miss Emily alone refused to let them fasten the metal numbers above her door and attach a mailbox to it. She would not listen to them.

Daily, monthly, yearly we watched the Negro grow grayer and more stooped, going in and out with the market basket. Each December we sent her a tax notice, which would be returned by the post office a week later, unclaimed. Now and then we would see her in one of the downstairs windows—she had evidently shut up the top floor of the house—like the carven torso of an idol in a niche, looking or not looking at us, we could never tell which. Thus she passed from generation to generation—dear, inescapable, impervious, tranquil, and perverse.

And so she died. Fell ill in the house filled with dust and shadows, with only a doddering Negro man to wait on her. We did not even know she was sick; we had long since given up trying to get any information from the Negro. He talked to no one, probably not even to her, for his voice had grown harsh and rusty, as if from disuse.

She died in one of the downstairs rooms, in a heavy walnut bed with a curtain, her gray head propped on a pillow yellow and moldy with age and lack of sunlight.

V

The Negro met the first of the ladies at the front door and let them in, with their hushed, sibilant voices and their quick, curious glances, and then he disappeared. He walked right through the house and out the back and was not seen again.

The two female cousins came at once. They held the funeral on the second day, with the town coming to look at Miss Emily beneath a mass of bought flowers, with the crayon face of her father musing profoundly above the bier and the ladies sibilant and macabre; and the very old men—some in their brushed Confederate uniforms—on the porch and the lawn, talking of Miss Emily as if she had been a contemporary of theirs, believing that they had danced with her and courted her perhaps, confusing time with its mathematical progression, as the old do, to whom all the past is not a diminishing road but, instead, a huge meadow which no winter ever quite touches, divided from them now by the narrow bottle-neck of the most recent decade of years.

Already we knew that there was one room in that region above stairs which no one had seen in forty years, and which would have to be forced. They waited until Miss Emily was decently in the ground before they opened it.

The violence of breaking down the door seemed to fill this room with pervading dust. A thin, acrid pall as of the tomb seemed to lie everywhere upon this room decked and furnished as for a bridal: upon the valance curtains of faded rose color, upon the rose-shaded lights, upon the dressing table, upon the delicate array of crystal and the man's toilet things backed with tarnished silver, silver so tarnished that the monogram was obscured. Among them lay a collar and tie, as if they had just been removed, which, lifted, left upon the surface a pale crescent in the dust. Upon a chair hung the suit, carefully folded; beneath it the two mute shoes and the discarded socks.

The man himself lay in the bed.

For a long while we just stood there, looking down at the profound and fleshless grin. The body had apparently once lain in the attitude of an embrace, but now the long sleep that outlasts love, that conquers even the grimace of love, had cuckolded him. What was left of him, rotted beneath what was left of the nightshirt, had become inextricable from the bed in which he lay; and upon him and upon the pillow beside him lay that even coating of the patient and biding dust.

Then we noticed that in the second pillow was the indentation of a head. One of us lifted something from it, and leaning forward, that faint and invisible dust dry and acrid in the nostrils, we saw a long strand of iron-gray hair.

Eudora Welty

(1909-   )

FROM Jackson, Mississippi, Eudora Welty casts a loving glance on the characters, events, and places of her native South. Her vision is deeper than it is wide, more gentle than violent, more delicate than heavy. Her photographer's eye focuses narrowly, almost squintingly, on choice details to highlight her realism in fictions which reach out to worlds far beyond Jackson, New Orleans, China Grove, or Farr's Gin. She writes of one region, but, like her contemporary and acknowledged model William Faulkner, she is more than a local colorist. "Location," she says, "is the ground conductor of all the currents of emotions and belief and moral conviction that charge out from the story in its course" ("Place in Fiction," *Three Papers on Fiction*, 1962). Place inspires her highly charged descriptions, but her sympathy and the shock she evokes give her that measure of texture and tone which make her a distinguished figure in modern American literature.

Eudora Welty was born and raised in Jackson, and she lives there still. Her education at Mississippi State College for Women, the University of Wisconsin, and Columbia University's Business School equipped her for more than her first full-time job, as a photographer and interviewer for the Works Progress Administration (1933–1936). From her photographs (published in *One Time, One Place*, 1971) she learned the eloquence of the human face and the human body in "a moment's glimpse"; in her stories, she gives us a "long look, a growing contemplation," an insight into the "unpredictable," yet common, feelings and gestures of her delightfully human vision (Preface to *One Time, One Place,* 1971).

There are no castles in Eudora Welty's post-Depression South, but there are plantation homes which bear the marks of an aristocratic past and a hopeless future. The Farrs' home in "Clytie," like Emily Grierson's in "A Rose for Emily," is a kind of "fallen monument," and its inhabitants a dying "tradition" (Faulkner's "A Rose for Emily"). Proud to the end, the Farrs willingly separate themselves from the townspeople and keep every shade drawn and every window closed as if in protection from the "common world" outside. Clytie's sister, Octavia, never ventures from upstairs; Mr. James Farr can't; and Gerald Farr shouldn't. They are living representations of the suffocation, disease, and death of their house. "Their faces came between her face and another," explains the reliable but detached narrator; the angry face of Octavia, the "apoplectic face" of the father, the drunken scowl of her brother, and the memory of the other brother with "the bullet hole through the forehead"—these grotesque physiognomies keep Clytie from finding a place full of happiness and love. Like "four wet black cedars, which smelled bitter as smoke," this family, individually and collectively, is isolated, decaying, unaware of the life-giving water in the sunken path below them. Clytie's duty to her family has become automatic and economically necessary. Her duty to herself is gradually obscured, even absorbed, by the grotesques she serves.

When Mr. Bobo, the nervous town barber, comes on Friday to shave Mr. James Farr, Clytie desperately and gently touches his face. He races from the hall; she, "pale as a ghost," runs to the rain barrel, as Octavia demands, and embraces it. The pathos of this act of hugging a familiar object as a friend gradually deteriorates into tragedy. Clytie sees herself in the water, recognizes the signs of suffering in her own face, and follows obediently the suggestion of Octavia's "monumental voice." The "kind, featureless depth" of the friendly rain barrel anticipates the welcoming river for Flannery O'Connor's Henry Ashfield and echoes the moment of true reflection for Mary Shelley's monster. Merging with self is a narcissistic response, but, for Clytie, it is "the only thing she could think of to do." No alternatives remain for Clytie; she has become no more than the grotesques of her strange family.

Welty's final antiseptic image of legs like tongs makes Clytie little more than another inanimate object without a face to be remembered or loved. Faceless, loveless, lifeless, Clytie submits to the dehumanizing forces beyond her control.

Clytie (1941)

It was late afternoon, with heavy silver clouds which looked bigger and wider than cotton fields, and presently it began to rain. Big round drops fell, still in the sunlight, on the hot tin sheds, and stained the white false fronts of the row of stores in the little town of Farr's Gin. A hen and her string of yellow chickens ran in great alarm across the road, the dust turned river-brown, and the birds flew down into it immediately, sitting out little pockets in which to take baths.

The bird dogs got up from the doorways of the stores, shook themselves down to the tail, and went to lie inside. The few people standing with long shadows on the level road moved over into the post office. A little boy kicked his bare heels into the sides of his mule, which proceeded slowly through the town toward the country.

After everyone else had gone under cover, Miss Clytie Farr stood still in the road, peering ahead in her nearsighted way, and as wet as the little birds.

She usually came out of the old big house about this time in the afternoon, and hurried through the town. It used to be that she ran about on some pretext or other, and for a while she made soft-voiced explanations that nobody could hear, and after that she began to charge up bills, which the postmistress declared would never be paid any more than anyone else's, even if the Farrs were too good to associate with other people. But now Clytie came for nothing. She came every day, and no one spoke to her any more: she would be in such a hurry, and couldn't see who it was. And every Saturday they expected her to be run over, the way she darted out into the road with all the horses and trucks.

It might be simply that Miss Clytie's wits were all leaving her, said the ladies standing in the door to feel the cool, the way her sister's had left her; and she would just wait there to be told to go home. She would have to wring out everything she had on—the waist and the jumper skirt, and the long black stockings. On her head was one of the straw hats from the furnishing store, with an old black satin ribbon pinned to it to make it a better hat, and tied under the chin. Now, under the force of the rain, while the ladies watched, the hat slowly began to sag down on each side until it looked even more absurd and done for, like an old bonnet on a horse. And indeed it was with the patience almost of a beast that Miss Clytie stood there in the rain and stuck her long empty arms out a little from her sides, as if she were waiting for something to come along the road and drive her to shelter.

In a little while there was a clap of thunder.

"Miss Clytie! Go in out of the rain, Miss Clytie!" someone called.

The old maid did not look around, but clenched her hands and drew them up under her armpits, and sticking out her elbows like hen wings, she ran out of the street, her poor hat creaking and beating about her ears.

"Well, there goes Miss Clytie," the ladies said, and one of them had a premonition about her.

Through the rushing water in the sunken path under the four wet black cedars, which smelled bitter as smoke, she ran to the house.

"Where the devil have you been?" called the older sister, Octavia from an upper window.

Clytie looked up in time to see the curtain fall back.

She went inside, into the hall, and waited, shivering. It was very dark and bare. The only light was falling on the white sheet which covered the solitary piece of furniture, an organ. The red curtains over the parlor door, held back by ivory hands, were still as tree trunks in the airless house. Every window was closed, and every shade was down, though behind them the rain could still be heard.

Clytie took a match and advanced to the stair post, where the bronze cast of Hermes was holding up a gas fixture; and at once above this, lighted up, but quite still, like one of the unmovable relics of the house, Octavia stood waiting on the stairs.

She stood solidly before the violet-and-lemon-colored glass of the window on the landing, and her wrinkled, unresting fingers took hold of the diamond cornucopia she always wore in the bosom of her long black dress. It was an unwithered grand gesture of hers, fondling the cornucopia.

"It is not enough that we are waiting here—hungry," Octavia was saying, while Clytie waited below. "But you must sneak away and not answer when I call you. Go off and wander about the streets. Common—common——!"

"Never mind, Sister," Clytie managed to say.

"But you always return."

"Of course. . . ."

"Gerald is awake now, and so is Papa," said Octavia, in the same vindictive voice—a loud voice, for she was usually calling.

Clytie went to the kitchen and lighted the kindling in the wood stove. As if she were freezing cold in June, she stood before its open door, and soon a look of interest and pleasure lighted her face, which had in the last years grown weather-beaten in spite of the straw hat. Now some dream was resumed. In the street she had been thinking about the face of a child she had just seen. The child, playing with another of the same age, chasing it with a toy pistol, had looked at her with such an open, serene, trusting expression as she passed by! With this small, peaceful face still in her mind, rosy like these flames, like an inspiration which drives all other thoughts away, Clytie had forgotten herself and had been obliged to stand where she was in the middle of the road. But the rain had come down, and someone had shouted at her, and she had not been able to reach the end of her meditations.

It had been a long time now since Clytie had first begun to watch faces, and to think about them.

Anyone could have told you that there were not more than 150 people in Farr's Gin, counting Negroes. Yet the number of faces seemed to Clytie almost infinite. She knew now to look slowly and carefully at a face; she was convinced that it was impossible to see it all at once. The first thing she discovered about a face was always that she had never seen it before. When she began to look at people's actual countenances there was no more familiarity in the world for her. The most profound, the most moving sight in the whole world must be a face. Was it possible to comprehend the eyes and the mouths of other people, which concealed she knew not what, and secretly asked for still another unknown thing? The mysterious smile of the old man who sold peanuts by the church gate returned to her; his face seemed for a moment to rest upon the iron door of the stove, set into the lion's mane. Other people said Mr. Tom Bate's Boy, as he called himself, stared away with a face as clean-blank as a water-melon seed, but to Clytie, who observed grains of sand in his eyes and in his old yellow lashes, he might have come out of a desert, like an Egyptian.

But while she was thinking of Mr. Tom Bate's Boy, there was a terrible gust of wind which struck her back, and she turned around. The long green window shade billowed and plunged. The kitchen window was wide open—she had done it herself. She closed it gently. Octavia, who never came all the way downstairs for any reason, would never have forgiven her for an open window, if she knew. Rain and sun signified ruin, in Octavia's mind. Going over the whole house, Clytie made sure that everything was safe. It was not that ruin in itself could distress Octavia. Ruin or encroachment, even upon priceless treasures and even in poverty, held no terror for her; it was simply some form of prying from without, and this she would not forgive. All of that was to be seen in her face.

Clytie cooked the three meals on the stove, for they all ate different things, and set the three trays. She had to carry them in proper order up the stairs. She frowned in concentration, for it was hard to keep all the dishes straight, to make them come out right in the end, as Old Lethy could have done. They had had to give up the cook long ago when their father suffered the first stroke. Their father had been fond of Old Lethy, she had been his nurse in childhood, and she had come back out of the country to see him when she heard he was dying. Old Lethy had come and knocked at the back door. And as usual, at the first disturbance, front or back, Octavia had peered down from behind the curtain and cried, "Go away! Go away! What the devil have you come *here* for?" And although Old Lethy and their father had both pleaded that they might be allowed to see each other, Octavia had shouted as she always did, and sent the intruder away. Clytie had stood as usual, speechless in the kitchen, until finally she had repeated after her sister, "Lethy, go away." But their father had not died. He was, instead, paralyzed, blind, and able only to call out in unintelligible sounds and to swallow liquids. Lethy still would come to the back door now and then, but they never let her in, and the old man no longer heard or knew enough to beg to see her. There was only one caller admitted to his room. Once a week the barber came by appointment to shave him. On this occasion not a word was spoken by anyone.

Clytie went up to her father's room first and set the tray down on a little marble table they kept by his bed.

"I want to feed Papa," said Octavia, taking the bowl from her hands.

"You fed him last time," said Clytie.

Relinquishing the bowl, she looked down at the pointed face on the pillow. Tomorrow was the barber's day, and the sharp black points, at their longest, stuck out like needles all over the wasted cheeks. The old man's eyes were half closed. It was impossible to know what he felt. He looked as though he were really far away, neglected, free. . . . Octavia began to feed him.

Without taking her eyes from her father's face, Clytie suddenly began to speak in rapid, bitter words to her sister, the wildest words that came to her head. But soon she began to cry and gasp, like a small child who has been pushed by the big boys into the water.

"That is enough," said Octavia.

But Clytie could not take her eyes from her father's unshaven face and his still-open mouth.

"And I'll feed him tomorrow if I want to," said Octavia. She stood up. The thick hair, growing back after an illness and dyed almost purple, fell over her forehead. Beginning at her throat, the long accordion pleats which fell the length of her gown opened and closed over her breasts as she breathed. "Have you forgotten Gerald?" she said. "And I am hungry too."

Clytie went back to the kitchen and brought her sister's supper. Then she brought her brother's.

Gerald's room was dark, and she had to push through the usual barricade. The smell of whisky was everywhere; it even flew up in the striking of the match when she lighted the jet.

"It's night," said Clytie presently.

Gerald lay on his bed looking at her. In the bad light he resembled his father.

"There's some more coffee down in the kitchen," said Clytie.

"Would you bring it to me?" Gerald asked. He stared at her in an exhausted, serious way.

She stooped and held him up. He drank the coffee while she bent over him with her eyes closed, resting.

Presently he pushed her away and fell back on the bed, and began to describe how nice it was when he had a little house of his own down the street, all new, with all conveniences, gas stove, electric lights, when he was married to Rosemary. Rosemary—she had given up a job in the next town, just to marry him. How had it happened that she had left him so soon? It meant nothing that he had threatened time and again to shoot her, it was nothing at all that he had pointed the gun against her breast. She had not understood. It was only that he had relished his contentment. He had only wanted to play with her. In a way he had wanted to show her that he loved her above life and death.

"Above life and death," he repeated, closing his eyes.

Clytie did not make an answer, as Octavia always did during these scenes, which were bound to end in Gerald's tears.

Outside the closed window a mockingbird began to sing. Clytie held back the curtain and pressed her ear against the glass. The rain had stopped. The bird's song sounded in liquid drops down through the pitch-black trees and the night.

"Go to hell," Gerald said. His head was under the pillow.

She took up the tray, and left Gerald with his face hidden. It was not necessary for her to look at any of their faces. It was their faces which came between.

Hurrying, she went down to the kitchen and began to eat her own supper.

Their faces came between her face and another. It was their faces which had come pushing in between, long ago, to hide some face that had looked back at her. And now it was hard to remember the way it looked, or the time when she had seen it first. It must have been when she was young. Yes, in a sort of arbor, hadn't she laughed, leaned forward . . . and that vision of a face—which was a little like all the other faces, the trusting child's, the innocent old traveler's, even the greedy barber's and Lethy's and the wandering peddlers' who one by one knocked and went unanswered at the door—and yet different, yet far more—this face had been very close to hers, almost familiar, almost accessible. And then the face of Octavia was thrust between, and at other times the apoplectic face of her father, the face of her brother Gerald and the face of her brother Henry with the bullet hole through the forehead. . . . It was purely for a resemblance to a vision that she examined the secret, mysterious, unrepeated faces she met in the street of Farr's Gin.

But there was always an interruption. If anyone spoke to her, she fled. If she saw she was going to meet someone on the street, she had been known to dart behind a bush and hold a small branch in front of her face until the person had gone by. When anyone called her by name, she turned first red, then white, and looked somehow, as one of the ladies in the store remarked, *disappointed*.

She was becoming more frightened all the time, too. People could tell because she never dressed up any more. For years, every once in a while, she could come out in what was called an "outfit," all in hunter's green, a hat that came down around her face like a bucket, a green silk dress, even green shoes with pointed toes. She would wear the outfit all one day, if it was a pretty day, and then next morning she would be back in the faded jumper with her old hat tied under the chin, as if the outfit had been a dream. It had been a long time now since Clytie had dressed up so that you could see her coming.

Once in a while when a neighbor, trying to be kind or only being curious, would ask her opinion about anything—such as a pattern of crochet—she would not run away; but, giving a thin trapped smile, she would say in a childish voice, "It's nice." But, the ladies always added, nothing that came anywhere close to the Farrs' house was nice for long.

"It's nice," said Clytie when the old lady next door showed her the new rosebush she had planted, all in bloom.

But before an hour was gone, she came running out of her house screaming, "My sister Octavia says you take that rosebush up! My sister Octavia says you take that rosebush up and move it away from our fence! If you don't I'll kill you! You take it away."

And on the other side of the Farrs lived a family with a little boy who was always playing in his yard. Octavia's cat would go under the fence, and he would take it and hold it in his arms. He had a song he sang to the Farrs' cat. Clytie would come running straight out of the house, flaming with her message from Octavia. "Don't you do that! Don't you do that!" she would cry in anguish. "If you do that again, I'll have to kill you!"

And she would run back to the vegetable patch and begin to curse.

The cursing was new, and she cursed softly, like a singer going over a song for the first time. But it was something she could not stop. Words which at first horrified Clytie poured in a full, light stream from her throat, which soon, nevertheless, felt strangely relaxed and rested. She cursed all alone in the peace of the vegetable garden. Everybody said, in something like deprecation, that she was only imitating her older sister, who used to go out to that same garden and curse in that same way, years ago, but in a remarkably loud, commanding voice that could be heard in the post office.

Sometimes in the middle of her words Clytie glanced up to where Octavia, at her window, looked down at her. When she let the curtain drop at last, Clytie would be left there speechless.

Finally, in a gentleness compounded of fright and exhaustion and love, an overwhelming love, she would wander through the gate and out through the town, gradually beginning to move faster, until her long legs gathered a ridiculous, rushing speed. No one in town could have kept up with Miss Clytie, they said, giving them an even start.

She always ate rapidly, too, all alone in the kitchen, as she was eating now. She bit the meat savagely from the heavy silver fork and gnawed the little chicken bone until it was naked and clean.

Halfway upstairs, she remembered Gerald's second pot of coffee, and went back for it. After she had carried the other trays down again and washed the dishes, she did not forget to try all the doors and windows to make sure that everything was locked up absolutely tight.

The next morning, Clytie bit into smiling lips as she cooked breakfast. Far out past the secretly opened window a freight train was crossing the bridge in the sunlight. Some Negroes filed down the road going fishing, and Mr. Tom Bate's Boy, who was going along, turned and looked at her through the window.

Gerald had appeared dressed and wearing his spectacles, and announced that he was going to the store today. The old Farr furnishing store did little business now, and people hardly missed Gerald when he did not come; in fact, they could hardly tell when he did because of the big boots strung on a wire, which almost hid the cagelike office. A little high-school girl could wait on anybody who came in.

Now Gerald entered the dining room.

"How are you this morning, Clytie?" he asked.

"Just fine, Gerald, how are you?"

"I'm going to the store," he said.

He sat down stiffly, and she laid a place on the table before him.

From above, Octavia screamed, "Where in the devil is my thimble, you stole my thimble, Clytie Farr, you carried it away, my little silver thimble!"

"It's started," said Gerald intensely. Clytie saw his fine, thin, almost black lips spread in a crooked line. "How can a man live in the house with women? How can he?"

He jumped up, and tore his napkin exactly in two. He walked out of the dining room without eating the first bite of his breakfast. She heard him going back upstairs into his room.

"My thimble!" screamed Octavia.

She waited one moment. Crouching eagerly, rather like a little squirrel, Clytie ate part of her breakfast over the stove before going up the stairs.

At nine Mr. Bobo, the barber, knocked at the front door.

Without waiting, for they never answered the knock, he let himself in and advanced like a small general down the hall. There was the old organ that was never uncovered or played except for funerals, and then nobody was invited. He went ahead, under the arm of the tiptoed male statue and up the dark stairway. There they were, lined up at the head of the stairs, and they all looked at him with repulsion. Mr. Bobo was convinced that they were every one mad. Gerald, even, had already been drinking, at nine o'clock in the morning.

Mr. Bobo was short and had never been anything but proud of it, until he had started coming to this house once a week. But he did not enjoy looking up from below at the soft, long throats, the cold, repelled, high-reliefed faces of those Farrs. He could only imagine what one of those sisters would do to him if he made one move. (As if he would!) As soon as he arrived upstairs, they all went off and left him. He pushed out his chin and stood with his round legs wide apart, just looking around. The upstairs hall was absolutely bare. There was not even a chair to sit down in.

"Either they sell away their furniture in the dead of night," said Mr. Bobo to the people of Farr's Gin, "or else they're just too plumb mean to use it."

Mr. Bobo stood and waited to be summoned, and wished he had never started coming to this house to shave old Mr. Farr. But he had been so surprised to get a letter in the mail. The letter was on such old, yellowed paper that at first he thought it must have been written a thousand years ago and never delivered. It was signed "Octavia Farr," and began without even calling him "Dear Mr. Bobo." What it said was: "Come to this residence at nine o'clock each Friday morning until further notice, where you will shave Mr. James Farr."

He thought he would go one time. And each time after that, he thought he would never go back—especially when he never knew when they would pay him anything. Of course, it was something to be the only person in Farr's Gin allowed inside the house (except for the undertaker, who had gone there when young Henry shot himself, but had never to that day spoken of it). It was not easy to shave a man as bad off as Mr. Farr, either—not anything like as easy as to shave a corpse or even a fighting-drunk field hand. Suppose you were like this, Mr. Bobo would say: you couldn't move your face; you couldn't hold up your chin, or tighten your jaw, or even bat your eyes when the razor came close. The trouble with Mr. Farr was his face made no resistance to the razor. His face didn't hold.

"I'll never go back," Mr. Bobo always ended to his customers. "Not even if they paid me. I've seen enough."

Yet here he was again, waiting before the sickroom door.

"This is the last time," he said. "By God!"

And he wondered why the old man did not die.

Just then Miss Clytie came out of the room. There she came in her funny, sideways walk, and the closer she got to him the more slowly she moved.

"Now?" asked Mr. Bobo nervously.

Clytie looked at his small, doubtful face. What fear raced through his little green eyes! His pitiful, greedy, small face—how very mournful it was, like a stray kitten's. What was it that this greedy little thing was so desperately needing?

Clytie came up to the barber and stopped. Instead of telling him that he might go in and shave her father, she put out her hand and with breath-taking gentleness touched the side of his face.

For an instant afterward, she stood looking at him inquiringly, and he stood like a statue, like the statue of Hermes.

Then both of them uttered a despairing cry. Mr. Bobo turned and fled, waving his razor around in a circle, down the stairs and out the front door; and Clytie, pale as a ghost, stumbled against the railing. The terrible scent of bay rum, of hair tonic, the horrible moist scratch of an invisible beard, the dense, popping green eyes—what had she got hold of with her hand! She could hardly bear it—the thought of that face.

From the closed door to the sickroom came Octavia's shouting voice.

"Clytie! Clytie! You haven't brought Papa the rain water. Where in the devil is the rain water to shave Papa?"

Clytie moved obediently down the stairs.

Her brother Gerald threw open the door of his room and called after her, "What now? This is a madhouse! Somebody was running past my room, I heard it. Where do you keep your men? Do you have to bring them home?" He slammed the door again, and she heard the barricade going up.

Clytie went through the lower hall and out the back door. She stood beside the old rain barrel and suddenly felt that this object, now, was her friend, just in time, and her arms almost circled it with impatient gratitude. The rain barrel was full. It bore a dark, heavy, penetrating fragrance, like ice and flowers and the dew of night.

Clytie swayed a little and looked into the slightly moving water. She thought she saw a face there.

Of course. It was the face she had been looking for, and from which she had been separated. As if to give a sign, the index finger of a hand lifted to touch the dark cheek.

Clytie leaned closer, as she had leaned down to touch the face of the barber.

It was a wavering, inscrutable face. The brows were drawn together as if in pain. The eyes were large, intent, almost avid, the nose ugly and discolored as if from weeping, the mouth old and closed from any speech. On either side of the head dark hair hung down in a disreputable and wild fashion. Everything about the face frightened and shocked her with its signs of waiting, of suffering.

For the second time that morning, Clytie recoiled, and as she did so, the other recoiled in the same way.

Too late, she recognized the face. She stood there completely sick at heart, as though the poor, half-remembered vision had finally betrayed her.

"Clytie! Clytie! The water! The water!" came Octavia's monumental voice.

Clytie did the only thing she could think of to do. She bent her angular body further, and thrust her head into the barrel, under the water, through its glittering surface into the kind, featureless depth, and held it there.

When Old Lethy found her, she had fallen forward into the barrel, with her poor ladylike black-stockinged legs up-ended and hung apart like a pair of tongs.

Flannery O'Connor
(1925-1964)

THE bare facts of Flannery O'Connor's life mirror the incongruity which enriches her fiction—"being Southern and being Catholic" ("The Catholic Novelist in the Protestant South"). From the first, she drew the "manners" of her narrative art—contradiction, irony, contrast, and dialect; from the second, she took the sense of "mystery" that imbues everything she wrote ("Writing Short Stories" and "On Her Own Work"). Her very limitations were sources of extraordinary strength; disease could not cripple her vision, nor could imminent death dissuade her from making her "habit of being" into a "habit of art." O'Connor's life and letters (*The Habit of Being*, ed. Sally Fitzgerald, 1979) challenge and inform readers by example and wisdom; her short stories and novels shock and intrigue them with horror and comedy. From the incongruities of realistic natural details and brilliant caricatures, emotional flatness and sensational violence, come the unities of a mind and art seldom matched in modern American literature.

Flannery O'Connor was born in Savannah, Georgia, and lived most of her life on a dairy farm in Milledgeville with her mother and flocks of fowl, peacocks being her favorites. When she was fifteen, her father died of a debilitating illness—lupus crythematosus,—which also afflicted her at the age of twenty-five and caused her death at thirty-nine. She attended Georgia State College for Women (1941–1945), and then left home for five years, first earning an M.F.A. from Iowa State University (1944–1947), then living at Yaddo writers' colony (1947–1948), in New York City (1949), and with Robert and Sally Fitzgerald at their home in Connecticut (1950). Lupus attacked her when she was en route to Milledgeville for Christmas in 1950; she remained there until her death in 1964. As her fiction gained its deserved acclaim (*Wise Blood*, 1952; *A Good Man Is Hard to Find*, 1955; and *The Violent Bear It Away*, 1960), she accepted several invitations to speak at colleges and universities, conferences and symposia. Her occasional prose from these meetings has been selected and edited by Sally and Robert Fitzgerald, in a useful volume appropriately entitled *Mystery and Manners* (1969). For her *Collected Stories* (1971), she was posthumously awarded the

National Book Award. Her life and art consistently exemplify Erwin Panofsky's description of High Gothic form: an "acceptance and ultimate reconciliation of contradictory possibilities" (*Gothic Architecture and Scholasticism*, 1951). From her earliest sketches to her last fiction, Flannery O'Connor reconciled and accepted grotesque caricatures and orthodox vision, light comedy and grim horror, meaningless life and meaningful death. The intensity of her strong faith and stern intellect gives her fictions the power of transcendence and the force of irony. In a comment on her artistic theory, she explains the incongruity simply: "If you can't make something out of a little experience, you probably won't be able to make it out of a lot. The writer's business is to contemplate experience, not to be merged in it" ("The Nature and Aim of Fiction").

With Harry Ashfield, the neglected child in "The River," we see (and even taste and smell) the staleness of the Ashfield apartment; it becomes literally a field of ashes. Like him, too, we appreciate the contrasting country setting with its "red clay road winding between banks of honeysuckle," even as we note the ominous "shadows of a wood" and "scum of gray cloud." Harry's truth that "You found out more when you left where you lived" is ours. We do not share, however, his confusion of the literal and symbolic, and we watch in horror as he acts out his simple faith in the paradoxical redemptive suicide. Behind Harry's point of view lies the sure control of the author, who controls our judgment through details which "accumulate meaning" until "they become symbolic in the way they work" ("Writing Short Stories"). The skeletonlike Mrs. Connin, the pigs as devils and man, the skeptical squint and single-eyed glance of grace, and the baptism of faith in the River of Life require of the reader an "anagogical vision," one capable of seeing "different levels of reality in one image or situation" ("The Nature and Aim of Fiction"). As O'Connor contemplates experience, so must we; and yet we do not merge in it but remain distant, like an audience at a play. The reader need not, O'Connor says, "identify himself with the character or feel compassion for the character or anything like that" ("The Nature and Aim of Fiction"). And we do not. The child's version is too simple for us, but we must admire his perception of moral and spiritual chaos: "Where he lived everything was a joke"; the baptism "was not a joke." Mr. Paradise's skeptical perspective on the healing is obviously demonic; Mrs. Connin's superstitious but unquestioning faith in it is skeletal; the Ashfields' reaction is materialistic; and Harry's identification with the fundamentalist preacher in name and action is naïve. No one character merits the reader's clear identification or approbation. Everyone in the story seems unreasonable and is.

O'Connor demands that the reader find reason in the unreasonable, mystery in the manners, belief in the shock of disbelief. The violent climax plunges us into the reality of "the central Christian mysteries," the reality of the moment of grace ("On Her Own Work"). For Harry, despite his naïveté, grace works; he succeeds in his "peculiar desire to find the kingdom of Christ" ("On Her Own Work"). By dramatizing his success at salvation, O'Connor affirms the religious enthusiasm of the South while she recognizes its grotesque or extreme features ("The Catholic Novelist in the Protestant South"). For both Flannery O'Connor and Bevel Summers, the sacrament of baptism and the sacramental vision of nature are central to human life. The ghosts of the "Christ-haunted" South in O'Connor's fiction are both fierce and instructive: by distortion and exaggeration, she reveals the value of belief in a "Christ-centered" universe ("The Grotesque in Southern Fiction"). To give baptism "some kind of emotional recognition of its significance," Flannery O'Connor deliberately jars the reader with her language, structure, and action. Her distortions are functional; her exaggeration purposeful ("Novelist and Believer"). In "The River" and throughout her fiction, hers "is not the kind of distortion that destroys; it is the kind that reveals or should reveal" ("Novelist and Believer"). In her splendid "habit of art" we cannot fail to recognize her "habit of being."

The River (1955)

The child stood glum and limp in the middle of the dark living room while his father pulled him into a plaid coat. His right arm was hung in the sleeve but the father buttoned the coat anyway and pushed him forward toward a pale spotted hand that stuck through the half-open door.

"He ain't fixed right," a loud voice said from the hall.

"Well then for Christ's sake fix him," the father muttered. "It's six o'clock in the morning." He was in his bathrobe and barefooted. When he got the child to the door and tried to shut it, he found her looming in it, a speckled skeleton in a long pea-green coat and felt helmet.

"And his and my carfare," she said. "It'll be twict we have to ride the car."

He went in the bedroom again to get the money and when he came back, she and the boy were both standing in the middle of the room. She was taking stock. "I couldn't smell those dead cigarette butts long if I was ever to come sit with you," she said, shaking him down in his coat.

"Here's the change," the father said. He went to the door and opened it wide and waited.

After she had counted the money she slipped it somewhere inside her coat and walked over to a watercolor hanging near the phonograph. "I know what time it is," she said, peering closely at the black lines crossing into broken planes of violent color. "I ought to. My shift goes on at 10 P.M. and don't get off till 5 and it takes me one hour to ride the Vine Street car."

"Oh, I see," he said; "well, we'll expect him back tonight, about eight or nine?"

"Maybe later," she said. "We're going to the river to a healing. This particular preacher don't get around this way often. I wouldn't have paid for that," she said, nodding at the painting, "I would have drew it myself."

"All right, Mrs. Connin, we'll see you then," he said, drumming on the door.

A toneless voice called from the bedroom, "Bring me an ice-pack."

"Too bad his mama's sick," Mrs. Connin said. "What's her trouble?"

"We don't know," he muttered.

"We'll ask the preacher to pray for her. He's healed a lot of folks. The Reverend Bevel Summers. Maybe she ought to see him sometime."

"Maybe so," he said. "We'll see you tonight," and he disappeared into the bedroom and left them to go.

The little boy stared at her silently, his nose and eyes running. He was four or five. He had a long face and bulging chin and half-shut eyes set far apart. He seemed mute and patient, like an old sheep waiting to be let out.

"You'll like this preacher," she said. "The Reverend Bevel Summers. You ought to hear him sing."

The bedroom door opened suddenly and the father stuck his head out and said, "Good-by, old man. Have a good time."

"Good-by," the little boy said and jumped as if he had been shot.

Mrs. Connin gave the watercolor another look. Then they went out into the hall and rang for the elevator. "I wouldn't have drew it," she said.

Outside the gray morning was blocked off on either side by the unlit empty buildings. "It's going to fair up later," she said, "but this is the last time we'll be able to have any preaching at the river this year. Wipe your nose, Sugar Boy."

He began rubbing his sleeve across it but she stopped him. "That ain't nice," she said. "Where's your handkerchief?"

He put his hands in his pockets and pretended to look for it while she waited. "Some people don't care how they send one off," she murmured to her reflection in the coffee shop window. "You pervide." She took a red and blue flowered handkerchief out of her pocket and stooped down and began to work on his nose. "Now blow," she said and he blew. "You can borry it. Put it in your pocket."

He folded it up and put it in his pocket carefully and they walked on to the corner and leaned against the side of a closed drugstore to wait for the car. Mrs. Connin turned up her coat collar so that it met her hat in the back. Her eyelids began to droop and she looked as if she might go to sleep against the wall. The little boy put a slight pressure on her hand.

"What's your name?" she asked in a drowsy voice. "I don't know but only your last name. I should have found out your first name."

His name was Harry Ashfield and he had never thought at any time before of changing it. "Bevel," he said.

Mrs. Connin raised herself from the wall. "Why ain't that a coincident!" she said. "I told you that's the name of this preacher!"

"Bevel," he repeated.

She stood looking down at him as if he had become a marvel to her. "I'll have to see you meet him today," she said. "He's no ordinary preacher. He's a healer. He couldn't do nothing for Mr. Connin though. Mr. Connin didn't have the faith but he said he would try anything once. He had this griping in his gut."

The trolley appeared as a yellow spot at the end of the deserted street.

"He's gone to the government hospital now," she said, "and they taken one-third of his stomach. I tell him he better thank Jesus for what he's got left but he says he ain't thanking nobody. Well I declare," she murmured, "Bevel!"

They walked out to the tracks to wait. "Will he heal me?" Bevel asked.

"What you got?"

"I'm hungry," he decided finally.

"Didn't you have your breakfast?"

"I didn't have time to be hungry yet then," he said.

"Well when we get home we'll both have us something," she said. "I'm ready myself."

They got on the car and sat down a few seats behind the driver and Mrs. Connin took Bevel on her knees. "Now you be a good boy," she said, "and let me get some sleep. Just don't get off my lap." She lay her head back and as he watched, gradually her eyes closed and her mouth fell open to show a few long scattered teeth, some gold and some darker than her face; she began to whistle and blow like a musical skeleton. There was no one in the car but themselves and the driver and when he saw she was asleep, he took out the flowered handkerchief and unfolded it and examined it carefully. Then he folded it up again and unzipped a place in the innerlining of his coat and hid it in there and shortly he went to sleep himself.

Her house was a half-mile from the end of the car line, set back a little from the road. It was tan paper brick with a porch across the front of it and a tin top. On the porch there were three little boys of different sizes with identical speckled faces and one tall girl who had her hair up in so many aluminum curlers that it glared like the roof. The three boys followed them inside and closed in on Bevel. They looked at him silently, not smiling.

"That's Bevel," Mrs. Connin said, taking off her coat. "It's a coincident he's named the same as the preacher. These boys are J. C., Spivey, and Sinclair, and that's Sarah Mildred on the porch. Take off that coat and hang it on the bed post, Bevel."

The three boys watched him while he unbuttoned the coat and took it off. Then they watched him hang it on the bed post and then they stood, watching the coat. They turned abruptly and went out the door and had a conference on the porch.

Bevel stood looking around him at the room. It was part kitchen and part bedroom. The entire house was two rooms and two porches. Close to his foot the tail of a light-colored dog moved up and down between two floor boards as he scratched his back on the underside of the house. Bevel jumped on it but the hound was experienced and had already withdrawn when his feet hit the spot.

The walls were filled with pictures and calendars. There were two round photographs of an old man and woman with collapsed mouths and another picture of a man whose eyebrows dashed out of two bushes of hair and clashed in a heap on the bridge of his nose; the rest of his face stuck out like a bare cliff to fall from. "That's Mr. Connin," Mrs. Connin said, standing back from the stove for a second to admire the face with him, "but it don't favor him any more." Bevel turned from Mr. Connin to a colored picture over the bed of a man wearing a white sheet. He had long hair and a gold circle around his head and he was sawing on a board while some children stood watching him. He was going to ask who that was when the three boys came in again and motioned for him to follow them. He thought of crawling under the bed and hanging onto one of the legs but the three boys only stood there, speckled and silent, waiting, and after a second he followed them at a little distance out on the porch and around the corner of the house. They started off through a field of rough yellow weeds to the hog pen, a five-foot boarded square full of shoats, which they intended to ease him over into. When they reached it, they turned and waited silently, leaning against the side.

He was coming very slowly, deliberately bumping his feet together as if he had trouble walking. Once he had been beaten up in the park by some strange boys when his sitter forgot him, but he hadn't known anything was going to happen that time until it was over. He began to smell a strong odor of garbage and to hear the noises of a wild animal. He stopped a few feet from the pen and waited, pale but dogged.

The three boys didn't move. Something seemed to have happened to them. They stared over his head as if they saw something coming behind him but he was afraid to turn his own head and look. Their speckles were pale and their eyes were still and gray as glass. Only their ears twitched slightly. Nothing happened. Finally, the one in the middle said, "She'd kill us," and turned, dejected and hacked, and climbed up on the pen and hung over, staring in.

Bevel sat down on the ground, dazed with relief, and grinned up at them.

The one sitting on the pen glanced at him severely. "Hey you," he said after a second, "if you can't climb up and see these pigs you can lift that bottom board off and look in thataway." He appeared to offer this as a kindness.

Bevel had never seen a real pig but he had seen a pig in a book and knew they were small fat pink animals with curly tails and round grinning faces and bow ties. He leaned forward and pulled eagerly at the board.

"Pull harder," the littlest boy said. "It's nice and rotten. Just life out thet nail."

He eased a long reddish nail out of the soft wood.

"Now you can lift up the board and put your face to the . . ." a quiet voice began.

He had already done it and another face, gray, wet and sour, was pushing into his, knocking him down and back as it scraped out under the plank. Something snorted over him and charged back again, rolling him over and pushing him up from behind and then sending him forward, screaming through the yellow field, while it bounded behind.

The three Connins watched from where they were. The one sitting on the pen held the loose board back with his dangling foot. Their stern faces didn't brighten any but they seemed to become less taut, as if some great need had been partly satisfied. "Maw ain't going to like him lettin out thet hawg," the smallest one said.

Mrs. Connin was on the back porch and caught Bevel up as he reached the steps. The hog ran under the house and subsided, panting, but the child screamed for five minutes. When she had finally calmed him down, she gave him his breakfast and let him sit on her lap while he ate it. The shoat climbed the two steps onto the back porch and stood outside the screen door, looking in with his head lowered sullenly. He was long-legged and humpbacked and part of one of his ears had been bitten off.

"Git away!" Mrs. Connin shouted. "That one yonder favors Mr. Paradise that has the gas station," she said. "You'll see him today at the healing. He's got the cancer over his ear. He always comes to show he ain't been healed."

The shoat stood squinting a few seconds longer and then moved off slowly. "I don't want to see him," Bevel said.

They walked to the river, Mrs. Connin in front with him and the three boys strung out behind and Sarah Mildred, the tall girl, at the end to holler if one of them ran out on the road. They looked like the skeleton of an old boat with two pointed ends, sailing slowly on the edge of the highway. The white Sunday sun followed at a little distance, climbing fast through a scum of gray cloud as if it meant to overtake them. Bevel walked on the outside edge, holding Mrs. Connin's hand and looking down into the orange and purple gulley that dropped off from the concrete.

It occurred to him that he was lucky this time that they had found Mrs. Connin who would take you away for the day instead of an ordinary sitter who only sat where you lived or went to the park. You found out more when you left where you lived. He had found out already this morning that he had been made by a carpenter named Jesus Christ. Before he had thought it had been a doctor named Sladewall, a fat man with a yellow mustache who gave him shots and thought his name was Herbert, but this must have been a joke. They joked a lot where he lived. If he had thought about it before, he would have thought Jesus Christ was a word like "oh" or "damn" or "God," or maybe somebody who had cheated them out of something sometime. When he had asked Mrs. Connin who the man in the sheet in the picture over her bed was, she had looked at him a while with her mouth open. Then she had said, "That's Jesus," and she had kept on looking at him.

In a few minutes she had got up and got a book out of the other room. "See here," she said, turning over the cover, "this belonged to my great grandmamma. I wouldn't part with it for nothing on earth." She ran her finger under some brown writing on a spotted page. "Emma Stevens Oakley, 1832," she said. "Ain't that something to have? And every word of it the gospel truth." She turned the next page and read him the name: "The Life of Jesus Christ for Readers Under Twelve." Then she read him the book.

It was a small book, pale brown on the outside with gold edges and a smell like old putty. It was full of pictures, one of the carpenter driving a crowd of pigs out of a man. They were real pigs, gray and sour-looking, and Mrs. Connin said Jesus had driven them all out of this one man. When she finished reading, she let him sit on the floor and look at the pictures again.

Just before they left for the healing, he had managed to get the book inside his innerlining without her seeing him. Now it made his coat hang down a little farther on one side than the other. His mind was dreamy and serene as they walked along and when they turned off the highway onto a long red clay road winding between banks of honeysuckle, he began to make wild leaps and pull forward on her hand as if he wanted to dash off and snatch the sun which was rolling away ahead of them now.

They walked on the dirt road for a while and then they crossed a field stippled with purple weeds and entered the shadows of a wood where the ground was covered with thick pine needles. He had never been in woods before and he walked carefully, looking from side to side as if he were entering a strange country. They moved along a bridle path that twisted downhill through crackling red leaves, and once, catching at a branch to keep himself from slipping, he looked into two frozen green-gold eyes enclosed in the darkness of a tree hole. At the bottom of the hill, the woods opened suddenly onto a pasture dotted here and there with black and white cows and sloping down, tier after tier, to a broad orange stream where the reflection of the sun was set like a diamond.

There were people standing on the near bank in a group, singing. Long tables were set up behind them and a few cars and trucks were parked in a road that came up by the river. They crossed the pasture, hurrying, because Mrs. Connin, using her hand for a shed over her eyes, saw the preacher already standing out in the water. She dropped her basket on one of the tables and pushed the three boys in front of her into the knot of people so that they wouldn't linger by the food. She kept Bevel by the hand and eased her way up to the front.

The preacher was standing about ten feet out in the stream where the water came up to his knees. He was a tall youth in khaki trousers that he had rolled up higher than the water. He had on a blue shirt and a red scarf around his neck but no hat and his light-colored hair was cut in sideburns that curved into the hollows of his cheeks. His face was all bone and red light reflected from the river. He looked as if he might have been nineteen years old. He was singing in a high twangy voice, above the singing on the bank, and he kept his hands behind him and his head tilted back.

He ended the hymn on a high note and stood silent, looking down at the water and shifting his feet in it. Then he looked up at the people on the bank. They stood close together, waiting; their faces were solemn but expectant and every eye was on him. He shifted his feet again.

"Maybe I know why you come," he said in the twangy voice, "maybe I don't."

"If you ain't come for Jesus, you ain't come for me. If you just come to see can you leave your pain in the river, you ain't come for Jesus. You can't leave your pain in the river," he said. "I never told nobody that." He stopped and looked down at his knees.

"I seen you cure a woman oncet!" a sudden high voice shouted from the hump of people. "Seen that woman git up and walk out straight where she had limped in!"

The preacher lifted one foot and then the other. He seemed almost but not quite to smile. "You might as well go home if that's what you come for," he said.

Then he lifted his head and arms and shouted, "Listen to what I got to say, you people! There ain't but one river and that's the River of Life, made out of Jesus' Blood. That's the river you have to lay your pain in, in the River of Faith, in the River of Life, in the River of Love, in the rich red river of Jesus' Blood, you people!"

His voice grew soft and musical. "All the rivers come from that one River and go back to it like it was the ocean sea and if you believe, you can lay your pain in that River and get rid of it because that's the River that was made to carry sin. It's a River full of pain itself, pain itself, moving toward the Kingdom of Christ, to be washed away, slow, you people, slow as this here old red water river round my feet.

"Listen," he sang, "I read in Mark about an unclean man, I read in Luke about a blind man, I read in John about a dead man! Oh you people hear! The same blood that makes this River red, made that leper clean, made that blind man stare, made that dead man leap! You people with trouble," he cried, "lay it in that River of Blood, lay it in that River of Pain, and watch it move away toward the Kingdom of Christ."

While he preached, Bevel's eyes followed drowsily the slow circles of two silent birds revolving high in the air. Across the river there was a low red and gold grove of sassafras with hills of dark blue trees behind it and an occasional pine jutting over the skyline. Behind, in the distance, the city rose like a cluster of warts on the side of the mountain. The birds revolved downward and dropped lightly in the top of the highest pine and sat hunch-shouldered as if they were supporting the sky.

"If it's this River of Life you want to lay your pain in, then come up," the preacher said, "and lay your sorrow here. But don't be thinking this is the last of it because this old red river don't end here. This old red suffering stream goes on, you people, slow to the Kingdom of Christ. This old red river is good to Baptize in, good to lay your faith in, good to lay your pain in, but it ain't this muddy water here that saves you. I been all up and down this river this week," he said. "Tuesday I was in Fortune Lake, next day in Ideal, Friday me and my wife drove to Lulawillow to see a sick man there. Them people didn't see no healing," he said and his face burned redder for a second. "I never said they would."

While he was talking a fluttering figure had begun to move forward with a kind of butterfly movement—an old woman with flapping arms whose head wobbled as if it might fall off any second. She managed to lower herself at the edge of the bank and let her arms churn in the water. Then she bent farther and pushed her face down in it and raised herself up finally, streaming wet; and still flapping, she turned a time or two in a blind circle until someone reached out and pulled her back into the group.

"She's been that way for thirteen years," a rough voice shouted. "Pass the hat and give this kid his money. That's what he's here for." The shout, directed out to the boy in the river, came from a huge old man who sat like a humped stone on the bumper of a long ancient gray automobile. He had on a gray hat that was turned down over one ear and up over the other to expose a purple bulge on his left temple. He sat bent forward with his hands hanging between his knees and his small eyes half closed.

Bevel stared at him once and then moved into the folds of Mrs. Connin's coat and hid himself.

The boy in the river glanced at the old man quickly and raised his fist. "Believe Jesus or the devil!" he cried. "Testify to one or the other!"

"I know from my own self-experience," a woman's mysterious voice called from the knot of people, "I know from it that this preacher can heal. My eyes have been opened! I testify to Jesus!"

The preacher lifted his arms quickly and began to repeat all that he had said before about the River and the Kingdom of Christ and the old man sat on the bumper, fixing him with a narrow squint. From time to time Bevel stared at him again from around Mrs. Connin.

A man in overalls and a brown coat leaned forward and dipped his hand in the water quickly and shook it and leaned back, and a woman held a baby over the edge of the bank and splashed its feet with water. One man moved a little distance away and sat down on the bank and took off his shoes and waded out into the stream; he stood there for a few minutes with his face tilted as far back as it would go, then he waded back and put on his shoes. All this time, the preacher sang and did not appear to watch what went on.

As soon as he stopped singing, Mrs. Connin lifted Bevel up and said, "Listen here, preacher, I got a boy from town today that I'm keeping. His mama's sick and he wants you to pray for her. And this is a coincident—his name is Bevel! Bevel," she said, turning to look at the people behind her, "same as his. Ain't that a coincident, though?"

There were some murmurs and Bevel turned and grinned over her shoulder at the faces looking at him. "Bevel," he said in a loud jaunty voice.

"Listen," Mrs. Connin said, "have you ever been Baptized, Bevel?"

He only grinned.

"I suspect he ain't ever been Baptized," Mrs. Connin said, raising her eyebrows at the preacher.

"Swang him over here," the preacher said and took a stride forward and caught him.

He held him in the crook of his arm and looked at the grinning face. Bevel rolled his eyes in a comical way and thrust his face forward, close to the preacher's. "My name is Bevvvuuuuul," he said in a loud deep voice and let the tip of his tongue slide across his mouth.

The preacher didn't smile. His bony face was rigid and his narrow gray eyes reflected the almost colorless sky. There was a loud laugh from the old man sitting on the car bumper and Bevel grasped the back of the preacher's collar and held it tightly. The grin had already disappeared from his face. He had the sudden feeling that this was not a joke. Where he lived everything was a joke. From the preacher's face, he knew immediately that nothing the preacher said or did was a joke. "My mother named me that," he said quickly.

"Have you ever been Baptized?" the preacher asked.

"What's that?" he murmured.

"If I Baptize you," the preacher said, "you'll be able to go to the Kingdom of Christ. You'll be washed in the river of suffering, son, and you'll go by the deep river of life. Do you want that?"

"Yes," the child said, and thought, I won't go back to the apartment then, I'll go under the river.

"You won't be the same again," the preacher said. "You'll count." Then he turned his face to the people and began to preach and Bevel looked over his shoulder at the pieces of the white sun scattered in the river. Suddenly the preacher said, "All right, I'm going to Baptize you now," and without more warning, he tightened his hold and swung him upside down and plunged his head into the water. He held him under while he said the words of Baptism and then he jerked him up again and looked sternly at the gasping child. Bevel's eyes were dark and dilated. "You count now," the preacher said. "You didn't even count before."

The little boy was too shocked to cry. He spit out the muddy water and rubbed his wet sleeve into his eyes and over his face.

"Don't forget his mamma," Mrs. Connin called. "He wants you to pray for his mamma. She's sick."

"Lord," the preacher said, "we pray for somebody in affliction who isn't here to testify. Is your mother sick in the hospital?" he asked. "Is she in pain?"

The child stared at him. "She hasn't got up yet," he said in a high dazed voice. "She has a hangover." The air was so quiet he could hear the broken pieces of the sun knocking in the water.

The preacher looked angry and startled. The red drained out of his face and the sky appeared to darken in his eyes. There was a loud guffaw from the bank and Mr. Paradise shouted, "Haw! Cure the afflicted woman with the hangover!" and began to beat his knee with his fist.

"He's had a long day," Mrs. Connin said, standing with him in the door of the apartment and looking sharply into the room where the party was going on. "I reckon it's past his regular bedtime." One of Bevel's eyes was closed and the other half closed; his nose was running and he kept his mouth open and breathed through it. The damp plaid coat dragged down on one side.

That would be her, Mrs. Connin decided, in the black britches— long black satin britches and barefoot sandals and red toenails. She was lying on half the sofa, with her knees crossed in the air and her head propped on the arm. She didn't get up.

"Hello, Harry," she said. "Did you have a big day?" She had a long pale face, smooth and blank, and straight sweet-potato-colored hair, pulled back.

The father went off to get the money. There were two other couples. One of the men, blond with little violet-blue eyes, leaned out of his chair and said, "Well Harry, old man, have a big day?"

"His name ain't Harry. It's Bevel," Mrs. Connin said.

"His name is Harry," *she* said from the sofa. "Whoever heard of anybody named Bevel?"

The little boy had seemed to be going to sleep on his feet, his head drooping farther and farther forward; he pulled it back suddenly and opened one eye; the other was stuck.

"He told me this morning his name was Bevel," Mrs. Connin said in a shocked voice. "The same as our preacher. We been all day at a preaching and healing at the river. He said his name was Bevel, the same as the preacher's. That's what he told me."

"Bevel!" his mother said. "My God! what a name."

"This preacher is named Bevel and there's no better preacher around," Mrs. Connin said. "And furthermore," she added in a defiant tone, "he Baptized this child this morning!"

His mother sat straight up. "Well the nerve!" she muttered.

"Furthermore," Mrs. Connin said, "he's a healer and he prayed for you to be healed."

"Healed!" she almost shouted. "Healed of what for Christ's sake?"

"Of your affliction," Mrs. Connin said icily.

The father had returned with the money and was standing near Mrs. Connin waiting to give it to her. His eyes were lined with red threads. "Go on, go on," he said, "I want to hear more about her affliction. The exact nature of it has escaped . . ." He waved the bill and his voice trailed off. "Healing by prayer is mighty inexpensive," he murmured.

Mrs. Connin stood a second, staring into the room, with a skeleton's appearance of seeing everything. Then, without taking the money, she turned and shut the door behind her. The father swung around, smiling vaguely, and shrugged. The rest of them were looking at Harry. The little boy began to shamble toward the bedroom.

"Come here, Harry," his mother said. He automatically shifted his direction toward her without opening his eye any farther. "Tell me what happened today," she said when he reached her. She began to pull off his coat.

"I don't know," he muttered.

"Yes you do know," she said, feeling the coat heavier on one side. She unzipped the innerlining and caught the book and a dirty handkerchief as they fell out. "Where did you get these?"

"I don't know," he said and grabbed for them. "They're mine. She gave them to me."

She threw the handkerchief down and held the book too high for him to reach and began to read it, her face after a second assuming an exaggerated comical expression. The others moved around and looked at it over her shoulder. "My God," somebody said.

One of the men peered at it sharply from behind a thick pair of glasses. "That's valuable," he said. "That's a collector's item," and he took it away from the rest of them and retired to another chair.

"Don't let George go off with that," his girl said.

"I tell you it's valuable," George said. "1832."

Bevel shifted his direction again toward the room where he slept. He shut the door behind him and moved slowly in the darkness to the bed and sat down and took off his shoes and got under the cover. After a minute a shaft of light let in the tall silhouette of his mother. She tiptoed lightly across the room and sat down on the edge of his bed. "What did that dolt of a preacher say about me?" she whispered. "What lies have you been telling today, honey?"

He shut his eye and heard her voice from a long way away, as if he were under the river and she on top of it. She shook his shoulder. "Harry," she said, leaning down and putting her mouth to his ear, "tell me what he said." She pulled him into a sitting position and he felt as if he had been drawn up from under the river. "Tell me," she whispered and her bitter breath covered his face.

He saw the pale oval close to him in the dark. "He said I'm not the same now," he muttered. "I count."

After a second, she lowered him by his shirt front onto the pillow. She hung over him an instant and brushed her lips against his forehead. Then she got up and moved away, swaying her hips lightly through the shaft of light.

He didn't wake up early but the apartment was still dark and close when he did. For a while he lay there, picking his nose and eyes. Then he sat up in bed and looked out the window. The sun came in palely, stained gray by the glass. Across the street at the Empire Hotel, a colored cleaning woman was looking down from an upper window, resting her face on her folded arms. He got up and put on his shoes and went to the bathroom and then into the front room. He ate two crackers spread with anchovy paste, that he found on the coffee table, and drank some ginger ale left in a bottle and looked around for his book but it was not there.

The apartment was silent except for the faint humming of the refrigerator. He went into the kitchen and found some raisin bread heels and spread a half jar of peanut butter between them and climbed up on the tall kitchen stool and sat chewing the sandwich slowly, wiping his nose every now and then on his shoulder. When he finished he found some chocolate milk and drank that. He would rather have had the ginger ale he saw but they left the bottle openers where he couldn't reach them. He studied what was left in the refrigerator for a while—some shriveled vegetables that she had forgot were there and a lot of brown oranges that she bought and didn't squeeze; there were three or four kinds of cheese and something fishy in a paper bag; the rest was a pork bone. He left the refrigerator door open and wandered back into the dark living room and sat down on the sofa.

He decided they would be out cold until one o'clock and that they would all have to go to a restaurant for lunch. He wasn't high enough for the table yet and the waiter would bring a highchair and he was too big for a highchair. He sat in the middle of the sofa, kicking it with his heels. Then he got up and wandered around the room, looking into the ashtrays at the butts as if this might be a habit. In his own room he had picture books and blocks but they were for the most part torn up; he found the way to get new ones was to tear up the ones he had. There was very little to do at any time but eat; however, he was not a fat boy.

He decided he would empty a few of the ashtrays on the floor. If he only emptied a few, she would think they had fallen. He emptied two, rubbing the ashes carefully into the rug with his finger. Then he lay on the floor for a while, studying his feet which he held up in the air. His shoes were still damp and he began to think about the river.

Very slowly, his expression changed as if he were gradually seeing appear what he didn't know he'd been looking for. Then all of a sudden he knew what he wanted to do.

He got up and tiptoed into their bedroom and stood in the dim light there, looking for her pocketbook. His glance passed her long pale arm hanging off the edge of the bed down to the floor, and across the white mound his father made, and past the crowded bureau, until it rested on the pocketbook hung on the back of a chair. He took a car-token out of it and half a package of Life Savers. Then he left the apartment and caught the car at the corner. He hadn't taken a suitcase because there was nothing from there he wanted to keep.

He got off the car at the end of the line and started down the road he and Mrs. Connin had taken the day before. He knew there wouldn't be anybody at her house because the three boys and the girl went to school and Mrs. Connin had told him she went out to clean. He passed her yard and walked on the way they had gone to the river. The paper brick houses were far apart and after a while the dirt place to walk on ended and he had to walk on the edge of the highway. The sun was pale yellow and high and hot.

He passed a shack with an orange gas pump in front of it but he didn't see the old man looking out at nothing in particular from the doorway. Mr. Paradise was having an orange drink. He finished it slowly, squinting over the bottle at the small plaid-coated figure disappearing down the road. Then he set the empty bottle on a bench and, still squinting, wiped his sleeve over his mouth. He went in the shack and picked out a peppermint stick, a foot long and two inches thick, from the candy shelf, and stuck it in his hip pocket. Then he got in his car and drove slowly down the highway after the boy.

By the time Bevel came to the field speckled with purple weeds, he was dusty and sweating and he crossed it at a trot to get into the woods as fast as he could. Once inside, he wandered from tree to tree, trying to find the path they had taken yesterday. Finally he found a line worn in the pine needles and followed it until he saw the steep trail twisting down through the trees.

Mr. Paradise had left his automobile back some way on the road and had walked to the place where he was accustomed to sit almost every day, holding an unbaited fishline in the water while he stared at the river passing in front of him. Anyone looking at him from a distance would have seen an old boulder half hidden in the bushes.

Bevel didn't see him at all. He only saw the river, shimmering reddish yellow, and bounded into it with his shoes and his coat on and took a gulp. He swallowed some and spit the rest out and then he stood there in water up to his chest and looked around him. The sky was a clear pale blue, all in one piece—except for the hole the sun made—and fringed around the bottom with treetops. His coat floated to the surface and surrounded him like a strange gay lily pad and he stood grinning in the sun. He intended not to fool with preachers any more but to Baptize himself and to keep on going this time until he found the Kingdom of Christ in the river. He didn't mean to waste any more time. He put his head under the water at once and pushed forward.

In a second he began to gasp and sputter and his head reappeared on the surface; he started under again and the same thing happened. The river wouldn't have him. He tried again and came up, choking. This was the way it had been when the preacher held him under—he had had to fight with something that pushed him back in the face. He stopped and thought suddenly: it's another joke, it's just another joke! He thought how far he had come for nothing and he began to hit and splash and kick the filthy river. His feet were already treading on nothing. He gave one low cry of pain and indignation. Then he heard a shout and turned his head and saw something like a giant pig bounding after him, shaking a red and white club and shouting. He plunged under once and this time, the waiting current caught him like a long gentle hand and pulled him swiftly forward and down. For an instant he was overcome with surprise; then since he was moving quickly and knew that he was getting somewhere, all his fury and his fear left him.

Mr. Paradise's head appeared from time to time on the surface of the water. Finally, far downstream, the old man rose like some ancient water monster and stood empty-handed, staring with his dull eyes as far down the river line as he could see.

Anne Sexton
(1928-1975)

BEFORE committing suicide in 1975, Anne Sexton had long weighed the merits of life and death. She confessed her inner debate in the books of poetry she produced: *To Bedlam and Part Way Back* (1960), *All My Pretty Ones* (1962), *Live or Die* (1967), *The Death Notebooks* (1974), and *The Awful Rowing Toward God* (1975; posthumous). In the mode of confessional poetry defined by Robert Lowell, with whom she studied, Sylvia Plath, whose fate haunted her, and W. D. Snodgrass, whose collection *Heart's Needle* (1959) moved her to courageous action, Anne Sexton wrote of her impulses toward suicide, her nervous breakdowns and stays in mental hospitals, her relations with her husband, her lover, and her two daughters, and her understanding of what it is to be a woman. Reviewers tended to compare her work unfavorably with the poetry of Lowell and Plath, judging it to be flawed by self-indulgence; but they all acknowledged both her suffering and the brutal honesty of her vision.

The heart of that vision was estrangement—her estrangement from the outside world, from her mind, and from her body. In the poem "Briar Rose (Sleeping Beauty)" from *Transformations* (1971), she wrestles with several kinds of estrangement, but especially with the simultaneous needs to disown and cling to the past. The poems in *Transformations* show her recognizing the desirability of greater indirection and distance in her work, for she poses as a middle-aged "witch" retelling, or "transforming," the tales of the Brothers Grimm. But in the different forms of alienation that the poems describe—from "Rumpelstiltskin," where the dwarf wants only "a living thing/to call his own," to "Rapunzel," where an old witch yearns for the young beauty of her lost beloved—Sexton's own agony of separation comes clearly across.

In an interview with Patricia Marx for the *Hudson Review* (Winter 1965–1966), Sexton emphasized the importance to her work of a letter written by Franz Kafka: "The books we need are the kind that act upon us like a misfortune, that make us suffer, like the death of someone we love more than ourselves. A book should serve as the axe for the frozen sea within us." She went on to say that poetry "should be a shock to the senses. It should almost hurt." The painful images in "Briar Rose"—the "eyes burnt by cigarettes," the "hole in my cheek," the rank honeysuckle, the "sleeping jellyfish," Edvard Munch's lithograph *The Scream*—challenge the complacency of modern suburban lives. The sardonic humor of the poem— "Presto! She's out of prison!"—gives a taste of desperation and terror to the sweetness of most fairy tales. The analogy of Briar Rose to a woman in the present undergoing a hypnotic voyage back to her past—and failing to escape the prison or come to comfortable terms with life—lends an almost mythic dimension to modern misery. The confusion of "Daddy" and the prince reveals the influence of Freudian concepts on Sexton's work. In this poem, and in all of *Transformations*, the "psychological Gothic," developed in the writings of such authors as James and Poe, undergoes another evolution to become the "psychoanalytic." Though Sexton was hagridden by ideas of death, and though, in the end, she chose to take her own life, a poem like "Briar Rose" is still affirmative in deserving the tribute Sexton offered to Elizabeth Bishop and Randall Jarrell: "Their work shocks me into being more alive." And that, perhaps, is the ultimate justification for the evil image.

Briar Rose (Sleeping Beauty) (1971)

Consider
a girl who keeps slipping off,
arms limp as old carrots,
into the hypnotist's trance,
into a spirit world
speaking with the gift of tongues.   5
She is stuck in the time machine,
suddenly two years old sucking her thumb,
as inward as a snail,
learning to talk again.
She's on a voyage.   10
She is swimming further and further back,
up like a salmon,
struggling into her mother's pocketbook.
Little doll child,
come here to Papa.   15

Sit on my knee.
I have kisses for the back of your neck.
A penny for your thoughts, Princess.
I will hunt them like an emerald.   20
Come be my snooky
and I will give you a root.
That kind of voyage,
rank as honeysuckle.

Once   25
a king had a christening
for his daughter Briar Rose
and because he had only twelve gold plates
he asked only twelve fairies
to the grand event.   30
The thirteenth fairy,
her fingers as long and thin as straws,
her eyes burnt by cigarettes,
her uterus an empty teacup,
arrived with an evil gift.   35
She made this prophecy:
The princess shall prick herself
on a spinning wheel in her fifteenth year
and then fall down dead.
Kaputt!   40
The court fell silent.
The king looked like Munch's *Scream*.
Fairies' prophecies,
in times like those,
held water.   45
However the twelfth fairy
had a certain kind of eraser
and thus she mitigated the curse
changing that death
into a hundred-year sleep.   50

The king ordered every spinning wheel
exterminated and exorcized.
Briar Rose grew to be a goddess
and each night the king
bit the hem of her gown   55
to keep her safe.
He fastened the moon up
with a safety pin
to give her perpetual light
He forced every male in the court   60

to scour his tongue with Bab-o
lest they poison the air she dwelt in.
Thus she dwelt in his odor.
Rank as honeysuckle.

On her fifteenth birthday   65
she pricked her finger
on a charred spinning wheel
and the clocks stopped.
Yes indeed. She went to sleep.
The king and queen went to sleep,   70
the courtiers, the flies on the wall.
The fire in the hearth grew still
and the roast meat stopped crackling.
The trees turned into metal
and the dog became china.   75
They all lay in a trance,
each a catatonic
stuck in the time machine.
Even the frogs were zombies.

Only a bunch of briar roses grew   80
forming a great wall of tacks
around the castle.
Many princes
tried to get through the brambles
for they had heard much of Briar Rose   85
but they had not scoured their tongues
so they were held by the thorns
and thus were crucified.
In due time
a hundred years passed   90
and a prince got through.
The briars parted as if for Moses
and the prince found the tableau intact.
He kissed Briar Rose
and she woke up crying: 95
Daddy! Daddy!
Presto! She's out of prison!
She married the prince
and all went well
except for the fear—   100
the fear of sleep.

Briar Rose
was an insomniac . . .

She could not nap
or lie in sleep   105
without the court chemist
mixing her some knock-out drops
and never in the prince's presence.
If it is to come, she said,
sleep must take me unawares   110
while I am laughing or dancing
so that I do not know that brutal place
where I lie down with cattle prods,
the hole in my cheek open.
Further, I must not dream   115
for when I do I see the table set
and a faltering crone at my place,
her eyes burnt by cigarettes
as she eats betrayal like a slice of meat.

I must not sleep   120
for while asleep I'm ninety
and think I'm dying.
Death rattles in my throat
like a marble.
I wear tubes like earrings.   125
I lie as still as a bar of iron.
You can stick a needle
through my kneecap and I won't flinch.
I'm all shot up with Novocain.
This trance girl   130
is yours to do with.
You could lay her in a grave,
an awful package,
and shovel dirt on her face
and she'd never call back: Hello there!   135
But if you kissed her on the mouth
her eyes would spring open
and she'd call out: Daddy! Daddy!
Presto!
She's out of prison.   140

There was a theft.
That much I am told.
I was abandoned.
That much I know.
I was forced backward.   145
I was forced forward.

I was passed hand to hand
like a bowl of fruit.
Each night I am nailed into place
and I forget who I am.   150
Daddy?
That's another kind of prison.
It's not the prince at all,
but my father
drunkenly bent over my bed,   155
circling the abyss like a shark,
my father thick upon me
like some sleeping jellyfish.

What voyage this, little girl?
This coming out of prison?   160
God help—
this life after death?

Edvard Munch's famous lithograph *The Scream*, mentioned in Anne Sexton's poem "Briar Rose (Sleeping Beauty)," shows a figure reacting with dramatic terror to an image of evil. COURTESY MUSEUM OF FINE ARTS, BOSTON.

Stephen King
(1947-   )

STEPHEN King is in a unique position to comment on the teacher's frequently-held opinion that her pupils are "little monsters." His experiences teaching English at Hampden Academy in his native Maine and creative writing at his *alma mater*, the University of Maine at Orono, gave him access to the world of Miss Sidley, the spinster-heroine of "Suffer the Little Children"; and they undoubtedly lend the force of conviction to her remark, "They are all monsters. I found out." King has focused on the adolescent or child in several of his major novels, including *Carrie* (1974), *The Shining* (1977), and *Firestarter* (1980). Sympathetic as his young protagonists often are, they possess preternatural powers that strike fear into the hearts of their elders. Their skills at telekinesis, clairvoyance, and pyrotechnics permit them to assume a mastery over the adult world that can result in mayhem and carnage. The aliens who have possessed the bodies of Miss Sidley's pupils, with their laughter like "river mud" and their eyes like "knife-struck egg yolks," use their grotesque ability at changing for purely evil purposes. They are far from being the innocents that Jesus summoned to him in *Mark* 10:14: "Suffer the little children to come unto me, and forbid them not: for of such is the kingdom of God." They are, rather, a source of agony much more potent and inscrutable than a bad back for the "constantly suffering" Miss Sidley.

In part, the teacher provokes her own doom by trying to conceal her weaknesses and by pretending, "like God," to know everything all at once. She cultivates in her pupils a respect for her omniscience by means of her "little tricks" and her "advantages." She has her teacherly secrets, and with them she plays upon the fear and hatred of her pupils. Teaching "was her game," and her undoing. She is a good player, but not so skilled as the possessed children, who have their own insidious "secrets." When she returns to her class around Halloween and finds even more children "hiding behind masks," she merely *thinks* she is ready for the game. Her pupil Robert is setting her up for defeat as he plays a more sinister game than dodgem ball. Unfortunately, Miss Sidley's loss is to be only the first in a series: the ending implies that Buddy Jenkins, whose "game" is psychiatry, will attempt to handle the children in the same unsuccessful way.

King is clearly working with the same ideas that inspired Henry James to write about children possessed by evil beings in *The Turn of the Screw*. In the frame to James's story, Douglas points out that the innocence usually associated with childhood lends a piquancy to the description of evil: "If the child gives the effect another turn of the screw, what do you say to *two* children—?" Or, as King would put it, what do you say to *twelve*? Of course, it is not certain that the children are evil, for King—like James—poses questions about sanity and madness, reality and illusion. Miss Sidley is initially skeptical about her perceptions of Robert and worried about losing her mind; she becomes convinced of the presence of evil during the incident in the lavatory, only to find her conviction again shaken by the appearance of the little boy she has shot. Mr. Hanning and Mrs. Crossen seem very sure that she is a psychopath. Buddy Jenkins undergoes a change of mind. These alternations between conviction and doubt in the characters parallel our own groping for the truth as we read. The technique is reminiscent not only of James's *Turn of the Screw* and "The Ghostly Rental," but also of Poe's "Fall of the House of Usher," Dickens' "Signal-Man," and Le Fanu's "Green Tea." The Gothic conventions for depicting evil are as old as Horace Walpole and as new as Stephen King. It is not surprising that the image of evil, though portrayed by countless authors for widely different audiences, remains very similar. In writing and reading about our terrified responses to the evil image, we show that we are all human beings. Are we not?

Suffer the Little Children (1972)

Miss Sidley was her name, and teaching was her game.

She was a small woman who had to reach on tiptoes to write on the highest level of the blackboard, which she was doing now. Behind her, none of the children giggled or whispered or munched on secret sweets held in cupped hands. They knew Miss Sidley too well. Miss Sidley knew instinctively who was chewing gum at the back of the room, who had a beanshooter in his pocket, who wanted to go to the bathroom to trade baseball cards rather than use the facilities. Like God, she seemed to know everything all at once.

She was graying, and the brace she wore to support her failing back was lined clearly against her print dress. Small, constantly suffering, gimlet-eyed woman. But they feared her. Her tongue was a school-yard legend. The eyes, when turned on a giggler or a whisperer, could turn the stoutest knees to water.

Now, writing the day's list of spelling words on the slate, she reflected that the success of her long teaching career could be summed and checked and proven by this one everyday action. She could turn her back on her pupils in confidence.

"Vacation," she said, pronouncing the word as she wrote it in her firm, no-nonsense script. "Edward, you will please use the word *vacation* in a sentence."

"I went on a vacation to New York City," Edward piped. Then, as Miss Sidley had taught, he repeated the word carefully. "Vay-cay-shun."

"Very good, Edward." She began on the next word.

She had her little tricks, of course; success, she firmly believed, depended as much upon taking note of little things as it did upon the big ones. She applied the principle constantly in the classroom, and it never failed.

"Jane," she said quietly.

Jane, who had been furtively perusing her Reader, looked up guiltily.

"Close that book right now, please." The book shut; Jane looked with pale, hating eyes at Miss Sidley's back. "And you will stay for fifteen minutes after the final bell."

Jane's lips trembled. "Yes, Miss Sidley."

One of her little tricks was the careful use of her glasses. The whole class was reflected to her in their thick lenses and she had always been thinly amused by their guilty, frightened faces when she caught them at their nasty little games.

Now she saw a phantomish, distorted Robert in the first row wrinkle his nose. She did not speak. Robert would hang himself if given just a little more rope.

"Tomorrow," she pronounced clearly. "Robert, you will please use the word *tomorrow* in a sentence." Robert frowned over the problem. The classroom was hushed and sleepy in the late September sun. The electric clock over the door buzzed a rumor of three o'clock dismissal just a half-hour away and the only thing that kept young heads from drowsing over their spellers was the silent, ominous threat of Miss Sidley's back.

"I am waiting, Robert."

"Tomorrow a bad thing will happen," Robert said. The words were perfectly innocuous, but Miss Sidley, with the seventh sense that all strict disciplinarians have, could sense a double meaning.

"Too-mor-row," Robert finished. His hands were folded neatly on the desk, and he wrinkled his nose again. He also smiled a tiny side-of-the-mouth smile. Miss Sidley was suddenly unaccountably sure Robert knew her little trick with the glasses.

Very well.

She began to write the next word with no comment of commendation for Robert, letting her straight body speak its own message. She watched carefully with one eye. Soon Robert would stick out his tongue or make that disgusting finger gesture, just to see if she really knew what he was doing. Then he would be punished.

The reflection was small, ghostly, and distorted. And she had all but the barest corner of her eye on the word she was writing.

Robert changed.

She caught just a corner of it, just a frightening glimpse of Robert's face changing into something . . . different.

She whirled around, face white, barely noticing the protesting stab of pain in her back.

Robert looked at her blandly, questioningly. His hands were neatly folded. The first signs of an afternoon cowlick showed at the back of his head. He did not look frightened.

I have imagined it, she thought. I was looking for something, and when there was nothing, I just made something up. However—

"Robert?" she asked. She had meant to be authoritative; the unspoken demand for confession. It did not come out that way.

"Yes, Miss Sidley?" His eyes were a very dark brown, like the mud at the bottom of a slow-running stream.

"Nothing."

She turned back to the board and a little whisper ran through the class.

"Be *quiet!*" her voice snapped. She turned again and faced them. "Another sound and we will all stay after school with Jane!" She addressed the whole class, but looked particularly at Robert. He looked back with childlike I-didn't-do-it innocence.

She turned to the board and began to write, not looking out of the corners of her glasses. The last half-hour dragged, and it seemed that Robert gave her a strange look on the way out. A look that said, *we have a secret, don't we?*

It wouldn't get out of her mind.

It seemed to be stuck like a tiny string of roast beef between two molars, a small thing, actually, but feeling as big as a cinderblock.

She sat down to her solitary dinner at five, poached eggs on toast, still thinking about it. She knew she was getting older and accepted the knowledge calmly. She was not going to be one of those old lady schoolteachers dragged kicking and screaming from their classrooms at the age of retirement. They reminded her of gamblers emotionally unable to leave the tables while they were losing. But *she* was not losing. She had always been a winner.

She looked down at her poached egg.

Hadn't she?

She thought of the well-scrubbed faces in her third grade classroom, and found Robert's face superimposed over them.

She got up and switched on a light.

Later, just before dropping off to sleep, Robert's face floated in front of her, smiling unpleasantly in the darkness behind her lids. The face began to change—

But before she saw exactly what it was changing into, she dropped off to sleep.

Miss Sidley spent an unrestful night and the next day her temper was short. She waited, almost hoped for a whisperer, a giggler, or perhaps even a note-passer. But the class was quiet—very quiet. They all stared at her unresponsively, and it seemed that she could feel the weight of their eyes on her like blind, crawling ants.

Now stop! she told herself sternly. She paused, controlling an urge to bite her lip. She was acting like a skittish girl just out of Seminary.

Again the day seemed to drag, and she believed she was more relieved than her charges when the dismissal bell rang. The children lined up in orderly rows at the door, boys and girls by height, hands dutifully linked.

"Dismissed," she said, and listened sourly as they shrieked down the hall and into the bright sunlight.

What was it? It was bulbous. It shimmered and it changed and it stared at me, yes, stared and grinned and it wasn't a child at all. It was old and it was evil and—

"Miss Sidley?"

Her head jerked up; a little *oh!* hiccupped involuntarily from her throat.

It was Mr. Hanning. He smiled apologetically. "Didn't mean to disturb you."

"Quite all right," she said, more curtly than she had intended. What had she been thinking? What was wrong with her?

"Would you mind checking the paper towels in the girls' lavatory?"

"Surely." She got up, placing her hands against the small of her back.

Mr. Hanning looked at her sympathetically. Save it, she thought. The old maid is not amused. Or even interested.

She brushed by Mr. Hanning and started down the hall to the girls' lavatory. A capering group of small boys, carrying scratched and pitted baseball equipment, grew silent at the sight of her and leaked out the door, where their cries began again.

Miss Sidley looked after them resentfully, reflecting that children had been different in her day. Not more polite—children have never had time for that—and not exactly more respectful of their elders; it was a kind of hypocrisy that had never been there before. A smiling quietness around adults that had never been there before. A kind of quiet contempt that was upsetting and unnerving. As if they were . . .

Hiding behind masks.

She pushed the thought away and went into the lavatory.

It was a small, tiled room with frosted glass windows, shaped like an L. The toilets were ranged along one bar, the sinks along both sides of the shorter bar.

As she checked along the paper towel containers, she caught a glimpse of her face in one of the mirrors and was startled into looking at it closely.

God.

There was a look that hadn't been there two days before, a frightened, watching look. With sudden shock she realized that the tiny, blurred reflection in her glasses coupled with Robert's pale, respectful face had gotten inside her and was festering.

The door opened and she heard two girls come in, giggling secretly about something. She was about to turn the corner and walk out past them when she heard her own name. She turned back to the washbowls and began checking the towel holders again.

"And then he—"

Soft giggles.

"She knows, but—"

More giggles, soft and sticky as melting soap.

"Miss Sidley is—"

Stop it! Stop that noise!

By moving slightly she could see their shadows, made fuzzy and ill-defined by the diffuse light filtering through the frosted windows, holding onto each other with girlish glee.

Another thought crawled up out of her mind.

They knew she was there.

Yes, they did, the little bitches. They knew.

She would shake them. Shake them until their teeth rattled and their giggles turned to wails and she would make them admit that they knew, they knew, they—

The shadows changed.

They seemed to elongate, to flow like dripping tallow, taking on strange, hunched shapes that made Miss Sidley cringe back against the porcelain washstands, her heart swelling in her chest.

But they went on giggling.

THE EVIL IMAGE

The voices changed, no longer girlish, now sexless and soulless, and quite, quite evil. A slow, turgid sound of mindless humor that flowed around the corner to her like river mud.

She stared at the hunched shadows and suddenly screamed at them. The scream went on and on, swelling in her head until it attained a pitch of lunacy. And then she fainted. The giggling, like the laughter of demons, followed her down into darkness.

She could not, of course, tell them the truth.

Miss Sidley knew this even as she opened her eyes and looked up at the anxious faces of Mr. Hanning and Mrs. Crossen. Mrs. Crossen was holding a bottle of sharp-smelling stuff under her nose. Mr. Hanning turned around and told the two little girls who were looking curiously at Miss Sidley to go on home now, please.

They both smiled at her, slow, we-have-a-secret smiles, and went out.

Very well. She would keep their secret. For a while. She would not have people thinking her insane. She would not have them thinking that the first feelers of senility had touched her early. She would play their game. Until she could expose their nastiness and rip it out. By the roots.

"I'm afraid I slipped," she said calmly, sitting up and ignoring the excruciating pain in her back. "A patch of wetness."

"This is awful," Mr. Hanning said. "Terrible. Are you—"

"Did the fall hurt your back, Emily?" Mrs. Crossen interrupted. Mr. Hanning looked at her gratefully.

Miss Sidley got up, her spine screaming in her body.

"No," she said. "In fact, something seems to have snapped back into place. It actually feels better."

"We can send for a—" Mr. Hanning began.

"No physician necessary. I'll just go on home." Miss Sidley smiled at him coolly.

"I'll get you a taxi."

"I always take the bus," Miss Sidley said. She walked out.

Mr. Hanning sighed and looked at Mrs. Crossen. "She *does* seem more like herself—"

The next day Miss Sidley kept Robert after school. He did nothing, so she simply accused him falsely. She felt no qualms; he was a monster, not a little boy. And she would make him admit it.

Her back was in agony. She realized Robert knew; he expected that would help him. But it wouldn't. That was another of her little advantages. Her back had been a constant pain to her for the last twelve years, and there had been times when it had been this bad— well, almost as bad—as this.

She closed the door, shutting the two of them in.

For a moment she stood still, training her gaze on Robert. She waited for him to drop his eyes. He didn't. He gazed back at her, and presently a little smile began to play around the corners of his mouth.

"Why are you smiling, Robert?" she asked softly.

"I don't know." Robert went on smiling.

"Tell me, please, Robert."

Robert said nothing. He went on smiling.

The outside sounds of children at play were far off, distant, dreamy. Only the hypnotic buzz of the wall clock was real.

"There's quite a few of us," Robert said suddenly, as if he were commenting on the weather.

It was Miss Sidley's turn to be silent.

"Eleven right here in this school." Robert went on smiling his small smile.

Quite evil, she thought, amazed. Very, incredibly evil.

"Please don't lie," she clearly. "Lies only make things worse."

Robert's smile grew wider; it became vulpine. "Do you want to see me change, Miss Sidley?" he asked. "Would you like to see it right out?"

Miss Sidley felt a nameless chill. "Go away," she said curtly. "And bring your mother and father to school with you tomorrow. We'll get this business straightened out." There. On solid ground again. She waited for his face to crumble, waited for the tears and the pleas to relent.

Robert's smile grew wider. He showed his teeth. "It will be just like Show and Tell, won't it, Miss Sidley? Robert—the *other* Robert —he liked Show and Tell. He's still hiding 'way, 'way down in my head." The smile curled at the corners of his mouth like charring paper. "Sometimes he runs around . . . it itches. He wants me to let him out."

"Go away," Miss Sidley said numbly. The buzzing of the clock seemed very loud.

Robert changed.

His face suddenly ran together like melting wax, the eyes flattening and spreading like knife-struck egg yolks, nose widening and yawning, mouth disappearing. The head elongated, and the hair was suddenly not hair but straggling, twitching growths.

Robert began to chuckle.

The slow, cavernous sound came from what had been his nose, but the nose was eating into the lower half of his face, nostrils meeting and merging into a central blackness like a huge, shouting mouth.

Robert got up, still chuckling, and behind it all she could see the last shattered remains of the other Robert, howling in maniac terror, screeching to be let out.

She ran.

She fled screaming down the corridor, and the few late-leaving pupils turned to look at her with large and uncomprehending eyes.

Mr. Hanning jerked open his door and looked out just as Miss Sidley plunged through the wide glass front doors, a wild, waving scarecrow silhouetted against the bright September sky.

He ran after her, Adam's apple bobbing convulsively. "Miss Sidley! *Miss Sidley!*"

Robert came out of the classroom and watched curiously.

Miss Sidley neither heard nor saw. She clattered down the walk and across the sidewalk and into the street with her screams trailing behind her like banners. There was a huge, blatting horn and then the bus was looming over her, the bus driver's face a plaster mask of fear. Air brakes whined and hissed like dragons in flight.

Miss Sidley fell, and the huge wheels shuddered to a smoking stop just eight inches from her frail, brace-armored body. She lay shuddering on the pavement, hearing the crowd gather around her.

She turned over and the children were staring down at her. They were ringed in a tight little circle, like mourners around an open grave. And at the head of the grave was Robert, his little face sober and solemn, ready to read the death rites and shovel the first spade of dirt over her face.

From far away, the bus driver's shaken babble: ". . . crazy or somethin' . . . my God, another half a foot . . ."

Miss Sidley stared numbly at the children. Their shadows covered her and blocked out the sun. Their faces were impassive. Some of them were smiling little secret smiles, and Miss Sidley knew that soon she would begin to scream again.

Then Mr. Hanning broke their tight noose and shooed them away.

Miss Sidley began to sob weakly.

She did not go back to her third grade for a month. She told Mr. Hanning calmly that she had not been feeling herself, and Mr. Hanning suggested that she go to a reputable, ah, doctor, and discuss the matter with him. Miss Sidley agreed that this was the only sensible and rational course. She also said that if the school board wished her resignation she would tender it immediately, although it would hurt her very much. Mr. Hanning, looking uncomfortable, said he doubted if that would be necessary.

The upshot of the matter was that Miss Sidley went back to her class in late October, once again ready to play the game and now knowing how to play it.

For the first week she let things go on as ever. It seemed the whole class now regarded her with hostile, shielded eyes. Robert smiled distantly at her from his first-row seat, and she did not have the courage to take him to task.

Once, while on playground duty, Robert walked over to her, holding a dodgem ball, smiling. "There's more of us now," he said. "Lots, lots more." A girl on the jungle gym looked across the playground at them and smiled, as if she had heard.

Miss Sidley smiled serenely, refusing to remember the face changing, mutating: "Why, Robert, whatever do you mean?"

But Robert only continued smiling and went back to his game. Miss Sidley knew the time had come.

She brought the gun to school in her handbag.

It had been her brother Jim's. He had taken it from a dead German shortly after the Battle of the Bulge. Jim had been gone ten years now. She had not opened the box that held the gun in more years than that, but when she did it was still there, gleaming dully. The four clips of shells were still in the box, too, and she loaded carefully the way Jim had showed her once.

She smiled pleasantly at her class; at Robert in particular. Robert smiled back and she could see the murky alienness swimming just below his skin, muddy, full of filth.

She never cared wondering just what was impersonating Robert, but she wished she knew if the real Robert was still inside. She did not wish to be a murderess. She decided that the real Robert must have died or gone insane, living inside the dirty, crawling thing that had chuckled at her in the classroom and sent her screaming into the street. So even if he was still alive, putting him out of his misery would be a mercy.

"Today we're going to have a Test," Miss Sidley said.

The class did not groan or shift apprehensively; they merely looked at her. She could feel their eyes, like weights. Heavy, smothering.

"It's a very special Test. I will call you down to the mimeographing room one by one and give you your Test. Then you may have a candy and go home for the day. Won't that be nice?"

They smiled empty smiles and said nothing.

"Robert, will you come first?"

Robert got up, smiling his little smile. He wrinkled his nose quite openly at her. "Yes, Miss Sidley."

Miss Sidley took her bag and they went down the empty, echoing corridor together, past the sleepy buzz of reciting classes coming from behind closed doors.

The mimeograph room was at the far end of the hall, past the lavatories. It had been soundproofed two years ago; the big machine was very old and very noisy.

Miss Sidley closed the door behind them and locked it.

"No one can hear you," she said calmly. She took the gun from her bag. "You or the gun."

Robert smiled innocently. "There are lots of us, though. Lots more than here." He put one small scrubbed hand on the paper-tray of the mimeograph machine. "Would you like to see me change, Miss Sidley?"

Before she could speak, the change began. Robert's face began to melt and shimmer into the grotesqueness beneath, and Miss Sidley shot him. Once. In the head.

He fell back against the paper-lined shelves and slid down to the floor, a little dead boy with a round black hole above the right eye.

He looked very pathetic.

Miss Sidley stood over him, breathing hard. Her scrawny cheeks were livid.

The huddled figure didn't move.

It was human.

It was Robert.

No!

It was all in your mind, Emily. All in your mind.

No! No, no, *no!*

She went back up to the room and began to lead them down, one by one. She killed twelve of them and would have killed them all if Mrs. Crossen hadn't come down for a package of composition paper.

Mrs. Crossen's eyes got very big; one hand crept up and clutched her mouth. She began to scream and she was still screaming when Miss Sidley reached her and put a hand on her shoulder. "It had to be done, Margaret," she said sadly to the screaming Mrs. Crossen. "It's terrible, but it had to. They are all monsters. I found out."

Mrs. Crossen stared at the gay-clothed little bodies scattered around the mimeograph and continued to scream.

The little girl whose hand Miss Sidley was holding began to cry steadily and monotonously.

"Change," Miss Sidley said. "Change for Mrs. Crossen. Show her it had to be done."

The girl continued to weep uncomprehendingly.

"Damn you, *change!*" Miss Sidley screamed. "Dirty bitch, dirty, crawling, filthy unnatural *bitch!* Change! God damn you, *change!*" She raised the gun. The little girl cringed, and then Mrs. Crossen was on her like a cat, and Miss Sidley's back gave way.

No trial.

The papers screamed for a trial, bereaved parents swore hysterical oaths against Miss Sidley, and the city sat back on its haunches in numb shock—

—*Twelve children!*

The State Legislature called for more stringent teacher examination tests, Summer Street School closed for a week of mourning, and Miss Sidley went quietly to an antiseptic madhouse in the next state. She was put in deep analysis, given the most modern drugs, introduced into daily work-therapy sessions. A year later, under strictly controlled conditions, Miss Sidley was put in an experimental encounter-therapy situation.

Buddy Jenkins was his name, psychiatry was his game.

He sat behind a one-way glass with a clipboard, looking into a room which had been outfitted as a nursery. On the far wall, the cow was jumping over the moon and the mouse was halfway up the clock. Miss Sidley sat in her wheelchair with a story book, surrounded by a group of soft, trusting, totally mindless retarded children. They smiled at her and drooled and touched her with small wet fingers while attendants at the next window watched for the first sign of an aggressive move.

For a time Buddy thought she responded well. She read aloud, stroked a girl's head, picked up a small boy when he fell over a toy block. Then she seemed to see something which disturbed her; a frown creased her brow and she looked away from the children.

"Take me away, please," Miss Sidley said, softly and tonelessly, to no one in particular.

And so they took her away. Buddy Jenkins watched the children watch her go, their eyes wide and empty, but somehow deep. One smiled, and another put his fingers in his mouth slyly. Two little girls clutched each other and giggled.

That night Miss Sidley cut her throat with a bit of broken mirror-glass, and Buddy Jenkins began to watch the children.

Suggestions for Further Reading in the Gothic Tradition

The following list does not presume to be comprehensive—only interesting:

Aiken, Conrad. *The Short Stories of Conrad Aiken* (1950).

Alcott, Louisa May. *Behind a Mask* (1975). *Plots and Counterplots* (1978).

Amis, Kingsley. *The Green Man* (1969).

Anderson, Sherwood. *Winesburg, Ohio* (1919).

Anson, Jay. *The Amityville Horror* (1977).

Ashford, Daisy. *The Young Visiters, or Mr. Salteenas Plan* (1919).

Austen, Jane. *Northanger Abbey* (1818).

Beckford, William. *Vathek* (1786).

Bierce, Ambrose. *Can Such Things Be?* (1893) *Ghost and Horror Stories of Ambrose Bierce*, ed. E. F. Bleiler (1964).

Blackwood, Algernon. *Ancient Sorceries and Other Stories* (1968). *The Insanity of Jones and Other Tales* (1966). *Tales of the Uncanny and Supernatural* (1962).

Blair, Robert. *The Poetical Works of Robert Blair* (1802).

Blake, William. *The Poetry and Prose of William Blake*, ed. David V. Erdman (1965).

Blatty, William Peter. *The Exorcist* (1971).

Brandon, Beatrice. *The Cliffs of Night* (1974).

Brent, Madeleine. *Moonraker's Bride* (1973). *Tregaron's Daughter* (1971).

Brontë, Charlotte. *Jane Eyre* (1848).

Brontë, Emily. *Wuthering Heights* (1847).

Brown, Charles Brockden. *Ormond: or, The Secret Witness* (1799). *Wieland: or, The Transformation; Together with Memoirs of Carwin the Biloquist, a Fragment* (1798).

Byfield, Barbara Ninde. *The Book of Weird* (1973).

Byron, George Gordon, Lord. *The Works of Lord Byron: Poetry*, ed. Ernest H. Coleridge. 7 vols. 1905, rpt. 1972.

Capote, Truman. *In Cold Blood* (1965). *The Grass Harp and A Tree of Night* (1945). *Other Voices, Other Rooms* (1948). *Music for Chameleons* (1980).

Carroll, Lewis. *The Hunting of the Snark* (1876).

Coleridge, Samuel Taylor. *The Poems of Samuel Taylor Coleridge,* ed. Ernest H. Coleridge (1912).

Collier, John. *Fancies and Goodnights* (1951). *The Touch of Nutmeg* (1943).

Collins, William Wilkie. *After Dark and Other Stories,* 2 vols. (1856). *The Haunted Hotel* and *My Lady's Money,* 2 vols. (1879). *The Moonstone* (1868).

Daniels, Dorothy. *The Spanish Castle* (1969).

De La Mare, Walter. *The Connoisseur* (1926). *On the Edge* (1930). *The Riddle* (1923). *The Wind Blows Over* (1936).

Dickens, Charles. *Christmas Books* (1852). *Christmas Stories* (1871).

Dinesen, Isak. *Seven Gothic Tales* (1934).

Eden, Dorothy. *Dark Water* (1963).

Ellin, Stanley. *The Blessington Method and Other Strange Tales* (1956).

Eyre, Marie. *Bury Me Not at Sea* (1974).

Faulkner, William. *As I Lay Dying* (1930). *Requiem for a Nun* (1951). *Sanctuary* (1931).

Gardner, John. *October Light* (1976).

Godwin, William. *The Adventures of Caleb Williams; or, Things as They Are* (1794).

Green, William Child. *The Maniac of the Desert* (1821). *The Prophecy of Duncannon* (1824).

Haining, Peter, ed. *Gothic Tales of Terror* (1972).

Hardy, Thomas. *Life's Little Ironies* (1894). *Selected Stories* (1966).

Hawthorne, Nathaniel. *The Complete Novels and Selected Tales of Nathaniel Hawthorne,* ed. Norman Holmes Pearson (1937).

Hoffmann, E. T. A. *The Best Tales of Hoffmann,* ed. E. F. Bleiler (1967).

Hogg, James. *The Private Memoirs and Confessions of a Justified Sinner* (1824).

Holland, Isabelle. *Trelawney* (1976).

Holt, Victoria. *Kirkland Revels* (1962). *Mistress of Mellyn* (1960).

Inge, William. *Good Luck, Miss Wyckoff* (1970).

Jackson, Shirley. *The Haunting of Hill House* (1959). *We Have Always Lived in the Castle* (1962). *The Magic of Shirley Jackson,* ed. Stanley Edgar Hyman, including "The Lottery" (1965).

James, Henry. *The Ghostly Tales of Henry James,* including *The Turn of the Screw* and *The Beast in the Jungle,* ed. Leon Edel (1963). *Stories of the Supernatural,* ed. Leon Edel (1971).

James, Montague Rhodes. *The Collected Ghost Stories* (1931). *Ghost*

Stories of an Antiquary (1904). *More Ghost Stories of an Antiquary* (1911).

Kafka, Franz. *The Castle* (1926). *Metamorphosis and Other Stories* (1937).

King, Stephen. *Carrie* (1974). *Firestarter* (1980). *The Dead Zone* (1979). *Salem's Lot* (1975). *The Shining* (1977). *The Stand* (1978).

Latham, Francis. *The Midnight Bell* (1798). *Mystery* (1800).

Le Fanu, Joseph Sheridan. *Best Ghost Stories of J. S. Le Fanu*, ed. E. F. Bleiler (1964). *Ghost Stories and Mysteries*, ed. E. F. Bleiler (1975).

Lewis, Matthew Gregory. *The Monk; a Romance* (1796). *Tales of Terror* (1799). *Tales of Wonder* (1801). *Venoni: or, the Novice of St. Mark's* (1808).

Lovecraft, H. P. *At the Mountains of Madness* (1964). *The Case of Charles Dexter Ward* (1941). *The Shuttered Room and Other Tales of Horror* (1970).

Lucie-Smith, Edward, ed. *The Penguin Book of Satirical Verse* (1967).

Macbeth, George, ed. *The Penguin Book of Sick Verse* (1963).

Machen, Arthur. *The Children of the Pool, and Other Stories* (1936). *The Great God Pan, and The Inmost Light* (1913). *The Hill of Dreams* (1907).

Maturin, Charles. *The Fatal Revenge; or, The Family of Montorio*, 3 vols. (1807). *Melmoth the Wanderer; a Tale* (1820).

McCullers, Carson. *The Ballad of the Sad Cafe and Other Stories* (1951). *The Heart Is a Lonely Hunter* (1940). *Reflections in a Golden Eye* (1945).

Melville, Herman. *Moby Dick* (1851).

Moore, John. *Zeluco: Various Views of Human Nature, Taken from Life and Manners, Foreign and Domestic.* 2 vols. (1786).

Oates, Joyce Carol. *By the North Gate* (1966). *Bellefleur* (1980). *Expensive People* (1968). *A Garden of Earthly Delights* (1967). *Wheel of Love* (1965).

O'Connor, Flannery. *Everything That Rises Must Converge* (1965). *A Good Man Is Hard to Find* (1955). *The Violent Bear It Away* (1960). *Wise Blood* (1952).

Ossian. *The Poems of Ossian*, trans. James Macpherson (1760).

Ostrander, Sheila and Lynn Shroeder. *Psychic Discoveries Behind the Iron Curtain* (1970).

Plath, Sylvia. *Ariel* (1968). *The Colossus* (1957). *The Bell Jar* (1963).

Poe, Edgar Allan. *The Complete Works of Edgar Allan Poe*, ed. James A. Harrison. 17 vols. (1965).

Prest, Thomas Peckett. *The Black Monk: or, The Secret of the Grey Turret* (1844). *Varney the Vampire* (1847).

Purdy, James. *Color of Darkness: Eleven Stories and a Novella* (1961). *Eustace Chisholm and the Works* (1967).

Radcliffe, Ann. *Gaston de Blondeville* (1826). *The Italian* (1797). *The Mysteries of Udolpho* (1794). *The Romance of the Forest* (1791). *A Sicilian Romance* (1790).

Reeve, Clara. *The Old English Baron; A Gothic Story* (1777).

Rhys, Jean. *Wide Sargasso Sea* (1966).

Rice, Anne. *Interview with the Vampire* (1976).

Rossner, Judith. *Looking for Mr. Goodbar* (1975).

Saki (Hector Hugh Monro). *Beasts and Super Beasts* (1914). *The Chronicles of Clovis* (1911). *The Bodley Head Saki*, ed. J. W. Lambert (1963). *Reginald in Russia* (1910).

Sexton, Anne. *All My Pretty Ones* (1962). *The Awful Rowing Toward God* (1975). *To Bedlam and Part Way Back* (1960). *Transformations* (1971).

Shelley, Mary Wollstonecraft. *Collected Tales and Stories*, ed. Charles Robinson (1976). *Frankenstein; or, The Modern Prometheus* (1818; 1831).

Shelley, Percy Bysshe. *The Complete Works*, ed. Roger Ingpen and Walter E. Peck (1965).

Stevenson, Robert Louis. *The Merry Men and Other Tales and Fables* (1887). *New Arabian Nights*, 2 vols. (1882). *The Strange Case of Dr. Jekyll and Mr. Hyde* (1886).

Stoker, Bram. *Dracula* (1897).

Straub, Peter. *Ghost Story* (1979).

Summers, Montague, ed. *The Supernatural Omnibus* (1931).

Tryon, Thomas. *The Other* (1971).

Vandergriff, Aola. *Wyndspelle* (1975).

Van Dyke, Henry. *Ladies of the Rachmaninoff Eyes* (1965).

Walpole, Horace. *The Castle of Otranto* (1764).

Wilde, Oscar. *The Picture of Dorian Gray* (1891).

Williams, Charles. *The Greater Trumps* (1950).

Williams, Tennessee. *Eight Mortal Ladies Possessed* (1971). *Hard Candy* (1954). *One Arm* (1948).

Wolf, Leonard, ed. *The Annotated Frankenstein* (1977).

Woolf, Virginia. *Orlando* (1928).

Yeats, W. B. *Collected Plays*, 2nd ed. (1952). *Collected Poems*, 2nd ed. (1950).

LARAMIE JR. HIGH IMC

About the Editors

Patricia L. Skarda, born in Clovis, New Mexico, and educated at Sweet Briar College, Texas Tech University, and The University of Texas at Austin (Ph.D., 1973), became an admirer of Gothic literature through Romantic poetry and Victorian fiction, which she has taught at Smith College since 1973. In 1978–1979 she held an ACE Fellowship in Academic Administration and spent the year at Carleton College, the Associated Colleges of the Midwest headquarters, Stanford University, and Trinity University in San Antonio. She is author of articles on the Romantic poets, Gerard Manley Hopkins, and Smith writers. Currently she is President of the Phi Beta Kappa Chapter at Smith.

Nora Crow Jaffe, who received her doctorate from Harvard in 1971, is Associate Professor of English at Smith College. A specialist in eighteenth-century literature, she is author of articles on Swift and Pope and of *The Poet Swift* (1977).

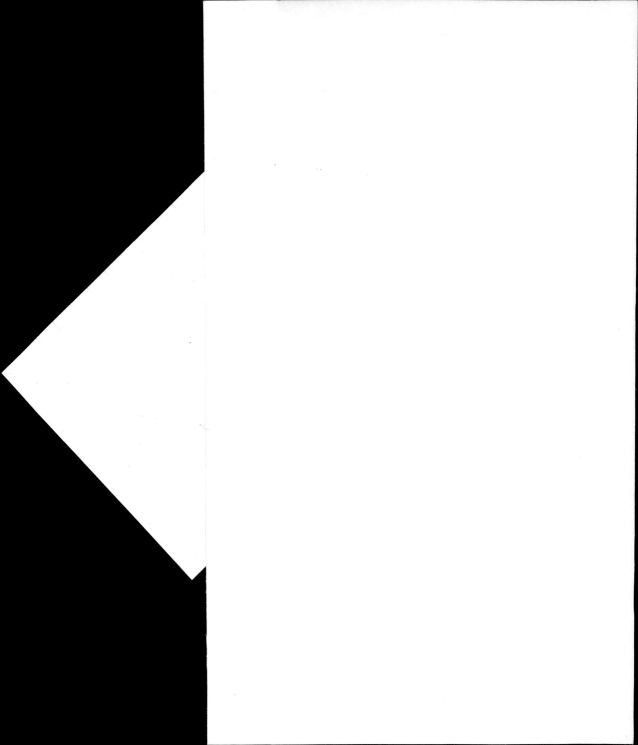

LARAMIE JR. HIGH IMC

DATE

JAN   5 1998
OCT   9 2003
NOV
MAY 2 5 2007
MAR 1 9

DEMCO 38-297